Map Collections in the United States and Canada

4th Edition
A Directory

David K. Carrington
and
Richard W. Stephenson,
Editors

Special Libraries Association
New York

Printed in the United States of America

Library of Congress Cataloging in Publication Data
Main entry under title:

Map collections in the United States and Canada.

   Includes index.
   1. Map collections—United States—Directories.
2. Map collections—Canada—Directories.   I. Carrington,
David K., 1938–   .   II. Stephenson, Richard W.,
1930–   .
GA193.U5M36   1985   026′.912′02573   84–27571
ISBN 0–87111–306–6

Preface

Work on the fourth edition of *Map Collections in the United States and Canada* began in the early Spring of 1983. The first mailing of some 1200 cover letters and questionnaires occurred in August of that year; a second, much smaller mailing was done in March 1984. Finally, in an attempt to obtain up-to-date information for as many map collections as possible, a telephone canvass, conducted by members of the SLA Geography and Map Division, took place in late June and early July 1984. These extensive solicitation efforts have resulted in the selection of 804 entries for inclusion in this edition. The initial mailing list was generated from entries in the third edition of the Directory, plus various United States map depository lists and other miscellaneous sources.

The questionnaire duplicates that which was used for the previous edition with the exception that each data field has been coded in order to facilitate computer inputting and manipulation of the information. Data obtained for the fourth edition have been stored on magnetic tape. It is anticipated that this will simplify greatly the preparation of future revisions of the Directory.

Entries in this edition, as in the previous editions, are arranged alphabetically by city within a state or province. Each page has a running title indicating the name of the state or province and entry numbers found on that page, an enhancement that will aid in the use of this new edition. The layout of the descriptive data is very much the same as in the previous edition. All data included have been taken directly from the questionnaires with the exception of a few Canadian entries. As before, numbers in the index refer to individual entries rather than to pages. All significant data found in the collection descriptions have been recorded except for regional and subject specializations. The index in the fourth edition was prepared by professional indexer Janet Kvamme.

The editors wish to express appreciation to the many individuals who provided information and assistance in the compilation of this edition. We especially wish to thank Michael J. Esposito, Editor, Non-Serial Publications, Special Libraries Association, who has been instrumental in coordinating the work among the printer, Port City Press, the indexer and the editors. In addition, the editors wish to thank the following SLA members who assisted in the time-consuming telephone canvass: Barbara Berthelsen, Robert Bier, Jr., Barbara Cox, James Flatness, Mary Fortney, Richard Fox, James Gillispie, Joanne Hansen, Alfred Herman, Barbara McCorkle, James Minton, Andrew Modelski, Anita Oser, Karl Proehl, Pamela Rau, Christine Reinhard, Marsha Selmer, Charlotte Slocum, Robert Sperling, Paul Stout, John Schroeder, Johnny Sutherland, Mai Treude, and Christine Windheuser. We also wish to thank Julia Pettross and Peggy Coates, Administrative Secretary and Assistant Secretary, respectively, of the Library of Congress, Geography and Map Division, for their assistance in typing the cover letters and questionnaire, and in preparing the address files and mailing labels.

David K. Carrington
Richard W. Stephenson

Abbreviations

AGS	American Geographical Society
DOS	Directorate of Overseas Surveys (Great Britain)
GSC	Geological Survey of Canada
LC	Library of Congress
NOS	National Ocean Service (United States)
NTS	National Topographic System (Canada)
USGS (Geol.)	United States Geological Survey Geologic Quadrangles
USGS (Topo.)	United States Geological Survey Topographic Quadrangles

Map Collections in the
United States
and Canada, 4th Edition

Map Collections in the United States

ALABAMA

Auburn

1. AUBURN UNIVERSITY
Ralph B. Draughon Library
Special Collections
Auburn, AL 36849
Established 1963.
Telephone: 205/826-4500.
Contact Person: G. E. Geiger, Libn. III.
Staff: 1 professional (full time); 2 non-professional (full time).
Size: 95,500 maps; 25 atlases; 1 globes; 40,000 aerial photographs; 210 reference books and gazetteers; 7 serials (titles received).
Annual Accessions: 4,000 maps; 5 atlases; 200–300 aerial photographs; 20 reference books and gazetteers.
Area Specialization: Alabama; southeastern United States.
Dates: pre-1800 (less than 1%); 1800-1899 (less than 1%); 1900 - (99%).
Classification System: DMA.
Collections Cataloged. (Some).
Depository for: DMA; USGS (Geol., topo.).
Serves: students; faculty; employees; public. Mon.–Thurs. 7:45 a.m.–10 p.m., Fri. 7:45–5 p.m.; Sat. 9 a.m.–6 p.m.; Sun. 1–10 p.m. (Seats 65; 400 readers served per month).
Interlibrary Loan Available.
Reproduction Facility: photocopy; microform.

Birmingham

2. BIRMINGHAM PUBLIC LIBRARY
Rucker Agee Cartographic Collection
2020 Park Place
Birmingham, AL 35203
Established 1964.
Telephone: 205/254-2534.
Contact Person: Virginia K. Scott, Head, Tutwiler Collection.
Size: 2995 maps; 655 atlases; 7 globes; 6 relief models; 130 aerial photographs; 2123 reference books and gazetteers; 8 serials (titles received); 1 microforms (no. of titles).
Area Specialization: southeastern United States; Alabama.
Subject Specialization: historical cartography; discovery and exploration; Civil War.
Special Cartographic Collections: Agee Collection; Woodward Collection—historical and regional maps from the Age of Discovery to the present.
Dates: pre-1800 (40%); 1800-1899 (50%); 1900 - (10%).
Classification System: Dewey.
Collections Cataloged.
Serves: public. Mon.–Thurs. 9 a.m.–8 p.m.; Fri. 9 a.m.–6 p.m.; Sat. 9–6 p.m.; Sun. 2–6 p.m. (Seats 2 (pre-1900); 30 (post-1900 & facsimiles)).
Reproduction Facility: photocopy.
Publications: *A List of Nineteenth Century Maps of the State of Alabama* (1973); *The Rucker Agee Collection of the Birmingham Public Library* (brochure); *A List of 16th, 17th, 18th century material in the Rucker Agee Map Collection* (1978); *Selected items from the Joseph H. Woodward II Collection of the Birmingham Public Library* (brochure).

3. SAMFORD UNIVERSITY
Harwell G. Davis Library
Special Collections
Birmingham, AL 35229
Established 1957.
Telephone: 205/870-2749.
Contact Person: Elizabeth C. Wells, Special Collections Libn.
Staff: 2 professional (full time); 2 non-professional (part time).
Size: 2,500 maps; 75 atlases; 1 globes; 51 relief models; 75 reference books and gazetteers; 5 microforms (no. of titles).
Annual Accessions: 30 maps; 2 atlases.
Area Specialization: Alabama; southeastern United States; Ireland.
Subject Specialization: local history; cities & counties; southeastern United States territorial development; Irish History.
Special Cartographic Collections: William H. Brantley Collection—18th & 19th century maps of Alabama and the Southeast; Albert E. Casey Collection—maps of Ireland, particularly from the Ordnance Survey.
Dates: pre-1800 (10); 1800-1899 (40); 1900 - (50).
Classification System: local system.
Collections Cataloged. (75%).
Depository for: USGS (Topo.); Alabama Development Office.
Serves: students; faculty; employees; public. Mon. 8 a.m.–9 p.m., Tues.–Fri. 8 a.m.–4:30 p.m. (Seats 40).
Interlibrary Loan Available. (restricted)
Reproduction Facility: photocopy; quickcopy; microform.
Publications: *Maps in the Samford University Library; An Annotated List 1977.*

Mobile

4. MOBILE PUBLIC LIBRARY
Special Collections
Gallalee Cartographic Collection
704 Government St.
Mobile, AL 36602
Established 1974.
Telephone: 205/438-7093.
Contact Person: Jay Higginbotham, Research Libn.
Staff: 1 professional (full time); 1 professional (part time).
Size: 300 maps; 3 atlases; 30 aerial photographs; 16 reference books and gazetteers.
Annual Accessions: 50 maps; 2 atlases; 10 aerial photographs; 10 reference books and gazetteers.
Area Specialization: Mobile Bay and Gulf Coast.
Subject Specialization: history (French, Spanish, British and American maps, 1520–1973).
Dates: pre-1800 (40%); 1800-1899 (40%); 1900 - (20%).

Classification System: local system.
Serves: public. Mon.–Fri. 9 a.m.–5 p.m.
Interlibrary Loan Available.
Reproduction Facility: quickcopy.

Montgomery

5. ALABAMA (STATE) DEPARTMENT OF ARCHIVES & HISTORY
624 Washington Ave.
Montgomery, AL 36106
Established March 2, 1901.
Telephone: 205/261-2500.
Contact Person: Richard J. Cox, Head, Archives and Records Division.
Size: 66 atlases; 33 reference books and gazetteers.
Area Specialization: Alabama; other southeastern states; Alabama towns, and counties.
Subject Specialization: Indian maps; military maps; forts; rivers and harbors of Alabama; topographical maps; county soil survey maps; railroad maps; historical maps.
Dates: pre-1800 (10%); 1800-1899 (40%); 1900 - (50%).
Collections not Cataloged.
Serves: employees; public. Mon.–Fri. 8 a.m.–5 p.m.; Sat. 9 a.m.–5 p.m. (Seats 35; 18 readers served per month).
Reproduction Facility: photocopy; quickcopy; microform.
Publications: Unpublished inventory.

University

6. UNIVERSITY OF ALABAMA
Department of Anthropology
P.O. Box 6135
University, AL 35486
Established 1968.
Telephone: 205/348-5947.
Contact Person: C. Earle Smith, Jr., Professor of Anthropology and Biology.
Size: 5,000 maps.
Annual Accessions: 300 maps.
Area Specialization: Alabama.
Subject Specialization: topography.
Dates: 1900 - (100%).
Classification System: Alphabetical.
Collections not Cataloged.
Depository for: USGS (Topo.).
Serves: students; faculty; employees; public. Mon.–Fri. 8 a.m.–4:45 p.m.
Reproduction Facility: photocopy.

7. UNIVERSITY OF ALABAMA
Geography/Winn-Dixie Map Library
202 Farrah Hall
University, AL 35486
Telephone: 205/348-5047.
Contact Person: Neal G. Lineback, Chairman and Professor of Geography Department.
Staff: 1 professional (part time).
Size: 80,000 maps; 25 atlases; 4 globes; 30 relief models; 4,000 aerial photographs.
Area Specialization: United States.
Subject Specialization: Energy resources.
Dates: 1900 - (100%).
Classification System: LC.
Collections Cataloged.
Depository for: DMA; USGS (Geol., topo.).
Serves: students; faculty; employees; public;. Mon.–Fri, 8–4:30 p.m. (Seats 25; 20 readers served per month).

8. UNIVERSITY OF ALABAMA
Main Library
Special Collections
University, AL 35486
Established 1945.
Telephone: 205/348-5512.
Contact Person: Joyce Lamonte, Curator, Special Collections.
Staff: 5 professional (full time); 2 non-professional (full time); 7 non-professional (part time).
Size: 90,000 maps.
Area Specialization: Alabama; southeastern United States.
Subject Specialization: topography; local history.
Special Cartographic Collections: Sanborn Fire Insurance Maps (Alabama); plats of the original surveys of Alabama.
Dates: pre-1800 (10); 1800-1899 (40); 1900 - (50).
Classification System: LC; local system.
Collections Cataloged. (35).
Depository for: DMA; NOS; USGS (Geol., topo.); Alabama Geological Survey.
Serves: students; faculty; employees; public. Mon.–Fri. 8 a.m.–5 p.m. (Thurs. to 10 p.m.). (Seats 35).
Interlibrary Loan Available. (restricted)
Reproduction Facility: quickcopy.

ALASKA

Anchorage

9. U.S. GEOLOGICAL SURVEY
National Cartographic Information Center
218 E Street
Anchorage, AK 99501
Established 1980.
Telephone: 907/271-4159.
Contact Person: Cheryl A. Hallam, Chief.
Staff: 4 professional (full time).
Size: 6,000 maps; 6 atlases; 50 relief models; 40,000 aerial photographs; 1,000 reference books and gazetteers; 6 serials (titles received); 20 microforms (no. of titles).
Area Specialization: Alaska; United States.
Subject Specialization: remote sensing and cartographic information.
Special Cartographic Collections: 35,000 Prints (Old Alaska Mapping Photography); USGS Alaska Autopositives (USGS 1:250,000 and 1:63,360 scale maps on Stable-base Mylars); 16mm Microfilm of Alaska High Altitude Photography; 16mm Microfilm of Satellite imagery (Landsat, Skylab); 16mm Microfilm of NASA Reconnaissance Photography; 35mm Microfilm of USGS Historical Maps; USGS Geodetic Control of Alaska.
Dates: 1800-1899 (1%); 1900 - (99%).
Classification System: Dewey;.
Collections Cataloged.
Collections not Cataloged. (95%).
Serves: public;. Mon.–Fri. 8 a.m.–5 p.m. (except Holidays). (Seats 12; 200 readers served per month).
Reproduction Facility: Ozalid, Xerox, Reader-Printers.

Fairbanks

10. ALASKA (STATE) DIVISION OF GEOLOGICAL AND GEOPHYSICAL SURVEYS
794 University Avenue
Fairbanks, AK 99701
Telephone: 907/474-7062.
Contact Person: Frank Larson, Publications Specialist.
Staff: 1 non-professional (part time).

Size: 500 maps; 4 atlases; 3,000 reference books and gazetteers.
Area Specialization: Alaska.
Subject Specialization: geology; geochemistry; hydrology; archaeology; history.
Dates: 1800-1899 (2%); 1900 - (98%).
Classification System: local system.
Collections not Cataloged.
Depository for: USGS (Geol.).
Serves: employees; public. Mon.–Fri., 8 a.m.–4:30 p.m. (Seats 4; 15 readers served per month).
Reproduction Facility: quickcopy.

11. UNIVERSITY OF ALASKA, FAIRBANKS
Elmer E. Rasmuson Library
Map Collection
310 Tanana Drive
Fairbanks, AK 99701
Telephone: 907/474-7624.
Contact Person: Pauline Gunter, Government Publications and Map Libn.
Staff: 1 professional (full time); 3 non-professional (full time).
Size: 7,762 maps; 495 atlases; 3 globes; 1 relief models; 500 aerial photographs; 350 reference books and gazetteers; 5 serials (titles received).
Annual Accessions: 350 maps; 40 atlases; 25 aerial photographs; 30 reference books and gazetteers; 1 serials (titles received).
Area Specialization: Alaska; Arctic Regions.
Dates: pre-1800 (5%); 1800-1899 (20%); 1900 - (75%).
Classification System: LC.
Collections Cataloged.
Depository for: NOS; USGS (Geol., topo.).
Serves: students; faculty; employees; public. Mon.–Fri. 8:30 am.–10:00 p.m.; Sat. 10 a.m.–6 p.m.; Sun. 1–5 p.m. (Seats 40).
Reproduction Facility: photocopy.

12. UNIVERSITY OF ALASKA, FAIRBANKS
Institute of Marine Science Library
905 Koyukuk Avenue North
Fairbanks, AK 99801
Established 1965.
Telephone: 907/474-7740.
Contact Person: Robert C. Williams, Institute Libn.
Staff: 1 professional (part time); 1 non-professional (part time).
Size: 1,600 maps; 52 atlases; 2 globes; 1 relief models; 20 aerial photographs; 30 reference books and gazetteers.
Annual Accessions: 20–30 maps; 5–10 atlases; 5–10 reference books and gazetteers.
Area Specialization: Polar Regions.
Dates: 1900 -.
Classification System: local system.
Collections Cataloged.
Serves: students; faculty; employees; public. Mon.–Fri. 8 a.m.–5 p.m. (Seats 20; 8–10 for maps readers served per month).
Interlibrary Loan Available.
Reproduction Facility: photocopy; microform.

Juneau

13. ALASKA DIVISION OF STATE LIBRARIES AND MUSEUMS
Alaska Historical Library
Pouch G
Juneau, AK 99811
Telephone: 907/465-2925.
Contact Person: Phyllis De Muth, Head, Reader Services.

Staff: 2 professional (part time); 1 non-professional (part time).
Size: 3,000 maps; 40 atlases; 1 relief models; 12 reference books and gazetteers; 1,000 microforms (no. of titles).
Area Specialization: Alaska; the Arctic.
Special Cartographic Collections: Sanborn fire insurance atlases of Alaska; the Dolgopolov Collection of Russian America and Pacific exploration materials (include maps).
Dates: 1900 - (95%).
Classification System: local system.
Collections Cataloged.
Depository for: USGS (Topo.); State depository.
Serves: public. Mon.–Fri. 8 a.m.–5 p.m. (Seats 12; 20 readers served per month).
Reproduction Facility: microform.
Publications: *U.S. National Fisheries Service Map Collection: A Guide to the Dolgopolov Collection in the Alaska Historical Library (includes maps); A Guide to the Alaska Packers Association Records, 1891–1970 (includes ca. 500 maps) (will loan in microfiche form).*

14. ALASKA (STATE) GEOLOGICAL & GEOPHYSICAL SURVEYS
Dept. of Natural Resources
Div. of Geo. & Geophysical Surveys
230 S. Franklin St., Rm 401
Juneau, AK 99801
Established 1959.
Telephone: 907/465-3400, ext. 39.
Contact Person: Judith Sigler, Natural Resource Technician II.
Staff: 1 professional (full time).
Area Specialization: Alaska.
Subject Specialization: Geology.
Special Cartographic Collections: Division of Geological & Geophysical Surveys Reports.
Dates: 1900 - (100%).
Classification System: local system.
Depository for: USGS (Geol., topo.); Alaska Geological & Geophysical Maps & Reports.
Serves: public. Mon.–Fri. 8 a.m.–4:30 p.m. (Seats 6; 25 readers served per month).
Reproduction Facility: quickcopy.

Ketchikan

15. ALASKA (STATE) DEPARTMENT OF NATURAL RESOURCES
Division of Mining
P.O. Box 7438
Ketchikan, AK 99901
Telephone: 907/225-4181.
Contact Person: Geraldine Zartman, Natural Resources Technician.
Staff: 1 professional (full time).
Size: 800 maps.
Area Specialization: Alaska.
Subject Specialization: mining.
Dates: 1900 - (100%).
Collections not Cataloged.
Depository for: USGS (Topo.).
Serves: public. Mon–Fri. 8 a.m.–12 noon, 1 p.m.–4 p.m. (Seats 6; 12 readers served per month).

Palmer

16. MATANUSKA-SUSITNA COMMUNITY COLLEGE
Library
Palmer, AK 99645
Established 1979.
Telephone: 907/745-4255.
Contact Person: Marcia Colson, Library Assistant.
Size: 150 maps; 5 atlases; 1 globes.
Annual Accessions: 0–1 atlases.
Area Specialization: Alaska; Washington; Oregon.
Dates: 1900 - (100%).
Collections not Cataloged.
Depository for: USGS (Topo.).
Serves: students; faculty; employees; public. Mon.–Thur. 9 a.m.–10 p.m., Fri. 9 a.m.–7 p.m. (Seats 12).
Reproduction Facility: photocopy.

ARIZONA

Flagstaff

17. MUSEUM OF NORTHERN ARIZONA
Library
Map Collection
Route 4, Box 720
Flagstaff, AZ 86001
Established 1928.
Telephone: 602/774-5211.
Contact Person: Dorothy House, Libn.
Staff: 1 professional (full time); 1 non-professional (full time); 1 non-professional (part time).
Size: 4,000 maps.
Area Specialization: southern Colorado Plateau.
Subject Specialization: anthropology; archaeology; geology; biology.
Dates: 1900 - (100%).
Classification System: unique local system.
Collections Cataloged.
Serves: employees; public. Mon.–Fri. 9 a.m.–5 p.m. (Seats 15).
Reproduction Facility: photocopy.

18. NORTHERN ARIZONA UNIVERSITY
North Center Library
Map Collection
C.U. Box 6022
Flagstaff, AZ 86011
Established 1965.
Telephone: 602/523-2171.
Contact Person: Robert H. Hassell, Reference Department Coordinator.
Staff: 1 professional (part time); 1 non-professional (part time).
Size: 19,447 maps; 647 atlases; 1 globes; 11 relief models; 195 reference books and gazetteers.
Annual Accessions: 1,109 maps; 35 atlases; 9 relief models; 18 reference books and gazetteers.
Area Specialization: Flagstaff; Coconino County; State of Arizona.
Subject Specialization: geology.
Dates: 1900 - (99.9%).
Classification System: LC.
Depository for: USGS (Geol., topo.).
Serves: students; faculty; employees; public;. Mon.–Fri. 7:30 a.m. to 11 p.m.; Sat. 8 a.m.–6 p.m.; Sun. 1–11:00 p.m. (Seats 50; 300 readers served per month).
Interlibrary Loan Available.
Reproduction Facility: photocopy; quickcopy.

Phoenix

19. ARIZONA (STATE) DEPARTMENT OF LIBRARY, ARCHIVES, AND PUBLIC RECORDS
Documents Division
Map Library
Phoenix, AZ 85007
Telephone: 602/255-4046.
Contact Person: Joanne M. Perry, Map Libn.
Staff: 1 professional (full time).
Size: 10,000 maps; 150 atlases; 20 reference books and gazetteers.
Area Specialization: Arizona; southwestern United States.
Depository for: USGS (Topo.); NCIC co-affiliate; GPO depository.
Serves: public; (legislature). Mon.–Fri. 8 a.m.–5 p.m.
Reproduction Facility: photocopy.

20. ARIZONA (STATE) DEPT. OF MINES AND MINERAL RESOURCES
Mineral Building, Fairgrounds
Phoenix, AZ 85007
Telephone: 602/255-3791.
Contact Person: John Jett, Director.
Size: 4,000 maps; 11 atlases; 5,000 reference books and gazetteers.
Area Specialization: Arizona.
Subject Specialization: mines and mining.
Special Cartographic Collections: mine and claim maps and sketches.
Serves: public.

21. PHOENIX PUBLIC LIBRARY
Arts and Humanities Division
12 East McDowell
Phoenix, AZ 85004
Established 1952.
Telephone: 602/262-4783.
Contact Person: Bill Kneedler, Head.
Staff: 2 professional (full time); 2 professional (part time).
Size: 3,750 maps; 50 atlases; 200 reference books and gazetteers.
Area Specialization: United States; Arizona; Mexico.
Dates: 1800-1899 (1%); 1900 - (99%).
Collections Cataloged. (20%). Mon.–Thurs. 9 a.m.–9 p.m.; Sat. Fri.–Sat. 9 a.m.–6 p.m.; Sun. 1–5 p.m. (50 readers served per month).
Reproduction Facility: photocopy.

Tempe

22. ARIZONA STATE UNIVERSITY
Noble Science and Engineering Library
Map Collection
Tempe, AZ 85287
Established 1970.
Telephone: 602/965-3582.
Contact Person: Rosanna Miller, Head, Map Collection.
Staff: 1 professional (full time); 3 non-professional (full time); 1 non-professional (part time).
Size: 100,000 maps; 1,055 atlases; 1 globes; 1,650 aerial photographs; 513 reference books and gazetteers; 12 serials (titles received).
Annual Accessions: 5,500 maps; 100 atlases; 175 aerial photographs; 30 reference books and gazetteers.
Area Specialization: Arizona; southwestern United States; Mexico.
Subject Specialization: topography; geology.
Dates: pre-1800 (1%); 1800-1899 (7%); 1900 - (92%).
Classification System: LC.

Collections not Cataloged.
Depository for: DMA; NOS; USGS (Geol., topo.).
Serves: students; faculty; employees; public. Mon.–Thur. 8 a.m.–8 p.m.; Fri. 8 a.m.–5 p.m.; Sun. 1–5 p.m. (Seats 26; 450 readers served per month).
Interlibrary Loan Available.
Reproduction Facility: photocopy; quickcopy.

Tucson

23. ARIZONA HISTORICAL SOCIETY/ARIZONA HERITAGE CENTER
Research Library
Map Section
949 East Second Street
Tucson, AZ 85719
Established 1884.
Telephone: 602/628-5774, ext. 9.
Contact Person: Jean S. Bock, Map Libn.
Staff: 1 professional (full time); 1 non-professional (part time).
Size: 3,000 maps.
Annual Accessions: 50 atlases.
Area Specialization: Arizona; southwestern United States; northern Mexico.
Subject Specialization: historical mines, missions and military.
Dates: pre-1800 (15%); 1800-1899 (75%); 1900 - (10%).
Classification System: local system; area subject headings.
Collections Cataloged. (80%).
Serves: public. Mon.–Fri. 10 a.m.–4 p.m.; Sat. 10 a.m.–1 p.m. (Seats 35; maybe 50 for maps readers served per month).
Reproduction Facility: photocopy; microform.

24. UNIVERSITY OF ARIZONA
Bureau of Geology and Mineral Technology
845 North Park Ave.
Tucson, AZ 85719
Established 1915.
Telephone: 602/621-7906.
Contact Person: Tom McGarvin, Research Assistant.
Staff: 2 professional (part time).
Size: 9,700 maps.
Area Specialization: Arizona and adjacent states.
Subject Specialization: geology; mines and mining; metallurgy.
Dates: 1800-1899 (10%); 1900 - (90%).
Classification System: USGS library system.
Collections not Cataloged.
Depository for: USGS (Geol., topo.).
Serves: students; faculty; public. Mon.–Fri. 8 a.m.–5 p.m. (Seats 6; 50 readers served per month).
Reproduction Facility: photocopy; microform.

25. UNIVERSITY OF ARIZONA
University Library
Map Collection
Tucson, AZ 85721
Established 1955.
Telephone: 602/621-2596.
Contact Person: James O. Minton, Head Map Libn.
Staff: 3 professional (full time); 1 non-professional (full time); 5 non-professional (part time).
Size: 165,000 maps; 2,000 atlases; 13 globes; 60 relief models; 16,331 aerial photographs; 1,300 reference books and gazetteers; 55 serials (titles received); 23 microforms (no. of titles).
Annual Accessions: 6,100 maps; 150 atlases; 1 globes; 100 reference books and gazetteers.

Area Specialization: Arizona; southwestern United States; Mexico.
Subject Specialization: topography; geology; mineral resources; history of the Southwest.
Special Cartographic Collections: Landsat: approx. 2,126 reels of 70 mm. negative film, providing complete coverage of land surfaces of the earth, images taken primarily between 1975 and 1977.
Dates: 1800-1899 (.5%); 1900 - (99.5%).
Classification System: LC.
Collections Cataloged. (100%).
Depository for: DMA; USGS (Geol., topo.).
Serves: students; faculty; employees; public;. Mon.–Fri. 8 a.m.–5 p.m.; Sat. 9 a.m.–1 p.m. (Seats 26; 600 readers served per month).
Interlibrary Loan Available.
Reproduction Facility: photocopy.
Publications: *UA Map News Monthly.*

ARKANSAS

Conway

26. UNIVERSITY OF CENTRAL ARKANSAS
Torreyson Library
Map Library
Conway, AR 72032
Telephone: 501/450-3164.
Contact Person: Paul L. Butt, Assistant Professor, Dept. of Geography.
Staff: 2 non-professional (part time).
Size: Estimate: 100,000 maps.
Area Specialization: United States.
Subject Specialization: topography.
Dates: 1900 - (100%).
Classification System: local system.
Collections Cataloged. (100%).
Depository for: USGS (Topo.).
Serves: students; faculty; employees; public. (Seats 6; about 50 readers served per month).

Fayetteville

27. UNIVERSITY OF ARKANSAS—UNIVERSITY LIBRARY
Reference Department
Map Collection
University of Arkansas
Fayetteville, AR 72701
Established 1975.
Telephone: 501/575-6645.
Contact Person: Alberta S. Bailey, Reference Libn.; Janet Dixon, Map Assistant.
Staff: 3 professional (part time); 2 non-professional (part time).
Size: 104,000 maps; 130 atlases; 1 globes; 6 relief models; 70 reference books and gazetteers; 1 serials (titles received); 510 microforms (no. of titles).
Annual Accessions: 3,500 maps.
Area Specialization: United States; Arkansas and surrounding states; continents and countries.
Subject Specialization: topography; geology; political.
Dates: 1800-1899 (10%); 1900 - (90%).
Classification System: LC.
Collections Cataloged. (90%).
Depository for: DMA; NOS; USGS (Geol., topo.); NOAA, CB, SCS, NFS, BLM, CIA, FEMA.

Serves: students; faculty; employees; public. Mon.–Thur. 7 a.m.–11 p.m.; Fri. 7 a.m.–6 p.m.; Sat. 9 a.m.–6 p.m.; Sun. 10 a.m.–11 p.m. (Seats 52; 100 readers served per month).
Reproduction Facility: photocopy.
Publications: *Map Collection Resource Guide—University of Arkansas Library* (guide).

State University

28. ARKANSAS STATE UNIVERSITY
Dean B. Ellis Library
Arkansas Room
P. O. Box 2040
State University, AR 72467
Telephone: 501/972-3077.
Contact Person: Kevin L. Cook, Documents Libn.
Staff: 1 professional (part time); 1 non-professional (part time).
Size: 800 maps.
Annual Accessions: 175 maps.
Area Specialization: Arkansas.
Dates: 1800-1899 (2%); 1900 - (98%).
Collections not Cataloged.
Depository for: USGS (Topo.).
Serves: students; faculty; employees; public;. Mon.–Fri. 7:30 a.m.–4:30 p.m.; Sat. By special arrangement; Sun. By special arrangement. (Seats 20; 25 readers served per month).
Reproduction Facility: photocopy.

CALIFORNIA

Arcata

29. HUMBOLDT STATE UNIVERSITY
Library
Map Collection
Arcata, CA 95521
Established 1965.
Telephone: 707/826-3416.
Contact Person: Robert L. Sathrum, Science Reference Libn.
Staff: 1 professional (part time); 1 non-professional (part time).
Size: 13,664 maps; 420 atlases; 3 globes; 25 relief models; 7,000 aerial photographs; 2 microforms (no. of titles).
Annual Accessions: 1,000 maps; 30 atlases.
Area Specialization: northwestern California.
Subject Specialization: natural resources; oceanography.
Dates: pre-1800 (less than 1%); 1800-1899 (less than 1%); 1900 - (99%). .
Classification System: LC.
Collections Cataloged. (15%).
Depository for: DMA; NOS; USGS (Geol., topo.).
Serves: students; faculty; employees; public. Mon.–Thurs. 7:30 a.m.–10 p.m.; Fri. 7:30 a.m.–5 p.m.; Sat. 1–5 p.m.; Sun. 1–10 p.m.
Interlibrary Loan Available.
Reproduction Facility: photocopy; microform.
Publications: *Atlas and Map Collection* (guide).

Bakersfield

30. KERN COUNTY LIBRARY
Reference Department
Geology-Mining-Petroleum Collection
1315 Truxtun Avenue
Bakersfield, CA 93301
Established 1945.
Telephone: 805/861-2136.
Contact Person: Mary Haas, Geology-Mining-Petroleum Libn.
Staff: 1 professional (part time).
Size: 8,121 maps.
Annual Accessions: 140 maps.
Area Specialization: California and western states.
Subject Specialization: topography (California); geology (California, western states).
Dates: 1900 - (100%).
Classification System: arranged by state and quadrangle name.
Collections not Cataloged.
Depository for: California Division of Mines and Geology.
Serves: public. Mon.—Thurs. 10 a.m.–9 p.m., Fri. 10 a.m.–6 p.m.; Sat. 10 a.m.–6 p.m. (Seats 10; 60 readers served per month).
Reproduction Facility: photocopy.

Berkeley

31. BERKELEY PUBLIC LIBRARY
Reference Department
2090 Kittredge
Berkeley, CA 94704
Established 1930.
Telephone: 415/644-6648.
Contact Person: Robert Saunderson, Reference Libn.
Staff: 1 professional (part time); 1 non-professional (part time).
Size: 7,000 maps; 280 atlases; 2 globes; 3 relief models; 22 reference books and gazetteers; 4 serials (titles received).
Annual Accessions: 200 maps; 15 atlases; 5 reference books and gazetteers.
Area Specialization: California; United States city and urban maps.
Subject Specialization: urban planning.
Special Cartographic Collections: USGS topographical maps for California (nearly complete and current).
Dates: 1800-1899 (1%); 1900 - (99%).
Classification System: Dewey.
Collections not Cataloged.
Collections not Cataloged. ((books are).
Serves: public. Mon.–Thurs. 10 a.m.–8 p.m., closed Friday; Sat. 10 a.m.–6 p.m.; Sun. 1–5 p.m. (Seats 50).
Reproduction Facility: photocopy; microform.

32. UNIVERSITY OF CALIFORNIA, BERKELEY
The Bancroft Library
Berkeley, CA 94720
Established 1859.
Telephone: 415/642-4940.
Contact Person: Philip Hoehn, Map Libn.
Staff: 1 professional (part time); 1 non-professional (part time).
Size: 20,487 maps; 500 atlases; 6 globes; 9 aerial photographs; 500 reference books and gazetteers; 2 serials (titles received); 1,500 microforms (no. of titles).
Annual Accessions: 300–400 maps; 5–10 atlases; 0–1 globes; 0–3 aerial photographs; 5–10 reference books and gazetteers; 20 microforms (no. of titles).

Area Specialization: California; Mexico; western North America; Central America; selective worldwide coverage before 1800.
Subject Specialization: land grants; mines and minerals.
Special Cartographic Collections: California land grant (rancho) case maps (1,400 sketch maps and surveys of California ranchos on deposit from U.S. District Court of Northern California); Alfred H. DeVries geographical collection (old maps, atlases and geographical works); University Archives collection (116 maps of the Berkeley campus, 1866 to date); Charles W. Weber map collection (200 maps, primarily 19th century California).
Dates: pre-1800 (25%); 1800-1899 (55%); 1900 - (20%).
Classification System: LC.
Collections Cataloged.
Serves: students; faculty; employees; public;. Mon.–Fri. 9 a.m.–5 p.m.; Sat. 1–5 p.m. (Seats 50; 45 readers served per month).
Interlibrary Loan Available. Approximately 25 percent of the Bancroft Library's cartographic materials are now housed in the General Library's Map Room (these are non-rare items) where reference service, shelving & retrieving, etc. are done. Perhaps 10–20 Map Room patrons per month use these Bancroft materials in Map Room. Note: Re ILL: Photocopies and microcopies are available to California libraries and to research libraries elsewhere.

33. UNIVERSITY OF CALIFORNIA, BERKELEY
Department of Geography
Berkeley, CA 94720
Telephone: 415/642-3903.
Contact Person: Margaret K. Riddall, Laboratory Assistant.
Staff: 1 non-professional (part time).
Size: 8,000 maps; 40 atlases; 5 globes; 60 relief models; 1,500 aerial photographs; 20 reference books and gazetteers.
Area Specialization: California; western United States; Latin America.
Dates: 1800-1899 (5%); 1900 - (95%).
Classification System: local system. Mon.–Fri. 8 a.m.–5 p.m. (50 readers served per month).
Reproduction Facility: quickcopy.

34. UNIVERSITY OF CALIFORNIA, BERKELEY
East Asiatic Library of the General Library
Map Collection (of the East Asiatic Library)
Berkeley, CA 94720
Telephone: 415/642-2556.
Contact Person: Donald H. Shively, Head, East Asiatic Library.
Size: 2,305 maps; about 100 aerial photographs; 90 reference books and gazetteers; 1 serials (titles received).
Annual Accessions: 10 reference books and gazetteers.
Area Specialization: old Japanese maps of the world (63); East Asia (77); and Japan (2,165).
Subject Specialization: Japanese cities (1100).
Special Cartographic Collections: collection of old Japanese maps, remarkable for having 205 maps made before 1801, 499 from 1801–67, and 1,601 from 1868–1912, most of which date from before 1895. All maps are folded, mostly printed by woodblock, but some are manuscripts, and later maps are copperplate.
Dates: pre-1800 (10%); 1800-1899 (65%); 1900 - (25%).
Classification System: local system.
Collections Cataloged.
Serves: students; faculty; employees; public;. Mon.–Fri. 9 a.m.–5 p.m. (Seats 12; 4 readers served per month).
Reproduction Facility: photocopy; microform.

35. UNIVERSITY OF CALIFORNIA, BERKELEY
General Library
Earth Sciences Library
Berkeley, CA 94720
Telephone: 415/642-4940.
Contact Person: John Creaser.
Staff: 1 non-professional (part time).
Size: 38,739 maps; 65 atlases; 1 globes; 6 reference books and gazetteers.
Annual Accessions: 1,100 maps.
Area Specialization: western United States.
Subject Specialization: geology; topography.
Dates: 1900 - (99%).
Classification System: local system.
Depository for: USGS (Geol., topo.).
Serves: students; faculty; employees; public. Mon.–Fri. 9 a.m.–5 p.m.; Tues., Wed. 7–9 p.m.; Sat. 1–5 p.m.; Sun. 1–5 p.m. (Seats 5).
Reproduction Facility: photocopy; quickcopy; microform.

36. UNIVERSITY OF CALIFORNIA, BERKELEY
General Library
Map Room
Berkeley, CA 94720
Established 1917.
Telephone: 415/642-4940.
Contact Person: Philip Hoehn, Map Libn.
Staff: 2 non-professional (full time); 1 professional (part time).
Size: 237,772 maps; 1,000 atlases; 3 globes; 300 relief models; 21,593 aerial photographs; 2,300 reference books and gazetteers; 200 serials (titles received); 6,425 microforms (no. of titles).
Annual Accessions: 8,000 maps; 100 atlases; 0–1 globes; 3 relief models; 1,000–8,000 aerial photographs; 150 reference books and gazetteers; 5 serials (titles received); 1,000–2,300 microforms (no. of titles).
Area Specialization: worldwide, with emphasis on the United States, particularly California and the West; Mexico; Central America; Togo.
Subject Specialization: topography.
Dates: pre-1800 (.5%); 1800-1899 (4.5%); 1900 - (95%).
Classification System: LC.
Collections Cataloged.
Depository for: DMA; NOS; USGS (Topo.); GPO.
Serves: students; faculty; employees; public. Mon.–Fri. 10 a.m.–5 p.m.; Sat. 1–5 p.m. (Seats 14; 450 readers served per month).
Interlibrary Loan Available.
Reproduction Facility: photocopy; quickcopy; microform; Photographs, slides.

37. UNIVERSITY OF CALIFORNIA, BERKELEY
Water Resources Center Archives
410 O'Brien Hall
Berkeley, CA 94720
Established 1957.
Telephone: 415/642-2666.
Contact Person: Gerald J. Giefer, Libn.
Staff: 1 professional (full time); 2 non-professional (part time).
Size: 5,400 maps.
Annual Accessions: 275 maps.
Area Specialization: California; The West; United States.
Subject Specialization: water resources; irrigation development.
Dates: 1800-1899 (1%); 1900 - (99%).
Classification System: local system.
Collections Cataloged.
Serves: students; faculty; employees; public. Mon.–Fri. 8 a.m.–5 p.m. (Seats 20; 1,200 readers served per month).
Publications: *Dictionary Catalog of the Water Resources Center Archives* (1970–).

Chico

38. CALIFORNIA STATE UNIVERSITY, CHICO
Geography Department
Map Room
Butte Hall, Room 518
Chico, CA 95929
Established 1972.
Telephone: 916/895-5969 or 5285.
Contact Person: Charles Nelson, Cartographic Technician.
Staff: 1 professional (full time); 3 non-professional (part time).
Size: 14,788 maps; 15 atlases; 7 globes; 106 relief models; 5,250 aerial photographs; 6 serials (titles received).
Annual Accessions: 265 maps; 100 aerial photographs.
Area Specialization: northeastern California.
Dates: 1800-1899 (1%); 1900 - (99%).
Classification System: LC (modified).
Collections not Cataloged.
Serves: students; faculty; employees; public. Mon.–Fri. 8 a.m.–12 noon, 1–5 p.m. (except June and July). (Seats 6; 1,000 readers served per month).
Reproduction Facility: photocopy; quickcopy; Diazo.

39. CALIFORNIA STATE UNIVERSITY, CHICO
Meriam Library
Map Section
1st & Normal Streets
Chico, CA 95929
Established 1970.
Telephone: 916/895-6803.
Contact Person: Joe Crotts, Map Libn.
Staff: 1 professional (full time); 1/2 non-professional (part time).
Size: 100,000 maps; 275 atlases; 2 globes; 83 relief models; 106 aerial photographs; 325 reference books and gazetteers; 5 serials (titles received).
Annual Accessions: 2,000 maps; 25 atlases; 15 aerial photographs; 20 reference books and gazetteers.
Area Specialization: California; western United States.
Subject Specialization: geology; land use; vegetation; soils; local history.
Dates: 1800-1899 (1%); 1900 - (99%).
Classification System: LC.
Collections Cataloged.
Depository for: DMA; NOS; USGS (Geol., topo.).
Serves: students; faculty; employees; public. Mon.–Thurs. 8 a.m.–10 p.m.; Fri. 8 a.m.–5 p.m.; Sat. 1–5 p.m.; Sun. 1–5 p.m. (Seats 75; 300 readers served per month).
Interlibrary Loan Available.
Reproduction Facility: quickcopy.
Publications: *Geologic Map Index to 7.5' and 15' Quadrangles of California, 1883–1983; Index to the Defense Mapping Agency-Army Map Services Catalogs. 1976; University Map Newsletter.*

Claremont

40. CLAREMONT COLLEGES
Honnold Library
Government Publications
9th & Dartmouth
Claremont, CA 91711
Established 1974.
Telephone: 714/621-8000, ext. 3861.
Contact Person: Julia Jacinto, Department Head.
Staff: 1 professional (part time).
Subject Specialization: Topographic maps.
Depository for: DMA; USGS (Geol.).

Serves: students; faculty; employees; public. Mon.–Thurs. 8 a.m.–10 p.m., Fri. 8 a.m.–5 p.m.; Sat. 9 a.m.–5 p.m.; Sun. 1–10 p.m.
Reproduction Facility: photocopy.

Cupertino

41. SANTA CLARA COUNTY FREE LIBRARY
Central Research
10400 Torre Avenue
Cupertino, CA 95014
Telephone: 408/253-6212.
Contact Person: Victor Tung, Libn. II.
Staff: 1 professional (full time); professional (part time).
Size: 1,886 maps.
Annual Accessions: 250 maps.
Area Specialization: United States.
Dates: 1900 - (100%).
Classification System: local system.
Collections not Cataloged.
Depository for: USGS (Topo.).
Serves: public.
Reproduction Facility: photocopy.

Davis

42. UNIVERSITY OF CALIFORNIA, DAVIS
Peter J. Shields Memorial Library
Map Collection
Davis, CA 95616
Established 1966.
Telephone: 916/752-1624.
Contact Person: David Lundquist, Map Libn.
Staff: 1 professional (part time); 1 non-professional (part time).
Size: 90,000 maps; 1,700 atlases; 2 globes; 45 relief models; 20,000 aerial photographs; 150 reference books and gazetteers; 7,000 microforms (no. of titles).
Annual Accessions: 15,000 maps.
Area Specialization: western North America; world.
Subject Specialization: agricultural and biological sciences; soils; vegetation; climate; land use.
Classification System: LC.
Collections Cataloged. (33%).
Depository for: DMA; USGS (Geol., topo.).
Serves: students; faculty; employees; public. Mon.–Fri. 8 a.m.–5 p.m.; Sat. 1–5 p.m.; Sun. 1–5 p.m. (Seats 30; 2,000 readers served per month).
Interlibrary Loan Available.
Reproduction Facility: quickcopy.

Fresno

43. CALIFORNIA STATE UNIVERSITY, FRESNO
Henry Madden Library
Map Library
Fresno, CA 93740
Telephone: 209/294-2405.
Contact Person: Herbert S. Fox, Map Libn.
Staff: 1 professional (part time); 2 non-professional (part time).
Size: 103,000 maps; 550 atlases; 5 globes; 30 relief models; 1,200 aerial photographs; 220 reference books and gazetteers; 5 microforms (no. of titles).
Annual Accessions: 3,000 maps; 60 atlases; 50 aerial photographs; 4 reference books and gazetteers; 1 microforms (no. of titles).
Area Specialization: Central California.

Dates: 1900 - (99%).
Classification System: LC.
Collections not Cataloged.
Depository for: DMA; USGS (Geol., topo.).
Serves: students; faculty; employees; public. (Seats 28; 210 readers served per month).
Interlibrary Loan Available.
Reproduction Facility: photocopy.
Publications: *Atlas and Map Acquisitions (annual); A Guide to Research in Geography.*

Fullerton

44. CALIFORNIA STATE UNIVERSITY, FULLERTON
Department of Geography
Map Library
Fullerton, CA 92634
Established 1963.
Telephone: 714/773-3161, ext. 3161.
Contact Person: Laurie S. MacDonald, Map Curator.
Staff: non-professional (full time); 1 non-professional (part time).
Size: 26 atlases; 8 globes; approx. 62 relief models.
Area Specialization: California and Orange County.
Dates: 1900 - (nearly 100%).
Classification System: local system.
Collections Cataloged.
Depository for: DMA.
Serves: students; faculty; employees; public; Campuses. Tues. 1–4 p.m., Wed. 9 a.m.–12 noon, Fri. 9 a.m.–1 p.m. (Seats 8; varies readers served per month).
Reproduction Facility: photocopy.

45. CALIFORNIA STATE UNIVERSITY, FULLERTON
Library
Collection for the History of Cartography
P.O. Box 4150
Fullerton, CA 92634
Established Oct. 22, 1971.
Telephone: 714/773-2964.
Contact Person: Roy V. Boswell, Curator.
Staff: 1 professional (full time); 1 non-professional (part time).
Size: 1,450 maps; 180 atlases; 1,400 reference books and gazetteers; 15 serials (titles received).
Annual Accessions: 150 maps; 20 atlases; 75 reference books and gazetteers; 2 serials (titles received).
Area Specialization: world; Western Hemisphere; Pacific Basin; European origin of the Americas.
Dates: pre-1800 (90%); 1800-1899 (9%); 1900 - (1%).
Classification System: LC.
Collections Cataloged. ((books only)).
Serves: students; faculty; public. Mon.–Fri. 9 a.m.–12 noon, 1–5 p.m. (hours may vary; phone for appointment) (Seats 2).
Reproduction Facility: quickcopy.
Publications: *California & Other Early Maps illustrating the History of Cartography, 1375–1873 (o.p.); Noteworthy Maps & Charts A.D. 1513–1774; The Iberian Origin of the Americas, Maps & Charts A.D. 1513–1851; British Battle Plans, Maps and Charts of the American Revolutionary War, 1775–1793; Collection for the History of Cartography; The English Origin of the Americas, Maps & Charts 1486–1808; The Grand Ocean; The East and Cathay.*

Glendale

46. GLENDALE CENTRAL LIBRARY
Reference Section
222 East Harvard
Glendale, CA 91250
Established ca. 1930.
Telephone: 818/956-2027.
Contact Person: Margaret V. Peterson, Reference Libn.
Staff: 1 professional (part time); 1 non-professional (part time).
Size: 3,000 maps; 80 atlases; 3 relief models; 3 aerial photographs; 4 reference books and gazetteers.
Annual Accessions: 200 maps; 1 atlases; 1 reference books and gazetteers.
Area Specialization: Southern California.
Subject Specialization: topography.
Special Cartographic Collections: historical maps of the City of Glendale.
Dates: pre-1800 (1%); 1800-1899 (1%); 1900 - (98%).
Classification System: local system.
Collections Cataloged.
Serves: students; faculty; employees; public. Mon.–Thurs. 10 a.m.–9 p.m.; Fri 10 a.m.–6 p.m.; Sat. Sat. 10 a.m.–6 p.m. (Seats 8; 40 readers served per month).
Interlibrary Loan Available. (restricted)
Reproduction Facility: photocopy.

Irvine

47. UNIVERSITY OF CALIFORNIA AT IRVINE
University Libraries
Main Library
Irvine, CA 92717
Telephone: 714/856-6836.
Contact Person: Julia Gelfand, Reference Libn. & Bibliographer.
Size: 2,000 maps; 2,000 atlases; 6 globes; 50 relief models; 250 aerial photographs; 400 reference books and gazetteers; 40 serials (titles received).
Area Specialization: California.
Subject Specialization: topography.
Classification System: local system.
Collections not Cataloged.
Depository for: USGS (Geol., topo.).
Serves: students; faculty; employees; public;. Mon.–Fri. 8 a.m.–12 midnight; Sat. 10–5 p.m.; Sun. 1–10 p.m. (Seats 8).
Reproduction Facility: photocopy.

La Jolla

48. UNIVERSITY OF CALIFORNIA, SAN DIEGO
Central University Library
Map Section C-075P
La Jolla,, CA 92093
Established 1968.
Telephone: 619/452-3338.
Contact Person: Larry Cruse, Head.
Staff: 1 professional (part time); 1 non-professional (full time); 3 non-professional (part time).
Size: 156,026 maps; 36 atlases; 2 globes; 1,712 aerial photographs; 455 reference books and gazetteers; 3,858 microforms (no. of titles).

Annual Accessions: 6,000 maps; 200 aerial photographs; 50 reference books and gazetteers; 1,000 microforms (no. of titles).
Area Specialization: United States; Mexico; Latin America.
Dates: pre-1800 (2%); 1800-1899 (8%); 1900 - (90%).
Classification System: LC.
Collections Cataloged. (100%).
Depository for: DMA; NOS; USGS (Geol., topo.); Automobile Club of Southern California; California State Automobile Club.
Serves: students; faculty; employees; public. Mon.–Fri. 8 a.m.–10 p.m.; Sat. 9 a.m–5 p.m.; Sun. 12 noon–10 p.m. (Seats 40; 300 readers served per month).
Interlibrary Loan Available.
Reproduction Facility: photocopy; microform.

49. UNIVERSITY OF CALIFORNIA, SAN DIEGO
Scripps Institution of Oceanography Library
Map Collection C-075C
La Jolla, California 92093
Established 1962.
Telephone: 619/452-3274.
Contact Person: Paul M. Leverenz, Map Collection Manager.
Size: 52,270 maps; 500 atlases; 2 globes.
Area Specialization: Charts: Global, emphasis on Pacific; Maps: Global, emphasis on N. & S. America.
Subject Specialization: oceanography and earth sciences.
Special Cartographic Collections: Nautical charts of global oceans by United States (NOS & DMA) and 36 foreign hydrographic agencies. Topographic and geologic maps of U.S., Mexico, Central and South America.
Dates: 1900 - (100%).
Classification System: LC.
Collections not Cataloged.
Depository for: NOS.
Serves: students; faculty; employees; public. Mon.–Fri. 8 a.m.–4 p.m.
Reproduction Facility: quickcopy.

Lodi

50. SAN JOAQUIN COUNTY HISTORICAL MUSEUM
11793 N. Micke Grove Road, P.O. Box 21
Lodi, CA 95240
Established 1968.
Telephone: 209/368-9154.
Contact Person: Debbie Mastel, Registrar.
Staff: 1 non-professional (part time).
Size: 300 maps; 400 aerial photographs.
Annual Accessions: 1–10 maps.
Area Specialization: San Joaquin County, California.
Subject Specialization: agriculture; urban development; reclamation; transportation.
Dates: 1900 -.
Classification System: local system.
Collections Cataloged. (50%).
Depository for: San Joaquin County.
Serves: public. Mon.–Fri. 8–5 (by appointment). (Seats 4; 3 readers served per month).
Reproduction Facility: quickcopy.

Long Beach

51. CALIFORNIA STATE UNIVERSITY, LONG BEACH
Department of Geography
Map Center
1250 Bellflower Blvd.
Long Beach, CA 90840
Telephone: 213/498-4977.
Contact Person: Rodney Steiner, Department Chairperson.
Staff: 1 non-professional (part time).
Size: 50,000 maps; 30 atlases; 5 globes; 10 relief models; 1,000 aerial photographs; 200 reference books and gazetteers.
Annual Accessions: 100 maps.
Area Specialization: Southern California; California; United States.
Subject Specialization: topography.
Dates: 1900 - (100%).
Classification System: DMA.
Collections Cataloged. (80%).
Depository for: DMA.
Serves: students; faculty; employees; public. (Seats 8; 30 readers served per month).

52. CALIFORNIA STATE UNIVERSITY, LONG BEACH
Library and Learning Resources
Reference and Instructional Services - Map Room
6101 East 7th Street
Long Beach, CA 90840
Telephone: 213/498-4026.
Staff: 1 professional (part time); 1 non-professional (part time).
Size: 22,544 maps; 550 atlases; 4 globes; 45 relief models; 350 aerial photographs; 400 reference books and gazetteers; 70 serials (titles received).
Annual Accessions: 2,000 maps; 30 atlases; 50 reference books and gazetteers.
Area Specialization: California; Arizona; Utah.
Subject Specialization: topography; geology.
Dates: 1900 -.
Classification System: LC.
Collections Cataloged.
Depository for: California Div. of Mines & Geology; U.S. Bureau of the Census.
Serves: students; faculty; employees; public. Mon.–Fri. 8 a.m.–9 p.m.; Sat. 9 a.m.–5 p.m.; Sun. 1 p.m.–9 p.m. (Seats 20; 250 readers served per month).
Reproduction Facility: photocopy.

53. LONG BEACH PUBLIC LIBRARY
Science and Technology Department
101 Pacific Avenue
Long Beach, CA 90802
Telephone: 213/437-2949.
Contact Person: Charles S. Vestal, General Libn. II.
Staff: 1 professional (part time).
Size: 10 atlases; 3 globes; 3 reference books and gazetteers.
Annual Accessions: 100 maps.
Area Specialization: California.
Subject Specialization: petroleum.
Special Cartographic Collections: have maps in a historical collection of Petroleum industry in California.
Dates: 1900 - (100%).
Collections not Cataloged.
Depository for: NOS; USGS (Topo.).
Serves: public. Mon. 10 a.m.–8 p.m.; Tues.–Fri. 10 a.m.–5:30 p.m.; Sat. 10 a.m.–5:30 p.m.; Sun. 1:30–5 p.m. (20 readers served per month).
Reproduction Facility: photocopy.

Los Angeles

54. CALIFORNIA STATE UNIVERSITY, LOS ANGELES
Geography Map Library
5151 State University Drive
Los Angeles, CA 90032
Telephone: 213/224-3851.
Contact Person: Dr. Vincent G. Mazzucchelli, Faculty Map Room Coordinator.
Staff: 4 non-professional (part time).
Size: 45,000 maps; 270 atlases; 5 globes; 55 relief models; 5,000 aerial photographs; 475 reference books and gazetteers; 9 serials (titles received); 50 microforms (no. of titles).
Annual Accessions: 300 maps.
Area Specialization: California; western United States.
Subject Specialization: geography.
Dates: 1800-1899 (2%); 1900 - (98%).
Classification System: LC modified.
Collections Cataloged. (100%).
Depository for: DMA; USGS (Topo.).
Serves: students; faculty; employees; public. Mon.–Thurs. 9 a.m.–6 p.m. (Seats 18).
Reproduction Facility: photocopy; quickcopy.

55. LOS ANGELES DEPARTMENT OF PUBLIC WORKS
Street Opening and Widening Division
Historical Map Section
200 N. Main St., Room 755 (Stop 901)
Los Angeles, CA 90012
Established Oct. 1969.
Telephone: 213/485-3034.
Contact Person: Bernice Kimball, Cartographer.
Staff: 1 professional (full time).
Size: 1,250 microforms (no. of titles).
Annual Accessions: 50 microforms (no. of titles).
Area Specialization: original city (pueblo) prior to 1940; L.A. county-wide maps; city-wide maps of Los Angeles.
Subject Specialization: City of Los Angeles, its public works, and ownerships; special attention to change in contours of the land.
Special Cartographic Collections: Official City Maps, 1849 to 1900—723 titles, microform.
Dates: 1800-1899 (69%); 1900 - (31%).
Classification System: By date, showing location and 21 categories of information.
Collections Cataloged. (100%).
Serves: students; employees; public. Mon.–Fri. 7:30 a.m.–4:15 p.m. (Seats 1; 10 readers served per month).
Reproduction Facility: quickcopy; microform; Photo reproduction by special order.
Publications: *Index to Historical Maps of Greater Los Angeles* (April 1983).

56. LOS ANGELES PUBLIC LIBRARY
History Dept.
Map Room
630 West 5th Street
Los Angeles, CA 90071
Established 1926.
Telephone: 213/626-7461, ext. 314, 311.
Contact Person: Dorothy R. Mewshaw, Map Libn.
Staff: 1 professional (part time); 1 non-professional (part time).
Size: 75,000 maps; 1,500 atlases; 1 globes; 6 relief models; 20 aerial photographs; 1,500 reference books and gazetteers; 10 serials (titles received); 200 microforms (no. of titles).
Annual Accessions: 3,400 maps; 75–100 atlases.
Area Specialization: Los Angeles; California.
Subject Specialization: topography; history; cultural geography.

Special Cartographic Collections: Defense Mapping (worldwide topographic maps); U.S.G.S. topographic maps (U.S. topo); U.S. National Ocean Survey charts (U.S. coastal waters).
Dates: pre-1800 (less than 1%); 1800-1899 (less than 1%); 1900 - (99%).
Classification System: Dewey.
Depository for: DMA; NOS; USGS (Topo.).
Serves: public. Mon, Wed., Fri., 10–5:30; Tues., Thurs., 12–8; Sat. 10–5:30.
Reproduction Facility: photocopy.

57. UNIVERSITY OF CALIFORNIA, LOS ANGELES
Geology-Geophysics Library
William C. Putnam Map Room
4697 Geology Bldg., UCLA
Los Angeles, CA 90024
Telephone: 213/825-1055.
Contact Person: Sara E. How, Head, Geology-Geophysics Library.
Staff: 1 non-professional (part time).
Size: 100,000 maps; 31 relief models.
Area Specialization: California; Nevada.
Subject Specialization: geology; geothermal resources; economic geology; structural geology; flood zones; gravity and magnetics.
Dates: 1900 - (100%).
Collections not Cataloged.
Depository for: USGS (Geol., topo.).
Serves: students; faculty; employees; public. Mon.–Fri. 8 a.m.–5 p.m. (by request).

58. UNIVERSITY OF CALIFORNIA, LOS ANGELES
Library
Map Library
Los Angeles, CA 90265
Established 1957.
Telephone: 213/825-3526.
Contact Person: Carlos B. Hagen, Director.
Staff: 1 professional (full time); 3 non-professional (full time).
Size: 507,097 maps; 2,550 atlases; 4 globes; 61 relief models; 10,424 aerial photographs; 5,566 reference books and gazetteers; 311 serials (titles received); 38 microforms (no. of titles).
Annual Accessions: 9–11,000 maps; 60 atlases; 100 aerial photographs; 180 reference books and gazetteers; 2 serials (titles received); 5 microforms (no. of titles).
Area Specialization: Latin America; Pacific Ocean; Near East; California.
Subject Specialization: computer cartography; map projections; city plans.
Special Cartographic Collections: city plans from all cities, especially from the last 100 years to the present.
Dates: 1800-1899 (20%); 1900 - (80%).
Classification System: LC.
Collections not Cataloged.
Depository for: DMA; DOS (Gt. Brit); GSC; NOS; NTS (Canada); USGS (Geol., topo.); New Zealand, Australia.
Serves: students; faculty; employees; public. Mon.–Fri. 10 a.m.–3 p.m. (Seats 6; 500 readers served per month).
Interlibrary Loan Available.
Reproduction Facility: photocopy.
Publications: *UCLA Map Library Newsletter and Selected Acquisitions* (2 times a year).

59. UNIVERSITY OF CALIFORNIA, LOS ANGELES
University Research Library
Department of Special Collections
Los Angeles, CA 90024
Established 1951.
Telephone: 213/825-4879.
Contact Person: Hilda Bohem, Libn.

Staff: 1 professional (part time).
Size: 2,200 maps; 100 atlases.
Annual Accessions: 10–15 maps.
Area Specialization: world; California; Pacific Coast.
Subject Specialization: history; land use; water resources.
Special Cartographic Collections: Stuart de Rothesay collection of continental maps, *ca.* 1715–1840; Pamphlet map collection, chiefly California and the West; Japanese map collection, 1616–1896; Pacific voyages and exploration.
Dates: pre-1800 (50%); 1800-1899 (45%); 1900 - (5%).
Classification System: LC; local system: maps are given unique collection numbers and are. listed in a finding guide; flat maps are cataloged by a system established by Harlow and Horn
Collections Cataloged.
Serves: students; faculty; employees; public. Mon.–Fri. 9 a.m.–5 p.m.; Sat. 9 a.m.–5 p.m. (Seats 12–15; 2–3 readers served per month).
Reproduction Facility: photocopy; quickcopy.

Menlo Park

60. U.S. GEOLOGICAL SURVEY
Library
345 Middlefield Road
Menlo Park, CA 94025
Established 1955.
Telephone: 415/323-8111, ext. 2208.
Contact Person: Eleanore E. Wilkins, Libn.
Staff: 4 professional (full time); 6 non-professional (full time); 5 non-professional (part time).
Size: 66,000 maps; 80 atlases; 3 globes; 25 relief models; 12,000 aerial photographs; 600 reference books and gazetteers; 50 serials (titles received).
Area Specialization: western United States; Pacific Basin.
Subject Specialization: geology; geophysics; hydrology; seismology; geomorphology; mineral resources.
Dates: 1800-1899 (10%); 1900 - (90%).
Classification System: USGS.
Collections Cataloged.
Depository for: USGS (Geol., topo.).
Serves: employees; public. Mon.–Fri. 7:45 a.m.–4:15 p.m. (Seats 20; 2,700 readers served per month).
Interlibrary Loan Available.
Reproduction Facility: photocopy.

Northridge

61. CALIFORNIA STATE UNIVERSITY, NORTHRIDGE
Department of Geography Map Library
18111 Nordhoff Street
Northridge, CA 91330
Established 1962.
Telephone: 818/885-3465.
Contact Person: Michael Swift, Map Curator.
Staff: 2 professional (full time).
Size: 350,000 maps; 900 atlases; 25 globes; 150 relief models; 30,000 aerial photographs; 2,500 reference books and gazetteers; 30 serials (titles received); 180 microforms (no. of titles).
Annual Accessions: 6,000 maps.
Area Specialization: United States; Canada; Western Hemisphere.
Subject Specialization: topography; geology.
Special Cartographic Collections: 145,000 Sanborn fire insurance maps dating from the early 1880's to the early 1960's (large-scale maps detailing building structures).
Dates: 1800-1899 (10%); 1900 - (90%).
Classification System: LC.
Collections not Cataloged.

Depository for: DMA; NTS (Canada); USGS (Geol., topo.).
Serves: students; faculty; employees; public. Mon.–Fri. 8:00 a.m.–5:00 p.m. (Seats 12; 500 readers served per month).

Oakland

62. OAKLAND PUBLIC LIBRARY
History & Literature Section
125-14th Street
Oakland, CA 94612
Telephone: 415/273-3136.
Contact Person: Donald Hausler, Libn.
Size: 75,000 maps; 50 atlases; 2 globes; 2 relief models; 100 aerial photographs; 100 reference books and gazetteers.
Annual Accessions: 3,000 maps; 5 atlases.
Area Specialization: Oakland; Alameda County; California.
Special Cartographic Collections: historical maps of Oakland, Alameda County, and California; U.S.G.S. maps (7.5 min. & 15 min.) of every state; maps published by Army Map Service and Defense Mapping Agency.
Dates: pre-1800 (1%); 1800-1899 (1%); 1900 - (98%).
Classification System: Dewey; DMA.
Collections Cataloged.
Depository for: DMA; USGS (Topo.).
Serves: public. Mon. 12 noon–8:30 p.m., Tues.–Thurs., 10 a.m.–8:30 p.m.; Fri., 10 a.m.–5; Sat. 10 a.m.–5:30 p.m. (Seats 60; 200 readers served per month).
Interlibrary Loan Available.
Reproduction Facility: photocopy.

Palo Alto

63. PALO ALTO CITY LIBRARY
1213 Newell Road
Palo Alto, CA 94303
Telephone: 415/329-2664.
Contact Person: Karen Rollin-Duffy.
Collections not Cataloged.
Depository for: USGS (Topo.).
Serves: public. Mon.–Fri. 10 a.m.–9 p.m.; Sat. 10 a.m.–6 p.m.; Sun. 1–5 p.m. (Seats 100+).
Reproduction Facility: photocopy.

Pasadena

64. CALIFORNIA INSTITUTE OF TECHNOLOGY
Division of Geological and Planetary Sciences 170-25
Geology Map Room
Pasadena, CA 91125
Established 1950.
Telephone: 213/356-6699.
Contact Person: Daphne Plane, Geology Libn.
Staff: 1 non-professional (part time).
Subject Specialization: geology; topography.
Collections Cataloged. ((geology maps only)).
Depository for: USGS (Geol., topo.); Australia; certain US state surveys.
Serves: students; faculty; employees; public. Mon.–Fri. 8 a.m.–12; 1–5 p.m. (60 readers served per month).
Reproduction Facility: quickcopy.

65. PASADENA PUBLIC LIBRARY
285 East Walnut Street
Pasadena, CA 91101
Telephone: 213/405-4054.
Contact Person: Mary Anne Hardy.
Staff: 1 professional (part time).

Size: 3,000 maps; 175 atlases; 1 relief models; 175 aerial photographs; 250 reference books and gazetteers.
Area Specialization: Pasadena and San Gabriel Valley, California.
Subject Specialization: local history.
Dates: 1800-1899 (10%); 1900 - (90%).
Depository for: USGS (Topo.); California State publications.
Serves: public. Mon.–Thurs. 9 a.m.–9 p.m.; Fri. 9 a.m.–6 p.m.; Sat. 9 a.m.–6 p.m.
Interlibrary Loan Available.
Reproduction Facility: photocopy.

Pleasant Hill

66. CONTRA COSTA COUNTY LIBRARY
Documents Section
1750 Oak Park Blvd.
Pleasant Hill, CA 94523
Established 1966.
Telephone: 415/944-3434.
Contact Person: Carmen Miller, Documents Libn.
Staff: 1 professional (full time); 1 non-professional (full time).
Size: 3,600 maps.
Annual Accessions: 200 maps.
Area Specialization: California; United States.
Subject Specialization: topography.
Dates: 1800-1899 (5%); 1900 - (95%).
Classification System: local system; alphabetical by series or type.
Collections not Cataloged.
Depository for: USGS (Topo.).
Serves: public. Mon.–Thurs. 10 a.m.–9 p.m.; Fri. 10 a.m.–6 p.m.; Sat. 10 a.m.–6 p.m. (Seats 40; 100 readers served per month).
Reproduction Facility: photocopy.

Pomona

67. POMONA PUBLIC LIBRARY
625 South Garey Avenue
Pomona, CA 91766
Telephone: Reference 714/620-2043; Special Collections 714/620-2026.
Contact Person: topographic maps: David Streeter, Supervisor, Special Collections; general maps: Garey Christmas, Libn. I.
Size: 4,000 maps; 70 atlases; 1 globes; 175 aerial photographs; 98 reference books and gazetteers; 1 serials (titles received).
Area Specialization: California.
Subject Specialization: topography.
Dates: 1900 - (100%).
Classification System: alphabetical.
Collections not Cataloged.
Depository for: USGS (Topo.).
Serves: students; faculty; employees; public;. Mon., Tues. 10 a.m.–9 p.m.; Wed. & Thurs. 10 a.m.–6 p.m.; Fri. 10 a.m.–5 p; Sat. 12 noon–5 p.m. (Seats 420; few readers served per month).
Interlibrary Loan Available.
Reproduction Facility: quickcopy.

Redlands

68. UNIVERSITY OF REDLANDS
Armacost Library
James Irvine Foundation Map Library
1200 E. Colton Avenue
Redlands, CA 92374
Established 1970.
Telephone: 714/793-2121, ext. 472.
Contact Person: Lynne Reasoner, Reference Services Libn.
Staff: 1 professional (part time); 1 non-professional (part time).
Size: 14,750 maps; 11 globes; 35 aerial photographs.
Annual Accessions: 675 maps.
Area Specialization: California; Arizona; Nevada; Oregon.
Dates: 1900 - (100%).
Classification System: LC.
Collections Cataloged. (10%).
Depository for: USGS (Topo.).
Serves: students; faculty; employees; public. Mon.–Thurs. 8 a.m.–10 p.m.; Fri. 8 a.m.–5 p.m. (Summer. hours: M–F 8 a.m.–5 p.m.) Sat. 10 a.m.–5 p.m.; 8–1 p.m.); Sun. 1 p.m.–10 p.m. Closed in summer months. (Seats 16).
Reproduction Facility: photocopy; microform.

Richmond

69. RICHMOND PUBLIC LIBRARY
Reference Division
Documents
Civil Center Plaza
Richmond, CA 94804
Telephone: 415/231-2125.
Contact Person: J. Berg, Documents Libn.; G. Miller, Pamphlet Libn.
Staff: 2 professional (part time); 1 non-professional (part time).
Size: 2,500 maps; 100 atlases; 40 reference books and gazetteers.
Area Specialization: California.
Subject Specialization: topography.
Classification System: Dewey.
Collections Cataloged.
Depository for: USGS (Topo.).
Serves: public. Mon.–Wed. 9 a.m.–9 p.m.; Thurs.–Fri. 9 a.m.–6 p.m.; Sat. 9–6 p.m.; Sun. 2–5 p.m.
Reproduction Facility: photocopy.

Riverside

70. UNIVERSITY OF CALIFORNIA, RIVERSIDE
Department of Earth Sciences
Map Collection
Riverside, CA 92521
Telephone: 714/787-3434.
Contact Person: Dr. Peter M. Sadler, Associate Professor of Geology.
Staff: 1 non-professional (part time).
Size: over 10,000 maps; 90 atlases; 140 relief models; over 1,000 aerial photographs.
Annual Accessions: 100 maps; 2 atlases.
Area Specialization: Southern California; Baja California; Nevada.
Subject Specialization: geology; topography.
Special Cartographic Collections: wall charts—250, cloth mounted, hanging, teaching maps.
Dates: 1800-1899 (1%); 1900 - (99%).
Collections Cataloged. (50%).
Serves: students; faculty. (25 readers served per month).

71. UNIVERSITY OF CALIFORNIA, RIVERSIDE
Library
Government Publications Department
P.O. Box 5900
Riverside, CA 92517
Telephone: 714/787-3226.
Contact Person: James Rothenberger, Head, Government Publications Department.
Size: 75,000 maps; 2,000 atlases; 500 reference books and gazetteers.
Classification System: LC.
Depository for: DMA; USGS (Topo.).
Serves: students; faculty; employees; public.

72. UNIVERSITY OF CALIFORNIA, RIVERSIDE
Physical Sciences Library
Riverside, CA 92517
Established 1960.
Telephone: 714/787-3511 or 3512.
Contact Person: Dick Vierich, Head Libn.; Carol Resco, Reference Libn.
Staff: 2 professional (full time); 4 non-professional (full time).
Size: 15,000+ maps.
Annual Accessions: 1,000 maps.
Area Specialization: western US-especially southern California; Arizona; Nevada.
Subject Specialization: geology; soil surveys.
Dates: 1900 - (99%).
Classification System: local system.
Depository for: USGS (Geol.); USGS open file reports on microfiche.
Serves: students; faculty; employees; public;. Mon.–Thurs. 8 a.m.–10 p.m.; Fri. 8 a.m.–8 p.m.; Sat. 1–6 p.m.; Sun. 1–10 p.m.
Interlibrary Loan Available.
Reproduction Facility: photocopy; microform.
Publications: Computer catalog—area, subject, author, series.

Sacramento

73. CALIFORNIA STATE ARCHIVES
1020 O Street, Room 130
Sacramento, CA 95814
Telephone: 916/445-4293.
Contact Person: John Burns, Chief of Archives.
Staff: 6 professional (full time); 8 non-professional (full time).
Size: 18,000 maps; 2,500 aerial photographs; 500 reference books and gazetteers.
Area Specialization: California.
Subject Specialization: history.
Special Cartographic Collections: Official records of state agencies.
Dates: 1800-1899 (10%); 1900 - (90%).
Classification System: Arranged by state agency (record group).
Collections Cataloged.
Depository for: California State agencies.
Serves: public. Mon.–Fri. 8 a.m.–5 p.m.
Reproduction Facility: quickcopy.

74. CALIFORNIA STATE LANDS COMMISSION
1807 13th Street
Sacramento, CA 95814
Contact Person: Roy Minnick, Senior Boundary Determination Officer.
Staff: 1 professional (full time); 1 professional (part time).
Size: 25,000 maps.
Annual Accessions: 300 maps.

Area Specialization: California.
Subject Specialization: boundary studies.
Dates: 1800-1899 (50%); 1900 - (50%).
Classification System: local system.
Collections Cataloged.
Serves: students; faculty; employees; public. Mon.–Fri. 9 a.m.–4 p.m. (Seats 10; 50 readers served per month).
Reproduction Facility: photocopy; quickcopy.
Publications: Guide to Hydrographic and Topographic Charts along the Coast of California; 2) Research Guide to Mexican and Spanish Land Grants in California.

75. CALIFORNIA STATE LIBRARY
Government Publications Section
P.O. Box 2037
Sacramento, CA 95809
Telephone: 916/322-4572.
Contact Person: Thomas K. Andersen, Head, Government Publications Section.
Staff: 6 professional (full time); 10 non-professional (full time); 1 professional (part time); 3 non-professional (part time).
Size: 100,000 maps; 150 atlases; 2 globes; 60 relief models.
Annual Accessions: 5,000 maps; 5 atlases; 1 relief models.
Area Specialization: California.
Dates: 1800-1899 (25%); 1900 - (75%).
Classification System: LC; Superintentent of Documents.
Collections Cataloged.
Depository for: USGS (Geol., topo.).
Classification System: Superintentent of Documents.
Serves: public. Mon.–Fri. 8 a.m.–5 p.m. (Seats 12; 50 readers served per month).
Reproduction Facility: quickcopy; Photostats (fee basis).

San Bernardino

76. CALIFORNIA STATE COLLEGE AT SAN BERNARDINO
Pfau Library
5500 State College Parkway
San Bernardino, CA 92407
Telephone: 714/887-7320.
Contact Person: Buckley Barrett, Asst. Head, Materials Services.
Staff: 1 professional (full time); 2 non-professional (full time).
Size: 12,845 maps.
Annual Accessions: 1,000 maps.
Area Specialization: California.
Subject Specialization: topography; navigation.
Dates: 1900 - (100%).
Classification System: LC.
Depository for: DMA; USGS (Geol., topo.).
Serves: students; faculty; public. Mon.–Thurs. 8 a.m.–10 p.m., Fri. 8 a.m.–5 p.m.; Sat. 9 a.m.–5 p.m.; Sun. 12 noon–8 p.m. (Seats 10).

San Diego

77. COUNTY OF SAN DIEGO
Department of Public Works
Survey Records—MS 0336
5555 Overland Avenue
San Diego, CA 92123
Telephone: 619/565-5404.
Contact Person: Charles F. Hartjen, Engineering Technician II.

Staff: 3 professional (full time); 1 non-professional (part time).
Size: 20,000 maps; 20,000 aerial photographs; 60,000 microforms (no. of titles).
Area Specialization: San Diego County.
Subject Specialization: subdivisions; parcel maps; records of survey; Government surveys; improvement plans; topographic maps; road surveys.
Dates: 1800-1899 (10%); 1900 - (90%).
Classification System: local system.
Collections Cataloged. (90%).
Serves: employees; public. Mon.–Fri. 8:00 a.m.–5:00 p.m. (Seats 6; 400 readers served per month).
Reproduction Facility: photocopy; microform.

78. SAN DIEGO PUBLIC LIBRARY
California Room
820 E Street
San Diego, CA 92101
Established 1882.
Telephone: 619/236-5834.
Contact Person: Rhoda E. Kruse, Senior Libn.
Size: 550 maps; 50 atlases; 6 aerial photographs; 20 reference books and gazetteers; 1 serials (titles received).
Annual Accessions: 6 maps; 2–3 atlases.
Area Specialization: San Diego City and County; California; Baja California; western United States.
Subject Specialization: history; transportation.
Special Cartographic Collections: Sanborn fire insurance maps for the city of San Diego; 1887, 1888, 1920–1940.
Dates: pre-1800 (1% (est.)); 1800-1899 (14% (est.)); 1900 - (85%).
Collections Cataloged. (30%).
Serves: students; faculty; employees; public. Mon.–Thurs. 10 a.m.–9 p.m.; Sat. 9:30 a.m.–5:30 p.m. (Seats 16).
Reproduction Facility: photocopy.

79. SAN DIEGO PUBLIC LIBRARY
Central Library
History Section
820 E Street
San Diego, CA 92101
Telephone: 619/236-5821.
Contact Person: Jean Hughes, Senior Libn.
Staff: 1 professional (part time).
Size: 2,000 maps; 50 atlases; 3 globes; 50 reference books and gazetteers.
Annual Accessions: 100 maps; 6 atlases; 6 reference books and gazetteers.
Dates: pre-1800 (1%); 1800-1899 (14%); 1900 - (85%).
Collections Cataloged. (15%). Mon.–Thurs. 10 a.m.–9 p.m.; Sat. 9:30 a.m.–5:30 a.m. (Seats 80).
Interlibrary Loan Available.
Reproduction Facility: photocopy.

80. SAN DIEGO PUBLIC LIBRARY
Science Section
Government Documents
820 E Street
San Diego, CA 92101
Established 1882.
Telephone: 619/236-5813.
Contact Person: Joanne Anderson, Senior Libn.
Staff: 1 professional (part time); 1 non-professional (part time).
Size: 24,961 maps; 9 relief models; 50 microforms (no. of titles).
Annual Accessions: 850 maps.
Area Specialization: western United States.
Subject Specialization: topography.
Dates: 1900 - (100%).
Classification System: local system.
Collections not Cataloged.

Depository for: USGS (Geol., topo.).
Serves: public. Mon.–Thurs. 10 a.m.–9 p.m., Fri. 9:30 a.m.–5:30 p.m.; Sat. 9:30 a.m.–5:30 p.m. (Seats 50).
Reproduction Facility: photocopy; microform.

81. SAN DIEGO STATE UNIVERSITY
University Library
Map Collection
San Diego, CA 92182
Telephone: 619/265-5832.
Contact Person: Muriel Strickland, Map Curator.
Staff: 1 professional (full time); 2–3 non-professional (part time).
Size: 130,000 maps; 600 atlases; 3 globes; 2 relief models; 200 aerial photographs; 200 reference books and gazetteers.
Annual Accessions: 3,500 maps; 10–20 atlases; 10–20 reference books and gazetteers.
Area Specialization: San Diego County.
Dates: 1800-1899 (Less than 1%); 1900 - (99%).
Classification System: local system.
Collections not Cataloged.
Depository for: DMA; USGS (Geol., topo.).
Serves: students; faculty; employees; public. Mon.–Fri. 8 a.m.–4:30 p.m. (Seats 10–12; 250 readers served per month).
Interlibrary Loan Available.
Reproduction Facility: quickcopy.

San Francisco

82. CALIFORNIA ACADEMY OF SCIENCES
J.W. Mailliard, Jr. Library
Golden Gate Park
San Francisco, CA 94118
Telephone: 415/221-4214, ext 275.
Contact Person: James E. Jackson, Asst. Libn.
Size: 35,000 maps; 25 relief models; 600 reference books and gazetteers; 3 serials (titles received).
Annual Accessions: 1,000 maps; 5 reference books and gazetteers.
Area Specialization: western North America; Baja California; South America and Galapagos Islands.
Special Cartographic Collections: Belvedere Collection-Baja California; maps and books.
Dates: pre-1800 (5%); 1800-1899 (20%); 1900 - (75%).
Classification System: LC; Dewey;.
Collections Cataloged. (35%).
Depository for: USGS (Geol., topo.); New Zealand Geological Survey.
Serves: students; faculty; employees; public; members. Mon.–Fri. 9 a.m.–5 p.m. (Seats 30; 100 readers served per month).
Interlibrary Loan Available.
Reproduction Facility: photocopy; quickcopy.

83. CALIFORNIA HISTORICAL SOCIETY, LIBRARY
2099 Pacific Avenue
San Francisco, CA 94109
Established 1922.
Telephone: 415/567-1848.
Contact Person: Bruce L. Johnson, Library Director.
Size: 3,000 maps; 75 atlases; 10 relief models; several thousands aerial photographs; 100 reference books and gazetteers.
Annual Accessions: 10 maps; 2 atlases; 1 relief models; 5 reference books and gazetteers.
Area Specialization: California; the Pacific Coast (Alaska to Baja California); western United States.
Subject Specialization: California and western United States history.

Dates: 1800-1899 (40%); 1900 - (60%).
Classification System: local system.
Collections Cataloged. (35%).
Serves: students; faculty; employees; public. Wed.–Fri. 10 a.m.–4 p.m.; Sat. 10 a.m.–4 p.m. (Seats 20–25).
Reproduction Facility: photocopy.

84. CALIFORNIA (STATE) DIVISION OF MINES AND GEOLOGY
Library
Ferry Building
San Francisco, CA 94111
Established 1950.
Telephone: 415/557-2292.
Contact Person: C.W. Jennings, Senior Geologist.
Staff: 1 non-professional (part time).
Size: several thousand maps; 100 atlases.
Area Specialization: California; United States.
Subject Specialization: geology; mines and minerals; topography.
Dates: 1800-1899 (5%); 1900 - (95%).
Classification System: local system.
Collections Cataloged. (100%).
Depository for: USGS (Geol., topo.).
Serves: employees; public. Mon.–Fri. 8:30 a.m.–4 p.m. (Seats 2; 4 readers served per month).
Reproduction Facility: photocopy.

85. MECHANICS' INSTITUTE LIBRARY
57 Post St.
San Francisco, CA 94104
Established 1907.
Telephone: 415/421-1750.
Contact Person: Kathryn McDevitt-Parks, Reference Libn.
Size: 1,000 maps; 75 atlases; 1 globes; 25 reference books and gazetteers.
Dates: 1800-1899 (5%); 1900 - (95%).
Classification System: Dewey.
Collections Cataloged.
Depository for: USGS (Geol.).
Serves: members. Mon.–Fri. 9 a.m.–9 p.m.; Sat. 9 a.m.–9 p.m.; Sun. 1–5 p.m. (Seats 50).
Reproduction Facility: photocopy.

86. SAN FRANCISCO PUBLIC LIBRARY
History and Social Sciences Department
Civic Center
San Francisco, CA 94102
Telephone: 415/558-4927.
Contact Person: Joan Casserly, Reference Libn.
Size: 45,000 maps; 310 atlases; 6 globes; 2 relief models; 700 reference books and gazetteers; 17 serials (titles received).
Annual Accessions: 3,000 maps; 19 atlases; 50 reference books and gazetteers.
Area Specialization: California.
Subject Specialization: local history; geography; geology; topography.
Special Cartographic Collections: California city and town street maps; United States and foreign cities street maps;.
Dates: 1800-1899 (25%); 1900 - (75%).
Classification System: Dewey.
Collections Cataloged. (25%).
Depository for: USGS (Geol., topo.).
Serves: public. Mon.–Fri. 10 a.m.–6 p.m.; Tues., Wed., & Thurs. 10 a.m.–9 p.m. Sat. 10 a.m.–6 p.m.; Sun. 1–5 p.m. (Seats 100; 1,000 readers served per month).
Reproduction Facility: photocopy.

87. SAN FRANCISCO STATE UNIVERSITY
Geography Department
Map Library, Room HLL 289
1600 Holloway Avenue
San Francisco, CA 94132
Established 1965.
Telephone: 415/469-1145.
Contact Person: Richard Montgomery, Map Libn.; Duncan Watry, Map Libn.
Staff: 2 professional (part time).
Size: 50,000 (approx.) maps; 100 atlases; 8 globes; 200 relief models; 2,500 aerial photographs.
Annual Accessions: 500 maps.
Area Specialization: western United States; San Francisco Bay area; Asia.
Subject Specialization: topography.
Special Cartographic Collections: California Historical USGS collection; complete collection of lunar surface satellite photo imagery.
Dates: 1900 - (100%).
Collections not Cataloged.
Depository for: USGS (Topo.).
Serves: students; faculty; employees; public. Mon.–Fri. 8:30 a.m.–4:30 p.m. (Seats 20; 300 readers served per month).

88. SAN FRANCISCO STATE UNIVERSITY
Library/Government Publications Services
Map and Atlas Collection
1630 Holloway Avenue
San Francisco, CA 94132
Established 1952.
Telephone: 415/469-1557.
Contact Person: Lavonne Jacobsen, Government Publications Coordinator.
Staff: 1 professional (part time); 1 non-professional (part time).
Size: 9,671 maps; 500 atlases; 12 globes.
Annual Accessions: 159 maps; 25 atlases.
Area Specialization: California.
Dates: 1800-1899 (1%); 1900 - (99%).
Classification System: LC; DMA.
Collections Cataloged.
Depository for: DMA; USGS (Topo.).
Serves: students; faculty; employees; public. Mon.–Thurs. 8 a.m.–10 p.m., Fri. 8 a.m.–5 p.m.; Sat. 1–5 p.m.; Sun. 1–5 p.m. (Seats 82).
Interlibrary Loan Available.
Reproduction Facility: photocopy; microform.
Publications: *Maps and Atlases: Information guide #20;* "*Government Publications: Information guide #14.*

89. THE SOCIETY OF CALIFORNIA PIONEERS
Library
Map Collection
456 McAllister Street
San Francisco, CA 94102
Telephone: 415/861-5278.
Contact Person: Grace E. Baker, Libn.
Area Specialization: California.
Subject Specialization: California counties.

90. STANDARD OIL COMPANY OF CALIFORNIA
Economics Staff
Geosciences Library—Room 1410
225 Bush Street
San Francisco, CA 94104
Telephone: 415/894-3370.
Contact Person: Peg Marshburn, Geosciences Libn.
Staff: 2 professional (part time); 3 non-professional (part time).
Size: 5,500 maps; 35 atlases; 225 reference books and gazetteers; 130 serials (titles received).
Annual Accessions: 125 maps.

Area Specialization: California; Alaska; foreign areas.
Subject Specialization: geosciences, especially petroleum geology.
Dates: 1900 - (100%).
Classification System: Dewey.
Collections Cataloged. (100%).
Serves: employees; public. Mon.–Fri. 8 a.m.–5 p.m. (Seats 25).
Interlibrary Loan Available.
Reproduction Facility: quickcopy; microform.

San Luis Obispo

91. CALIFORNIA POLYTECHNIC STATE UNIVERSITY
Government Documents and Maps Department
San Luis Obispo, CA 93407
Established 1977.
Telephone: 805/546-1364.
Contact Person: Chi Su Kim, Head.
Staff: 1 professional (part time).
Size: 18,185 maps; 430 atlases; 2 globes; 47 relief models; 61 aerial photographs.
Annual Accessions: 368 maps; 25 atlases.
Area Specialization: California.
Subject Specialization: planning maps; soils; topography.
Classification System: LC.
Collections Cataloged.
Depository for: USGS (Geol.).
Serves: students; faculty; employees; public. Mon.–Fri. 7:30–10 p.m.; Sat. 7:30 a.m.–5 p.m.; Sun. 1–10 p.m. (Seats 50).
Reproduction Facility: photocopy; microform.

Santa Ana

92. SANTA ANA PUBLIC LIBRARY
Reference/Reader Advisor Section
26 Civic Center Plaza
Santa Ana,, CA 92701
Telephone: 714/834-4845.
Contact Person: Paul Wang, Reference Libn.

Santa Barbara

93. UNIVERSITY OF CALIFORNIA, SANTA BARBARA
Library
Map and Imagery Laboratory
Santa Barbara, CA 93106
Established 1967.
Telephone: 805/961-2779.
Contact Person: Larry Carver, Department Head.
Staff: 1 professional (full time); 3 non-professional (full time); 10 non-professional (part time).
Size: 300,000 maps; 1,800 atlases; 9 globes; 300 relief models; 1,500,000 aerial photographs; 700 reference books and gazetteers; 25 serials (titles received); 21,000 microforms (no. of titles).
Annual Accessions: 15,000 maps; 25 atlases; 10,000 aerial photographs; 10 reference books and gazetteers; 1 serials (titles received); 4,000 microforms (no. of titles).
Subject Specialization: physical sciences; topography; bathymetry; natural resources; land-use; urban planning; satellite multispectral imagery.
Special Cartographic Collections: Landsat-2 Imagery Collection—1.2 million; 70 mm master negative multispectral images covering much of the world from 11/75 to 11/78; California imagery collection: 250,000 frames of high/medium altitude color infrared, color; B/W aerial photography, specializing in the tri-county area, the Central

Valley, and the Pacific coast; EROS Data Center Browse Files: Complete sets of all microform materials at EROS Data Center; 16 mm copies of CIR, color, B/W of NASA United States imagery; 16 mm B/W Landsat imagery; 35 mm Thematic Mapper color composite slides; all microindexes for aerial photography; Remote sensing/cartographic interpretation and information transfer laboratory and training available to all patrons.
Dates: 1800-1899 (1%); 1900 - (99%).
Classification System: LC (modified)*.
Collections Cataloged.
Depository for: DMA; NOS; USGS (Geol., topo.).
Serves: students; faculty; employees; public. Mon.–Thurs. 8 a.m.–5, 7–10 p.m.; Fri. 8 a.m.–5 p.m. (Seats 90; 3,000 readers served per month).
Interlibrary Loan Available. (selected)
Reproduction Facility: photocopy; microform; Hasselblad, polaroid, and 35 mm copy camera systems.
Collections not Cataloged.
Depository for: USGS (Topo.).
Serves: public. Mon.–Fri. 9 a.m.–9 p.m.; Sat. 9 a.m.–6 p.m.; Sun. 1–5 p.m.
Reproduction Facility: photocopy.

Santa Clara

*95. UNIVERSITY OF SANTA CLARA
Orradre Library
Santa Clara, CA 95053
Established 1974.
Telephone: 405/984-4415.
Contact Person: Lorraine Bazan.
Staff: 1 professional (part time).
Size: 4,351 maps; 200 atlases.
Annual Accessions: 250 maps.
Area Specialization: California.
Subject Specialization: national forests; topography.
Dates: 1900 - (100%).
Classification System: LC.
Depository for: USGS (Topo.).
Serves: students; faculty; employees; public. Mon.–Fri. 8 a.m.–12 midnight; Sat. 9 a.m.–5 p.m.; Sun. 12 noon–12 midnight. (Seats 6).

Santa Cruz

96. UNIVERSITY OF CALIFORNIA, SANTA CRUZ
University Library
Map Collection
McHenry Library, UCSC
Santa Cruz, CA 95064
Established 1966.
Telephone: 408/429-2364.
Contact Person: Stanley D. Stevens, Map Libn.
Staff: 1 professional (full time).
Size: 130,000 maps; 650 atlases; 5 globes; 135 relief models; 18,106 aerial photographs; 700 reference books and gazetteers; 8,900 microforms (no. of titles).
Annual Accessions: 5,000 maps; 10 atlases; 3,000 aerial photographs; 10 reference books and gazetteers; 500 microforms (no. of titles).
Area Specialization: Monterey Bay region of California which encompasses 5 counties: Monterey, San Benito, San Mateo, Santa Clara, Santa Cruz.
Subject Specialization: and ownership; early topographic maps for region; aerial photography (every flight of entire region from 1925).
Special Cartographic Collections: Frederick A. Hihn Collection (19th century-late land ownership of Santa Cruz County).

*Note: Item No. 94 has been dropped from the directory.

Dates: 1800-1899 (10%); 1900 - (90%).
Classification System: LC.
Collections Cataloged. (1%).
Depository for: DMA; NTS (Canada); USGS (Geol., topo.).
Serves: students; faculty; employees; public. Mon.–Fri. 9 a.m.–5 p.m. (Seats 20; 175 readers served per month).
Interlibrary Loan Available.
Reproduction Facility: quickcopy.
Publications: *Catalog of Aerial Photos in the Map Collection of the University Library. 1979.* (o.p.); *Catalog of Maps Mounted for Classroom Use. 1979.*(o.p.).

Santa Monica

97. SANTA MONICA PUBLIC LIBRARY
Map Collection
1343 Sixth Street
Santa Monica, CA 90401
Established 1965.
Telephone: 213/451-5751, ext. 52.
Contact Person: H. Gera Freeman, Reference Libn.
Size: 1,839 maps; 42 atlases; 2 globes; 2 relief models; 20 reference books and gazetteers.
Annual Accessions: 20–100 maps; 1–5 atlases.
Area Specialization: southern California.
Subject Specialization: travel and recreation.
Dates: 1900 -.
Classification System: local system.
Collections not Cataloged.
Serves: public. Mon.–Thurs. 10 a.m.–9 p.m.; Fri. 10 a.m.–5:30 p.m.; Sat. 10 a.m.–5:30 p.m. (Seats 250; 100 readers served per month).
Reproduction Facility: photocopy.

Stanford

98. STANFORD UNIVERSITY
Cecil H. Green Library, General Reference Department
Central Map Collection
Stanford, CA 94305
Established 1952.
Telephone: 415/497-1811.
Contact Person: Karyl Tonge, Library Specialist.
Staff: 2 non-professional (part time).
Size: 78,000 maps; 60–65 atlases; ca. 350 reference books and gazetteers; 10 serials (titles received).
Annual Accessions: ca. 500–1,000 maps.
Special Cartographic Collections: 18th and 19th century maps of Europe, Asia, Africa and the Americas; German "captured" maps of Europe and North Africa.
Dates: 1900 - (80%).
Classification System: LC.
Collections Cataloged. (75%).
Depository for: DMA; USGS (Topo.).
Serves: students; faculty; employees; public. Mon.–Thurs. 9 a.m.–11:30 (or by appointment). (Seats 20; 30–40 readers served per month).
Interlibrary Loan Available.
Reproduction Facility: photocopy.
Publications: *SUL Guide #21—Map Collections* (guide).

99. STANFORD UNIVERSITY
Libraries
Branner Earth Sciences Library
Stanford, CA 94305
Established 1915.
Telephone: 415/497-1093.
Contact Person: Charlotte Derksen, Libn.; Michael Noga, Map Specialist.

Staff: 1 professional (full time); 2 non-professional (full time); 10 non-professional (part time).
Size: 85,000 maps; 240 atlases; 10 relief models; 530 reference books and gazetteers; 14,000 serials (titles received); 19 microforms (no. of titles).
Annual Accessions: 4,500 maps; 25 atlases; 30 reference books and gazetteers; 100 serials (titles received); 1 microforms (no. of titles).
Area Specialization: Africa; Latin America; Alpine/Himalayan Region; New Zealand; Canada; Japan; France.
Subject Specialization: geology; geophysics; hydrogrology; mineral resources; soils.
Special Cartographic Collections: Broken Hill Mine—Australia (including reports and folded maps on geology and the mine itself); J.C. Branner's collection on geology and mining in Brazil, including folded maps, 1848–1940.
Dates: 1800-1899 (2%); 1900 - (98%).
Classification System: LC.
Collections not Cataloged.
Depository for: GSC; USGS (Geol., topo.).
Serves: students; faculty; employees; public. Mon.–Thurs. 8 a.m.–10 p.m.; Fri. 8 a.m.–6 p.m.; Sat. 10 a.m.–5 p.m.; Sun. 1–10 p.m. (Seats 135).
Interlibrary Loan Available.
Reproduction Facility: photocopy; microform.
Publications: *Map series and serials in Branner Earth Sciences Library A guide to Branner Earth Sciences Library Map Collections.*

Stockton

100. SAN JOAQUIN DELTA COLLEGE
Goleman Library
5151 Pacific Avenue
Stockton, CA 95207
Established 1960.
Telephone: 209/474-5138.
Contact Person: Evia B. Moore, Periodicals Libn.
Size: 4,140 maps; 24 atlases; 1 globes; 50 reference books and gazetteers; 10 serials (titles received).
Annual Accessions: 150 maps.
Area Specialization: California.
Classification System: Geological materials are filed by their number as they arrive;. all other maps are in alphabetical order
Collections not Cataloged.
Depository for: USGS (Geol., topo.).
Serves: students; faculty; employees; public. Mon.–Thurs. 8 a.m.–8 p.m., Fri. 8 a.m.–2:30 p.m. (Seats 522).
Interlibrary Loan Available.
Reproduction Facility: photocopy.

101. STOCKTON-SAN JOAQUIN COUNTY PUBLIC LIBRARY
605 N. El Dorado
Stockton, CA 95204
Established 1880.
Telephone: 209/944-8221.
Contact Person: Amoes Hunt.
Size: 6,000 maps.
Annual Accessions: 250 maps.
Area Specialization: California and San Joaquin County.
Special Cartographic Collections: USGS Depository Collections for California, Nevada, Washington, Oregon & Hawaii—topographic maps only.
Dates: 1800-1899 (2%); 1900 - (98%).
Collections not Cataloged.
Depository for: USGS (Topo.).
Serves: public. Mon., Wed., Thurs. 10 a.m.–9 p.m., Tues.,. Fri. 10 a.m.–6 p.m. (Seats 80).
Reproduction Facility: photocopy.

Turlock

102. CALIFORNIA STATE COLLEGE, STANISLAUS
Library
800 W. Monte Vista Ave.
Turlock, CA 95380
Established 1960.
Telephone: 209/667-3233.
Contact Person: Judith A. Tamimi, Reference Libn.
Staff: 1 professional (part time).
Size: 3,000 maps; 350 atlases; 1 globes; 3 relief models;
30 reference books and gazetteers.
Annual Accessions: varies–ca. 100 maps; 25 atlases; 2–3
reference books and gazetteers.
Area Specialization: California.
Subject Specialization: comprehensive.
Collections not Cataloged.
Serves: students; faculty; employees; public. Mon.–Thurs.
7:30 a.m.–11 p.m., Fri. 7:30 a.m.–5:00 p.m.; Sat. 9 a.m.–5
p.m.; Sun. 1–9 p.m. (Seats 225).
Interlibrary Loan Available.
Reproduction Facility: photocopy; microform.
Publications: *Index to Map Collection. Index to Atlas
Collection.*

Whittier

103. WHITTIER COLLEGE
Department of Geology
Fairchild Aerial Photograph Collection
Whittier, CA 90608
Established 1965.
Telephone: 213/693-0771, ext. 363.
Contact Person: William B. Wadsworth, Chairman,
Department of Geology.
Staff: 2 non-professional (part time).
Size: 300,000 aerial photographs.
Area Specialization: California, particularly southern
California and metropolitan areas.
Subject Specialization: aerial photography.
Dates: 1900 - (100%).
Classification System: local system (Fairchild flight
numbers referenced to mosaic. indexes of flights)
Collections Cataloged.
Depository for: Calif. Div. Mines & Geology.
Serves: students; faculty; public. hours vary. (Seats 20; 10
readers served per month).
Interlibrary Loan Available. (on a service-fee basis only)
Publications: *The Fairchild Aerial Photography Collection at
Whittier College* (brochure).

COLORADO

Boulder

104. UNIVERSITY OF COLORADO, BOULDER
University Libraries
Map Library
Campus Box 184
Boulder, CO 80309
Established 1970.
Telephone: 303/492-7578.
Contact Person: David M. Fagerstom, Head, Science, Earth
Science, and Map Libraries.
Size: 123,000 maps; 10 atlases; 250 aerial photographs.
Annual Accessions: 2,500 maps.
Area Specialization: Colorado; United States.

Dates: pre-1800 (5%); 1800-1899 (10%); 1900 - (85%).
Classification System: local system.
Collections not Cataloged.
Depository for: DMA; USGS (Geol., topo.); U.S. Forestry
Service.
Serves: students; faculty; employees; public. Mon.–Thurs. 10
a.m.–5 p.m., 7–9 p.m., Fri. 9 a.m.–5 p.m. (Seats 20; 250
readers served per month).
Interlibrary Loan Available.
Reproduction Facility: photocopy; microform.

Colorado Springs

105. U.S. AIR FORCE ACADEMY
Department of Geography
Map Depository
Colorado Springs, CO 80840
Established 1962.
Telephone: 303/472-3067 or 3068.
Contact Person: Captain Stanley T. Slaydon, Officer-In-
Charge, Map Depository.
Staff: 2 non-professional (full time).
Size: 50,000 maps; 5 atlases; 5 globes; 200 relief models;
500 aerial photographs; 144 reference books and
gazetteers; 1 serials (titles received).
Annual Accessions: 3,000 maps; 1 serials (titles received).
Area Specialization: comprehensive.
Subject Specialization: geography; history.
Dates: 1800-1899 (5%); 1900 - (95%).
Classification System: local system.
Collections Cataloged.
Depository for: DMA; DOS (Gt. Brit); GSC; NOS; USGS
(Geol., topo.); CIA, National Geographic.
Serves: students; faculty. Mon.–Fri. 7 a.m.–4 p.m.
Reproduction Facility: photocopy.

106. UNIVERSITY OF COLORADO, COLORADO SPRINGS
Library
Map Collection
Austin Bluffs Parkway
Colorado Springs, CO 80933-7150
Established 1980.
Telephone: 303/593-3290.
Contact Person: Mary Ellen Haug, Instructor Adjunct.
Size: 3,816 maps; 140 atlases; 80 reference books and
gazetteers; 4 serials (titles received).
Annual Accessions: 5% maps; 5% atlases; 5% reference
books and gazetteers.
Area Specialization: Colorado.
Subject Specialization: geology; geography; topography.
Dates: 1800-1899 (5%); 1900 - (95%).
Classification System: LC; GPO classification system.
Collections Cataloged. (10%).
Depository for: USGS (Geol., topo.).
Serves: students; faculty; public. Mon.–Fri. 8 a.m.–10:30
p.m.; Sat. 9 a.m.–5 p.m.; Sun. 1–5 p.m. (Seats 4; 50
readers served per month).
Interlibrary Loan Available.

Denver

107. COLORADO HISTORICAL SOCIETY
Books and Ephemera
1300 Broadway
Denver, CO 80203
Telephone: 303/866-2305.
Contact Person: Alice L. Sharp, Libn.
Size: 3,000 maps; 77 atlases; 14 relief models.
Area Specialization: Colorado.

Subject Specialization: history of Colorado.
Classification System: LC.
Collections Cataloged. (20%).
Serves: students; faculty; employees; public. Tues.–Fri. 10 a.m.–4:30 p.m.; Sat. 10 a.m.–4:30 p.m. (Seats 26; 175 readers served per month).
Reproduction Facility: photocopy.

108. DENVER PUBLIC LIBRARY
Government Publications Department
1357 Broadway
Denver, CO 80203
Telephone: 303/571-2130.
Contact Person: Donna Koepp, Map Specialist.
Staff: 1 professional (full time).
Size: 87,700 maps; 1,150 atlases; 2 globes; 7 relief models; 3,500 aerial photographs; 120 reference books and gazetteers; 10 serials (titles received); 1,000 microforms (no. of titles).
Area Specialization: Denver; Colorado; front range of the Rocky Mountains.
Dates: 1900 - (100%).
Classification System: LC; DMA.
Collections Cataloged.
Depository for: DMA; USGS (Topo.).
Serves: public. Mon.–Wed. 10 a.m.–9 p.m., Fri. 10 a.m.–5:30 p.m.; Sat. 10 a.m.–5:30 p.m. (Seats 18).
Interlibrary Loan Available. (restricted)
Reproduction Facility: photocopy; microform.

109. DENVER PUBLIC LIBRARY
Western History Department
1357 Broadway
Denver, CO 80203
Telephone: 303/571-2013.
Contact Person: Lynn Taylor, Senior Libn.
Staff: 1 professional (part time).
Size: 5,000 maps; 50 atlases; 30 reference books and gazetteers; 1 serials (titles received).
Annual Accessions: 200 maps; 5 atlases; 5 reference books and gazetteers.
Area Specialization: Colorado; United States west of the Mississippi.
Subject Specialization: mining; real estate atlases.
Special Cartographic Collections: Rocky Mountain Fuel Co. map coll.; Colorado Towns Fire Insurance Atlas.
Dates: pre-1800 (5%); 1800-1899 (45%); 1900 - (50%).
Classification System: LC.
Collections Cataloged.
Serves: students; faculty; employees; public. Mon.–Wed. 10 a.m.–9 p.m., Fri. 10–5:30 p.m.; Sat. 10:00 a.m.–5:30 p.m. (Seats 50; 50 readers served per month).
Reproduction Facility: photocopy.

110. U.S. GEOLOGICAL SURVEY
Denver Library
Box 25046, Denver Federal Center
Denver, CO 80225
Established 1948.
Telephone: 303/236-1000.
Contact Person: Cheryl Sund, Reference Libn.
Staff: 1 professional (part time); 2 non-professional (part time).
Size: 110,000 maps; 125 atlases; 4 globes; 60 relief models.
Annual Accessions: 3,000 maps; 5 atlases.
Area Specialization: United States.
Subject Specialization: earth sciences.
Special Cartographic Collections: collection of manuscript maps made by USGS geologists in connection with their field work (housed in Field Records Section of the library).
Dates: 1800-1899 (5%); 1900 - (95%).
Classification System: local system.

Collections Cataloged.
Depository for: USGS (Geol., topo.).
Serves: employees; public. Mon.–Fri. 7:30 a.m.–4 p.m. (Seats 15; 200 readers served per month).
Interlibrary Loan Available.
Reproduction Facility: photocopy; quickcopy.

Durango

111. FORT LEWIS COLLEGE
Library
Durango, CO 81307
Telephone: 303/247-7914.
Contact Person: Monica Engle, Maps & Documents Libn.
Staff: 1 professional (part time).
Size: 4,000 maps; 75 atlases; 2 globes; 50 reference books and gazetteers.
Annual Accessions: 500 maps; 5 atlases; 5 reference books and gazetteers.
Area Specialization: Colorado; western United States.
Subject Specialization: geology.
Dates: pre-1800 (1%); 1800-1899 (2%); 1900 - (97%).
Classification System: LC.
Collections Cataloged.
Depository for: USGS (Geol., topo.).
Serves: students; faculty; employees; public. Mon.–Fri. 8 a.m.–11 p.m.; Sat. 10 a.m.–4 p.m.; Sun. 2–10 p.m. (Seats 10).
Interlibrary Loan Available.
Reproduction Facility: photocopy; quickcopy.

Fort Collins

112. COLORADO STATE UNIVERSITY
CSU Libraries
Fort Collins, CO 80523
Established 1968.
Telephone: 303/491-1833.
Staff: 1 professional (part time); 1 non-professional (part time).
Size: 24,905 maps; 30 atlases; 2 globes; 12 relief models; 35 aerial photographs.
Annual Accessions: 2,000 maps.
Area Specialization: Alaska; western United States.
Subject Specialization: topography.
Dates: pre-1800 (1%); 1800-1899 (2%); 1900 - (97%).
Classification System: LC.
Collections Cataloged. (10%).
Depository for: USGS (Topo.).
Serves: students; public. (Seats 8; 300–350 readers served per month).
Interlibrary Loan Available.
Publications: Guide to maps in CSU library.

Golden

113. COLORADO SCHOOL OF MINES
Arthur Lakes Library
Map Room
Golden, CO 80401
Telephone: 303/273-3697.
Contact Person: Mary Lynette Larsgaard, Map Libn.
Staff: 1 professional (full time); 1 professional (part time); student help (40–80 hours per week) non-professional (part time).
Size: 116,418 maps; 5 globes; 30 relief models; 2,000 aerial photographs; 4 microforms (no. of titles).

Annual Accessions: 8,000 maps; 2 relief models; 400 aerial photographs; 1 microforms (no. of titles).
Area Specialization: Colorado.
Subject Specialization: geology; mines.
Special Cartographic Collections: Oil well completion cards (120,000 items).
Dates: 1800-1899 (1%); 1900 - (99%).
Classification System: LC.
Collections Cataloged. (92%).
Depository for: DMA; NOS; USGS (Geol., topo.); BLM.
Serves: students; faculty; employees; public;. Mon.–Fri. 7:30 a.m.–11 p.m.; Sat. 9 a.m.–5 p.m.; Sun. 1–11 p.m. (Seats 25; 110 readers served per month).
Interlibrary Loan Available.
Reproduction Facility: photocopy.
Publications: *Recently Cataloged Maps & Atlases; Map Room (leaflet); Finding a Geologic Map in the Map Room, Arthur Lakes Library, Colorado School of Mines*

Littleton

114. MARATHON OIL COMPANY
Research Center Library
7400 South Broadway
Littleton, CO 80122
Established 1956.
Telephone: 303/794-2601, ext. 338.
Contact Person: Kristine M. Palumbo, Associate Technical Libn.
Staff: 2 professional (full time); 1 non-professional (part time).
Size: 9,000 maps; 55 atlases; 10 reference books and gazetteers; 3 serials (titles received).
Area Specialization: North America.
Subject Specialization: geology; petroleum; oceanography.
Dates: 1800-1899 (2%); 1900 - (98%).
Classification System: LC.
Collections Cataloged.
Serves: employees. Mon.–Fri. 8:00 a.m.–4:30 p.m.

Pueblo

115. UNIVERSITY OF SOUTHERN COLORADO
Library
2200 Bonforte Blvd.
Pueblo, CO 81001
Established 1965.
Telephone: 303/549-2451.
Contact Person: Kirstine St. Jernholm, Reference Libn.; Dan Sullivan, Catalog Libn.
Staff: 1 professional (part time).
Size: 7,000 maps; 5 relief models; 693 reference books and gazetteers.
Annual Accessions: 200 maps.
Area Specialization: Colorado; Wyoming; Utah; Arizona; New Mexico; Kansas.
Subject Specialization: geology; hydrology.
Special Cartographic Collections: USGS topographic (1:24,000 and 1:62,500) on depository for states listed above.
Dates: 1900 - (100%).
Classification System: LC; local system.
Collections not Cataloged.
Depository for: DMA; USGS (Geol., topo.).
Serves: students; faculty; employees; public. Mon.–Fri. 7 a.m.–9 p.m.; Sun. 1–9 p.m. (Seats 25).
Reproduction Facility: photocopy.

CONNECTICUT

Bridgeport

116. BRIDGEPORT PUBLIC LIBRARY
925 Broad Street
Bridgeport, CT 06604
Telephone: 203/576-7403.
Area Specialization: Connecticut; Bridgeport.
Subject Specialization: topography; local history.
Serves: public. Mon. and Wed. 9 a.m.–9 p.m.; Tues., Thurs. and Fri. 9 a.m.–5 p.m. Sat. 9 a.m.–5 p.m.
Reproduction Facility: photocopy; microform.

Hartford

117. CONNECTICUT HISTORICAL SOCIETY
1 Elizabeth Street
Hartford, CT 06105
Established 1825.
Telephone: 203/236-0861 ext. 27.
Contact Person: Florence Crofut, Curator, Rare Books & Manuscripts.
Staff: 1 professional (full time).
Size: 350 maps; 70 atlases; 700 aerial photographs; 100 reference books and gazetteers.
Area Specialization: Connecticut; northeastern United States.
Dates: pre-1800 (5%); 1800-1899 (75%); 1900 - (20%).
Classification System: local system.
Collections Cataloged. (33%).
Depository for: Metropolitan District (water and sewage—Hartford area).
Serves: public. Mon.–Fri. 9 a.m.–5 p.m. (Seats 28; 10 readers served per month).
Reproduction Facility: photocopy; microform.
Publications: Typed list: Panoramic views of Connecticut. Thompson, Edmund. *Maps of Connecticut.* 2 vols. 1800; 1801–1860. Windham, 1940, 1942.

118. CONNECTICUT STATE LIBRARY
Archives, History & Genealogy Unit
231 Capitol Avenue
Hartford, CT 06110
Contact Person: Theodore O. Wohlsen, Jr., Unit Head.
Staff: 4 professional (part time); 2 non-professional (part time).
Size: 200 lin. ft. maps; 66 lin. ft. aerial photographs; 5–10 serials (titles received).
Annual Accessions: .5 lin. ft. maps; 5 atlases; 15 reference books and gazetteers.
Area Specialization: Connecticut: New England.
Subject Specialization: history.
Special Cartographic Collections: William Brownell Goodwin Collection, 1934–1949 (Record Group 69:15); early maps and atlases, c. 1482–1850; Connecticut town maps.
Classification System: Dewey; local system for State Government Publications.
Collections Cataloged. (50%).
Depository for: USGS (Topo.).
Serves: students; faculty; employees; public;. 8:30 a.m.–5 p.m.; Sat. 9 a.m.–1 p.m. (Seats 35; 12 readers served per month).
Reproduction Facility: photocopy; Camera stand in research room. Researchers must have their own. camera and film.

119. HARTFORD PUBLIC LIBRARY
Reference Department
500 Main Street
Hartford, CT 06103
Telephone: 203/525-9121.
Contact Person: Martha D. Nolan, Reference Libn. Head.
Size: 32,150 maps; 150 atlases.
Annual Accessions: 200 maps.
Dates: 1800-1899 (5%); 1900 - (95%).
Classification System: LC.
Collections not Cataloged.
Depository for: DMA; USGS (Topo.).
Serves: students; faculty; employees; public. Mon.–Thurs. 9 a.m.–9 p.m., Fri. 9 a.m.–5 p.m.; Sat. 9 a.m.–5 p.m.
Reproduction Facility: quickcopy.

120. TRINITY COLLEGE
Watkinson Library
Map collection
300 Summit Street
Hartford, CT 06106
Established 19th century.
Telephone: 203/527-3151, ext. 307.
Contact Person: Dr. Jeffrey H. Kaimowitz, Curator.
Size: 700 maps; 185 atlases; 100 reference books and gazetteers.
Area Specialization: eastern United States.
Subject Specialization: discovery and exploration.
Dates: pre-1800 (15%); 1800-1899 (75%); 1900 - (10%).
Classification System: Watkinson Library.
Collections Cataloged.
Serves: students; faculty; employees; public. Mon.–Fri. 8:30 a.m.–4:30 p.m. (Seats 24; 150 readers served per month).
Reproduction Facility: photocopy; quickcopy; microform.

Middletown

121. WESLEYAN UNIVERSITY
Earth & Environmental Sciences Department
Middletown, CT 06457
Telephone: 203/347-9411.
Contact Person: Peter C. Patton, Assoc. Prof.
Staff: 1 non-professional (part time).
Size: 13,000 maps; 15 atlases; 3 globes; 50 relief models; 500 aerial photographs.
Annual Accessions: 100–200 maps.
Area Specialization: United States.
Subject Specialization: geology; geography.
Dates: 1800-1899 (10%); 1900 - (90%).
Classification System: local system.
Collections Cataloged. (60%).
Serves: students; faculty; employees. Mon.–Fri. 8 a.m.–5 p.m.
Reproduction Facility: Mapograph.

122. WESLEYAN UNIVERSITY
Science Library
Middletown, CT 06457
Telephone: 203/347-9411, ext. 2113, 2818.
Contact Person: William Calhoon, Science Libn.
Staff: 1 non-professional (part time).
Size: 125,000 maps; 130 atlases; 2 globes; 125 reference books and gazetteers; 5 serials (titles received).
Annual Accessions: 3,000 maps; 2 atlases; 1 reference books and gazetteers; 5 serials (titles received).
Area Specialization: United States.
Dates: 1800-1899 (10%); 1900 - (90%).
Classification System: LC.
Collections not Cataloged.
Depository for: DMA; USGS (Topo.).

Serves: students; faculty; employees; public. Mon.–Fri. 7 a.m.–2 a.m.; Sat. 9 a.m.–12 midnight; Sun. 10 a.m.–2 a.m. (Seats 6; 5 readers served per month).
Reproduction Facility: photocopy.

Mystic

123. MYSTIC SEAPORT
G. W. Blunt White Library
Charts Department
Greenmanville Avenue
Mystic, CT 06355
Established 1968.
Telephone: 203/572-0711, ext. 291.
Contact Person: Virginia Allen, Custodian of Charts.
Staff: 2 non-professional (part time).
Size: 260; (4,600 charts) maps.
Area Specialization: North America; Europe.
Subject Specialization: navigation.
Dates: pre-1800 (1%); 1800-1899 (43%); 1900 - (56%).
Classification System: Boggs-Lewis.
Collections Cataloged.
Serves: public. Mon.–Thurs. 9 a.m.–5 p.m.
Publications: *Guide to the G. W. Blunt White Library* (guide).

New Britain

124. CENTRAL CONNECTICUT STATE UNIVERSITY
Department of Geography
Map Depository
1615 Stanley Street
New Britain, CT 06050
Established 1967–1968.
Telephone: 203/827-7218.
Contact Person: Dr. James N. Snaden, Professor of Geography.
Staff: 2 professional (part time).
Size: 22,000 maps; 5 atlases; 2 globes; 10 relief models; 1,000 aerial photographs; 100 reference books and gazetteers.
Annual Accessions: 500 maps; 10 aerial photographs; 5 reference books and gazetteers.
Area Specialization: Europe; Asia; United States; Latin America.
Subject Specialization: topography; hydrology.
Dates: 1900 - (100%).
Classification System: DMA.
Collections Cataloged.
Depository for: DMA; USGS (Topo.).
Serves: students; faculty; employees; public. by appointment only. (Seats 50).
Reproduction Facility: photocopy.

New Haven

125. SOUTHERN CONNECTICUT STATE UNIVERSITY
Hilton C. Buley Library
Reference Department
501 Crescent Street
New Haven, CT 06515
Established 1977.
Telephone: 203/397-4511.
Contact Person: Thomas C. Clarie, Head, Reference Department.
Size: 3,850 maps; 330 atlases; 3 globes.
Annual Accessions: 700 maps; 35 atlases.
Subject Specialization: New England.

Dates: 1900 - (100%).
Classification System: local system.
Collections not Cataloged.
Depository for: DMA; USGS (Topo.).
Serves: students; faculty; employees; public. Mon.–Fri. 8 a.m.–4 p.m. (Seats 25; 260 readers served per month).
Reproduction Facility: photocopy; quickcopy.

126. YALE UNIVERSITY
Geology Library
210 Whitney Avenue, P.O. Box 6666
New Haven, CT 06511
Established 1964.
Telephone: 203/436-2480.
Contact Person: Harry D. Scammell, Libn.
Staff: 1 professional (full time); 2 non-professional (full time); 4 non-professional (part time).
Size: 170,000 maps.
Annual Accessions: 5,000 maps.
Area Specialization: comprehensive.
Subject Specialization: geology.
Dates: 1800-1899 (1%); 1900 - (99%).
Classification System: local system.
Collections Cataloged. (100%).
Depository for: USGS (Geol.).
Serves: students; faculty; employees. Mon.–Fri. 8:30 a.m.–5:00 p.m. (Seats 40).
Interlibrary Loan Available.
Reproduction Facility: photocopy.

127. YALE UNIVERSITY
Sterling Memorial Library
Map Collection
Box 1603A Yale Station
New Haven, CT 06520
Established 1930.
Telephone: 203/436-8638.
Contact Person: Barbara B. McCorkle, Map Curator.
Staff: 1 non-professional (full time); 1 non-professional (part time).
Size: 185,000 maps; 2,500 atlases; 20 globes; 50 relief models; 450 reference books and gazetteers; 14 serials (titles received).
Annual Accessions: 3,500 maps; 50 atlases; 50 reference books and gazetteers.
Area Specialization: New England; United States; England; Europe; Asia.
Subject Specialization: history.
Special Cartographic Collections: a collection of 15,000 maps published before 1850.
Classification System: local system.
Collections Cataloged. (65%).
Depository for: DMA; NOS; USGS (Topo.).
Serves: students; faculty; employees; public. Mon.–Fri. 10 a.m.–12 noon; 1–5 p.m. (Seats 12; 70 readers served per month).
Reproduction Facility: photocopy; quickcopy; microform.
Publications: *Yale University Library Information Leaflets: The Map Collection* (handout).

Storrs

128. UNIVERSITY OF CONNECTICUT
University Library
Map Library, U-5M
19 Fairfield Road
Storrs, CT 06268
Established 1967.
Telephone: 203/486-4539.
Contact Person: Thornton P. McGlamery, Map Libn.
Staff: 1 professional (full time).

Size: 100,000 maps; 6 atlases; 9,000 aerial photographs; 1,000 reference books and gazetteers; 5 serials (titles received); 80 microforms (no. of titles).
Annual Accessions: 6,000 maps.
Area Specialization: United States; New England; Connecticut.
Subject Specialization: topography; geology.
Special Cartographic Collections: Petersen collection (photostats of New England towns, villages, school districts from 1840–1875); Microform collection of Connecticut bird's-eye-views.
Dates: 1800-1899 (5%); 1900 - (95%).
Classification System: LC.
Collections Cataloged. (90%).
Depository for: DMA; USGS (Geol., topo.); Metropolitan District (Hartford area).
Serves: students; faculty; employees; public. Mon.–Fri. 9 a.m.–5 p.m. (Seats 20; 400 readers served per month).
Interlibrary Loan Available.
Reproduction Facility: photocopy.
Publications: Information brochure
Telephone: University of Connecticut.

DELAWARE

Dover

129. DELAWARE STATE ARCHIVES
Bureau of Archives and Records Management
Hall of Records
Dover, DE 19901
Established ca. 1905.
Telephone: 302/736-5318.
Contact Person: Joanne A. Mattern, Supervisor, Archives Branch.
Staff: 2 professional (part time).
Size: 450 maps; 15 atlases; 100 aerial photographs; 15 reference books and gazetteers; 2 microforms (no. of titles).
Annual Accessions: 5 maps.
Area Specialization: Delaware and surrounding areas.
Subject Specialization: history of Delaware; records of State government.
Dates: pre-1800 (25%); 1800-1899 (50%); 1900 - (25%).
Classification System: local system.
Collections Cataloged. (95%).
Depository for: USGS (Geol., topo.); All state agencies.
Serves: students; faculty; employees; public;. Tues.–Fri. 8.30 a.m.–12; 1–4:15 p.m.; Sat. 8 a.m.–12:30 p.m.; 1:00–3:45 p.m. (Seats 12; 171 readers served per month).
Reproduction Facility: photocopy; microform.

Newark

130. UNIVERSITY OF DELAWARE
Morris Library
Government Documents/Maps Office
Newark, DE 19711
Established 1967.
Telephone: 302/451-2238.
Contact Person: Rebecca C. Knight, Head, Government Documents/Maps Office.
Staff: 1 professional (full time); 3 non-professional (full time).
Size: 86,533 maps; 2 globes; 250 reference books and gazetteers.
Annual Accessions: 3,000 maps; 25 reference books and gazetteers.
Area Specialization: United States.

Dates: 1800-1899 (2%); 1900 - (98%).
Classification System: LC.
Collections not Cataloged.
Depository for: DMA; NOS; USGS (Geol., topo.).
Serves: students; faculty; employees; public;. Mon.–Thurs. 8:30 a.m.–12 midnight; Sat. 9 a.m.–10 p.m.; Sun. 11 a.m.–12:30 a.m. (Seats 20).
Interlibrary Loan Available.
Reproduction Facility: photocopy; quickcopy.

Wilmington

131. ELEUTHERIAN MILLS-HAGLEY FOUNDATION
Hagley Museum and Library
P.O. Box 3630, Greenville
Wilmington, DE 19807
Established 1961.
Telephone: 302/658-2400.
Contact Person: Richmond D. Williams, Deputy Director for Library Administration.
Size: 2,425 maps; ca. 225 atlases; ca. 15,000 aerial photographs; ca. 280 reference books and gazetteers.
Annual Accessions: ca. 20 maps; ca. 5 atlases; 5 reference books and gazetteers.
Area Specialization: Mid Atlantic States; Delaware; Pennsylvaniva; Maryland; New Jersey.
Subject Specialization: business; economic and technological history; railroad; coal and petroleum industries; pre-Revolutionary French history; insurance industry.
Special Cartographic Collections: Dallin Aerial Survey Company collection: ca. 15,000 aerial photographs (in Pictorial Collections Dept.).
Dates: pre-1800 (ca. 20%); 1800-1899 (ca. 35%); 1900 - (ca. 45%).
Classification System: LC; local system.
Collections Cataloged.
Serves: employees; public. Mon.–Fri. 8:30 a.m.–4:30 p.m.; Sat. 2nd Sat. of each month. (Seats 12; 50 readers served per month).
Interlibrary Loan Available.
Reproduction Facility: photocopy; microform; Photography.

132. HISTORICAL SOCIETY OF DELAWARE
505 Market Street
Wilmington, DE 19801
Established 1865.
Telephone: 302/655-7161.
Contact Person: Dr. Barbara Benson, Director of Libraries.
Staff: .75 professional (full time).
Size: 1,500 maps; 50 atlases; few reference books and gazetteers.
Annual Accessions: 12 maps; few reference books and gazetteers.
Area Specialization: Delaware.
Subject Specialization: land survey maps; city and town maps.
Dates: pre-1800 (75%); 1800-1899 (15%); 1900 - (10%).
Classification System: local system.
Collections Cataloged. (100%).
Serves: students; faculty; employees; public;. Mon. 1–9 p.m.; Tues–Fri. 9 a.m.–5 p.m. (Seats 30; 100 readers served per month).
Reproduction Facility: photocopy; quickcopy.

133. WILMINGTON INSTITUTE FREE LIBRARY
Reference Department
10th and Market Street
Wilmington, DE 19801
Established 1789.
Telephone: 302/571-7416.
Contact Person: Larry Manuel, Head, Reference Dept.

Staff: 1 professional (full time).
Size: 2,500 maps; 25 atlases; 3 reference books and gazetteers.
Annual Accessions: 5 atlases.
Area Specialization: Delaware.
Dates: pre-1800 (25%); 1800-1899 (25%); 1900 - (50%).
Classification System: Dewey.
Collections Cataloged. (100%).
Serves: students; faculty; employees; public;. Mon. 9 a.m.–9 p.m., Tues.–Thurs. 9 a.m.–6 p.m.,. Fri. 9 a.m.–5 p.m. Sat. 9 a.m.–5 p.m. (Seats 75).
Interlibrary Loan Available.
Reproduction Facility: photocopy; quickcopy.

DISTRICT OF COLUMBIA

134. DISTRICT OF COLUMBIA PUBLIC LIBRARY
Georgetown Regional Branch Library
Peabody Room
Wisconsin Avenue & R Street, N.W.
Washington, D.C. 20007
Established 1935.
Telephone: 202/727-1353.
Contact Person: Robert W. Lyle, Curator.
Staff: 1 professional (full time).
Size: ca. 50 maps.
Area Specialization: Georgetwon D.C.
Subject Specialization: Georgetown D.C.
Collections not Cataloged.
Serves: public. Mon. & Fri. 1:30–5:30 p.m., Tues. 9:30 a.m.–1:30 p.m.,. Wed. 1–9 p.m.

135. DISTRICT OF COLUMBIA PUBLIC LIBRARY
Martin Luther King Memorial Library
History Division
901 G St., N.W.
Washington, D.C. 20001
Telephone: 202/727-1161.
Contact Person: Eleanor A. Bartlett, Chief, History Division.
Staff: 2 professional (part time).
Size: 5,713 maps; 250 atlases; 1 globes.
Annual Accessions: 175 maps; 20 atlases.
Dates: 1900 - (100%).
Classification System: Dewey.
Collections Cataloged. (Atlases).
Collections not Cataloged. (Maps).
Depository for: USGS (Topo.).
Serves: public. Mon.–Thurs. 9 a.m.–9 p.m., Fri. 9 a.m.–5:30 p.m.; Sat. 9 a.m.N–5:30 p.m.; Sun. 1–5 p.m. (Seats 107; 100 readers served per month).
Reproduction Facility: photocopy.

136. DISTRICT OF COLUMBIA PUBLIC LIBRARY
Martin Luther King Memorial Library
Washingtoniana Division
901 G Street N.W.
Washington, D.C. 20001
Established 1928.
Telephone: 202/727-1213.
Contact Person: Kathryn Ray, Asst. Chief Washingtoniana Division.
Staff: 5 professional (part time); 2 non-professional (part time).
Size: 1,000 maps.
Area Specialization: Washington, D.C. metropolitan area.
Subject Specialization: Washington, D.C.
Special Cartographic Collections: Washington, D.C. real estate atlases 1887–1976.

Dates: 1800-1899 (30%); 1900 - (60%).
Classification System: local system.
Collections Cataloged.
Serves: public. Mon.–Thurs. 9 a.m.–9 p.m., Fri. 9 a.m.–5:30 p.m.; Sat. 9 a.m.–5:30 p.m.; Sun. 1–5 p.m. (closed during summer). (Seats 50).
Reproduction Facility: photocopy.

137. GEORGE WASHINGTON UNIVERSITY
Gelman Library
Reference Department
2130 H Street, N.W.
Washington, D.C. 20052
Established 1976.
Telephone: 202/676-6047.
Contact Person: Barbara Maxwell, Government Documents/Reference Libn.
Staff: 1 professional (part time).
Size: 15,600 maps; 50 atlases; 1 globes.
Subject Specialization: topography.
Dates: 1900 - (100%).
Classification System: DMA; USGS quadrangles alphabetically arranged by state and sheet. name
Collections not Cataloged.
Depository for: DMA; USGS (Topo.); GPO.
Serves: students; faculty; public. Mon.–Thurs. 8:30–10 p.m.; Fri. 8:30 a.m.–6 p.m.; Sat. 10 a.m.–6 p.m.; Sun. 12 noon–10 p.m. (Seats 4; 2 readers served per month).
Reproduction Facility: quickcopy.

138. METROPOLITAN WASHINGTON COUNCIL OF GOVERNMENTS
Metropolitan Information Center
1875 Eye Street, N.W., Suite 200
Washington, D.C. 20006
Telephone: 202/223-6800, ext. 230.
Contact Person: Peggy Simon, Information Center Manager.
Staff: 1 professional (full time).
Area Specialization: District of Columbia metropolitan area.
Subject Specialization: urban planning.
Depository for: USGS (Topo.).
Serves: students; faculty; employees; public;. Mon.–Fri. 9 a.m.–5 p.m. (Seats 8).
Reproduction Facility: photocopy.

139. NATIONAL CAPITAL PLANNING COMMISSION
Office of Carto and Graphic Services
1325 G Street, N.W.
Washington, D.C. 20576
Established 1965.
Telephone: 202/724-0211.
Contact Person: Andrea J. Zenthe, Cartotechnician.
Staff: 1 professional (part time); 1 non-professional (part time).
Size: 300,000 maps; 15 atlases; 600 aerial photographs; 35,000 microforms (no. of titles).
Annual Accessions: 2,500 maps; 1,200 microforms (no. of titles).
Area Specialization: Washington, D.C. metropolitan area.
Subject Specialization: planning maps.
Dates: pre-1800 (2%); 1800-1899 (8%); 1900 - (90%).
Classification System: geographic location; subject numbers.
Collections Cataloged.
Serves: employees; public. Mon.–Fri. 8 a.m.–5 p.m. (Seats 5).
Interlibrary Loan Available.
Reproduction Facility: microform; Ozalid.

140. NATIONAL GEOGRAPHIC SOCIETY
Map Library
1146 16th Street, N.W.
Washington, D.C. 20036
Established 1940.
Telephone: 301/921-1401.
Contact Person: Margery K. Barkdull, Map Libn.
Staff: 1 professional (full time); 2 non-professional (full time).
Size: 105,000 maps; 600 atlases; 204 relief models; 250 aerial photographs; 800 reference books and gazetteers; 7 serials (titles received).
Annual Accessions: 1,000 maps; 50 atlases.
Dates: 1800-1899 (1%); 1900 - (99%).
Classification System: LC (some atlases); local system.
Collections Cataloged. (90%).
Depository for: DMA; NTS (Canada); USGS (Topo.).
Serves: employees; public. Mon.–Fri. 8:30 a.m.–5:00 p.m. (Seats 8).
Interlibrary Loan Available. (restricted)
Reproduction Facility: quickcopy.

141. ORGANIZATION OF AMERICAN STATES
Columbus Memorial Library
17th & Constitution, N.W.
Washington, D.C. 20006
Telephone: 202/789-3832.
Contact Person: Guillermo J. Paz, Libn.
Staff: 1 professional (full time).
Area Specialization: Latin America.
Subject Specialization: economic and social geography.
Dates: 1900 - (100%).
Classification System: LC.
Collections Cataloged. (100%).
Serves: students; faculty; employees; public. Mon.–Fri. 9 a.m.–5:15 p.m. (Seats 4).
Reproduction Facility: quickcopy.

142. U.S. DEFENSE MAPPING AGENCY HYDROGRAPHIC/TOPOGRAPHIC CENTER
Scientific Data Department
Support Division
6500 Brookes Lane
Washington, D.C. 20315
Established 1940.
Telephone: 202/227-2080.
Contact Person: Frank P. Lozupone, Chief, Support Division.
Staff: 59 professional (full time); 20 non-professional (full time).
Size: 1,179,656 maps; 250 atlases; 27,690 reference books and gazetteers; 850 serials (titles received).
Annual Accessions: 58,000 maps; 35 atlases; 560 reference books and gazetteers; 40 serials (titles received).
Area Specialization: comprehensive.
Subject Specialization: cartography; engineering; geodesy; hydrography; photogrammetry; topopgraphy.
Special Cartographic Collections: bathymetric, geodetic, nautical charts, and topographic maps.
Classification System: Topographic Data Library System (TDLS); Automated Nautical. Chart Information File (ANCIF)
Collections Cataloged
Serves: employees; by special arrangement. Mon.–Fri. 8:30 a.m.–3 p.m. (Seats Limited).
Reproduction Facility: photocopy; quickcopy; microform.
Publications: *Bi-weekly Accessions List; Annual List of Periodicals Currently Received.*

143. U.S. LIBRARY OF CONGRESS
Geography and Map Division
Washington, D.C. 20540
Established 1897.
Telephone: 202/287-8530 (administration); 202/287-6277. (reference)
Telephone: 202/287-8530
Contact Person: John A. Wolter, Chief.
Staff: 23 professional (full time); 12 non-professional (full time); 2 professional (part time); 1 non-professional (part time).
Size: 3,800,000 maps; 47,000 atlases; 300 globes; 2,258 relief models; 650 aerial photographs; 8,000 reference books and gazetteers; 195 serials (titles received); 58,000 microforms (no. of titles).
Annual Accessions: 56,697 maps; 1,522 atlases; 18 globes; 230 reference books and gazetteers; 5 serials (titles received).
Subject Specialization: comprehensive.
Special Cartographic Collections: American Congress on Surveying and Mapping's Map Design Competition Collection; American Map Collection; Melville Eastham Collection; William Faden Collection; Ethel M. Fair Collection; Millard Fillmore Collection; Peter Force Collection; Thaddeus M. Fowler Collection; Henry Harrisse Collection; Hauslab-Liechtenstein Collection; John Hills Collection; John L. Hines Collection; Jedediah Hotchkiss Collection; Richard Howe Collection; Arthur W. Hummel Collection; Andrew Jackson Collection (Blair Collection); Johann Georg Kohl Collection; Lewis and Clark Collection; Woodbury Lowery Collection; Pierre Ozanne Collection; Panama Canal Company Collection; Walter W. Ristow Map Christmas Card Collection; Rochambeau Collection; Albert Ruger Collection; Sanborn Fire Insurance Map Collection; William Tecumseh Sherman Collection; Ephraim George Squier Collection; Vellum Chart Collection; Langdon Warner Collection.
Dates: pre-1800 (5%); 1800-1899 (20%); 1900 - (75%).
Classification System: LC.
Collections Cataloged. (maps 10%; atlases 90%).
Depository for: DMA; DOS (Gt. Brit); GSC; NOS; NTS (Canada); USGS (Geol., topo.); Official depository for all Federal map producing agencies.
Serves: public. Mon.–Fri. 8:30 a.m.–5 p.m.; Sat. 8:30–12:30 p.m. (Seats 36; 2,626 readers served per month).
Interlibrary Loan Available.
Reproduction Facility: photocopy; quickcopy; microform; color transparencies.
Publications: Information brochure and publication list available upon request.

144. U.S. NATIONAL ARCHIVES & RECORDS SERVICE
Cartographic & Architectural Branch
Washington, D.C. 20408
Established 1934.
Telephone: 703/756-6700.
Contact Person: William H. Cunliffe, Chief.
Staff: 6 professional (full time); 5 non-professional (full time); 3 non-professional (part time).
Size: 2,000,000 maps; 200 atlases; 100 relief models; 10,000,000 aerial photographs; 500 reference books and gazetteers; 25 serials (titles received); 25 microforms (no. of titles).
Annual Accessions: varies maps; varies atlases; varies globes; varies relief models; varies aerial photographs; varies reference books and gazetteers; varies serials (titles received); varies microforms (no. of titles).
Area Specialization: United States; other countries (Western Europe, Latin America, Pacific Basin) in which U.S. government has active interest.
Subject Specialization: U.S. history; history of cartography.
Special Cartographic Collections: Maps: Corps of Engineers (19th century exploration, military activities,

engineering projects); General Land Office (township plats, field notes); Bureau of Indian Affairs (Indian Land Cessions and reservations); Census Bureau (enumeration district maps, 1900–1960); Navy Hydrographic Office and Coast and Geodetic Survey (nautical charts); State Department (International Boundary Commissions and American Commission to Negotiate Peace, WWI); Panama Canal Company; Aerial Photographs: Agriculture Department (U.S. 1930's & 1940's); Defense Intelligence Agency (U.S. 1940's–1960's; Captured German Prints, WW II, Europe).
Dates: pre-1800 (5%); 1800-1899 (45%); 1900 - (50%).
Classification System: Archival arrangement by record groups and federal agency. created classification system
Collections Cataloged. (70%).
Depository for: DMA; NOS; USGS (Geol., topo.).
Serves: public. Mon.–Fri. 8 a.m.–4:30 p.m. (Seats 25; 150 readers served per month).
Reproduction Facility: photocopy; quickcopy;.
Publications: *Guide to Cartographic Records in the National Archives;* list of other publications available upon request.

145. WORLD BANK
Cartography Division
Cartography Library
1818 H Street N.W.
Washington, D.C. 20433
Established 1976.
Telephone: 202/676-0229.
Contact Person: Christine S. Windheuser, Cartographic Libn.
Staff: 1 professional (full time); 1 non-professional (full time).
Size: 20,000 maps; 200 atlases; 1 globes; 300 reference books and gazetteers; 20 serials (titles received).
Annual Accessions: 1,500 maps; 10 atlases; 20 reference books and gazetteers.
Area Specialization: developing nations of Asia, Africa and South America.
Subject Specialization: basic small and medium scale topographic and planometric maps.
Special Cartographic Collections: National Atlases of Developing Countries; Archival collection of World Bank report maps; Satellite tape and image collection.
Dates: 1900 - (100%).
Classification System: Natural Language Titling.
Collections Cataloged.
Serves: employees. Mon.–Fri. 8 a.m.–4:30 p.m. (150 readers served per month).
Reproduction Facility: photocopy.

FLORIDA

Boca Raton

146. FLORIDA ATLANTIC UNIVERSITY
S.E. Wimberly Library
Reference Department
P.O. Box 3092
Boca Raton, FL 33431
Established 1964.
Telephone: 305/395-3785.
Contact Person: Linda Wiler, Head, Reference Dept.
Staff: 1 professional (part time); 1 non-professional (part time).
Area Specialization: Florida.
Subject Specialization: topography.
Special Cartographic Collections: Broward County, Florida aerial photography; U.S. Geological Survey topographic quadrangles.

Dates: 1900 - (100%).
Classification System: Arranged in LC order but not classified.
Collections Cataloged. (Books—Yes; Maps—No).
Depository for: USGS (Topo.).
Serves: students; faculty; employees; public;. Mon.–Thurs. 8 a.m.–12 midnight; Fri. 8 a.m.–6 p.m.; Sat. 9 a.m.–6 p.m.; Sun. 12 noon–12 midnight.
Reproduction Facility: photocopy; microform.

Coral Gables

147. UNIVERSITY OF MIAMI
Geography Department
Map Library
Coral Gables, FL 33146
Telephone: 305/284-4087.
Contact Person: Dr. Donald L. Capone, Professor.
Staff: 1 professional (full time); 1 non-professional (part time).
Size: 45,000 maps; 100 atlases; 25 globes; 200 relief models; 5,000 aerial photographs; 100 reference books and gazetteers.
Annual Accessions: 1,000 maps; 5 atlases; 10 relief models; 500 aerial photographs; 10 reference books and gazetteers.
Area Specialization: North America; South America.
Subject Specialization: topography.
Dates: pre-1800 (1%); 1800-1899 (2%); 1900 - (97%).
Classification System: AGS.
Collections Cataloged. (50%).
Depository for: DMA.

Deland

148. STETSON UNIVERSITY
DuPont-Ball Library
Government Documents
421 North Boulevard
Deland, FL 32720
Established 1950.
Telephone: 904/734-4121, ext. 216.
Contact Person: Sims Kline, Director.
Size: 3,200 maps; 150 atlases; 1 globes; 50 reference books and gazetteers.
Annual Accessions: 175 maps; 20 atlases; 5 reference books and gazetteers.
Area Specialization: Florida.
Subject Specialization: topography.
Dates: 1900 - (100%).
Classification System: LC for Atlases.
Depository for: USGS (Topo.).
Serves: students; faculty; employees. Mon.–Fri. 8 a.m.–11 p.m.; Sat. 9 a.m.–5 p.m.; Sun. 1–11 p.m. (Seats 20; 15 readers served per month).
Reproduction Facility: photocopy; microform.

Gainesville

149. UNIVERSITY OF FLORIDA
P. K. Yonge Library of Florida History
Map Collection
404 Library West, University of Florida
Gainesville, FL 32611
Established 1944.
Telephone: 904/392-0319.
Contact Person: Elizabeth Alexander, Libn.

Staff: 2 professional (full time); 2 non-professional (part time).
Size: 1,875 maps; 25 reference books and gazetteers.
Annual Accessions: 90 maps; 1 reference books and gazetteers.
Area Specialization: Florida; Gulf Coast; West Indies; southeastern United States.
Subject Specialization: history.
Special Cartographic Collections: Public Record Office maps of Florida and the southeastern United States (photocopies); Archivo General de Indias maps of Florida and the southeastern United States (photocopies).
Dates: pre-1800 (30%); 1800-1899 (40%); 1900 - (30%).
Classification System: local system.
Serves: public. Mon.–Fri. 8 a.m.–4:45 p.m. (Seats 2; 20 readers served per month).

150. UNIVERSITY OF FLORIDA
University Libraries
Map Library
Gainesville, FL 32611
Established 1948/1973.
Telephone: 904/392-0803.
Contact Person: Dr. HelenJane Armstrong, Map Libn.
Staff: 1 professional (full time); 1 non-professional (full time); 1 professional (part time); 5 non-professional (part time).
Size: 334,785 maps; 745 atlases; 17 globes; 94 relief models; 169,131 aerial photographs; 1,084 reference books and gazetteers; 8 serials (titles received); 38 microforms (no. of titles).
Annual Accessions: 8,000 maps; 25 atlases; 3,000 aerial photographs; 25 reference books and gazetteers.
Area Specialization: Comprehensive; Latin America and Florida emphasis.
Subject Specialization: Comprehensive.
Special Cartographic Collections: Remote Sensing Imagery Collection-1236 hardocpy, 13 slides; NASA Aerial Film Library-456 (9" rolls) & 111 (70mm film)-low level, color, CIR, B&W; Florida Cities Sanborn Collection; Erwin Raisz Collection-personal maps and books.
Dates: pre-1800 (.5%); 1800-1899 (.5%); 1900 - (99%).
Classification System: LC.
Collections Cataloged.
Depository for: DMA; NOS; USGS (Geol., topo.).
Serves: students; faculty; employees; public. Mon.–Fri. 8:30 a.m.–5 p.m. (Seats 32; 1,060 readers served per month).
Interlibrary Loan Available. restricted
Reproduction Facility: photocopy.
Publications: *Map Resources of Africa* (brochure); *Map Resources of Latin America* (brochure-in progress).

Lake Alfred

151. INSTITUTE OF FOOD AND AGRICULTURAL SCIENCES
Remote Sensing-Aerial Photographic Archives
700 Experiment Station Road
Lake Alfred, FL 33850
Established 1982.
Telephone: 813/956-1151, ext 271.
Contact Person: Dr. Carlos H. Blazquez, Associate Professor.
Staff: $1/2$ professional (full time); $1/2$ non-professional (full time).
Size: 1,000 maps; 5,000 aerial photographs.
Annual Accessions: 100 maps; 600/biennially aerial photographs; 300 aerial photographs.
Area Specialization: Florida.
Subject Specialization: citrus areas.
Dates: 1900 - (100%).
Classification System: USDA system.

Collections Cataloged.
Depository for: USGS (Topo.).
Serves: faculty; scientific investigators. By appointment. (Seats 10; 20 readers served per month).
Interlibrary Loan Available. (by special arrangement)

Miami

152. FLORIDA INTERNATIONAL UNIVERSITY
Library
Documents Section
Tamiami Campus
Miami, FL 33199
Contact Person: J. Hortensia Rodriguez, Documents Libn.
Staff: 1 professional (full time); 1 non-professional (part time).
Size: 7,344 maps; 300 atlases; 2 globes; 5 reference books and gazetteers.
Annual Accessions: 100 maps; 5 atlases; 5 reference books and gazetteers.
Area Specialization: southeastern United states.
Subject Specialization: topography.
Dates: 1900 - (100%).
Collections not Cataloged.
Depository for: USGS (Topo.).
Serves: students; faculty; employees; public. Mon.–Thurs. 8 a.m.–11 p.m.; Fri. 8 a.m.–8 p.m.; Sat. 9 a.m.–8 p.m.; Sun. 1–11 p.m. (Seats 20; 10 readers served per month).
Interlibrary Loan Available.
Reproduction Facility: Xerox.

153. MIAMI-DADE PUBLIC LIBRARY
Main Library
General Reference Department, Florida Collection
One Biscayne Boulevard
Miami, FL 33132
Telephone: 305/579-5001.
Contact Person: Arlene Freier, General Reference, Libn. I; Sam Boldrick, Florida Collection, Libn. II.
Staff: 2 professional (part time); 2 non-professional (part time).
Size: 1,500 maps; 110 atlases; 2 globes; 300 aerial photographs; 15 reference books and gazetteers.
Annual Accessions: 150 maps; 5 atlases; 1 reference books and gazetteers.
Area Specialization: southeastern United States; Caribbean.
Subject Specialization: topography.
Special Cartographic Collections: meteorology (hurricanes).
Dates: pre-1800 (Florida 25%); 1800-1899 (Florida 25%); 1900 - (Florida 50%).
Classification System: local system: Alphabetical by political unit (governmental. unit)
Collections not Cataloged.
Depository for: USGS (Geol., topo.).
Serves: students; faculty; employees; public. Mon.–Fri. 9 a.m.–6 p.m.; Sat. 9 a.m.–6 p.m.; Sun. October to May 1 p.m.–5 p.m. (Seats 24; 20 readers served per month).
Interlibrary Loan Available. (copies)
Reproduction Facility: photocopy; photograph, blue print.

Pensacola

154. UNIVERSITY OF WEST FLORIDA
John C. Pace Library
Pensacola, FL 32504
Established 1967.
Telephone: 904/474-2414.
Contact Person: Bob Perdue, Reference Libn.

Staff: 1 professional (part time); 1 non-professional (part time).
Size: 13,000 maps; 250 atlases; 2 globes; 3,000 aerial photographs; 100 reference books and gazetteers; 10 serials (titles received); 5 microforms (no. of titles).
Annual Accessions: 300 maps; 20 atlases; 30 aerial photographs; 10 reference books and gazetteers; 1 serials (titles received).
Area Specialization: western Florida; Gulf Coast.
Subject Specialization: history.
Special Cartographic Collections: depository for USGS (Geol—Florida, Alabama, and Georgia), and NOS Gulf Coast Nautical charts; maintains a collection of original and reproduction maps of the historical cartography of west Florida.
Dates: pre-1800 (5%); 1800-1899 (10%); 1900 - (85%).
Classification System: local system.
Depository for: NOS; USGS (Geol.).
Serves: students; faculty; employees; public. Mon.–Thurs. 8 a.m.–10:30 p.m., Fri. 8 a.m.–5 p.m.; Sat. 8 a.m.–5 p.m.; Sun. 1–10 p.m. (Seats 20; 150 readers served per month).
Reproduction Facility: photocopy; microform.
Publications: *Basic Information Sources: Maps* (guide).

Tallahassee

155. FLORIDA (STATE) BUREAU OF GEOLOGY
Library
903 West Tennessee Street
Tallahassee, FL 32304
Telephone: 904/488-9380, ext. 35.
Contact Person: Alison M. Lewis, Libn.
Staff: 1 professional (full time); 1 non-professional (part time).
Size: 12,500 maps; 25 atlases; 614 aerial photographs; 2,400 reference books and gazetteers; 35 serials (titles received).
Annual Accessions: 200 maps; 30 reference books and gazetteers.
Area Specialization: Florida.
Subject Specialization: geology; topography.
Dates: 1800-1899 (1%); 1900 - (99%).
Collections not Cataloged.
Depository for: DOS (Gt. Brit); NTS (Canada); USGS (Geol., topo.).
Serves: public. Mon.–Fri. 8a.m.–5 p.m. (Seats 5; 200 readers served per month).
Interlibrary Loan Available.
Reproduction Facility: photocopy.

156. FLORIDA STATE UNIVERSITY
Documents-Maps-Micromaterials Department
Maps Department
Tallahassee, FL 32306
Established 1947.
Telephone: 904/644-6061.
Contact Person: Marianne Donnell, Maps Libn.
Staff: 1 professional (full time).
Size: 136,000 maps; 2,065 atlases; 15 globes; 12 relief models; 650 reference books and gazetteers; 14 serials (titles received); 3 microforms (no. of titles).
Annual Accessions: 5,000 maps; 125 atlases; 35 reference books and gazetteers; 1 serials (titles received).
Area Specialization: Florida; southeastern United states.
Subject Specialization: history; topography; geology.
Dates: pre-1800 (10%); 1800-1899 (15%); 1900 - (75%).
Classification System: LC.
Collections Cataloged.
Depository for: DMA; NOS; USGS (Geol., topo.).
Serves: students; faculty; employees; public;. Mon.–Thurs. 8 a.m.–12 midnight; Fri. 8 p.m.–10 p.m.; Sat. 10 a.m.–10 p.m.;

Sun. 1 p.m.–12 midnight. (Seats 52; 500 readers served per month).
Interlibrary Loan Available.
Reproduction Facility: photocopy.
Publications: Monthly acquisitions list.

GEORGIA

Athens

Tampa

157. UNIVERSITY OF SOUTH FLORIDA
Library
Documents
Tampa, FL 33620
Established 1962.
Telephone: 813/961-6935.
Contact Person: Julia Schwartz, Documents Libn.
Staff: 1 non-professional (part time).
Size: 66,342 maps; 500 atlases; 1 globes; 3 relief models; 500 reference books and gazetteers; 3 serials (titles received); 700 microforms (no. of titles).
Annual Accessions: 2,000 maps; 350 microforms (no. of titles).
Dates: 1900 - (100%).
Classification System: LC.
Collections not Cataloged.
Depository for: DMA; USGS (Topo.).
Serves: students; faculty; employees; public;. Mon.–Fri. 8 a.m.–11 p.m.; Sat. 8 a.m.–5 p.m.; Sun. 1–11 p.m. (Seats 50; 120 readers served per month).
Interlibrary Loan Available.
Reproduction Facility: photocopy; microform.

158. UNIVERSITY OF SOUTH FLORIDA, LIBRARY
Special Collections
Florida Map Collections
Tampa, FL 33620
Established 1962.
Telephone: 813/974-2731.
Contact Person: Paul Eugen Camp, Associate Libn., Special Collections.
Staff: 2 professional (full time); 4 non-professional (full time).
Size: ca. 1,500 maps; ca. 50 atlases; 1 globes; 45 reference books and gazetteers.
Annual Accessions: variable maps; variable atlases; variable reference books and gazetteers.
Area Specialization: Florida.
Subject Specialization: Florida history.
Special Cartographic Collections: Florida (pre-1900)- collection is divided into original and facsimile sections; 19th Century Florida nautical charts; Superseded USGS topo maps; Florida highway maps to 1970; Florida Historical Society Collection of maps of Florida.
Dates: pre-1800 (25%); 1800-1899 (45%); 1900 - (30%).
Classification System: local system.
Collections Cataloged.
Depository for: USGS (Topo.); Fla. State Highway Maps.
Serves: students; faculty; employees; public;. Mon.–Thurs. 8 a.m.–9 p.m.; Fri. 8 a.m.–5 p.m.; Sun. 1 p.m.–5 p.m. (Seats 30; 150 readers served per month).
Reproduction Facility: photocopy.

159. UNIVERSITY OF GEORGIA
Department of Geography
Athens, GA 30602
Telephone: 404/542-2856.
Contact Person: Dr. James Fisher, Chairman.
Staff: 1 non-professional (part time).
Size: 4,000 maps.
Area Specialization: Georgia; southeastern United States.
Subject Specialization: topography.
Classification System: local system.
Serves: students; faculty.

160. UNIVERSITY OF GEORGIA
Libraries
Special Collections Division
Athens, GA 30602
Established 1939.
Telephone: 404/542-7123.
Contact Person: Robert M. Willingham, Jr., Curator, Rare Books and Manuscripts.
Staff: 1 professional (part time); 1 non-professional (part time).
Size: 2,400 maps; 25 atlases; 125 reference books and gazetteers.
Annual Accessions: 40 maps; 1 atlases; 10 reference books and gazetteers.
Area Specialization: southeastern United States; British Isles.
Subject Specialization: Confederate imprints.
Dates: pre-1800 (30%); 1800-1899 (45%); 1900 - (25%).
Classification System: local system.
Collections Cataloged. (100%).
Serves: students; faculty; employees; public. Mon.–Fri. 8 a.m.–6 p.m.; Sat. 9 a.m.–6 p.m. (Seats 10; 15 readers served per month).
Reproduction Facility: photocopy; microform.

161. UNIVERSITY OF GEORGIA
Science Library
Map Collection
Athens, Georgia 30602
Established 1948.
Telephone: 404/542-4535.
Contact Person: Johnnie D. Sutherland, Curator of Maps.
Staff: 2 professional (full time); 1 non-professional (full time); 3 non-professional (part time).
Size: 291,165 maps; 800 atlases; 6 globes; 40 relief models; 192,068 aerial photographs; 400 reference books and gazetteers; 6 serials (titles received); 10 microforms (no. of titles).
Annual Accessions: 10,000 maps; 50 atlases; 6,000 aerial photographs; 50 reference books and gazetteers.
Area Specialization: Georgia; southeastern United States; Central and South America; Europe.
Subject Specialization: topography; geology; soils; vegetation.
Special Cartographic Collections: Sanborn Fire Insurance Map Collection (7,000+ sheets).
Dates: 1800-1899 (2%); 1900 - (98%).
Classification System: LC.

Collections Cataloged. (85%).
Depository for: DMA; NOS; USGS (Geol., topo.); Georgia Department of Transportation.
Serves: students; faculty; employees; public. Mon.–Thurs. 8 a.m.–10 p.m.; Fri. 8 a.m.–6 p.m.; Sat. 1 p.m.–6 p.m.; Sun. 1 p.m.–10 p.m. (Seats 25; 700 readers served per month).
Interlibrary Loan Available.
Reproduction Facility: photocopy; quickcopy.
Publications: *Sanborn Fire Insurance Maps* (List); *Air Photos of Georgia* (List); *Atlases in Map Collection* (List); *Newsletter/Acquisitions List; Guide to Map Collection.*

Atlanta

162. GEORGIA INSTITUTE OF TECHNOLOGY
Price Gilbert Memorial Library
Department of Government Documents and Maps
225 North Avenue
Atlanta, Georgia 30332
Established 1946.
Telephone: 404/894-4538, 4519.
Contact Person: Barbara J. Walker, Librarian-Assistant Professor.
Staff: 2 professional (full time); 1 non-professional (full time); 7 non-professional (part time).
Size: 127,000 sheets maps; 900 atlases; 4 globes; 75 relief models; 5 vols. aerial photographs; 500 reference books and gazetteers; 10 microforms (no. of titles).
Annual Accessions: 3,900 sheets maps; 20 atlases.
Area Specialization: Georgia; southeastern United States.
Subject Specialization: topography; geology; transportation; city planning; architecture.
Special Cartographic Collections: Joan Blaeu *Grooten Atlas* - 9 folio volumes - Dutch Text.
Dates: pre-1800 (5%); 1800-1899 (5%); 1900 - (90%).
Classification System: LC.
Collections Cataloged.
Depository for: DMA; NOS; USGS (Geol., topo.).
Serves: students; faculty; employees; public. Mon.–Thurs. 8 a.m.–12 midnight; Fri. 8 a.m.–6 p.m.; Sat. 9 a.m.–6 p.m.; Sun. 2–12 Midnight. (Seats 50 (Government Documents and Maps)).
Interlibrary Loan Available.
Reproduction Facility: photocopy; quickcopy; microform.

163. GEORGIA (STATE) SURVEYOR GENERAL DEPARTMENT
Cartographic Collection
Archives and Records Building, 330 Capitol Avenue
Atlanta, GA 30334
Established 1964.
Telephone: 404/656-2367, ext. 68.
Contact Person: Marion R. Hemperley, Deputy Surveyor General of Georgia.
Staff: 4 professional (full time).
Size: 10,000 maps; 50 atlases; 15 relief models; 250 aerial photographs; 100 reference books and gazetteers; 10 microforms (no. of titles).
Annual Accessions: 100 maps; 5 atlases; 5 reference books and gazetteers.
Area Specialization: Georgia; southeastern United States.
Subject Specialization: original base surveys for Georgia, 1805–1832.
Special Cartographic Collections: Dr. John H. Goff Collection of southern place names and historic places.
Dates: pre-1800 (20); 1800-1899 (65); 1900 - (15).
Classification System: local system.
Collections Cataloged. (100%).
Depository for: USGS (Topo.).

Serves: students; faculty; employees; public. Mon.–Fri. 8 a.m.–4:30 p.m. (Seats 35; 300 readers served per month).
Reproduction Facility: photocopy.
Publications: *Descriptive Inventory No. 1: Records of the Town of Columbus; Descriptive Inventory No. 2: John H. Goff Collection; Descriptive Inventory No. 3: Records of the Town of Macon; Catalog of Pre-Nineteenth Century Maps, 1260–1799; Nineteenth Century Maps, 1800–1849.*

164. GEORGIA STATE UNIVERSITY
Pullen Library
Reference Department
100 Decatur Street, SE
Atlanta, GA 30303
Telephone: 404/658-2186.
Contact Person: Gayle Christian, Reference and Map Libn.
Staff: 1 professional (part time); 1 non-professional (part time).
Size: 8,000 maps; 225 atlases; 1 globes.
Area Specialization: Georgia; southeastern United States.
Subject Specialization: urban.
Special Cartographic Collections: Sanborn Fire Insurance Maps/Georgia (microform).
Dates: 1900 - (99%).
Classification System: LC; GPO.
Collections Cataloged. (20%).
Depository for: USGS (Geol., topo.).
Serves: students; faculty; employees; public. Mon.–Fri. 8 a.m.–10 p.m.; Sat. 9 a.m.–6 p.m.; Sun. 12 noon–6 p.m.
Reproduction Facility: photocopy.

Carrollton

165. WEST GEORGIA COLLEGE
Irvine Sullivan Ingram Library
Map Collection
Carrollton, GA 30118
Established 1968.
Telephone: 404/834-1370.
Contact Person: Virginia Ruskell, Head of Reference.
Staff: 1 professional (part time).
Size: 11,377 maps; 46 atlases; 3 globes; 3 reference books and gazetteers.
Annual Accessions: 804 maps.
Area Specialization: United States; southeastern United States.
Subject Specialization: geography; geology.
Classification System: LC.
Collections Cataloged.
Depository for: USGS (Topo.).
Serves: students;. faculty; employees; public. Mon.–Thurs. 7:30 a.m.–10 p.m.; Fri. 7:30 a.m.–5 p.m.; Sat. 10 a.m.–5 p.m.; Sun. 3 p.m.–10 p.m. (Seats 12).
Interlibrary Loan Available.
Reproduction Facility: photocopy.

Columbus

166. COLUMBUS COLLEGE
Simon Schwob Memorial Library
Map Section
Algonquin Drive
Columbus, GA 31993
Established 1982.
Telephone: 404/568-2042.

Contact Person: Merne H. Posey, Documents Libn.
Staff: 1 professional (part time); 1 non-professional (part time).
Size: 1,200 maps.
Annual Accessions: around 800 maps.
Area Specialization: southeastern United States.
Subject Specialization: topography; geology; history; city street maps; state maps; European and Asian city and country maps.
Dates: pre-1800 (2%); 1800-1899 (10%); 1900 - (88%).
Classification System: In-house, based on LC.
Collections Cataloged.
Depository for: USGS (Geol.).
Serves: students; faculty; employees; public. Mon.–Thurs. 8:00 a.m.–11:00 p.m.; Fri. 8:00 a.m.–5:15 p.m.; Sat. 1–6 p.m.; Sun. 2–8 p.m. (50–75 readers served per month).
Reproduction Facility: photocopy; microform.

Douglas

167. SOUTH GEORGIA COLLEGE
William S. Smith Library
Douglas, GA 31533
Telephone: 912/384-1100, ext. 290.
Contact Person: Judy Kipp, Assistant Libn. for Technical Services.
Staff: 1 professional (part time); 1 non-professional (part time).
Size: 16,700 maps.
Annual Accessions: 800–900 maps.
Dates: 1900 - (100%).
Classification System: local system.
Collections not Cataloged.
Serves: students; faculty; public. Mon.–Thur. 8 a.m.–10 p.m.; Fri 8:00 a.m.–5:00 p.m. Summer hours:. Mon.–Fri. 8 a.m.–7 p.m. Sun. 3–8:00 p.m.
Reproduction Facility: photocopy.

Savannah

168. GEORGIA HISTORICAL SOCIETY
501 Whitaker Street
Savannah, GA 31499
Telephone: 912/944-2128.
Contact Person: Anne Smith, Archivist.
Staff: 2 professional (full time); 2 non-professional (full time); 2 non-professional (part time).
Area Specialization: Georgia; southeastern United States.
Collections Cataloged. (50%).
Depository for: USGS (Topo.).
Serves: students; faculty; public. Mon.–Fri. 10 a.m.–5 p.m. (Seats 35; 50 readers served per month).
Reproduction Facility: quickcopy.

Statesboro

169. GEORGIA SOUTHERN COLLEGE
Library
Landrum Box 8074
Statesboro, GA 30460
Telephone: 912/681-5645.
Contact Person: Orion Harrison, Head Reference Libn.
Size: 4,933 maps.
Dates: 1900 - (99%).
Classification System: local system.
Collections not Cataloged.
Depository for: NOAA.

Serves: students; faculty. Mon.–Fri. 8 a.m.–9 p.m.; Sat. 9 a.m.–5 p.m.; Sun. 2–9 p.m. (Seats 30; 4–5 readers served per month).
Reproduction Facility: photocopy.

Valdosta

170. VALDOSTA STATE COLLEGE
Library
Government Documents and Maps
Valdosta, GA 31698
Telephone: 912/333-5943.
Contact Person: Jane Zahner, Documents Libn.
Staff: 1 professional (part time).
Size: 750 maps; 35 atlases; 1 globes; 30 aerial photographs; 15 reference books and gazetteers.
Annual Accessions: 300 maps; 2 atlases; 5 reference books and gazetteers.
Area Specialization: Georgia; southeastern United States.
Special Cartographic Collections: Holtzendorff Map Collection—Early Georgia History and Geography; Bennett Collection—Includes early survey maps of South Georgia.
Dates: pre-1800 (3%); 1800-1899 (5%); 1900 - (92%).
Classification System: local system.
Collections Cataloged. (8%).
Depository for: USGS (Topo.).
Serves: students; faculty; employees; public;. Mon.–Thurs. 8 a.m.–10 p.m.; Fri. 8 a.m.–5 p.m.; Sat. 11 a.m.–5 p.m.; Sun. 2 p.m.–10 p.m. (Seats 80; 15 readers served per month).
Interlibrary Loan Available.
Reproduction Facility: photocopy.

HAWAII

Hilo

171. UNIVERSITY OF HAWAII AT HILO
Library
Government Documents Department
1400 K
Hilo, HI 96720
Telephone: 808/961-9525.
Contact Person: T. H. Minn, Government Documents Libn.
Size: 669 maps; 1 globes.
Area Specialization: Hawaii.
Dates: 1900 - (100%).
Classification System: local system: Arranged by regions.
Collections not Cataloged.
Serves: students; faculty; employees; public. Mon.–Fri. 7:45 a.m.–10 p.m.; Sun. 1–10 p.m. (Seats 16; 5 readers served per month).
Interlibrary Loan Available.
Reproduction Facility: photocopy; microform.

Honolulu

172. BERNICE P. BISHOP MUSEUM
Library
Geography and Map Division
P.O. Box 19000-A
Honolulu, HI 96817
Established 1960.
Telephone: 808/847-3511, ext. 144.
Contact Person: Lee S. Mottler, Geographer.
Staff: 1 professional (full time); 1 professional (part time).

Size: 20,000 maps; 450 atlases; 8 globes; 20 relief models; 70,000 aerial photographs; 1,700 reference books and gazetteers; 6 serials (titles received); 12 microforms (no. of titles).
Area Specialization: Hawaii; Pacific Ocean; Southeast Asia.
Subject Specialization: place name research; hydrography; biogeography; topography.
Special Cartographic Collections: Aerial photographs of the Pacific Islands during World War II; Manuscript charts and archaeological surveys; Printed maps of Early Pacific Explorations.
Dates: pre-1800 (3%); 1800-1899 (12%); 1900 - (85%).
Classification System: local system.
Collections Cataloged. (60%).
Depository for: DMA; USGS (Topo.).
Serves: students; faculty; employees; public;. Mon.–Fri. 8 a.m.–4 p.m. (Seats 6; 25 readers served per month).
Reproduction Facility: photocopy; photographic copy via in-house laboratory.

173. HAWAII INSTITUTE OF GEOPHYSICS
Library
Room 252
2525 Correa Road
Honolulu, HI 96822
Established 1963.
Telephone: 808/948-7040.
Contact Person: Patricia Price, Libn.
Size: 8,000 maps; 25 atlases; 2 globes; 20 aerial photographs; 10 microforms (no. of titles).
Annual Accessions: 20 maps.
Area Specialization: Pacific Ocean area; Hawaii.
Subject Specialization: topography; bathymetry; geology.
Dates: 1800-1899 (2%); 1900 - (98%).
Classification System: local system.
Collections Cataloged. (99%).
Serves: students; faculty; employees; public. Mon.–Fri. 7:30 a.m.–5:45 p.m. (Seats 40; 50 readers served per month).
Interlibrary Loan Available.
Reproduction Facility: photocopy.

174. HAWAII STATE ARCHIVES
Iolani Palace Grounds
Honolulu, HI 96813
Telephone: 808/548-2355.
Contact Person: Richard F. Thompson, Libn.
Staff: 1 professional (part time).
Size: 2,025 maps; 1,000 aerial photographs.
Annual Accessions: 15 maps.
Area Specialization: Hawaiian Islands.
Dates: pre-1800 (Less than 1%); 1800-1899 (10%); 1900 - (90%).
Classification System: Island-Area-Date.
Collections Cataloged. (100%). Mon.–Fri. 7:45 a.m.–4:30 p.m. except state holidays. (Seats 25; 5 readers served per month).
Reproduction Facility: photocopy.

175. HAWAII STATE LIBRARY
Hawaii and Pacific Section
478 South King Street
Honolulu, HI 96813
Telephone: 808/548-2346.
Contact Person: Proserfina Strona, Head.
Staff: 3 professional (part time); 1 non-professional (part time).
Size: 1,000 maps; 12 atlases; 1 relief models; 500 aerial photographs.
Area Specialization: Hawaii; Pacific Ocean; Australia; New Zealand; Philippines.
Dates: pre-1800 (1%); 1800-1899 (1%); 1900 - (98%).
Collections not Cataloged.

Serves: students; faculty; employees; public. Mon., Wed., Fri. 9 a.m.–5 p.m.; Tues. & Thurs. 9 a.m.–8 p.m.; Sat. 9 a.m.–5 p.m. (Seats 12; 25 readers served per month).
Interlibrary Loan Available.
Reproduction Facility: photocopy.

176. HAWAII STATE LIBRARY
Language, Literature & History Section
478 S. King Street
Honolulu, HI 96734
Established 1913.
Telephone: 808/548-2695.
Contact Person: Arlene Kita, Libn.
Staff: 1 professional (full time).
Size: 2,000 est. maps; 25-30 est. atlases; 1 globes; 10-20 est. reference books and gazetteers; 1 serials (titles received).
Area Specialization: emphasis on U.S. cities and counties, but also covers other countries and their cities.
Classification System: local system.
Collections not Cataloged.
Depository for: Maps from these agencies are usually ordered. by the Hawaiian and Pacific Section and housed in the Language, Literature, History Section. The Government Documents Section, a partial depository, does not house the maps. Mon.–Fri. 9 a.m.–5 p.m.; Sat. 9 a.m.–5 p.m.
Reproduction Facility: photocopy.

177. HAWAIIAN HISTORICAL SOCIETY
Library
560 Kawaiahao St.
Honolulu, HI 96813
Established 1892.
Telephone: 808/537-6271.
Contact Person: Barbara E. Dunn, Libn.
Staff: 1 professional (full time).
Area Specialization: Hawaii and the Pacific Basin.
Subject Specialization: history.
Dates: pre-1800 (10%); 1800-1899 (80%); 1900 - (10%).
Collections not Cataloged.
Serves: public. Mon.–Fri 10 a.m.–4 p.m. (Seats 14; 100 readers served per month).

178. UNIVERSITY OF HAWAII AT MANOA
Library
Map Collection
2550 The Mall
Honolulu, HI 96822
Telephone: 808/948-8539.
Contact Person: Mabel Suzuki, Library Technician.
Staff: 1 non-professional (full time); 1 non-professional (part time).
Size: 105,000 maps; 12 atlases; 1 globes; 20 relief models; 4,600 aerial photographs; 60 reference books and gazetteers; 3 serials (titles received).
Annual Accessions: 5,000 maps.
Area Specialization: Hawaii; Pacific; Asia.
Subject Specialization: comprehensive.
Dates: pre-1800 (.5%); 1800-1899 (.5%); 1900 - (99%).
Classification System: LC; Superintendent of Documents.
Collections Cataloged. (85%).
Depository for: DMA; NOS; USGS (Geol., topo.); GPO.
Serves: students; faculty; employees; public. Mon.–Fri. 8:30 a.m.–4:30 p.m. (Seats 14; 200 readers served per month).
Reproduction Facility: photocopy; microform; Photography.

IDAHO

Boise

179. IDAHO STATE HISTORICAL SOCIETY
325 West State Street
Boise, ID 83702
Established 1886.
Telephone: 280/334-3356.
Contact Person: Larry R. Jones, Historian.
Staff: 1 professional (full time); 1 professional (part time).
Size: 10,000 maps; 6 atlases; 15 relief models; 100 aerial photographs; 50 reference books and gazetteers.
Annual Accessions: 50-100 maps.
Area Specialization: Idaho; Pacific Northwest.
Subject Specialization: history.
Dates: 1800-1899 (10); 1900 - (90).
Classification System: LC; local system filed alphabetically and by subject.
Collections not Cataloged.
Serves: public. Mon.–Fri. 8 a.m.–5 p.m. (Seats 15; 100 readers served per month).
Reproduction Facility: photocopy.

180. BOISE STATE UNIVERSITY
Library
Map Department
1910 University Drive
Boise, ID 83725
Established 1971.
Telephone: 208/385-3958.
Contact Person: Don P. Haacke, Map Libn.
Staff: 1 professional (full time); 1 non-professional (full time).
Size: 101,500 maps; 108 atlases; 3 globes; 93 relief models; 78,000 aerial photographs; 197 reference books and gazetteers; 8 serials (titles received).
Annual Accessions: 3,997 maps; 3 relief models; 2,000 aerial photographs; 5 reference books and gazetteers.
Area Specialization: Pacific Northwest; United States.
Subject Specialization: geology; public lands; transportation.
Dates: 1800-1899 (2%); 1900 - (98%).
Classification System: LC.
Collections Cataloged.
Depository for: NOS; USGS (Geol., topo.).
Serves: students; faculty; employees; public. Mon.–Fri. 8 a.m.–10 p.m.; Sat. 9 a.m.–5 p.m.; Sun. 1–9 p.m. (Seats 24; 135 readers served per month).
Interlibrary Loan Available.
Reproduction Facility: photocopy.

Moscow

181. UNIVERSITY OF IDAHO
Library
Map Collection
Moscow, ID 83842
Telephone: 208/885-6344.
Contact Person: Dennis Baird, Social Science Libn.
Staff: 1 professional (part time); 1 non-professional (part time).
Size: 126,173 maps; 400 atlases; 1 globes; 20,000 aerial photographs; 300 reference books and gazetteers.
Annual Accessions: 2,100 maps; 25 atlases; 1,000 aerial photographs; 10 reference books and gazetteers.
Area Specialization: Idaho; Pacific Northwest.
Subject Specialization: forestry; geology.
Special Cartographic Collections: National forest maps, pre-1930.

Dates: 1800-1899 (2%); 1900 - (98%).
Classification System: LC.
Collections Cataloged. (35%).
Depository for: DMA; USGS (Geol., topo.); Hemispheric Mapping Program.
Serves: students; faculty; employees; public;. Mon.–Fri. 8 a.m.–10 p.m.; Sat. 9 a.m.–5 p.m.; Sun. 1–10 p.m. (Seats 20; 600 readers served per month).
Reproduction Facility: photocopy; microform.
Publications: *University of Idaho Library Guide 11: Map Collection; University of Idaho Library Guide 38: How to Find a Geologic Map.*

Pocatello

182. IDAHO STATE UNIVERSITY
Eli M. Oboler Library
Map Collection
Pocatello, ID 83209
Established Pre-1948.
Telephone: 208/236-3212.
Contact Person: Gary Domitz, Reference and Archives Libn.
Staff: 1 professional (part time); 1 non-professional (part time).
Size: 36,831 maps; 120 atlases; 10 relief models; 380 reels microforms (no. of titles).
Annual Accessions: 1,000 maps.
Area Specialization: western United States.
Subject Specialization: topography.
Dates: 1900 - (100%).
Classification System: LC; DMA; local system.
Collections not Cataloged.
Depository for: DMA; USGS (Geol., topo.).
Serves: students; faculty; employees; public;. Mon.–Thurs. 7:45 a.m.–10:30 p.m., Fri 7:45 a.m.–5 p.m.; Sat. 9 a.m.–5 p.m.; Sun. 2–10:30 p.m. (Seats 24; 50 readers served per month).
Interlibrary Loan Available.
Reproduction Facility: photocopy.

183. POCATELLO PUBLIC LIBRARY
812 E. Clark
Pocatello, ID 83201
Established 1979.
Telephone: 208/232-1263.
Contact Person: Janet K. Wright, Adult Services Libn.
Staff: 1 professional (part time).
Size: 1,000 maps; 24 atlases; 1 globes; 1 relief models; 1 aerial photographs; 10 reference books and gazetteers.
Annual Accessions: 40 maps.
Area Specialization: Idaho.
Subject Specialization: topography.
Special Cartographic Collections: U.S.G.S. Maps— topographic quadrangle maps issued for state of Idaho.
Dates: 1900 - (100%).
Classification System: local system.
Collections not Cataloged.
Depository for: USGS (Topo.).
Serves: public. Sat. 10 a.m.–6 p.m. (Seats 45).
Reproduction Facility: photocopy.

Rexburg

184. RICKS COLLEGE
David O. McKay Learning Resources Center
Map Collection
Rexburg, ID 83440
Established 1956.
Telephone: 208/356-2351.
Contact Person: Gale D. Reeser, Humanities/Map Libn.
Staff: 2 professional (full time); 8 non-professional (part time).
Size: 13,459 maps; 163 atlases; 6 globes; 15 relief models; 181 reference books and gazetteers; 4 serials (titles received); 200 microforms (no. of titles).
Annual Accessions: 283 maps.
Area Specialization: Idaho; Pacific Northwest.
Subject Specialization: geology.
Dates: pre-1800 (1%); 1800-1899 (1%); 1900 - (98%).
Classification System: LC.
Collections Cataloged. (50%).
Depository for: USGS (Topo.).
Serves: students; faculty; employees; public. Mon.–Fri. 7 a.m.–10 p.m.; Sat. 7 a.m.–10 p.m. (Seats 100; 15 readers served per month).
Interlibrary Loan Available.
Reproduction Facility: photocopy.

ILLINOIS

Aurora

185. AURORA PUBLIC LIBRARY
Adult Services Department
One East Benton St.
Aurora, IL 60506
Established 1900's.
Telephone: 312/896-9761.
Contact Person: Kathryn Tutor, Adult Services Assistant.
Staff: 1 professional (full time); 1 non-professional (full time).
Size: 500 maps; 20 atlases; 1 globes; 1 aerial photographs; 20 reference books and gazetteers.
Annual Accessions: 50 maps.
Dates: 1900 - (100%).
Classification System: Alphabetically by quadrangle.
Collections not Cataloged.
Depository for: USGS (Topo.). Mon.–Fri. 9 a.m.–9 p.m.; Sat. 9 a.m.–6 p.m. (Seats 89).
Reproduction Facility: photocopy.

Carbondale

186. SOUTHERN ILLINOIS UNIVERSITY AT CARBONDALE
Morris Library, Science Division
Map Library
Carbondale, IL 62901
Established 1954.
Telephone: 618/453-2700.
Contact Person: Jean M. Ray, Map and Assistant Science Libn.
Staff: 1 professional (part time); 4 non-professional (part time).
Size: 158,000 maps; 1,000 atlases; 6 globes; 300 relief models; 47,000 aerial photographs; 1,000 reference books and gazetteers; 25 serials (titles received); 2 microforms (no. of titles).

Annual Accessions: 5,000 maps; 20 atlases; 5 relief models; 150 aerial photographs; 25 reference books and gazetteers; 2 serials (titles received).
Area Specialization: Southern Illinois; Mississippi Valley.
Subject Specialization: geology; Illinois plat books.
Special Cartographic Collections: Sang Collection—64 early maps of North America, especially the Mississippi Valley, 1584-1840.
Dates: pre-1800 (1%); 1800-1899 (1%); 1900 - (98%).
Classification System: LC.
Collections Cataloged. (95%).
Depository for: DMA; NOS; USGS (Geol., topo.); Illinois Dept. of Transportation; Illinois State Geological Survey.
Serves: students; faculty; employees; public. Mon.–Thurs. 7:45 a.m.–11 p.m.; Fri. 7:45 a.m.–9 p.m.; Sat. 11 a.m.–6 p.m.; Sun. 1–11 p.m. (Seats 35; 200 readers served per month).
Interlibrary Loan Available.
Reproduction Facility: quickcopy.
Publications: guide.

Champaign

187. ILLINOIS STATE GEOLOGICAL SURVEY
Library
Map Room
615 E. Peabody
Champaign, IL 61820
Telephone: 217/344-1481, ext. 261.
Contact Person: Mary Krick, Libn.
Staff: 1 non-professional (full time).
Size: 27,500 maps; 10 atlases; 1 globes; 6,000 aerial photographs; 30 reference books and gazetteers.
Annual Accessions: 1,000 maps.
Area Specialization: Illinois; midwestern United States.
Subject Specialization: geology; mineral resources.
Dates: pre-1800 (1%); 1800-1899 (4%); 1900 - (95%).
Collections Cataloged.
Depository for: USGS (Geol., topo.).
Serves: public. Mon.–Fri. 8 a.m.–12 noon, 1–5 p.m. (Seats).

Charleston

188. EASTERN ILLINOIS UNIVERSITY
Booth Library
Reference Department, Map Collection
Charleston, IL 61920
Telephone: 217/581-6072.
Contact Person: Robert Chen, Coordinator of Documents Services.
Size: 24,558 maps; 1 globes; 5 relief models.
Area Specialization: Illinois.
Subject Specialization: geography; topography.
Dates: 1900 - (100%).
Classification System: LC.
Collections Cataloged. (85%).
Depository for: DMA; USGS (Geol., topo.); GPO.
Serves: students; faculty; employees; public. Mon.–Thurs. 8 a.m.–10 p.m.; Fri. 9–5 p.m.; Sat. 9 a.m.–5 p.m.; Sun. 2–10 p.m. (Seats 30).
Interlibrary Loan Available. (Restricted)
Reproduction Facility: photocopy.

Chicago

189. CHICAGO HISTORICAL SOCIETY
Library
Map Collection
Clark Street at North Avenue
Chicago, IL 60614
Established 1856.
Telephone: 312/642-4600.
Contact Person: Grant T. Dean, Associate Libn.
Staff: 1 professional (part time); 1 non-professional (part time).
Size: 9,500 maps; 313 atlases; 54 globes; 1,000 aerial photographs; 350 reference books and gazetteers.
Annual Accessions: 50 maps; 10 reference books and gazetteers.
Area Specialization: Chicago and its environs.
Dates: pre-1800 (5%); 1800-1899 (60%); 1900 - (35%).
Classification System: LC.
Collections Cataloged. (40%).
Serves: public. Tues.–Sat. 9:30 a.m.–4:30 p.m. (Seats 38; 10 readers served per month).
Reproduction Facility: photocopy.

190. CHICAGO PUBLIC LIBRARY
Government Publications Department
425 N. Michigan Avenue
Chicago, IL 60611
Telephone: 312/269-3002.
Contact Person: Robert Baumruk, Department Head.
Staff: 1 professional (part time); 2 non-professional (part time).
Size: 56,215 maps; 25 atlases; 100 reference books and gazetteers.
Annual Accessions: 1,000 maps; 2 reference books and gazetteers.
Area Specialization: United States.
Subject Specialization: topography.
Dates: 1900 - (100%).
Collections not Cataloged.
Depository for: DMA; USGS (Geol., topo.).
Serves: public. Mon.–Thurs. 9–7; Fri. 9–6; Sat. 9–5. (Seats 23; 25 readers served per month).
Interlibrary Loan Available.
Reproduction Facility: photocopy; microform.

191. CHICAGO PUBLIC LIBRARY
Social Sciences and History Information Center
History Section
425 North Michigan Avenue
Chicago, IL 60611
Telephone: 312/269-2830.
Contact Person: Donald M. Mosser, Libn. II.
Staff: 1 professional (part time).
Size: 2,000 maps; 90 atlases; 80 reference books and gazetteers.
Annual Accessions: 150 (mostly replacements) maps; 5 atlases; 10 reference books and gazetteers.
Area Specialization: provide public with general coverage over the entire world; concentration on road maps for the states, cities, countries and cities in other countries.
Dates: pre-1800 (20%); 1800-1899 (20%); 1900 - (60%).
Classification System: LC.
Collections Cataloged.
Serves: students; employees; public. Mon.–Thurs. 9 a.m.–7 p.m., Fri. 9 a.m.–6 p.m.; Sat. 9–5. (Seats 50).
Reproduction Facility: photocopy.

192. FIELD MUSEUM OF NATURAL HISTORY
Department of Geology
Map Library
Roosevelt Road and Lake Shore Drive
Chicago, IL 60605
Established 1893.
Contact Person: B. G. Woodland, Curator of Petrology.
Staff: 2 non-professional (part time).
Size: 100,000 maps.
Annual Accessions: 2,500 maps.
Area Specialization: North America.
Subject Specialization: geology.
Dates: 1900 - (100%).
Collections not Cataloged.
Depository for: USGS (Geol., topo.).
Serves: employees; public. Mon.–Fri. 8:30 a.m.–4:30 p.m. (10 readers served per month).
Reproduction Facility: photocopy.

193. ILLINOIS INSTITUTE OF TECHNOLOGY
Library
Documents Department
3300 S. Federal Street
Chicago, IL 60616
Telephone: 312/567-3888.
Contact Person: Nancy Roberts, Documents Libn.
Staff: 1 professional (part time); 1 non-professional (part time).
Size: 40,000 maps; 20 atlases; 1 globes; 100 reference books and gazetteers.
Annual Accessions: 2,000 maps; 2 atlases; 10 reference books and gazetteers.
Dates: 1900 - (100%).
Classification System: Dewey.
Collections not Cataloged.
Depository for: DMA; USGS (Topo.).
Serves: students; faculty; employees; public. Mon.–Thurs. 8:30 a.m.–10 p.m.; Fri. 8:30 a.m.–5 p.m.; Sat. 8:30 a.m.–5 p.m.; Sun. 2–10 p.m. (Seats 500).
Reproduction Facility: photocopy; microform.

194. LOYOLA UNIVERSITY OF CHICAGO
E. M. Cudahy Memorial Library
6525 N. Sheridan Road
Chicago, IL 60626
Established 1976.
Telephone: 312/274-3787.
Contact Person: Roy H. Fry, Coordinator of Public Services.
Staff: 1 professional (part time).
Size: 350 maps.
Collections not Cataloged.
Depository for: USGS (Topo.).
Serves: students; faculty; employees; public.
Staff: Mon.–Fri. 8:30 a.m.–5 p.m. professional (full time). (Seats 10; 5 readers served per month).
Reproduction Facility: photocopy.

195. THE NEWBERRY LIBRARY
Special Collections
Map Section
60 W. Walton Street
Chicago, IL 60610
Established 1887.
Telephone: 312/943-9090, ext. 208.
Contact Person: Robert W. Karrow, Jr., Curator of Maps.
Staff: 2 professional (full time).
Size: 13,000 maps; 1,600 atlases; 2 globes; 1,600 reference books and gazetteers; 70 serials (titles received); 50 microforms (no. of titles).
Annual Accessions: 200 maps; 35 atlases; 70 reference books and gazetteers; 1 serials (titles received); 10 microforms (no. of titles).

Area Specialization: The Americas; western Europe.
Subject Specialization: history of cartography.
Special Cartographic Collections: Ayer Collection: Disc. & explor. of Americas; Portolan charts; Ptolemy Novacco coll.: 16th-century maps printed in Italy; Graff coll.: Trans-Mississippi West.
Dates: pre-1800 (75%); 1800-1899 (20%); 1900 - (5%).
Classification System: LC.
Collections Cataloged. (40%).
Serves: students; faculty; employees; public. Tues.–Fri. 9 a.m.–6 p.m.; Sat. 9 a.m.–6 p.m. (Seats 5; 15 readers served per month).
Reproduction Facility: photocopy; quickcopy; microform.
Publications: Selected list of publications: *Index to Maps in the Graff Collection of Western Americana; Checklist of Printed Maps of the Middle West to 1900; Mapping the American Revolutionary War; Mapping the Great Lakes Region: Motive and Method; Mapline* (quarterly newsletter).

196. RAND MCNALLY & CO.
Map Library
P.O. Box 7600
Chicago, IL 60680
Established 1957.
Telephone: 312/673-9100, ext. 516.
Contact Person: Joseph Rockey, Supervisor of Library Services.
Staff: 1 professional (full time); 1 non-professional (part time).
Size: 95,000 maps; 1,500 atlases; 10 globes; 5,000 reference books and gazetteers; 75 serials (titles received).
Annual Accessions: 2,500 maps; 75 atlases; 250 reference books and gazetteers.
Area Specialization: United States; Canada.
Subject Specialization: place Names; topography; transportation; cartographic methods.
Dates: 1800-1899 (5%); 1900 - (95%).
Classification System: local system.
Collections Cataloged. (90%).
Serves: employees;. Mon.–Fri. 8:30 a.m.–4:30 p.m. (Seats 2).
Interlibrary Loan Available.
Reproduction Facility: photocopy.

197. UNIVERSITY OF CHICAGO
Regenstein Library
Map Collection
1100 E. 57th Street
Chicago, IL 60637
Established 1931.
Telephone: 312/962-8761.
Contact Person: Christopher Winters, Map Libn.
Staff: 1 professional (part time); 1 non-professional (full time); 2 non-professional (part time).
Size: 275,000 maps; 1,500 atlases; 3 globes; 32 relief models; 9,500 aerial photographs; 600 reference books and gazetteers; 10 serials (titles received); 40 microforms (no. of titles).
Annual Accessions: 7,000 maps; 25 atlases; 50 reference books and gazetteers; 1 serials (titles received); 10 microforms (no. of titles).
Area Specialization: United States; Canada; western Europe; U.S.S.R.; South Asia; the Far East.
Subject Specialization: topography; geology; urban geography; transportation; land use.
Special Cartographic Collections: 19th century county atlas collection—a 200 title collection of original editions of county atlases especially strong for the Midwestern United States; extensive collection of 19th century street maps for western European cities and towns.
Dates: pre-1800 (4%); 1800-1899 (21%); 1900 - (75%).
Collections not Cataloged.

Depository for: DMA; GSC; NOS; USGS (Geol., topo.); G.P.O. (selective).
Serves: students; faculty; employees; public. Mon.–Fri. 9 a.m.–5 p.m.; Sat. 9 a.m.–12 noon. (Seats 16; 150 readers served per month).
Interlibrary Loan Available.
Reproduction Facility: photocopy; microform; Photography.
Publications: *Maps (a guide to the collection).*

198. UNIVERSITY OF ILLINOIS AT CHICAGO CIRCLE
University Library
Map Section
801 S. Morgan
Chicago, IL 60680
Established 1946.
Telephone: 312/996-5277.
Contact Person: Marsha L. Selmer, Map Libn.
Staff: 1 professional (full time); 1 non-professional (full time); 2 non-professional (part time).
Size: 121,631 maps; 589 atlases; 2 globes; 7 relief models; 136 reference books and gazetteers; 2 serials (titles received); 2 microforms (no. of titles).
Annual Accessions: 4,497 maps; 27 atlases; 5 reference books and gazetteers.
Area Specialization: Chicago; Illinois; North Central United States.
Subject Specialization: topography; geology.
Special Cartographic Collections: Antiquarian map collection: Illinois, 19th century; Great Lakes area, 17th & 18th century; Eastern Europe & the Russian Empire, 16th to 19th century. Aerial photomaps: Chicago; northeastern Illinois.
Dates: pre-1800 (.2%); 1800-1899 (.2%); 1900 - (99.6%).
Classification System: LC.
Collections Cataloged. (99%).
Depository for: DMA; USGS (Geol., topo.).
Serves: students; faculty; employees; public. Mon.–Fri. 8:30 a.m.–5 p.m. (Seats 25; 169 readers served per month).
Interlibrary Loan Available.
Reproduction Facility: photocopy.
Publications: Information brochure—*Chicago in Maps.*

DeKalb

199. NORTHERN ILLINOIS UNIVERSITY
Map Library
Room 222, Davis Hall
DeKalb, IL 60115
Established 1966.
Telephone: 815/753-1813.
Contact Person: Mrs. Marian Hunter, Library Technical Assistant III.
Staff: 1 non-professional (full time); 8 non-professional (part time).
Size: 172,800 maps; 1,500 atlases; 10 globes; 45 relief models; 655 aerial photographs; 43 serials (titles received).
Annual Accessions: 4,500 maps; 100 atlases.
Area Specialization: northern Illinois; North America; Southeast Asia.
Dates: 1900 - (99%).
Classification System: LC; DMA.
Collections Cataloged.
Depository for: DMA; DOS (Gt. Brit); NOS; NTS (Canada); USGS (Geol., topo.).
Serves: students; faculty; employees; public. Mon.–Wed.: 8 a.m.–9 p.m.; Thurs.-Fri.: 8 a.m.–5 p.m. (Seats 38).
Interlibrary Loan Available.
Reproduction Facility: photocopy.
Publications: *Selected Acquisitions List N.I.U. Map Library.*

Edwardsville

200. SOUTHERN ILLINOIS UNIVERSITY AT EDWARDSVILLE

Lovejoy Library
Social Sciences/Map Library
Edwardsville, IL 62026
Established 1966.
Telephone: 618/692-2422.
Contact Person: Marvin Soloman, Social Sciences Libn.
Staff: 1 professional (full time); 1 professional (part time); 1 non-professional (full time).
Size: 134,000 maps; 500 atlases; 4 relief models; 6,145 aerial photographs; 400 reference books and gazetteers.
Annual Accessions: 4,000 maps; 25 atlases; 20 reference books and gazetteers.
Area Specialization: United States; St. Louis area.
Subject Specialization: topography.
Dates: 1800-1899 (1%); 1900 - (99%).
Classification System: LC.
Collections Cataloged.
Depository for: USGS (Geol., topo.).
Serves: students; faculty; employees; public. Mon.–Fri. 8 a.m.–11 p.m.; Sat. 8 a.m.–6 p.m.; Sun. 11:30 a.m.–10 p.m. (Seats 10; 100 readers served per month).
Interlibrary Loan Available.
Reproduction Facility: photocopy.

Elgin

201. GAIL BORDEN PUBLIC LIBRARY

200 N. Grove
Elgin, IL 60120
Established 1969.
Telephone: 312/742-2411.
Contact Person: Ann Schneck, Reference Libn.
Staff: 1 professional (part time).
Size: 4,197 maps; 83 atlases; 3 globes.
Area Specialization: Illinois and adjoining states.
Subject Specialization: geology.
Dates: pre-1800 (1%); 1800-1899 (1%); 1900 - (98%).
Collections not Cataloged.
Depository for: USGS (Topo.).
Serves: public. Mon.–Thurs. 9 a.m.–9 p.m. (winter) Fri 9–5:30 p.m.; Sat. 9 a.m.–5:30 p.m.; Sun. 2–5 p.m. (Sept–May). (Seats 150).
Reproduction Facility: photocopy.

Evanston

202. NORTHWESTERN UNIVERSITY

Grant Memorial Library of Geology
Locy Hall
Evanston, IL 60201
Telephone: 312/492-5525.
Contact Person: Janet Ayers, Geology Libn.
Staff: 1 professional (part time); 2 non-professional (part time).
Size: 5,860 maps.
Depository for: USGS (Geol.).
Serves: public. Mon.–Fri. 1–5 p.m. (Oct–May).
Reproduction Facility: photocopy.

203. NORTHWESTERN UNIVERSITY

University Library
Map Collection
1935 Sheridan Road
Evanston, IL 60201
Established 1948.
Telephone: 312/492-7603.

Contact Person: Mary Fortney, Map Libn.
Staff: 1 professional (part time); 1 non-professional (full time); 1 non-professional (part time).
Size: 170,104 maps; 2,085 atlases; 3 globes; 27 relief models; 1,540 aerial photographs; 18 serials (titles received).
Annual Accessions: 3,600 maps; 24 atlases; 20 reference books and gazetteers; 43 serials (titles received).
Dates: pre-1800 (1%); 1800-1899 (2%); 1900 - (97%).
Classification System: LC; Dewey.
Collections Cataloged. (90%).
Depository for: DMA; NOS; USGS (Topo.).
Serves: students; faculty; employees; public. Mon.–Fri. 10 a.m.–5 p.m. also Tues. 7–10:00. (Seats 19; 180 readers served per month).
Interlibrary Loan Available.
Reproduction Facility: quickcopy.

Kankakee

204. OLIVET NAZARENE COLLEGE

Benner Library
Kankakee, IL 60901
Established 1974.
Telephone: 815/939-5145.
Contact Person: Lynette Christensen, Reference/Catalog Libn.
Staff: 1 professional (part time); 1 non-professional (part time).
Size: 7,500 maps.
Annual Accessions: 500 maps.
Area Specialization: Illinois; midwestern United States.
Classification System: local system.
Collections Cataloged. (100%).
Depository for: USGS (Geol., topo.).
Serves: students; faculty; employees; public. Mon., Tues., Thurs., 8 a.m.–10 p.m. Wed. 8 a.m.–6 p.m., 8:15–10 p.m.; Fri. 8 a.m.–5 p.m., 7–9:30 p.m. Sat. 9 a.m.–10 p.m. (Seats 6).
Interlibrary Loan Available.
Reproduction Facility: photocopy.
Publications: *Guide to the Use of Room 131 (Map Room) 1979* (guide).

Macomb

205. WESTERN ILLINOIS UNIVERSITY

Maps
Macomb, IL 61455
Telephone: 309/298-1171.
Contact Person: John Bergen, Professor of Geography and Map Curator.
Staff: 1 professional (part time); 1 non-professional (full time); 4 non-professional (part time).
Size: 150,000 maps; 2,000 atlases; 2 globes; 50 relief models; 13,000 aerial photographs; 5,000 reference books and gazetteers; 50 serials (titles received).
Annual Accessions: 6,000 maps; 50-100 atlases; 500 reference books and gazetteers.
Area Specialization: Illinois.
Dates: pre-1800 (0.5%); 1800-1899 (2.5%); 1900 - (97%).
Classification System: local system.
Collections Cataloged. (90%).
Depository for: DMA; USGS (Geol., topo.); Illinois Department of Transportation.
Serves: students; faculty; employees; public;. Mon.–Fri. 8 a.m.–4:30 p.m. (Seats 30-40; 300 readers served per month).
Interlibrary Loan Available.
Reproduction Facility: photocopy.

Monmouth

206. MONMOUTH COLLEGE
Hewes Library
Monmouth, IL 61462
Telephone: 309/457-2031.
Contact Person: Skip Burhans, Reference/Government Documents Libn.
Staff: 1 professional (full time); 1 non-professional (part time).
Size: 50,000 maps; 28 atlases; 1 reference books and gazetteers.
Annual Accessions: 1,000 maps.
Area Specialization: United States.
Subject Specialization: geology; topography.
Dates: 1900 - (100%).
Collections not Cataloged.
Depository for: USGS (Geol., topo.).
Serves: students; faculty; employees; public. Mon.–Fri. 8 a.m.–12 midnight; Sat. 9 a.m.–5 p.m.; Sun. 1–10 p.m. (Seats 50; 10 readers served per month).
Interlibrary Loan Available. (restricted)
Reproduction Facility: photocopy; microform.

Normal

207. ILLINOIS STATE UNIVERSITY
Milner Library
Map Room
School & College Streets
Normal, IL 61761
Established 1964.
Telephone: 309/438-3486.
Contact Person: William W. Easton, Map Libn. Associate Professor.
Staff: 1 professional (full time); 3 non-professional (part time).
Size: 274,000 maps; 2,500 atlases; 10 globes; 20,000 aerial photographs; 250 reference books and gazetteers; 100 microforms (no. of titles).
Annual Accessions: 15,250 maps; 60 atlases; 100 aerial photographs; 40 reference books and gazetteers; 10 microforms (no. of titles).
Area Specialization: Illinois; Alaska; United States; Canada; Spain; Japan; Australia.
Subject Specialization: topography; geology; oceanography.
Special Cartographic Collections: U.S.G.S. Folio Atlases (complete); News Maps-World War II-Army Information Branch-complete.
Dates: pre-1800 (5%); 1800-1899 (10%); 1900 - (85%).
Classification System: LC (modified).
Collections Cataloged. (30%).
Depository for: DMA; NOS; NTS (Canada); USGS (Geol., topo.); Australia Department of Natural Development.
Serves: students; faculty; employees; public;. Mon. 8 a.m.–10 p.m.; Tues.–Fri. 8 a.m.–5 p.m. (Seats 28).
Interlibrary Loan Available.
Reproduction Facility: photocopy. Departments

Peoria

208. PEORIA PUBLIC LIBRARY
Reference and Business, Science and Technology
107 NE Monroe St
Peoria, IL 61602
Telephone: 309/672-8858 or 8844.
Contact Person: Joyce Johnson, Head, Reference Department; Jean Shrier, Head, Business, Science, Technology Dept.
Size: 65,322 maps; 141 atlases; 3 globes; 73 reference books and gazetteers.
Area Specialization: Peoria.
Subject Specialization: travel; topography.
Dates: pre-1800 (a few); 1800-1899 (some); 1900 - (most of the collection).
Classification System: Dewey; SuDoc (National Park Service). Vertical File subject headings
Collections Cataloged. (10%).
Depository for: USGS (Topo.).
Serves: public. Mon.–Thurs. 9 a.m.–9 p.m., Fri. 9 a.m.–6 p.m.; Sat. 9 a.m.–6 p.m. (except in summer).
Interlibrary Loan Available.
Reproduction Facility: photocopy.

Rock Island

209. AUGUSTANA COLLEGE
Department of Geography
David M. Loring Map Library
Rock Island, IL 61201
Established 1943–44.
Telephone: 309/794-7303.
Contact Person: Dr. Norman Moline, Associate Professor of Geography.
Size: 60,000 maps.
Area Specialization: midwestern United States; Scandinavia.
Subject Specialization: climate; geology; hydrology; topography; transportation.
Special Cartographic Collections: "Se Garden Därhemma" map collection (maps of Scandinavian countries, established by a donation to the college by the Swedish American Line and Mr. Thorsten Hanson.
Dates: 1800-1899 (2%); 1900 - (98%).
Classification System: LC.
Collections Cataloged.
Depository for: DMA; USGS (Geol., topo.).
Serves: students; faculty; public. Mon.–Fri. 8 a.m.–5 p.m. (Seats 4; 100 readers served per month).
Interlibrary Loan Available.
Reproduction Facility: photocopy.

Springfield

210. ILLINOIS STATE HISTORICAL LIBRARY
Old State Capitol
Springfield, IL 62706
Established 1889.
Telephone: 217/782-4836.
Staff: professional (full time).
Size: 2,000 maps; 400 atlases; 100 reference books and gazetteers; 6 serials (titles received); 2 microforms (no. of titles).
Area Specialization: Illinois.
Subject Specialization: history; Civil War; Lincoln.
Dates: pre-1800 (5%); 1800-1899 (60%); 1900 - (35%).
Classification System: local system.
Collections Cataloged. Mon.–Fri. 8:30 a.m.–5:00 p.m. (Seats 48).
Reproduction Facility: photocopy; microform.

211. ILLINOIS STATE LIBRARY
Centennial Bldg.
Springfield, IL 62756
Telephone: 217/782-7523.
Contact Person: Arlyn Sherwood, Map Libn.
Staff: 1 professional (full time); 1 non-professional (part time).

Size: 95,000 maps; 2,650 atlases; 500 reference books and gazetteers; 85 serials (titles received); 10 microforms (no. of titles).
Annual Accessions: 3,350 maps; 50 atlases; 30 reference books and gazetteers; 5 microforms (no. of titles).
Area Specialization: Illinois.
Special Cartographic Collections: 19th century Illinois county atlases; official Illinois highway maps, 1921– to date; Illinois county highway maps, 1937–to date.
Dates: 1800-1899 (5%); 1900 - (95%).
Classification System: LC.
Collections Cataloged. (40%).
Depository for: USGS (Geol., topo.); GPO.
Serves: students; faculty; employees; public;. Mon.–Fri 8 a.m.–4:30 p.m. (Seats 32; 30 readers served per month).
Interlibrary Loan Available.
Reproduction Facility: photocopy.
Publications: Sherwood, Arlyn. "Maps in the Illinois State Library." In *Illinois Libraries,* vol. 58 #2, February 1976, pp. 160-179.

Urbana

212. UNIVERSITY OF ILLINOIS
Geology Library
1301 W. Green
Urbana, IL 61801
Telephone: 217/333-1266.
Contact Person: Diana L. Walter, LTA II.
Staff: 1 non-professional (full time).
Size: 20,000 maps; 10 reference books and gazetteers; 600 serials (titles received).
Annual Accessions: 1,000 maps.
Area Specialization: United States.
Subject Specialization: geology; hydrology; tectonics geomorphology; energy resources.
Dates: pre-1800 (1%); 1800-1899 (2%); 1900 - (97%).
Collections Cataloged.
Depository for: USGS (Geol.).
Serves: students; faculty; employees; public. Mon.–Fri. 9 a.m.–5 p.m. (Seats 5; 215 readers served per month).
Interlibrary Loan Available.

213. UNIVERSITY OF ILLINOIS AT URBANA-CHAMPAIGN
Illinois Historical Survey
1408 W. Gregory Dr.
Urbana, IL 61801
Established 1910.
Telephone: 217/333-1777.
Staff: 1 professional (full time); 1 non-professional (full time); 1/2 non-professional (part time).
Size: 1,700 maps; 80 atlases; 50 reference books and gazetteers.
Annual Accessions: 10-20 maps; 1-3 atlases; 1-5 reference books and gazetteers.
Area Specialization: Illinois; Old Northwest; Mississippi River Valley; French Canada.
Subject Specialization: history (Illinois and the Midwest).
Special Cartographic Collections: Karpinski Collection— over 500 photocopies of maps in various French archival depositories.
Dates: pre-1800 (33%); 1800-1899 (33%); 1900 - (33%).
Classification System: local system.
Serves: students; faculty; employees; public. Mon.–Fri. 9 a.m.–5 p.m. (Seats 16).
Reproduction Facility: quickcopy; microform.

214. UNIVERSITY OF ILLINOIS
University Library
Map and Geography Library
1408 West Gregory Drive
Urbana, IL 61801
Established 1944.
Telephone: 217/333-0827.
Contact Person: David A. Cobb, Map and Geography Libn.
Staff: 2 professional (full time); 1 non-professional (full time); 8 non-professional (part time).
Size: 319,000 maps; 2,700 atlases; 7 globes; 46 relief models; 144,000 aerial photographs; 15,000 reference books and gazetteers; 815 serials (titles received); 600 microforms (no. of titles).
Annual Accessions: 10,000 maps; 100 atlases; 2,000 aerial photographs; 600 reference books and gazetteers; 50 microforms (no. of titles).
Area Specialization: Illinois; Great Lakes; United States; Canada; Europe.
Subject Specialization: comprehensive (excepting geology).
Special Cartographic Collections: Sanborn Fire Insurance maps of Illinois cities; 19th and 20th century atlases of counties and states in Midwest; Illinois aerial photography; NCIC microfiche data; Freeman collection of Early Maps of America; Lybyer collection of Maps of the Near East; Schmidt collection of Lewis Evans maps: Cavagna collection of Italian maps.
Dates: pre-1800 (5%); 1800-1899 (10%); 1900 - (85%).
Classification System: LC.
Collections Cataloged. (90%).
Depository for: DMA; NOS; NTS (Canada); USGS (Topo.).
Serves: students; faculty; employees; public. Mon.–Thurs. 9 a.m.–5 p.m., 7–10 p.m.; Fri, 9 a.m.–5 p.m.; Sat. 1–4 p.m.; Sun. 1–5 p.m.; 7–10 p.m. (Seats 20; 1,000 readers served per month).
Interlibrary Loan Available.
Reproduction Facility: photocopy; quickcopy; microform.
Publications: *Biblio* (accession list); *Collection Development Statement; State Atlases: An Annotated Bibliography; Collection Guide; Sanborn Fire Insurance Maps in the Map & Geography Library; INFO 1-A List of Illinois County Atlases; INFO 2-List of Aerial Photographs.*

INDIANA

Bloomington

215. INDIANA UNIVERSITY
Geography and Map Library
Kirkwood Hall Room 301
Bloomington, IN 47405
Established 1946.
Telephone: 812/335-1108.
Contact Person: Daniel T. Seldin, Head, Geography and Map Library.
Staff: 1 professional (full time); 1 non-professional (full time); 3 non-professional (part time).
Size: 211,000 maps; 1,600 atlases; 5 globes; 150 relief models; 1,000 aerial photographs; 8,000 reference books and gazetteers; 190 serials (titles received); 8,009 microforms (no. of titles).
Annual Accessions: 3,000 maps; 10-15 atlases; 850 reference books and gazetteers; 10 serials (titles received); 100 microforms (no. of titles).
Area Specialization: Indiana; Soviet Union; Eastern Europe.
Subject Specialization: geography; topography.
Special Cartographic Collections: Indiana Census Maps; Indiana Sanborn Fire Insurance Maps; Alfred C. Kinsey Map Collection.
Dates: 1800-1899 (7%); 1900 - (93%).

Classification System: AGS.
Collections not Cataloged.
Depository for: DMA; NOS; USGS (Topo.).
Serves: students; faculty; employees; public;. Mon.–Fri. 8 a.m.–5 p.m. Mon.–Thurs 7–10 p.m. Sun. 7–10 p.m. (Seats 12; 20 for maps readers served per month).
Interlibrary Loan Available.
Reproduction Facility: quickcopy.
Publications: Library handbook (out of print); Current Acquisitions list (quarterly).

216. INDIANA UNIVERSITY
Geology Library
1005 E. 10th Street
Bloomington, IN 47405
Telephone: 812/335-7170.
Staff: 1 non-professional (part time).
Size: 250,000 maps; 1 globes.
Annual Accessions: 5,000 maps.
Area Specialization: United States.
Subject Specialization: geology.
Dates: 1900 - (95%).
Collections not Cataloged.
Depository for: USGS (Geol., topo.); state geological surveys.
Serves: students; faculty; employees; public;. Mon.–Fri. 8 a.m.–11 p.m.; Sat. 8 a.m.–5 p.m. (Seats 78).
Interlibrary Loan Available.
Reproduction Facility: photocopy.

217. INDIANA UNIVERSITY
Lilly Library
Bloomington, IN 47405-3301
Established 1960.
Telephone: 812/335-2452.
Contact Person: David Warrington, Head, Reference and Reader's Services.
Staff: 1 professional (part time).
Size: 620, including 100 manuscript maps maps; 200 atlases; 125 reference books and gazetteers.
Area Specialization: Indiana; United States; London.
Subject Specialization: local history; European history.
Special Cartographic Collections: Maps of the Trans-Mississippi West in the Ellison collection of Western Americana; Extensive atlas collection, strong in Ptolemy and Ortelius.
Dates: pre-1800 (20%); 1800-1899 (78%); 1900 - (2%).
Classification System: LC; maps not classified.
Collections Cataloged. (95% (atlases)).
Serves: students; faculty; employees; public. Mon.–Thurs. 9 a.m.–10 p.m.; Fri 9 a.m.–5 p.m.; Sat. 9 a.m.–12 Noon. (Seats 24; 5 readers served per month).
Reproduction Facility: photocopy; microform.
Publications: Bennett, Josiah, "The Cartographic Treasures of the Lilly Library," in *The Map Collector,* no. 22, March 1983, pp. 30-35.

Fort Wayne

218. ALLEN COUNTY PUBLIC LIBRARY
Main Library
Business and Technology Department
900 Webster Street, Box 2270
Fort Wayne, IN 46801
Established 1964.
Telephone: 219/424-7241.
Contact Person: John N. Dickmeyer, Department Manager.
Staff: 6 professional (full time); 1 non-professional (full time).
Size: 8,743 maps; 210 atlases.
Annual Accessions: 900 maps; 2 atlases.

Area Specialization: Indiana and Contiguous States.
Subject Specialization: topography.
Special Cartographic Collections: Contour lake maps of Indiana.
Dates: 1800-1899 (.1%); 1900 - (99.9%).
Collections not Cataloged.
Depository for: USGS (Topo.).
Serves: public. Mon.–Thurs. 9 a.m.–9 p.m.; Fri. 9 a.m.–6 p.m.; Sat. 9 a.m.–6 p.m.; Sun. 1–6 p.m. (Labor Day through Memorial Day only). (Seats 16; 30 readers served per month).
Reproduction Facility: photocopy.

219. INDIANA UNIVERSITY - PURDUE UNIVERSITY AT FORT WAYNE
Earth and Space Sciences Department
Map Collection
2101 East Coliseum Blvd.
Ft. Wayne, IN 46805
Established 1981.
Telephone: 219/482-5372.
Contact Person: Dr. Soon Kim, Assistant Professor, Earth and Space Sciences.
Staff: 1 professional (part time).
Area Specialization: Indiana.
Dates: 1900 - (100%).
Collections not Cataloged.
Depository for: DMA; USGS (Geol., topo.).
Serves: students; faculty; employees; public. Mon.–Fri. 8 a.m.–5 p.m. (Seats 5).
Reproduction Facility: photocopy.

Gary

220. INDIANA UNIVERSITY NORTHWEST
Library
Map Collection
3400 Broadway
Gary, IN 46408
Established 1969.
Telephone: 219/980-6608.
Contact Person: Richard B. Reich, Documents Library.
Staff: 1 non-professional (part time).
Size: 17,000 maps; 60 atlases; 1 globes; 60 reference books and gazetteers.
Annual Accessions: 1,500 maps; 3 atlases; 10 reference books and gazetteers.
Dates: 1900 - (100%).
Collections not Cataloged.
Depository for: USGS (Geol., topo.).
Serves: students; faculty; employees; public. Mon.–Fri. 8 a.m.–5 p.m.; Sat. 8:30 a.m.–5 p.m. (Seats 10; 2 readers served per month).

Greencastle

221. DEPAUW UNIVERSITY
Roy O. West Library
Government Documents
Box 137
Greencastle, IN 46135
Telephone: 317/658-4514.
Contact Person: Cathie Bean, Reference Assistant.
Staff: 1 non-professional (full time); 1 non-professional (part time).
Size: 25,000 maps.

Area Specialization: United States.
Dates: 1900 - (100%).
Classification System: alphabetical by state and quadrangle.
Collections not Cataloged.
Depository for: USGS (Topo.).
Serves: students; faculty; employees; public;. Mon.–Fri. 7:50 a.m.–11:30 p.m.; Sat. 9:30 a.m.–5:00 p.m.; Sun. 12:00–11:30 p.m. (Seats 50).
Reproduction Facility: photocopy.

Hanover

222. HANOVER COLLEGE
Department of Geology
Hanover, IN 47243
Telephone: 812/866-2151, ext. 393.
Contact Person: Stanley M. Totten, Professor of Geology.
Staff: 1 non-professional (part time).
Size: 10,000 maps.
Annual Accessions: 500 maps.
Subject Specialization: topography; geology.
Dates: 1900 - (100%).
Collections not Cataloged.
Depository for: USGS (Geol., topo.).
Serves: students; faculty; employees; public. Mon.–Fri. 8 a.m.–5 p.m. (Seats 8).
Interlibrary Loan Available.

Indianapolis

223. INDIANA HISTORICAL SOCIETY
Library
315 West Ohio Street
Indianapolis, IN 46202
Established 1934.
Telephone: 317/232-1879.
Contact Person: Leigh Darbee, Head, Reference and Bibliographic Services.
Staff: 1 professional (part time).
Size: 800 maps; 160 atlases; 100 reference books and gazetteers.
Annual Accessions: 15 maps; 3 atlases; 10 reference books and gazetteers.
Area Specialization: Indiana; Ohio Valley; Old Northwest Territory.
Subject Specialization: Indians.
Dates: pre-1800 (20%); 1800-1899 (70%); 1900 - (10%).
Classification System: LC.
Collections Cataloged. (6%).
Serves: students; faculty; employees; public. Mon.–Fri. 8:30 a.m.–5 p.m.; Sat. 8:30 a.m.–4 p.m., Sept. to May. (Seats 24; 200 readers served per month).
Reproduction Facility: photocopy; microform.

224. INDIANA STATE LIBRARY
Indiana Division
140 North Senate Avenue
Indianapolis, IN 46204
Telephone: 317/232-3668.
Contact Person: Byron Swanson, Reference Libn.
Staff: 5 professional (part time); 1 non-professional (part time).
Size: 4,772 maps; 447 atlases; 7,000 aerial photographs; 102 reference books and gazetteers; 24 microforms (no. of titles).
Area Specialization: Indianapolis; Indiana.
Subject Specialization: plat books and atlases of Indiana counties.

Special Cartographic Collections: Sanborn fire insurance maps of Indiana cities; Baist's real estate atlases of Indianapolis.
Dates: pre-1800 (5%); 1800-1899 (15%); 1900 - (80%).
Classification System: Dewey.
Collections Cataloged. (100%).
Depository for: USGS (Topo.).
Serves: public. Mon.–Fri. 8:15 a.m.–5 p.m. (Seats 30; 100 readers served per month).
Reproduction Facility: microform.

225. INDIANA UNIVERSITY - PURDUE UNIVERSITY AT INDIANAPOLIS
University Library
Government Documents Department
815 West Michigan St.
Indianapolis, IN 46202
Telephone: 317/264-4447, ext. 19.
Contact Person: Francis Brey, Government Documents/Map Libn.
Staff: 1 professional (part time); 4 non-professional (part time).
Size: 25,254 maps.
Area Specialization: Indiana.
Dates: 1900 - (100%).
Classification System: LC.
Collections not Cataloged.
Depository for: USGS (Geol., topo.).
Serves: students; faculty; employees; public. Mon.–Thur. 8 a.m.–10 p.m.,. Fri. 8 a.m.–5 p.m. Sat. 8 a.m.–5 p.m.; Sun. 12 Noon–7 p.m. (Seats 8).
Reproduction Facility: photocopy.

Muncie

226. BALL STATE UNIVERSITY
Department of Library Service
Map Collection
Muncie, IN 47306
Established 1976.
Telephone: 317/285-1097.
Contact Person: Paul W. Stout, Map Libn. and Assistant Professor of Library Service.
Staff: 1 professional (full time); 1 non-professional (full time); 1 non-professional (part time).
Size: 102,514 maps; 1,310 atlases; 2 globes; 21 relief models; 528 aerial photographs; 420 reference books and gazetteers; 25 serials (titles received); 31 microforms (no. of titles).
Annual Accessions: 10,000 maps; 140 atlases.
Area Specialization: Indiana.
Subject Specialization: cities; roads; bicycle maps; university campus maps.
Dates: 1900 - (99%).
Classification System: LC.
Collections not Cataloged.
Depository for: DMA; USGS (Geol., topo.); Indiana Geological Survey.
Serves: students; faculty; employees; public. Mon.–Fri. 8 a.m.–5 p.m. (Seats 16; 460 readers served per month).
Interlibrary Loan Available.
Reproduction Facility: photocopy.
Publications: *Guide to Ball State University Libraries Map Collection* (guide).

Notre Dame

227. UNIVERSITY OF NOTRE DAME
Memorial Library
Microtext Reading Room
Notre Dame, IN 46556
Telephone: 219/239-6450.
Contact Person: Pamela Paidle, Library Technical Assistant.
Staff: 2 professional (part time); 1 non-professional (full time); 3 non-professional (part time).
Size: 100,000 maps.
Annual Accessions: 4,000 maps.
Subject Specialization: topography.
Collections not Cataloged.
Depository for: DMA; USGS (Topo.).
Serves: students; faculty; employees; public. Mon.–Thurs. 8 a.m.–11 p.m., Fri 8 a.m.–10 p.m.; Sat. 9 a.m.–10 p.m.; Sun. 1–11 p.m. (Seats 16; 10 readers served per month).
Reproduction Facility: quickcopy.

Rensselaer

228. SAINT JOSEPH'S COLLEGE
Department of Earth Science
Rensselaer, IN 47978
Established 1963.
Telephone: 219/866-7111.
Contact Person: Michael E. Davis, Associate Professor of Geology.
Staff: 1 professional (part time); 2 non-professional (part time).
Size: 100,000 maps; 10 atlases; 20 relief models; 300 aerial photographs.
Annual Accessions: 700 maps.
Subject Specialization: geology; topography; river surveys.
Collections not Cataloged.
Depository for: USGS (Geol., topo.).
Serves: students; faculty; public.
Reproduction Facility: quickcopy.

Richmond

229. EARLHAM COLLEGE
Wildman Science Library
Box 72
Richmond, IN 47374
Established 1972.
Telephone: 317/962-6561, ext. 245.
Contact Person: Sara Woolpy, Science Libn.
Staff: 1 professional (full time); 3 non-professional (part time).
Size: 9,500 maps; 25 atlases; 1 globes; 30 reference books and gazetteers.
Annual Accessions: 520 maps.
Area Specialization: Indiana; Ohio; Kentucky; western United States.
Subject Specialization: geology; forestry.
Dates: 1800-1899 (1%); 1900 - (99%).
Classification System: AGS.
Collections Cataloged.
Depository for: USGS (Geol., topo.).
Serves: students; faculty; employees; public;. Mon.–Thurs. 8 a.m.–11 p.m., Fri. 8 a.m.–10 p.m.; Sat. 10 a.m.–5 p.m.; Sun. 12:30 p.m.–11 p.m. (Seats 12; 15 readers served per month).
Reproduction Facility: photocopy.

Terre Haute

230. INDIANA STATE UNIVERSITY
Dr. John Oliver Geography Map Library
6th & Chestnut Streets
Terre Haute, IN 47809
Established 1962.
Telephone: 812/232-6311.
Contact Person: Ed Ellis, Curator.
Size: 160,000 maps; 6,000 aerial photographs.
Annual Accessions: 300 maps; 400 aerial photographs.
Area Specialization: United States; Canada.
Subject Specialization: topography.
Dates: 1800-1899 (5%); 1900 - (95%).
Classification System: .
Collections not Cataloged.
Depository for: DMA; USGS (Geol., topo.).
Serves: students; faculty. (Seats 30; 100 readers served per month).
Reproduction Facility: photocopy.

Valparaiso

231. VALPARAISO UNIVERSITY
Henry F. Moellering Memorial Library
Valparaiso, IN 46383
Established early 1950's.
Telephone: 219/464-5482.
Contact Person: Elmer B. Hess, Documents/Map Libn.
Staff: 1 professional (full time); 1 non-professional (part time).
Size: 90,000+ maps; 1 globes.
Annual Accessions: 3,000 maps.
Area Specialization: United States.
Subject Specialization: topography.
Dates: 1900 - (100%).
Collections not Cataloged.
Depository for: DMA; USGS (Geol., topo.).
Serves: students; faculty; employees; public. Mon.–Fri. 8 a.m.–11 p.m.; Sat. 9 a.m.–5 p.m.; Sun. 1–11 p.m. (Seats 5; 5 readers served per month).
Reproduction Facility: photocopy.
Publications: "Map Projections".

West Lafayette

232. PURDUE UNIVERSITY
Geosciences Department
Map Room (103)
West Lafayette, IN 47902
Established 1970.
Contact Person: Prof. Wilton N. Melhorn, Curator of Map Room.
Staff: 1 professional (part time); 1 non-professional (part time).
Size: 30,000 maps; 50 atlases; 82 relief models; 2,000 aerial photographs.
Annual Accessions: 300 maps; 2 relief models; 10 aerial photographs.
Area Specialization: United States.
Subject Specialization: topography; geology; hydrography; mineral resources.
Special Cartographic Collections: geologic quadrangle map series for State of Tennessee.
Dates: 1800-1899 (5%); 1900 - (95%).
Classification System: Dewey.
Collections Cataloged. (5%).
Depository for: USGS (Geol.); Indiana Geological Survey.

Serves: students; faculty. Mon.–Fri. 10:30 a.m.–12:30 a.m. (Seats 10; 20 readers served per month).
Reproduction Facility: photocopy.

233. PURDUE UNIVERSITY
Libraries
Map Collection
Stewart Center
West Lafayette, IN 47907
Established 1946.
Telephone: 317/494-2906.
Contact Person: Mrs. Anne Black, Library Assistant IV.
Staff: 1 non-professional (full time); 1 non-professional (part time).
Size: 118,000 maps; 400 atlases; 1 globes; 25 relief models; 275 reference books and gazetteers.
Annual Accessions: 4,000 maps; 5 atlases; 10 reference books and gazetteers.
Area Specialization: Indiana; United States; Canada.
Subject Specialization: topography.
Special Cartographic Collections: *Theatrum Orbis Terrarum,* world cartography-facsimile atlases, 1477-1776; *Serial Atlas Of the Marine Environment,* marine geology, 1963-1974; *Atlas Catalan de 1375,* Spanish manuscripts; *Portugaliae Monumenta Cartographica,* history of Portuguese cartography.
Dates: pre-1800 (1%); 1800-1899 (1%); 1900 - (98%).
Classification System: Dewey (atlases, gazetteers, reference books only).
Collections not Cataloged.
Depository for: DMA; NTS (Canada); USGS (Topo.); U.S. Army Corps of Engineers river charts.
Serves: students; faculty; employees; public. Mon.–Fri. 8 a.m.–5 p.m. (Seats 15; 100 readers served per month).
Interlibrary Loan Available.
Reproduction Facility: photocopy.

IOWA

Ames

234. IOWA STATE UNIVERSITY
Library
Map Room
Ames, IA 50011
Established 1948.
Telephone: 515/294-3956.
Contact Person: Marilyn K. Moody, Map Bibliographer.
Staff: 1 non-professional (full time); 1 professional (part time).
Size: 76,659 maps; 1,048 atlases; 9 globes; 18 relief models; 20,332 aerial photographs; 350 reference books and gazetteers; 30 serials (titles received).
Annual Accessions: 3,760 maps; 50 atlases; 1,000 aerial photographs; 25 reference books and gazetteers; 5 serials (titles received).
Area Specialization: U.S.; Iowa.
Special Cartographic Collections: Iowa State Planning Board W.P.A. plans, charts, maps.
Dates: 1900 - (100%).
Classification System: LC.
Collections Cataloged. (20%).
Depository for: DMA; NOS; USGS (Topo.).
Serves: students; faculty; employees; public. Mon.–Fri. 8 a.m.–5 p.m.; Mon.–Thurs. 7–10 p.m.; Sun. 2–6 p.m. (Seats 20; 258 readers served per month).
Interlibrary Loan Available.
Reproduction Facility: quickcopy.
Publications: *Index to Cataloged Maps in the Map Room.*

Cedar Falls

235. UNIVERSITY OF NORTHERN IOWA
Library
Documents and Maps
Cedar Falls, IA 50613
Established 1970.
Telephone: 319/273-6327.
Contact Person: Patrick J. Wilkinson, Documents and Maps Libn.
Staff: 1 professional (part time); 1.5 non-professional (part time).
Size: 30,000 maps; 25 atlases; 5 globes; 2 relief models; 250 aerial photographs; 300 reference books and gazetteers; 1 serials (titles received); 14 microforms (no. of titles).
Annual Accessions: 1,500 maps; 2 atlases; 20 aerial photographs; 10-15 reference books and gazetteers; 1 microforms (no. of titles).
Area Specialization: Iowa.
Dates: 1800-1899 (10%); 1900 - (90%).
Classification System: LC; 50% classified LC; 50% large scale U.S.G.S. topo's organized by state and quad n.
Collections Cataloged. (50%).
Depository for: USGS (Geol., topo.).
Serves: students; faculty; employees; public. Mon.–Thurs. 7:30 a.m.–5:00 p.m., 6:00 p.m.–9:00 p.m.,. Fri. 7:30 a.m.-5 p.m. Sun. 6 p.m.–9 p.m. (Seats 20; 125 readers served per month).
Interlibrary Loan Available.
Reproduction Facility: photocopy.
Publications: (1)*Maps Collection* (A "How to" guide to the UNI Map Collection) *Selected List of Government Publications & Maps* (Issued 4-6 times a year).

Council BLuffs

236. FREE PUBLIC LIBRARY
200 Pearl Street
Council BLuffs, IA 51501
Telephone: 712/323-7553.
Contact Person: Mildred K. Smock, Library Director.
Staff: 5 professional (part time); 3 non-professional (part time).
Area Specialization: Council Bluffs area; midwestern United States.
Dates: 1900 - (95%).
Classification System: local system.
Collections not Cataloged.
Depository for: USGS (Topo.).
Serves: public. Mon.–Thurs. 9:30 a.m.–9 p.m., Fri 9:30 a.m.–6 p.m.; Sat. 9:30 a.m.–5 p.m.; Sun. 1–4:30 p.m. (Seats 24).
Interlibrary Loan Available.
Reproduction Facility: photocopy.

Decorah

237. LUTHER COLLEGE
Preus Library
Decorah, IA 52101
Established 1861.
Telephone: 319/387-1163.
Contact Person: Elizabeth Kaschins, Reference Libn.
Staff: 3 professional (part time); 1 non-professional (part time).
Size: 1,000 maps; 400 atlases; 10 globes; 100 reference books and gazetteers.
Annual Accessions: 20 maps.

Area Specialization: Decorah (Iowa); Winneshiek County (Iowa); Iowa.
Dates: 1800-1899 (1%); 1900 - (99%).
Classification System: LC.
Collections Cataloged.
Depository for: Iowa state publications (includes some maps).
Serves: students; faculty; employees; public. Mon.–Thurs. 7:30 a.m.–11:30 p.m., Fri. 7:30 a.m.–10 p.m.; Sat. 9 a.m.–5 p.m.; Sun. 1:30–11:30 p.m. (Seats 12).
Reproduction Facility: photocopy.

Des Moines

238. DRAKE UNIVERSITY
Cowles Library
Government Publications Department
28th & University Avenue
Des Moines, IA 50311
Established 1968.
Telephone: 515/271-2814.
Contact Person: James S. Leonardo, Government Publications Libn.
Staff: 1 professional (full time); 1 non-professional (full time).
Size: 1,200 maps; 1 globes; 100 reference books and gazetteers.
Annual Accessions: 50 maps.
Area Specialization: Iowa.
Dates: 1900 - (100%).
Classification System: alphabetical by map title.
Collections not Cataloged.
Depository for: USGS (Topo.).
Serves: public. Mon.–Thurs. 7:30 a.m.–12 midnight; Fri. 7:30 a.m.–10 p.m.; Sat. 8 a.m.–8 p.m.; Sun. 1 p.m.–12 midnight. (Seats 40; 450-500 readers served per month).
Reproduction Facility: photocopy.

239. IOWA STATE HISTORICAL DEPARTMENT
State Archives of Iowa
E. 7th & Court Avenue
Des Moines, IA 50265
Telephone: 515/281-3007.
Contact Person: Edward N. McConnell, State Archivist.
Staff: 3 professional (full time); 1 non-professional (part time).
Size: 3,550 approx. maps; 2 atlases; 1,000 aerial photographs; 8,209 approx. microforms (no. of titles).
Area Specialization: Iowa.
Special Cartographic Collections: Original land surveys; Sanborn Fire Insurance maps.
Dates: 1800-1899 (65%); 1900 - (35%).
Classification System: local system.
Serves: students; faculty; employees; public;. Mon.–Fri. 8 a.m.–4:30 p.m. (Seats 10; 20 readers served per month).
Reproduction Facility: photocopy; microform.
Publications: *Fire insurance maps of Iowa cities and towns—A List of Holdings.*

240. IOWA STATE LIBRARY
Information Services
E. 12th and Grand, Historical Buidling
Des Moines, IA 50319
Telephone: 515/281-4102.
Contact Person: Linda Mauer, Library Associate.
Staff: 1 professional (part time).
Area Specialization: Iowa.
Subject Specialization: topography; census maps.
Collections not Cataloged.
Serves: employees; public. Mon.–Fri. 8 a.m.–4 p.m. (Seats 16; 10 readers served per month).
Reproduction Facility: photocopy; quickcopy.

Dubuque

241. CARNEGIE-STOUT PUBLIC LIBRARY
11th & Bluff Streets
Dubuque, IA 52001
Telephone: 819/556-8270.
Contact Person: Elizabeth Dunn, Reference Libn.
Staff: professional (part time).
Size: 800 maps; 10 atlases.
Annual Accessions: 80 maps.
Area Specialization: Iowa; Dubuque County; Dubuque.
Collections not Cataloged.
Depository for: USGS (Topo).
Serves: students; faculty; employees; public;. Mon.–Thurs. 9 a.m.–9 p.m.; Sat. 9 a.m.–5 p.m.; Sun. 1:N5 p.m. Sept-May.
Reproduction Facility: photocopy.

242. LORAS COLLEGE
Wahlert Memorial Library
14th & Alta Vista
Dubuque, IA 52001
Established 1968.
Telephone: 319/588-7164.
Contact Person: Robert Klein, Libn.
Staff: 1 professional (part time).
Size: 3,151 maps.
Annual Accessions: 275 maps.
Area Specialization: Iowa; Illinois; Wisconsin.
Dates: 1900 - (100%).
Collections Cataloged.
Depository for: USGS (Topo.).
Serves: students; faculty; employees; public. Mon.–Fri. 8 a.m.–11:30 p.m.; Sat. 10 a.m.–5 p.m.; Sun. 12 Noon–11:30 p.m. (Seats 200).
Reproduction Facility: photocopy.

Iowa City

243. IOWA (STATE) GEOLOGICAL SURVEY
123 N. Capitol
Iowa City, IA 52242
Telephone: 319/338-1173.
Contact Person: Donald L. Koch, State Geologist.
Size: 900 maps.
Area Specialization: Iowa.
Subject Specialization: topography.
Depository for: USGS (Topo.).
Serves: public. Mon.–Fri. 8 a.m.–4:30 p.m.

244. STATE HISTORICAL SOCIETY OF IOWA
Library
402 Iowa Avenue
Iowa City, IA 52240
Contact Person: Nancy E. Kraft.
Staff: 1 professional (part time); 1 non-professional (part time).
Size: 1,200 maps; 400 atlases; 20 reference books and gazetteers; 3 serials (titles received); 4,500 microforms (no. of titles).
Area Specialization: Iowa.
Subject Specialization: geology.
Special Cartographic Collections: Sanborn fire insurance maps of Iowa cities.
Dates: 1800-1899 (65%); 1900 - (35%).
Classification System: LC.
Collections Cataloged. (40%).
Serves: students; faculty; public.

Reproduction Facility: photocopy; quickcopy.
Publications: *Fire insurance maps of Iowa cities and towns; A list of holdings. 1983.*

245. UNIVERSITY OF IOWA
Geology Library
136 Trowbridge Hall
Iowa City, IA 52242
Telephone: 319/353-4225.
Contact Person: Louise S. Zipp, Geology Libn.
Staff: 1 professional (full time); 1 non-professional (full time); 4 non-professional (part time).
Size: 83,042 maps; 1 globes.
Annual Accessions: 3,500 maps.
Area Specialization: North America.
Subject Specialization: earth sciences; topography.
Dates: 1800-1899 (2%); 1900 - (98%).
Classification System: local system.
Collections not Cataloged.
Depository for: USGS (Geol., topo.).
Serves: students; faculty; employees; public. Mon.–Thurs. 8 a.m.–10 p.m.; Fri. 8 a.m.–5 p.m.; Sat. 1–5 p.m.; Sun. 1–5 p.m., 6–10 p.m. (Seats 36).
Interlibrary Loan Available.

246. UNIVERSITY OF IOWA, LIBRARIES
Special Collections Department
Map Collection
Iowa City, IA 52242
Established 1965.
Telephone: 319/353-4467.
Contact Person: Richard S. Green, Map Libn.
Staff: 1 professional (full time); 4 non-professional (part time).
Size: 99,301 maps; 1,971 atlases; 3 globes; 35 relief models; 97,000 aerial photographs; 1,362 reference books and gazetteers; 50 serials (titles received); 1,108 microforms (no. of titles).
Annual Accessions: 3,000 maps; 100 atlases; 1 globes; 1 relief models; 500 aerial photographs; 50 reference books and gazetteers; 5 serials (titles received); 25 microforms (no. of titles).
Area Specialization: Iowa; midwestern United States; Canada.
Special Cartographic Collections: Fire insurance maps of Iowa cities and towns (over 4,300 microfiche).
Dates: pre-1800 (0.003%); 1800-1899 (0.1%); 1900 - (99.9%).
Classification System: LC.
Collections Cataloged.
Depository for: DMA; NOS; NTS (Canada); USGS (Topo.); Iowa (State Government);. GPO (Library system is a regional depository)
Serves: public. Mon.–Fri. 8–12 noon, 1–5 p.m. (Seats 32; 500 readers served per month).
Interlibrary Loan Available.
Reproduction Facility: photocopy; microform.

Ottumwa

247. OTTUMWA PUBLIC LIBRARY
129 N. Court St.
Ottumwa, IA 52501
Telephone: 515/682-7563.
Contact Person: Jerry Geib, Director.
Staff: 2 professional (part time); 1 non-professional (part time).
Size: 320 maps; 20 atlases; 1 globes; 3 reference books and gazetteers.
Annual Accessions: 5 maps; less than 1 atlases; less than 1 reference books and gazetteers.

Area Specialization: State of Iowa.
Subject Specialization: topography.
Dates: pre-1800 (1%); 1800-1899 (1%); 1900 - (98%).
Classification System: Dewey.
Depository for: USGS (Topo.).
Serves: public. Mon.–Wed. 9 a.m.–6 p.m., Thurs. 9 a.m.–9 p.m., Fri. 9 a.m.–6 p.m. (Seats 28; 10 readers served per month).
Reproduction Facility: quickcopy; microform.

Waterloo

248. GROUT MUSEUM OF HISTORY AND SCIENCE
503 South Street
Waterloo, IA 50701
Established 1956.
Telephone: 319/234-6357.
Contact Person: Mary B. Miller, Archivist.
Staff: 1 non-professional (full time).
Size: 135 maps; 23 atlases; 2 globes; 5 aerial photographs.
Area Specialization: Waterloo, Iowa; Blackhawk County, Iowa; Iowa.
Dates: 1800-1899 (40%); 1900 - (60%).
Classification System: Dewey.
Collections Cataloged. (50%).
Serves: students; employees; public. Tues.–Fri. 9:30–4:30 p.m.; Sat. 1–4 p.m. (Seats 8; 15-20 readers served per month).
Reproduction Facility: photocopy.

KANSAS

Hutchinson

249. HUTCHINSON PUBLIC LIBRARY
Reference Department
901 North Main
Hutchinson, KS 67501
Established 1970.
Telephone: 316/663-5441.
Contact Person: Marilyn Dean Mitchell, Department Head.
Staff: 1 professional (part time); 4 non-professional (part time).
Size: 1,405 maps; 38 atlases; 33 reference books and gazetteers; 110 microforms (no. of titles).
Annual Accessions: 15-20 maps; 3 atlases; 4 reference books and gazetteers; 5 microforms (no. of titles).
Area Specialization: Kansas.
Subject Specialization: topography.
Dates: 1900 - (100%).
Classification System: local system.
Collections not Cataloged.
Depository for: USGS (Topo.).
Serves: students; employees; public. Mon.–Fri. 9 a.m.–9 p.m.; Sat. 9 a.m.–6 p.m.; Sun. 1–5 p.m. (Seats 15; 20 readers served per month).
Reproduction Facility: photocopy; microform.

Lawrence

250. UNIVERSITY OF KANSAS
KU Map Library
T.R. Smith Map Collection
Room 112, Kenneth Spencer Research Library
Lawrence, KS 66045
Established 1947.
Telephone: 913/864-4420.
Contact Person: Richard L. Embers, Curator of Maps.
Staff: 1 professional (full time); 3 non-professional (part time).
Size: 224,195 maps; 10 globes; 36 relief models; 400 aerial photographs; 2,561 reference books and gazetteers; 119 serials (titles received); 5 microforms (no. of titles).
Annual Accessions: 9,562 maps; 30 aerial photographs; 73 reference books and gazetteers; 48 (number of active titles) serials (titles received).
Area Specialization: comprehensive collection with specialization for Kansas, North America, South East Asia, and Europe.
Subject Specialization: Geology; topography; population; recreation; transportation.
Special Cartographic Collections: Historical Maps Collection: Pre-1800 maps, rare original and facsimiles, 880 maps. Kansas Collection: Pre-1900 maps of Kansas and the midwest region, 9,300 maps.
Dates: 1800-1899 (10%); 1900 - (90%).
Classification System: T.R. Smith system.
Collections Cataloged. (90%).
Depository for: DMA; USGS (Geol., topo.).
Serves: students; faculty; employees; public. Mon.–Fri. 8 a.m.–5 p.m.; Sat. 9 a.m.–1 p.m. (during school). (Seats 20; 325 readers served per month).
Interlibrary Loan Available.
Reproduction Facility: photocopy; tracing machine.
Publications: *Guide for Readers-Map Library* (guide); *Annotated Mediagraphy of Old Maps in the KU Map Library* (in process).

251. UNIVERSITY OF KANSAS, LIBRARIES
Kansas Collection
Lawrence, KS 66045
Telephone: 913/864-4274.
Contact Person: Sheryl Williams, Curator.
Staff: 2 professional (full time); 3 non-professional (full time).
Size: 9,332 maps; 23,706 serials (titles received); 1,077 microforms (no. of titles).
Annual Accessions: 20 maps; 5,500 issues serials (titles received); 55 microforms (no. of titles).
Area Specialization: Kansas; Great Plains region.
Subject Specialization: railroads; Indian lands; urban planning.
Special Cartographic Collections: Sanborn maps for Kansas towns—plat atlases for many counties in Kansas and Missouri.
Dates: 1800-1899 (80%); 1900 - (20%).
Classification System: local system.
Collections Cataloged. (65%).
Serves: students; faculty; employees; public. Mon.–Fri. 8 a.m.–5 p.m.; Sat. 9 a.m.–1 p.m. (Only when classes are in session). (Seats 16 for maps; 190 readers served per month).
Reproduction Facility: photocopy; microform.
Publications: card catalog in the collection.

Manhattan

252. KANSAS STATE UNIVERSITY
Documents Department
Manhattan, KS 66506
Telephone: 913/532-6516, ext. 28.
Contact Person: John L. Johnson, Libn.
Size: 100,000 maps; 625 atlases; 1 globes; 600 aerial photographs.
Annual Accessions: 4,000 maps; 30 atlases; 50 aerial photographs.
Area Specialization: Kansas; Great Plains.
Dates: 1800-1899 (10%); 1900 - (90%).
Classification System: LC.
Collections Cataloged.
Depository for: USGS (Geol., topo.); GPO.
Serves: students; faculty; employees; public. Mon.–Fri. 8 a.m.–10 p.m.; Sat. 9 a.m.–5 p.m.; Sun. 2–10 p.m. (Seats 6; 130-150 readers served per month).
Interlibrary Loan Available.
Reproduction Facility: photocopy; microform.

Topeka

253. KANSAS STATE HISTORICAL SOCIETY
Manuscript Department
Map Division
120 West 10th Avenue
Topeka, KS 66612
Established 1875.
Telephone: 913/296-4793.
Contact Person: Bob Knecht, Assistant Manuscripts Curator.
Staff: 1 professional (part time).
Size: 12,966 maps.
Annual Accessions: 875 maps.
Area Specialization: Kansas; the Great Plains; western United States.
Subject Specialization: general maps; railroads; roads and trails; counties; cities; Indian lands; explorations.
Dates: pre-1800 (less than 1%); 1800-1899 (60%); 1900 - (40%).
Classification System: local system.
Collections Cataloged.
Depository for: USGS (Topo.).
Serves: students; faculty; employees; public. Mon.–Fri. 9 a.m.–5 p.m. (Seats 28; 15-20 readers served per month).
Reproduction Facility: photocopy; quickcopy; microform.
Publications: *Preliminary Guide to the Unpublished Records and Papers in the Kansas State Historical Society That Relate to Country Schools: Maps* (1981).

254. KANSAS STATE LIBRARY
3rd floor Capital
Topeka, KS 66612
Telephone: 913/296-3296.
Contact Person: Marc Galbraith, Director of Reference.
Staff: 1 professional (full time).
Dates: 1900 - (100%).
Classification System: local system.
Depository for: USGS (Topo.).
Serves: employees; public. Mon.–Fri. 8 a.m.–5 p.m. (Seats 20).
Interlibrary Loan Available.
Reproduction Facility: photocopy; quickcopy.

Wichita

255. WICHITA PUBLIC LIBRARY
Reference Department
Map Section
223 South Main Street
Wichita, KS 67202
Established 1977.
Telephone: 316/262-0611.
Contact Person: Larry A. Vos, Map Reference Libn.
Staff: 1 professional (part time).
Size: 20,000 maps; 95 atlases; 3 globes; 2 relief models; 45 reference books and gazetteers.
Annual Accessions: 200 maps; 8 atlases; 5 reference books and gazetteers.
Area Specialization: Kansas.
Dates: 1800-1899 (2%); 1900 - (98%).
Classification System: LC.
Collections Cataloged.
Depository for: USGS (Topo.).
Serves: public. Mon.–Thurs 8:30 a.m.–9 p.m.; Fri 8:30 a.m.–5:30 p.m.; Sat. 8:30 a.m.–5:30 p.m.; Sun. 1–5 p.m.
Interlibrary Loan Available.
Reproduction Facility: photocopy.

256. WICHITA STATE UNIVERSITY
Geology Department
Wichita, KS 67208
Established 1926.
Telephone: 316/689-3140.
Contact Person: Dr. Daniel F. Merriam, Professor of Geology.
Size: 50,000 maps; 150 atlases.
Area Specialization: Kansas; Oklahoma; Colorado.
Subject Specialization: geology.
Dates: 1800-1899 (5%); 1900 - (95%).
Collections not Cataloged.
Serves: students; faculty. by request.
Reproduction Facility: quickcopy.

257. WICHITA STATE UNIVERSITY
Special Collections Department
Wichita, KS 67208
Telephone: 316/689-3590.
Contact Person: Michael T. Kelly, Curator of Special Collections.
Size: 250 maps; 75 atlases.
Annual Accessions: 5 maps; 1 atlases.
Area Specialization: Kansas.
Subject Specialization: land ownership.
Special Cartographic Collections: plat books of Kansas counties.
Dates: pre-1800 (5%); 1800-1899 (95%).
Classification System: local system.
Collections Cataloged.
Serves: students; faculty; public. Mon.–Fri. 8:00 a.m.–12 noon, 1–5 p.m. (Seats 6; 50 readers served per month).
Reproduction Facility: photocopy; microform.

KENTUCKY

Berea

258. BEREA COLLEGE
Geology Department
College Box 1105
Berea, KY 40404
Established 1920.
Telephone: 606/986-9341, ext. 598.

Contact Person: Z. L. Lipchinsky, Chairman.
Staff: 1 professional (full time); 1 non-professional (part time).
Size: 2,000 maps; 200 atlases; 10 globes; 30 relief models; 100 aerial photographs; 5 reference books and gazetteers.
Annual Accessions: 200 maps; 2 atlases; 1 reference books and gazetteers.
Area Specialization: Appalachian area.
Subject Specialization: topography; geology.
Dates: 1800-1899 (10%); 1900 - (90%).
Classification System: AMS.
Collections Cataloged.
Depository for: USGS (Geol., topo.).
Serves: students; faculty; public. Mon.–Fri. 8 a.m.–5 p.m. (Seats 12; 3 readers served per month).
Interlibrary Loan Available.
Reproduction Facility: photocopy.

Bowling Green

259. WESTERN KENTUCKY UNIVERSITY
Kentucky Library and Museum
Bowling Green, KY 42101
Established 1931.
Telephone: 502/745-2592.
Contact Person: Constance A. Mills, Reference Libn.
Staff: 1 professional (full time).
Size: 1,050 maps; 45 atlases; 2 globes; 1 relief models; 10 aerial photographs; 25 reference books and gazetteers; 1 serials (titles received).
Annual Accessions: 50 maps; 1 atlases; 1 reference books and gazetteers.
Area Specialization: Kentucky; Virginia; Ohio River Valley.
Subject Specialization: history.
Dates: pre-1800 (12%); 1800-1899 (23%); 1900 - (65%).
Classification System: local system.
Collections Cataloged. (90%).
Depository for: USGS (Geol., topo.).
Serves: students; faculty; employees; public. Mon.–Fri. 8 a.m.–4:30 p.m.; Sat. 9 a.m.–4:30 p.m. (Seats 30; 125 readers served per month).
Reproduction Facility: photocopy.

Frankfort

260. KENTUCKY HISTORICAL SOCIETY
Library
P.O. Box H Broadway
Frankfort, KY 40602
Telephone: 502/564-3016.
Contact Person: Mary E. Winter, Photo/Archivist.
Staff: 1 professional (full time).
Size: 900 maps; 30 atlases; 6 aerial photographs.
Area Specialization: Kentucky state and counties; southeastern United States.
Dates: 1800-1899 (75%); 1900 - (25%).
Classification System: local system.
Collections Cataloged. (60%).
Serves: students; faculty; employees; public. Mon.–Fri. 8 a.m.–4:30 p.m. (Seats 10; 20-30 readers served per month).
Reproduction Facility: photocopy; microform.

261. KENTUCKY (STATE) DEPARTMENT OF COMMERCE
Department of Research
Division of Map Sales
133 Holmes Street
Frankfort, KY 40601
Established 1948.
Telephone: 502/564-4715.

Contact Person: Bill Howard, Office Supervisor.
Staff: 3 professional (full time).
Size: 100,000 maps; 125,000 aerial photographs; 7,000 serials (titles received).
Area Specialization: Kentucky.
Subject Specialization: geology; industry.
Collections Cataloged.
Depository for: USGS (Geol., topo.).
Serves: public. Mon.–Fri. 8 a.m.–4:30 p.m.

Lexington

262. UNIVERSITY OF KENTUCKY
Geology Library
Geology Library Map Collection
100 Bowman Hall
Lexington, KY 40506
Established 1923.
Telephone: 606/257-8359 or 5730.
Contact Person: Vivian S. Hall, Geology Libn.
Staff: 1 professional (part time); 3 non-professional (part time).
Size: 98,900 maps; 25 atlases; 1 globes; 10 reference books and gazetteers; 4 serials (titles received).
Annual Accessions: 3,900 maps.
Area Specialization: Kentucky; southeastern United States.
Subject Specialization: earth Sciences (geology).
Special Cartographic Collections: tectonics, coal, petroleum, and other mineral resources; topography and geology.
Dates: 1800-1899 (1%); 1900 - (99%).
Classification System: local system: a one card geographical system devised by the. librarian
Collections Cataloged. (75%).
Depository for: USGS (Geol., topo.).
Serves: students; faculty; employees; public. Mon.–Thurs. 8:00 a.m.–10:00 p.m.; Fri. 8 a.m.–4:30 p.m.; Sat. 1–5:00 p.m.; Sun. 1–5:00 p.m. (Seats 47; 2,000 readers served per month).
Reproduction Facility: photocopy; microform.
Publications: monthly acquisition list.

263. UNIVERSITY OF KENTUCKY
MIK Library
Map Collection
Lexington, KY 40506
Established 1972.
Telephone: 606/257-1853.
Contact Person: Gwen Curtis, Head.
Staff: 1 non-professional (full time); 3 non-professional (part time).
Size: 44,277 maps; 770 atlases; 1 globes; 26 relief models; 25,057 aerial photographs; 465 reference books and gazetteers; 5 serials (titles received); 151 microforms (no. of titles).
Annual Accessions: 1,000 maps; 20 atlases; 5,100 aerial photographs; 20 reference books and gazetteers; 1 serials (titles received); 118 microforms (no. of titles).
Area Specialization: Kentucky; southeastern United States.
Special Cartographic Collections: Sanborn insurance maps of Kentucky cities.
Dates: pre-1800 (5%); 1800-1899 (20%); 1900 - (75%).
Classification System: LC.
Collections Cataloged. (10%).
Depository for: DMA; Ky. Geological Survey.
Serves: students; faculty; employees; public. Mon.–Fri. 10 a.m.–4:30 p.m. (Seats 16; 158 readers served per month).
Interlibrary Loan Available.
Reproduction Facility: photocopy; microform.
Publications: *Selected Acquisitions Bulletin.*

Louisville

264. THE FILSON CLUB
118 W. Breckinridge St.
Louisville, KY 40203
Established 1884.
Telephone: 502/582-3727.
Contact Person: Dorothy Rush, Libn.
Size: 800 maps.
Area Specialization: Kentucky and adjacent states.
Subject Specialization: history (Kentucky).
Dates: pre-1800 (10%); 1800-1899 (50%); 1900 - (40%).
Classification System: Dewey.
Collections Cataloged.
Serves: public. Mon.–Fri. 9 a.m.–5 p.m.; Sat. 9 a.m.–12 noon. (Seats 18; 650 readers served per month).
Reproduction Facility: photocopy.

265. UNIVERSITY OF LOUISVILLE
Ekstrom Library
Reference Department
Louisville, KY 40292
Telephone: 502/588-6747.
Contact Person: Joan ten Hoor, Reference Libn.
Staff: 1 professional (part time); 1 non-professional (part time).
Size: 11,000 maps.
Area Specialization: Kentucky.
Subject Specialization: topography; geology.
Collections not Cataloged.
Depository for: DMA; USGS (Geol., topo.).
Serves: students; faculty; employees; public. Mon.–Thurs. 8 a.m.–10 p.m.; Sat. 9 a.m.–5 p.m.; Sun. 1–9 p.m.
Interlibrary Loan Available.
Reproduction Facility: photocopy.

LOUISIANA

Baton Rouge

266. LOUISIANA STATE UNIVERSITY
Department of Geography and Anthropology
Cartographic Information Center
Baton Rouge, LA 70803
Telephone: 504/388-6247.
Contact Person: Joyce Nelson, map Curator.
Staff: 1 professional (full time); 4 non-professional (part time).
Size: 420,000 maps; 50 atlases; 15 globes; 100 relief models; 80,000 aerial photographs; 8 reference books and gazetteers.
Annual Accessions: 5,000 maps.
Area Specialization: Gulf Coast; southeastern United States; Latin America.
Subject Specialization: earth Sciences; geology.
Special Cartographic Collections: Sanborn fire insurance maps of Louisiana.
Dates: pre-1800 (less than 1%); 1800-1899 (less than 1%); 1900 - (99%).
Classification System: local system.
Collections not Cataloged.
Depository for: DMA; NOS; USGS (Geol., topo.).

Serves: students; faculty; employees; public;. Thurs. 8 a.m.–4:30 p.m., Fri. 8 a.m.–12 noon. (Seats 20; 150 readers served per month).
Reproduction Facility: quickcopy.

267. LOUISIANA STATE UNIVERSITY
Middleton Library
Department of Archives and Manuscripts
Baton Rouge, LA 70803
Telephone: 505/388-2240.
Contact Person: M. Stone Miller, Jr., Dept. Head.
Staff: 2 professional (full time); 2 non-professional (full time).
Size: 500 maps.
Annual Accessions: 20 maps.
Area Specialization: Lower Mississippi Valley: southern United States.
Subject Specialization: history; sociology; economics; culture.
Dates: pre-1800 (15%); 1800-1899 (60%); 1900 - (25%).
Classification System: local system.
Collections Cataloged.
Serves: students; faculty; employees; public. Mon.–Fri. 7:30 a.m.–4 p.m.; Sat. 8 a.m.–12 Noon. (Seats 18; ca. 75 readers served per month).
Reproduction Facility: photocopy; quickcopy; microform.

268. LOUISIANA STATE UNIVERSITY
Middleton Library
Louisiana Room
Baton Rouge, LA 70803
Established 1935.
Telephone: 504/388-2575.
Contact Person: Evangeline Mills Lynch, Libn. and Head of Louisiana Room.
Staff: 1 professional (full time); 1 professional (part time); 1 non-professional (full time); 11 non-professional (part time).
Size: 1,185 maps; 142 atlases.
Area Specialization: Louisiana; Territory of Orleans; Lower Mississippi Valley.
Subject Specialization: comprehensive for Louisiana.
Special Cartographic Collections: Sanborn fire insurance maps for Louisiana towns.
Classification System: LC.
Serves: students; faculty; employees; public. Mon.–Fri. 7:30 a.m.–4 p.m.; Sat. 8 a.m.–12 Noon; Sun. 7–9 p.m. (Seats 30).
Reproduction Facility: photocopy; quickcopy; microform.

269. SOUTHERN UNIVERSITY
John B. Cade Library
Reference Department
Swan Avenue
Baton Rouge, LA 70813
Telephone: 504/771-4990.
Size: 60 maps; 50 atlases; 1 globes; 16 reference books and gazetteers.
Annual Accessions: 5 atlases.
Area Specialization: Baton Rouge; Louisiana; United States; world.
Classification System: LC.
Collections Cataloged.
Depository for: DMA; USGS (Geol., topo.).
Serves: students; faculty; employees; public. Mon.–Thurs. 8 a.m.–12 midnight, Fri. 8 a.m.–5 p.m.; Sat. 8:00 a.m.–5 p.m.; Sun. 2:00 p.m.–12 midnight.
Reproduction Facility: photocopy.

New Orleans

270. LOUISIANA STATE MUSEUM
Louisiana Historical Center
Cartographic Division
400 Esplanade Avenue, Old U.S. Mint
New Orleans, LA 70116
Established 1906.
Telephone: 504/568-8216.
Contact Person: Joseph D. Castle, Curator of Maps, Manuscripts and Rare Books.
Staff: 4 professional (full time); 1 non-professional (full time).
Size: 3,500 maps; 22 atlases; 78 reference books and gazetteers; 4 serials (titles received); 1 microforms (no. of titles).
Annual Accessions: 75 maps; 1 atlases; 2 reference books and gazetteers; 1 serials (titles received).
Area Specialization: Louisiana; North America.
Subject Specialization: Louisiana; Colonial North America.
Special Cartographic Collections: Solis & Helen Seiferth Cartographic Collection (primarily Louisiana and North America) Sanborn fire insurance maps 1867-1950--Louisiana (microform).
Dates: pre-1800 (70%); 1800-1899 (15%); 1900 - (15%).
Classification System: local system: Museum accession number.
Serves: students; faculty; employees; public. Mon.–Fri. 8:45 a.m.–4:45 p.m. (Seats 24; 50-75 readers served per month).
Reproduction Facility: photocopy; quickcopy.
Publications: *Guide to the Cartographic Collection of the Louisiana State Museum* (in press).

271. NEW ORLEANS PUBLIC LIBRARY
Louisiana Division
219 Loyola Avenue
New Orleans, LA 70140
Established 1958.
Telephone: 504/596-2610.
Contact Person: Wayne M. Everard, Libn. I.
Staff: 3 professional (full time); 1 professional (part time); 3 non-professional (full time); 1 non-professional (part time).
Size: 2,800 maps; 118 atlases; 16,700 aerial photographs; 25 reference books and gazetteers; 12 microforms (no. of titles).
Annual Accessions: 50 maps; 5 atlases.
Area Specialization: Louisiana; Mississippi River; northern Gulf of Mexico; New Orleans.
Special Cartographic Collections: City Archives Collection (property surveys and street plans, 1700-present).
Dates: pre-1800 (1%); 1800-1899 (9%); 1900 - (90%).
Classification System: local system.
Collections Cataloged. (75%).
Serves: students; faculty; employees; public. Tues.–Fri. 10 a.m.–6 p.m.; Sat. 10 a.m.–6 p.m. (Seats 60; 50 readers served per month).
Reproduction Facility: photocopy; microform.

272. TULANE UNIVERSITY
Howard-Tilton Memorial Library
Government Documents Department
7001 Freret Street
New Orleans, LA 70118
Telephone: 504/865-5683.
Staff: 2 non-professional (part time).
Size: 98,200 maps; 500 aerial photographs.
Annual Accessions: 1,800 maps; 100 aerial photographs.
Area Specialization: United States.
Subject Specialization: topography.
Dates: 1800-1899 (2%); 1900 - (98%).
Collections not Cataloged.
Depository for: DMA; USGS (Topo.).

Serves: public. Mon.–Thurs. 8:30 a.m.–9 p.m.; Fri. 8:30 a.m.–5 p.m.; Sat. 10 a.m.–5 p.m.; Sun. 1–9 p.m. (8 readers served per month).
Reproduction Facility: photocopy.

273. TULANE UNIVERSITY
Latin American Library
7001 Freret Street
New Orleans, LA 70118
Established 1924.
Telephone: 504/865-5681.
Contact Person: Martha B. Robertson, Library Assistant.
Staff: 1 non-professional (part time).
Size: 2,300 maps; 250 atlases; 15 aerial photographs; 100 reference books and gazetteers; 35 serials (titles received).
Area Specialization: Mexico; Central America; South America.
Subject Specialization: archeology; history.
Special Cartographic Collections: Frederick L. Hoffman Collection (852 maps on Mexico, Central America & South America); Frank Keller Collection (150 maps on South America).
Dates: pre-1800 (20%); 1800-1899 (30%); 1900 - (50%).
Classification System: local system.
Collections Cataloged.
Serves: students; faculty; employees; public. Mon.–Fri. 8 a.m.–5 p.m.; Sat. 10 a.m.–5 p.m. (Seats 45; 10 readers served per month).
Reproduction Facility: photocopy; quickcopy.
Publications: *An Inventory of the Collections of the Middle American Research Institute: no. 4: Maps in the Library of the Middle American Research Institute.* New Orleans: The Institute, Tulane University, 1941; *No. 3: Maps in the Frederick L. Hoffman Collection.* New Orleans: The Institute, Tulane University, 1939.

274. UNIVERSITY OF NEW ORLEANS
Library
Government Documents Division
Lakefront
New Orleans, LA 70005
Telephone: 504/286-6547.
Contact Person: Frances W. Skiffington, Head of Government Documents.
Staff: 2 professional (full time); 1 non-professional (full time); 2 non-professional (part time).
Size: 12,850 maps; 85 atlases; 2 globes; 35 reference books and gazetteers.
Annual Accessions: 1,100 maps; 4 atlases; 2 reference books and gazetteers.
Area Specialization: southern United States.
Subject Specialization: geology; topography.
Dates: 1900 - (100%).
Classification System: local system.
Collections not Cataloged.
Depository for: USGS (Geol., topo.).
Serves: students; faculty; employees; public. Mon.–Fri. 7:45 a.m.–10 p.m.; Sat. 7:45 a.m.–6 p.m.; Sun. 1–10 p.m. (Seats approx. 50; 100 readers served per month).
Interlibrary Loan Available.
Reproduction Facility: photocopy.

Ruston

275. LOUISIANA TECH UNIVERSITY
Prescott Memorial Library
Government Documents Department
Ruston, LA 71272-0046
Established 1983.
Telephone: 318/257-4962.

Contact Person: Stephen Henson, Government Documents Libn.
Staff: 1 professional (full time); 2 non-professional (full time).
Size: 3,000 maps.
Area Specialization: Louisiana; Texas; Mississippi; Arkansas.
Subject Specialization: topography; geology.
Dates: 1900 - (100%).
Classification System: local system.
Collections Cataloged. (20%).
Depository for: USGS (Geol., topo.).
Serves: students; faculty; employees; public. Mon.–Thurs. 7 a.m.–11 p.m.; Fri. 7 a.m.–5 p.m.; Sat. 9 a.m.–4 p.m.; Sun. 2–11 p.m. (Seats 30).
Interlibrary Loan Available.
Reproduction Facility: photocopy.

MAINE

Bangor

276. BANGOR PUBLIC LIBRARY
145 Harlow Street
Bangor, ME 04401
Telephone: 207/947-8336.
Contact Person: Susan Wight, Head, Adult Services.
Staff: 1 professional (full time).
Size: 24,250 maps; 475 atlases; 4 globes; 40 aerial photographs; 30 reference books and gazetteers.
Annual Accessions: 250 maps; 12 atlases; 5 reference books and gazetteers.
Area Specialization: Maine.
Dates: 1800-1899 (25%); 1900 - (75%).
Classification System: Dewey.
Collections Cataloged. (100%).
Depository for: USGS (Geol.).
Serves: students; faculty; employees; public;. Mon.–Fri. 9 a.m.–9 p.m. (Summer hours 9 a.m.–7 p.m.); Sat. 9 a.m.–5 p.m. (Seats 25).
Reproduction Facility: photocopy; quickcopy.

Brunswick

277. BOWDOIN COLLEGE LIBRARY
Map Collection
Brunswick, ME 04011
Telephone: 207/725-8731, ext. 298.
Contact Person: Elda Takugi, Documents Libn.
Staff: 1 professional (part time); 1 non-professional (part time).
Size: 60,000 maps; 100 atlases; 75 reference books and gazetteers.
Area Specialization: Maine.
Special Cartographic Collections: World War II maps.
Dates: 1900 - (100%).
Classification System: LC; DMA.
Collections not Cataloged. (10).
Depository for: DMA; USGS (Geol., topo.).
Serves: students; faculty; employees; public. Mon.–Fri. 8:30 a.m.–12 midnight; Sat. 8:30–12 midnight; Sun. 10 a.m.–12 midnight.
Reproduction Facility: photocopy; microform.

Lewiston

278. BATES COLLEGE
Ladd Library
Lewiston, ME 04240
Established 1976.
Telephone: 207/786-6263.
Contact Person: LaVerne Winn, Reference Libn.
Staff: 1 professional (part time).
Size: 2,000 maps; 1 globes.
Area Specialization: New England.
Subject Specialization: geology.
Special Cartographic Collections: Lewiston ward maps.
Dates: 1900 - (100%).
Classification System: LC; local system.
Depository for: USGS (Geol., topo.).
Serves: public. Mon.–Fri. 8:30 a.m.–10 p.m.
Interlibrary Loan Available.
Reproduction Facility: photocopy.

Orono

279. UNIVERSITY OF MAINE AT ORONO
Raymond H. Fogler Library
Government Documents Department
Orono, ME 04469
Established 1907.
Telephone: 207/581-1680.
Contact Person: Francis R. Wihbey, Dept. Head.
Staff: 1 professional (full time); 3 non-professional (full time).
Size: 39,000 maps; 379 atlases; 13 relief models; 267 reference books and gazetteers; 9 serials (titles received); 4,000 microforms (no. of titles).
Annual Accessions: 4,700 maps; 4-10 atlases; 1 relief models; 5 reference books and gazetteers; 1,500 microforms (no. of titles).
Area Specialization: United States; New England; Canada.
Special Cartographic Collections: USDA Soil Conservation Service *Soil Surveys*; U.S. Fish and Wildlife Service *Ecological Characterization of Coastal Maine.*
Dates: 1800-1899 (1%); 1900 - (99%).
Classification System: DMA (DMA maps only); By agency-assigned serial number; otherwise by geographic name within series.
Collections Cataloged. (2%).
Depository for: DMA; NOS; NTS (Canada); USGS (Geol., topo.).
Serves: students; faculty; employees; public. Mon.–Fri. 8 a.m.–4:30 p.m. (Seats 29; 400 readers served per month).
Interlibrary Loan Available.
Reproduction Facility: photocopy; microform.

280. UNIVERSITY OF MAINE AT ORONO
Raymond H. Fogler Library
Special Collections Department
Orono, ME 04469
Established 1970.
Telephone: 207/581-1688.
Contact Person: Eric S. Flower, Head.
Size: 2,000 maps; 10 atlases; 5 aerial photographs; 5 reference books and gazetteers.
Annual Accessions: 50 maps; 1 atlases.
Area Specialization: Maine.
Subject Specialization: local history.
Dates: 1800-1899 (27%); 1900 - (73%).
Classification System: by cartographer or Agency responsible.
Collections Cataloged.
Depository for: Maine State Agency publications.

Serves: students; faculty; employees; public. Mon.–Fri. 8 a.m.–4:30 p.m.; Sun. 1–5 p.m. (Seats 20; 400 readers served per month).
Reproduction Facility: photocopy; microform.
Publications: *List of Maps Held in the Special Collections Department, Raymond H. Fogler Library, University of Maine, Orono, Maine* (1974).

Portland

281. MAINE HISTORICAL SOCIETY
Imprints Library
485 Congress St.
Portland, ME 04101
Established 19th century.
Telephone: 207/774-1822.
Contact Person: Margaret McCain, Libn.
Area Specialization: Maine.
Classification System:
Collections Cataloged.
Serves: members of MHS. Mon., Tues., Wed., Fri., 9 a.m.–5 p.m.; Thurs. 9 a.m.–8:30 p.m.; Sat. 2nd Sat. of each month 9 a.m.–5 p.m. (Seats 20; 320 readers served per month).
Reproduction Facility: photocopy.

282. PORTLAND PUBLIC LIBRARY
Government Documents
5 Monument Square
Portland, ME 04101
Telephone: 207/773-4761, ext. 121.
Contact Person: John Long, Documents Libn.
Staff: 1 professional (part time); 1 non-professional (part time).
Size: 5,000 maps; 120 atlases; 1 globes; 150 reference books and gazetteers.
Annual Accessions: 200 maps; 4-5 atlases; 2-3 reference books and gazetteers.
Area Specialization: United States.
Subject Specialization: topography.
Dates: 1900 - (100%).
Collections not Cataloged.
Depository for: USGS (Topo.).
Serves: public. Mon., Wed., Fri. 9 a.m.–6 p.m.; Tues., Thurs. 12 noon–9 p.m.; Sat. 9 a.m.–5 p.m. (Seats 33; 15 readers served per month).
Reproduction Facility: photocopy.

MARYLAND

Annapolis

283. MARYLAND HALL OF RECORDS COMMISSION
Archives
College Avenue & St. John's Street
Annapolis, MD 21404
Established 1935.
Telephone: 301/269-3914.
Contact Person: Nancy M. Bramucci, Archivist III.
Staff: 1 professional (full time).
Size: 1,707 maps; 21 atlases; 36 cubic ft. aerial photographs; 1 microforms (no. of titles).
Area Specialization: Middle Atlantic States.
Subject Specialization: Chesapeake Bay region.
Special Cartographic Collections: Huntingfield Corporation Collection [MdHRG1399]-reference collection of privately owned maps of Maryland 1565-1891; USGS topographical maps of Maryland [MdHRG1427-1214].

Dates: pre-1800 (43%); 1800-1899 (33%); 1900 - (24%).
Collections Cataloged.
Depository for: maps produced by Md. State agencies.
Serves: students; faculty; employees; public. Mon.–Fri. 8:30 a.m.–4:30 p.m.; Sat. 8:30 a.m.–4:30 p.m. (Seats 30; 938 readers served per month).
Reproduction Facility: photocopy; microform.
Publications: Russell Morrison, Edward C. Papenfuse, Nancy M. Bramucci and Robert J.H. Janson-Lapaline. *On the Map: An Exhibit and Catalogue of Maps Relating to Maryland and the Chesapeake Bay honoring George Washington at the beginning of the Third Century of Washington College at Chestertown, Maryland February 21– March 6, 1983* (Huntingfield Corporation, 1983) Edward C. Papenfuse and Joseph M. Coale III. *The Hammond-Harwood Atlas of Historical Maps of Maryland 1608-1908* (Baltimore: The Johns Hopkins University Press, 1982).

Baltimore

284. ENOCH PRATT FREE LIBRARY
General Information Department
400 Cathedral Street
Baltimore, MD 21201
Established 1933.
Telephone: 301/396-5472.
Contact Person: Marion V. Bell, Head.
Staff: 1 professional (full time); 1 non-professional (full time).
Size: 101,362 maps; 3 globes.
Annual Accessions: 2,500 maps.
Area Specialization: United States; western Europe.
Dates: 1800-1899 (10%); 1900 - (90%).
Classification System: combined classification system.
Collections Cataloged. (50%).
Depository for: DMA; NOS; USGS (Geol., topo.).
Serves: public. Mon.–Thurs. 10 a.m.–9 p.m.; Fri. 9 a.m.–5 p.m.; Sat. 9 a.m.–5 p.m.; Sun. 1–5 p.m. (Seats 60; 65 readers served per month).
Interlibrary Loan Available.
Reproduction Facility: photocopy.
Publications: guide.

285. JOHNS HOPKINS UNIVERSITY
Milton S. Eisenhower Library
Government Publications/Maps/Law Department
34 at Charles Street
Baltimore, MD 21218
Established 1964.
Telephone: 301/338-8360.
Contact Person: Jim Gillispie, Head Government Publications/Maps/Law Dept.; Bill Johnson, Map Supervisor.
Staff: 2 professional (full time); 1 professional (part time); 3 non-professional (full time).
Size: 183,301 maps; 685 atlases; 1 globes; few relief models; 313 reference books and gazetteers; 2 serials (titles received).
Annual Accessions: 3,000 maps; 50 atlases; 25 reference books and gazetteers.
Area Specialization: United States; Maryland.
Subject Specialization: geology; topography.
Dates: 1800-1899 (20%); 1900 - (80%).
Classification System: LC.
Collections Cataloged. (80%).
Depository for: USGS (Geol., topo.); Maryland Geological Survey Maps.
Serves: students; faculty; employees; public. Mon.–Fri. 8:30 a.m.–5 p.m. (Seats 24 (GOVT. PUBS/MAPS/LAW READING ROOM)).
Interlibrary Loan Available. restricted

Reproduction Facility: photocopy.
Publications: guide.

286. JOHNS HOPKINS UNIVERSITY
Milton S. Eisenhower Library
Peabody Department
17 East Mount Vernon Place
Baltimore, MD 21202
Established 1878.
Telephone: 301/659-8197.
Contact Person: Lyn Hart, Peabody Libn.
Staff: 2 professional (full time); 1 professional (part time); 3 non-professional (full time); 2 non-professional (part time).
Area Specialization: Baltimore; Maryland; Europe.
Subject Specialization: local history; atlases of the 16th-19th centuries.
Classification System: Dewey; local system.
Collections Cataloged. (80%).
Serves: students; faculty; employees; public. Mon.–Fri. 9 a.m.–5 p.m.; Sat. 9 a.m.–5 p.m. except June, July, August. (Seats 100; 500 readers served per month).
Interlibrary Loan Available.
Reproduction Facility: photocopy.

287. JOHNS HOPKINS UNIVERSITY
Milton S. Eisenhower Library
Special Collections Division, The John Work Garrett Collection
4545 North Charles Street
Baltimore, MD 21210
Established 1952.
Telephone: 301/338-7641.
Contact Person: Jane Katz, John Work Garrett Libn.
Staff: 1 professional (full time); 1 non-professional (part time).
Size: 450 maps; 35 atlases; 2 globes; 38 reference books and gazetteers.
Area Specialization: Maryland; Virginia; Pennsylvania; world.
Dates: pre-1800 (98.5%); 1800-1899 (1.5%).
Serves: students; faculty; employees; public. Mon.–Fri. 9 a.m.–5 p.m. (Seats 6; 1-2 readers served per month).
Reproduction Facility: photocopy.

288. MARYLAND HISTORICAL SOCIETY
Prints and Photographs Division
201 West Monument Street
Baltimore, MD 21201
Established 1844.
Telephone: 301/685-3750, ext. 76.
Contact Person: Ms. Laurie A. Baty, Prints and Photographs Libn.
Staff: 2 professional (full time).
Size: 3,000 maps; 25 reference books and gazetteers; 4 serials (titles received).
Annual Accessions: 30 maps; 2 reference books and gazetteers.
Area Specialization: Baltimore; Maryland; Mid-Atlantic States; Chesapeake Bay.
Dates: pre-1800 (10%); 1800-1899 (45%); 1900 - (45%).
Classification System: local system.
Collections Cataloged.
Depository for: USGS (Geol., topo.).
Serves: public. Tues.–Fri. 11 a.m.–4:30 p.m.; Sat. 9 a.m.–4:30 p.m. (Seats 4; 10 readers served per month).
Reproduction Facility: photocopy.
Publications: Maryland Historical Society. *The Mapping of Maryland 1590-1914: An Overview* (Baltimore, 1982).

Catonsville

289. UNIVERSITY OF MARYLAND BALTIMORE COUNTY
Albin O. Kuhn Library and Gallery
5401 Wilkens Avenue
Catonsville, MD 21228
Established 1971.
Telephone: 301/455-2232.
Contact Person: Patricia Stegall, Reference Libn.
Staff: 1 professional (part time).
Size: 4,385 maps; 361 atlases; 2 globes.
Annual Accessions: 300 maps.
Area Specialization: State of Maryland.
Dates: 1900 - (99%).
Classification System: LC.
Collections Cataloged.
Depository for: USGS (Topo.); State of Maryland Road
Maps.
Serves: students; faculty; employees; public. Mon.–Thurs. 8
a.m.–11 p.m., Fri. 8 a.m.–6 p.m.; Sat. 10 a.m.–4 p.m.; Sun.
1–9 a.m.
Reproduction Facility: photocopy.

College Park

290. UNIVERSITY OF MARYLAND
McKeldin Library
Documents/Maps Room
College Park, MD 20742
Telephone: 301/454-3034.
Contact Person: Lola N. Warren, Acting Head.
Staff: 2 professional (full time); 3 non-professional (full
time).
Size: 90,000 maps; 300 atlases; 25 relief models; 30 aerial
photographs; 350 reference books and gazetteers; 10
serials (titles received); 1 microforms (no. of titles).
Annual Accessions: 1,000 maps; 10 atlases; 5-10 aerial
photographs; 20 reference books and gazetteers; 10 serials
(titles received); 1 microforms (no. of titles).
Dates: 1800-1899 (5%); 1900 - (95%).
Classification System: SuDoc.
Collections Cataloged. (2%).
Depository for: DMA; USGS (Topo.).
Serves: students; faculty; employees; public. Mon.–Fri. 8
a.m.–11 p.m.; Sat. 10 a.m.–6 p.m.; Sun. 12 noon–11 p.m.
(Seats 90; 75 readers served per month).
Reproduction Facility: photocopy.

Frostburg

291. FROSTBURG STATE COLLEGE
Library
Document and Map Department
Frostburg, MD 21532
Established 1968.
Telephone: 301/689-4423.
Contact Person: Harry O. Davis, Document and Map Libn.
Staff: 1 professional (part time); 2 non-professional (part
time).
Size: 31,000 maps; 3 globes; 30 relief models; 25
reference books and gazetteers.
Annual Accessions: 1,400 maps; 4 reference books and
gazetteers.
Area Specialization: Maryland; Middle Atlantic States;
United States; Canada; Mexico.
Dates: 1800-1899 (1%); 1900 - (99%).
Classification System: LC; DMA.
Collections not Cataloged.
Depository for: DMA; USGS (Topo.).

Serves: students; faculty; employees; public. Mon.–Fri. 8:30
a.m.–10 p.m.; Sat. 1–5 p.m.; Sun. 1–10 p.m. (Seats 15).
Interlibrary Loan Available.
Reproduction Facility: photocopy.

Riverdale

292. U.S. NATIONAL OCEAN SERVICE
Map Library
6501 Lafayette Avenue
Riverdale, MD 20737
Established 1945.
Telephone: 301/436-6977.
Contact Person: Robert C. Hansen, Technical Information
Specialist.
Staff: 1 professional (full time); 4 non-professional (full
time); 1 non-professional (part time).
Size: 400,000 maps; 20 atlases; 2 relief models; 1,000
aerial photographs; 100 reference books and gazetteers; 10
serials (titles received); 5 microforms (no. of titles).
Annual Accessions: 4,000 maps.
Area Specialization: United States coastal waters.
Subject Specialization: hydrography; topography.
Special Cartographic Collections: nautical charts.
Dates: 1800-1899 (20%); 1900 - (80%).
Classification System: .
Collections Cataloged. (5%).
Depository for: NOS; NTS (Canada); USGS (Topo.); U.S.
county highway maps.
Serves: employees; public. Mon.–Fri. 8 a.m.–4:30 p.m.
Interlibrary Loan Available.
Reproduction Facility: photocopy; quickcopy.

Rockville

293. U.S. NATIONAL OCEAN SERVICE
6001 Executive Blvd.
Rockville, MD 20852
Telephone: 301/443-8408.
Contact Person: George Mastrogianis, Chief, Data Control
Section.
Staff: 1 professional (full time); 5 non-professional (full
time).
Size: 25,000 maps.
Area Specialization: United States contiguous coastline and
possessions.
Subject Specialization: hydrographic and topographic
(shoreline) surveys.
Classification System: local system.
Serves: students; faculty; employees; public;. Mon.–Fri. 8
a.m.–4:30 p.m. (Seats 10).
Reproduction Facility: photocopy.

294. U.S. NATIONAL OCEANIC AND ATMOSPHERIC ADMINISTRATION
Library and Information Service Division
6009 Executive Blvd.
Rockville, MD 20852
Telephone: 301/443-8330.
Area Specialization: comprehensive.
Subject Specialization: meteorology; climatology.
Special Cartographic Collections: extensive collection of
daily weather maps from most of the countries in the
world.
Serves: students; faculty; employees; public;. Mon.–Fri. 8
a.m.–4:30 p.m.
Reproduction Facility: quickcopy.

Towson

295. TOWSON STATE UNIVERSITY
Geography Dept.
College of Liberal Arts
York Rd.
Towson, MD 21204
Established 1970.
Telephone: 301/321-2963.
Contact Person: Marshall Stevenson, Assistant Professor of Geography.
Staff: 1 professional (part time); 1 non-professional (part time).
Size: 100 atlases; 5 globes; 85 relief models; 400 aerial photographs.
Annual Accessions: 200-250 maps.
Area Specialization: Maryland; Middle Atlantic States.
Subject Specialization: general.
Special Cartographic Collections: historical maps of Baltimore and Maryland.
Dates: 1800-1899 (5%); 1900 - (95%).
Classification System: LC.
Collections Cataloged. (100%).
Depository for: DMA; USGS (Geol., topo.).
Serves: students; faculty; employees; public. Mon.–Fri. 9 a.m.–4 p.m. (Seats 10; 10-15 readers served per month).

MASSACHUSETTS

Amherst

296. AMHERST COLLEGE
Library
Amherst, MA 01002
Telephone: 413/542-2319.
Contact Person: Floyd S. Merritt, Reference Libn.
Staff: 1 non-professional (part time).
Size: 60,000 maps; 485 atlases; 4 globes; 3 relief models; 220 reference books and gazetteers; 25 microforms (no. of titles).
Annual Accessions: 1,150 maps; 10 atlases; 15 reference books and gazetteers; 25 microforms (no. of titles).
Area Specialization: United States.
Dates: 1900 - (95%).
Classification System: LC; Dewey.
Collections not Cataloged.
Depository for: DMA; USGS (Geol., topo.).
Serves: students; faculty; employees; public. Mon.–Fri. 8:30 a.m.–9 p.m.; Sat. 9 a.m.–4 p.m. (Seats 6; 25 readers served per month).
Reproduction Facility: photocopy.

297. UNIVERSITY OF MASSACHUSETTS-AMHERST
University Library
Map Collection
Amherst, MA 01003
Established 1973.
Telephone: 413/545-2397.
Contact Person: Paul Shepard, Map Assistant.
Staff: 1 non-professional (full time); 1 non-professional (part time).
Size: 105,000 maps; 6 relief models.
Annual Accessions: 3,000 maps.
Dates: 1800-1899 (2%); 1900 - (98%).
Collections Cataloged. (1%).
Depository for: DMA; USGS (Geol., topo.).
Serves: students; faculty; public. Mon.–Fri. 8:30 a.m.–5 p.m. (Seats 12; 300 readers served per month).
Interlibrary Loan Available.

Boston

298. THE BOSTON ATHENAEUM
Reference/Research Department
10½ Beacon Street
Boston, MA 02108
Established 1807.
Telephone: 617/227-0270, ext. 22,20.
Contact Person: Cynthia English, Lisa Backman, Stephen Nonack, Reference Libns.
Staff: 4 professional (part time).
Size: 4,000 maps; 1,000 atlases; 5 globes; 100 reference books and gazetteers; 1 serials (titles received).
Area Specialization: Boston; New England.
Dates: pre-1800 (20%); 1800-1899 (60%); 1900 - (20%).
Classification System: LC; Cutter.
Collections Cataloged. (95%).
Depository for: USGS (Topo.).
Serves: employees; (members, guest researchers). Mon.–Fri. 9 a.m.–5:30 p.m.; Sat. 9–4 (Oct.–May). (Seats 12; 20 readers served per month).
Reproduction Facility: photocopy; microform.

299. THE BOSTONIAN SOCIETY
Library
Map Collection
15 State St., 3rd Floor
Boston, MA 02109
Established 1882.
Telephone: 617/242-5614.
Contact Person: Mary Leen, Libn.
Staff: 1 professional (full time); 1 professional (part time).
Size: 300 maps; 40 atlases; 50 aerial photographs; 5,000 reference books and gazetteers; 15 serials (titles received).
Area Specialization: Boston.
Subject Specialization: history of Boston; biographical material on prominent Bostonians.
Dates: pre-1800 (25%); 1800-1899 (60%); 1900 - (15%).
Classification System: LC.
Collections Cataloged.
Serves: public. Mon.–Fri. 9:30 a.m.–4:30 p.m. (Seats 8; 65 readers served per month).
Reproduction Facility: photographs.

300. INSURANCE LIBRARY ASSOCIATION
156 State Street
Boston, MA 02109
Telephone: 617/227-2087.
Contact Person: Jean Lucey, Libn.
Staff: 2 professional (full time); 1 professional (part time).
Size: 7,000 maps.
Area Specialization: New England.
Special Cartographic Collections: Sanborn fire insurance maps for most New England town and cities excluding Boston.
Dates: 1800-1899 (2%); 1900 - (98%).
Collections Cataloged.
Serves: public. Mon.–Fri. 9 a.m.–5 p.m.
Reproduction Facility: photocopy.

301. MASSACHUSETTS HISTORICAL SOCIETY
1154 Boylston Street
Boston, MA 02215
Established 1791.
Telephone: 617/536-1608.
Contact Person: John D. Cushing, Libn.
Size: 5,000 maps; 200 atlases.
Area Specialization: Massachusetts; New England.
Dates: pre-1800 (10%); 1800-1899 (89%); 1900 - (1%).
Classification System: local system.
Collections Cataloged. Mon.–Fri. 9 a.m.–4:45 p.m.
Reproduction Facility: photocopy.

302. MASSACHUSETTS STATE LIBRARY
Special Collections Department
341 State House
Boston, MA 02133
Established State Library established 1826.
Telephone: 617/727-2595.
Contact Person: Brenda Howitson, Chief.
Staff: 1 professional (full time); 1 non-professional (full time).
Size: 15,000 maps; 1,000 atlases; 250 reference books and gazetteers.
Annual Accessions: 300 maps; 10-15 reference books and gazetteers.
Area Specialization: Massachusetts; New England.
Subject Specialization: town and county maps and atlases of Massachusetts.
Special Cartographic Collections: Sanborn fire insurance maps-Massachusetts; Panoramic view maps-Massachusetts.
Dates: pre-1800 (5%); 1800-1899 (65%); 1900 - (30%).
Classification System: local system.
Collections Cataloged.
Depository for: NOS; USGS (Geol., topo.).
Serves: public. Mon.-Fri. 9 a.m.-5 p.m. (Seats 15; 40+ readers served per month).
Publications: Unpublished guides to atlases, Sanborn insurance maps, and panoramic view maps are available in the Library.

303. SOCIETY FOR THE PRESERVATION OF NEW ENGLAND ANTIQUITIES
Library
141 Cambridge Street
Boston, MA 02193
Telephone: 617/227-3956.
Contact Person: Elinor Reichlin.
Staff: 1 professional (full time); 1/2 professional (part time).
Size: 500 maps; 50 atlases; 50 aerial photographs.
Annual Accessions: ca. 125 atlases.
Area Specialization: Boston and Vicinity: Massachusetts.
Subject Specialization: cities; towns.
Dates: 1800-1899 (90%); 1900 - (10%).
Classification System: .
Collections Cataloged.
Serves: students; faculty; employees; public. Mon.-Fri. 9:30 a.m.-5 p.m. (by appointment); Sat.; Sun. (Seats 10; For all purposes, 60-70 readers served per month).
Reproduction Facility: photocopy.
Publications: *Guide to Boston and vicinity maps* (guide).

304. UNIVERSITY OF MASSACHUSETTS-BOSTON
Library and Geography and Earth Sciences Department
Harbor Campus
Boston, MA 02125
Telephone: 617/929-7633 or 8550.
Contact Person: Francis Schlesinger, Document Libn.; Richard Gelpke, Professor, Geography and Earth Sciences Dept.
Staff: 2 professional (part time).
Size: 40,000 maps; 100 atlases; 24 globes; 100 relief models; 200 aerial photographs.
Area Specialization: United States.
Dates: 1900 - (100%).
Collections not Cataloged.
Depository for: DMA; NOS; USGS (Topo.).
Serves: students; faculty; public. Mon.-Thurs. 8 a.m.-10 p.m., Fri. 8 a.m.-5 p.m.; Sun. 1-8 p.m.
Reproduction Facility: photocopy; microform.

Bridgewater

305. BRIDGEWATER STATE COLLEGE
Clement C. Maxwell Library
Government Documents
Shaw Road
Bridgewater, MA 02324
Established 1975.
Telephone: 617/697-1394.
Contact Person: Ms. Ratna Chandrasekhar, Library Assistant.
Staff: 1 professional (part time); 1 non-professional (part time).
Size: 9,477 maps; 203 atlases; 2 globes; 58 reference books and gazetteers; 16 serials (titles received).
Annual Accessions: 759 maps; 10 atlases; 4 reference books and gazetteers.
Area Specialization: Massachusetts.
Subject Specialization: topography; nautical sciences.
Classification System: DMA.
Collections not Cataloged.
Depository for: DMA; USGS (Geol., topo.).
Serves: students; faculty; employees; public. Mon.-Fri. 7:45 a.m.-11:00 p.m.; Sat. 8:30 a.m.-4 p.m.; Sun. 1-10 p.m. (Seats 60; 20 readers served per month).
Reproduction Facility: photocopy.

Buzzards Bay

306. MASSACHUSETTS MARITIME ACADEMY
Capt. Charles H. Hurley Library
Nantucket Way
Buzzards Bay, MA 02532
Telephone: 617/759-5761, ext. 350.
Contact Person: CDR Maurice Bosse, Director, Library Services.
Staff: 2 professional (full time); 1 professional (part time); 2 non-professional (full time).
Size: 190 maps; 10 atlases; 1 globes; 260 serials (titles received); 145 microforms (no. of titles).
Special Cartographic Collections: 850 nautical charts.
Classification System: local system.
Collections Cataloged.
Depository for: NOS.
Serves: students; faculty; employees. Mon.-Thurs. 8 a.m.-11 p.m.; Fri. 8 a.m.-5 p.m.; Sun. 4 p.m.-N:11 p.m.
Reproduction Facility: photocopy.

Cambridge

307. HARVARD UNIVERSITY
Geological Sciences Library
Map Collection
24 Oxford St.
Cambridge, MA 02138
Telephone: 617/495-2029.
Contact Person: Constance Wick, Libn.
Staff: 1 professional (part time); 1 non-professional (part time).
Size: 15,000 maps; 50 atlases; 50 reference books and gazetteers.
Area Specialization: United States.
Subject Specialization: geology.
Dates: 1800-1899 (5%); 1900 - (95%).
Classification System: LC.
Collections Cataloged. (50%).
Depository for: DOS (Gt. Brit); GSC; USGS (Geol.).
Serves: students; faculty; employees; public. Mon.-Fri. 9 a.m.-5 p.m. (Seats 10; 20 readers served per month).
Reproduction Facility: photocopy.

308. HARVARD UNIVERSITY
Pusey Library
Harvard Map Collection
Cambridge, MA 02138
Established 1818.
Telephone: 617/495-2417.
Contact Person: Dr. Frank E. Trout, Curator of Maps.
Staff: 1 professional (full time); 4 professional (part time); 2 non-professional (full time).
Size: 500,000 maps; 6,100 atlases; 2,900 reference books and gazetteers.
Area Specialization: comprehensive.
Subject Specialization: antiquarian; modern topographic world-wide 1:50,000 coverage; city plans.
Dates: pre-1800 (30%); 1800-1899 (10%); 1900 - (60%).
Classification System: LC geographical code & chronological sequence.
Collections Cataloged.
Depository for: DMA; NOS; USGS (Topo.).
Serves: students; faculty; employees; public. Mon.–Fri. 9 a.m.–1 p.m.; 2–5 p.m. (Seats 16).
Reproduction Facility: photocopy; microform; Photography, Slides.

309. MASSACHUSETTS INSTITUTE OF TECHNOLOGY
Science Library
Boston Stein Club Map Room
Room 14S-100
Cambridge, MA 02139
Established 1951.
Telephone: 617/253-5685.
Contact Person: Jean T. Eaglesfield, Lindgren Libn.
Size: 66,000 maps; 50 atlases; 3 globes; 100 reference books and gazetteers; 1 serials (titles received).
Annual Accessions: 2,000 maps; 1 atlases; 3 reference books and gazetteers.
Area Specialization: United States.
Subject Specialization: topography.
Dates: 1900 - (100%).
Classification System: LC.
Collections not Cataloged.
Depository for: DMA; USGS (Topo.).
Serves: students; faculty; employees; public. Mon.–Fri. 8:30 a.m.–11 p.m.; Sat. 11 a.m.–6 p.m.; Sun. 1–11 p.m. (Seats 44; 300 readers served per month).
Interlibrary Loan Available.
Reproduction Facility: photocopy; quickcopy.
Publications: *Maps and Atlases in MIT Libraries* (guide).

310. MASSACHUSETTS INSTITUTE OF TECHNOLOGY
Lindgren Library
Theodore Edward Schwarz Memorial Map Room
Room 54-200
Cambridge, MA 02139
Established 1938.
Telephone: 617/253-5679.
Contact Person: Jean T. Eaglesfield, Lindgren Libn.
Staff: 1 professional (full time); 1.5 non-professional (full time).
Size: 10,000 maps; 350 atlases; 4 globes.
Annual Accessions: 200 maps; 5 atlases.
Area Specialization: United States; comprehensive.
Subject Specialization: geology; geophysics; oceanography; meteorology.
Dates: 1800-1899 (10%); 1900 - (80%).
Classification System: LC.
Collections Cataloged. (25%).
Depository for: DMA; USGS (Geol.).
Serves: students; faculty; employees; public. Mon.–Fri. 8:30 a.m.–11 p.m.; Sat. 11 a.m.–6 p.m.; Sun. 1–11 p.m. (Seats 10; 5 readers served per month).

Interlibrary Loan Available.
Reproduction Facility: photocopy.
Publications: *Maps and Atlases in MIT Libraries* (guide).

311. MASSACHUSSETS INSTITUTE OF TECHNOLOGY
Rotch Library
Room 7-238
100 Massachusetts Avenue
Cambridge, MA 02139
Telephone: 617/253-7052.
Contact Person: Rona Gregory, Collections Manager.
Size: 1,200 maps; 75 atlases; 2 globes; 100 aerial photographs; 5 reference books and gazetteers; 350 microforms (no. of titles).
Annual Accessions: 75-100 maps; 3-5 atlases.
Area Specialization: Boston; Massachusetts.
Subject Specialization: urban planning; census maps.
Special Cartographic Collections: Sanborn fire insurance atlases of Greater Boston.
Dates: 1800-1899 (1%); 1900 - (99%).
Classification System: LC.
Collections Cataloged. (20%).
Depository for: U.S. Census.
Serves: students; faculty; employees; public. Mon.–Fri. 8:30 a.m.–10 p.m.; Sat. 11 a.m.–6 p.m.; Sun. 2–10 p.m.
Reproduction Facility: quickcopy; microform.

Medford

312. TUFTS UNIVERSITY
Wessell Library
Government Publications, Microforms, Maps Department
Medford, MA 02155
Telephone: 617/628-5000, ext. 2094.
Contact Person: David C. R. Heisser, Documents Libn.
Staff: 2 professional (part time); 1 non-professional (part time).
Size: 95,000 maps.
Annual Accessions: 2,500 maps.
Area Specialization: United States.
Subject Specialization: topography; geology.
Dates: 1900 - (95%).
Classification System: local system.
Collections not Cataloged.
Depository for: USGS (Geol., topo.); some other USGS, DMA, CIA, USDA series received on deposit from Superintendent o.
Serves: students; faculty; employees; public. Mon.–Fri 9 a.m.–10 p.m. (shorter summer hours); Sat. 9 a.m.–5 p.m.; Sun. 10 a.m.–10 p.m. (Seats 14; 10-15 readers served per month).
Reproduction Facility: photocopy.

New Bedford

313. FREE PUBLIC LIBRARY
Melville Whaling Room
613 Pleasant St.
New Bedford, MA 02740
Telephone: 613/999-6291, ext. 23.
Contact Person: Paul A. Cyr, Curator of Special Collections.
Staff: 1 professional (full time); 1 non-professional (full time).
Size: 646 maps.
Area Specialization: southeastern Massachusetts; oceans.
Subject Specialization: whaling.
Dates: pre-1800 (1%); 1800-1899 (75%); 1900 - (24%).
Collections not Cataloged.

Serves: public. Mon.–Fri. 9 a.m.–5 p.m.; Sat. 9 a.m.–5 p.m. (Seats 18).
Reproduction Facility: photocopy.

314. OLD DARTMOUTH HISTORICAL SOCIETY
Whaling Museum Library
18 Johnny Cake Hill
New Bedford, MA 02740
Established Society established 1903.
Telephone: 617/997-0046.
Contact Person: Virginia M. Adams, Libn.
Staff: 2 professional (full time); 1 professional (part time); 1 non-professional (full time); 21 volunteers non-professional (part time).
Size: 650 maps.
Area Specialization: oceans of the world; southeastern Massachusetts.
Subject Specialization: whaling: history of New Bedford area.
Dates: pre-1800 (negligible); 1800-1899 (75%); 1900 - (25%).
Collections not Cataloged. Mon.–Fri. 9 a.m.–5 p.m. (Seats 18; 14 readers served per month).
Reproduction Facility: photocopy.

North Dartmouth

315. SOUTHEASTERN MASSACHUSETTS UNIVERSITY
Library Communication Center
Reference Department
North Dartmouth, MA 02747
Established 1965.
Telephone: 617/999-8679.
Contact Person: Paige Gibbs, Reference Libn.
Staff: 1 professional (part time); 3 non-professional (part time).
Size: 6,085 maps; 116 atlases; 10 reference books and gazetteers.
Annual Accessions: 40 maps; 5 atlases; 1 reference books and gazetteers.
Area Specialization: North and South America.
Subject Specialization: nautical charts.
Special Cartographic Collections: circa 1850, 1880, 1920 maps of New Bedford and Fall River, Mass.
Dates: 1800-1899 (2); 1900 - (98).
Classification System: LC; DMA; NOAA.
Collections Cataloged. (90%).
Depository for: DMA; GSC; NOS; USGS (Topo.).
Serves: students; faculty; employees; public. Mon.–Fri. 8:30 a.m.–11 p.m.; Sat. 9:30 a.m.–5 p.m.; Sun. 2–9:30 p.m. (Seats 18; 300 readers served per month).
Interlibrary Loan Available.
Reproduction Facility: photocopy; microform; slides.

Northampton

316. FORBES LIBRARY
Reference Department
Northampton Map Collection
20 West Street
Northampton, MA 01060
Established 1894.
Telephone: 413/584-8399, 8550.
Contact Person: Elise Bernier-Feeley, Reference Libn.
Staff: 1 professional (full time); 1 non-professional (part time).
Size: 2,940 maps; 41 atlases; 1 globes; 160 reference books and gazetteers.

Annual Accessions: 60 maps; 3 atlases; 12 reference books and gazetteers.
Area Specialization: Northampton; Hampshire County, Mass.
Subject Specialization: local history.
Dates: pre-1800 (2%); 1800-1899 (3%); 1900 - (95%).
Classification System: Cutter.
Collections Cataloged.
Depository for: USGS (Topo.).
Serves: public. Mon.–Thurs. 9 a.m.–9 p.m.; Fri. 9 a.m.–5 p.m.; Sat. 9 a.m.–5 p.m.
Reproduction Facility: photocopy; Microfilm Microprint.

317. SMITH COLLEGE
Department of Geology
Burton Hall
Northampton, MA 01063
Established 1950.
Telephone: 413/584-2700, ext. 697.
Contact Person: Robert M. Newton, Assistant Professor.
Staff: 2 non-professional (part time).
Size: 175,000 maps; 200 reference books and gazetteers.
Annual Accessions: 1,000 maps.
Area Specialization: United States.
Subject Specialization: geology.
Dates: 1800-1899 (1); 1900 - (99%).
Classification System: local system.
Collections not Cataloged.
Depository for: USGS (Geol., topo.).
Serves: students; faculty; employees; public. Mon.–Fri 8 a.m.–4 p.m. (Seats 2; 5-10 readers served per month).

Salem

318. ESSEX INSTITUTE
James Duncan Phillips Library
132 Essex Street
Salem, MA 01970
Telephone: 617/744-3390.
Contact Person: Mary M. Ritchie, Assistant Libn.
Size: 1,200 maps; 120 atlases; 100 reference books and gazetteers.
Area Specialization: Essex County; Mass.; New England.
Subject Specialization: American history and culture.
Dates: 1800-1899 (80%).
Classification System: Dewey; local system.
Collections Cataloged.
Serves: students; public; members ($2.00 per day fee charged to non-members). Mon.–Fri. 9 a.m.–4:30 p.m. (Seats 16; 5 readers served per month).
Reproduction Facility: photocopy.

319. SALEM STATE COLLEGE
Library
Lafayette Street
Salem, MA 01970
Established 1974.
Telephone: 617/745-0556, ext. 2607.
Contact Person: Glenn Macnutt, Circulation Libn.
Staff: 1 professional (part time).
Size: 70,000 maps.
Annual Accessions: 3,000 maps.
Area Specialization: United States.
Special Cartographic Collections: U.S.G.S. topographic maps, geologic maps, orthophotoquads, land use and land cover maps, hydrologic atlases, planetary photomosaics and maps.
Collections not Cataloged.
Depository for: USGS (Geol., topo.).

Serves: students; faculty; employees; public. Mon.–Fri. 9 a.m.–4 p.m. (Seats 8; 30 readers served per month). No **Reproduction Facility:** photocopy.

South Hadley

320. MOUNT HOLYOKE COLLEGE
Department of Geography and Geology
College Street
South Hadley, MA 01075
Established Ca. 1920.
Telephone: 413/538-2278.
Contact Person: Dr. Peter M. Enggass, Chairman.
Staff: 1 non-professional (full time); 1 non-professional (part time).
Size: 8,000 maps; 200 atlases; 3 globes; 20 relief models; 300 aerial photographs; 50 reference books and gazetteers; 10 serials (titles received).
Annual Accessions: 400 maps; 4-6 atlases.
Area Specialization: Latin America; Caribbean; America; Europe; South Asia.
Dates: 1900 - (100%).
Classification System: AGS.
Collections Cataloged.
Depository for: USGS (Geol., topo.).
Serves: students; faculty; employees; public. Mon.–Fri. 8:30 a.m.–4 p.m. (Seats 2-4; 15 readers served per month).
Interlibrary Loan Available.

Wellesley

321. BABSON COLLEGE
Map Museum
Babson Park
Wellesley, MA 02157
Established 1925.
Telephone: 617/235-1200, ext. 232.
Contact Person: Dirk A. D. Smith, Curator.
Staff: 1 professional (full time); 2 professional (part time).
Area Specialization: United States.
Special Cartographic Collections: Museum contains the world's largest relief map of the U.S. in natural vegetation colors as would be seen from 700 miles in space on August 20th at 2:00 p.m. The map measures 65 feet from Maine to California and is set on a curve accurate at that scale.
Serves: students; faculty; employees; public;. 10:00 a.m.– 5:00 p.m.; Sat. same; Sun. same.

322. WELLESLEY COLLEGE
Geology Department
Wellesley, MA 02181
Telephone: 617/235-0320, ext 3092.
Contact Person: Martha Gordon, Curator/Technical Secretary.
Staff: 1 non-professional (part time).
Area Specialization: U.S.
Subject Specialization: geology, topography.
Collections not Cataloged.
Depository for: DMA; USGS (Geol., topo.).
Serves: students; faculty; employees; public. by appointment.
Reproduction Facility: quickcopy.

Williamstown

323. WILLIAMS COLLEGE
Geological Library
Williamstown, MA 01267
Established 1900.
Telephone: 413/597-2221.
Contact Person: Reinhard Wobus, Professor of Geology.
Staff: non-professional (full time); non-professional (part time).
Size: 60,000 maps; 3 globes; 6,500 reference books and gazetteers; 50 serials (titles received).
Area Specialization: United States.
Subject Specialization: Geology.
Dates: 1900 -.
Classification System: LC; Superintendent of Documents.
Collections Cataloged.
Depository for: USGS (Topo.).
Serves: students; faculty; employees; public. Mon.–Fri. 8:30 a.m.–4:30 p.m. (Seats 25).
Reproduction Facility: photocopy.

Woods Hole

324. WOODS HOLE OCEANOGRAPHIC INSTITUTION
Data Library, McLean Laboratory
Quissett Campus
38 Water Street
Woods Hole,, MA 02543
Established 1956.
Telephone: 617/548-1400, ext. 2471.
Contact Person: William M. Dunkle, Data Libn.
Staff: 2 professional (full time); 1 non-professional (part time).
Size: 30,000 charts, 20,000 maps maps; 1,000 atlases; 3 globes; 12 relief models; 500 aerial photographs; 150 reference books and gazetteers.
Annual Accessions: 500 charts, 200 maps maps; 75 atlases; 10 aerial photographs; 10 reference books and gazetteers.
Area Specialization: World oceans and coastal regions; United States and possessions.
Subject Specialization: oceanography; geology; bathymetry; hydrography; topography; climatology; ocean floor photographs.
Special Cartographic Collections: New England Coastal Chart and Maps; Climatological data for New England from 1896 to present; world collection of DMA charts; U.S. Geological Survey quadrangle maps of New England including New York.
Dates: 1800-1899 (1%); 1900 - (99%).
Classification System: DMA; National Ocean Service System.
Collections Cataloged.
Depository for: DMA; NOS; USGS (Geol., topo.).
Serves: students; faculty; employees; public; local laboratories. Mon.–Fri. 8 a.m.–5 p.m. (Seats 10; 300 readers served per month).
Reproduction Facility: photocopy; quickcopy; microform; flow Camera for continuous scientific records.

Worcester

325. AMERICAN ANTIQUARIAN SOCIETY
Department of Graphic Arts
185 Salisbury Street
Worcester, MA 01609
Established 1812.
Telephone: 617/755-5221.

Contact Person: Georgia Brady Bumgardner, Curator of Graphic Arts.
Size: 10,000 maps; 450 atlases; 4 globes; 350 reference books and gazetteers; 7 serials (titles received).
Annual Accessions: 10 maps; 5 atlases; 5-10 reference books and gazetteers.
Area Specialization: New England; Massachusetts; Worcester.
Dates: pre-1800 (20%); 1800-1899 (80%).
Classification System: local system.
Collections not Cataloged.
Serves: students; faculty; public. Mon.–Fri. 9 a.m.–5 p.m. (5 readers served per month).
Reproduction Facility: photocopy; microform; photography.

326. CLARK UNIVERSITY
Graduate School of Geography
Map Library
950 Main Street
Worcester, MA 01610
Established 1925.
Telephone: 617/793-7322.
Contact Person: Charlotte Slocum, Map and Geography Libn.
Staff: 1 professional (full time); 6 non-professional (part time).
Size: 137,000 maps; 510 atlases; 10 globes; 50 relief models; 7,300 aerial photographs; 415 reference books and gazetteers; 45 serials (titles received); 35 microforms (no. of titles).
Annual Accessions: 3,750 maps; 40 atlases; 1 globes; 1 relief models; 20 aerial photographs; 50 reference books and gazetteers; 3 serials (titles received); 20 microforms (no. of titles).
Area Specialization: New England; Africa; Central America.
Dates: pre-1800 (3%); 1800-1899 (15%); 1900 - (82%).
Classification System: LC modified.
Collections Cataloged.
Depository for: DMA; USGS (Geol., topo.); U.S. Forest Service.
Serves: students; faculty; employees; public. Mon.–Fri. 8:45 a.m.–4:45 p.m. (Seats 20; 150 readers served per month).
Interlibrary Loan Available.
Reproduction Facility: photocopy.
Publications: *Map Library Guide* (guide); *Clark Geophile* (newsletter), miscellaneous subject bibliographies.

MICHIGAN

Albion

327. ALBION COLLEGE
Stockwell Memorial Library
602 E. Cass St.
Albion, MI 49224
Established 1983.
Telephone: 517/629-5511, ext 384.
Contact Person: Carolyn Gaswick, Periodicals and Government Documents Libn.
Staff: 1 professional (part time); 1 non-professional (part time).
Size: 3,000 maps; 3-10 atlases; 25 reference books and gazetteers.
Annual Accessions: 500 maps; 3 atlases; 10 reference books and gazetteers.
Area Specialization: Michigan.
Subject Specialization: general.
Dates: 1900 - (100%).
Classification System: LC.
Collections Cataloged. (90%).

Depository for: DMA; USGS (Geol., topo.).
Serves: students; faculty; employees; public. Mon.–Fri. 8 a.m.–12 midnight; Sat. 9 a.m.–11 p.m.; Sun. 1–12 midnight. (Seats 20; 15 readers served per month).
Reproduction Facility: photocopy.

Allendale

328. GRAND VALLEY STATE COLLEGE
Zumberge Library
Allendale, MI 49401
Established 1965.
Telephone: 616/895-7611.
Contact Person: Robert Beasecker, Reference Libn.
Staff: 1 professional (part time); 1 non-professional (part time).
Size: 46,400 maps.
Annual Accessions: ca. 2,000 maps.
Area Specialization: Michigan; United States.
Subject Specialization: topography; geology.
Dates: 1900 - (100%).
Classification System: local system: by region or state.
Collections not Cataloged.
Depository for: NOS; USGS (Geol., topo.).
Serves: students; faculty; employees; public. Mon.–Thurs. 8 a.m.–12 midnight; Fri. 8 a.m.–6 p.m.; Sat. 12:30–9 p.m.; Sun. 1–12 midnight. (Seats 42).
Reproduction Facility: photocopy; microform.

Alma

329. ALMA COLLEGE
Library
Alma, MI 48801
Telephone: 517/463-7227.
Contact Person: Priscilla Perkins, Technical Services Libn.
Staff: professional (part time); non-professional (part time).
Depository for: USGS (Topo.).
Serves: students; faculty; employees; public. hours vary.
Reproduction Facility: photocopy.

Ann Arbor

330. MICHIGAN (STATE) DEPARTMENT OF NATURAL RESOURCES, INSTITUTE FOR FISHERIES RESEARCH
Library
212 Museums Annex Building
Ann Arbor, MI 48109
Established 1930's.
Telephone: 313/663-3554.
Contact Person: Barbara A. Lowell, Department Executive.
Staff: 1 professional (part time).
Size: 400 maps.
Area Specialization: Michigan inland lakes.
Subject Specialization: inland lakes maps.
Dates: 1900 -.
Collections not Cataloged.
Serves: students; faculty; employees; public. Mon.–Fri. 8 a.m.–12 noon, 1–5 p.m. (Seats 1–2).

331. UNIVERSITY OF MICHIGAN
Bentley Historical Library, Michigan Historical Collections
1150 Beal Ave.
Ann Arbor, MI 48109-2113
Established 1935.
Telephone: 313/764-3482.
Contact Person: Leonard A. Coombs, Printed Works Archivist.

Staff: 1 professional (part time).
Size: 3,500 maps; 225 atlases; 100 aerial photographs; 30 reference books and gazetteers; 5 microforms (no. of titles).
Annual Accessions: 70 maps; 10 atlases.
Area Specialization: Michigan; Great Lakes region.
Subject Specialization: history.
Special Cartographic Collections: Manuscript field notes and maps of early state geologists of Michigan and of Michigan lumber companies; photolithographic copies of original land surveys of Michigan, 1800-1850; military maps relating to American intervention in North Russia, 1918-1919.
Dates: pre-1800 (2%); 1800-1899 (73%); 1900 - (25%).
Classification System: local system.
Collections Cataloged.
Serves: students; faculty; employees; public. Mon.–Fri. 8:30 a.m.–5 p.m.; Sat. 9 a.m.–12:30 p.m. (Sept.–May). (Seats 16; 23 readers served per month).
Reproduction Facility: photocopy; microform.

332. UNIVERSITY OF MICHIGAN
Harlan Hatcher Graduate Library
Map Library
825 Hatcher Library
Ann Arbor, MI 48109-1205
Telephone: 313/764-0407.
Staff: 1 professional (full time); 2 professional (part time); 1 non-professional (full time).
Size: 300,000 maps; 5,000 atlases; 5 globes; 2,500 aerial photographs; 3,000 reference books and gazetteers; 20 serials (titles received); 20 microforms (no. of titles).
Annual Accessions: 8,000-10,000 maps; 100 atlases; 1 globes; 100 aerial photographs; 200 reference books and gazetteers; 1 serials (titles received).
Area Specialization: Michigan; Great Lakes; Canada; Europe; Middle East; East Asia.
Subject Specialization: geology; economic; social-cultural geography; transportation.
Special Cartographic Collections: A set of 5000 glass slides showing economic, political and cultural subjects of the world from about 1900 through 1930.
Dates: pre-1800 (3); 1800-1899 (7); 1900 - (90).
Classification System: LC; local system.
Collections Cataloged. (97%).
Depository for: DMA; NOS; USGS (Geol., topo.).
Serves: students; faculty; employees; public. Mon.–Fri. 1–5:00 p.m., 6:30–9:30 p.m. (fall/winter semesters). (Seats 50; 350 readers served per month).
Interlibrary Loan Available. (some restrictions)
Reproduction Facility: photocopy; quickcopy; microform.

333. UNIVERSITY OF MICHIGAN
William L. Clements Library
Map Division
909 S. University Ave.
Ann Arbor, MI 48109
Established 1931.
Telephone: 313/764-2347.
Contact Person: David Bosse, Map Libn.
Staff: 1 professional (full time).
Size: 36,000 maps; few hundred atlases.
Area Specialization: The Americas, ca. 1942-ca. 1870.
Classification System: local system.
Collections Cataloged. Mon.–Fri 10:30–12 noon, 1–5 p.m.
Publications: Brun, Christian. *Guide to the manuscript maps in the William L. Clements Library.* Ann Arbor, U. of M., 1959; Marshall, Douglas W. *Research catalog of maps of America to 1860.* 4 vols., Boston, GLK. Hall, 1972.

Berrien Springs

334. ANDREWS UNIVERSITY
James White Library
Periodical Department
Berrien Springs, MI 49104
Contact Person: Robert Pierson, Geography Dept.; Kit Watts, Periodical Libn.
Staff: 2 professional (part time).
Size: 30,000 maps; 268 atlases; 67 reference books and gazetteers; 8 serials (titles received).
Annual Accessions: 2,000 maps.
Area Specialization: United States.
Dates: 1900 - (100%).
Classification System: LC; local system.
Collections not Cataloged.
Depository for: USGS (Geol., topo.).
Serves: students; faculty; employees. by appointment (map area). (Seats 8; 6 readers served per month).
Reproduction Facility: photocopy.

Detroit

335. DETROIT HISTORICAL MUSEUM
Architectural History Division
5401 Woodward
Detroit, MI 48202
Established 1928.
Telephone: 313/297-9362.
Contact Person: James E. Conway, Curator.
Staff: 1 professional (part time).
Size: 60 maps; 15 atlases; 2 globes; 10 aerial photographs; 15 reference books and gazetteers.
Area Specialization: Detroit; Michigan; North America.
Subject Specialization: road maps; transportation.
Dates: pre-1800 (10%); 1800-1899 (40%); 1900 - (50%).
Collections Cataloged. (90%).
Serves: students; employees. Mon.–Fri. 8:30 a.m.–4 p.m. (by appointment). (Seats 3).
Reproduction Facility: photocopy.

336. DETROIT PUBLIC LIBRARY
Burton Historical Collection
5201 Woodward Avenue
Detroit, MI 48202
Established 1914.
Telephone: 313/833-1000, ext. 341.
Contact Person: Mrs. Alice C. Dalligan, Chief.
Staff: 7 professional (full time); 3 non-professional (full time).
Size: 4,000 maps.
Area Specialization: Great Lakes; Old Northwest Territory.
Dates: pre-1800 (45%); 1800-1899 (50%); 1900 - (5%).
Classification System: Dewey (modified).
Collections Cataloged.
Serves: public. (Seats 54).
Reproduction Facility: photocopy.
Publications: *The Burton Historical Collection of the Detroit Public Library* (information brochure); *Maps of Michigan and the Great Lakes, 1545–1845, from the Private Collection of Renville Wheat with Additions from the Burton Historical Collection* (1967). 1949; maps collected since 1865 and cataloged and classified since 1915.

337. DETROIT PUBLIC LIBRARY

History and Travel Department
Map Room
5201 Woodward Avenue
Detroit, MI 48202
Established Map Room established 1956; History and Travel Dept.,.
Telephone: 313/833-1445 or 1446.
Staff: 1 professional (full time); 3 professional (part time); 1 non-professional (part time).
Size: 161,318 maps; 3,658 atlases; 13 globes; 37 relief models; 25 aerial photographs; 2,170 reference books and gazetteers; 25 serials (titles received); 5 microforms (no. of titles).
Annual Accessions: 4,000 maps; 150 atlases; 100 reference books and gazetteers; 10 microforms (no. of titles).
Area Specialization: Detroit; Michigan; Great Lakes Region; Canada.
Subject Specialization: topography; history of cartography; street maps; general political maps.
Special Cartographic Collections: Sanborn Fire Insurance maps of Michigan dating from 1883 to early 1960's covering over 300 Michigan cities; Ready reference map collection of street and political maps of countries, states, region (consists of ca. 8,235 maps).
Dates: pre-1800 (1%); 1800-1899 (14%); 1900 - (85%).
Classification System: LC; Dewey.
Collections Cataloged. (90%).
Depository for: DMA; GSC; NOS; USGS (Geol., topo.); GPO.
Serves: students; faculty; employees; public. Tues., Thurs., Fri., 9:30 a.m.–5:30 p.m. Wed., 1–9 p.m.; Sat. 9:30 a.m.–5:30 p.m. (Seats 22; 200 readers served per month).
Interlibrary Loan Available.
Reproduction Facility: photocopy; quickcopy; microform.
Publications: *The Detroit Public Library's Map Collection* by June C. Harris.

East Lansing

338. MICHIGAN STATE UNIVERSITY

Main Library
Map Library
East Lansing, MI 48824
Telephone: 517/353-4593.
Contact Person: Diana H. Rivera, Libn. I.
Staff: 1 professional (full time); 1 professional (part time); 1 non-professional (part time).
Size: 137,730 maps; 2,280 atlases; 3 globes; 300 reference books and gazetteers; 7 serials (titles received).
Annual Accessions: 4,500 maps; 120 atlases; 30 reference books and gazetteers.
Area Specialization: Michigan; United States; Africa; Canada; Mexico; Latin America.
Subject Specialization: topography; geology; agriculture.
Dates: 1800-1899 (5%); 1900 - (95%).
Classification System: AGS primary.
Collections Cataloged.
Depository for: DMA; USGS (Geol., topo.); Canadian Land Use.
Serves: students; faculty; employees; public;. (Seats 30–36).
Interlibrary Loan Available.
Reproduction Facility: photocopy; microform.
Publications: *Map Line* (acquisitions list); *A Guide to Cartographic Resources in the MSU Libraries* (guide).

Flint

339. FLINT JOURNAL

Editorial Library
200 East First Street
Flint, MI 48502
Telephone: 313/767-0660.
Contact Person: David Larzelere, Libn.
Size: 800 maps; 25 atlases; 1 globes; 400 aerial photographs; 3 reference books and gazetteers.
Annual Accessions: 50 maps; 2 atlases; 50 aerial photographs.
Area Specialization: Flint; Genesee County, Michigan.

Grand Rapids

340. GRAND RAPIDS PUBLIC LIBRARY

Michigan and Family History Department
60 Library Plaza, N.E.
Grand Rapids, MI 49503
Established 1904.
Telephone: 616/456-4424.
Contact Person: Gordon Olson, City Historian.
Staff: 2 professional (full time); 1 professional (part time); 1 non-professional (full time).
Size: 2,200 maps; 500 atlases; 200 reference books and gazetteers; 60 microforms (no. of titles).
Annual Accessions: 100 maps; 20 atlases; 15 reference books and gazetteers; 5 microforms (no. of titles).
Area Specialization: Grand Rapids; Kent County; Michigan.
Dates: 1800-1899 (10%); 1900 - (90%).
Collections Cataloged. (50%).
Depository for: USGS (Topo.).
Serves: public. Tues., Wed. 12 noon–9 p.m.; Thurs.–Sat. 9 a.m.–5:30 p.m. (Seats 45; 130 readers served per month).
Reproduction Facility: photocopy.

Kalamazoo

341. WESTERN MICHIGAN UNIVERSITY

Waldo Library
Map Library
Kalamazoo, MI 49008
Established 1968.
Telephone: 616/383-4952, ext. 24.
Contact Person: Michael McDonnell, Maps and Documents Reference Libn.
Staff: 1 professional (part time); 1 non-professional (full time).
Size: 164,602 maps; 950 atlases; 5 globes; 3 relief models; 300 reference books and gazetteers; 5 serials (titles received).
Annual Accessions: 6,000 maps; 10 atlases; 10 reference books and gazetteers.
Area Specialization: Michigan; Great Lakes; United States.
Subject Specialization: topography; geology.
Dates: 1800-1899 (5%); 1900 - (95%).
Classification System: LC (modified).
Collections Cataloged. (85%).
Depository for: DMA; GSC; NOS; USGS (Geol., topo.); U.S. Soil Surveys.
Serves: students; faculty; employees; public. Mon.–Thurs. 8 a.m.–11:30 p.m., Fri. 8 a.m.–6 p.m.; Sat. 9 a.m.–6 p.m.; Sun. 12 noon–11:30 p.m. (Seats 10; 800 readers served per month).
Reproduction Facility: photocopy; microform.

Lansing

342. LIBRARY OF MICHIGAN
Information & Government Services
735 E. Michigan Ave., Box 30007,
Lansing, MI 48909
Telephone: 517/373-1593.
Contact Person: Judith Dow, Reference Libn.
Size: 5,000 maps.
Annual Accessions: 50 maps.
Area Specialization: Michigan; Great Lakes Region; Old Northwest.
Dates: pre-1800 (2%); 1800-1899 (40%); 1900 - (58%).
Collections not Cataloged.
Depository for: NOS; USGS (Topo.).
Serves: students; faculty; employees; public. Mon.–Fri. 1:00 p.m.–5:00 p.m.

343. MICHIGAN (STATE) DEPARTMENT OF NATURAL RESOURCES
Geological Survey Division
Library
Stevens T. Mason Building
Lansing, MI 48909
Established 1837.
Telephone: 517/373-1256.
Contact Person: Irvin V. Kuehner, Staff Specialist/Libn.
Staff: 1 professional (part time).
Size: 3,500 maps; 10 atlases; 6 relief models; 5,000 aerial photographs; 50 reference books and gazetteers; 20 serials (titles received); 150 microforms (no. of titles).
Annual Accessions: 300 maps; 3 atlases; 100 aerial photographs; 10 reference books and gazetteers; 20 serials (titles received); 50 microforms (no. of titles).
Area Specialization: Michigan; Michigan Basin; Lake Superior Basin; Great Lakes.
Subject Specialization: geology; geography; mineral, water and fuel resources; environmental protection.
Special Cartographic Collections: U.S. Geological Survey topographic quadrangles; Michigan mine maps; oil and gas field maps.
Dates: 1800-1899 (5); 1900 - (95).
Collections not Cataloged.
Depository for: GSC; USGS (Geol., topo.); State geologic surveys and Department of Natural Resources. Mon.–Fri. 8 a.m.–5 p.m. (Seats 14; 15 readers served per month).
Reproduction Facility: quickcopy; microform.
Publications: *Circular 16, Annotated List of Publications of the Michigan Geological Survey 1838–1977* (available from DNR Information Services Center, Lansing, Michigan 48909); *Publication List; Maps (List) Available from the Geological Survey* .

344. STATE OF MICHIGAN, ARCHIVES
History Division
3405 North Logan
Lansing, MI 48918
Established 1913.
Telephone: 517/373-0512.
Contact Person: LeRoy Barnett, Reference Archivist.
Staff: professional (part time).
Size: 1,000,000 maps; 30 atlases; 6 reference books and gazetteers.
Annual Accessions: 100 maps; 1 atlases.
Area Specialization: Michigan.
Subject Specialization: municipal plat maps; township and range land surveys; transportation surveys; geology; town and county maps; rural land surveys.
Special Cartographic Collections: rural property inventories (1935–1940) which show each tract of land in the state plus a plan of the major structure thereon (this contsitues

the bulk of our cartographic holdings). Also have 70,000 plats of urban areas (additions, subdivisions, etc.).
Dates: pre-1800 (1%); 1800-1899 (9%); 1900 - (90%).
Classification System: local system.
Collections Cataloged.
Serves: students; faculty; employees; public;. Mon.–Fri. 8 a.m.–5 p.m. (Seats 6; 5 readers served per month).
Reproduction Facility: quickcopy.

Marquette

345. MARQUETTE COUNTY HISTORICAL SOCIETY
J. M. Longyear Research Library
213 North Front Street
Marquette, MI 49855
Established 1937.
Telephone: 906/226-3571.
Contact Person: Edna Paulson, Libn.
Staff: 1 professional (part time).
Size: 1,100 maps; 20 atlases; 350 reference books and gazetteers.
Area Specialization: Upper Peninsula of Michigan; North Central States; Great Lakes, especially Lake Superior.
Subject Specialization: communities; railroads; geology; rivers; roads.
Dates: 1800-1899 (75%); 1900 - (25%).
Classification System: Dewey.
Collections Cataloged.
Serves: public. Mon.–Fri. 9 a.m.–12 noon; 1 p.m.–4:30 p.m. (Seats 8; 30 readers served per month).
Reproduction Facility: photocopy.

346. NORTHERN MICHIGAN UNIVERSITY
Olson Library, Learning Research Center
Documents and Maps
Marquette, MI 49855
Established 1965.
Telephone: 906/227-2112.
Contact Person: John Berens, Documents and Map Libn.
Staff: 1 professional (part time); 1 non-professional (part time).
Size: 30,000 maps; 400 atlases; 6 globes; 5,000 aerial photographs; 200 reference books and gazetteers; 20 serials (titles received).
Annual Accessions: 2,000 maps; 25 atlases; 100 aerial photographs; 30 reference books and gazetteers.
Area Specialization: Michigan.
Subject Specialization: geology; land use.
Dates: 1900 - (100%).
Classification System: DMA; SuDocs for depository maps.
Collections not Cataloged.
Depository for: DMA; NOS; USGS (Geol., topo.).
Serves: students; faculty; employees; public. Mon.–Fri. 8 a.m.–5 p.m. (Seats 40; 70 readers served per month).
Interlibrary Loan Available.
Reproduction Facility: photocopy; quickcopy.

Mount Pleasant

347. CENTRAL MICHIGAN UNIVERSITY
Clarke Historical Library
Mount Pleasant, Michigan 48859
Telephone: 517/774-3352.
Contact Person: William Miles, Bibliographer.
Staff: 3 professional (part time); 3 non-professional (part time).

Size: 2,700 maps; 370 atlases; 125 reference books and gazetteers; 150 microforms (no. of titles).
Annual Accessions: 200 maps; 20 atlases; 15 reference books and gazetteers; 10 microforms (no. of titles).
Area Specialization: Great Lakes; Old Northwest Territory; Michigan.
Subject Specialization: history; history of cartography.
Special Cartographic Collections: lithographic bird's-eye views of Michigan cities and towns.
Dates: pre-1800 (25%); 1800-1899 (60%); 1900 - (15%).
Classification System: local system.
Collections Cataloged. (70%).
Serves: students; faculty; employees; public. Mon.–Fri. 8 a.m.–5 p.m.; Sat. 9 a.m.–1 p.m. (Seats 50; 250 readers served per month).
Reproduction Facility: photocopy; quickcopy; microform.
Publications: *Annual Report to Map Accessions and Collections* .

Mt. Pleasant

348. CENTRAL MICHIGAN UNIVERSITY
Library
Documents Department
Mt. Pleasant, MI 48859
Established 1958.
Telephone: 517/774-3414.
Contact Person: David B. Shirley, Documents Libn.
Staff: 1 professional (full time); 1 non-professional (full time).
Size: 27,500 maps; 300 atlases; 3 globes; 25 aerial photographs; 90 reference books and gazetteers; 12 serials (titles received).
Annual Accessions: 3,500 maps; 25 atlases; 10 reference books and gazetteers.
Area Specialization: Western Hemisphere.
Subject Specialization: Geology.
Dates: 1800-1899 (2%); 1900 - (98%).
Classification System: LC.
Collections Cataloged. (100%).
Depository for: DMA; NOS; USGS (Geol., topo.).
Serves: students; faculty; employees; public. Mon.–Fri. 8:00 a.m.–12 midnight. (Seats 100).
Reproduction Facility: photocopy; quickcopy; microform.

Ypsilanti

349. EASTERN MICHIGAN UNIVERSITY
Center of Educational Resources
Map Library
Ypsilanti, MI 48197
Established 1945.
Telephone: 313/487-3191.
Contact Person: Joanne Hansen, Coordinator, Science and Technology Division.
Staff: 4 professional (part time); 1 non-professional (part time).
Size: 37,705 maps; 1,000 atlases; 2 globes; 8 relief models; 2,000 aerial photographs; 300 reference books and gazetteers; 5 serials (titles received).
Annual Accessions: 2,000 maps; 30 atlases; 20 reference books and gazetteers.
Area Specialization: United States; Michigan.
Special Cartographic Collections: tourist and road map file of 13,496 uncataloged items.
Dates: pre-1800 (1%); 1800-1899 (2%); 1900 - (97%).

Classification System: local system.
Collections Cataloged.
Depository for: DMA; NOS; USGS (Geol., topo.).
Serves: students; faculty; employees; public. Mon.–Thurs. 8:30 a.m.–5:00 p.m., 6:00 p.m.–9:30 p.m. (Seats 36; 350 readers served per month).
Reproduction Facility: photocopy.

MINNESOTA

Bemidji

350. BEMIDJI STATE UNIVERSITY
Department of Geography
Division of Social and Behavioral Sciences
Bemidji, MN 56601
Established 1970.
Telephone: 218/755-2880.
Contact Person: Dr. Peter L. Smith, Chairperson, Department of Geography.
Staff: 1 non-professional (part time).
Size: 24,000 maps; 30 atlases; 8 globes; 250 relief models; 104,000 aerial photographs; 8 reference books and gazetteers.
Annual Accessions: 100 maps; 3 atlases; 1 reference books and gazetteers.
Area Specialization: Minnesota; Canada; world.
Subject Specialization: topography.
Special Cartographic Collections: topographic maps of Great Britain (1;63,360).
Dates: 1800-1899 (1%); 1900 - (99%).
Classification System: DMA; local system.
Collections Cataloged. (90%).
Depository for: DMA; USGS (Geol., topo.).
Serves: students; faculty; employees; public. (Seats 15; 45 readers served per month).

Collegeville

351. ST. JOHN'S UNIVERSITY
Alcuin Library
Collegeville, MN 56321
Established ca. 1945.
Telephone: 612/363-2117.
Contact Person: Carol P. Johnson, Systems Libn.
Staff: professional (full time); professional (part time).
Size: 14,000 maps; 50 atlases; 100 reference books and gazetteers.
Annual Accessions: 200 maps.
Area Specialization: Minnesota.
Dates: 1900 - (100%).
Classification System: LC; SuDocs.
Collections Cataloged. (85%).
Depository for: DMA; USGS (Geol., topo.).
Serves: students; faculty; employees; public. Mon.–Thurs. 8 a.m.–midnight; Fri. 8 a.m.–9 p.m.; Sat. 10 a.m.–9 p.m.; Sun. 1 p.m.–12 midnight. (Seats 450).
Reproduction Facility: photocopy; microform.
Publications: *Guide to Maps in Alcuin Library* (leaflet).

Duluth

352. DULUTH PUBLIC LIBRARY
Reference and Information Services
520 West Superior Street
Duluth, MN 55802
Telephone: 218/723-3802.
Contact Person: Joann Koellen, Head, Reference &
Information Services.
Staff: 2 professional (part time).
Size: ca. 2,000 maps; 150 atlases.
Area Specialization: United States.
Subject Specialization: topography.
Dates: 1800-1899 (1%); 1900 - (99%).
Classification System: local system.
Collections not Cataloged.
Depository for: USGS (Topo.).
Serves: students; faculty; employees; public.
Reproduction Facility: photocopy.

353. UNIVERSITY OF MINNESOTA-DULUTH
Sociology, Anthropology, Geography
Duluth, MN 55811
Established 1970.
Contact Person: Fred Witzig, Professor of Geography.
Staff: non-professional (part time).
Size: 3,000 maps; 1 globes; 2 relief models; 200 aerial
photographs; 40 reference books and gazetteers.
Annual Accessions: 200 maps.
Area Specialization: Upper midwest.
Subject Specialization: topography.
Dates: 1900 -.
Classification System: LC.
Collections Cataloged.
Depository for: USGS (Topo.).
Serves: students; faculty; employees; public. (Seats 2; 12
readers served per month).

Mankato

354. MANKATO STATE UNIVERSITY
Memorial Library
Map Room
Mankato, MN 56001
Established 1969.
Telephone: 507/389-6201.
Contact Person: Russell K. Amling, Maps and Microforms
Libn.
Staff: 1 professional (full time); 5 non-professional (part
time).
Size: 96,000 maps; 500 atlases; 13 globes; 38 relief
models; 18,000 aerial photographs; 180 reference books
and gazetteers; 1,000,000 microforms (no. of titles).
Annual Accessions: 4-10,000 maps; 12 atlases; 2,000
aerial photographs; 6 reference books and gazetteers;
10,000+ microforms (no. of titles).
Area Specialization: Blue Earth County; Minnesota.
Subject Specialization: History; Geography.
Dates: 1800-1899 (1%); 1900 - (99%).
Classification System: LC.
Collections Cataloged.
Depository for: DMA; NOS; USGS (Geol., topo.).
Serves: students; faculty; employees; public;. Mon.–Thurs.
7:45 a.m.–11:45 p.m., Fri 7:45 a.m.–4:30 p.m.; Sat. 10 a.m.–
5 p.m.; Sun. 1 p.m.–11:45 p.m. (Seats 30).
Interlibrary Loan Available.
Reproduction Facility: photocopy; quickcopy; microform.

Minneapolis

355. MINNEAPOLIS PUBLIC LIBRARY AND INFORMATION CENTER
History and Travel Department
300 Nicollet Mall
Minneapolis, MN 55401
Telephone: 612/372-6537.
Contact Person: Robert K. Bruce, Dept. Head.
Size: 3,500 maps; 1,400 atlases; 1 globes; 14 serials (titles
received).
Area Specialization: U.S.
Subject Specialization: travel.
Dates: 1900 - (98%).
Depository for: USGS (Topo.).
Serves: students; faculty; employees; public. Mon.–Thurs.
9:00 a.m.–9 p.m.; Fri. 9:00 a.m.–5:30 p.m.; Sat. 9:00–5:30
p.m.
Reproduction Facility: photocopy.

356. UNIVERSITY OF MINNESOTA
O. M. Wilson Library
James Ford Bell Library
309 19th Ave. South
Minneapolis, MN 55455
Established 1953.
Telephone: 612/373-2888.
Contact Person: John Parker, Curator; Carol Urness,
Assistant Curator.
Staff: 2 professional (full time); 1 non-professional (part
time).
Area Specialization: world-wide, pre 1800.
Dates: pre-1800 ().
Classification System: local system (chronological, author).
Collections Cataloged.
Serves: students; faculty; employees; public;. Mon.–Fri. 8
a.m.–5 p.m. (Seats 20).
Reproduction Facility: photocopy; microform.
Publications: *The James Ford Bell Library* (Boston, G.K.
Hall, 1981).

357. UNIVERSITY OF MINNESOTA
O. M. Wilson Library
Map Library
309 19th Avenue
Minneapolis, MN 55455
Telephone: 612/373-2825.
Contact Person: Mai Treude, Map Librarian/Associate
Professor.
Staff: 1 professional (full time); 1 non-professional (full
time); 1 professional (part time).
Size: 214,377 maps; 3,930 atlases; 3 globes; 154,519 aerial
photographs; 33 serials (titles received).
Annual Accessions: 4,000 maps; 100 atlases; 2,000 aerial
photographs; 2 serials (titles received).
Area Specialization: comprehensive.
Special Cartographic Collections: Early maps of
Minnesota (pre 1900); Ames Library of South Asia—mostly
pre-1900 maps of India and South Asia; Aerial photographs
of Minnesota, 1937 to date.
Dates: 1900 - (80%).
Classification System: LC; Dewey (books).
Collections Cataloged.
Depository for: DMA; NTS (Canada); USGS (Topo.).
Serves: students; faculty; employees; public;. Mon., Tues.,
Thurs., Fri. 9 a.m.–5 p.m., Wed. 1–8 p.m. (Seats 52).
Reproduction Facility: photocopy.
Publications: Map Library information brochure; *Catalog of
Aerial Photography in the Map Division, Wilson Library.* St.
Paul, Minnesota State Planning Agency, 1977. 50 pages;
*Windows to the Past: A Bibliography of Minnesota County
Atlases.* Minneapolis, Center for Urban and Regional Affairs,

Univ. of Minn., 1980 187 pages. (This work contains the holdings of the Map Library); *Introduction to the Map Library* (seven minutes slide/tape show about the Map Library at University of Minnesota; (Available on loan).

358. UNIVERSITY OF MINNESOTA
Winchell Library of Geology
204 Pillsbury Hall, 310 Pillsbury Drive SE
Minneapolis, MN 55116
Telephone: 612/373-4052.
Contact Person: Marie Dvorzak, Head, Winchell Library of Geology.
Size: 75,000 maps; 45 atlases; 15 reference books and gazetteers.
Annual Accessions: 1,500 approximately maps; 2 or 3 atlases; 1 reference books and gazetteers.
Area Specialization: United States, Canada (geological maps only).
Subject Specialization: geology and related topics (i.e. tectonics, mineral, metallogenic, structure).
Dates: 1800-1899 (less than 1%); 1900 - (99%).
Collections not Cataloged.
Depository for: USGS (Geol.).
Serves: students; faculty; employees; public. Mon.–Fri. 8:00–4:30 M–F. (Seats 32).
Reproduction Facility: photocopy.

Northfield

359. CARLETON COLLEGE
Department of Geology
Map Library
Northfield, MN 55057
Established 1932.
Telephone: 507/645-4431.
Contact Person: Timothy D. Vick, Technical Director of Geology.
Staff: 1 professional (part time); 6-8 non-professional (part time).
Size: 80,000 maps; 10 atlases; 3 globes; 25 relief models; 1,000 aerial photographs; 20 reference books and gazetteers.
Annual Accessions: 2,000 maps; 1 atlases; 50 aerial photographs; 2 reference books and gazetteers.
Area Specialization: United States.
Subject Specialization: topography.
Dates: 1900 - (100%).
Classification System: DMA.
Collections Cataloged.
Depository for: DMA; USGS (Topo.).
Serves: students; faculty; employees; public. Mon.–Fri. 1 p.m.–4 p.m. (Seats 25; 50 readers served per month).
Reproduction Facility: quickcopy.

St. Cloud

360. ST. CLOUD STATE UNIVERSITY
Learning Resources Services
Government Documents/Map Section
St. Cloud, MN 56301
Telephone: 612/252-2401.
Contact Person: Lawrence R. Busse, Government Documents/Map Librarian.
Staff: 1 professional (full time); 1 non-professional (full time); 12 non-professional (part time).
Size: 80,000 maps.
Annual Accessions: 1,500 maps.
Area Specialization: Minnesota, midwestern United States.
Classification System: local system.

Collections not Cataloged.
Depository for: USGS (Geol., topo.).
Serves: students; faculty; employees; public. Mon.–Fri. 7:30 a.m.–11 p.m.; Sat. 9 a.m.–5 p.m.; Sun. 2–10 p.m. (Seats 125; 1,000 readers served per month).
Reproduction Facility: photocopy.

St. Paul

361. MINNESOTA HISTORICAL SOCIETY
Map Library
Collections Division
690 Cedar Street
St. Paul, MN 55101
Established 1974.
Telephone: 612/296-4543.
Contact Person: Jon L. Walstrom, Map Libn.
Staff: 1 professional (full time).
Size: 30,000 maps; 1,150 atlases; 50 aerial photographs; 150 reference books and gazetteers.
Annual Accessions: 500 maps; 40 atlases; 5 reference books and gazetteers.
Area Specialization: Minnesota; Middle West; United States; Canada; North America.
Subject Specialization: history of Minnesota and Mid-West.
Special Cartographic Collections: Sanborn, Rascher and Insurance Services Office of Minnesota Fire Insurance maps for 900 Minnesota cities from 1875 to 1970; Minnesota bird's-eye views.
Dates: pre-1800 (10%); 1800-1899 (40%); 1900 - (50%).
Classification System: LC.
Collections not Cataloged.
Depository for: USGS (Topo.).
Serves: students; faculty; employees; public. Mon.–Fri. 8:30 a.m.–5 p.m.; Sat. 8:30 a.m.–5 p.m. (Seats 4; 65 readers served per month).
Reproduction Facility: photocopy.

362. ST. PAUL PUBLIC LIBRARY
Social Sciences and Literature Reference
90 West 4th Street
St. Paul, MN 55102
Established 1917.
Telephone: 612/292-6307.
Contact Person: Patricia Ethier, Libn. II.
Staff: professional (full time); 50% professional (part time).
Size: 1,500-2,000 maps; 1 globes.
Area Specialization: North America.
Subject Specialization: roads (travel).
Dates: 1800-1899 (5%); 1900 - (95%).
Classification System: local system.
Collections not Cataloged.
Depository for: USGS (Topo.).
Serves: students; faculty; employees; public. Mon. and Thurs. 9 a.m.–9 p.m.; Tues., Wed., Fri. 9 a.m.–5:30 p.m.; Sat. 9 a.m.–5:30 p.m., Sept.–May only.
Reproduction Facility: photocopy.

363. UNIVERSITY OF MINNESOTA
Minnesota Geological Survey Library
2642 University Avenue
St. Paul, MN 55114
Established 1974.
Telephone: 612/373-3372.
Contact Person: Lynn Swanson, Sr. Library Assistant.
Staff: 1 non-professional (full time).
Size: 3,000 maps; 22 atlases; 3,000 aerial photographs; 350 reference books and gazetteers; 130 serials (titles received); 1,500 microforms (no. of titles).

Annual Accessions: 200 maps; 1-2 atlases; 5-10 aerial photographs; 5-10 reference books and gazetteers; 5-10 serials (titles received); 5-10 microforms (no. of titles).
Area Specialization: Minnesota and surrounding states and provinces of Canada.
Subject Specialization: geology: (bedrock, surficial, geophysics, hydrogeology, engineering geology).
Dates: 1800-1899 (5%); 1900 - (95%).
Classification System: Dewey.
Collections Cataloged.
Depository for: USGS (Geol., topo.).
Serves: students; faculty; employees; public; industry. 8 a.m.–4:30 p.m. Mon.–Fri. (Seats 8; 80 readers served per month).
Reproduction Facility: photocopy.

St. Peter

364. GUSTAVUS ADOLPHUS COLLEGE
Geography
St. Peter, MN 56082
Established ca. 1946.
Telephone: 507/931-7312, 7313.
Contact Person: Robert T. Moline, Professor of Geography.
Staff: 2 professional (part time); 1 non-professional (part time).
Size: 49,000 maps; 12 atlases; 6 globes; 250 relief models; 800 aerial photographs; 70 reference books and gazetteers.
Annual Accessions: 800 maps; 1 or 2 relief models; 8 or 10 aerial photographs.
Area Specialization: North America; Europe; East Asia.
Subject Specialization: topography; urban planning.
Dates: 1800-1899 (7%); 1900 - (93%).
Classification System: LC.
Collections Cataloged. (90%).
Depository for: DMA; USGS (Geol., topo.).
Serves: students; faculty; employees; public. Mon.–Fri. 7:30 a.m.–5 p.m.; Sat. 9:00–12 noon; Sun. Irregular. (Seats 10).
Reproduction Facility: photocopy.

MISSISSIPPI

Jackson

365. MISSISSIPPI (STATE) BUREAU OF GEOLOGY
Library
2525 N. West Street
Jackson, MS 39216
Telephone: 601/354-6228.
Contact Person: Carolyn Woodley, Libn.
Staff: 1 professional (full time); 1 non-professional (part time).
Size: 13,000 maps; 200 atlases.
Area Specialization: Mississippi and adjacent states.
Subject Specialization: geology; mineral resources; paleontology; water resources; environmental geology.
Special Cartographic Collections: U.S. Geological Survey Map Series: Geologic Quadrangle, Geophysical Investigation, Hydrologic Atlas, Miscellaneous Field Studies; Topographic maps for Mississippi, Alabama, Arkansas, Tennessee, Louisiana, and Alabama. Flood Plain Maps: U.S.G.S. and Federal Insurance Administration Flood Hazard Boundary Maps for the state of Mississippi.
Dates: 1800-1899 (2%); 1900 - (98%).
Classification System: local system.
Collections not Cataloged.
Depository for: USGS (Geol., topo.).

Serves: students; faculty; employees; public. Mon.–Fri. 8 a.m.–5 p.m. (Seats 4; 75 readers served per month).
Interlibrary Loan Available.
Reproduction Facility: photocopy.
Publications: Agency list of publications.

366. MISSISSIPPI (STATE) DEPARTMENT OF ARCHIVES AND HISTORY
Special Collections
100 S. State Street
Jackson, MS 39205
Established 1902.
Telephone: 601/359-1424.
Contact Person: Martha McBee, Archivist.
Size: c.7,000 maps; c.25 atlases; c.2,500 aerial photographs; c.30 reference books and gazetteers; c.5 serials (titles received); 9 reels microforms (no. of titles).
Annual Accessions: c.15 maps.
Area Specialization: Mississippi.
Dates: pre-1800 (15%); 1800-1899 (45%); 1900 - (40%).
Classification System: local system.
Collections Cataloged.
Serves: public. Mon.–Fri. 8 a.m.–5 p.m.; Sat. 8:30 a.m.–4:30 p.m. (Seats 25).
Reproduction Facility: photocopy.

Mississippi State

367. MISSISSIPPI STATE UNIVERSITY
Library
Physical & Biology Sciences
P.O. Drawer 5408
Mississippi State, MS 39762
Telephone: 601/325-3060.
Contact Person: Mary Downey, Head, Physical & Biological Sciences.
Staff: 1 professional (full time); 1 professional (part time); 1 (15 students) non-professional (part time).
Size: 10 globes; 400 reference books and gazetteers.
Area Specialization: Mississippi.
Subject Specialization: topography.
Dates: 1900 - (100%).
Collections not Cataloged.
Depository for: DMA; USGS (Geol., topo.).
Serves: students; faculty; employees; public. Mon.–Thurs. 8 a.m.–11:30 p.m., Fri. 8 a.m.–5 p.m.; Sat. 9 a.m.–6 p.m.; Sun. 2–11:30 p.m. (50 readers served per month).
Interlibrary Loan Available.
Reproduction Facility: quickcopy.

University

368. UNIVERSITY OF MISSISSIPPI
Williams Library
Documents Department
University, MS 38677
Telephone: 601/232-5857.
Contact Person: Dr. Annie E. Mills, Assoc. Prof. & Documents Libn.
Staff: 2 non-professional (part time).
Size: 40,000+ maps.
Annual Accessions: c 2,500 maps.
Area Specialization: United States.
Special Cartographic Collections: USGS topo maps.
Dates: 1900 - (100%).
Classification System: Superintendent of Documents.
Depository for: DMA; USGS (Topo.).

Serves: students; faculty; employees; public. Mon. 8 a.m.–8 p.m., Tues.–Fri. 8 a.m.–4:30 p.m.; Sat. 10 a.m.–12 midnight. (Seats 35).
Reproduction Facility: photocopy.

Vicksburg

369. U.S. MISSISSIPPI RIVER COMMISSION
P.O. Box 80
Vicksburg, MS 39180
Telephone: 601/634-5878.
Contact Person: Ms. Tony Erves, Clerk.
Staff: 1 professional (full time); 1 non-professional (part time).
Size: 500 maps.
Area Specialization: lower Mississippi River Basin.
Subject Specialization: navigation and flood control.
Special Cartographic Collections: USGS quadrangle maps of the area immediately bordering the Mississippi River from Cairo, Ill. to the Gulf of Mexico.
Dates: 1800-1899 (1); 1900 - (99).
Serves: employees; public. Mon.–Fri. 8 a.m.–4:45 p.m. (Seats 2).

MISSOURI

Cape Girardeau

370. SOUTHEAST MISSOURI STATE UNIVERSITY
Kent Library
Map Collection
Cape Girardeau, MO 63701
Established ca. 1960's.
Telephone: 314/651-2243.
Contact Person: J. Robert Willingham, Non-print Cataloger.
Staff: 1 professional (full time).
Size: 1,000 maps; 200 atlases; 1 globes; 75 aerial photographs.
Annual Accessions: 50 maps; 5 atlases; 10 aerial photographs.
Area Specialization: Missouri and adjacent states.
Subject Specialization: topography.
Dates: 1900 - (100%).
Collections not Cataloged.
Depository for: USGS (Topo.); GPO; NOAA.
Serves: students; faculty; public. Mon.–Fri. 8 a.m.–5 p.m. (Seats 4; 20 readers served per month).
Reproduction Facility: photocopy.

Columbia

371. STATE HISTORICAL SOCIETY OF MISSOURI
Map Collection
1020 Lowry
Columbia, MO 65201
Established 1899–1900.
Telephone: 314/882-7083.
Contact Person: Dr. Richard S. Brownlee, Director.
Staff: 5 professional (part time).
Size: 1,500 maps; 395 atlases; 5,000 reference books and gazetteers.
Annual Accessions: 100 maps; 10 atlases.
Area Specialization: Missouri; western United States.
Subject Specialization: railroads.

Special Cartographic Collections: USGS topographic maps (Missouri only); aerial photographs (Missouri counties only); depository for publications of the State of Missouri.
Dates: pre-1800 (1%); 1800-1899 (75%); 1900 - (24%).
Classification System: Dewey; local system.
Collections Cataloged. (80%).
Depository for: USGS (Topo.); State of Missouri official publications.
Serves: public. Mon.–Fri. 8 a.m.–4:30 p.m. (Seats 45; 750 readers served per month).
Reproduction Facility: photocopy; quickcopy.

372. UNIVERSITY OF MISSOURI—COLUMBIA
Elmer Ellis Library
Geography—History—Philosophy
Columbia, MO 65201
Established 1954.
Telephone: 314/882-6824.
Contact Person: Anne Edwards, Libn.
Staff: 1 professional (full time); 1 non-professional (full time).
Size: 32,000 maps; 40 atlases; 1 globes; 30 reference books and gazetteers.
Annual Accessions: 300 maps; 2 atlases; 2 reference books and gazetteers.
Area Specialization: Missouri; Europe.
Subject Specialization: topography.
Special Cartographic Collections: Sanborn Fire Insurance maps of Missouri.
Dates: 1800-1899 (5%); 1900 - (95%).
Classification System: LC.
Collections Cataloged. (50%).
Depository for: DMA.
Serves: students; faculty; employees; public. Mon.–Fri. 9 a.m.–5 p.m. (Seats 16; 35 readers served per month).
Interlibrary Loan Available.
Reproduction Facility: photocopy.

373. UNIVERSITY OF MISSOURI—COLUMBIA
Geography Department
Map Collection
Stewart Hall
Columbia, MO 65211
Established 1950.
Telephone: 314/882-8370.
Contact Person: Walter A. Schroeder, Chairman, Department of Geography.
Size: 4,200 maps; 166 atlases; 4 globes; 20 relief models; 200 aerial photographs; 100 reference books and gazetteers; 1,382 microforms (no. of titles).
Area Specialization: Missouri.
Subject Specialization: physical geography; land use; water resources.
Dates: 1800-1899 (2%); 1900 - (98%).
Serves: students; faculty; employees; public. Mon.–Fri. 8 a.m.–5 p.m. (Seats 15; 120 readers served per month).
Reproduction Facility: photocopy; quickcopy.

374. UNIVERSITY OF MISSOURI—COLUMBIA
Geology Library
201 Geology Building
Columbia, MO 65211
Telephone: 314/882-4860.
Contact Person: Robert Heidlage, Head.
Size: 100,000 maps; 650 atlases; 2 globes.
Annual Accessions: 4,000–5,000 maps.
Area Specialization: North America; South Africa; India; Australia.
Subject Specialization: 75% of topography collection is topographic (U.S.G.S. 7:SUP/$_2$, 15 minute, 1:250,000, 1:1,000,000 series); the rest is geologic with exception of USGS Land-use series.
Dates: 1800-1899 (5%); 1900 - (95%).

Classification System: LC.
Collections not Cataloged.
Depository for: GSC; USGS (Geol., topo.); Missouri Geological Survey, Geological Survey of S. Africa, India,. Australia, and several Australian states, and New Zealand
Serves: students; faculty; employees; public;. Mon.–Fri. 8 a.m.–5 p.m. (Seats 8).
Interlibrary Loan Available.
Publications: Acquisitions List.

Kansas City

375. KANSAS CITY PUBLIC LIBRARY
Main Library
Map Room
311 E. 12th Street
Kansas City, MO 64106
Established 1900.
Telephone: 816/221-2685, ext. 150, 152.
Contact Person: Fiona Fuhri, Reference Coordinator.
Staff: 1 professional (part time); 2 non-professional (part time).
Size: 60,000 maps.
Annual Accessions: 3,000 maps.
Dates: 1900 - (100%).
Collections not Cataloged.
Depository for: USGS (Topo.).
Serves: public. Mon.–Fri. 9 a.m.–5 p.m.; Sat. 9 a.m.–5 p.m. (25–50 readers served per month).
Reproduction Facility: photocopy.

376. LINDA HALL LIBRARY
Documents Department
5109 Cherry Street
Kansas City, MO 64110
Established 1946.
Telephone: 816/363-4600.
Contact Person: Bruce B. Cox, Documents Libn.
Staff: 1 professional (part time); 1 non-professional (part time).
Size: 64,000 maps.
Annual Accessions: 500 maps.
Area Specialization: United States.
Subject Specialization: geology.
Dates: 1900 - (100%).
Collections not Cataloged.
Depository for: USGS (Geol., topo.).
Serves: public. Mon. 9 a.m.–8:30 p.m.; Tues–Fri. 9 a.m.–5 p.m.; Sat. 10 a.m.–4 p.m.
Reproduction Facility: photocopy; microform.

Rolla

377. MISSOURI (STATE) DEPARTMENT OF NATURAL RESOURCES
Division of Geology and Land Survey
Geological Library
111 Fairgrounds Road
Rolla, MO 65401
Established 1853.
Telephone: 314/364-1752.
Contact Person: Marcia Cussins, Libn.
Staff: 1 professional (full time); 1 professional (part time).
Size: 13,000 maps; 220 atlases; 75,000 aerial photographs; 3,100 microforms (no. of titles).
Annual Accessions: 200 maps; 3 atlases; 500 aerial photographs; 500 microforms (no. of titles).
Area Specialization: Missouri.

Subject Specialization: geology; topography; caves; aerial photographs.
Special Cartographic Collections: unpublished area geologic maps, structural geology maps, economic geology maps, etc. (Missouri); unpublished cave maps (Missouri); rare, out-of-print geologic maps published by the Missouri Geological Survey; out-of-print topographic maps (Missouri);.
Dates: 1800-1899 (5%); 1900 - (95%).
Classification System: local system.
Collections Cataloged.
Depository for: USGS (Geol., topo.).
Serves: students; faculty; employees; public. Mon.–Fri. 8 a.m.–5 p.m. (Seats 4; 130 readers served per month).
Interlibrary Loan Available. (reproductions and most published maps) (Unpublished archival originals)
Reproduction Facility: photocopy; microform.
Publications: Index to Areal Geologic Maps of Missouri, 1890–1984 (I.C.29); Missouri D.N.R.—D.G.L.S. List of Publications; Index to topographic maps of Missouri.

378. MISSOURI (STATE) DEPARTMENT OF NATURAL RESOURCES
Division of Geology & Land Survey
Land Survey Repository
111 Fairgrounds Road
Rolla, MO 65401
Established 1972.
Telephone: 314/364-1752.
Contact Person: Jack C. McDermott, Chief of Land Records Repository.
Staff: 2 professional (full time); 2 non-professional (part time).
Size: 300 maps; 215 atlases; 1,000 aerial photographs; 200/250,000 microforms (no. of titles).
Annual Accessions: 50 maps; 2 atlases; 900 aerial photographs; 5,000 microforms (no. of titles).
Area Specialization: Missouri.
Subject Specialization: land Survey maps, notes and related information.
Special Cartographic Collections: collection of otherwise unpublished Survey Information and related areas.
Dates: pre-1800 (0.5%); 1800-1899 (25%); 1900 - (74.5%).
Classification System: local system.
Collections Cataloged.
Depository for: USGS (Topo.).
Serves: students; faculty; employees; public;. Mon.–Fri. 8 a.m.–5 p.m. (Seats 4; 20 readers served per month).
Reproduction Facility: photocopy; microform.
Publications: Repository Catalogue; Standards of Practice; Current Reference Sheets.

379. UNIVERSITY OF MISSOURI—ROLLA
Curtis Laws Wilson Library
Rolla, MO 65401
Telephone: 314/341-4007.
Size: 1,500 maps; 100 atlases; 1 globes; 100 aerial photographs; 50 reference books and gazetteers.
Annual Accessions: 20 maps; 5 atlases; 2 reference books and gazetteers.
Area Specialization: Missouri.
Collections not Cataloged.
Depository for: DMA; USGS (Geol., topo.).
Serves: students; faculty; employees; public;. Mon.–Fri. 8 a.m.–12 midnight; Sat. 8 a.m.–5 p.m.; Sun. 2–12 midnight. (Seats 12; 10 readers served per month).
Interlibrary Loan Available.
Reproduction Facility: photocopy.

380. UNIVERSITY OF MISSOURI—ROLLA
Geology Library
Rolla, MO 65401
Established 1910.
Telephone: 314/341-4616.

Contact Person: A.C. Spreng.
Staff: 1 professional (full time).
Size: 10,250 maps; 50 atlases; 4 globes; 5 relief models; 12 reference books and gazetteers.
Annual Accessions: 400 maps; 2 reference books and gazetteers.
Area Specialization: Missouri.
Subject Specialization: geology.
Dates: 1900 - (100%).
Classification System: DMA.
Collections not Cataloged.
Depository for: DMA; USGS (Geol., topo.).
Serves: public. Mon.–Fri. 8 a.m.–5 p.m. (Seats 25; 150 readers served per month).
Interlibrary Loan Available.
Reproduction Facility: photocopy.

St. Louis

381. MISSOURI HISTORICAL SOCIETY
Research Library
Jefferson Memorial Building/Forest Park
St. Louis, MO 63112
Telephone: 314/361-1424.
Contact Person: Stephanie A. Klein, Libn.-Archivist.
Size: ca. 2,000 maps; 200 atlases.
Annual Accessions: 5–20 maps.
Area Specialization: St. Louis; Missouri.
Dates: pre-1800 (est. 5%); 1800-1899 (est. 60%); 1900 - (est. 35%).
Classification System: local system.
Serves: public; Members. Tues.–Fri 9:30 a.m.–4:45 p.m. (Seats 16).
Reproduction Facility: photocopy; photographs available through pictorial history department.

382. ST. LOUIS PUBLIC LIBRARY
History and Genealogy Department
1301 Olive Street
St. Louis, MO 63103
Established 1865.
Telephone: 314/241-2288, ext. 385.
Contact Person: Noel C. Holobeck, Chief Libn.
Staff: 3 professional (part time).
Size: 106,678 maps; 325 atlases; 1 globes; 525 reference books and gazetteers; 5 serials (titles received).
Annual Accessions: 2,582 maps; 5–15 atlases.
Area Specialization: United States; Missouri; St. Louis.
Dates: pre-1800 (1%); 1800-1899 (15–20%); 1900 - (75–80%).
Classification System: LC; Dewey.
Collections Cataloged. (50%).
Depository for: DMA; USGS (Geol., topo.).
Serves: public. Mon. 9 a.m.–9 p.m.; Tues.–Fri. 9 a.m.–5 p.m.; Sat. 9 a.m.–5 p.m. (Seats 42; 100–110 readers served per month).
Reproduction Facility: photocopy.
Publications: *Maps in the St. Louis Public Library*, by Mildred Boatman. (St. Louis, 1931).

383. ST. LOUIS UNIVERSITY
Pius XII Memorial Library
Government Documents
3655 West Pine Blvd.
St. Louis, MO 63108
Telephone: 314/658-3105.
Contact Person: Mr. John Waide, Reference Libn.
Staff: 1 professional (full time); 3 professional (part time).
Size: 100,000 maps; 200 atlases; 500 aerial photographs; 100 reference books and gazetteers.

Annual Accessions: 4,000 maps; 5 atlases; 50 aerial photographs; 5 reference books and gazetteers.
Area Specialization: Missouri; Illinois.
Subject Specialization: topography.
Dates: 1900 - (100%).
Collections not Cataloged.
Depository for: USGS (Geol.).
Serves: students; faculty; employees; public. Mon.–Fri. 8:30 a.m.–5 p.m. (20 readers served per month).
Reproduction Facility: photocopy.

384. U.S. DEFENSE MAPPING AGENCY AERONAUTICAL CENTER
Cartographic Data Base Division
Library Branch
3200 South Second Street
St. Louis, MO 63118
Telephone: 314/263-4841.
Contact Person: James Tancock, Chief, Library Branch.
Staff: 1 professional (full time); 5 non-professional (full time).
Size: 150,000 maps; 100,000 microforms (no. of titles).
Area Specialization: Comprehensive.
Subject Specialization: aerial charting data.
Dates: 1900 - (100%).
Classification System: DMA.
Collections Cataloged.
Serves: employees; Special arrrangement. Mon.–Fri. 6:30 a.m.–3 p.m.
Reproduction Facility: photocopy.

385. WASHINGTON UNIVERSITY
Earth and Planetary Sciences Library
St. Louis, MO 63130
Established 1927.
Telephone: 314/889-5406.
Contact Person: Deborah Hartwig, Libn.
Staff: 1 professional (full time); 1 non-professional (full time).
Size: 76,716 maps; 98 atlases; 1 globes; 97 reference books and gazetteers; 249 serials (titles received); 800 microforms (no. of titles).
Annual Accessions: 2,500 maps.
Area Specialization: Missouri.
Subject Specialization: geology; geophysics; geochemistry; petrology; mineralogy; lunar geology; remote sensing; paleontology; micropaleontology.
Collections not Cataloged.
Depository for: DMA; USGS (Geol., topo.).
Serves: students; faculty; employees; public. Mon.–Thurs. 8:30 a.m.–9 p.m.; Fri. 8:30 a.m.–5 p.m.; Sat. 9 a.m.–12 noon. (Seats 30; 200 readers served per month).
Interlibrary Loan Available.
Reproduction Facility: photocopy.
Publications: Information brochure.

Springfield

386. SOUTHWEST MISSOURI STATE UNIVERSITY
Duane G. Meyer Library
Map Collection
901 South Kings Street
Springfield, MO 65804-0095
Established August 1980.
Telephone: 417/836-5104.
Contact Person: James A. Coombs, Map Libn.
Staff: 1 professional (full time); 7 non-professional (part time).
Size: 86,470 maps; 776 atlases; 2 globes; 6 relief models; 33,022 aerial photographs; 132 reference books and

gazetteers; 18 serials (titles received); 10 microforms (no. of titles).

Annual Accessions: 5,000 maps; 20 atlases; 1 globes; 2 relief models; 300 aerial photographs; 45 reference books and gazetteers; 2 serials (titles received); 4 microforms (no. of titles).

Area Specialization: Ozark Plateau.

Dates: pre-1800 (1%); 1800-1899 (7%); 1900 - (92%).

Classification System: LC.

Collections Cataloged. (10%).

Depository for: DMA; USGS (Geol., topo.); GPO; Missouri state map publications.

Serves: students; faculty; employees; public. Mon.–Thurs. 8 a.m.–10 p.m., Fri. 8 a.m.–5 p.m.; Sat. 10 a.m.–3 p.m.; Sun. 2–7 p.m. (Seats 15; 125 readers served per month).

Interlibrary Loan Available.

Reproduction Facility: photocopy; microform.

Warrensburg

387. CENTRAL MISSOURI STATE UNIVERSITY

Ward Edwards Library
Warrensburg, MO 64093
Telephone: 816/429-4141.
Contact Person: Michael Lee.
Depository for: DMA.

MONTANA

Billings

388. EASTERN MONTANA COLLEGE

Library
Documents/Serials/Maps Department
1500 N. 30th Street
Billings, MT 59101
Established 1976.
Telephone: 406/657-1664.
Contact Person: Aaron Hause, Documents/Serials/Maps Libn.
Staff: 1 professional (part time); 1 non-professional (part time).
Size: 41,597 maps.
Annual Accessions: 120 maps.
Area Specialization: Montana.
Subject Specialization: topography.
Dates: 1900 - (100%).
Classification System: local system.
Collections not Cataloged.
Depository for: USGS (Topo.).
Serves: students; faculty; employees; public. (Seats 20; 10 readers served per month).
Interlibrary Loan Available.
Reproduction Facility: photocopy.

389. PARMLY BILLINGS LIBRARY

510 N. Broadway
Billings, MT 59102
Telephone: 406/657-8290.
Contact Person: Linda Weirather, Public Services Coordinator.
Staff: 1 professional (part time).
Size: 300–400 maps; 10 reference books and gazetteers.
Area Specialization: Montana.
Subject Specialization: topography; geology.
Special Cartographic Collections: original map of Yellowstone watershed by scout Yellowstone Kelly, ink on linen, 1870's.

Dates: 1900 -.
Classification System: Dewey.
Collections not Cataloged.
Serves: public. Tues.–Fri. 1–5 p.m.; Sat. 1–5 p.m. (Seats 12; 150 readers served per month).
Interlibrary Loan Available.
Reproduction Facility: photocopy; microform.

Bozeman

390. MONTANA STATE UNIVERSITY

Dept of Earth Sciences
Map Library
Bozeman, MT 59717
Telephone: 406/994-3331.
Contact Person: Dr. Stephan G. Custer.
Staff: 1 professional (part time).
Size: 40,000 maps; 40 atlases; 6 globes; 25,000 aerial photographs; 30 reference books and gazetteers.
Annual Accessions: 1,500 maps; 5 atlases; 2,500 aerial photographs; 5 reference books and gazetteers.
Area Specialization: North America; South America.
Subject Specialization: topography; geology; agriculture; transportation.
Depository for: DMA; USGS (Geol., topo.).
Interlibrary Loan Available.

Butte

391. MONTANA COLLEGE OF MINERAL SCIENCE AND TECHNOLOGY

Library
Butte, MT 59701
Established 1900.
Telephone: Located in Documents Collection at present: 406/496-4286.
Contact Person: Elizabeth Morrissett, Head Libn.
Staff: 1 non-professional (part time).
Size: 75,000 maps; 10 atlases; 3 globes; 10 relief models; 25 reference books and gazetteers; 750 serials (titles received).
Annual Accessions: 2,000 maps; 1 atlases; 1 reference books and gazetteers; 5 serials (titles received).
Area Specialization: Montana.
Subject Specialization: geology; geophysics; geochemistry; mining and metallurgy; mineral resources; environmental engineering.
Collections not Cataloged.
Depository for: DMA; USGS (Geol., topo.).
Serves: students; faculty; employees; public;. Mon.–Fri. 7:30 a.m.–11 p.m.; Sat. 9 a.m.–5 p.m.; Sun. 3:30–10:30 p.m. (Seats 300; 25 readers served per month).
Interlibrary Loan Available.
Reproduction Facility: photocopy. collection first in 1974.

Helena

392. MONTANA HISTORICAL SOCIETY

Library
225 N. Roberts Street
Helena, MT 59620
Established Maps collected since 1865. Organized into a more-or-less coherent.
Telephone: 406/444-2681.
Contact Person: Robert M. Clark, Libn.
Staff: 3 professional (part time); 1 non-professional (part time).

Size: 12,500 maps; 125 atlases; 1 globes; 3 relief models; 35 reference books and gazetteers; 2 serials (titles received); 2 microforms (no. of titles).
Annual Accessions: 200 maps; 2 atlases; 1–2 reference books and gazetteers.
Area Specialization: Montana.
Subject Specialization: Montana history; discovery and exploration.
Special Cartographic Collections: Sanborn fire insurance maps for Montana towns and cities; manuscript maps on Montana history.
Dates: 1800-1899 (40%); 1900 - (60%).
Classification System: local system; alphabet size/location designator and. sequential numbering.
Collections Cataloged. (90%).
Depository for: USGS (Topo.); Montana state agencies.
Serves: public. Mon.–Fri. 8 a.m.–5 p.m.; Sat. 9 a.m.–5 p.m. (Seats 30; 300 readers served per month).
Reproduction Facility: photocopy.
Publications: *Catalog of the Map Collection, Montana Historical Society* (Helena, Mt. 1983); Eight sheet microfiche of card catalog (duplicated on request).

Missoula

393. UNIVERSITY OF MONTANA
Mansfield Library
Documents Division
Missoula, MT 59812
Telephone: 406/243-4564.
Contact Person: Constance M. Piquette, Map Libn. & Library Technician/Documents.
Staff: 1 professional (full time); 1 non-professional (part time).
Size: 82,000 maps; 250 atlases; 3 globes; 8 relief models; 400 aerial photographs; 240 reference books and gazetteers; 3 microforms (no. of titles).
Annual Accessions: 3,500 maps; 10 atlases; 2 relief models; 5 reference books and gazetteers; 1 microforms (no. of titles).
Area Specialization: Montana; Pacific Northwest; The West; United States; Western Canada.
Subject Specialization: geology; forestry; history; geography; topography.
Special Cartographic Collections: historical Maps of Montana & the West; USGS topographic quadrangles of the United States; USGS open-file reports for Montana; Western Montana orthophotoquads; false color composite Landsat scenes of Montana.
Dates: pre-1800 (1%); 1800-1899 (5%); 1900 - (94%).
Classification System: LC.
Collections Cataloged.
Depository for: DMA; USGS (Geol., topo.).
Serves: students; faculty; employees; public;. Mon.–Fri. 8 a.m.–5 p.m. (Seats 15; 200 readers served per month).
Reproduction Facility: photocopy.
Publications: Piquette, Constance M. *Indexed, Annotated Cartobibliography of the University of Montana Mansfield Library Historical Map Collection.* 1983. Piquette, Constance M. 'Montana and Vicinity, a select and indexed listing of U.S. Geological Survey Open-File Reports Issued Between 1974 and Sept. of 1980.' *Western Association of Map Libraries. Information Bulletin.* Vol. 14 No. 1, Nov. 1982, pp. 56–67.

NEBRASKA

Lincoln

394. NEBRASKA STATE HISTORICAL SOCIETY
Library
1500 R Street
Lincoln, NE 68508
Established 1878 (library established).
Telephone: 402/471-4750, 4751.
Contact Person: Ann Reinert, Libn.
Staff: 3 professional (part time).
Size: 3,500 maps; 400 atlases; 30 reference books and gazetteers; 1 serials (titles received); 9 microforms (no. of titles).
Area Specialization: Nebraska, pre-1800 to present.
Subject Specialization: local history.
Special Cartographic Collections: Sanborn fire insurance maps of Nebraska (563 sets); Nebraska land owner maps & atlases; 13 Birds-eye-views of Nebraska.
Dates: pre-1800 (1%); 1800-1899 (60%); 1900 - (39%).
Classification System: Dewey (modified).
Collections Cataloged. (100%).
Depository for: State of Nebraska publications (including maps).
Serves: public. Mon.–Fri. 8 a.m.–5 p.m.; Sat. 8 a.m.–5 p.m. (20 readers served per month).
Reproduction Facility: photocopy.
Publications: *Checklist of Printed Maps of the Middle West to 1900: V. 12 Nebraska.* Reinert, Ann. "Historical Maps of Nebraska." v. 14 no. 1 (Spring 1983) of Nebraska Library Association Quarterly pp. 4–10.

395. UNIVERSITY OF NEBRASKA—LINCOLN
Geology Library
303 Morrill Hall
Lincoln, NE 68588
Established 1895.
Telephone: 402/472-2653.
Contact Person: Agnes Adams, Assistant Professor.
Staff: 1 professional (full time); 1 non-professional (full time); 2 professional (part time).
Size: 65,000 maps; 350 atlases; 1,000 reference books and gazetteers; 700 serials (titles received).
Annual Accessions: 3,000 maps.
Area Specialization: western United States; Antarctica.
Subject Specialization: geology, hydrology.
Dates: 1800-1899 (10%); 1900 - (90%).
Classification System: LC.
Collections Cataloged. (50%).
Depository for: USGS (Geol., topo.).
Serves: students; faculty; employees; public. Mon.–Fri. 8 a.m.–5 p.m., 7 p.m.–10 p.m.; Sat. 9 a.m.–12 noon. (Seats 70; 1,200 readers served per month).
Interlibrary Loan Available.

396. UNIVERSITY OF NEBRASKA—LINCOLN
University Libraries
Love Library Map Collection
Lincoln, NE 68588-0410
Telephone: 402/472-2525.
Contact Person: Virginia Moreland, Assistant Professor, University Libraries.
Staff: 1 professional (part time).
Size: 30,000 maps; 2 globes.
Area Specialization: Nebraska; Great Plains states.
Dates: 1800-1899 (1%); 1900 - (99%).
Classification System: DMA; local system.
Collections not Cataloged.
Depository for: DMA; other GPO maps, census, etc.

Serves: students; faculty; employees; public;. Mon.–Fri. 8 a.m.–5 p.m., 6–9 p.m.; Sat. 10 a.m.–5 p.m.; Sun. 1:30–9 p.m. (Seats 24).
Interlibrary Loan Available.
Reproduction Facility: photocopy.

Omaha

397. OMAHA PUBLIC LIBRARY
Business/Science/Technology Department
Documents
215 South 15 Street
Omaha, NE 68102
Established 1945 (Approx).
Telephone: 402/444-4817.
Contact Person: Janet Davenport, Documents Libn.
Staff: 1 professional (part time); 3 non-professional (part time).
Size: 52,091 maps.
Annual Accessions: 3,000 maps.
Area Specialization: United States.
Subject Specialization: topography.
Dates: 1800-1899 (less than 1%); 1900 - (99%).
Classification System: GPO maps: SuDocs classification; USGS maps: alphabetical by state.
Collections not Cataloged.
Depository for: USGS (Topo.).
Serves: public. Mon.–Fri. 9 a.m.–8:30 p.m. (summer hours vary); Sat. 9 a.m.–5:30 p.m. (30–50 readers served per month).
Reproduction Facility: photocopy.

398. UNIVERSITY OF NEBRASKA—OMAHA,
University Library
Reference Map & Atlas Collection
60th & Dodge Streets
Omaha, NE 68182
Established 1972.
Telephone: 402/554-2661.
Contact Person: John Davis Hill, Science Reference Libn.
Staff: 1 professional (part time); 1 non-professional (part time).
Size: 12,500 maps; 300 atlases; 1 globes; 10 reference books and gazetteers; 5 serials (titles received).
Annual Accessions: 600 maps; 10 atlases; 2 reference books and gazetteers.
Area Specialization: Afghanistan; Central Great Plains.
Subject Specialization: topography; geology.
Dates: 1800-1899 (1%); 1900 - (99%).
Classification System: local system.
Collections not Cataloged.
Depository for: USGS (Geol., topo.).
Serves: public. Mon.–Thurs. 9 a.m.–10 p.m.; Fri. 9 a.m.–5 p.m.; Sat. 9 a.m.–5 p.m.; Sun. 1–9 p.m. (Seats 20; 30–50 readers served per month).
Reproduction Facility: photocopy.
Publications: *Library Facts: Maps and Atlases* by John Hill, Sept. 1982.

NEVADA

Carson City

399. NEVADA STATE LIBRARY
Public Services Division
401 North Carson Street
Carson City, NV 89710
Telephone: 702/885-5160.

Area Specialization: Nevada and California.
Subject Specialization: topography.
Serves: public. Mon.–Fri. 8 a.m.–5 p.m.

Reno

400. UNIVERSITY OF NEVADA, RENO
Mines Library
Reno, NV 89557
Established 1978.
Telephone: 702/784-6596.
Contact Person: Linda P. Newman, Map Libn.
Staff: 1 professional (part time); 3 non-professional (part time).
Size: 97,400 maps; 15 atlases; 1 globes; 2 relief models; 46 reference books and gazetteers; 8 serials (titles received).
Annual Accessions: 3,500 maps; 1 atlases; 5 reference books and gazetteers.
Area Specialization: Nevada; western United States.
Subject Specialization: topography; geology.
Dates: 1800-1899 (5%); 1900 - (95%).
Classification System: DMA; local system.
Collections Cataloged. (15%).
Depository for: DMA; USGS (Geol., topo.); Nevada Bureau of Mines & Geology.
Serves: students; faculty; employees; public. Mon.–Thurs. 8 a.m.–10 p.m., Fri. 8 a.m.–5 p.m.; Sat. 1–5 p.m.; Sun. 1–5 p.m., 7–10 p.m. (Seats 12; 510 readers served per month).
Interlibrary Loan Available.
Reproduction Facility: photocopy.
Publications: *Books and Maps Received in the Mines Library* (quarterly); *Maps, Library Information Leaflet, No. 14* (guide).

NEW HAMPSHIRE

Concord

401. NEW HAMPSHIRE HISTORICAL SOCIETY
30 Park Street
Concord, NH 03301
Established 1823.
Telephone: 603/225-3381.
Contact Person: William Copeley, Associate Libn.
Staff: 1 professional (part time).
Size: 1,200 maps; 50 atlases; 50 reference books and gazetteers.
Annual Accessions: 10 maps; 1 atlases; 1 reference books and gazetteers.
Area Specialization: New Hampshire.
Dates: pre-1800 (10%); 1800-1899 (70%); 1900 - (20%).
Classification System: Dewey (modified).
Collections Cataloged. (100%).
Serves: public. Mon.–Fri. 9 a.m.–4:30 p.m.; Sat. 9–4:30 (Oct–May). (Seats 20).
Reproduction Facility: quickcopy; photograph.

402. NEW HAMPSHIRE STATE LIBRARY
Reference Department
20 Park Street
Concord, NH 03301
Telephone: 603/271-2394.
Contact Person: Stella Scheckter, Head, Reference Dept.
Area Specialization: New Hampshire.
Depository for: USGS (Geol.).
Serves: public.
Interlibrary Loan Available.
Reproduction Facility: quickcopy.

Hanover

403. DARTMOUTH COLLEGE
Baker Library
Map Room
Hanover, NH 03755
Telephone: 603/646-2579.
Contact Person: John F. Berthelsen, Map Curator.
Staff: 1 professional (full time); 2 non-professional (part time).
Size: 129,000 maps; 2,900 atlases; 25 globes; 300 relief models; 350 aerial photographs; 500 reference books and gazetteers; 15 serials (titles received).
Annual Accessions: 4,400 maps; 35 atlases; 25 reference books and gazetteers; 1 serials (titles received).
Area Specialization: Hanover; New Hampshire; Vermont; New England; Northeastern States; United States; Polar; Arctic Regions; USSR; Central America.
Subject Specialization: historical cartography; geology; topography.
Special Cartographic Collections: Stefansson (Polar and Arctic Regions); Karpinski (American Maps from European Collections); Scavenious (Maps of the American Revolution).
Dates: pre-1800 (3%); 1800-1899 (9%); 1900 - (88%).
Classification System: LC.
Collections Cataloged. (96%).
Depository for: DMA; NTS (Canada); USGS (Geol., topo.).
Serves: students; faculty; employees; public. Mon.–Fri. 8 a.m.–4:30 p.m. (Seats 14).
Interlibrary Loan Available.
Reproduction Facility: photocopy.

Keene

404. KEENE STATE COLLEGE
Geography Department
Keene, NH 03431
Telephone: 603/352-1909, ext. 256.
Contact Person: Klaus Bayr, Professor of Geography.

Manchester

405. MANCHESTER CITY LIBRARY
Reference Department
405 Pine Street
Manchester, NH 03104
Established 1855.
Telephone: 603/624-6550.
Contact Person: Betty H. Carr, Coordinator, Information Services.
Size: 1,500 maps; 50 atlases; 6 globes; 12 reference books and gazetteers.
Annual Accessions: 100 maps.
Area Specialization: Manchester; New Hampshire; New England.
Dates: pre-1800 (1%); 1800-1899 (24%); 1900 - (75%).
Collections not Cataloged.
Depository for: USGS (Topo.).
Serves: students; faculty; employees; public. Summer: Mon., Tues., Thurs. 9 a.m.–9 p.m., Wed., Fri. 9 a.m.–6 p.m.; Winter: Mon, Tues, Thurs., 9 a.m.–9 p.m., Wed, Fri. 9 a.m.–5:30 p.m.; Sat. Winter: 9 a.m.–5 p.m. (Seats 50; 25 readers served per month).
Reproduction Facility: photocopy; quickcopy.

406. MANCHESTER HISTORIC ASSOCIATION
Library
129 Amherst St.
Manchester, NH 03104
Established 1896.
Telephone: 603/622-7531.
Contact Person: Elizabeth Lessard, Libn.
Staff: 2 professional (full time).
Size: 2,500 maps; 12 atlases; 2 globes; 8 aerial photographs; 6 reference books and gazetteers.
Area Specialization: Manchester, New Hampshire.
Special Cartographic Collections: Amoskeag Mfg Co.: Merrimack River, Amoskeag canals, street plans, Profiles, plot plans, building plans; Amoskeag Industries, Inc.: Amoskeag Millyard, plot plans, street plans, industrial development plans; Manchester, N.H.: street plans, development plans.
Dates: pre-1800 (less than 1%); 1800-1899 (95%); 1900 - (5%).
Classification System: local system.
Collections Cataloged. (70%).
Serves: students; public. Tues–Fri. 9 a.m.–4 p.m.; Sat. 10 a.m.–4 p.m. (Seats 6; 30 readers served per month).
Reproduction Facility: photocopy; quickcopy.

407. SAINT ANSELM COLLEGE
Geisel Library
St. Anselm Drive
Manchester, NH 03102
Telephone: 603/669-1030, ext. 240.
Contact Person: Barbara C. Gannon, Reference Director.
Staff: 1 professional (part time).
Size: 300 maps; 30 atlases; 1 globes; 40 reference books and gazetteers.
Annual Accessions: 30 maps.
Area Specialization: New Hampshire.
Dates: 1900 - (100%).
Classification System: LC.
Collections Cataloged.
Depository for: USGS (Geol.).
Serves: students; faculty; employees; public;. Mon.–Fri. 8 a.m.–Midnight; Sat. 9 a.m.–5 p.m.; Sun. 1 p.m.–Midnight. (Seats 20).
Interlibrary Loan Available.
Reproduction Facility: photocopy.

Nashua

408. NASHUA PUBLIC LIBRARY
Reference Dept.
2 Court Street
Nashua, NH 03060
Telephone: 603/883-4141.
Contact Person: Florence Shepard, Supervisor Adult Services.
Size: 100 maps; 20 atlases; 3 reference books and gazetteers.
Area Specialization: New Hampshire; Nashua.
Subject Specialization: history.
Special Cartographic Collections: New Hampshire county maps in book form.
Dates: 1800-1899 (20%); 1900 - (75%).
Classification System: Dewey.
Collections Cataloged.
Serves: students; faculty; employees; public. Mon.–Fri. 8:30 a.m.–9 p.m.; Sat. 8:30 a.m.–5:30 p.m.; Sun. 1–5 p.m. (Sep–Apr only).
Reproduction Facility: photocopy.

NEW JERSEY

Bloomfield

409. BLOOMFIELD PUBLIC LIBRARY
Reference Department
90 Broad St.
Bloomfield, NJ 07003
Established 1965.
Contact Person: Ina Campbell, Head, Reference Dept.
Staff: 1 professional (part time); 2 non-professional (part time).
Size: 6 vertical file drawers maps; 60 atlases; 1 globes; 25 reference books and gazetteers; 5 serials (titles received).
Annual Accessions: 300 maps; 2 atlases.
Area Specialization: United States; Essex County, New Jersey; New York State.
Subject Specialization: history; political geography.
Special Cartographic Collections: Several historical maps of Bloomfield.
Dates: 1800-1899 (2%); 1900 - (98%).
Classification System: local system.
Collections Cataloged. (Books only).
Depository for: selective govt. depository.
Serves: students; faculty; employees; public. Mon.–Tues, Wed. 9 a.m.–9 p.m., Thurs., Fri. 9 a.m.–5 p.m.; Sat. 9 a.m.–5 p.m. (Seats 62; 50 readers served per month).
Interlibrary Loan Available.
Reproduction Facility: photocopy.

Convent Station

410. GENERAL DRAFTING CO., INC.
Library
Canfield Road
Convent Station, NJ 07961
Telephone: 201/538/7600, ext. 227.
Contact Person: Allen Freeman, Libn.
Staff: 1 professional (part time).
Size: 25,000 maps; 2,500 aerial photographs; 2,000 (including atlases) reference books and gazetteers.
Area Specialization: United States.
Subject Specialization: roads; travel.
Dates: 1900 - (100%).
Collections not Cataloged.
Serves: employees. Mon.–Fri. 8 a.m.–5 p.m. (Seats 3; 400 readers served per month).

East Orange

411. EAST ORANGE PUBLIC LIBRARY
21 So. Arlington Avenue
East Orange, NJ 07018
Telephone: 201/266-5612.
Contact Person: Mr. J. Robert Starkey, Reference Libn.
Staff: 1 professional (part time).
Size: 1,800 maps; 70 atlases; 3 globes; 1 relief models; 4 reference books and gazetteers.
Annual Accessions: 75 maps; 3 atlases.
Area Specialization: East Orange, New Jersey.
Subject Specialization: local history.
Dates: 1800-1899 (1%); 1900 - (99%).
Classification System: Dewey.
Collections Cataloged.
Serves: public. Mon., Tues., Thurs, 9 a.m.–9 p.m.; Wed., 9 a.m.–6 p.m.;. Fri. 10 a.m.–6 p.m. Sat. 9 a.m.–5 p.m.; Sun. 1 a.m.–5 p.m. (exc. summer). (Seats 142).
Reproduction Facility: photocopy.

Glassboro

412. GLASSBORO STATE COLLEGE
Savitz Library
Main Floor
US Route 322
Glassboro, NJ 08028
Established 1975.
Telephone: 609/893-6302.
Contact Person: William A. Garrabrant, Science & Technology Subject Specialist.
Staff: 1 professional (part time); 1 non-professional (part time).
Size: 600 maps; 75 atlases; 4 globes; 550 reference books and gazetteers; 20 serials (titles received).
Annual Accessions: 75 maps; 5 atlases; 1 globes; 50 reference books and gazetteers; 2 serials (titles received).
Area Specialization: southern Delaware River valley; southern New Jersey.
Special Cartographic Collections: Stewart Collection (contains maps of Jerseyana and the Revolutionary War).
Dates: pre-1800 (20); 1900 - (80).
Classification System: LC 80; Dewey 20.
Collections Cataloged. (80%).
Depository for: State of New Jersey.
Serves: students; faculty; employees; public;. Mon.–Thurs. 8 a.m.–10 p.m., Fri. 8 a.m.–6 p.m.; Sat. 9 a.m.–5 p.m.; Sun. 2 p.m.–9 p.m. (Seats 400; 22,000 readers served per month).
Interlibrary Loan Available. books only
Reproduction Facility: photocopy; microform.

Jersey City

413. JERSEY CITY PUBLIC LIBRARY
New Jersey Room
472 Jersey Avenue
Jersey City, NJ 07302
Established 1889.
Telephone: 201/547-4503.
Contact Person: Joan Doherty, NJ Room Libn.
Staff: 2 professional (full time); 1 non-professional (full time).
Size: 500 maps; 50 atlases; 30 aerial photographs; 13 reference books and gazetteers; 5 microforms (no. of titles).
Annual Accessions: 10 maps; 1 atlases; 5 aerial photographs; 1 microforms (no. of titles).
Area Specialization: Hudson County, NJ.
Subject Specialization: topography; insurance; roads.
Dates: pre-1800 (10%); 1800-1899 (40%); 1900 - (50%).
Classification System: Dewey; local system.
Collections Cataloged. (60%).
Depository for: USGS (Topo.).
Serves: students; public. Mon.–Fri. 9 a.m.–5 p.m.; Sat. 10 a.m.–5 p.m. except summer. (Seats 16).
Reproduction Facility: photocopy; microform.

Maplewood

414. HAMMOND INCORPORATED
Editorial Department Library
515 Valley Street
Maplewood, NJ 07040
Established 1945.
Telephone: 201/763-6000.
Contact Person: Ernest J. Dupuy, Libn.
Staff: 1 professional (full time).
Size: 13,000 maps; 750 atlases; 4 globes; 16 relief models; 8,000 reference books and gazetteers; 160 serials (titles received).

Annual Accessions: 450 maps; 35 atlases; 150 reference books and gazetteers.
Subject Specialization: history; travel; geography; earth science; space science; demography; biblical archaeology; anthropology.
Special Cartographic Collections: USGS topographic quadrangles (partial); United States 1:250,000 series; World IMW series; U.S. and foreign road maps; United States and Canadian province administrative maps; Aeronautical charts (United States and World).
Dates: 1800-1899 (.5%); 1900 - (99.5%).
Classification System: AGS (modified).
Collections Cataloged. (50%).
Serves: employees.
Publications: *Hammond Report* (ca. 2 issues per year).

New Brunswick

415. RUTGERS UNIVERSITY
Alexander Library
College Ave.
New Brunswick, NJ 08903
Telephone: 201/932-7007.
Contact Person: Ilona Caparros, Public Services Libn.—Maps and Microforms.
Dates: 1900 - (100%).
Classification System: local system.
Collections not Cataloged.
Depository for: Census maps.
Serves: students; faculty; employees; public.
Interlibrary Loan Available.
Reproduction Facility: photocopy.

416. RUTGERS UNIVERSITY
Alexander Library
Department of Special Collections and Archives
New Brunswick, NJ 08903
Established ca. 1930.
Telephone: 201/932-7510, 7049.
Contact Person: Ronald L. Becker, Curator of Manuscripts and Rare Books.
Staff: 1 professional (full time); 1 non-professional (full time); 1 professional (part time).
Size: 4,500 maps; 270 atlases; 3 globes; 1 relief models; 25 aerial photographs; 30 reference books and gazetteers.
Annual Accessions: 50 maps; 2 atlases.
Area Specialization: New Jersey.
Subject Specialization: topography; land use.
Special Cartographic Collections: Charles Hartman (18–20th Century manuscript South Jersey property & tax maps); Alan F. Guldi (20th Century American Service Station road maps); Delaware and Raritan Canal Commission (early 20th century manuscript canal maps); Daniel B. Frazier Company (19th–20th Century manuscript maps of Jersey shore).
Dates: pre-1800 (15%); 1800-1899 (50%); 1900 - (35%).
Classification System: SPINDEX Control Number.
Collections Cataloged. (65%).
Serves: students; faculty; employees; public. Mon., Tues., Thurs., Fri. 9 a.m.–5 p.m., Wed. 9 a.m.–9 p.m.; Sat. 12 noon–6 p.m. (Seats 25; 350 readers served per month).
Reproduction Facility: photocopy.

Newark

417. NEW JERSEY HISTORICAL SOCIETY
Library
230 Broadway
Newark, NJ 07104
Established 1845.
Telephone: 201/483-3939, ext. 37.
Contact Person: Kathleen Stavec, Reference Libn.
Staff: 4 professional (full time); 1 non-professional (full time); 1 professional (part time).
Size: 1,250 maps; 150 atlases.
Annual Accessions: 10 maps.
Area Specialization: New Jersey.
Subject Specialization: history of New Jersey, 17th century to present.
Dates: pre-1800 (20); 1800-1899 (60); 1900 - (20).
Classification System: Dewey; flat maps unclassified.
Collections Cataloged. (90%).
Serves: public. Mon.–Fri. 9:30 a.m.–4:15 p.m.; Sat. 9:30 a.m.–4:15 p.m. (Seats 15 (map room)).
Reproduction Facility: photocopy.

418. NEWARK PUBLIC LIBRARY
Humanities Department
5 Washington Street
Newark, NJ 07101
Telephone: 201/733-7820.
Contact Person: Simone Galik, Libn., Reference Dept.
Staff: 1 professional (part time); 3 non-professional (part time).
Size: 18,000 maps; 600 atlases; 200 reference books and gazetteers.
Annual Accessions: 800 maps; 10–20 atlases.
Area Specialization: New Jersey; New York; United States.
Dates: pre-1800 (10%); 1800-1899 (10%); 1900 - (80%).
Classification System: local system.
Collections not Cataloged. ((alphabeti).
Depository for: DMA; NOS; USGS (Geol., topo.); U.S. Army Corps of Engineers.
Serves: public. Mon., Wed., Thurs., 9 a.m.–9 p.m.; Tues., Fri. 9 a.m.–5:30 p.m.; Sat. 9 a.m.–5 p.m. (Seats 150).
Reproduction Facility: quickcopy; own camera.

Piscataway

419. RUTGERS UNIVERSITY
Library of Science and Medicine
Reference department
Busch Campus
Piscataway, NJ 08854
Established 1978.
Telephone: 201/932-2895.
Contact Person: Susan Goodman, Map Libn.
Staff: 1 professional (part time); 1 non-professional (part time).
Size: 100,000 maps; 180 atlases; 300 reference books and gazetteers.
Annual Accessions: 3,000 maps; 3 atlases.
Area Specialization: New Jersey; Middle Atlantic states.
Subject Specialization: geology; soils; topography.
Dates: 1900 - (100%).
Classification System: local system.
Collections not Cataloged.
Depository for: DMA; USGS (Geol., topo.).
Serves: students; faculty; employees; public. Mon.–Thurs. 8 a.m.–1 a.m., Fri. 8 a.m.–10 p.m.; Sat. 10 a.m.–6 p.m.; Sun. 12 noon–1 a.m.
Reproduction Facility: photocopy.

Plainfield

420. PLAINFIELD PUBLIC LIBRARY
Eighth Street at Park Avenue
Plainfield, NJ 07060
Established Ca. 1940.
Telephone: 201/757-1111.
Contact Person: Mrs. Dorothea Tutwiler, Reference Libn.
Staff: 1 professional (part time).
Size: 1,000 maps; 55 atlases; 1 globes; 46 reference books and gazetteers.
Annual Accessions: 50 maps; 1 atlases; 1 reference books and gazetteers.
Area Specialization: New Jersey.
Dates: 1800-1899 (1%); 1900 - (99%).
Classification System: Dewey.
Collections Cataloged. (75%).
Serves: public. Mon.–Fri. 9 a.m.–9 p.m.; Sat. 9 a.m.–5 p.m. (Seats 140).
Interlibrary Loan Available. (restricted)
Reproduction Facility: photocopy; microform.

Princeton

421. PRINCETON UNIVERSITY
Geology Library
Map Collection
Guyot Hall
Princeton, NJ 08544
Telephone: 609/452-3247.
Contact Person: Patricia Gaspari-Bridges, Map Libn.
Staff: 1 professional (full time); 1 non-professional (part time).
Size: 127,000 maps; 500 atlases; 8 globes; 8 relief models; 200 aerial photographs; 250 reference books and gazetteers; 5 serials (titles received); 5 microforms (no. of titles).
Annual Accessions: 2,000 maps; 25 atlases; 1 globes; 25 aerial photographs; 25 reference books and gazetteers; 1 serials (titles received); 2 microforms (no. of titles).
Area Specialization: United States.
Subject Specialization: geology; topography.
Dates: 1800-1899 (.5%); 1900 - (99.5%).
Classification System: LC.
Collections not Cataloged.
Depository for: USGS (Geol., topo.).
Serves: students; faculty; employees; public. Mon.–Fri. 9 a.m.–5 p.m. (Seats 17; 200 readers served per month).
Reproduction Facility: photocopy.

422. PRINCETON UNIVERSITY
Rare Books and Special Collections
Richard Halliburton Map Collection
Princeton, NJ 08544
Established 1948.
Telephone: 609/452-3214.
Contact Person: Lawrence E. Spellman, Curator of Maps.
Staff: 1 professional (full time); 3 non-professional (part time).
Size: 230,000 maps; 400 atlases; 25 globes; 60 relief models; 1,000 aerial photographs; 2,000 reference books and gazetteers; 40 serials (titles received).
Annual Accessions: 8,500 maps; 20 atlases; 1 globes; 50 aerial photographs; 75 reference books and gazetteers.
Area Specialization: New Jersey; United States.
Subject Specialization: transportation; regional history; urban development.
Special Cartographic Collections: American Revolutionary War.
Dates: pre-1800 (2%); 1800-1899 (5%); 1900 - (93%).

Classification System: DMA (modified).
Collections not Cataloged.
Depository for: DMA; NOS; USGS (Topo.).
Serves: students; faculty; employees; public. Mon.–Fri. 9 a.m.–4 p.m. (Seats 15; 350 readers served per month).
Interlibrary Loan Available.
Reproduction Facility: photocopy; quickcopy.

Shrewsbury

423. MONMOUTH COUNTY LIBRARY
Eastern Branch
State Highway 35
Shrewsbury, NJ 07701
Telephone: 201/842-5995.
Contact Person: Mrs. E. Dawn Burke, Reference Libn.
Area Specialization: New England; Middle Atlantic States.
Subject Specialization: topography; hydrography.
Collections not Cataloged.
Depository for: USGS (Topo.).
Serves: public. Mon.–Thurs. 9 a.m.–9 p.m., Fri. 9 a.m.–5 p.m.; Sat. 9 a.m.–5 p.m.
Reproduction Facility: photocopy.

Trenton

424. NEW JERSEY DEPARTMENT OF STATE
Division of Archives and Records Management
Archives Section
185 W. State Street CN307
Trenton, NJ 08625
Telephone: 609/292-6260.
Contact Person: Karl Niederer, Supervising Archivist.
Size: 2,000 maps; 200 aerial photographs.
Area Specialization: New Jersey.
Special Cartographic Collections: Manuscript Collection—Department of Environmental Protection: Morris Canal and Banking Company—Over 500 maps and drawings of the Morris Canal; N.J. Geological Survey Maps—154 maps 1880s–1950s; N.J. Department of State—Railroad, Turnpike and Canal Maps—800 maps.
Dates: pre-1800 (15%); 1800-1899 (70%); 1900 - (15%).
Classification System: local system.
Collections Cataloged.
Depository for: NJGS & manuscript maps.
Serves: students; faculty; employees; public. Mon.–Fri. 8:30 a.m.–4:30 p.m.; Sat. 9 a.m.–5 p.m. (Seats 25; 300 readers served per month).
Reproduction Facility: photocopy; Will send materials to photograph company for reproduction.

425. NEW JERSEY GEOLOGICAL SURVEY
Trenton, NJ 08625
Established 1865.
Telephone: 609/292-2576.
Contact Person: William P. Graff, Cartographer.
Staff: 1 professional (part time).
Size: 2,000 maps; 25 atlases; 4,000 aerial photographs.
Annual Accessions: 50 maps.
Area Specialization: New Jersey.
Subject Specialization: geology; topography.
Special Cartographic Collections: New Jersey Topographic Atlas sheet series.
Dates: 1800-1899 (30%); 1900 - (70%).
Classification System: local system.
Collections Cataloged. (50%).
Depository for: NOS; USGS (Topo.).
Serves: public. Mon.–Fri. 8 a.m.–4:30 p.m. (Seats 2; 5 readers served per month).
Reproduction Facility: photocopy.

426. TRENTON STATE COLLEGE
Geography Department
Map Library
Trenton, NJ 08625
Established 1947.
Telephone: 609/771-2415.
Contact Person: John F. Fox, Professor.
Staff: 1 professional (part time).
Size: 10,000 maps; 14 atlases; 12 globes; 20 relief models; 100 aerial photographs; 50 reference books and gazetteers.
Annual Accessions: 500 maps; 5 relief models; 10 aerial photographs; 10 reference books and gazetteers.
Area Specialization: United States.
Subject Specialization: topography.
Dates: 1900 - (100%).
Depository for: DMA.
Serves: students; faculty; public.

NEW MEXICO

Albuquerque

427. ALBUQUERQUE PUBLIC LIBRARY
Special Collections
423 Central N.E.
Albuquerque, NM 87102
Telephone: 505/766-5009.
Contact Person: Laurel E. Drew, Special Collections Libn.
Staff: 1 professional (part time).
Size: 500 maps; 50 atlases; 40 reference books and gazetteers.
Area Specialization: Albuquerque; New Mexico.
Subject Specialization: genealogy; local history.
Dates: 1800-1899 (1%); 1900 - (98%).
Collections not Cataloged.
Serves: public. Tues. and Thurs., 12:30–8 p.m.; Wed., Fri. 9:30 a.m.–5:30 p.m.; Sat. 9:30 a.m.–5:30 p.m. (Seats 100; 400 readers served per month).
Reproduction Facility: photocopy; microform.

428. U.S. GEOLOGICAL SURVEY
Water Resources Division
505 Marquette NW, Rm 720
Albuquerque, NM 87102
Telephone: 505/766-1284.
Contact Person: Rise Pappas, Libn.
Staff: 1 professional (part time); 1 non-professional (part time).
Size: 6,000 maps; 75 serials (titles received).
Area Specialization: New Mexico.
Subject Specialization: hydrography.
Dates: 1800-1899 (5%); 1900 - (95%).
Collections not Cataloged.
Depository for: USGS (Geol., topo.).
Serves: employees; public. Mon.–Thurs. 8:30 a.m.–5 p.m. (Seats 4; 400 readers served per month).

429. UNIVERSITY OF NEW MEXICO
Department of Geology
Northrop Hall
Albuquerque, NM 87131
Telephone: 505/277-4204.
Contact Person: Dr. Stephen G. Wells, Associate Professor of Geology.
Staff: 1 non-professional (part time).
Size: 5,000 maps; 10,000 aerial photographs.
Annual Accessions: 50–100 maps.

Area Specialization: New Mexico; Southwest United States.
Subject Specialization: topography; geology.
Dates: pre-1800 (4%); 1800-1899 (5–7%); 1900 - (90%).
Collections Cataloged. (10%).
Depository for: USGS (Geol.).
Serves: students; faculty; public.

430. UNIVERSITY OF NEW MEXICO
Zimmerman Library
Government Publications and Maps Department
Albuquerque, NM 87131
Established 1975.
Telephone: 505/277-4567.
Contact Person: Heather Rex, Map Specialist.
Staff: 1 non-professional (full time); 2 (students) non-professional (part time).
Size: 107,000 maps; 800 atlases; 3 globes; 40 relief models; 6,800 aerial photographs; 600 reference books and gazetteers; 10 serials (titles received); 1 microforms (no. of titles).
Annual Accessions: 5,000 maps; 130 atlases; 500 aerial photographs; 80 serials (titles received); 150 (fiche) microforms (no. of titles).
Area Specialization: New Mexico; southwestern United States.
Subject Specialization: topography; geology; forestry; land use.
Special Cartographic Collections: Sanborn Fire Insurance Maps (1,000) of many New Mexico towns; New Mexico Road Maps from 1910.
Dates: 1800-1899 (1%); 1900 - (99%).
Classification System: LC.
Collections not Cataloged.
Depository for: DMA; NOS; USGS (Geol., topo.); NM Bureau of Mines and Mineral Resources; United States Forest Service;. United States Bureau of Land Managment
Serves: students; faculty; employees; public. Mon.–Fri. 8:30 a.m.–4 p.m. (Seats 18; 200 readers served per month).
Interlibrary Loan Available.
Reproduction Facility: photocopy.
Publications: "Selected Map Room Acquisitions" (section of monthly *Government Publications Newsltter*); "Introduction to the Map Room", brochure.

Las Cruces

431. NEW MEXICO STATE UNIVERSITY
Library
Special collections
Las Cruces, NM 88001
Telephone: 505/646-3238.
Contact Person: Christine Myers, Special Collections Libn.
Staff: 1 professional (part time); 1 non-professional (part time).
Size: 40,000 maps; 200 atlases; 2 globes; 100 reference books and gazetteers.
Area Specialization: New Mexico.
Subject Specialization: geology; topography.
Depository for: DMA; USGS (Geol., topo.).
Serves: students; faculty; public.
Reproduction Facility: quickcopy.

Las Vegas

432. NEW MEXICO HIGHLANDS UNIVERSITY
Donnelly Library
Las Vegas, NM 87701
Telephone: 505/425-7511, ext. 404.
Contact Person: Karen Jaggers, Associate Libn.

Staff: 1 professional (full time); 1 non-professional (full time); 1 non-professional (part time).
Size: 11,700 maps; 171 atlases; 1 globes; 12 relief models; 118 aerial photographs; 33 reference books and gazetteers.
Annual Accessions: 1,400 maps.
Area Specialization: Western United States; New Mexico and adjoining states.
Dates: 1800-1899 (1%); 1900 - (99%).
Collections not Cataloged.
Depository for: USGS (Geol., topo.).
Serves: students; faculty; employees; public. Mon.–Thurs. 8 a.m.–10 p.m., Fri. 8 a.m.–11 p.m.; Sat. 8 a.m.–5 p.m.; Sun. 2–10 p.m. (Seats 30; 40 readers served per month).
Reproduction Facility: photocopy.

Portales

433. EASTERN NEW MEXICO UNIVERSITY
Golden Library
Map Division
Portales, NM 88130
Telephone: 505/562-2624.
Contact Person: E. A. Richter, Ref. Libn.; Laura H. McGuire, Docs. Libn.; Mary Lee Morris, Cataloger.
Staff: 3 professional (part time); 2 non-professional (part time).
Size: 6,655 maps; 195 atlases; 1 globes; 78 relief models; 10 aerial photographs; 185 reference books and gazetteers.
Annual Accessions: 100 maps; 5–10 atlases; 5 relief models; 10 reference books and gazetteers.
Area Specialization: New Mexico.
Dates: pre-1800 (1%); 1800-1899 (1%); 1900 - (98%).
Classification System: LC; Superintendent of Documents.
Collections Cataloged. (35%).
Depository for: DMA; GPO.
Serves: students; faculty; employees; public;. Mon.–Fri. 7:30 a.m.–11:30 p.m.; Sat. 10 a.m.–5 p.m.; Sun. 2–11:30 p.m. (Seats 35; not available readers served per month).
Interlibrary Loan Available.
Reproduction Facility: photocopy.

Santa Fe

434. MUSEUM OF NEW MEXICO
History Library
P.O. Box 2087
Santa Fe, NM 87503
Established 1885.
Telephone: 505/827-6474.
Contact Person: Stephany Eger, Libn.
Staff: 1 professional (full time).
Size: 3,000 maps.
Annual Accessions: 50 maps.
Area Specialization: New Mexico; southwestern United States.
Subject Specialization: Spanish colonial maps.
Dates: pre-1800 (30%); 1800-1899 (30%); 1900 - (40%).
Classification System: Dewey (modified).
Collections Cataloged. Tues.–Fri. 9 a.m.–12 noon, 1–5 p.m.; Sat. 9 a.m.–12 noon. (Seats 20; 100 readers served per month).
Reproduction Facility: photocopy.

435. NEW MEXICO STATE LIBRARY
325 Don Gaspar
Santa Fe, NM 85703
Contact Person: Michael Miller, Southwest Libn.
Staff: 1 professional (full time); 1 non-professional (full time).

Size: 500 maps; 15 atlases; 10 reference books and gazetteers.
Area Specialization: New Mexico.
Subject Specialization: arts; natural resources.
Collections not Cataloged.
Depository for: USGS (Topo.); GPO.
Serves: employees; public. Mon.–Fri. 8 a.m.–5 p.m. (Seats 15; 6 readers served per month).
Reproduction Facility: quickcopy; microform.

Socorro

436. NEW MEXICO INSTITUTE OF MINING AND TECHNOLOGY
Martin Speare Memorial Library
Socorro, NM 87801
Telephone: 505/835-5614.
Contact Person: Betty Reynolds, Director.
Staff: 2 non-professional (full time).
Size: 5,079 maps; 80 atlases; 20 reference books and gazetteers.
Serves: public. Mon.–Thurs. 8 a.m.–5 p.m.; Sat. 10 a.m.–5 p.m.; Sun. 10 a.m.–11 p.m.
Reproduction Facility: photocopy.

Taos

437. KIT CARSON MEMORIAL FOUNDATION, INC.
Historical Research Library and Archives
P.O. Drawer B
Taos, NM 87571
Established 1952.
Telephone: 505/758-4741.
Contact Person: Jack K. Boyer, Director.
Staff: 1 non-professional (full time).
Size: 430 maps; 10 atlases; 2 relief models; 20 aerial photographs; 10 reference books and gazetteers.
Annual Accessions: 15 maps.
Area Specialization: western United States.
Subject Specialization: early military; fur trade; southwest trails.
Dates: pre-1800 (25%); 1800-1899 (50%); 1900 - (25%).
Classification System: local system.
Collections Cataloged.
Serves: employees; public. Mon.–Fri. 8 a.m.–5 p.m. (Seats 2).

NEW YORK

Albany

438. NEW YORK STATE DEPARTMENT OF TRANSPORTATION
Map Information Unit
State Campus, Bldg. 4, Room 105
Albany, NY 12232
Established 1969.
Telephone: 518/457-3555.
Contact Person: Paul G. Hein, Senior Cartographer.
Staff: 3 professional (full time); 1 non-professional (full time).
Size: 7,000 maps; 100,000 aerial photographs.
Annual Accessions: 200 maps.
Area Specialization: New York State.

Special Cartographic Collections: 1:24,000 scale planimetric, general base and topographic maps of New York State.
Dates: 1800-1899 (1%); 1900 - (99%).
Classification System: Alphabetical by quadrangle names.
Collections Cataloged. (50%).
Depository for: NOS; USGS (Topo.).
Serves: students; faculty; employees; public;. Mon.–Fri. 8:30 a.m.–4:30 p.m. (Seats 5; 350 readers served per month).

439. NEW YORK STATE LIBRARY
Manuscripts and Special Collections
Cultural Education Center, Empire State Plaza
Albany, NY 12230
Established 1818.
Telephone: 518/474-6282.
Contact Person: James Corsaro, Senior Libn.
Staff: 4 professional (part time); 2 non-professional (part time).
Size: 175,000 maps; 1,000 atlases; 3 globes; 60 relief models; 50 aerial photographs; 600 reference books and gazetteers; 1–5 serials (titles received); USGS topos. only microforms (no. of titles).
Annual Accessions: ca. 2,000 maps; ca. 50 atlases; 30 reference books and gazetteers; 1–2 serials (titles received).
Area Specialization: New York State; northeastern United States; United States; North America; World.
Subject Specialization: history; cadastral maps; and geology of New York State.
Special Cartographic Collections: James Hall Papers Map Collection (historical geology); Cherry Hill Map Collection (Capital District region).
Dates: pre-1800 (2%); 1800-1899 (20%); 1900 - (78%).
Classification System: Dewey.
Collections Cataloged.
Depository for: DMA; DOS (Gt. Brit); NOS; USGS (Geol., topo.).
Serves: students; faculty; employees; public. Mon.–Fri. 9 a.m.–5 p.m. (Seats ca. 15 for maps and atlases).
Reproduction Facility: photocopy; microform; Photostat.

440. STATE UNIVERSITY OF NEW YORK AT ALBANY
University Library—Government Publications
1400 Washington Avenue
Albany, NY 12222
Established 1974.
Telephone: 518/457-8564.
Contact Person: Tae M. Lee, U.S. Documents Specialist.
Staff: 2 professional (part time); 1 non-professional (part time).
Size: 18,000 maps; 250 atlases; 125 reference books and gazetteers.
Annual Accessions: 200 maps; 10 atlases; 15 reference books and gazetteers.
Area Specialization: United States.
Dates: 1800-1899 (5%); 1900 - (95%).
Classification System: LC; alphabetical arrangement.
Collections Cataloged. (10%).
Depository for: USGS (Geol., topo.).
Serves: students; faculty; employees; public. Mon.–Fri. 9 a.m.–10 p.m.; Sat. 9 a.m.–6 p.m.; Sun. 12 noon–10 p.m. (Seats 8).

Alfred

441. ALFRED UNIVERSITY
Department of Geology
Alfred, NY 14802
Established 1968.
Telephone: 607/871-2203.

Contact Person: Dr. R. Laurence Davis, Assoc. Professor of Geology.
Staff: 1 non-professional (part time).
Size: 5,000 maps; 3,000 serials (titles received).
Annual Accessions: 100 maps; 100 serials (titles received).
Area Specialization: New York; northeast United States.
Subject Specialization: geology.
Dates: 1900 - (100).
Classification System: local system.
Collections Cataloged.
Depository for: USGS (Geol., topo.).
Serves: students; faculty; employees; public. on request. (Seats 3; 10 readers served per month).
Interlibrary Loan Available.
Reproduction Facility: photocopy.

Amherst

442. STATE UNIVERSITY OF NEW YORK AT BUFFALO
Science and Engineering Library
University Libraries Map Collection
Capen Hall
Amherst, NY 14260
Established 1978.
Telephone: 716/636-2946.
Contact Person: Ernest L. Woodson, Maps/Geology Libn.
Staff: 1 professional (part time); 1 non-professional (part time).
Size: 160,000 maps; 1,000 atlases; 25 relief models; 5,000 aerial photographs; 200 reference books and gazetteers.
Annual Accessions: 6,400 maps; 10 atlases; 1 relief models; 600 aerial photographs; 10 reference books and gazetteers.
Area Specialization: New York State.
Subject Specialization: topography; glaciology; political geography; computer mapping.
Special Cartographic Collections: topographic maps of New York State at all scales.
Dates: 1800-1899 (2%); 1900 - (98%).
Classification System: LC.
Collections Cataloged. (5% (est.)).
Depository for: DMA; NOS; NTS (Canada); USGS (Geol., topo.).
Serves: students; faculty; employees; public. Mon.–Thurs. 8 a.m.–11:45 p.m., Fri. 8 a.m.–9 p.m.; Sat. 9 a.m.–9 p.m.; Sun. 12 noon–10 p.m. (Seats 52; 500 readers served per month).
Interlibrary Loan Available.
Reproduction Facility: photocopy; microform.
Publications: *Maps; University Libraries Map Collection;* (brochure) *How to locate maps, charts, remote-sensing imagery, and atlases in Map Room* (guide).

Binghamton

443. STATE UNIVERSITY OF NEW YORK AT BINGHAMTON
Science Library
Map Room
Vestal Parkway
Binghamton, NY 13901
Established 1973.
Telephone: 607/798-2219.
Contact Person: Robin Petrus, Map Libn.
Staff: 1 professional (part time); 2 non-professional (part time).
Size: 76,500 maps; 700 atlases; 5 globes; 2,000 aerial photographs; 100 reference books and gazetteers.
Annual Accessions: 4,200 maps; 10 atlases; 1 aerial photographs.
Area Specialization: United States.

Subject Specialization: geology.
Dates: 1800-1899 (1%); 1900 - (99%).
Classification System: AGS.
Collections Cataloged. (20%).
Depository for: DMA; NOS; USGS (Geol., topo.).
Serves: students; faculty; public. Mon.–Fri. 8:30 a.m.–12 midnight; Sat. 10 a.m.–6 p.m.; Sun. 2 p.m.–12 midnight. (Seats 15; 200 readers served per month).
Interlibrary Loan Available.
Reproduction Facility: photocopy.
Publications: *Map Room Resources* (guide).

Blue Mt. Lake

444. ADIRONDACK MUSEUM LIBRARY
Blue Mt. Lake, NY 12812
Established 1956.
Telephone: 518/352-7311.
Contact Person: Jerold Pepper, Libn.
Staff: 1 professional (full time).
Size: 1,200 maps; 70 atlases; 25 reference books and gazetteers.
Annual Accessions: 50 maps; 5 atlases; 3 reference books and gazetteers.
Area Specialization: northern New York State.
Subject Specialization: Adirondack Park.
Dates: pre-1800 (15%); 1800-1899 (35%); 1900 - (50%).
Classification System: .
Collections Cataloged. (95%).
Serves: students; faculty; employees; public. Mon.–Fri. 9 a.m.–5 p.m. (by appointment). (Seats 2; 20 readers served per month).
Interlibrary Loan Available.
Reproduction Facility: photocopy.

Brooklyn

445. BROOKLYN COLLEGE, CUNY
Geology Department
Map Room
Bedford Ave. & Ave. H
Brooklyn, NY 11210
Established 1957.
Telephone: 212/780-5415.
Contact Person: John Cashman, College Lab Technician.
Staff: 1 professional (full time).
Size: 1,000 maps; 50 aerial photographs.
Annual Accessions: 50 maps; 10 aerial photographs.
Area Specialization: New York, New Jersey, Massachusetts, Vermont, Pennsylvania.
Subject Specialization: topography; geology; hydrology.
Dates: 1900 - (100).
Classification System: local system.
Collections Cataloged.
Depository for: USGS (Geol., topo.).
Serves: students; faculty; employees; public. Mon.–Fri. 9 a.m.–5 p.m. (Seats 25; 20 readers served per month).
Reproduction Facility: photocopy; quickcopy.

446. BROOKLYN HISTORICAL SOCIETY
128 Pierrepont Street
Brooklyn, NY 11201
Telephone: 718/MA4-0890.
Contact Person: Lucinda Manning, Head Libn.
Staff: 3 professional (full time); 6 non-professional (part time).
Size: 750 maps and atlases maps.
Area Specialization: Long Island; Brooklyn; New York City; Kings County.

Subject Specialization: local history; genealogy.
Classification System: local system.
Collections Cataloged. (Indexed).
Serves: public. Tues.–Fri. 9 a.m.–5 p.m.; Sat. 9 a.m.–5 p.m. (Seats 50; 1,835 per year readers served per month).
Reproduction Facility: quickcopy.

447. BROOKLYN PUBLIC LIBRARY
History Division
Map Collection
Grand Army Plaza
Brooklyn, NY 11238
Established 1961.
Telephone: 212/780-7794.
Contact Person: Mr. Tsugio Yoshinaga, Map Libn.
Staff: 1 professional (part time); 1 non-professional (part time).
Size: 80,000 maps; 850 atlases; 1 globes; 12 relief models; 35 aerial photographs; 800 reference books and gazetteers; 30 serials (titles received).
Annual Accessions: 2,000 maps; 10 atlases; 25 reference books and gazetteers.
Area Specialization: Brooklyn; New York State.
Subject Specialization: local history.
Dates: 1900 - (95%).
Classification System: AGS.
Collections Cataloged. (50%).
Depository for: DMA; USGS (Topo.).
Serves: students; faculty; employees; public. Mon.–Thurs. 9 a.m.–8 p.m.; Fri. 10 a.m.–6 p.m.; Sat. 10 a.m.–6 p.m.; Sun. 1 p.m.–5 p.m. (Seats 90; 65 readers served per month).
Reproduction Facility: photocopy.

Buffalo

448. BUFFALO AND ERIE COUNTY HISTORICAL SOCIETY
25 Nottingham Court
Buffalo, NY 14216
Established 1862.
Telephone: 716/873-9644.
Contact Person: Dr. Herman Sass, Senior Libn.
Staff: 1 professional (full time); 2 professional (part time).
Size: 1,000 maps; 100 atlases; 50 aerial photographs.
Area Specialization: Buffalo and surrounding areas.
Dates: 1800-1899 (100%).
Classification System: Dewey; local system.
Collections Cataloged.
Serves: public. Wed., Thur., Fri. 10 a.m.–5 p.m.; Sat. 12 noon–5 p.m. (Seats 15; 300 readers served per month).
Reproduction Facility: photographic.
Publications: Card catalog.

449. BUFFALO AND ERIE COUNTY PUBLIC LIBRARY
Lafayette Square
Buffalo, NY 14222
Established 1870's.
Telephone: 716/856-7525, ext. 256.
Contact Person: Catherine Mishler, Libn.
Staff: 1 professional (part time).
Size: 80,000 maps; 800 atlases; 1 globes; 10 relief models; 150 reference books and gazetteers; 15 serials (titles received).
Annual Accessions: 2–3,000 maps; 30 atlases; 12 reference books and gazetteers.
Area Specialization: Buffalo; Erie County; western New York State.
Subject Specialization: history; map reading and interpretation.
Dates: pre-1800 (15%); 1800-1899 (35%); 1900 - (50%).
Classification System: Boggs-Lewis; DMA.
Collections Cataloged. (75%).

Depository for: DMA; USGS (Geol., topo.); U.S. GPO.
Serves: public. Mon. and Thurs. 9 a.m.–9 p.m., Tues., Wed.
Fri. 9 a.m.–6 p.m.; Sat. 9 a.m.–6 p.m. (Seats 78).
Reproduction Facility: photocopy.

Clinton

450. HAMILTON COLLEGE
Department of Geology
Clinton, NY 13323
Established 1930.
Telephone: 315/859-7212.
Contact Person: Donald B. Potter, Chairman, Geology
Department.
Staff: 3 non-professional (part time).
Area Specialization: United States.
Subject Specialization: topography; geology.
Collections not Cataloged.
Depository for: USGS (Geol., topo.).
Serves: students; faculty; employees; public. Mon.–Fri. 8:30
a.m.–5 p.m. (Seats 10; 30 readers served per month).

Geneseo

451. STATE UNIVERSITY OF NEW YORK COLLEGE AT GENESEO
Milne Library
Map Collection
Geneseo, NY 14454
Established 1968.
Telephone: 716/245-5595.
Contact Person: Polly Stapley, Assistant Reference Libn.
Staff: 1 professional (part time); 1 non-professional (part
time).
Size: 4,000 maps; 250 est. atlases; 30 est. reference books
and gazetteers.
Annual Accessions: ca. 200 maps; 5 est. atlases; 5 est.
reference books and gazetteers.
Area Specialization: New York State; Genesee Valley
region.
Subject Specialization: local history.
Dates: 1800-1899 (.3%); 1900 - (99.7%).
Classification System: local system.
Collections Cataloged. (approx. 50%).
Depository for: USGS (Topo.).
Serves: students; faculty; employees; public. Mon.–Thurs. 8
a.m.–11 p.m.; Fri. 8 a.m.–10 p.m. Hours vary when classes
are not in session. Sat. 9 a.m.–9 p.m.; Sun. 12 noon–11
p.m. (30 readers served per month).
Reproduction Facility: quickcopy.

Geneva

452. HOBART AND WILLIAM SMITH COLLEGES
Demarest Library
Geneva, NY 14456
Telephone: 315/789-5500, ext. 349.
Contact Person: Gary Thompson, Head, Public Services.
Staff: 2 (each devotes approx. 5% of his time) professional
(part time).
Size: 5,498 maps; 141 atlases; 10 relief models; 150
reference books and gazetteers; 4 serials (titles received).
Annual Accessions: 300 maps; 20 atlases.
Area Specialization: New York State; Pennsylvania.
Subject Specialization: geology.
Dates: 1900 - (95%).
Classification System: LC.
Collections Cataloged.

Depository for: USGS (Geol., topo.).
Serves: students; faculty; employees; public. Mon.–Fri. 8:30
a.m.–10 p.m.; Sat. 8:30 a.m.–10 p.m.; Sun. 10 a.m.–11:30
p.m.
Reproduction Facility: quickcopy.

Hamilton

453. COLGATE UNIVERSITY
Everett Case Library
Hamilton, NY 13346
Telephone: 315/824-1000, ext. 304.
Contact Person: Frank Dugan, Documents Libn.
Staff: 1 professional (part time).
Size: 30,000 maps; 100 atlases; 1 globes; 3 relief models;
200 reference books and gazetteers; 30 serials (titles
received).
Area Specialization: New York State; Asia; China.
Subject Specialization: Geology.
Special Cartographic Collections: Early New York State
county atlases.
Dates: 1800-1899 (.5%); 1900 - (99.5%).
Classification System: local system.
Collections not Cataloged.
Depository for: DMA; USGS (Geol., topo.).
Serves: students; faculty; employees; public. Mon.–Fri. 8.m.–
12 midnight; Fri. 8 a.m.–11 p.m.; Sat. 10 a.m.–11 p.m.; Sun.
12 noon–12 midnight. (Seats 50).
Reproduction Facility: quickcopy.

Hempstead

454. HOFSTRA UNIVERSITY
Library
Documents and Map Collections
Hempstead, NY 11550
Established 1969.
Telephone: 516/560-5972.
Contact Person: Vincent Jennings, Associate Professor of
Library Services (Documents.
Staff: 1 professional (part time); 2 non-professional (part
time).
Size: 50,000 maps; 1 serials (titles received).
Annual Accessions: 2,000 maps.
Area Specialization: United States.
Subject Specialization: topography.
Dates: 1900 - (100%).
Collections not Cataloged.
Depository for: USGS (Topo.).
Serves: students; faculty; employees; public. Mon.–Tues. 9
a.m.–9 p.m.; Wed.–Fri. 9 a.m.–5 p.m.; Sat. 12–5 p.m.; Sun.
12–5 p.m. (Seats 2; 20 readers served per month).
Reproduction Facility: photocopy.

Ithaca

455. CORNELL UNIVERSITY
College of Agriculture and Life Services
Resource Information Laboratory
Ithaca, NY 14853
Telephone: 607/256-6520.
Contact Person: Eugenia M. Barnaba, Manager.
Staff: 5 professional (full time).
Size: 10,000 maps; 70,000 aerial photographs.
Area Specialization: New York State.
Subject Specialization: land use; agriculture; natural
resources, and community development.
Dates: 1900 - (100%).

Classification System: local system.
Collections Cataloged.
Depository for: N.Y. State Dept. of Agriculture and Markets; N.Y. State Dept. of Commerce; U.S. Dept of Interior, Fish and Wildlife Service
Serves: students; faculty; employees; public.
Reproduction Facility: diazo.

456. CORNELL UNIVERSITY
John M. Olin Library
Department of Maps, Microtexts, Newspapers
Ithaca, NY 14853
Established 1949.
Telephone: 607/256-5258.
Contact Person: Barbara Berthelsen, Map Libn.
Staff: 1 professional (full time); 3 (2 students) non-professional (part time).
Size: 153,360 maps; 2,600 atlases; 10 globes; 25 relief models; 927 reference books and gazetteers; 4 serials (titles received); 3 microforms (no. of titles).
Annual Accessions: ±5,000 maps; ±100 atlases; 1 globes; 1 relief models; ±100 reference books and gazetteers.
Area Specialization: Southeast Asia; New York State; world.
Subject Specialization: comprehensive.
Special Cartographic Collections: Hartmann Collection (S.E. Asia with emphasis on Vietnam); Wason (China, East Asia); Echols (Southeast Asia); Jared Sparks (American Revolution).
Dates: pre-1800 (0.5%); 1800-1899 (1%); 1900 - (98.5%).
Classification System: LC.
Collections Cataloged. (90%).
Depository for: DMA; GSC; USGS (Geol., topo.).
Serves: students; faculty; employees; public. Mon.–Thurs. 8 a.m.–10 p.m.; Fri. 8 a.m.–6 p.m.; Sat. 9 a.m.–6 p.m.; Sun. 1 p.m.–10 p.m. (Seats 38; 135 readers served per month).
Interlibrary Loan Available. (On a case by case basis)
Reproduction Facility: photocopy; quickcopy.

457. CORNELL UNIVERSITY
Remote Sensing Program
Ithaca, NY 14853
Telephone: 607/256-4330.
Contact Person: Warren R. Philipson, Associate Prof.
Size: 600,000 aerial photographs.
Area Specialization: Northeastern United States.
Collections not Cataloged.
Serves: students; faculty; employees; public. Mon.–Fri. 9 a.m.–4 p.m.

458. DEWITT HISTORICAL SOCIETY
116 North Cayuga Street
Ithaca, NY 14850
Telephone: 607/273-8284.
Contact Person: Amy Humber, Archivist.
Staff: 1 professional (part time).
Size: 250 maps; 15 atlases.
Area Specialization: Tompkins County; Ithaca.
Subject Specialization: local history; genealogy.
Classification System: local system.
Collections Cataloged.
Serves: public. Tues–Fri. 12:30–5 p.m.; Sat. 12:30–5 p.m. (Seats 6; 100 readers served per month).
Reproduction Facility: photocopy.

Jamaica

459. QUEENS BOROUGH PUBLIC LIBRARY
History, Travel and Biography Division
89-11 Merrick Blvd.
Jamaica, NY 11432
Established 1970.
Telephone: 212/990-0762.
Contact Person: Deborah Hammur, Head, Supervising Libn.
Staff: 5 professional (full time); 3 non-professional (full time).
Size: 6,000 maps; 255 atlases; 1 globes; 30 relief models; 200 reference books and gazetteers; 6 serials (titles received).
Area Specialization: World; United States; New York State; New York City.
Subject Specialization: history; travel; cities.
Dates: pre-1800 (15%); 1800-1899 (20%); 1900 - (65%).
Classification System: Modified DDC, alphanumeric arrangement.
Collections Cataloged. (50%).
Depository for: USGS (Topo.).
Serves: public. Mon.–Fri. 10 a.m.–8:45 p.m.; Sat. 10 a.m.–5:15 p.m. (Seats 92; 90 readers served per month).
Reproduction Facility: photocopy.

460. QUEENS BOROUGH PUBLIC LIBRARY
Long Island Division
89-11 Merrick Boulevard
Jamaica, NY 11432
Telephone: 212/990-0770.
Contact Person: Nicholas Falco, Head.
Size: 5,400 maps; 135 atlases; 175 aerial photographs; 30 reference books and gazetteers.
Area Specialization: Long Island.
Subject Specialization: history; topography; real estate; surveys.
Dates: pre-1800 (5%); 1800-1899 (40%); 1900 - (45%).
Classification System: local system (geographical and chronological arrangement).
Collections Cataloged. (60%).
Serves: public. Mon. and Fri., 10 a.m.–9 p.m.; Tues.–Thurs. 10 a.m.–6 p.m.; Sat. 10 a.m.–5:30 p.m. (Seats 24; 125 readers served per month).
Reproduction Facility: quickcopy.

New York

461. AMERICAN ALPINE CLUB
113 East 90th Street
New York, NY 10128
Contact Person: Patricia Fletcher, Libn.
Staff: 1 professional (part time).
Size: 1,200 maps; 25 atlases; 10 relief models; 5 reference books and gazetteers; 100 serials (titles received).
Area Specialization: alpine and polar regions.
Subject Specialization: mountains; mountaineering.
Dates: 1800-1899 (40%); 1900 - (60%).
Classification System: local system.
Collections Cataloged. (100%).
Serves: public. Mon.–Fri. 10 a.m.–4 p.m. (Seats 6; 100 readers served per month).
Reproduction Facility: quickcopy.
Publications: *American Alpine Journal* (annual since 1929); *Accidents in N.A. mountaineering* (annual since 1951); Quarterly newsletter for members.

462. CITY COLLEGE OF NEW YORK
Dept. of Earth and Planetary Sciences
137th Street and Convent Avenue
New York, NY 10031
Established ca. 1928.
Telephone: 212/690-6984.
Contact Person: Dr. Simon Schaffel, Professor-Deputy
Chairman.
Staff: 1-2 professional (part time); 3-4 non-professional (part
time).
Size: 10,000 maps; 500 atlases; 10 globes; 50 relief
models; 2,500 aerial photographs.
Annual Accessions: 100 maps; 15 atlases; 25 aerial
photographs.
Area Specialization: United States; New York; New Jersey;
Pennsylvania; New England.
Subject Specialization: geology.
Dates: 1800-1899 (10%); 1900 - (90%).
Classification System: local system.
Collections Cataloged.
Collections not Cataloged. (100%).
Serves: students; faculty; employees; public;. Mon.–Fri. 12
a.m.–5 p.m.
Interlibrary Loan Available.
Reproduction Facility: photocopy; quickcopy.

463. COLUMBIA UNIVERSITY
Lehman Library
Map Room, Room 213
420
New York, NY 10027
Telephone: 212/280-5002.
Contact Person: Brian May, Documents Libn.
Staff: 1-2 non-professional (part time).
Size: 180,000 maps; 400 atlases; 6 globes; 100 relief
models; 200 reference books and gazetteers.
Annual Accessions: 2,600 maps.
Dates: 1900 - (95%).
Classification System: LC (books); local system.
Collections Cataloged. ((books)).
Depository for: DMA; NTS (Canada); USGS (Geol., topo.).
Serves: students; faculty; employees; public. Mon.–Thurs. 9
a.m.–7 p.m.; Fri. 9 a.m.–5 p.m.; Sat. 12 Noon–5 p.m.; Sun.
12 Noon–5 p.m. (Seats 6; 125 readers served per month).
Reproduction Facility: quickcopy; Light table.

464. ENGINEERING SOCIETIES LIBRARY
345 East 47th St.
New York, NY 10017
Established 1913.
Telephone: 212/705-7611.
Contact Person: S. K. Cabeen, Director.
Staff: 13 professional (full time); 27 non-professional (full
time).
Size: 12,548 maps; 25 atlases.
Annual Accessions: 100 maps.
Subject Specialization: geology; mining.
Dates: pre-1800 (5%); 1800-1899 (25%); 1900 - (70%).
Classification System: UDC.
Collections Cataloged.
Serves: public. Mon.–Thurs. 9 a.m.–7 p.m.; Fri. (and during
the summer) 9 a.m.–5 p.m. (Seats 55).
Reproduction Facility: photocopy; quickcopy; microform.

465. EXPLORERS CLUB
James B. Ford Library
Edmund Hillary Map Room
46 East 70 Street
New York, NY 10024
Telephone: 212/628-8383.
Contact Person: Janet Baldwin, Chairman, Library
Committee.

Size: ca. 5,000 maps; 50 atlases; 50 serials (titles
received).
Annual Accessions: 200 maps.
Dates: 1900 - (95%).
Collections not Cataloged.
Serves: public; members. By appointment only. (Seats 4-5).
Interlibrary Loan Available.
Reproduction Facility: quickcopy; microform;.

466. HISPANIC SOCIETY OF AMERICA
613 West 155th Street
New York, NY 10032
Telephone: 212/926-2234.
Contact Person: Lydia A. Dufour, Associate Curator of
Iconography.
Size: 2,000 maps; 12 atlases; 30 globes.
Area Specialization: Spain; Portugal.
Dates: pre-1800 (45%).
Collections Cataloged.
Serves: public. Tues.–Fri. 1–4:30 p.m.; Sat. 10:30 a.m.–4:30
p.m.
Publications: *Portolan charts.. descriptive list of those
belonging to the Hispanic Society of American (New York,
1911); Facsimiles of Portolan charts belonging to the
Hispanic Society of America* (New York, 1916).

467. NEW YORK HISTORICAL SOCIETY
Library
170 Central Park West
New York, NY 10024
Established 1804.
Telephone: 212/873-3400.
Contact Person: Larry E. Sullivan, Libn.
Size: 30,000 maps; 2,000 atlases; 5 globes; 1,000
reference books and gazetteers.
Area Specialization: New York City; New York State; pre-
1800 North America.
Subject Specialization: Revolutionary War; New York City
insurance and real estate atlases.
Special Cartographic Collections: Erskine-DeWitt
manuscripts of the American Revolutionary War period.
Dates: pre-1800 (30%); 1800-1899 (60%); 1900 - (10%).
Classification System: Local system (LC modified).
Serves: public. Tues.–Fri. 10 a.m.–5 p.m.; Sat. 10 a.m.–5
p.m. (Seats 40).
Reproduction Facility: microform.
Publications: Larry E. Sullivan, "The Cartographic
Resources of the New York Historical Society," *The Map
Collector* (Forthcoming).

468. NEW YORK PUBLIC LIBRARY
Map Division
Fifth Avenue and 42nd Street
New York, NY 10018
Established 1898.
Telephone: 212/930-0588.
Contact Person: Alice C. Hudson, Chief.
Staff: 4 professional (full time); 2 non-professional (part
time).
Size: 350,000 maps; 10,700 atlases; 6 globes; 30 relief
models; 88 aerial photographs; 3,300 reference books and
gazetteers; 25 serials (titles received).
Annual Accessions: 3,500 maps; 100 atlases; 5 aerial
photographs; 60 reference books and gazetteers; 2 serials
(titles received).
Area Specialization: Comprehensive.
Subject Specialization: history of cartography; techniques
of map making.
Special Cartographic Collections: Rare 17th and 18
century atlases and maps; United States county and real
estate atlases.
Dates: pre-1800 (20%); 1800-1899 (30%); 1900 - (50%).
Classification System: local system.

Collections Cataloged.
Depository for: DMA; NOS; NTS (Canada); USGS (Geol., topo.); GPO.
Serves: public. Mon., Wed., Fri. 10 a.m.–6 p.m., Tues. 10 a.m.–9 p.m.; Sat. 10 a.m.–6 p.m. (Seats 30; 750 readers served per month).
Reproduction Facility: photocopy; quickcopy; microform; photography.
Publications: occasional lists, articles and bibliographical studies in New York Public Library *Bulletin; Dictionary Catalog of the Map Division* (Boston, G.K. Hall, 1971) 10 v.

469. UNION THEOLOGICAL SEMINARY
Burke Library
Missionary Research Library Collection
3041 Broadway
New York, NY 10027
Telephone: 212/662-7100, ext. 270.
Contact Person: Richard D. Spoor, Director.
Size: 600 maps; 135 atlases.
Subject Specialization: Christian missions.
Serves: public.
Interlibrary Loan Available.

470. UNITED NATIONS
Dag Hammarskjold Library
Map Collection
New York, NY 10017
Established 1946.
Telephone: 212/754-7425.
Contact Person: Michael Dulka, Map Libn.
Staff: 1 professional (full time); 1 non-professional (full time).
Size: 80,000 maps; 1,500 atlases; 3 globes; 30 relief models; 3,000 reference books and gazetteers; 20 serials (titles received).
Annual Accessions: 1,400 maps; 10 atlases; 50 reference books and gazetteers.
Area Specialization: world.
Subject Specialization: political geography; toponymy.
Dates: 1800-1899 (1%); 1900 - (99%).
Classification System: O.S.S.
Collections not Cataloged.
Depository for: DOS (Gt. Brit).
Serves: U.N. Secretariat, delegations, and other accredited persons. Mon.–Fri. 9 a.m.–5:30 p.m. (Seats 28; 300 readers served per month).
Reproduction Facility: photocopy.

Oneonta

471. NEW YORK STATE UNIVERSITY COLLEGE
Milne Library
Map Collection
Oneonta, NY 13820
Established 1975.
Telephone: 607/431-3454.
Contact Person: Diana Carolyn Ice, Assistant Head of Cataloging and Map Libn.
Staff: 1 professional (part time).
Size: 17,388 maps; 1,004 atlases; 2 relief models; 172 reference books and gazetteers; 1 serials (titles received); 14 microforms (no. of titles).
Annual Accessions: 1,871 maps; 3 atlases; 11 reference books and gazetteers; 7 microforms (no. of titles).
Dates: 1900 - (100%).
Classification System: LC.
Collections Cataloged. (100%).
Depository for: DMA; NOS.

Serves: students; faculty; employees; public. Mon.–Fri. 8–4:30 on demand. (Seats 25; 5-10 readers served per month).
Reproduction Facility: photocopy.
Publications: Milne Library Information Series: Nuber 15 Map Collection (brochure).

Palisades

472. COLUMBIA UNIVERSITY
Lamont-Doherty Geological Observatory
Palisades, NY 10964
Established 1982.
Telephone: 914/359-2900, ext. 208.
Contact Person: Susan Klimley, Geological Sciences Libn.
Size: 1,000 maps; 31 serials (titles received).
Annual Accessions: 100 maps; 5 serials (titles received).
Subject Specialization: geology.
Dates: 1900 - (100%).
Classification System: local system.
Collections not Cataloged.
Depository for: USGS (Geol.).
Serves: students; faculty; employees. Mon.–Fri. 9 a.m.–5 p.m.
Interlibrary Loan Available.
Reproduction Facility: photocopy.

Plattsburgh

473. STATE UNIVERSITY COLLEGE
Feinberg Library
Government Documents Collection
Plattsburgh, NY 12901
Established 1968.
Telephone: 518/564-3180.
Contact Person: Joseph G. Swinyer, Documents Libn.
Staff: 1 professional (full time); 2 non-professional (full time).
Size: 4,225 maps.
Annual Accessions: 300 maps.
Area Specialization: New York; New Hampshire; Vermont.
Subject Specialization: topography.
Dates: 1900 - (100%).
Classification System: Alphabetical by state and quadrangle.
Collections not Cataloged.
Depository for: USGS (Topo.).
Serves: students; faculty; employees; public. Mon.–Fri. 8 a.m.–11:30 p.m.; Sat. 12 noon–10 p.m.; Sun. 12 noon–11:30 p.m. (Seats 24; 100 readers served per month).
Interlibrary Loan Available.
Reproduction Facility: photocopy.

Potsdam

474. STATE UNIVERSITY COLLEGE OF ARTS AND SCIENCE, POTSDAM
Crumb Library
Pierrepont Ave.
Potsdam, NY 13676
Established mid 1960's.
Telephone: 315/267-2486.
Contact Person: Nancy C. Eldblom, Associate Libn. (Documents and Maps).
Staff: 1 professional (part time); 2 non-professional (part time).
Size: 4,300 maps.
Annual Accessions: 150 maps.

Area Specialization: New York State.
Dates: 1800-1899 (1%); 1900 - (99%).
Classification System: LC; Most maps not classified—merely arranged by place.
Collections Cataloged. (1%).
Depository for: USGS (Geol., topo.); GPO.
Serves: students; faculty; employees; public;. Mon.–Thurs. 7:45 a.m.–11 p.m.; Fri. 7:45 a.m.–9 p.m.; Sat. 10:00 a.m.–11:00 p.m.; Sun. 10 a.m.–11 p.m. (Seats 765).
Interlibrary Loan Available.
Reproduction Facility: photocopy; microform.

Poughkeepsie

475. VASSAR COLLEGE
Geology Map Library
Poughkeepsie, NY 12601
Telephone: 914/452-7000, ext. 2177.
Contact Person: John H. Johnsen, Department Chairman.
Staff: 4 non-professional (part time).
Size: 20,000 maps; 100 atlases; 5 globes; 10 relief models; 100 aerial photographs.
Annual Accessions: 2,600 maps.
Subject Specialization: geology; topography.
Dates: 1800-1899 (5%); 1900 - (95%).
Classification System: local system.
Collections not Cataloged.
Depository for: DMA; USGS (Geol., topo.).
Serves: students; faculty; employees; public. Mon.–Fri. 7:30 a.m.–5 p.m. (50 readers served per month).
Reproduction Facility: quickcopy.

476. VASSAR COLLEGE LIBRARY
Special Collections
Poughkeepsie, NY 12601
Telephone: 914/452-7000, ext 2135.
Contact Person: Lisa Browar, Curator of Rare Books and Manuscripts.
Size: 200 maps; 40 atlases.
Special Cartographic Collections: Laskar Collection of antique atlases and maps.
Dates: 1800-1899 (85% (including pre-1800 materials)); 1900 - (15%).
Collections not Cataloged.
Serves: students; faculty; employees; public. Mon.–Fri. 8:30 a.m.–12 noon, 1–5 p.m.

Schenectady

477. UNION COLLEGE
Schaffer Library
Schenectady, NY 12308
Telephone: 518/370-6281.
Contact Person: Zina Shevchik, Documents Libn.
Size: 35,000 maps.
Area Specialization: United States east of the Mississippi.
Subject Specialization: topography.
Dates: 1800-1899 (5%); 1900 - (95%).
Classification System: local system.
Collections not Cataloged.
Depository for: USGS (Topo.). Mon.–Fri. 8:30 a.m.–11 p.m.; Sat. 9 a.m.–5 p.m.; Sun. 12 Noon–11 p.m.
Interlibrary Loan Available.
Reproduction Facility: quickcopy.

Staten Island

478. STATEN ISLAND HISTORICAL SOCIETY
441 Clark Avenue
Staten Island, NY 10306
Telephone: 718/351-1617.
Contact Person: Steve Barto, Archivist.
Staff: 2 professional (full time); 1 non-professional (part time).
Area Specialization: Staten Island.
Subject Specialization: regional and local history; genealogy.
Special Cartographic Collections: manuscript maps from Richmond County Clerk's office; real-estate maps; aerial photos mainly of Staten Island from 1920's to 1960's.
Classification System: local system.
Collections Cataloged.
Serves: public. Mon.–Fri. 9 a.m.–5 p.m. (by appointment).
Reproduction Facility: photocopy; quickcopy.

479. STATEN ISLAND INSTITUTE OF ARTS AND SCIENCES
Library
75 Stuyvesant Place
Staten Island, NY 10301
Telephone: 718/727-1135.
Contact Person: Eloise Beil, Archivist.
Staff: 2 professional (full time); 1 professional (part time).
Size: 12,000 maps; 57 atlases; 150 aerial photographs; 15 reference books and gazetteers.
Subject Specialization: local histroy; local natural science.
Special Cartographic Collections: Sanderson Smith Collection-early maps (world coverage) 16th–20th century.
Dates: pre-1800 (30%); 1800-1899 (33%); 1900 - (37%).
Classification System: local system.
Collections Cataloged. (90%).
Serves: public. Mon.–Fri. 9 a.m.–5 p.m. (by appointment). (Seats 2-4; 350 annual readers served per month).
Interlibrary Loan Available. (restricted)
Reproduction Facility: photocopy; quickcopy.

Stony Brook

480. STATE UNIVERSITY OF NEW YORK AT STONY BROOK
Melville Library
Map Collection
Stony Brook, NY 11794
Established 1972.
Telephone: 516/246-5975.
Contact Person: Barbara Shupe, Map Libn.
Staff: 1 professional (full time).
Size: 87,500 maps; 457 atlases; 5 globes; 300 aerial photographs; 675 reference books and gazetteers; 8 serials (titles received); 35 microforms (no. of titles).
Annual Accessions: 4,000 maps; 50 atlases; 1 globes; 50 aerial photographs; 50 reference books and gazetteers.
Area Specialization: Long Island; New York State.
Dates: 1800-1899 (1%); 1900 - (99%).
Classification System: LC.
Collections Cataloged. ((monographs and serials)).
Collections not Cataloged. ((maps)).
Depository for: DMA; NOS; USGS (Geol., topo.).
Serves: students; faculty; employees; public. Mon.–Fri. 8:30 a.m.–12 midnight; Sat. 10 a.m.–6 p.m.; Sun. 2 p.m.–12 midnight. (Seats 70; 280 readers served per month).
Interlibrary Loan Available.
Reproduction Facility: photocopy; microform.
Publications: "Map collection" (information brochure).

Syracuse

481. SYRACUSE UNIVERSITY
Ernest S. Bird Library
Map Collection
Waverly Avenue
Syracuse, NY 13210
Established 1935.
Telephone: 315/423-4176, 4158.
Contact Person: Mary Anne Waltz, Geography and Maps Libn.
Staff: 1 professional (full time); 1 non-professional (full time); 1 non-professional (part time).
Size: 135,000 maps; 1,100 atlases; 5 globes; 15 relief models; 10 aerial photographs; 150 reference books and gazetteers; 30 serials (titles received); 10 microforms (no. of titles).
Annual Accessions: 4000 maps; 15 atlases; 10 reference books and gazetteers; 5 serials (titles received).
Area Specialization: New York State; United States; northeastern United States.
Subject Specialization: topography; geology; urban planning.
Dates: 1800-1899 (1%); 1900 - (99%).
Classification System: LC; OSS.
Collections Cataloged. (40%).
Depository for: DMA; USGS (Geol., topo.); GPO.
Serves: students; faculty; employees; public. Mon.–Fri. 8 a.m.–10 p.m. (limited service in evening); Sat. 10 a.m.–6 p.m. (limited); Sun. 10 a.m.–10 p.m. (limited). (Seats 50; 200 readers served per month).
Interlibrary Loan Available.
Reproduction Facility: photocopy; microform.
Publications: Selected atlases (by state) in the atlas collection; Map Collection—maps of special interest and frequent use; SU Libraries Information Bullentin—Map Collection; Guide to Geo-Abstracts.

Troy

482. RENSSELAER POLYTECHNIC INSTITUTE
Library
Troy, NY 12181
Telephone: 518/266-8315.
Contact Person: Irving Stevens, Circulation Libn.
Staff: 1 professional (part time).
Size: 50,000 maps; 50 atlases.
Annual Accessions: 2,000 maps.
Area Specialization: United States.
Dates: 1900 - (100%).
Classification System: DMA.
Collections not Cataloged.
Depository for: DMA; USGS (Topo.).
Serves: students; faculty; employees; public. Mon.–Thurs. 7:30 a.m.–12 midnight; Fri. 7:30 a.m.–10 p.m.; Sat. 9 a.m.–10 p.m.; Sun. 12 noon–12 midnight. (10-12 readers served per month).
Reproduction Facility: quickcopy.

Utica

483. UTICA PUBLIC LIBRARY
303 Genesee Street
Utica, NY 13501
Telephone: 315/735-2279.
Contact Person: Elizabeth Pattengill, Reference Libn.
Staff: 2 professional (full time); 1 professional (part time).
Size: ca. 11,000 maps.

Area Specialization: Utica; Oneida County; New York State.
Subject Specialization: local history; genealogy.
Special Cartographic Collections: J.S. Mann-Utica land parcels (late 1900's).
Classification System: local system.
Depository for: USGS (Topo.).
Serves: public. Mon., Wed., Thurs. 9 a.m.–9 p.m. Tues., Fri. 9 a.m.–5:30 p.m.; Sat. 9 a.m.–5 p.m. (except July & August). (10 readers served per month).
Reproduction Facility: quickcopy.

West Point

484. U.S. MILITARY ACADEMY
Library
West Point, NY 10996
Established 1816.
Telephone: 914/938-2954.
Contact Person: Mrs. Marie T. Capps, Map & Manuscript Libn.
Staff: 1 professional (full time).
Size: 5,000 maps; 500 atlases; 3 globes; 2 relief models; 500 aerial photographs; 100 reference books and gazetteers; 15 serials (titles received).
Area Specialization: West Point; New York State; United States; Europe.
Special Cartographic Collections: Gilmer Collection (Civil War); Kruger Collection (World War II—Pacific area); Lasher Collection (Revolutionary War).
Dates: pre-1800 (36%); 1800-1899 (38%); 1900 - (26%).
Classification System: Dewey.
Collections Cataloged. (90%).
Serves: students; faculty; employees; public. Mon.–Fri. 8 a.m.–4:30 p.m. (Seats 16; 5 readers served per month).
Reproduction Facility: photocopy; quickcopy.

NORTH CAROLINA

Boone

485. APPLACHIAN STATE UNIVERSITY
Community Planning and Geography
Boone, NC 28608
Established 1970.
Telephone: 704/262-3001.
Contact Person: Dr. H. Daniel Stillwell, Professor-Geography.
Staff: 1 professional (part time); 6 non-professional (part time).
Size: 75,000 (plus 300 wall maps) maps; 800 atlases; 20 globes; 100 relief models; 11,500 aerial photographs; 5 serials (titles received).
Area Specialization: Appalachia.
Subject Specialization: natural hazards; urban planning.
Dates: 1800-1899 (2%); 1900 - (98%).
Classification System: .
Collections not Cataloged.
Depository for: DMA; USGS (Geol., topo.).
Serves: students; faculty; employees; public. Mon.–Fri. 8 a.m.–5 p.m. (Seats 30; 50 readers served per month).
Interlibrary Loan Available.
Reproduction Facility: quickcopy.

Buies Creek

486. CAMPBELL UNIVERSITY
Carrie Rich Memorial Library
Map and Atlas Collection
Buies Creek, NC 27506
Established 1965.
Telephone: 919/893-4111, ext. 238.
Contact Person: Karen Dickerson, Reference Libn.
Staff: 1 professional (full time).
Size: 14,000 maps; 50 atlases; 1 globes; 1 relief models;
25 reference books and gazetteers.
Annual Accessions: 1,000 maps; 5 atlases; 5 reference
books and gazetteers.
Area Specialization: North Carolina; southeastern United
States.
Dates: 1900 -.
Classification System: local system.
Collections not Cataloged.
Depository for: USGS (Geol., topo.).
Serves: students; faculty; employees; public;. Mon.–Fri. 7:50
a.m.–10:45 p.m.; Sat. 9:30 a.m.–12:30 p.m.; Sun. 6–10:15
p.m. (Seats 6; 15-20 readers served per month).
Interlibrary Loan Available.
Reproduction Facility: photocopy.

Chapel Hill

487. UNIVERSITY OF NORTH CAROLINA AT CHAPEL HILL
Geology Library
Mitchell Hall 029A
Chapel Hill, NC 27514
Established 1964.
Telephone: 919/962-2386.
Contact Person: Miriam L. Sheaves, Libn.
Staff: 1 professional (full time); 1 non-professional (part
time).
Size: 102,948 maps; 320 est. atlases; 3 globes; 850 est.
reference books and gazetteers; 700 serials (titles received);
106 microforms (no. of titles).
Annual Accessions: 3,300 maps; 15 atlases; 25 reference
books and gazetteers; 16 microforms (no. of titles).
Area Specialization: United States; southeastern United
States.
Subject Specialization: geology; geophysics; mineral
resources.
Special Cartographic Collections: 20 LANDSAT color
composite photo images of North Carolina and surrounding
areas.
Dates: 1800-1899 (2%); 1900 - (98%).
Classification System: LC.
Collections Cataloged. (100%).
Depository for: USGS (Geol., topo.).
Serves: students; faculty; employees; public. Mon.–Thurs. 8
a.m.–9 p.m.; Fri. 8 a.m.–5 p.m.; Sun. 3–9 p.m. (Seats 25;
1,000 (estimate) readers served per month).
Interlibrary Loan Available.
Reproduction Facility: photocopy.
Publications: *Guide to the Map Collection of the UNC
Geology Library.*

488. UNIVERSITY OF NORTH CAROLINA AT CHAPEL HILL
Wilson Library
Maps Collection
Chapel Hill, NC 27514
Established ca. 1943.
Telephone: 919/962-3028.
Contact Person: Celia D. Poe, Map Libn.
Staff: 1 professional (full time).

Size: 90,000 maps; 1,175 atlases; 2 globes; 110 relief
models; 910 reference books and gazetteers; 11 serials
(titles received); 5 microforms (no. of titles).
Annual Accessions: 2,200 maps; 30 atlases; 30 reference
books and gazetteers; 1 serials (titles received); 1
microforms (no. of titles).
Area Specialization: North Carolina; southeastern United
States; Latin America; eastern Africa; eastern Europe.
Subject Specialization: topography; local history.
Dates: pre-1800 (1%); 1800-1899 (5%); 1900 - (94%).
Classification System: LC; Dewey.
Collections Cataloged. (90% volumes, 1% maps).
Depository for: DMA; NOS; USGS (Geol., topo.).
Serves: students; faculty; employees; public. Mon.–Fri. 8
a.m.–5 p.m. (Seats 10; 85 readers served per month).
Interlibrary Loan Available. (restricted)
Reproduction Facility: photocopy; quickcopy; microform.

489. UNIVERSITY OF NORTH CAROLINA AT CHAPEL HILL
Wilson Library
North Carolina Collection
Chapel Hill, NC 27514
Established 1844.
Telephone: 919/962-1172.
Contact Person: Alice R. Cotten, Assistant Curator.
Size: 4,218 maps; 3,000 serials (titles received); 10,884
microforms (no. of titles).
Annual Accessions: 100 maps; 300 microforms (no. of
titles).
Area Specialization: North Carolina.
Subject Specialization: North Carolina.
Dates: pre-1800 (20%); 1800-1899 (30%); 1900 - (50%).
Classification System: Dewey modified.
Collections Cataloged. (99%).
Serves: students; faculty; employees; public. Mon.–Fri. 8
a.m.–5 p.m. (Seats 30; 2,000 readers served per month).
Reproduction Facility: microform.

Charlotte

490. UNIVERSITY OF NORTH CAROLINA AT CHARLOTTE
J. Murrey Atkins Library
Documents Department
Charlotte, NC 28223
Telephone: 704/597-2243.
Contact Person: Beverly Davis, Technical Asst.
Staff: 1 professional (full time); 3 non-professional (full
time); 1 non-professional (part time).
Size: 24,000 maps.
Annual Accessions: 1,000 maps.
Dates: 1900 - (100%).
Classification System: local system.
Collections not Cataloged.
Depository for: DMA; USGS (Geol., topo.).
Serves: students; faculty; employees; public;. Mon.–Thurs. 8
a.m.–11 p.m.; Fri. 8 a.m.–6 p.m.; Sat. 9 a.m.–5 p.m.; Sun.
2–11 p.m. (Seats 80; 1200 readers served per month).
Reproduction Facility: photocopy.

Cullowhee

491. WESTERN CAROLINA UNIVERSITY
Hunter Library
Map Room
Cullowhee, NC 28723
Established 1982.
Telephone: 704/227-7362.
Contact Person: Anita K. Oser, Reference and Map Libn.

Staff: 1 professional (part time); 1 non-professional (part time).
Size: 57,000 maps; 280 atlases; 3 globes; 1 relief models; 515 aerial photographs; 40 reference books and gazetteers.
Annual Accessions: 3,500 maps; 5 atlases; 5 aerial photographs; 10 reference books and gazetteers.
Area Specialization: North Carolina; Jamaica; Swaziland; southeastern United States.
Dates: 1800-1899 (1%); 1900 - (99%).
Classification System: LC.
Collections Cataloged. (2%).
Depository for: DMA; USGS (Geol., topo.).
Serves: students; faculty; employees; public. Mon.–Fri. 9 a.m.–5 p.m. (Seats 10; 30 readers served per month).
Interlibrary Loan Available.
Reproduction Facility: photocopy.

Durham

492. DUKE UNIVERSITY
Perkins Library
Public Documents and Maps Department
Durham, NC 27706
Established 1948.
Telephone: 919/684-2380, 5435.
Staff: 1 professional (part time); 1 non-professional (part time).
Size: 62,100 maps; 50 atlases; 1 globes; 35 relief models; 100 aerial photographs; 175 reference books and gazetteers; 2 serials (titles received); 2 microforms (no. of titles).
Annual Accessions: 4,000 maps; 2 atlases; 2 reference books and gazetteers.
Area Specialization: Southeastern states.
Subject Specialization: topography; geology.
Dates: 1800-1899 (1%); 1900 - (99%).
Classification System: LC; Dewey; DMA; Superintendent of Documents.
Collections not Cataloged.
Depository for: DMA; USGS (Geol., topo.).
Serves: students; faculty; employees; public. Mon.–Thurs. 8 a.m.–5, 7–10 p.m., Fri. 8 a.m.–5 p.m.; Sat. 9 a.m.–5 p.m.; Sun. 2–10 p.m. (Seats 50).
Interlibrary Loan Available.
Reproduction Facility: photocopy.
Publications: *Guide to Maps in Perkins Library* (guide).

493. NORTH CAROLINA CENTRAL UNIVERSITY
James E. Shepard Memorial Library
1801 Fayetteville Street
Durham, NC 27707
Telephone: 919/683-6475.
Size: 1,500 maps; 98 atlases; 3 globes; 30 reference books and gazetteers.
Annual Accessions: 250 maps; 3 atlases; 2 reference books and gazetteers.
Area Specialization: United States.
Dates: pre-1800 (5%); 1800-1899 (5%); 1900 - (90%).
Classification System: LC; Dewey; DMA.
Depository for: DMA.
Serves: students; faculty; employees; public. Mon.–Thurs. 8 a.m.–11 p.m., Fri. 8 a.m.–10 p.m.; Sun. Sun. 6–10 p.m.
Reproduction Facility: photocopy.

Greensboro

494. UNIVERSITY OF NORTH CAROLINA AT GREENSBORO
Jackson Library
Reference Department
Greensboro, NC 27412
Established 1974.
Telephone: 919/379-5419.
Contact Person: Nancy B. Ryckman, Assistant Reference Libn.
Staff: 1 professional (part time).
Size: 5,000 maps; 4 globes.
Annual Accessions: 400 maps; 5-10 atlases; 20-30 reference books and gazetteers.
Area Specialization: North Carolina and contiguous states.
Subject Specialization: polical geography; topography.
Dates: 1900 - (99%+).
Classification System: local system: informal geographic arrangement.
Collections Cataloged. (60%).
Depository for: DMA; USGS (Topo.).
Serves: students; faculty; employees; public. Mon.–Thurs. 8 a.m.–11 p.m., Fri. 8 a.m.–9 p.m.; Sat. 9 a.m.–5 p.m.; Sun. 1–11 p.m. (Seats 6; 15-20 readers served per month).
Reproduction Facility: photocopy.

Greenville

495. EAST CAROLINA UNIVERSITY
Geography Department
Greenville, NC 27834
Established 1957.
Telephone: 919/757-6230.
Contact Person: Palmyra Leahy, Map curator.
Staff: 1 professional (part time); 2 non-professional (part time).
Size: 80,000 maps.
Annual Accessions: 1,000 maps.
Area Specialization: United States.
Subject Specialization: topography; bathymetry.
Dates: 1900 - (100%).
Classification System: local system.
Depository for: DMA; NOS; USGS (Topo.).
Serves: students; faculty; employees; public;. (Seats 5; 30 readers served per month).

Raleigh

496. NORTH CAROLINA (STATE) DEPARTMENT OF CULTURAL RESOURCES
Division of Archives and History
Archives and Records Section
109 E. Jones Street
Raleigh, NC 27611
Established 1903.
Telephone: 919/733-3952.
Contact Person: George Stevenson, Reference Unit Supervisor.
Size: 4000 maps.
Area Specialization: North Carolina; North Carolina counties.
Special Cartographic Collections: Superintendent of Pubic Instruction maps (swamplands of eastern N.C., 19th Cent.); Eric Norden Map Collection (swamplands of eastern N.C., 20th cent.); Sanborn insurance maps, N.C. towns, 20th century.
Dates: pre-1800 (16%); 1800-1899 (64%); 1900 - (20%).
Classification System: local system.
Collections Cataloged.

Serves: public. Tues.–Fri. 8–5:30; Sat. 8:30 a.m.–5:30 p.m. (Seats 48).
Reproduction Facility: photocopy.

497. NORTH CAROLINA GEOLOGICAL SURVEY
North Carolina (State) Department of Natural Resources and Community Development
512 N. Salisbury Street
Raleigh, NC 27611
Telephone: 919/733-2423.
Contact Person: Billie J. Flynt, Jr., Cartographer.
Staff: 1 non-professional (full time).
Size: 3,500 maps; 10 atlases; 1 globes; 5,000 aerial photographs; 12 reference books and gazetteers; 2,000 microforms (no. of titles).
Area Specialization: North Carolina.
Subject Specialization: topography, geology.
Dates: 1800-1899 (1%); 1900 - (99%).
Classification System: alphabetical according to type.
Collections not Cataloged.
Depository for: USGS (Topo.).
Serves: students; faculty; employees; public. 8 a.m.–5 p.m. (Seats 5; 25 readers served per month).
Interlibrary Loan Available.
Reproduction Facility: photocopy; Blueprint.
Publications: *List of Publications of the N.C. Geological Survey* (1983); *Index to Surficial-Geologic Mapping 1895–1982, Geophysical Mapping, Geologic Fieldtrip Guidebooks, Ground-Water Reports in North Carolina* (1982).

498. NORTH CAROLINA STATE MUSEUM OF NATURAL HISTORY
H. H. Brimley Memorial Library
Southeastern Maps Collection
102 N. Salisbury Street, P.O. Box 27647
Raleigh, NC 27611
Telephone: 919/733-7451, ext. 4.
Contact Person: Dr. John E. Cooper, Director of Research & Collections.
Size: ca. 5,000 maps; 15 atlases; 1 relief models; ca. 200 aerial photographs; 50 reference books and gazetteers.
Area Specialization: Southeastern United States.
Subject Specialization: topography land forms; geology; hydrology.
Classification System: local system.
Collections not Cataloged.
Depository for: USGS (Topo.).
Serves: students; faculty; employees; public.
Interlibrary Loan Available.
Reproduction Facility: photocopy.

499. NORTH CAROLINA STATE UNIVERSITY
D.H. Hill Library
Documents Department
Box 7111
Raleigh, NC 27695-7111
Telephone: 919/737-3280.
Contact Person: Lisa A. Newman, Documents Libn.
Staff: 1 professional (part time); 1 non-professional (part time).
Size: 8,500 maps; 35 atlases; 1 globes.
Annual Accessions: 200 maps; 2 atlases.
Area Specialization: North Carolina.
Subject Specialization: nautical charts; topography; national forest; aeronautical charts.
Special Cartographic Collections: FAO/UNESCO soil maps of the world North Carolina topographic maps.
Dates: 1900 - (99%).
Collections not Cataloged.
Depository for: DMA; NOS; USGS (Topo.).

Serves: students; faculty; employees; public. 8 a.m.–10 p.m., Fri. 8 a.m.–6 p.m.; Sat. 9 a.m.–5:30 p.m.; Sun. 1–10:00 p.m. (Seats 4-5; 100 readers served per month).
Reproduction Facility: photocopy.

500. NORTH CAROLINA STATE UNIVERSITY
Department of Marine, Earth and Atmospheric Sciences
Departmental Reading Room—Library
P.O. Box 8208
Raleigh, NC 27659-8208
Telephone: 919/737-2212.
Contact Person: Anna H. Wuest, Libn.
Staff: 1 non-professional (part time).
Size: 11,286 maps.
Area Specialization: North Carolina; Virginia; Tennessee.
Subject Specialization: geology; geophysics; economics; hydrology; land use.
Dates: 1800-1899 (1%); 1900 - (99%).
Collections not Cataloged.
Depository for: USGS (Geol., topo.).
Serves: students; faculty; employees. Mon.–Fri. 8:30 a.m.–5 p.m. (8:30–12:30 with staff). (Seats 20; 300 readers served per month).
Reproduction Facility: photocopy.

Salisbury

501. CATAWBA COLLEGE
Corriher-Linn-Black Library
2300 West Innes Street
Salisbury, NC 28144
Established 1970.
Telephone: 704/637-4449.
Contact Person: Dr. Betty Sell, Director of Library Services.
Staff: 4 professional (part time); 2 non-professional (part time).
Size: 5,223 maps; 81 atlases; 123 aerial photographs; 152 reference books and gazetteers; 3 serials (titles received); 1,185 microforms (no. of titles).
Annual Accessions: ca.200 maps; 2 atlases; ca.30 aerial photographs; 2 reference books and gazetteers; ca. 50 microforms (no. of titles).
Area Specialization: North Carolina and neighboring states.
Subject Specialization: geology; geography; census.
Dates: 1800-1899 (1%); 1900 - (99%).
Collections Cataloged. (7%).
Depository for: USGS (Geol., topo.).
Serves: students; faculty; employees; public. Mon.–Thurs. 8 a.m.–9:30 p.m.; Sun. 1:30–9:30 p.m. (Seats 110; ca. 60 readers served per month).
Interlibrary Loan Available.
Reproduction Facility: photocopy; microform.

Winston-Salem

502. WAKE FOREST UNIVERSITY
Z. Smith Reynolds Library
Reference Department
Box 7777, Reynolds Station
Winston-Salem, NC 27109
Established 1879.
Telephone: 919/761-5480.
Contact Person: Mrs. Patricia Giles, Dept. Head.
Staff: 3 professional (full time).
Size: ca. 5,200 maps; ca. 50 atlases; 1 globes; ca. 10 reference books and gazetteers.
Annual Accessions: ca. 100 maps; ca. 3 atlases; ca. 2 reference books and gazetteers.
Classification System: local system.
Depository for: USGS (Topo.).

Serves: students; faculty; employees; public. Mon.–Fri. 9 a.m.–11 p.m.; Sat. 9 a.m.–5 p.m.; Sun. 1–4 p.m. (Seats 50; 12 readers served per month).
Reproduction Facility: photocopy.

NORTH DAKOTA

Fargo

503. NORTH DAKOTA STATE UNIVERSITY
The Library
Map Collection
Fargo, ND 58105
Established 1968.
Telephone: 701/237-8889.
Contact Person: Aileen Buck, Maps/Reference Libn.
Staff: 1 professional (part time); 1 non-professional (part time).
Size: 70,000 maps; 160 atlases; 2 globes; 5 reference books and gazetteers; 5 serials (titles received).
Annual Accessions: 2,500 maps.
Area Specialization: North Dakota.
Classification System: .
Collections Cataloged. (10%).
Depository for: DMA; USGS (Geol., topo.).
Serves: students; faculty; employees; public;. Mon.–Fri. 8 a.m.–10 p.m.; Sat. 10 a.m.–5 p.m.; Sun. 1–9 p.m. (Seats 24; 150-200 readers served per month).
Interlibrary Loan Available.
Reproduction Facility: photocopy; microform.

Grand Forks

504. UNIVERSITY OF NORTH DAKOTA
Geography Department
Map Library
Grand Forks, ND 58202
Telephone: 701/777-4246.
Contact Person: Dr. Kang-tsung Chang, Chairman.
Staff: 1 non-professional (part time).
Size: 35,000 maps; 30 atlases; 15 globes; 500 aerial photographs; 20 reference books and gazetteers.
Annual Accessions: 300 maps; 5 atlases; 100 aerial photographs; 2 reference books and gazetteers.
Dates: 1900 - (100%).
Classification System: local system.
Collections Cataloged.
Depository for: DMA.
Serves: students; faculty; employees; public. Mon.–Fri. 8:30 a.m.–4:30 p.m. (Seats 15; 5 readers served per month).
Reproduction Facility: photocopy.

505. UNIVERSITY OF NORTH DAKOTA
Libraries
Geology Branch
326 Leonard Hall
Grand Forks, ND 58201
Telephone: 701/777-3221.
Contact Person: Mrs. Holly Gilbert, Geolibn.
Staff: 1 professional (part time); 1 non-professional (part time).
Size: 67,000 maps; 50 atlases; 1 globes; 6,000 aerial photographs.
Annual Accessions: 4,000 maps.
Area Specialization: North Dakota; United States; Canada.
Subject Specialization: geology.
Classification System: LC (modified).
Collections Cataloged. (20%).

Depository for: USGS (Geol., topo.). Mon.–Fri. 8 a.m.–12 noon, 1–4:30 p.m. (Seats 20; 30 readers served per month).
Reproduction Facility: photocopy.

Minot

506. MINOT STATE COLLEGE
Earth Science Department
Map Library
Cyril Moore Hall
Minot, ND 58701
Established 1968.
Telephone: 701/857-3070.
Contact Person: Eric Clausen, Professor of Earth Sciences.
Staff: 2 non-professional (part time).
Size: 30,000 maps; 2 globes; 100 relief models; 2,500 aerial photographs; 5 serials (titles received).
Annual Accessions: 2,500 maps; 100 aerial photographs.
Area Specialization: Northern Great Plains; Rocky Mountains.
Subject Specialization: geology; topography.
Dates: 1900 - (100%).
Classification System: local system.
Collections Cataloged. (10%).
Depository for: USGS (Geol., topo.).
Serves: students; faculty; employees; public. Mon.–Fri. 8 a.m.–5 p.m. (Seats 20).
Interlibrary Loan Available. (restricted)
Publications: *Guide to the Minot State College Map Library* (guide).

OHIO

Akron

507. UNIVERSITY OF AKRON
Bierce Library
Reference Department
Akron, OH 44325
Established ca. 1964.
Telephone: 216/375-7234.
Contact Person: Claudia Salem, Head, Reference Department.
Staff: non-professional (full time); non-professional (part time).
Size: 7,000 maps; 700 atlases; 4 globes; 30 relief models; 10 reference books and gazetteers; 1 serials (titles received).
Area Specialization: Ohio.
Special Cartographic Collections: Historic Urban Plans (entire series).
Dates: pre-1800 (10%); 1800-1899 (15%); 1900 - (75%).
Classification System: LC.
Collections Cataloged.
Depository for: GPO.
Serves: students; faculty; employees; public. Mon.–Fri. 7:30 a.m.–9:30 p.m.; Sat. 7:30 a.m.–9:30 p.m. (Summer 9 a.m.–3 p.m.); Sun. 7:30 a.m.–9:30 p.m. (Summer 12 noon–6 p.m.). (Seats 35; 80 readers served per month).
Reproduction Facility: photocopy.
Publications: *Guide to the map room* .

Athens

508. OHIO UNIVERSITY
Alden Library
Map Collection
Athens, OH 45701
Established 1956.
Telephone: 614/594-5240.
Contact Person: Theodore S. Foster, Head, Microform, Map, & Nonprint Dept.
Staff: 1 professional (part time); 1 non-professional (part time).
Size: 131,062 maps; 912 atlases; 8 globes; 2 relief models; 1,200 aerial photographs; 221 reference books and gazetteers; 4 serials (titles received); 6 microforms (no. of titles).
Annual Accessions: 2,500 maps; 25 atlases; 15 reference books and gazetteers.
Area Specialization: S.E. Asia; Africa; Latin America; United States.
Subject Specialization: topography; land use; geology; earth resources.
Special Cartographic Collections: World War II Japanese Maps; Indonesia.
Dates: 1800-1899 (10%); 1900 - (90%).
Classification System: LC.
Collections Cataloged. (15%).
Depository for: DMA; USGS (Geol., topo.); GPO.
Serves: students; faculty; employees; public. Mon.–Fri. 8 a.m.–12 midnight; Sat. 12 noon–10 p.m.; Sun. 12 noon–12 midnight. (Seats 16; 120 readers served per month).
Interlibrary Loan Available.
Reproduction Facility: photocopy; microform.

Bowling Green

509. BOWLING GREEN STATE UNIVERSITY
Jerome Library
Map Library
Bowling Green, OH 43403
Telephone: 419/372-2156.
Contact Person: Evron Collins, Popular Culture/Map Libn.
Size: 40,000 maps; 220 atlases; 4 globes; 200 reference books and gazetteers; 4 serials (titles received); 2 microforms (no. of titles).
Annual Accessions: 2,000 maps; 15 atlases; 1 globes; 50 reference books and gazetteers; 1 serials (titles received).
Area Specialization: Ohio; Michigan; Indiana; Arizona; New Mexico; Utah; Colorado.
Dates: pre-1800 (5%); 1800-1899 (5%); 1900 - (90%).
Classification System: LC.
Collections Cataloged. (10%).
Depository for: DMA; NOS; USGS (Geol., topo.).
Serves: students; faculty; employees; public. Mon.–Fri. 9 a.m.–5 p.m.; Tues. until 10 p.m.; Sun. 1–10 p.m. (Seats 20; 100 readers served per month).
Interlibrary Loan Available.
Reproduction Facility: photocopy.
Publications: library guide.

Canton

510. STARK COUNTY DISTRICT LIBRARY
Reference Department
Map Collection
715 Market Avenue North
Canton, OH 44702
Established early 1960's.
Telephone: 216/452-0665, ext. 225.

Contact Person: Penny L. Marshall, Head, Reference Dept.
Staff: 3 professional (full time); 1 professional (part time); 1 non-professional (full time).
Size: 5,000 maps; 100 atlases; 1 globes; 200 aerial photographs; 100 reference books and gazetteers.
Annual Accessions: 250 maps; 15 atlases; 50 reference books and gazetteers.
Area Specialization: Canton; Stark County, Ohio; United States; world.
Subject Specialization: topography; transportation; travel.
Dates: 1900 - (100%).
Classification System: local system.
Collections not Cataloged.
Serves: students; faculty; employees; public. Mon.–Thurs. 9 a.m.–9 p.m.; Fri. 9 a.m.–5 p.m.; Sat. Sat 9 a.m.–5 p.m. (Seats 50).
Reproduction Facility: photocopy; microform.

Cincinnati

511. CINCINNATI HISTORICAL SOCIETY
Eden Park
Cincinnati, OH 45202
Established 1831.
Telephone: 513/241-4622.
Contact Person: Laura L. Chace, Head Libn.
Staff: 5 professional (full time); 3 non-professional (full time); 2 professional (part time).
Size: 2,700 maps; 75 atlases; 100 aerial photographs; 20 reference books and gazetteers.
Annual Accessions: 20 maps; 3 atlases.
Area Specialization: Cincinnati; Ohio; Old Northwest Territory.
Subject Specialization: land ownership.
Dates: 1800-1899 (75%); 1900 - (25%).
Classification System: Dewey.
Collections Cataloged.
Serves: public; Society. Tues.–Fri. 9 a.m.–4:30 p.m.; Sat. 9 a.m.–4:30 p.m. (Seats 35).
Reproduction Facility: photocopy.

512. PUBLIC LIBRARY OF CINCINNATI AND HAMILTON COUNTY
History Department
Map Collection
800 Vine Street, Library Square
Cincinnati, OH 45202-2071
Established 1955.
Telephone: 513/369-6909.
Contact Person: Carl G. Marquette Jr., Map Libn.
Staff: 1 professional (full time); 1 non-professional (full time).
Size: 137,951 maps; 1,250 atlases; 3 globes; 10 relief models; 125 aerial photographs; 750 reference books and gazetteers; 20 serials (titles received); 10 microforms (no. of titles).
Annual Accessions: 3,500 maps; 50 atlases; 50 reference books and gazetteers; 2 serials (titles received); 2 microforms (no. of titles).
Area Specialization: Cincinnati; Hamilton County; Ohio.
Special Cartographic Collections: old map of Cincinnati and Hamilton County; 19th century cadastral atlases of Ohio and contiguous states.
Dates: pre-1800 (5%); 1800-1899 (15%); 1900 - (80%).
Classification System: Dewey atlases and books only.
Collections Cataloged. (atlases and books only).
Depository for: DMA; NOS; USGS (Geol., topo.).
Serves: students; faculty; employees; public. Mon.–Fri. 9 a.m.–9 p.m.; Sat. 9 a.m.–9 p.m. (Seats 62; 150 readers served per month).
Reproduction Facility: photocopy.

513. UNIVERSITY OF CINCINNATI
Library, Geography Department
608 Swift Hall
Cincinnati, OH 45221
Telephone: 513/475-4332.
Contact Person: Richard A. Spohn, Geography
Bibliographer.
Staff: 1 professional (full time).
Size: 25,000 maps.
Annual Accessions: 100-300 maps.
Subject Specialization: topography.
Dates: 1900 - (100%).
Collections not Cataloged.
Depository for: DMA.
Serves: students; faculty. (Seats 18).
Reproduction Facility: photocopy.

514. UNIVERSITY OF CINCINNATI
Library, Geology Department
224 Old Tech Building
Cincinnati, OH 45221
Telephone: 513/475-4332.
Contact Person: Richard A. Spohm, Head, Geology Library.
Staff: 1 professional (full time).
Size: 80,000 maps; 2,000 aerial photographs.
Annual Accessions: 300-500 maps.
Area Specialization: Ohio; Kentucky; Indiana; Latin
America.
Subject Specialization: topography, geology.
Dates: 1900 - (100%).
Collections not Cataloged.
Depository for: GSC; USGS (Geol., topo.).
Serves: students; faculty; employees; public. Mon.–Thurs. 8
a.m.–10 p.m., Fri. 8 a.m.–5 p.m.; Sat. 1 p.m.–6 p.m.; Sun. 3
p.m.–9 p.m. (Seats 5).
Reproduction Facility: photocopy.

Cleveland

515. CASE WESTERN RESERVE UNIVERSITY
Sears Library
Special Materials
10900 Euclid Avenue
Cleveland, OH 44106
Telephone: 216/368-6602.
Contact Person: Gladys Smiley, Reference/Special
Materials Libn.
Staff: 1 professional (part time); 2 non-professional (part
time).
Size: 37,000 maps.
Annual Accessions: 1,300 maps.
Area Specialization: United States; Ohio.
Subject Specialization: topography; geology.
Dates: 1800-1899 (5%); 1900 - (95%).
Classification System: local system.
Collections not Cataloged.
Depository for: USGS (Geol., topo.).
Serves: students; faculty; employees; public. Mon.–Thurs 8
a.m.–12 midnight, Fri. 8 a.m.–5:30 p.m.; Sat. 9 a.m.–6 p.m.;
Sun. 2–12 midnight. (Seats 5).
Reproduction Facility: photocopy.
Publications: *Guide to use of geological survey maps*
(guide).

516. CLEVELAND PUBLIC LIBRARY
General Reference
Map Collection
325 Superior Avenue
Cleveland, OH 44114-1271
Established 1869.
Telephone: 216/623-2880.

Contact Person: Maureen Farrell, Head of Map Collection.
Staff: 1 professional (part time); 1 non-professional (full
time); 1 non-professional (part time).
Size: 111,133 maps; 1,088 atlases; 3 globes; 7 relief
models; 5 aerial photographs; 865 reference books and
gazetteers; 33 serials (titles received); 34 microforms (no. of
titles).
Annual Accessions: 5,700 maps; 55 atlases; 50 reference
books and gazetteers.
Area Specialization: North America; Great Lakes Region;
Ohio; Cuyahoga County.
Subject Specialization: topography; geology; history of
cartography.
Special Cartographic Collections: Karpinski reproductions
French Archive series of early American maps; Ohio County
Atlases (original and microfilm);.
Dates: pre-1800 (3%); 1800-1899 (5%); 1900 - (92%).
Classification System: LC.
Collections Cataloged. (100%).
Depository for: DMA; NOS; USGS (Geol., topo.); Ohio
Library Depository.
Serves: public. Mon.–Fri. 9 a.m.–6 p.m.; Sat. 9 a.m.–6 p.m.
(Seats 6; 275 readers served per month).
Interlibrary Loan Available.
Reproduction Facility: photocopy; quickcopy; microform.

517. CLEVELAND STATE UNIVERSITY
Library
1860 E. 22nd Street
Cleveland, OH 44115
Established 1964.
Telephone: 216/687-2490.
Contact Person: Henry E. York, Social Sciences Libn.
Staff: 1 professional (part time); 2 non-professional (part
time).
Size: 42,000 maps; 325 atlases; 2 globes.
Annual Accessions: 3,000 maps.
Area Specialization: Cleveland; United States.
Dates: 1900 - (99%).
Classification System: LC.
Collections Cataloged. ((purchased maps only)).
Depository for: USGS (Topo.).
Serves: students; faculty; employees; public. Mon.–Thurs.
7:30 a.m.–10:30 p.m.; Fri. 7:30 a.m.–5 p.m.; Sat. 10–5 p.m.;
Sun. 2–6 p.m.
Interlibrary Loan Available.
Reproduction Facility: photocopy.
Publications: *List of Atlases* .

518. WESTERN RESERVE HISTORICAL SOCIETY
History Library
10825 East Boulevard
Cleveland, OH 44106
Established 1867.
Telephone: 216/721-5722.
Contact Person: Kermit J. Pike, Director.
Staff: 5 professional (part time).
Size: 3,000 maps; 600 atlases; 3 globes; 18,000 aerial
photographs; 200 reference books and gazetteers.
Annual Accessions: 10 maps; 10 atlases; 10 reference
books and gazetteers.
Subject Specialization: exploration; Civil War; Ohio
(Western Reserve and Cleveland).
Dates: pre-1800 (10%); 1800-1899 (50%); 1900 - (40%).
Classification System: local system.
Collections Cataloged. (90%).
Serves: students; faculty; employees; public. Tues.–Fri. 9
a.m.–5 p.m.; Sat. 9 a.m.–5 p.m. (Seats 40; 900 readers
served per month).
Reproduction Facility: photocopy; microform.

Columbus

519. OHIO HISTORICAL SOCIETY
Library
Archives-Library Division
1982 Velma Avenue
Columbus, OH 43211
Established Early 20th Century.
Telephone: 614/466-1500.
Contact Person: Stephen Gutgesell, Map & Newspaper Libn.
Staff: 1 professional (part time).
Size: 15,000 maps; 500 atlases; 500 aerial photographs; 50 reference books and gazetteers.
Area Specialization: Ohio.
Subject Specialization: transportation.
Dates: pre-1800 (10%); 1800-1899 (45%); 1900 - (45%).
Classification System: local system.
Collections Cataloged. (75%).
Depository for: Ohio state documents.
Serves: public. Tues.–Fri. 9 a.m.–5 p.m.; Sat. 9 a.m.–5 p.m. (Seats 66).
Reproduction Facility: photocopy; quickcopy; microform.

520. OHIO STATE UNIVERSITY
Main Library
Map Library, Room 200
1858 Neil Avenue Mall
Columbus, OH 43210
Telephone: 614/422-2393.
Contact Person: George P. Schoyer, Libn.
Staff: 1 professional (part time); 1 non-professional (part time).
Size: 118,541 maps; 835 atlases; 1 globes; 10 relief models; 700 reference books and gazetteers; 10 serials (titles received).
Annual Accessions: 2,800 maps; 110 atlases; 130 aerial photographs; 2 serials (titles received).
Area Specialization: Ohio.
Subject Specialization: topography; economic geography; history.
Dates: 1800-1899 (10%); 1900 - (90%).
Classification System: LC.
Depository for: DMA; NOS; NTS (Canada); USGS (Topo.); CIA.
Serves: students; faculty; employees; public. Mon.–Fri. 8:30 a.m.–5:30 p.m. (Seats 21; 200 readers served per month).
Reproduction Facility: photocopy.
Publications: *Quarterly List of New Map Library Acquisitons*

521. OHIO STATE UNIVERSITY
Orton Memorial Library of Geology
155 South Oval Drive
Columbus, OH 43210
Established 1942.
Telephone: 614/422-2428.
Contact Person: Regina A. Brown, Head, Orton Mem. Lib. of Geology.
Staff: 1 non-professional (part time).
Size: 77,278 maps; 610 serials (titles received); 36 microforms (no. of titles).
Area Specialization: comprehensive.
Subject Specialization: geology; soils; physical oceanography.
Collections not Cataloged.
Depository for: USGS (Geol., topo.).
Serves: students; faculty; employees; public. Mon.–Thurs. 8 a.m.–5 p.m., 7–10 p.m.; Sat. 10 a.m.–2 p.m.; Sun. 2–6 p.m.
Reproduction Facility: photocopy; microform.
Publications: Monthly accessions list.

522. PUBLIC LIBRARY OF COLUMBUS AND FRANKLIN COUNTY
Biography, History and Travel Division
96 South Grant Avenue
Columbus, OH 43213
Established 1974.
Telephone: 614/222-7154.
Contact Person: Sam Roshon, Subject Specialist.
Staff: 2 non-professional (part time).
Size: 1,850 maps; 90 atlases; 1 globes; 62 aerial photographs; 30 reference books and gazetteers; 1 microforms (no. of titles).
Annual Accessions: 15 maps.
Area Specialization: Old Nortwest Territory; Ohio; Franklin Co., Ohio; Columbus, Ohio.
Special Cartographic Collections: railroad maps of Ohio; annexation maps of Columbus; zoning maps of Columbus; maps of all incorporated Ohio municipalities; Franklin County land ownership maps; Columbus and Franklin Co. maps, 1856–1984.
Dates: 1800-1899 (3%); 1900 - (97%).
Classification System: local system.
Collections not Cataloged.
Depository for: USGS (Topo.).
Serves: public; Government officials. Mon.–Thurs. 9 a.m.–9 p.m.; Fri. 9 a.m.–6 p.m.; Sat. 9 a.m.–6 p.m. (Seats 16).
Reproduction Facility: photocopy; microform.

523. STATE LIBRARY OF OHIO
Documents Dept.
65 South Front St.
Columbus, OH 43215
Telephone: 614/462-7051.
Contact Person: Clyde Hordusky, Documents specialist.
Staff: 1 professional (full time); 3 non-professional (full time).
Size: ca. 60,000 maps.
Area Specialization: Ohio and contiguous states.
Subject Specialization: topography.
Dates: 1800-1899 (ca. 5%); 1900 - (ca. 95%).
Classification System: local system.
Collections not Cataloged.
Depository for: USGS (Topo.).
Serves: employees; public. Mon.–Thurs. 8 a.m.–5 p.m., Fri. 9 a.m.–5 p.m. (Seats 15; 20 readers served per month).
Interlibrary Loan Available.
Reproduction Facility: quickcopy.

Dayton

524. DAYTON AND MONTGOMERY COUNTY PUBLIC LIBRARY
Social Sciences Division
215 East Third Street
Dayton, OH 45402
Telephone: 513/224-1651, ext. 272.
Staff: 2 professional (part time).
Size: 70,000 maps; 450 atlases; 1 globes; 5 relief models; 160 aerial photographs; 50 reference books and gazetteers.
Area Specialization: Dayton, Ohio, Ohio Miami Valley.
Dates: 1800-1899 (2%); 1900 - (98%).
Classification System: local system.
Collections not Cataloged.
Depository for: USGS (Topo.).
Serves: students; faculty; employees; public. Mon.–Fri. 9 a.m.–9 p.m. (Seats 80).
Reproduction Facility: photocopy.

525. DAYTON MUSEUM OF NATURAL HISTORY
2629 Ridge Ave.
Dayton, OH 45414
Established 1900.
Telephone: 513/275-7431.
Contact Person: Diana Morse, Curator of Geology.
Staff: 1 professional (full time).
Size: 8,000 maps.
Annual Accessions: 150 maps.
Area Specialization: Ohio; Kentucky; Indiana; Michigan; Pennsylvania; West Virgina.
Subject Specialization: topography and geology.
Dates: 1900 - (100%).
Classification System: USGS map numbers and index.
Collections Cataloged. (100%).
Depository for: USGS (Geol., topo.).
Serves: employees; public. Mon.–Fri. 9 a.m.–6 p.m. (Seats 15; 25 readers served per month).

526. WRIGHT STATE UNIVERSITY
University Library, Reference Department
Map Collection
Colonel Glenn Highway
Dayton, OH 45435
Established 1964.
Telephone: 513/873-2925.
Contact Person: Kathryn Reynolds, Reference Libn.
Staff: 1 professional (part time); 1 non-professional (part time).
Size: 29,000 maps; 92 atlases; 180 reference books and gazetteers.
Area Specialization: Ohio; United States.
Subject Specialization: Topagraphy; geology.
Dates: 1800-1899 (1T%%); 1900 - (99%).
Classification System: local system.
Depository for: USGS (Geol., topo.).
Serves: students; faculty; employees; public. Mon.–Thurs. 8 a.m.–11 p.m., Fri 8 a.m.–6 p.m.; Sat. 9 a.m.–5 p.m.; Sun. 1–9 p.m. (Seats 12).
Reproduction Facility: photocopy.
Publications: We have an approx. 650 page computer printout listing all of our map holdings and their locations.

Delaware

527. OHIO WESLEYAN UNIVERSITY
Geology-Geography Dept Map Library
Delaware, OH 43015
Established ca. 1925.
Telephone: 614/369-4431, ext. 900.
Contact Person: David H. Hickcox, Asst. Professor.
Staff: 1 non-professional (part time).
Size: 3,000 maps.
Annual Accessions: 100 maps.
Area Specialization: Ohio.
Subject Specialization: topography.
Dates: 1900 - (100%).
Classification System: alphabetical by quadrangle.
Collections not Cataloged.
Depository for: USGS (Topo.).
Serves: students; faculty; employees; public. by appointment. (5 readers served per month).
Reproduction Facility: photocopy.

Kent

528. KENT STATE UNIVERSITY
map Library
Kent, OH 44242
Established 1967.
Telephone: 216/672-2017.
Contact Person: Julia Canan, Map Library Supervisor.
Staff: 1 non-professional (full time).
Size: 160,000 maps; 1,208 atlases; 75 relief models; 389 reference books and gazetteers; 1 serials (titles received).
Annual Accessions: 1,000 maps; 6 reference books and gazetteers.
Area Specialization: Ohio; United States; Canada; USSR.
Subject Specialization: topography; soils; geology.
Special Cartographic Collections: Sanborn insurance maps of cities of Ohio.
Dates: 1800-1899 (2%); 1900 - (98%).
Classification System: LC.
Collections Cataloged. (20%).
Depository for: DMA; NOS; USGS (Geol., topo.); Ohio Division of Lands & Soils.
Serves: students; faculty; employees; public. Mon.–Fri. 8 a.m.–12 noon, 1–5 p.m. (Seats 10; 50 readers served per month).

Oxford

529. MIAMI UNIVERSITY
Brill Science Library
Map Room
Oxford, OH 45056
Established 1978.
Telephone: 513/529-7526.
Contact Person: Inka Blazek, Library Associate II.
Staff: 4 professional (full time); 3 (graduate assistants) professional (part time); 6 non-professional (full time); 35 (student assistants) non-professional (part time).
Size: 55,000 maps; 25 atlases; 1 globes; 1,000 aerial photographs; 4,000 reference books and gazetteers; 1,600 serials (titles received); 1,000 microforms (no. of titles).
Annual Accessions: 4,500 maps; 4 atlases.
Area Specialization: Ohio; Indiana; Illinois; Kentucky; Wyoming.
Subject Specialization: biology; geology.
Special Cartographic Collections: early Ohio topographic 1:64,000, AMS- most recent series; USGS-topographic all states, GQ, I and miscellaneous series; all national forests and national parks.
Dates: 1800-1899 (5%); 1900 - (95%).
Classification System: LC; DMA; geographic area and subject.
Depository for: DMA; USGS (Geol., topo.).
Serves: students; faculty; employees; public. Mon.–Fri. 8 a.m.–10:30 p.m.; Sat. 1–5:00 p.m.; Sun. 1–10:30 p.m. (Seats 750; 50,000 readers served per month).
Interlibrary Loan Available.
Reproduction Facility: photocopy; microform.
Publications: Acquisition list.

Toledo

530. TOLEDO-LUCAS COUNTY PUBLIC LIBRARY
History, Travel and Biography Department
325 North Michigan Street
Toledo, OH 43624
Telephone: 419/255-7055.
Contact Person: Donald Barnette, Head, History, Travel and Biography Department.

Staff: 3 professional (full time); 1 professional (part time).
Size: 120,000 maps; 400 atlases; 3 globes; 200 reference books and gazetteers; 5 serials (titles received); 2 microforms (no. of titles).
Annual Accessions: 200 maps; 24 atlases; 20 reference books and gazetteers.
Area Specialization: United States; Toledo and Vicinity.
Subject Specialization: local history.
Dates: 1800-1899 (15%); 1900 - (85%).
Classification System: Dewey (reference books and atlases).
Collections Cataloged. ((reference books and atlases)).
Depository for: DMA; USGS (Geol., topo.).
Serves: public. Mon.–Thurs. 9 a.m.–9 p.m.; Fri. 9 a.m.–5:30 p.m.; Sat. 9 a.m.–5:30 p.m. (Seats 36; 400 readers served per month).
Reproduction Facility: photocopy; quickcopy; microform.

531. UNIVERSITY OF TOLEDO

William S. Carlson Library
Map Collection
2801 West Bancroft Street
Toledo, OH 43606
Established 1956.
Telephone: 419/537-2865.
Contact Person: G. Robert McLean, Asst. Professor of Library Administration and Map.
Staff: 1 professional (full time); 3 non-professional (part time).
Size: 124,000 maps; 69 atlases; 3 globes; 10 relief models; 75 aerial photographs; 275 reference books and gazetteers; 2 serials (titles received); 217 microforms (no. of titles).
Annual Accessions: 4,000 maps.
Area Specialization: United States; Ohio; Europe.
Subject Specialization: topography; geology.
Dates: 1800-1899 (1%); 1900 - (99%).
Classification System: LC.
Collections Cataloged. (45%).
Depository for: DMA; NOS; USGS (Geol., topo.); GPO.
Serves: students; faculty; employees; public. Mon.–Thurs. 8 a.m.–12 midnight, Fri. 7:30 a.m.–8 p.m.; Sat. 9 a.m.–8 p.m.; Sun. 1–12 midnight. (Seats 8; 122 readers served per month).
Reproduction Facility: photocopy; quickcopy; microform; Tracing.
Publications: *Map Collection Guide* .

Yellow Springs

532. ANTIOCH COLLEGE

Geology Department
USGS Map Library
Yellow Springs, OH 45387
Established 1930.
Telephone: 513/767-7331, ext. 580.
Contact Person: Peter Townsend, Professor of Earth Sciences.
Staff: 1 non-professional (part time).
Annual Accessions: .
Collections not Cataloged.
Depository for: USGS (Geol., topo.).
Serves: students; faculty; employees; public. Mon.–Fri. 8:30 a.m.–4:45 p.m. (5 readers served per month).
Interlibrary Loan Available.
Reproduction Facility: photocopy.

Youngstown

533. PUBLIC LIBRARY OF YOUNGSTOWN AND MAHONING COUNTY

305 Wick Avenue
Youngstown, OH 44503
Established 1940.
Telephone: 216/744-8636.
Contact Person: Deborah McCullough, Head, General Reference Dept.; Orrin Cole, Head, Science and Industry Dept.
Staff: 2 professional (part time).
Size: 3,400 maps; 200 atlases; 25 reference books and gazetteers; 8 serials (titles received); 200-300 microforms (no. of titles).
Annual Accessions: 1,000 maps; 10 atlases; 2 reference books and gazetteers; 2 serials (titles received); 30 microforms (no. of titles).
Area Specialization: Youngstown, Ohio; Pennsylvania; Indiana; Illinois; Kentucky.
Subject Specialization: topography; geology; local history.
Special Cartographic Collections: Mahoning River-Army Corps of Engineers collection Lake to River Canal Project Maps, 1920-.
Dates: 1800-1899 (40%); 1900 - (60%).
Classification System: Dewey.
Collections not Cataloged.
Depository for: USGS (Geol., topo.).
Serves: students; faculty; employees; public. Mon., Tues. 9 a.m.–8 p.m.; Wed 9 a.m.–5:30 p.m.; Sat. 9 a.m.–5:30 p.m. (Seats 50; 50 readers served per month).
Reproduction Facility: photocopy; quickcopy; microform.

OKLAHOMA

Edmond

534. CENTRAL STATE UNIVERSITY

Library
Map Collection
100 N. University
Edmond, OK 73034
Established 1972.
Telephone: 405/341-2980, ext. 496.
Contact Person: Fritz A. Buckallew, Map Libn.
Staff: 1 professional (part time).
Size: 32,000 maps.
Annual Accessions: 4,000 maps.
Area Specialization: Oklahoma.
Subject Specialization: history.
Dates: pre-1800 (1%); 1800-1899 (3%); 1900 - (96%).
Collections Cataloged. (20%).
Depository for: USGS (Topo.).
Serves: students; faculty; employees; public. Mon.–Fri. 7:30 a.m.–11 p.m.; Sat. 10 a.m.–6 p.m.; Sun. 2–11 p.m. (Seats 12; 35 readers served per month).
Interlibrary Loan Available.
Reproduction Facility: photocopy.

Lawton

535. MUSEUM OF THE GREAT PLAINS

Special Collections
601 Ferris, P.O. Box 68
Lawton, OK 73502
Established 1960.
Telephone: 405/353-5675.

Contact Person: Paula Williams, Special Collections Curator.
Staff: 1 professional (full time); 1 professional (part time).
Size: 20,000 maps; 18,000 reference books and gazetteers; 150 serials (titles received).
Area Specialization: Great Plains region.
Subject Specialization: history.
Special Cartographic Collections: historical maps of Oklahoma and Southwest—original and photographic copies.
Dates: 1800-1899 (5%); 1900 - (95%).
Classification System: LC.
Collections Cataloged.
Depository for: USGS (Geol., topo.).
Serves: public. Mon.–Fri. 8 a.m.–5 p.m. (Seats 8).
Reproduction Facility: photocopy; quickcopy.
Publications: *Great Plains Journal* published by the Museum. (Publications brochure available upon request).

Norman

536. UNIVERSITY OF OKLAHOMA
Geology Library
830 Van Vleet Oval Room 103
Norman, OK 73019
Established 1950's.
Telephone: 405/325-6451.
Contact Person: Claren M. Kidd, Geology Libn.
Staff: 1 professional (part time); 1 non-professional (part time).
Size: 89,000 maps; 170 atlases; 2 globes; 3 relief models; 200 reference books and gazetteers; 5 serials (titles received); 4 microforms (no. of titles).
Annual Accessions: 5200 maps; 5 atlases; 10 reference books and gazetteers.
Area Specialization: Oklahoma, United States.
Subject Specialization: geology; geophysics; oil & gas; other minerals.
Dates: 1800-1899 (5%); 1900 - (95%).
Classification System: .
Collections Cataloged. (50%).
Depository for: DMA; USGS (Geol., topo.); other state & national geological surveys.
Serves: students; faculty; employees; public. Mon.–Fri. 8 a.m.–5 p.m.; Mon.–Thurs. 7–10 p.m.; Sat. 10 a.m.–2 p.m.; Sun. 2–5 p.m. (Seats 50 (total library); map users only, 50 readers served per month).
Interlibrary Loan Available.
Reproduction Facility: photocopy.

Oklahoma City

537. OKLAHOMA HISTORICAL SOCIETY
Research Library
Wiley Post Historical Building
Oklahoma City, OK 73105
Established Society established 1893.
Telephone: 405/521-2491.
Contact Person: Edward C. Shoemaker, Supervisor of Technical Services.
Staff: 1 professional (full time).
Size: 300 maps; 30 atlases; 25 reference books and gazetteers.
Area Specialization: Indian and Oklahoma Territory; Oklahoma; trans-Mississippi West.
Dates: 1800-1899 (55%); 1900 - (45%).
Collections not Cataloged.
Serves: public. 9 a.m.–4:30 p.m. (Seats 50; 3-5 readers served per month).
Reproduction Facility: photocopy.

Stillwater

538. OKLAHOMA STATE UNIVERSITY
Library
Map Room
Stillwater, OK 74078
Established 1950's.
Telephone: 405/624-6311.
Contact Person: Heather M. Lloyd, Reference Libn.
Staff: 1 professional (part time); 1 non-professional (full time); 1 non-professional (part time).
Size: 102,303 maps; 64,048 aerial photographs; ca. 150 reference books and gazetteers; 8 serials (titles received).
Annual Accessions: 5,000 maps; 4,000 aerial photographs; ca. 20 reference books and gazetteers.
Area Specialization: Oklahoma; southwestern United States.
Subject Specialization: topography; geology; transportation; agriculture; soils; local history.
Dates: 1800-1899 (.2%); 1900 - (99.8%).
Classification System: LC; DMA.
Collections not Cataloged.
Depository for: DMA; USGS (Geol., topo.); GPO regional depository library.
Serves: students; faculty; employees; public;. Mon–Fri. 8 a.m.–5 p.m. (Seats 14; 80 readers served per month).
Reproduction Facility: photocopy.
Publications: *Map Collection, Oklahoma State Unversity Library*, (brochure).

Tulsa

539. THOMAS GILCREASE INSTITUTE OF AMERICAN HISTORY & ART
1400 North 25th West Avenue
Tulsa, OK 74127
Established 1955.
Telephone: 918/582-3122.
Contact Person: Sarah Hirsch, Libn.
Staff: 1 professional (full time).
Size: 300 maps; 50 atlases; 100 reference books and gazetteers; 10 serials (titles received).
Area Specialization: Oklahoma and the trans-Mississippi West.
Subject Specialization: discovery and exploration; settlement of the American West.
Dates: pre-1800 (10%); 1800-1899 (50%); 1900 - (40%).
Collections not Cataloged.
Serves: public. Mon.–Fri. 9 a.m.–5 p.m. by Appointment. (Seats 8; 35 readers served per month).
Reproduction Facility: photocopy.

540. TULSA CITY-COUNTY LIBRARY
Business and Technology Department
400 Civic Center
Tulsa, OK 74103
Telephone: 918/581-5211.
Contact Person: Craig Buthod, Head.
Staff: 8 professional (full time); 4 non-professional (full time).
Size: 75,000 maps.
Annual Accessions: 1,600 maps.
Area Specialization: Western United States.
Subject Specialization: topography; geology; petroleum.
Special Cartographic Collections: General Land Office original survey maps (covering portions of 19 states); A.I. Levorsen gift collection (Foreign geology).
Dates: 1900 - (99%).
Depository for: USGS (Geol., topo.).

Serves: public. Mon.–Thurs. 9 a.m.–9 p.m.; Fri. 9 a.m.–5 p.m.; Sat. 9 a.m.–5 p.m.; Sun. 1–5 p.m. (Seats 100).
Interlibrary Loan Available.
Reproduction Facility: photocopy.

541. UNIVERSITY OF TULSA
McFarlin Library
600 South College
Tulsa, OK 74104
Telephone: 918/592-6000, ext. 2874.
Contact Person: Steven J. Nobles, Public Services Libn.
Staff: 1 professional (full time); 1 non-professional (full time).
Area Specialization: United States.
Subject Specialization: geology; topography.
Depository for: DMA; USGS (Geol., topo.).
Serves: students; faculty; employees. Mon.–Fri. 7–12 Midnight; Sat. 10 a.m.–8 p.m.; Sun. 1–12:00 midnight. (Seats 30).
Interlibrary Loan Available.
Reproduction Facility: photocopy; microform.

OREGON

Ashland

542. SOUTHERN OREGON STATE COLLEGE
Library
Map Collection
1250 Siskiyou Blvd.
Ashland, OR 97520
Established 1970.
Telephone: 503/482-6445.
Contact Person: Harold M. Otness, Acquisitions-Map Libn.
Staff: 1 professional (part time).
Size: 26,000 maps; 150 atlases; 1 globes; 200 aerial photographs; 50 reference books and gazetteers.
Annual Accessions: 500 maps; 10 atlases; 5 reference books and gazetteers.
Area Specialization: Oregon; west coast of United States.
Dates: 1900 - (99%).
Classification System: LC (modified).
Collections Cataloged. (15%).
Depository for: USGS (Topo.).
Serves: students; faculty; employees; public. 8 a.m.–10 p.m.; Sat. 1–5 p.m.; Sun. 2–10 p.m. (Seats 12).
Interlibrary Loan Available.
Reproduction Facility: photocopy.

Bend

543. CENTRAL OREGON COMMUNITY COLLEGE
Library/Media Services
2600 NW College Way
Bend, OR 97701-5998
Telephone: 503/382-6112, ext. 242.
Contact Person: Larry Fogg, Circulation Assistant.
Staff: 1 non-professional (part time).
Size: 3,000 maps; 50 atlases; 1 globes; 2 relief models.
Area Specialization: Oregon; Alaska.
Subject Specialization: topography.

Special Cartographic Collections: early 20th century central Oregon city maps.
Dates: 1900 - (100%).
Classification System: local system.
Collections not Cataloged.
Depository for: USGS (Topo.).
Serves: students; faculty; employees; public. 8 a.m.–9 p.m. Mon.–Thurs; 8 a.m.–4 p.m. Fri.; Sun. 3–9 p.m. (Seats 14).
Reproduction Facility: photocopy.
Publications: Alphabetical listing of collection (guide).

Corvallis

544. OREGON STATE UNIVERSITY
William Jasper Kerr Library
Map Room
Corvallis, Oregon 97331
Established 1954.
Telephone: 503/754-2971.
Staff: 1 professional (full time).
Size: 142,300 maps; 588 atlases; 4 globes; 42 relief models; 11,086 aerial photographs; 520 reference books and gazetteers; 3 serials (titles received); 1 microforms (no. of titles).
Annual Accessions: 3,100 maps; 60 atlases; 200 aerial photographs; 40 reference books and gazetteers.
Area Specialization: Pacific Northwest.
Subject Specialization: geology.
Special Cartographic Collections: Sanborn fire insurance maps of Oregon—178 cities and towns, 1884–1930; Oregon national forest maps; U.S.G.S. topographic sheets (60', 30', & 15' series) of the U.S. (of historical interest).
Dates: 1800-1899 (1%); 1900 - (99%).
Classification System: LC.
Collections Cataloged.
Depository for: DMA; NOS; USGS (Geol., topo.); various state agencies.
Serves: students; faculty; employees; public. Mon.–Thurs. 10–12; 1–5; 7–9; Fri. 10–12; 1–5; Sat. 10–2. (Seats 32; 337 readers served per month).
Interlibrary Loan Available.
Reproduction Facility: photocopy.
Publications: *Oregon State University Library Information Bulletin: Map Room.*

Eugene

545. UNIVERSITY OF OREGON
Map Library
165 Condon Hall
Eugene, OR 97403
Established 1967.
Telephone: 503/686-3051.
Contact Person: Peter L. Stark, Map Libn.
Staff: 1 professional (full time); 1 non-professional (full time).
Size: 225,000 maps; 3,000 atlases; 3 globes; 215 relief models; 300,000 aerial photographs; 250 reference books and gazetteers; 6 serials (titles received); 10 microforms (no. of titles).
Annual Accessions: 8,000 maps; 100 atlases; 5 relief models; 12,000 aerial photographs; 37 reference books and gazetteers.
Area Specialization: Oregon; Pacific Northwest; Latin America: Eastern Europe; Soviet Union; West Africa.
Subject Specialization: history of Pacific Northwest; biogeography; topography.

Special Cartographic Collections: mounted wall maps, world-wide coverage, 526 items; official and gas station road maps, pre WWII, approx. 700 items.
Dates: pre-1800 (.4%); 1800-1899 (9.6%); 1900 - (90%).
Classification System: LC.
Collections Cataloged.
Depository for: DMA; NOS; USGS (Geol., topo.).
Serves: students; faculty; employees; public. Mon.–Thurs. 8 a.m.–9 p.m.; Fri 8 a.m.–5 p.m.; Sun. 12 noon–5 p.m. (Seats 20; 700 readers served per month).
Interlibrary Loan Available.
Reproduction Facility: photocopy.
Publications: select acquisitions list 2 times a year.

Klamath Falls

546. OREGON INSTITUTE OF TECHNOLOGY
Library
Map Collection
Oretech Br. P.O.
Klamath Falls, OR 97601
Established 1965.
Telephone: 503/882-6321, ext. 182.
Contact Person: Robert Weber, Public Services Libn.
Staff: 1 professional (full time); 1 professional (part time).
Size: 2,150 maps; 150 atlases; 1 globes; 20 relief models; 750 aerial photographs.
Annual Accessions: 300 maps; 5 atlases.
Area Specialization: Oregon.
Special Cartographic Collections: geodetic diagrams of Oregon and northern California.
Dates: 1900 - (100%).
Classification System: local system.
Collections Cataloged.
Depository for: USGS (Geol., topo.).
Serves: students; faculty; employees; public. Mon.–Thurs. 7:30 a.m.–10 p.m., Fri 7:30–5 p.m.; Sat. 8 a.m.–5 p.m.; Sun. 6–10 p.m. (20 readers served per month).
Reproduction Facility: photocopy.

LaGrande

547. EASTERN OREGON STATE COLLEGE
Library
Map Library
LaGrande, OR 97850
Established 1965.
Telephone: 503/963-1546.
Contact Person: Verl A. Anderson, Map Libn.
Staff: 1 professional (part time); 2 non-professional (part time).
Size: 6,000 maps; 118 atlases; 2 globes; 20 relief models; 36,000 aerial photographs; 25 reference books and gazetteers; 16 serials (titles received).
Annual Accessions: 500 maps; 10 atlases; 6,000 aerial photographs; 10 reference books and gazetteers.
Area Specialization: Eastern Oregon.
Dates: 1800-1899 (1%); 1900 - (99%).
Classification System: LC.
Collections Cataloged. (85%).
Depository for: USGS (Topo.); Oregon Stabilization & Conservation Service aerial photographs.
Serves: students; faculty; employees; public. Mon.–Fri. 7:30 a.m.–10:00 p.m.; Sat. 1–5 p.m.; Sun. 7–11 p.m. (Seats 50; 100 readers served per month).
Interlibrary Loan Available.
Reproduction Facility: photocopy.

Portland

548. LIBRARY ASSOCIATION OF PORTLAND (MULTNOMAH COUNTY LIBRARY)
Central Library
Literature and History Department
801 S. W. Tenth Avenue
Portland, OR 97205
Telephone: 503/223-7201.
Contact Person: Barbara J. Kahl, Dept. Head.
Staff: 1 professional (part time); 1 non-professional (part time).
Size: 85,571 maps; 300 atlases; 1 globes; 23 relief models; 706 aerial photographs; 600 reference books and gazetteers; 6 serials (titles received); 1 microforms (no. of titles).
Annual Accessions: 1,000 maps.
Area Specialization: Oregon; Washington; Northwest Territory.
Dates: pre-1800 (less than 1%); 1800-1899 (5%); 1900 - (95%).
Classification System: Dewey.
Depository for: DMA; USGS (Topo.).
Serves: public. Mon.–Fri. 10 a.m.–9 p.m.; Tues.–Thurs. 10 a.m.–5:30 p.m.; Sat. 10 a.m.–5:30 p.m. (Seats 6; 400 readers served per month).
Reproduction Facility: photocopy; microform.
Publications: *Portland History* (brochure).

549. OREGON HISTORICAL SOCIETY
Library
Maps Department
1230 S. W. Park Avenue
Portland, OR 97205
Established ca. 1900.
Telephone: 503/222-1741, ext. 32.
Contact Person: Elizabeth Winroth, Maps Libn.
Staff: 1 professional (full time).
Size: 15,000 maps; 110 atlases; 1 globes; 17 relief models; 50 reference books and gazetteers; 15 serials (titles received).
Annual Accessions: 1,000 maps; 4 atlases.
Area Specialization: Oregon; Pacific Northwest; Alaska; North Pacific rim countries; Siberia.
Special Cartographic Collections: maritime and overland explorations of the Pacific Northwest (pre-1850); western explorations of North America (pre-1850).
Dates: pre-1800 (5%); 1800-1899 (15%); 1900 - (80%).
Classification System: LC.
Collections not Cataloged.
Depository for: USGS (Topo.); Oregon State Highway Division.
Serves: students; faculty; employees; public;. Mon.–Fri., 10:00 a.m.–4:45 p.m.; Sat. 10 a.m.–4:45 p.m. (Seats 4; 60 readers served per month).
Reproduction Facility: photocopy.

550. OREGON (STATE) DEPARTMENT OF GEOLOGY AND MINERAL INDUSTRIES
1005 State Office Building
Portland, OR 97201
Established 1940.
Telephone: 503/229-5580.
Contact Person: Klaus Neuendorf.
Staff: 1 professional (part time).
Area Specialization: Oregon; western states.
Subject Specialization: geology.
Dates: 1800-1899 (0.1%); 1900 - (99.9%).
Collections Cataloged. (20%).
Depository for: USGS (Geol.).
Serves: students; employees; public. 8:30 a.m.–12 noon; 1–4:30 p.m. (Seats 1; 50 readers served per month).

Interlibrary Loan Available. from Oregon State Library, Salem
Reproduction Facility: arrangements can be made.
Publications: Schumacher, *Index to published geologic mapping in Oregon, 1898–1979.*.

551. PORTLAND STATE UNIVERSITY
Library
Map Room
P.O. Box 1151
Portland, OR 97207
Established 1960.
Telephone: 503/229-4904.
Contact Person: Jerome DeGraaff, Social Science Libn.
Staff: 2 professional (part time); 2 non-professional (part time).
Size: 14,000 maps; 850 atlases; 2 globes; 30 reference books and gazetteers; 20 serials (titles received).
Annual Accessions: 1,000 maps.
Area Specialization: World alpine and cold weather regions.
Dates: 1900 - (100%).
Classification System: LC.
Collections Cataloged. (25%).
Depository for: DMA.
Serves: students; faculty; employees; public;. Mon.–Thurs. 8 a.m.–10 p.m.; Fri. 8 a.m.–6 p.m.; Sat. 10 a.m.–6 p.m.; Sun. 12 noon–7 p.m.
Interlibrary Loan Available.
Reproduction Facility: photocopy; microform.

Salem

552. OREGON STATE LIBRARY
State Library Building
Salem, OR 97310
Established 1905.
Telephone: 503/378-4277.
Contact Person: Richard Myers, Government Documents Supervisor.
Staff: 2 professional (part time); 1 non-professional (part time).
Size: 20,000 maps; 400 atlases; 1 globes; 25 relief models; 100 reference books and gazetteers.
Area Specialization: Oregon; western United States.
Subject Specialization: topography.
Dates: 1800-1899 (3%); 1900 - (97%).
Classification System: Dewey; Supt. of Docs. system and local system.
Collections Cataloged. (10%).
Depository for: DMA; USGS (Geol., topo.).
Serves: students; faculty; employees; public;. Mon.–Fri. 11 a.m.–5 p.m. (Seats 50 (not exclusively for map patrons); 30 readers served per month).
Interlibrary Loan Available.
Reproduction Facility: photocopy; microform.

PENNSYLVANIA

Bethlehem

553. LEHIGH UNIVERSITY
Linderman
Government Library
Bethlehem, PA 18015
Telephone: 215/861-3050.
Collections Cataloged.
Depository for: USGS (Geol.).

Serves: students; faculty; employees; public. Mon.–Fri. 8 a.m.–12 midnight; Sat. 8 a.m.–12 midnight; Sun. 12 noon–12 midnight.
Interlibrary Loan Available.
Reproduction Facility: photocopy.

554. MORAVIAN COLLEGE
Reeves Library
Main Street and Elizabeth Avenue
Bethlehem, PA 18018
Established 1957.
Telephone: 215/861-1440.
Contact Person: Dr. Joseph J. Gerencher, Jr., Associate Professor of Earth Sciences.
Staff: 1 professional (part time).
Size: 20,000 maps; 30 atlases; 10 globes; 200 relief models; 50 aerial photographs; 30 reference books and gazetteers.
Annual Accessions: 300 maps.
Area Specialization: DMA for the world; USGS for the United States with most coverage of Pennsylvania and surrounding states.
Subject Specialization: topography.
Dates: 1900 - (100%).
Classification System: DMA.
Collections not Cataloged.
Depository for: DMA; USGS (Topo.).
Serves: students; faculty; employees; public. (Seats 3-4; 5 readers served per month).
Reproduction Facility: photocopy.

Bryn Mawr

555. BRYN MAWR COLLEGE
Department of Geology
Bryn Mawr, PA 19010
Established prior to 1960.
Telephone: 215/645-5115.
Contact Person: Dr. Maria Luisa Crawford, Chairman.
Staff: 1 non-professional (part time).
Size: 11,400 (plus all U.S.G.S. topographic quadrangles) maps; 20 atlases; 2 globes; 15 relief models; 20 reference books and gazetteers.
Subject Specialization: topography; geology.
Classification System: alphabetical.
Collections not Cataloged.
Depository for: DMA; NTS (Canada); USGS (Geol., topo.).
Serves: students; faculty; employees; public. Mon.–Fri. 9 a.m. to 4:00 p.m. (Seats 2; 15 readers served per month).
Reproduction Facility: photocopy.

Carlisle Barracks

556. U.S. ARMY WAR COLLEGE
Library
Map Collection
Carlisle Barracks, PA 17013-5050
Established 1955.
Telephone: 717/245-4311.
Contact Person: Richard L. Weary, Map and Micrographics Libn.
Staff: 1 professional (part time).
Size: 41,183 maps; 20 atlases; 1,100 relief models; 12 reference books and gazetteers; 7 serials (titles received).
Annual Accessions: 2,154 maps.
Area Specialization: comprehensive.
Dates: 1900 - (100%).
Classification System: local system.
Collections not Cataloged.

Serves: students; faculty; employees. Mon.–Fri. 12:30–4:30 p.m. (Seats 20; 55 readers served per month).

Clarion

557. CLARION UNIVERSITY OF PENNSYLVANIA
Carlson Library
Clarion, PA 16214
Established 1966.
Telephone: 814/226-2303.
Contact Person: John G. Mager, Cataloger.
Staff: 1 professional (part time); 1 non-professional (part time).
Size: 1,600 maps; 45 atlases; 2 globes; 30 reference books and gazetteers; 5 serials (titles received).
Annual Accessions: 25 maps; 5 atlases; 5 reference books and gazetteers.
Area Specialization: Pennsylvania; Clarion County and Borough, Pennsylvania.
Subject Specialization: topography.
Dates: 1800-1899 (1%); 1900 - (99%).
Classification System: LC.
Collections Cataloged.
Serves: students; faculty; employees; public. Mon.–Thurs. 8 a.m.–10 p.m.; Fri. 8 a.m.–5 p.m.; Sat. 11 a.m.–5 p.m.; Sun. 2–10 p.m. (Seats 50).
Interlibrary Loan Available.
Reproduction Facility: photocopy.

Gettysburg

558. GETTYSBURG COLLEGE
Musselman Library
Audio-Visual Department
Gettysburg, PA 17325
Telephone: 717/334-3131, ext. 370.
Contact Person: David T. Hedrick, Audio-Visual Services Libn.
Staff: 1 professional (part time).
Size: 1,600 maps.
Annual Accessions: 50 maps.
Special Cartographic Collections: Stuckenberg Collection of 900 16th to 19th century maps of Europe and Western Hemisphere.
Dates: pre-1800 (40%); 1800-1899 (10%); 1900 - (50%).
Classification System: LC.
Collections Cataloged. (pre 1900, 25%;). post 1900, 100%
Serves: students; faculty; employees; public. Mon.–Fri. 8:30 a.m.–4:30 p.m.
Reproduction Facility: photocopy.

Harrisburg

559. PENNSYLVANIA (STATE) DEPARTMENT OF ENVIRONMENTAL RESOURCES
Bureau of Topographic and Geologic Survey
Library
916 Executive House Apts.
Harrisburg, PA 17120
Established ca. 1875.
Telephone: 717/783-8077.
Contact Person: Mrs. Sandra Blust, Libn.
Staff: 1 non-professional (part time).
Size: 85,000 maps; 9 atlases; 1 globes; 12 relief models; 170,000 aerial photographs; 900 reference books and gazetteers; 98 serials (titles received); 9 microforms (no. of titles).
Area Specialization: Pennsylvania.

Subject Specialization: geology; geochemistry; paleontology; geophysics; geomorphology; coal geology; hydrology; mineralogy.
Special Cartographic Collections: manuscript maps of geologic studies of Pennsylvania; historical maps of Pennsylvania; complete topographic collection of Pennsylvania.
Dates: pre-1800 (1%); 1800-1899 (9%); 1900 - (90%).
Classification System: LC.
Collections Cataloged.
Depository for: USGS (Geol., topo.).
Serves: students; faculty; employees; public. Mon.–Fri. 8 a.m.–4 p.m. (Seats 30; 175 readers served per month).
Interlibrary Loan Available.
Reproduction Facility: quickcopy; microform.

560. PENNSYLVANIA (STATE) HISTORICAL AND MUSEUM COMMISSION
Bureau of Archives and History
Division of Archives and Manuscripts
P.O. Box 1026
Harrisburg, PA 17108
Established 1903.
Telephone: 717/787-2701.
Contact Person: Linda A. Ries, Associate Archivist.
Staff: 1 professional (part time); 1 non-professional (part time).
Size: 885 maps; 15 atlases; 41 cu. ft. aerial photographs.
Annual Accessions: 5 maps.
Area Specialization: Pennsylvania.
Subject Specialization: canals; highways; industry; railroads; cities; towns; counties.
Dates: pre-1800 (30%); 1800-1899 (35%); 1900 - (35%).
Classification System: local system.
Collections Cataloged.
Depository for: USGS (Topo.).
Serves: students; faculty; employees; public;. Mon.–Fri. 8:30 a.m.–4:45 p.m. (Seats 30; 12 readers served per month).
Reproduction Facility: photocopy; quickcopy; microform.
Publications: *Descriptive List of the Map Collection in the Pennsylvania State Archives* compiled by Martha L. Simonetti, Harrisburg, PHMC, 1976.

561. PENNSYLVANIA (STATE) HISTORICAL AND MUSEUM COMMISSION
Division of Land Records
"A" 15 Archives Building
Harrisburg, PA 17120
Telephone: 717/787-5989, 7180.
Contact Person: Edward Price, Director.
Size: 510 maps.
Annual Accessions: 10 maps.
Area Specialization: Pennsylvania counties.
Subject Specialization: original land grants of the Penns and the Commonwealth of Pennsylvania.
Dates: pre-1800 (80%); 1800-1899 (20%).
Depository for: Commonwealth of Pennsylvania.
Serves: public. Mon.–Fri. 8:30 a.m.–4:45 p.m.
Reproduction Facility: Diazo.

562. PENNSYLVANIA STATE LIBRARY
General Library Bureau
Reference Section
Box 1601
Harrisburg, PA 17126
Contact Person: Terry Tilden, Reference Libn.
Staff: 1 professional (full time); 1 non-professional (part time).
Size: 7,000 maps; 2 globes.
Area Specialization: Pennsylvania.
Subject Specialization: local history.
Classification System: local system (DDC and LC modified).

Collections Cataloged. (50%).
Depository for: USGS (Topo.).
Serves: public. Mon., Wed., Thurs., Fri. 8:30 a.m.–5 p.m.; Tues. 8:30 a.m.–8:30 p.m.
Reproduction Facility: photocopy; microform.

Haverford

563. HAVERFORD COLLEGE
James P. Magill Library
Treasure Room
Haverford, PA 19072
Established 1957.
Telephone: 215/896-1161.
Contact Person: Diana Alten, Manuscripts Cataloger.
Staff: 1 non-professional (part time).
Size: 250 maps; 50 atlases.
Annual Accessions: 10-15 maps.
Area Specialization: Pennsylvania.
Subject Specialization: historical Philadelphia; Quaker settlements, burial sites, meetinghouses, etc.; Indian tribal locations.
Dates: pre-1800 (30%); 1800-1899 (40%); 1900 - (30%).
Classification System: local system (by collection).
Collections Cataloged.
Serves: students; faculty; employees; public. Mon.–Fri. 9 a.m.–12:30 p.m., 1:30–4:30 p.m. (Seats 18; 2 map collection readers/month readers served per month).
Reproduction Facility: photocopy.

Indiana

564. INDIANA UNIVERSITY OF PENNSYLVANIA
Department of Geography & Regional Planning
Map and Image Library
16 Leonard Hall
Indiana, PA 15705
Established 1960.
Telephone: 412/357-2250.
Contact Person: Dr. John D. Stephens, Associate Professor of Geography.
Staff: 1 professional (full time); 2 non-professional (part time).
Size: 15,500 maps; 75 atlases; 20 globes; 250 relief models; 5,200 aerial photographs; 180 reference books and gazetteers; 10 serials (titles received).
Annual Accessions: 1,500 maps; 25 atlases; 500 aerial photographs; 25 reference books and gazetteers.
Area Specialization: Pennsylvania and Middle Atlantic Region; United States; Canada; Caribbean, Latin America.
Subject Specialization: physical geography; human geography; regional planning; cartography.
Special Cartographic Collections: digital cartographic and imagery data (terrain models, Census Dime files, and Landsat data); cartographic and image-processing software (available on-line through Library's computing facilities).
Dates: 1800-1899 (1%); 1900 - (99%).
Classification System: Dewey (for monographs and atlases); local system (for maps and imagery).
Collections Cataloged. (60%).
Depository for: USGS (Topo.).
Serves: students; faculty; employees; public. Mon.–Fri. 10 a.m.–4 p.m. (during semesters). (Seats 18; 150 readers served per month).
Reproduction Facility: microprocessor, color graphics display screen, and matrix printer.

Kutztown

565. KUTZTOWN UNIVERSITY
Rohrbach Library
Map Collection
Kutztown, PA 19530
Established 1967.
Telephone: 215/683-4480.
Contact Person: Mrs. Anita T. Sprankle, Non-Book Materials Libn.
Staff: 1 professional (part time).
Size: 13,000 maps; 4 globes; 480 relief models; 390 aerial photographs; 2 microforms (no. of titles).
Annual Accessions: 500 maps; 10 relief models; 20 aerial photographs.
Area Specialization: Pennsylvania; United States.
Subject Specialization: topography; city planning.
Dates: 1800-1899 (1%); 1900 - (99%).
Classification System: Boggs-Lewis.
Collections Cataloged.
Depository for: USGS (Topo.).
Serves: students; faculty; employees; public. Mon.–Thurs. 7:45 a.m.–11 p.m., Fri. 7:45 a.m.–11 p.m.; Sat. 11 a.m.–5 p.m.; Sun. 2–11 p.m. (Seats 24; 150 readers served per month).
Reproduction Facility: photocopy.
Publications: *Rohrbach Library Map Collection* (information brochure).

Lancaster

566. LANCASTER MENNONITE HISTORICAL SOCIETY
2215 Millstream Road
Lancaster, PA 17602
Established 1964.
Telephone: 717/393-9745.
Contact Person: Lloyd Zeager, Libn.
Staff: 1 professional (full time); 1 professional (part time); 1 non-professional (full time); 1 non-professional (part time).
Size: ca. 200 maps; 80 titles atlases.
Area Specialization: Southeastern Pennsylvania.
Subject Specialization: patentee and warrantee maps; township maps; U.S. Geological Survey maps.
Dates: 1800-1899 (50%); 1900 - (50%).
Classification System: LC (for atlases).
Collections not Cataloged.
Serves: public. Tues.–Fri. 8:30 a.m.–4:30 p.m.; Sat. 8:30–4:30. (Seats 20; 150-200 readers served per month).
Reproduction Facility: photocopy.

Lewisburg

567. BUCKNELL UNIVERSITY
Ellen Clarke Bertrand Library
Reference Department
Lewisburg, PA 17837
Established 1976.
Telephone: 717/524-1462.
Contact Person: Patricia A. Peroni, Assistant Reference Libn.
Staff: 1 professional (part time); 1 non-professional (part time).
Size: 3,119 maps; 1 globes.
Area Specialization: Pennsylvania.
Dates: 1800-1899 (less than 1%); 1900 - (almost 100%).
Classification System: LC.
Collections Cataloged. (100%).
Depository for: USGS (Geol., topo.); GPO.

Serves: students; faculty; employees; public. Mon.–Fri. 7:45 a.m.–12 midnight; Sat. 9 a.m.–10 p.m.; Sun. 12 noon–12 midnight. (Seats 30; 50 readers served per month).
Interlibrary Loan Available.
Reproduction Facility: photocopy.

Meadville

568. CRAWFORD COUNTY HISTORICAL SOCIETY
848 North Main Street
Meadville, PA 16335
Established 1888.
Telephone: 814/724-6080.
Contact Person: Robert D. Ilisevich, Libn.
Staff: 2 professional (part time); 1 non-professional (full time).
Size: 400 maps; 10 atlases; 10 aerial photographs; 25 reference books and gazetteers.
Annual Accessions: 10 maps.
Area Specialization: Crawford County, PA.
Subject Specialization: history; transportation.
Dates: pre-1800 (10%); 1800-1899 (30%); 1900 - (60%).
Collections not Cataloged.
Serves: public. 1–5 p.m.; Sat. 10–1. (Seats 8; 80 readers served per month).
Reproduction Facility: photocopy; microform.

Millersville

569. MILLERSVILLE UNIVERSITY
Geography Department
Map Library
Millersville, PA 17551
Established 1963.
Telephone: 717/872-3557.
Contact Person: A. C. Lord.
Staff: professional (part time); non-professional (part time).
Size: 65,000 maps; 20 atlases; 10 globes; 25 relief models; 200 aerial photographs.
Annual Accessions: 100 maps.
Area Specialization: Pennsylvania; New York; New Jersey; Delaware; Maryland.
Subject Specialization: topography.
Dates: 1800-1899 (.1%); 1900 - (99.9%).
Classification System: .
Collections not Cataloged.
Depository for: DMA; USGS (Topo.).
Serves: students; faculty; employees; public. Mon.–Fri. 8 a.m.–3 p.m. (Seats 14; 20 readers served per month).

New Castle

570. NEW CASTLE PUBLIC LIBRARY
Reference Department
207 E. North Street
New Castle, PA 16101
Telephone: 412/658-6659, ext. 24.
Contact Person: Marcia A. Morelli, Reference Libn.
Staff: 1 professional (part time).
Size: 1,500 maps; 40 atlases; 5 globes.
Area Specialization: New Castle and Lawrence County, PA.
Subject Specialization: topography.
Dates: 1800-1899 (5%); 1900 - (95%).
Classification System: local system.
Collections Cataloged.
Depository for: USGS (Topo.).
Serves: public. Mon.–Fri. 8:30 a.m.–9 p.m.; Sat. 8:30 a.m.–5:30 p.m. (Seats 50).
Reproduction Facility: photocopy; microform.

Philadelphia

571. FREE LIBRARY OF PHILADELPHIA
Map Collection
Logan Square
Philadelphia, PA 19103
Established 1927.
Telephone: 215/686-5397.
Contact Person: Richard Boardman, Map Libn.
Staff: 1 professional (full time); 1 non-professional (full time).
Size: 133,000 maps; 3,000 atlases; 15 globes; 24 relief models; 100 aerial photographs; 3,000 reference books and gazetteers; 21 serials (titles received); 2 microforms (no. of titles).
Annual Accessions: ca. 3,000 maps; 50 atlases; 100 reference books and gazetteers; 1 serials (titles received).
Area Specialization: Philadelphia; Pennsylvania; Northeastern & Middle Atlantic States.
Subject Specialization: cartography; geography; map librarianship.
Special Cartographic Collections: William G. Kelso collection of Jansson-Visscher maps of America; fire insurance atlases of Philadelphia; Pennsylvania county atlases; maps of imaginary lands.
Dates: pre-1800 (10%); 1800-1899 (40%); 1900 - (50%).
Classification System: local system (titling).
Collections Cataloged. (27%).
Depository for: DMA; USGS (Topo.).
Serves: public. Mon.–Fri. 9 a.m.–5 p.m. (Seats 12; 150 readers served per month).
Reproduction Facility: photocopy; microform.

572. HISTORICAL SOCIETY OF PENNSYLVANIA
Manuscripts Department
1300 Locust Street
Philadelphia, PA 19107
Established 1824.
Telephone: 215/732-6200, ext. 17.
Contact Person: Peter J. Parker, Chief of Manuscripts.
Staff: 4 professional (part time).
Size: 7,600 maps; 350 atlases; 60 aerial photographs; 50 reference books and gazetteers; 2 serials (titles received).
Annual Accessions: 10 maps; 5 aerial photographs; 2 reference books and gazetteers.
Area Specialization: North America (17th & 18th Centuries); Middle Atlantic States; Southern States trans-Mississippi West.
Subject Specialization: Revolutionary War; Mason & Dixon Line; railroads and canals (Middle Atlantic States).
Special Cartographic Collections: Chew Collection of Mason & Dixon materials; A. A. Humphreys Collection of Civil War maps and railroad maps of 1850s; maritime atlases.
Dates: pre-1800 (30%); 1800-1899 (60%); 1900 - (10%).
Classification System: AGS for maps; local classification of atlases.
Collections Cataloged. (80%).
Serves: public. Mon. 1–9 p.m.; Tues.–Fri. 9 a.m.–5 p.m. (Seats 20; 180 (includes all department readers) readers served per month).
Reproduction Facility: photocopy; quickcopy; microform.

573. THE LIBRARY COMPANY OF PHILADELPHIA
Print Department
1314 Locust Street
Philadelphia, PA 19107
Established 1731.
Telephone: 215/546-3181.

Contact Person: Kenneth Finkel, Curator of Prints.
Staff: 1 professional (full time); 1 non-professional (full time).
Size: 2,000 maps; 150 atlases; 2 globes; 4,800 aerial photographs; 30 reference books and gazetteers.
Area Specialization: United States; Pennsylvania; Philadelphia.
Dates: pre-1800 (5%); 1800-1899 (40%); 1900 - (55%).
Collections Cataloged. (25%).
Serves: students; faculty; employees; public. Mon.–Fri. 9 a.m.–4:45 p.m. (Seats 6; 140 readers served per month).
Interlibrary Loan Available. select
Reproduction Facility: photocopy; quickcopy; microform; slides.

574. TEMPLE UNIVERSITY
Samuel Paley Library
Map Unit
Philadelphia, PA 19122
Established 1967.
Telephone: 215/787-8213, ext. 33.
Contact Person: Ida G. Ginsburgs, Map and Reference Libn.
Staff: 1 professional (part time); 1 non-professional (part time).
Size: 61,835 maps; 676 atlases; 1 globes; 215 reference books and gazetteers; 6 serials (titles received).
Annual Accessions: 4,500 maps; 45 atlases; 15 reference books and gazetteers.
Area Specialization: eastern United States.
Subject Specialization: topography.
Dates: 1800-1899 (5%); 1900 - (95%).
Classification System: AGS.
Collections Cataloged. (25%).
Depository for: DMA; USGS (Geol., topo.).
Serves: students; faculty; employees; public. Mon.–Fri. 9 a.m.–9 p.m.; Sat. 9 a.m.–5 p.m.; Sun. 12 noon–8 p.m. (Seats 12).
Interlibrary Loan Available.
Reproduction Facility: quickcopy.

575. UNIVERSITY OF PENNSYLVANIA
Geology Department
Hayden Hall, D4
Philadelphia, PA 19104
Established 1900.
Telephone: 215/898-5156.
Contact Person: Carol Faul, Map Libn.
Staff: 1 professional (full time); 1 professional (part time); 2 non-professional (full time); 2 non-professional (part time).
Size: 100,000 maps.
Annual Accessions: 1,000 maps.
Area Specialization: United States; Canada.
Dates: 1800-1899 (5%); 1900 - (95%).
Collections not Cataloged.
Depository for: DMA; NOS; NTS (Canada); USGS (Geol., topo.).
Serves: students; faculty; employees. (Seats 12; 60 readers served per month).
Reproduction Facility: photocopy.

Pittsburgh

576. CARNEGIE LIBRARY OF PITTSBURGH
Science and Technology Department
4400 Forbes Avenue
Pittsburgh, PA 15213
Established circa 1900.
Telephone: 412/622-3138.
Contact Person: Catherine M. Brosky, Head.
Size: 5,000 maps.

Area Specialization: United States.
Subject Specialization: topography; geology.
Dates: 1900 - (100%).
Classification System: local system.
Collections Cataloged.
Depository for: USGS (Geol., topo.).
Serves: public. Mon., Tues., Fri. 9 a.m.–9 p.m.; Wed, Thurs. 9–5:30 p.m.; Sat. 9 a.m.–9 p.m.; Winter 9a.m.–9 p.m. Summer; Sun. 2–5 p.m.
Reproduction Facility: photocopy; telefacsimile.

577. HISTORICAL SOCIETY OF WESTERN PENNSYLVANIA
Archives Department
4338 Bigelow Blvd.
Pittsburgh, PA 15213
Established 1914.
Telephone: 412/681-5533.
Contact Person: Ruth S. Reid, Archivist.
Staff: 1 professional (full time).
Size: 1425 maps; 125 atlases; 1 relief models; 10 aerial photographs; 48 reference books and gazetteers; 3 serials (titles received).
Annual Accessions: 50 maps; 10 atlases; 1 aerial photographs; 5 reference books and gazetteers.
Area Specialization: western Pennsylvania; eastern Ohio; northern West Virginia.
Subject Specialization: Land ownership.
Dates: pre-1800 (10%); 1800-1899 (70%); 1900 - (20%).
Classification System: local system.
Collections Cataloged.
Serves: students; faculty; employees; public. Tues.–Fri. 9:30 a.m.–4:30 p.m.; Sat. 9:30 a.m.–4:30 p.m. (Seats 36; 40 readers served per month).
Reproduction Facility: photocopy;.

578. UNIVERSITY OF PITTSBURGH
Darlington Memorial Library
601 Cathedral of Learning
Pittsburgh, PA 15260
Established 1937.
Telephone: 412/624-4491.
Contact Person: Dennis K. Lambert, Libn.
Staff: 1 professional (part time); 1 non-professional (part time).
Size: 901 maps; 69 atlases; 30 reference books and gazetteers.
Area Specialization: Pennsylvania; United States.
Dates: pre-1800 (30%); 1800-1899 (60%); 1900 - (10%).
Classification System: LC (atlases).
Collections Cataloged.
Serves: students; faculty; employees. Mon.–Fri. 1–5 p.m. (Seats 20).
Reproduction Facility: photocopy.

579. UNIVERSITY OF PITTSBURGH
Hillman Library
G-8 Hillman Library, University of Pittsburgh
Pittsburgh, PA 15260
Telephone: 412/624-4449.
Contact Person: Jean R. Aiken, Information Libn.
Staff: 1 professional (part time); 1 non-professional (part time).
Size: 77,000 maps.
Annual Accessions: 2,300 maps.
Classification System: LC.
Collections Cataloged. (15%).
Depository for: DMA; NOS; USGS (Topo.).
Serves: students; faculty; employees; public.
Reproduction Facility: photocopy.

Shippensburg

580. SHIPPENSBURG UNIVERSITY
Ezra Lehman Memorial Library
Government Documents Collection
Shippensburg, PA 17257
Established 1980.
Telephone: 717/532-1634.
Contact Person: Katherine Warkentin, Documents Libn.
Staff: 1 professional (part time); 1 non-professional (part time).
Size: 2,004 maps.
Area Specialization: Pennsylvania; United States.
Dates: 1900 - (100%).
Classification System: .
Collections not Cataloged.
Depository for: USGS (Topo.).
Serves: students; faculty; employees; public. (Seats 18).
Reproduction Facility: photocopy; microform.

Slippery Rock

581. SLIPPERY ROCK UNIVERSITY OF PENNSYLVANIA
Department of Geography & Environmental Studies
Slippery Rock, PA 16057
Established 1962.
Telephone: 412/794-7310, ext. 5310.
Contact Person: Dr. Paul F. Rizza, Department Chairperson.
Staff: 1 non-professional (part time).
Size: 22,000 maps; 21 atlases; 25 relief models; 240 aerial photographs; 17 reference books and gazetteers.
Area Specialization: Pennsylvania.
Dates: 1900 - (100%).
Classification System: local system.
Collections Cataloged.
Depository for: DMA; USGS (Geol., topo.).
Serves: students; faculty; employees; public. Mon.–Fri. 9 a.m.–4 p.m. (Seats; 12 readers served per month).
Interlibrary Loan Available.

Swarthmore

582. SWARTHMORE COLLEGE
Library
Swarthmore, PA 19081
Telephone: 215/447-7492.
Contact Person: Sue Williamson, Government Documents Libn.
Size: 15,000 maps; 184 atlases; 3 globes; 16 reference books and gazetteers.
Annual Accessions: 225 maps.
Area Specialization: Pennsylvania; Delaware; Maryland.
Subject Specialization: geology; Quaker history.
Special Cartographic Collections: British Ordnance Survey maps.
Depository for: USGS (Geol.).
Serves: public.
Interlibrary Loan Available.
Reproduction Facility: photocopy.

University Park

583. PENNSYLVANIA STATE UNIVERSITY
Pattee Library
Maps Section
University Park, PA 16802
Established 1947.
Telephone: 814/863-0094.
Contact Person: Karl H. Proehl, Map Libn.
Staff: 1 professional (full time); 2 professional (part time); 2 non-professional (full time); 8-10 non-professional (part time).
Size: 273,232 maps; 2,488 atlases; 8 globes; 177 relief models; 52 aerial photographs; 963 reference books and gazetteers; 27 serials (titles received); 5 microforms (no. of titles).
Annual Accessions: 8,000 maps; 28 atlases; 3 relief models; 4 aerial photographs; 20 reference books and gazetteers; 2 microforms (no. of titles).
Area Specialization: Pennsylvania; United States; Canada; western and central Europe.
Subject Specialization: topography; urban planning; transportation; place name studies; map reading and interpretation literature.
Special Cartographic Collections: Sanborn fire insurance maps of Pennsylvania towns and cities.
Dates: 1900 - (100%).
Classification System: LC.
Collections Cataloged.
Depository for: DMA; NOS; NTS (Canada); USGS (Topo.).
Serves: students; faculty; employees; public. Mon.–Thurs. 7:45 a.m.–12 midnight; Fri. 7:45 a.m.–9 p.m.; Sat. 7:45 a.m.–9 p.m.; Sun. 12 noon–12 midnight. (Seats 52; 1,606 readers served per month).
Interlibrary Loan Available.
Reproduction Facility: photocopy; microform.
Publications: *New Acquisitions/Cartographic Notes* (quarterly); *Pennsylvania Maps and Atlases in the Pennsylvania State University Libraries* by Ruby Miller; *Guide to Pennsylvania State University Maps Section.*.

West Chester

584. WEST CHESTER UNIVERSITY
Francis Harvey Green Library
Document and Map Department
West Chester, PA 19383
Established 1978.
Telephone: 215/436-2869.
Contact Person: Mary Ann Burns Duffy, Document and Map Libn.
Staff: 1 professional (full time); 1 non-professional (full time).
Size: 4,468 maps; 255 atlases; 2 globes; 12 relief models; 200 aerial photographs; 400 reference books and gazetteers.
Annual Accessions: 300 maps; 20 atlases; 20 reference books and gazetteers.
Area Specialization: Pennsylvania; Mid-Atlantic States.
Dates: pre-1800 (1%); 1800-1899 (2%); 1900 - (97%).
Classification System: LC.
Collections Cataloged.
Depository for: DMA; USGS (Topo.).
Serves: students; faculty; employees; public. Mon.–Fri. 9 a.m.–10 p.m.; Sat. 9 a.m.–5 p.m.; Sun. 2-10 p.m. (Seats 20 persons; 120 persons readers served per month).
Interlibrary Loan Available.
Reproduction Facility: photocopy; microform.
Publications: *Annual Acquisition List.*

PUERTO RICO

Rio Piedras

585. UNIVERSITY OF PUERTO RICO
General Library
Documents Room
Rio Piedras, PR 00931
Telephone: 764-0000, ext. 3514.
Contact Person: Ms. Angeles M. Reyes, Libn.
Staff: 1 professional (part time).
Size: 17,057 maps; 55 atlases; 1 globes; 40 reference books and gazetteers.
Annual Accessions: 500 (approx.) maps.
Subject Specialization: topography; geology.
Dates: 1900 -.
Classification System: DMA.
Collections not Cataloged.
Depository for: DMA; USGS (Geol., topo.).
Serves: students; faculty; employees; public;. Mon.–Wed. 7:30 a.m.–7:00 p.m.;. Thurs.–Fri. 7:30 a.m.–5:00 p.m. Mon.–Wed. 7:30 a.m.–7:00 p.m. Sat. 8:00 a.m.–12:00 p.m. (Seats 18; 300 readers served per month).
Reproduction Facility: photocopy.

RHODE ISLAND

Kingston

586. UNIVERSITY OF RHODE ISLAND
University Library
Special Collections
Kingston, RI 02881
Telephone: 401/792-2594.
Contact Person: David C. Maslyn, Head, Special Collections.
Size: 13,000 maps.
Annual Accessions: 130 maps.
Subject Specialization: topography.
Classification System: DMA.
Collections not Cataloged.
Depository for: DMA.
Serves: students; faculty; employees; public. Mon.–Fri. 9 a.m.–4 p.m.
Reproduction Facility: photocopy.

Newport

587. NEWPORT HISTORICAL SOCIETY
Library
82 Touro St.
Newport, RI 02840
Established 1854.
Telephone: 401/846-0813.
Contact Person: Thomas G. Brennan, Libn./Curator of Photographs & Maps.
Staff: 1 professional (full time).
Area Specialization: Newport; Acquidneck Island.
Collections not Cataloged.
Serves: public. Tues.–Fri. 9:30 a.m.–4:30 p.m. (Sept.–June); Sat. 9:30 a.m.–12 noon (Sept.–June). (Seats 10 persons; 30-50 readers served per month).
Reproduction Facility: photocopy; microform.

Providence

588. BROWN UNIVERSITY
John Carter Brown Library
Box 1894
Providence, RI 02912
Established ca. 1846.
Telephone: 401/863-2725.
Contact Person: Susan L. Danforth, Curator of Maps.
Staff: 1 professional (full time).
Size: 1,300 maps; 300 atlases; 20 (gores) globes; 900 reference books and gazetteers.
Annual Accessions: 20 maps; 10 atlases.
Area Specialization: Oceanic exploration; colonial North and South America; Arctic; Antarctic.
Subject Specialization: late medieval cosmography; exploration and discovery ca. 1450–1800; North and South American settlement, colonization, development, economy; maritime history.
Dates: pre-1800 (90%); 1800-1899 (9%); 1900 - (1%).
Classification System: local system.
Collections Cataloged.
Serves: students; faculty; employees. Mon.–Fri. 8:30 a.m.–5 p.m.; Sat. 8:30 a.m.–12 noon. (Seats 2; 15 readers served per month).
Reproduction Facility: photocopy; microform.
Publications: *The Blathwayt Atlas*, 2v., 1970-1975. *Opportunities for Research in the John Carter Brown Library*.

589. BROWN UNIVERSITY
Rockefeller Library
Prospect and College Streets
Providence, RI 02912
Telephone: 401/863-2167.
Classification System: LC; Boggs-Lewis; SuDoc system.
Collections Cataloged.
Depository for: DMA.
Serves: students; faculty; employees; Depository access.
Reproduction Facility: photocopy; microform.

590. BROWN UNIVERSITY
Sciences Library
Waterman and Thayer Streets
Providence, RI 02912
Telephone: 401/863-3333.
Contact Person: Patricia E. Galkowski, Reference Libn.
Staff: 1 professional (part time).
Size: 70,000 maps.
Annual Accessions: 3,000 maps.
Dates: 1900 - (99%).
Classification System: LC; Boggs-Lewis.
Collections Cataloged. (30%).
Depository for: USGS (Geol., topo.).
Serves: students; faculty; employees; public. Mon.–Fri. 9 a.m.–5 p.m. (Seats 6).
Reproduction Facility: photocopy.
Publications: *A Guide to Locating Maps in the Sciences Library* (guide).

591. PROVIDENCE PUBLIC LIBRARY
150 Empire Street
Providence, RI 02903
Telephone: 401/521-7722.
Area Specialization: east coast of North America; Rhode Island.
Subject Specialization: local history.
Special Cartographic Collections: Harris Collection (Civil War).
Depository for: USGS (Topo.).
Serves: public.
Reproduction Facility: photocopy.

592. RHODE ISLAND HISTORICAL SOCIETY
Library
Graphics Department
121 Hope Street
Providence, RI 02906
Established 1822.
Telephone: 401/331-8575.
Contact Person: Maureen Taylor, Graphics Curator.
Staff: 2 professional (full time).
Size: 2,765 maps; 127 atlases; 30 reference books and gazetteers.
Annual Accessions: 30 maps; 2 atlases; 2 reference books and gazetteers.
Area Specialization: Rhode Island.
Subject Specialization: same.
Special Cartographic Collections: Potter Collection: Early Manuscript maps of Narragansett, R.I.; Carrington Collection: China Trade maps.
Dates: pre-1800 (25%); 1800-1899 (50%); 1900 - (25%).
Classification System: local system.
Collections Cataloged. (33%).
Depository for: USGS (Geol., topo.).
Serves: students; faculty; employees; public. Labor Day– Memorial Day: Tues. 9 a.m.–5 p.m.; Wed.–Sat. 9 a.m.–6 p.m.; Su. Tues.–Thurs. 9 a.m.–6 p.m. (Seats 4–6; 30 readers served per month).
Reproduction Facility: photocopy.
Publications: Chapin, Howard M. *Checklist of Maps of Rhode Island.* Providence, R.I.: Preston and Rounds, 1918. Chapin, Howard M. *Cartography of Rhode Island,* Providence, 1915.

SOUTH CAROLINA

Clemson

593. CLEMSON UNIVERSITY
Robert Muldrow Cooper Library
Public Documents Unit
Clemson, SC 29631
Established 1945.
Telephone: 803/656-3024, ext. 34.
Contact Person: Maureen Harris, Head, Public Documents Unit.
Staff: 1 professional (part time); 4 non-professional (part time).
Size: 30,000 maps; 40 atlases; 5 relief models; 20 reference books and gazetteers; 25 serials (titles received).
Annual Accessions: 1,000 maps; 5 atlases; 2 reference books and gazetteers.
Subject Specialization: agriculture.
Dates: 1900 - (100%).
Classification System: LC; SuDocs for U.S. government maps.
Collections Cataloged. (50%).
Depository for: DMA; USGS (Geol., topo.).
Serves: students; faculty; employees; public. Mon.–Fri. 8 a.m.–10 p.m.; Sat. 10 a.m.–6 p.m.; Sun. 1–10:00 p.m. (10 readers served per month).
Interlibrary Loan Available.
Reproduction Facility: photocopy.

Columbia

594. SOUTH CAROLINA (STATE) DEPARTMENT OF ARCHIVES AND HISTORY
P.O. Box 11669, Capitol Station
Columbia, SC 29211
Established 1950.
Telephone: 803/758-5816.
Contact Person: Michael Stauffer, Archivist II.
Staff: 1 professional (part time).
Size: 160,000 maps; 6 atlases; 1 relief models; 17 reference books and gazetteers; 2 serials (titles received).
Annual Accessions: 75 maps.
Area Specialization: South Carolina; southeastern United States.
Subject Specialization: township plans; Indian lands; forts; canals; roads; railroads; soils; topography.
Special Cartographic Collections: original surveys for the John Wilson Map and the Mills Atlas.
Dates: pre-1800 (25%); 1800-1899 (50%); 1900 - (25%).
Classification System: local system.
Collections Cataloged.
Depository for: S.C. Secretary of State.
Serves: students; faculty; employees; public;. Mon.–Fri. 9 a.m.–9 p.m.; Sat. 9 a.m.–6 p.m.; Sun. 1–9 p.m. (Seats 35).
Reproduction Facility: photocopy; quickcopy; microform.

595. SOUTH CAROLINA GEOLOGICAL SURVEY
Harbison Forest Road
Columbia, SC 29210
Established 1957.
Telephone: 803/758-6431.
Contact Person: Agnes Streeter, Administrative Specialist.
Staff: 1 non-professional (full time).
Size: 4,500 maps; 40 atlases; 1,500 aerial photographs; 100 reference books and gazetteers.
Annual Accessions: 100 maps.
Area Specialization: South Carolina.
Subject Specialization: geology; geography.
Dates: 1900 - (100).
Depository for: USGS (Geol., topo.).
Serves: employees; public. Mon.–Fri. 8 a.m.–5 p.m. (Seats 10; 50 readers served per month).

596. UNIVERSITY OF SOUTH CAROLINA
Map Library
Columbia, SC 29208
Established 1897.
Telephone: 803/777-2802.
Contact Person: David C. McQuillan, Map Libn.
Staff: 1 professional (full time); 3 non-professional (part time).
Size: 180,000 maps; 1,500 atlases; 3 globes; 73 relief models; 60,000 aerial photographs; 2,000 reference books and gazetteers; 15 serials (titles received); 1 microforms (no. of titles).
Annual Accessions: 5,000 maps; 25 atlases; 1,500 aerial photographs; 100 reference books and gazetteers; 1 microforms (no. of titles).
Area Specialization: South Carolina; southeastern United States.
Subject Specialization: topography; cities; roads.
Dates: 1800-1899 (5%); 1900 - (95%).
Classification System: LC.
Collections Cataloged. (40%).
Depository for: DMA; USGS (Geol., topo.); GPO (through Gov. Doc. collection in Thomas Cooper Library).
Serves: students; faculty; employees; public. Mon.–Fri. 8:30 a.m.–5:00 p.m. (Seats 25; 100 readers served per month).
Reproduction Facility: quickcopy.

597. UNIVERSITY OF SOUTH CAROLINA
South Caroliniana Library
Columbia, SC 29208
Established 1940.
Telephone: 803/777-3132.
Contact Person: Eleanor Richardson, Reference Libn.
Staff: 1 professional (part time).
Size: 1,485 maps; 18 atlases; 15 aerial photographs; 20 reference books and gazetteers.
Annual Accessions: 15 maps.
Area Specialization: South Carolina; southeastern United States.
Special Cartographic Collections: Kendall Map Collection; Sanborn fire insurance maps (S.C. cities).
Dates: pre-1800 (23); 1800-1899 (33); 1900 - (44).
Classification System: local system.
Collections Cataloged. (100%).
Serves: students; faculty; employees; public. Mon., Wed., Fri. 8:30 a.m.–5 p.m. Tues., Thurs. 8:30 a.m.–8:00 p.m.; Sat. Sat. 8:30 a.m.–5 p.m. (Seats 50).
Reproduction Facility: quickcopy.
Publications: *Kendall Collection Catalog.*

SOUTH DAKOTA

Brookings

598. SOUTH DAKOTA STATE UNIVERSITY
H. M. Briggs Library
Documents Department
Brookings, SD 57007-1098
Established 1900.
Telephone: 605/688-5106.
Contact Person: Bang Kim, Documents Libn.
Staff: 1 professional (full time); 1 non-professional (full time).
Size: 65,965 maps; 100 atlases; 1 globes; 100 reference books and gazetteers.
Annual Accessions: 3,000 maps.
Subject Specialization: topography.
Dates: 1800-1899 (5%); 1900 - (95%).
Classification System: LC; local system.
Collections Cataloged.
Depository for: DMA; USGS (Topo.).
Serves: students; faculty; employees; public. Mon.–Fri. 7:45 a.m.–11:30 p.m.; Sat. 10 a.m.–9 p.m.; Sun. 1–11:30 p.m. (Seats 50).
Interlibrary Loan Available. restricted
Reproduction Facility: photocopy.

Pierre

599. HISTORICAL RESOURCE CENTER
500 East Capitol
Pierre, SD 57501
Established 1901.
Telephone: 605/773-3615.
Area Specialization: South Dakota; Dakota Territory.
Special Cartographic Collections: Sanborn fire insurance maps.
Collections not Cataloged.
Depository for: S.D. state highway maps.
Serves: students; faculty; employees; public. Mon.–Fri. 8 a.m.–5 p.m. (1 readers served per month).
Reproduction Facility: photocopy.

Rapid City

600. SOUTH DAKOTA SCHOOL OF MINES AND TECHNOLOGY
Devereaux Library
Map Collection
500 East St. Joseph Street
Rapid City, SD 57701
Established Circa mid-1970's.
Telephone: 605/394-2419.
Contact Person: Philip F. McCauley, Curator of Special Collections and Archivist of th.
Staff: 1 professional (part time); 1 non-professional (part time).
Size: c. 7,000-8,000 maps; c. 50-60 atlases; 1 globes; 5 aerial photographs; c. 200 reference books and gazetteers; 5 serials (titles received); 25 microforms (no. of titles).
Annual Accessions: c. 1,000 maps; c. 5-10 atlases.
Area Specialization: South Dakota and adjoining states.
Subject Specialization: Black Hills area of eastern Wyoming and western South Dakota.
Dates: 1800-1899 (10%); 1900 - (90%).
Classification System: LC.
Collections Cataloged.
Depository for: USGS (Geol., topo.); GPO (selective).
Serves: students; faculty; employees; public;. (Seats 14; 100+ readers served per month).
Interlibrary Loan Available.
Reproduction Facility: photocopy.

Vermillion

601. UNIVERSITY OF SOUTH DAKOTA
I.D. Weeks Library
Vermillion, SD 57069
Established 1975.
Telephone: 605/677-5371.
Contact Person: John Van Balen, Public Services Libn.
Staff: 1 professional (part time); 1 non-professional (part time).
Size: 24,000 maps; 156 atlases; 5 globes; 2 relief models; 37 reference books and gazetteers; 2 serials (titles received); 5 microforms (no. of titles).
Annual Accessions: 2,000 maps; 12 atlases; 3 reference books and gazetteers.
Area Specialization: South Dakota; northern Great Plains region.
Subject Specialization: geology.
Special Cartographic Collections: historical (rare) map collection of South Dakota and Northern Great Plains region.
Dates: 1800-1899 (2%); 1900 - (98%).
Classification System: LC.
Collections Cataloged. (99%).
Depository for: DOS (Gt. Brit); NTS (Canada); USGS (Geol., topo.); Australia Geological Survey.
Serves: students; faculty; employees; public. Mon.–Fri. 8 a.m.–5 p.m. (Seats 10; 20 readers served per month).
Interlibrary Loan Available.
Reproduction Facility: photocopy.
Publications: *Historical Maps in the Richardson Archives.* (1982) 104 pp. *South Dakota Topographic Maps and Selected Place Names Index.* (1983) 341 pp. *Maps in Earth Science Publications.* (1983) 130 pp.

TENNESSEE

Chattanooga

602. CHATTANOOGA-HAMILTON COUNTY BICENTENNIAL LIBRARY
Local History and Genealogy Department
1001 Broad Street
Chattanooga, TN 37402
Telephone: 615/757-5317.
Contact Person: Clara W. Swann, Head.
Staff: 1 professional (full time); 3 non-professional (full time); 1 non-professional (part time).
Size: 600 maps; 8 atlases; 3 relief models; 17 aerial photographs; 5 reference books and gazetteers.
Annual Accessions: 10 maps.
Area Specialization: Chattanooga; Hamilton County; Tennessee; Georgia.
Subject Specialization: historical maps.
Dates: pre-1800 (5%); 1800-1899 (45%); 1900 - (50%).
Classification System: local system (alaphabetical by location).
Collections Cataloged. (100%).
Serves: public. Mon.–Thurs. 9 a.m.–9 p.m.; Fri. 9 a.m.–6 p.m.; Sat. 9 a.m.–6 p.m. (Seats 20; 1,500 readers served per month).
Reproduction Facility: photocopy.

603. TENNESSEE VALLEY AUTHORITY
Mapping Services Branch
Map Information and Records Unit
101 Haney Building
Chattanooga, TN 37401
Established 1936.
Telephone: 615/751-5404.
Contact Person: Jack L. Dodd, Civil Engineer.
Staff: 1 professional (full time); 4 non-professional (full time).
Size: 14,800 (total collection including multiple copies maps; 2 atlases; 21 relief models; 1,100,000 aerial photographs; 105 reference books and gazetteers.
Annual Accessions: 425 maps; 20,000 aerial photographs.
Area Specialization: Tennessee River watershed; and selected adjacent areas.
Subject Specialization: topography; hydrography; navigation; recreation; geology; land use; remote sensing.
Dates: 1900 - (100%).
Classification System: local system.
Collections Cataloged. (85%).
Serves: employees; public. Mon.–Fri. 8 a.m.–4:45 p.m.
Reproduction Facility: photocopy; quickcopy; microform.
Publications: Price catalog; Index to Topographic Maps available through TVA; Index to Navigation Charts; Index to Recreation Maps.

Clarksville

604. AUSTIN PEAY STATE UNIVERSITY
Felix G. Woodward Library
Information Services Department
601 E. College Street
Clarksville, TN 37044
Telephone: 615/648-7346.
Contact Person: Anne C. May, Head, Information Services Dept.
Staff: 1 professional (full time); 1 non-professional (full time).
Size: 1,207 maps; 50 atlases; 1 globes; approx. 50 reference books and gazetteers; 8 serials (titles received).

Annual Accessions: approx. 175 maps; 2 atlases; 5 reference books and gazetteers.
Area Specialization: Tennessee.
Subject Specialization: geology.
Dates: pre-1800 (1%); 1800-1899 (4%); 1900 - (90%).
Classification System: local system.
Collections not Cataloged.
Depository for: USGS (Topo.).
Serves: students; faculty; employees; public;. Mon.–Thurs. 7:30 a.m.–10 p.m., Fri. 7:30 a.m.–4:30 p.m.; Sat. 10 a.m.–5 p.m.; Sun. 3–10 p.m. (Seats 30).
Reproduction Facility: photocopy; microform.

Cookeville

605. TENNESSEE TECHNOLOGICAL UNIVERSITY
Jere Whitson Memorial Library
Cookeville, TN 38505
Established 1974.
Telephone: 615/528-3217.
Contact Person: Jean Moore, Documents Libn.
Staff: 1 professional (full time).
Size: 27,590 maps; 74 atlases.
Annual Accessions: 2,700 maps; 5 atlases.
Area Specialization: United States.
Subject Specialization: topography; geology.
Dates: 1900 - (100%).
Classification System: alphabetical by state and quadrangle.
Collections not Cataloged.
Depository for: USGS (Geol., topo.).
Serves: students; faculty; employees; public. Mon.–Fri. 8 a.m.–12 midnight; Sat. 1–6 p.m.; Sun. 1 p.m.–12 midnight. (Seats 230).
Reproduction Facility: photocopy; microform.

Jefferson City

606. CARSON-NEWMAN COLLEGE
Geology Department
Jefferson City, TN 37760
Established 1975.
Telephone: 615/475-3781, ext. 251.
Contact Person: Dr. Edward T. Freels, Professor of Geography and Geology.
Staff: non-professional (part time).
Size: 8–10,000 maps.
Annual Accessions: 1,500 maps.
Area Specialization: United States; eastern United States.
Dates: 1900 - (100%).
Classification System: local system.
Collections not Cataloged.
Depository for: USGS (Topo.); Tennessee Div of Geology.
Serves: students; faculty; employees; public. On Demand. (Seats 2; 4–5 readers served per month).
Interlibrary Loan Available.

Johnson City

607. EAST TENNESSEE STATE UNIVERSITY
Sherrod Library
Map Collection
Box 22450A
Johnson City, TN 37614
Established 1968.
Telephone: 615/929-5334.
Contact Person: Stephen Patrick, Government Documents/Law Libn.

Staff: 1 professional (part time); 1 non-professional (part time).
Size: 50,000 maps.
Annual Accessions: 500 maps.
Area Specialization: Tennessee.
Subject Specialization: topography; geology.
Dates: 1900 - (100%).
Classification System: Superintendent of Documents system.
Collections not Cataloged.
Depository for: DMA; USGS (Geol., topo.); Tennessee. Dept of Conservation. Division of Geology.
Serves: students; faculty; employees; public;. Mon.–Thurs. 8 a.m.–10:30 p.m.; Fri. 8 a.m.–4:30 p.m.; Sat. 9 a.m.–5 p.m.; Sun. 1–10:30 p.m. (Seats 8; 30 readers served per month).
Reproduction Facility: photocopy.

Knoxville

608. TENNESSEE VALLEY AUTHORITY MAP SALES
400 West Summmit Hill Drive
WPA-3
Knoxville, TN 37902
Telephone: 615/632-2717.
Contact Person: Harold Donahue, Materials Clerk, Property and Supply.
Staff: 2 professional (full time).
Size: 22,000 maps; 100 atlases; 25 relief models; 200 reference books and gazetteers.
Annual Accessions: 20 maps; 5 atlases; 3 relief models.
Area Specialization: Tennessee and contiguous states.
Subject Specialization: planimetry; flood control; topography; navigation.
Dates: pre-1800 (less 1%); 1800-1899 (less 1%); 1900 - (99%).
Classification System: local system.
Collections not Cataloged.
Serves: students; faculty; employees; public;. Mon.–Fri. 8 a.m.–4:30 p.m.
Publications: *Selected list of Maps and Charts*; *TVA Maps—Map Catalog*.

609. UNIVERSITY OF TENNESSEE (KNOXVILLE)
Geography Department
Map Library
Knoxville, TN 37996
Telephone: 615/974-4315.
Contact Person: Dr. Leonard W. Brinkman, Associate Professor of Geography.
Staff: 1 professional (part time); 3 non-professional (part time).
Size: 250,000 maps; 125 atlases; 100 relief models; 100 reference books and gazetteers.
Annual Accessions: 5,000–6,000 maps; 5–10 atlases; 5–10 reference books and gazetteers.
Area Specialization: United States.
Subject Specialization: topography; geology.
Dates: 1800-1899 (10%); 1900 - (90%).
Classification System: local system.
Collections not Cataloged.
Depository for: DMA; USGS (Geol., topo.).
Serves: students; faculty; employees; public. Mon.–Fri. 9 a.m.–4:15 p.m. (60 readers served per month).

Memphis

610. MEMPHIS AND SHELBY COUNTY PUBLIC LIBRARY AND INFORMATION CENTER
1850 Peabody Avenue
Memphis, TN 38104
Telephone: 901/725-8816.
Size: 68,781 maps.
Collections not Cataloged.
Depository for: USGS (Topo.).
Serves: public. Mon.–Thurs. 9 a.m.–9 p.m.; Fri. 9 a.m.–6 p.m.; Sat. 9 a.m.–6 p.m.; Sun. 1–5 p.m.
Interlibrary Loan Available.
Reproduction Facility: photocopy.

611. MEMPHIS STATE UNIVERSITY
University Library
Government Documents and Maps Library
Memphis, TN 38119
Established 1976.
Telephone: 901/454-2206.
Contact Person: Eric Wedig, Assistant Government Documents Libn.
Staff: 1 professional (full time); 1 non-professional (part time).
Size: 120,000 maps; 350 atlases; 3 globes; 100 aerial photographs; 200 reference books and gazetteers; 100 microforms (no. of titles).
Annual Accessions: 2,500 maps; 10 atlases; 5 reference books and gazetteers; 10 microforms (no. of titles).
Area Specialization: midsouthern United States; western Europe; Central America.
Subject Specialization: topography.
Dates: 1800-1899 (4%); 1900 - (96%).
Classification System: local system.
Collections not Cataloged.
Depository for: DMA; USGS (Topo.).
Serves: students; faculty; employees; public;. Mon.–Fri. 8 a.m.–10 p.m.; Sat. 1–6 p.m.; Sun. 1–6 p.m. (Seats 15; 30 readers served per month).
Interlibrary Loan Available.
Reproduction Facility: quickcopy; microform.
Publications: *User Guide to Government Documents* (guide).

Nashville

612. TENNESSEE STATE LIBRARY AND ARCHIVES
403 7th Avenue North
Nashville, TN 37219
Telephone: 615/741-2561.
Contact Person: Fran Schell, Reference Libn.; Marylin Bell, Senior Archivist.
Size: 83,000 maps; 70 atlases.
Area Specialization: Tennessee; southeastern United States.
Dates: pre-1800 (3%); 1800-1899 (60%); 1900 - (37%).
Classification System: LC.
Collections Cataloged.
Depository for: USGS (Topo.).
Serves: students; faculty; employees; public. Mon.–Fri. 8 a.m.–4:30 p.m.; Sat. 8 a.m.–4:30 p.m.
Reproduction Facility: photocopy; microform.

613. VANDERBILT UNIVERSITY
Science Library
Map Room
419 21st Ave. South
Nashville, TN 37240-0007
Telephone: 615/322-2775.

Contact Person: Cris Robinson, Library Assistant.
Staff: 1 non-professional (part time).
Size: 120,000 maps.
Annual Accessions: 4,000 maps.
Area Specialization: Tennessee; southeastern United States.
Subject Specialization: topography; geology; history.
Special Cartographic Collections: Mississippi River maps & atlas—MRC & Corps of Engineers, ca. 1880–1945; TVA planimetric maps—224 sheets ca. 1935, scale 1:24000; Tennessee River maps—Corps of Engineers & USGS, ca. 1850–1930.
Dates: pre-1800 (1%); 1800-1899 (4%); 1900 - (95%).
Collections not Cataloged.
Depository for: NOS; USGS (Geol., topo.).
Serves: students; faculty; employees; public; all card holders. (Seats 12; 15 readers served per month).
Reproduction Facility: photocopy.

TEXAS

Alpine

614. SUL ROSS STATE UNIVERSITY
Geology Department
Alpine, TX 79832
Established 1975.
Telephone: 915/837-8259.
Contact Person: Dennis O. Nelson, Chairman, Geology Department.
Staff: 1 non-professional (part time).
Size: 20,000 maps; 25 atlases; 3 globes; 20 relief models; 500 aerial photographs.
Annual Accessions: 600 maps; 50 aerial photographs.
Area Specialization: southwestern United States.
Dates: 1900 - (100%).
Classification System: local system: alphabetical by state.
Collections not Cataloged.
Depository for: USGS (Geol., topo.).
Serves: students; faculty; employees; public. Mon.–Fri. 8 a.m.–12 noon–1–5 p.m. (20 readers served per month).

Arlington

615. UNIVERSITY OF TEXAS AT ARLINGTON
The Library
Cartographic History Library
P.O. Box 19497
Arlington, TX 76019
Established 1978.
Telephone: 817/273-3393.
Contact Person: Dr. Charles C. Colley, Director of Special Collections.
Staff: 1 professional (full time); 4 non-professional (full time); 2 non-professional (part time).
Size: 4,000 maps; 230 atlases; 3 globes; 20 aerial photographs; 750 reference books and gazetteers; 9 serials (titles received).
Annual Accessions: 75 maps; 10 atlases; 75 reference books and gazetteers.
Area Specialization: New World exploration; Gulf Coast.
Dates: pre-1800 (75%); 1800-1899 (23%); 1900 - (2%).
Classification System: local system.
Collections Cataloged. (80%).
Serves: students; faculty; employees; public. Mon.–Fri. 8 a.m.–5 p.m. (by appointment); Sat. 10 a.m.–2 p.m. (Seats 20; 10 readers served per month).
Reproduction Facility: photocopy.

616. UNIVERSITY OF TEXAS AT ARLINGTON
Library
Documents Department
P.O. Box 19497
Arlington, TX 76019
Established 1963.
Telephone: 817/273-3391, ext. 4970.
Contact Person: Pamela A. Morris, Head Documents Libn.
Staff: 2 professional (full time); 3 non-professional (full time); 2 non-professional (part time).
Size: 8,451 maps.
Area Specialization: Texas; United States.
Subject Specialization: geology; topography; water resources.
Dates: 1800-1899 (2%); 1900 - (98%).
Classification System: LC; Superintendent of Documents Classification, Texas Documents. Classification
Collections Cataloged. (5%).
Serves: students; faculty; employees; public. Mon.–Thurs. 8 a.m.–10:00 p.m., Fri. 8 a.m.–5:00 p.m.; Sat. 10 a.m.–6 p.m.; Sun. 1–9 p.m. (Seats 144).
Interlibrary Loan Available.
Reproduction Facility: photocopy; microform.

Austin

617. UNIVERSITY OF TEXAS AT AUSTIN
General Libraries
Barker Texas History Center
Richardson Hall
Austin, TX 78712
Established 1945.
Telephone: 512/471-5961, 7521.
Contact Person: Dr. Don E. Carlton.
Staff: 1 non-professional (part time).
Size: 25,000 maps; 45 atlases; 15 reference books and gazetteers.
Annual Accessions: 20 maps.
Area Specialization: Texas; southwestern United States.
Special Cartographic Collections: Joseph E. Taulman and Earl Vandale collections (Texas history and geography); George McClendon Collection (maps of Europe, 1635–1854); Sanborn fire insurance map collection.
Dates: pre-1800 (10%); 1800-1899 (70%); 1900 - (20%).
Classification System: LC.
Collections Cataloged.
Serves: students; public; university. Mon.–Fri. 8 a.m.–5 p.m.; Sat. 8 a.m.–5 p.m. (Seats 35; 50 readers served per month).
Reproduction Facility: photocopy.
Publications: *Texas in Maps,* by James P. Bryan and Walter K. Hanak (Austin, 1961).

618. UNIVERSITY OF TEXAS AT AUSTIN
General Libraries, Geology Library
Tobin International Geological Map Collection
GEO 302
Austin, TX 78712
Telephone: 512/471-1257.
Contact Person: Chestalene Pintozzi, Geology Libn.
Staff: 1 professional (part time); 1 non-professional (part time).
Size: 29,540 maps; 5 atlases; 1 globes; 5 reference books and gazetteers.
Annual Accessions: 1,021 maps.
Area Specialization: Texas; southeastern United States; western United States; United States; Mexico.
Subject Specialization: geology.
Dates: 1800-1899 (2%); 1900 - (98%).
Classification System: LC.
Collections not Cataloged.

Depository for: USGS (Geol., topo.).
Serves: students; faculty; employees; public;. Mon.–Thurs.; 8 a.m.–10 p.m.; Fri. 8 a.m.–6 p.m.; Sat. 9 a.m.–5 p.m.; Sun. 2–10 p.m. (Seats 14; 200 readers served per month).
Reproduction Facility: photocopy.

619. UNIVERSITY OF TEXAS AT AUSTIN.
The General Libraries
Nettie Lee Benson Latin American Collection
Sid Richardson Hall 1.109
Austin, TX 78712
Established 1921.
Telephone: 512/471-3818.
Contact Person: Laura Gutiérrez-Witt, Head Libn.
Staff: 5 professional (full time); 8 non-professional (full time); 1 professional (part time); 31 non-professional (part time).
Size: 18,000 maps.
Annual Accessions: 200 maps.
Area Specialization: Latin America, especially Mexico, Brazil, Peru, Colombia, Central America.
Subject Specialization: history.
Special Cartographic Collections: Gondra Collection maps of early Paraguay; hand-painted maps of the 16th century *relaciones geográficas,* census reports from New Spain to the King of Spain.
Dates: pre-1800 (20%); 1800-1899 (20%); 1900 - (60%).
Classification System: LC.
Collections not Cataloged.
Serves: students; faculty; employees; public. Mon.–Fri. 9 a.m.–5 p.m; Sat. 1–5 p.m. (Seats 12–15; 5–10 readers served per month).
Reproduction Facility: photocopy; microform.

620. UNIVERSITY OF TEXAS AT AUSTIN
Perry-Castaneda Library
Map Collection
Austin, TX 78712
Established 1977.
Telephone: 512/471-5944.
Contact Person: John Tongate, Acting Map Libn.
Staff: 1 professional (part time); 2 non-professional (part time).
Size: 172,000 maps; 300 atlases; 2 globes; 30 relief models; 160 reference books and gazetteers; 2 serials (titles received).
Annual Accessions: 9,500 maps; 10 atlases; 5 reference books and gazetteers.
Area Specialization: comprehensive.
Subject Specialization: comprehensive.
Dates: 1800-1899 (1%); 1900 - (99%).
Classification System: LC.
Collections Cataloged. (10%).
Depository for: DMA; NOS; USGS (Topo.);.
Serves: students; faculty; employees; public. Mon.–Fri. 8 a.m.–12 midnight (staffed 8 a.m.–5 p.m.); Sat. 9 a.m.–12 midnight; Sun. 12 noon–12 midnight. (Seats 50; 250 readers served per month).
Reproduction Facility: photocopy; microform.
Publications: *How To Find a Map in PCL* (guide).

College Station

621. TEXAS A&M UNIVERSITY
Sterling C. Evans Library
Map Department
College Station, TX 77843
Established est. 1970.
Telephone: 409/845-1024.
Contact Person: Judy Rieke, Head, Map Dept.

Staff: 2 non-professional (full time); 2 professional (part time); 5 non-professional (part time).
Size: 82,608 maps; 1,000 atlases; 10 globes; 8 relief models; 1,100 aerial photographs; 500 reference books and gazetteers; 6 serials (titles received); 4 microforms (no. of titles).
Annual Accessions: 5,000 sheets maps; 200 atlases; 50 reference books and gazetteers.
Area Specialization: Texas.
Subject Specialization: geology; soils; petroleum.
Dates: 1800-1899 (5%); 1900 - (95%).
Classification System: LC.
Collections Cataloged.
Depository for: DMA; NOS; USGS (Geol., topo.); Pan American Institute of Geography & History (PAIGH).
Serves: students; faculty; employees; public. Mon.–Thurs. 8 a.m.–11 p.m., Fri. 8 a.m.–8 p.m.; Sat. 9 a.m.–6 p.m.; Sun. 12 noon–11 p.m. (Seats 20; 800 readers served per month).
Interlibrary Loan Available.
Reproduction Facility: photocopy.

Dallas

622. DALLAS PUBLIC LIBRARY
Government Publications Division
Map Collection
1515 Young Street
Dallas, TX 75201
Established August 1976.
Telephone: 214/749-4176.
Contact Person: Emily Matteucci, Map Libn.
Staff: 1 professional (full time); 3 non-professional (part time).
Size: 22,000 maps; 217 atlases; 2 globes; 1 relief models; 870 aerial photographs; 328 reference books and gazetteers; 25 serials (titles received); 31 microforms (no. of titles).
Annual Accessions: 5,000 maps; 50 atlases; 50 reference books and gazetteers.
Area Specialization: Texas.
Subject Specialization: geology; petroleum; soils.
Dates: 1900 - (100%).
Classification System: LC (maps); Dewey (books).
Collections Cataloged. (10%).
Depository for: USGS (Topo.); PAIGH, GPO.
Serves: public. Mon.–Thurs. 9 a.m.–9 p.m., Fri. 9 a.m.–5 p.m.; Sat. 9 a.m.–5 p.m.; Sun. 1–5 p.m. (Seats 15; 280 readers served per month).
Interlibrary Loan Available.
Reproduction Facility: photocopy; microform. Division.

623. MOBIL RESEARCH AND DEVELOPMENT CORPORATION.
Dallas Research
Technical Information
13777 Midway Road
Dallas, TX 75234
Established 1955.
Telephone: 214/851-8143.
Contact Person: Dudley B. Schoolfield, Cataloger.
Staff: 1 professional (full time); 1 professional (part time).
Size: 1,900 maps; 30 atlases; 1 globes.
Annual Accessions: 300 maps; 6 atlases.
Area Specialization: western United States; Alaska.
Subject Specialization: geology; mineral resources.
Dates: 1900 - (100%).
Classification System: local system: faceted classification involves use of Dewey. Decimal classification and relative index.
Collections Cataloged.

Serves: employees; by arrangement. Mon.–Fri. 7:30 a.m.–4:15 p.m. (Seats 16).
Interlibrary Loan Available.
Reproduction Facility: photocopy.
Publications: Indexes to the library's topographic map collection.

624. SOUTHERN METHODIST UNIVERSITY
Science/Engineering Library
Edwin J. Foscue Map Library
Dallas, TX 75275
Established 1961.
Telephone: 214/692-2285.
Contact Person: Dorothy Fouts, Map Custodian.
Staff: 1 non-professional (full time); 1 non-professional (part time).
Size: 180,000 maps; 225 atlases; 1 globes; 1 relief models; 3,550 aerial photographs; 550 reference books and gazetteers; 10 serials (titles received).
Annual Accessions: 3,500 maps; 5 atlases; 25 reference books and gazetteers.
Area Specialization: Texas; New Mexico; Oklahoma; Colorado; Arkansas.
Subject Specialization: geology; agriculture; climatology; soils; water resources.
Classification System: LC.
Collections Cataloged.
Depository for: DMA; NOS; USGS (Geol., topo.).
Serves: students; faculty; employees; public. Mon.–Fri. 8 a.m.–4:30 p.m. (Seats 25; 50 readers served per month).
Interlibrary Loan Available.
Reproduction Facility: photocopy.

Denton

625. NORTH TEXAS STATE UNIVERSITY
Willis Library
Maps and Microforms—Room 437
Box 5188, N.T. Station
Denton, TX 76203
Telephone: 817/565-2763.
Contact Person: Dr. David R. Lindsey, LA III.
Staff: 2 non-professional (full time); 3 non-professional (part time).
Size: 12,833 maps; 600 atlases; 2 globes; 158 reference books and gazetteers.
Annual Accessions: 350 maps; 10 reference books and gazetteers.
Area Specialization: Texas.
Subject Specialization: topography.
Dates: 1900 - (90%).
Depository for: USGS (Topo.).
Serves: students; faculty; employees; public. Mon.–Thurs. 9 a.m.–9 p.m., Fri. 9 a.m.–6 p.m.; Sat. 11 a.m.–6 p.m.; Sun. 2–6 p.m. (Seats 16; 20 readers served per month).
Reproduction Facility: photocopy.
Publications: Index to topographic maps.

El Paso

626. UNIVERSITY OF TEXAS AT EL PASO
Government Documents & Maps Department
Map Section
Campus
El Paso, TX 79968
Established 1973.
Telephone: 915/747-5685.
Contact Person: Fred Lohrman, Maps Assistant.

Staff: 1 professional (full time); 2 non-professional (part time).
Size: 75,900 maps; 50 atlases; 5 globes; 7 relief models; 200 aerial photographs; 300 reference books and gazetteers; 2 serials (titles received).
Annual Accessions: 3,065 maps; 10 atlases; 25 reference books and gazetteers.
Area Specialization: Texas; New Mexico; Mexico; Arizona; southwestern United States.
Subject Specialization: geology; topography.
Special Cartographic Collections: D.G.G.T.N. topographic maps set of Mexico (1:50,000 & 1:250,000); D.G.G.T.N. geologic maps set of Mexico (1:50,000 & 1:250,000).
Dates: pre-1800 (1%); 1800-1899 (5%); 1900 - (94%).
Classification System: T.R. Smith cataloging system (from University of Kansas).
Collections Cataloged. (100%).
Depository for: DMA; NOS; USGS (Geol., topo.); U.S. Bureau of Census.
Serves: students; faculty; employees; public. Mon.–Thurs. 8 a.m.–10 p.m., Fri. 8 a.m.–5 p.m.; Sat. 10 a.m.–6 p.m.; Sun. 1–10 p.m. (Seats 14; 85 readers served per month).
Interlibrary Loan Available.
Reproduction Facility: photocopy; quickcopy; microform.
Publications: *Carto—Points* (acquistions list).

Fort Worth

627. FORT WORTH PUBLIC LIBRARY
Business & Technology
Earth Sciences Collection
300 Taylor Street
Fort Worth, TX 76102
Established pre-1962.
Telephone: 817/870-7727.
Contact Person: John R. McCracken, Manager, Business & Technology.
Staff: 3 professional (full time); 5 non-professional (part time).
Size: 18,000 maps; 35 atlases; 1 globes; 1 aerial photographs; 35,000 serials (titles received).
Subject Specialization: earth sciences.
Collections Cataloged. (100%).
Depository for: USGS (Topo.).
Serves: public. Mon.–Thurs. 9 a.m.–9 p.m., Fri. 10 a.m.–6 p.m.; Sat. 10 a.m.–6 p.m. (Seats 22; 600 readers served per month).
Reproduction Facility: photocopy.

Galveston

628. ROSENBERG LIBRARY
Galveston & Texas History Center;
Rare Books Room
2310 Sealy
Galveston, TX 77551
Telephone: 409/763-8854.
Contact Person: Jane Kenamore, Archivist.
Staff: 2 professional (full time); 1 non-professional (full time); 1 professional (part time).
Size: 1,050 maps; 30 atlases; 3 globes.
Annual Accessions: 20 maps; 2 atlases.
Area Specialization: Texas and upper Gulf Coast.
Dates: pre-1800 (30%); 1800-1899 (40%); 1900 - (30%).
Classification System: local system.
Collections Cataloged. (100%).
Serves: public. Tues.–Fri. 10 a.m.–5 p.m.; Sat. 10 a.m.–5 p.m. (Seats 20; 10 readers served per month).
Reproduction Facility: photocopy.
Publications: guide (forthcoming).

Houston

629. RICE UNIVERSITY
Fondren Library
Government Documents and Microforms Dept.
6100 South Main
Houston, TX 77005
Established 1958.
Telephone: 713/527-8101, ext. 2587.
Contact Person: Barbara Kile, Head.
Staff: 1 professional (full time); 1 non-professional (full time).
Size: 20,000 maps.
Subject Specialization: geology.
Dates: 1900 -.
Classification System: LC; DMA.
Collections Cataloged.
Depository for: DMA; USGS (Geol., topo.).
Serves: students; faculty; employees; public. Mon.–Fri. 8 a.m.–5 p.m. (Seats 12).
Interlibrary Loan Available.
Reproduction Facility: photocopy.

Lubbock

630. TEXAS TECH UNIVERSITY
Library
Map Collection
Lubbock, TX 79409
Established 1983.
Telephone: 806/742-2236.
Contact Person: Barbara Geyer, Reference Libn.— Science/Map Libn.
Staff: 1 professional (part time); 1 non-professional (part time).
Size: 4,000 maps; 125 atlases; 1 globes; 1 relief models; 40 reference books and gazetteers; 1 serials (titles received).
Annual Accessions: 300 maps; 15 atlases; 10 reference books and gazetteers; 1 serials (titles received).
Area Specialization: southern High Plains; Great Plains; southern Rocky Mountains; southwestern United States; Latin America.
Subject Specialization: comprehensive.
Dates: 1800-1899 (2%); 1900 - (98%).
Classification System: LC.
Collections Cataloged.
Depository for: USGS (Geol., topo.).
Serves: students; faculty; employees; public. (Seats 8).
Interlibrary Loan Available.
Reproduction Facility: photocopy.

Midland

631. MIDLAND COUNTY PUBLIC LIBRARY
Petroleum Dept.
Box 1191
Midland, TX 79701
Established 1959.
Telephone: 915/683-2708, ext. 29.
Staff: 1 professional (full time); 1 non-professional (part time).
Size: 7,590 maps.
Annual Accessions: 350 maps.
Area Specialization: Permian Basin of New Mexico and Texas; southwestern United States.
Subject Specialization: geology; petroleum.

Dates: 1800-1899 (1%); 1900 - (99%).
Collections Cataloged. (30%).
Depository for: USGS (Geol., topo.).
Serves: public. Mon.–Fri. 9 a.m.–6 p.m.; Sat. 9 a.m.–6 p.m. (Seats 14; 325 readers served per month).
Interlibrary Loan Available.
Reproduction Facility: photocopy.
Contact Person: Mrs. Leroy Wegner, Special Collection Libn.

Richardson

632. UNIVERSITY OF TEXAS AT DALLAS
Eugene McDermott Library
Government Documents Area
P.O.Box 830643
Richardson, TX 75083-0643
Established 1972.
Telephone: 214/690-2918.
Contact Person: Ellen Derey Safley, Government Documents Libn.
Staff: 2 professional (full time); 2 non-professional (part time).
Size: 19,891 maps; 100 atlases; 3 relief models; 200 aerial photographs; 5 reference books and gazetteers; 10,000 microforms (no. of titles).
Annual Accessions: 1,000 maps; 10 atlases.
Area Specialization: Texas; Louisiana; Arkansas; Utah; Colorado; Arizona; California; Nevada; New Mexico; Oklahoma.
Subject Specialization: topography; geology.
Dates: 1900 - (99%).
Classification System: LC; geographical.
Collections Cataloged. (66%).
Depository for: USGS (Topo.).
Serves: students; faculty; employees; public. Mon.–Thurs. 9 a.m.–6 p.m., Fri. 9 a.m.–5 p.m.; Sat. 10 a.m.–3 p.m.; Sun. 2–7 p.m. (Seats 10; 25 readers served per month).
Reproduction Facility: photocopy; microform.

Waco

633. BAYLOR UNIVERSITY
Moody Library
Documents and Maps Department
P.O. Box 6307
Waco, TX 76706
Established 1943.
Telephone: 817/755-2111, Ext. 6735.
Contact Person: William L. Olbrich, Head, Documents Dept.
Staff: 1 professional (full time); 1 non-professional (part time).
Size: 20,000 maps.
Annual Accessions: 1,000 maps.
Area Specialization: Texas.
Subject Specialization: topography; population studies.
Dates: 1800-1899 (1%); 1900 - (99%).
Collections not Cataloged.
Depository for: DMA; USGS (Topo.).
Serves: students; faculty; employees; public;. Mon.–Fri. 8 a.m.–10 p.m.; Sat. 9 a.m.–1 p.m.; Sun. 2–10 p.m. (Seats 20; 1,000 readers served per month).
Interlibrary Loan Available.
Reproduction Facility: photocopy; microform.

634. BAYLOR UNIVERSITY
The Texas Collection
Fifth Street and Speight Avenue
Waco, TX 76706
Established 1930s.
Telephone: 817/755-1268.
Contact Person: Kent Keeth, Director.
Staff: 1 professional (part time); 1 non-professional (part time).
Size: 8,000+ maps; 50 atlases; 3 globes; 37 reference books and gazetteers.
Annual Accessions: varies maps.
Area Specialization: Texas.
Subject Specialization: history; transportation; coasts; topography; cities and counties.
Special Cartographic Collections: J. P. Bryan Collection: printed maps of Texas, 1656–1900; William A. Blakley Collection: printed maps of Texas, 1820–1890; Frances Poage Collection (dynamic): printed maps of Texas, 1860–.
Dates: pre-1800 (2); 1800-1899 (20); 1900 - (78).
Classification System: local system.
Collections not Cataloged.
Serves: students; faculty; employees; public;. Mon.–Fri. 9 a.m.–5 p.m.; Sat. 9 a.m.–12 noon during terms. (Seats 36).
Reproduction Facility: photocopy; microform.

UTAH

Cedar City

635. SOUTHERN UTAH STATE COLLEGE
Special Collections
Cedar City, UT 84720
Established about 1975.
Contact Person: Inez S. Cooper, Special Collections Libn./curator/archivist.
Area Specialization: southern Utah; Utah; the West.
Subject Specialization: history; exploration; mines and minerals.
Special Cartographic Collections: William R. Palmer Collection of manuscript and published maps of the west; Dr. Morris A. Shirts manuscript maps of the various locations of Cedar City, Utah; Laurence C. Cooper Collection of maps of the Glen Canyon of the Colorado area and others; Kenneth R. Benson Collection of forest maps showing the old lumber trail in the Cedar City, Utah area; Indian Homelands (Palmer & others) Wm. A. Rieske maps & charts "Indians of North America".
Dates: 1800-1899; 1900 -.
Collections not Cataloged.
Serves: students; faculty; employees; public;. Mon.–Fri. 9 a.m.–4 p.m. (until June 1). (Seats 10).
Reproduction Facility: photocopy.

Logan

636. UTAH STATE UNIVERSITY
Merrill Library
Documents and Maps
Logan, UT 84322
Established 1950.
Telephone: 801/750-2682.
Contact Person: Karlo K. Mustonen, Senior Libn.; Stephen C. Weiss, Affiliate Libn.
Staff: 2 professional (full time); 1 non-professional (full time); 3 professional (part time).

Size: 53,707 maps; 210 atlases; 1 globes; 7 relief models; 24,400 aerial photographs; 24 reference books and gazetteers.
Annual Accessions: 6,000 maps; 12 atlases; 500 aerial photographs; 2 reference books and gazetteers.
Area Specialization: Utah; the West.
Subject Specialization: geology; hydrology; forestry.
Special Cartographic Collections: Claypool Collection—geologic maps; Special Collections Dept—western history; hydrology and irrigation.
Dates: 1800-1899 (5%); 1900 - (95%).
Classification System: LC.
Collections Cataloged. (15%).
Depository for: DMA; NOS; USGS (Geol., topo.).
Serves: students; faculty; employees; public. Mon.–Thurs. 7 a.m.–12 p.m., Fri. 7 a.m.–8 p.m.; Sat. 10 a.m.–5 p.m.; Sun. 1–12 p.m. (200 readers served per month).
Interlibrary Loan Available.
Reproduction Facility: photocopy; microform.

Provo

637. BRIGHAM YOUNG UNIVERSITY
Harold B. Lee Library
Map Collection
Provo, UT 84602
Established 1952.
Telephone: 801/378-4482.
Contact Person: Riley Moffat, Map Libn.
Staff: 1 professional (full time); 2 non-professional (part time).
Size: 150,000 maps; 4,900 atlases; 12 globes; 70 relief models; 1,200 aerial photographs; 8 serials (titles received); 94,500 microforms (no. of titles).
Annual Accessions: 10,000 maps; 300 atlases.
Area Specialization: Utah; United States; Canada.
Subject Specialization: history.
Dates: pre-1800 (1%); 1800-1899 (9%); 1900 - (90%).
Classification System: LC; Dewey pre 1977 atlases and gazetteers.
Collections Cataloged. (100% (except USGS guadrangles and road maps)).
Depository for: DMA; USGS (Geol.); several state and foreign geological surveys.
Serves: students; faculty; employees; public. Mon.–Fri. 8 a.m.–10 p.m.; Sat. 9 a.m.–6 p.m. (Seats 20; 500 readers served per month).
Interlibrary Loan Available.
Reproduction Facility: photocopy; microform.
Publications: *Selected Aquisitions* (3 times a year); general guide; area bibliographies.

Salt Lake City

638. GENEALOGICAL LIBRARY OF THE CHURCH OF JESUS CHRIST OF LATTER-DAY SAINTS
50 East North Temple Street
Salt Lake City, UT 84150
Established 1894.
Telephone: 801/531-3416.
Contact Person: Delbert Roach, Maps Libn.
Staff: 1 professional (full time).
Size: 8,000 maps; 500 atlases; 500 reference books and gazetteers; 100 microforms (no. of titles).
Annual Accessions: 250 maps; 25 atlases; 25 reference books and gazetteers; 10 microforms (no. of titles).
Area Specialization: comprehensive.
Subject Specialization: topography; political geography.
Dates: pre-1800 (5%); 1800-1899 (45%); 1900 - (50%).
Classification System: Dewey (modified).

Collections Cataloged.
Serves: employees; public. Mon. 7:30–6 p.m.; Tues.–Fri. 7:30 am.–10 p.m.; Sat. 7:30 a.m.–5 p.m. (1,500 readers served per month).
Reproduction Facility: photocopy; microform.
Publications: *Genealogical Library Catalog.*.

639. SALT LAKE CITY PUBLIC LIBRARY
Business/Science Department
209 E. 500 S.
Salt Lake City, UT 84111
Established 1904.
Telephone: 801/363-5733, ext. 255.
Contact Person: Sharon Peters, Business/Science Libn.
Staff: 1 professional (part time); 1 non-professional (part time).
Size: 5,281 maps; 132 atlases; 1 globes; 2 (Landsat) aerial photographs; 30 reference books and gazetteers; 2 serials (titles received); 1 microforms (no. of titles).
Annual Accessions: 200 maps; 22 atlases.
Area Specialization: Utah.
Special Cartographic Collections: Stansbury expedition.
Dates: 1800-1899 (1%); 1900 - (100%).
Classification System: modified Sears subject headings.
Collections not Cataloged.
Depository for: USGS (Topo.).
Serves: students; faculty; employees; public. Mon.–Fri. 9 a.m.–9 p.m.; Sat. 9 a.m.–6 p.m.; Sun. 1–5 p.m. October–April, closed May–September. (Seats 24).
Interlibrary Loan Available.
Reproduction Facility: photocopy.

640. UNIVERSITY OF UTAH
Marriott Library
Science and Engineering Division, Map Collection
Salt Lake City, UT 84112
Established 1950.
Telephone: 801/581-7533.
Contact Person: Barbara Cox, Associate Libn.
Staff: 1 non-professional (full time); 1 professional (part time).
Size: 115,000 maps; 650 atlases; 4 globes; 30 relief models; 1,200 aerial photographs; 150 reference books and gazetteers.
Annual Accessions: 3,500 maps; 40 atlases; 5 aerial photographs; 15 reference books and gazetteers.
Area Specialization: Internmountain West; Middle East (southwestern Asia, north Africa).
Subject Specialization: geology.
Dates: 1800-1899 (5%); 1900 - (95%).
Classification System: LC.
Collections Cataloged. (100%).
Depository for: DMA; USGS (Geol., topo.).
Serves: students; faculty; employees; public. Mon.–Thurs. 7:30 a.m.–11 p.m., Fri. 7:30–6 p.m.; Sat. 11 a.m.–6 p.m.; Sun. 11 a.m.–11 p.m. (Seats 7).
Interlibrary Loan Available.
Reproduction Facility: photocopy.
Publications: *Map Collection* (guide); major accessions listed in *New Books List* issued by Science and Engineering Library.

641. UNIVERSITY OF UTAH
Marriott Library
Special Collections
Salt Lake City, UT 84112
Established 1953.
Telephone: 801/581-8863.
Contact Person: Ruth R. Yeaman, Reference Libn., Maps and Rare Books.
Staff: 2 professional (part time).
Size: 10,000 maps; 14 atlases; 2 relief models; 6 aerial photographs; 6 reference books and gazetteers.

Area Specialization: Utah; southwestern and western United States.
Subject Specialization: Utah and western United States history; exploration and discovery.
Special Cartographic Collections: Sanborn fire insurance maps of Utah cities.
Dates: pre-1800 (2%); 1800-1899 (49%); 1900 - (49%).
Classification System: LC 73%; Dewey 2%; Superintendent of Documents.
Collections Cataloged. (20%).
Serves: students; faculty; employees; public. Mon.–Thurs. 8 a.m.–10 p.m.; Fri. 8 a.m.–5 p.m.; Sat. 11 a.m.–6 p.m. (Seats 29; 189 readers served per month).
Reproduction Facility: photocopy; microform.

642. UTAH STATE HISTORICAL SOCIETY
Library
Map and Photo Collection
300 Rio Grande
Salt Lake City, UT 84101
Established 1897.
Telephone: 801/533-5755.
Contact Person: Susan Whetstone, Map/Photo Libn.
Staff: 1 professional (full time).
Size: 26,000 maps; 300 aerial photographs.
Annual Accessions: 1,200 maps.
Area Specialization: Utah.
Subject Specialization: history.
Dates: 1800-1899 (25%); 1900 - (75%).
Classification System: local system.
Collections not Cataloged.
Depository for: USGS (Topo.).
Serves: public. Mon.–Fri. 9 a.m. –5 p.m. (Seats 25; 11 readers served per month).
Reproduction Facility: photocopy.

Vernal

643. UTAH FIELD HOUSE OF NATURAL HISTORY
Reference Library
Maps Section
235 East Main Street
Vernal, UT 84078
Established 1948.
Telephone: 801/789-3799.
Contact Person: Alden H. Hamblin, Park Manager.
Staff: 1 non-professional (part time).
Size: 1,300 maps; 1 atlases; 30 aerial photographs; 1 reference books and gazetteers.
Annual Accessions: 10 maps; 10 aerial photographs.
Area Specialization: uinta Basin; uinta Mountain area of Utah.
Subject Specialization: topography; geology.
Dates: 1900 - (100%).
Collections not Cataloged.
Serves: students; faculty; employees; public. Mon.–Fri. 9 a.m.–5 p.m. (Seats 4; 2 readers served per month).

VERMONT

Burlington

644. UNIVERSITY OF VERMONT
Bailey/Howe Library
Map Room
Burlington, VT 05405-0036
Established 1968.
Telephone: 802/656-2020, ext. 34.

Contact Person: Suzanne Clark, Head, Documents/Maps Department.
Staff: 1 professional (part time); 1 non-professional (part time).
Size: 150,000 maps; 425 atlases; 1 globes; 6,000 aerial photographs; 275 reference books and gazetteers.
Annual Accessions: 4,500 maps; 10 atlases; 7 reference books and gazetteers.
Area Specialization: Vermont; United States; Canada.
Special Cartographic Collections: John Johnson ms. maps/surveys of northern Vermont towns, 1795–1842.
Classification System: AGS.
Collections Cataloged.
Depository for: DMA; NOS; NTS (Canada); USGS (Geol., topo.).
Serves: students; faculty; employees; public. Mon.–Fri. 10:30 a.m.–4 p.m., 7–10 p.m.; Sat. 1–5 p.m.; Sun. 1–5 p.m. (Seats 16; 250 readers served per month).
Interlibrary Loan Available.
Reproduction Facility: photocopy.
Publications: *Guide to the Cartographic Resources in the UVM Bailey/Howe Library Map Room* (in progress).

Middlebury

645. MIDDLEBURY COLLEGE
Department of Geography
Map Library
402 Science Center
Middlebury, VT 05753
Established 1945.
Telephone: 802/388-3711, ext. 5563.
Contact Person: Robert R. Churchill, Chairman, Department of Geography.
Staff: 2 non-professional (full time); 1 non-professional (part time).
Size: 200,000 maps; 50 relief models; 2,500 aerial photographs; 20 reference books and gazetteers.
Annual Accessions: 1,000 maps; 50 aerial photographs; 1–2 reference books and gazetteers.
Area Specialization: comprehensive.
Dates: 1900 - (100%).
Classification System: Local system.
Collections Cataloged. (50%).
Depository for: DMA; USGS (Geol., topo.).
Serves: students; faculty; employees; public. Mon.–Fri. 8 a.m.–4 p.m. (Seats 10; 100 readers served per month).
Interlibrary Loan Available.
Reproduction Facility: photocopy.

Montpelier

646. VERMONT HISTORICAL SOCIETY
Library
Pavilion Building, 109 State Street
Montpelier, VT 05602
Established 1838.
Telephone: 802/828-2291.
Contact Person: Mrs. Reidun D. Nuquist, Libn.
Staff: 1 professional (full time); 1 professional (part time); 1 non-professional (part time).
Size: 1,000 maps; 60 atlases; 3 globes; 3 microforms (no. of titles).
Area Specialization: Vermont; New England; eastern New York; parts of Canada adjacent to New England.
Subject Specialization: historical maps relating to above areas.

Special Cartographic Collections: James Wilson globes (in museum collection).
Dates: pre-1800 (20%); 1800-1899 (60%); 1900 - (20%).
Classification System: Dewey.
Collections Cataloged. (90%).
Serves: public. Mon.–Fri. 8 a.m.–4:40 p.m. (except state holidays). (Seats 20 (entire library); 500 (all library users) readers served per month).
Reproduction Facility: photocopy.
Publications: David Allan Cobb, *Vermont Maps Prior to 1900: An Annotated Cartiobibliography*. Montpelier, Vt.: Vermont Historical Society, 1971. (Published as Vol. 39 (summer and fall of 1971), nos. 3 & 4 of *Vermont History*, Proceedings of the Vermont Historical Society.).

647. VERMONT (STATE) DEPARTMENT OF LIBRARIES
Law and Documents Unit
111 State Street
Montpelier, VT 05602
Telephone: 802/828-3268.
Contact Person: Vivian Bryan, Division Director.
Staff: 2 professional (full time); 2 non-professional (full time).
Size: 200 maps; 50 atlases; 1 globes; 800 aerial photographs; 5 reels microforms (no. of titles).
Area Specialization: Vermont.
Dates: 1900 -.
Classification System: By labelled drawers.
Collections Cataloged.
Depository for: USGS (Geol., topo.).
Serves: public. Mon.–Fri. 7:45 a.m.–4:30 p.m. (Seats 24; 425 readers served per month).
Interlibrary Loan Available.
Reproduction Facility: photocopy; microform.

Northfield

648. NORWICH UNIVERSITY
Military College of Vermont
Chaplin Memorial Library
South Main Street
Northfield, VT 05663
Established 1978.
Telephone: 802/485-5011, ext. 248/289.
Contact Person: Mrs. Jacqueline S. Painter, Documents Libn.
Staff: 1 professional (part time); 1 non-professional (part time).
Size: 1,570 maps; 26 atlases; 3 globes; 52 reference books and gazetteers; 6 serials (titles received).
Annual Accessions: 300 maps; 5 atlases; 10 reference books and gazetteers.
Area Specialization: New England; New York state.
Subject Specialization: topography; geology.
Dates: 1900 - (100%).
Classification System: local system.
Collections not Cataloged.
Depository for: USGS (Geol.).
Serves: students; faculty; employees; public. Mon.–Fri. 8 a.m.–12 midnight; Sat. 11 a.m.–11 p.m.; Sun. 11 a.m.–12 midnight.
Reproduction Facility: photocopy.

VIRGINIA

Blacksburg

649. VIRGINIA POLYTECHNIC INSTITUTE AND STATE UNIVERSITY
University Libraries
Geology Library
3040 Derring Hall
Blacksburg, VA 24061
Established ca. 1974.
Telephone: 703/961-6101.
Contact Person: John D. Crissinger, Geology and Map Libn.
Staff: 1 professional (part time); 1 non-professional (part time).
Size: 15,000 maps; 50 atlases; 25 relief models; 33,500 aerial photographs.
Area Specialization: geology.
Dates: 1900 - (100%).
Classification System: LC.
Collections not Cataloged.
Depository for: USGS (Geol.); Virginia Division of Mineral Resources.
Serves: students; faculty; employees; public. Mon.–Thurs. 8 a.m.–10 p.m., Fri. 8 a.m.–5 p.m.; Sat. varies; Sun. 10 a.m.–2 p.m. (Seats 40).
Interlibrary Loan Available.
Reproduction Facility: photocopy.
Publications: New acquisitions list.

650. VIRGINIA POLYTECHNIC INSTITUTE AND STATE UNIVERSITY
University Libraries/Carol M. Newman Library
Map Collection
Blacksburg, VA 24061
Telephone: 703/961-5589 (Reference desk).
Contact Person: John D. Crissinger, Geology and Map Libn.
Staff: 1 professional (part time); 3 non-professional (part time).
Size: 115,000 maps; 41 relief models.
Area Specialization: Virginia.
Dates: 1800-1899 (5%); 1900 - (95%).
Classification System: LC.
Collections not Cataloged.
Depository for: DMA; NTS (Canada); USGS (Topo.); GPO.
Serves: students; faculty; employees; public. Mon.–Thurs. 7:30 a.m.–12 midnight, Fri. 7:30 a.m.–10 p.m.; Sat. 9 a.m.–10 p.m.; Sun. 11 a.m.–12 midnight. (Seats 8).
Interlibrary Loan Available.
Reproduction Facility: photocopy.

651. VIRGINIA POLYTECHNIC INSTITUTE AND STATE UNIVERSITY
University Libraries/Carol M. Newman Library
Special Collections
Blacksburg, VA 24061
Telephone: 703/961-6308.
Contact Person: Glenn McMullen, Special Collections Libn.
Staff: 2 professional (full time); 1 non-professional (full time).
Size: 500 maps; 20 atlases; 20 reference books and gazetteers.
Special Cartographic Collections: Virginia Civil War battlefield maps; Virginia coal mine maps, 1840–1920; Virginia railroad maps, 1840–1920.
Dates: 1800-1899 (50%); 1900 - (50%).

Classification System: LC.
Collections Cataloged. (50).
Serves: students; faculty; employees; public. Mon.–Fri. 9 a.m.–4:30 p.m. (Seats 20).
Reproduction Facility: photocopy.

Bridgewater

652. BRIDGEWATER COLLEGE
Alexander Mack Memorial Library
Government Documents and Maps Department
Bridgewater, VA 22812
Established ca. 1920.
Telephone: 703/828-2501, ext. 511.
Contact Person: Dr. Buu Duong, Government Documents Libn.
Staff: 1 professional (part time); 2 non-professional (part time).
Size: 1,400 maps; 50 atlases; 3 globes; 2 relief models; 4 reference books and gazetteers.
Area Specialization: Virginia and contiguous states.
Dates: 1900 - (100%).
Classification System: local system.
Collections Cataloged. ((atlases)).
Depository for: USGS (Topo.).
Serves: students; faculty; employees; public. Mon.–Fri. 8 a.m.–11 p.m. (Seats 50; ca. 350 readers served per month).
Interlibrary Loan Available.
Reproduction Facility: photocopy.

Charlottesville

653. UNIVERSITY OF VIRGINIA
Alderman Library
Documents Section, Map Collection Center
Charlottesville, VA 22901
Telephone: 703/924-3133.
Contact Person: Walter L. Newsome, Documents Libn.
Staff: 2 professional (part time); 1 non-professional (part time).
Size: 567 reference books and gazetteers.
Dates: 1900 - (90%).
Classification System: AGS; DMA.
Collections not Cataloged.
Depository for: DMA; USGS (Geol., topo.).
Serves: students; faculty; public. Mon.–Fri. 8 a.m.–10 p.m.; Sat. 8 a.m.–6 p.m.
Reproduction Facility: photocopy; microform.

Fairfax

654. GEORGE MASON UNIVERSITY
Fenwick Library
4400 University Drive
Fairfax, VA 22030
Established 1963.
Telephone: 703/323-2605.
Contact Person: Helen Grissom, Coordinator, AV/Nonbook Materials.
Staff: 1 professional (full time); 1 professional (part time); 7 non-professional (part time).
Size: over 75,000 maps; 45 atlases; 1 globes; 15 reference books and gazetteers; 1 microforms (no. of titles).
Area Specialization: United States.

Subject Specialization: geography; geology; topography.
Special Cartographic Collections: U.S. Census maps; CIA maps of foreign countries; C. Harrison Mann collection of late 1500's to late 1800's maps of America including atlases, some state road and city maps.
Dates: pre-1800 (less than 1%); 1800-1899 (less than 1%); 1900 - (99%).
Classification System: LC (ref. books); local system.
Collections Cataloged.
Collections not Cataloged. (5%).
Depository for: USGS (Topo.).
Serves: students; faculty; employees; public. Mon.–Thurs. 7:30 a.m.–12 p.m., Fri. 7:30 a.m.–6 p.m.; Sat. 9 a.m.–5 p.m.; Sun. 1–9 p.m. (Seats 12).
Reproduction Facility: photocopy.

Falls Church

655. AMERICAN AUTOMOBILE ASSOCIATION
Library
8111 Gatehouse Road
Falls Church, VA 22047
Established 1955.
Telephone: 703/222-6466.
Contact Person: Sue Williams, Libn.
Size: 1,700 maps; 6 atlases.
Annual Accessions: 60 maps.
Area Specialization: North America.
Subject Specialization: roads.
Dates: 1900 -.
Collections not Cataloged.
Serves: employees; researchers. Mon.–Fri. 8:30 a.m.–5 p.m.
Reproduction Facility: quickcopy.

Gloucester Point

656. VIRGINIA INSTITUTE MARINE SCIENCE
Library
Gloucester Point, VA 23062
Telephone: 804/642-2111.
Contact Person: Susan Barrick, Library Director.
Staff: 2 professional (full time).
Size: 5,000 charts maps; 50 atlases; 20 reference books and gazetteers.
Area Specialization: Chesapeake Bay; Virginia; Atlantic coast.
Subject Specialization: marine sciences.
Classification System: National Ocean Survey.
Collections not Cataloged.
Depository for: NOS; USGS (Topo.).
Serves: students; faculty; employees; public. Mon.–Fri. 8 a.m.–4:30 p.m. (Seats 20).
Interlibrary Loan Available.
Reproduction Facility: photocopy.

Hampden-Sydney

657. HAMPDEN-SYDNEY COLLEGE
Eggleston Library
Hampden-Sydney, VA 23943
Telephone: 804/223-4381, Ext. 190.
Contact Person: Alan Zoellner, Reference Libn.
Size: 887 maps; 61 atlases; 156 reference books and gazetteers.
Annual Accessions: 50 maps; 5 atlases; 5–10 reference books and gazetteers.
Area Specialization: Virginia.
Subject Specialization: topography.

Dates: 1900 - (100%).
Classification System: LC.
Collections Cataloged. (25%).
Depository for: USGS (Topo.).
Serves: students; faculty; employees; public. Mon.–Fri. 8 a.m.–12 midnight; Sat. 8:30 a.m.–5 p.m.; Sun. 12 noon–12 midnight.
Reproduction Facility: photocopy.

Lexington

658. VIRGINIA MILITARY INSTITUTE
Geology Department
Lexington, VA 24450
Established ca. 1870.
Telephone: 703/463-6331.
Contact Person: Commander Ronald Erchul, Associate Professor of Geology.
Staff: 1 professional (part time).
Size: ca. 1,500 maps.
Area Specialization: Virginia and contiguous states.
Subject Specialization: topograhy.
Dates: 1900 - (100%).
Classification System: local system.
Collections not Cataloged.
Depository for: USGS (Topo.).
Serves: students; faculty; employees; public. Mon.–Fri. 8 a.m.–4 p.m. (Seats 4).
Reproduction Facility: photocopy.

Newport News

659. CHRISTOPHER NEWPORT COLLEGE
Capt. John Smith Library
50 Shoe Lane
Newport News, VA 23606
Established 1983.
Telephone: 804/599-7132.
Contact Person: Hugh J. Treacy, Reference/Instruction Libn.
Staff: 1 non-professional (part time).
Size: 866 maps.
Annual Accessions: 10 maps; 80 aerial photographs.
Area Specialization: Virginia.
Subject Specialization: topography.
Dates: 1900 - (100%).
Classification System: local system.
Collections not Cataloged.
Collections Cataloged. (100%).
Depository for: USGS (Topo.).
Serves: students; faculty; employees; public. Mon.–Thurs. 8 a.m.–10:30 p.m., Fri. 8 a.m.–4:45 p.m.; Sat. 11 a.m.–5 p.m.; Sun. 1–8 p.m. (Seats 24).
Reproduction Facility: photocopy.

660. MARINERS' MUSEUM
Library
Newport News, VA 23606
Established 1930.
Telephone: 804/595-0368.
Contact Person: Mr. Ardie L. Kelly, Libn.
Staff: 2 professional (full time); 2 non-professional (full time).
Size: 1,625 maps; 230 atlases; 8 globes.
Subject Specialization: maritime and naval history; nautical charts.
Dates: 1800-1899 (90%); 1900 - (10%).
Classification System: local system.
Collections Cataloged.

Serves: public. Mon.–Fri. 9 a.m.–5 p.m.; Sat. 9 a.m.–5 p.m. (Seats 15; 150 readers served per month).
Reproduction Facility: photocopy.
Publications: *Catalog of Maps, Ships' Papers and Logbooks.* Boston, G.K. Hall, 1964.

Norfolk

661. OLD DOMINION UNIVERSITY
Physics and Geographical Sciences
Map Reference Library
P.O. Box 6173
Norfolk, VA 23508
Telephone: 804/440-4141.
Contact Person: Henry Stewart.
Staff: 1 non-professional (part time).
Size: 3,500 maps.
Area Specialization: Virginia; Maryland; North Carolina; South Carolina.
Subject Specialization: topography.
Dates: 1900 - (100%).
Classification System: local system.
Collections not Cataloged.
Depository for: USGS (Topo.).
Serves: students; faculty; employees; public. Mon.–Fri. 8 a.m.–4 p.m. (Seats 5; 25 readers served per month).
Reproduction Facility: photocopy; quickcopy.

Portsmouth

662. PORTSMOUTH NAVAL SHIPYARD MUSEUM
Marshall W. Butt Library
2 High Street, P.O. Box 248
Portsmouth, VA 23705
Established 1949.
Telephone: 804/393-8591.
Contact Person: Alice C. Hanes, Curator. by appointment only.
Reproduction Facility: quickcopy.

Radford

663. RADFORD UNIVERSITY
Department of Geography
Map Collection
Radford University Station, P.O. Box 5811
Radford, VA 24142
Established 1960's.
Telephone: 703/731-5254.
Contact Person: Dr. Beund H. Kuennecke, Associate Professor of Geography.
Staff: 1 non-professional (full time); 2 professional (part time).
Size: 35,000 maps; 25 globes; 25 relief models; 10,000 aerial photographs.
Annual Accessions: 800 maps; 200 aerial photographs.
Area Specialization: Virginia; eastern United States.
Subject Specialization: topography; land use.
Dates: 1900 - (100%).
Classification System: local system.
Collections Cataloged.
Depository for: USGS (Topo.).
Serves: students; faculty; employees; public. Mon.–Fri. 8 a.m.–5 p.m. (Seats 6; 40 readers served per month).
Reproduction Facility: photocopy.

Reston

664. U.S. GEOLOGICAL SURVEY
Library
950 National Center
Reston, VA 22092
Established 1882.
Telephone: 703/860-6671; FTS 928-6671.
Contact Person: Barbara A. Chappell, Chief, Reference & Circulation.
Staff: 3 professional (full time); 1 non-professional (full time); 1 professional (part time); 1 non-professional (part time).
Size: 290,000 maps; 600 atlases; 7 globes; 200 relief models; 1,000 reference books and gazetteers; 50 serials (titles received); 50 microforms (no. of titles).
Annual Accessions: 8,000 maps; 30 atlases; 50 reference books and gazetteers; 1 serials (titles received); 2 microforms (no. of titles).
Area Specialization: comprehensive.
Subject Specialization: geology; geophysics; earth sciences; mineral resources; water resources.
Dates: 1800-1899 (2%); 1900 - (98%).
Classification System: USGS.
Collections Cataloged. (15%).
Depository for: DMA; DOS (Gt. Brit); GSC; USGS (Geol., topo.).
Serves: employees; public. Mon.–Fri. 7:15 a.m.–4:15 p.m. (Seats 80; 200 readers served per month).
Interlibrary Loan Available.
Reproduction Facility: photocopy.

665. U.S. GEOLOGICAL SURVEY
National Cartographic Information Center
507, U.S. Geological Survey, National Center
Reston, VA 22092
Established 1919.
Telephone: 703/860-6045.
Contact Person: Alan R. Stevens, Chief.
Staff: 17 professional (full time); 21 non-professional (full time); 6 non-professional (part time).
Size: 165,000 maps; 1,500,000 (on microfilm) aerial photographs; 20,000 microforms (no. of titles).
Annual Accessions: 5,000 maps; 1,000 aerial photographs; 2,000 microforms (no. of titles).
Area Specialization: United States and possessions; Antarctica; Moon; Planetary.
Subject Specialization: cartography; topograhy; remote sensing; geodetic control; geography.
Special Cartographic Collections: Map roll microfilm— 165,000 frames of current and historical USGS topographic, river survey, flood prone area and special maps; DMA current and historical maps; National Wetlands Inventory maps; maps from other federal and state agencies. Data base describing map, aerial, photo, and space imagery holdings of federal, state, and non-governmental agencies.
Dates: 1800-1899 (1%); 1900 - (99%).
Classification System: local system.
Collections Cataloged.
Serves: students; faculty; employees; public. Mon.–Fri. 7:45 a.m.–4:15 p.m. (Seats 5; 120 readers served per month).
Reproduction Facility: photocopy; quickcopy; microform.
Publications: Brochures, indexes and other publications available on request.

Richmond

666. MUSEUM OF THE CONFEDERACY
Brockenbrough Library
1201 East Clay Street
Richmond, VA 23219
Established 1896.
Telephone: 804/649-1861.
Contact Person: Cathy Carlson, Curator of Manuscripts.
Staff: 1 professional (full time).
Size: 225 maps.
Area Specialization: southeastern United States.
Subject Specialization: Civil War history.
Dates: 1800-1899 (100%).
Collections not Cataloged.
Serves: students; faculty; employees; public. Mon.–Fri. 10 a.m.–5 p.m. (Seats 4; 20 readers served per month).
Reproduction Facility: photocopy.

667. VALENTINE MUSEUM
Library
1015 E. Clay St.
Richmond, VA 23219-1590
Established 1930.
Telephone: 804/649-0711.
Contact Person: Sarah Shields, Curator.
Staff: 2 professional (full time); 1 professional (part time).
Size: ca. 400 maps; 25 atlases.
Area Specialization: city of Richmond & environs.
Dates: 1800-1899 (70%); 1900 - (30%).
Classification System: local system.
Collections Cataloged.
Serves: students; faculty; employees; public. Mon.–Fri. 10 a.m.–5 p.m. (by appointment). (Seats 2; 30 readers served per month).
Reproduction Facility: photocopy; quickcopy.

668. VIRGINIA HISTORICAL SOCIETY
Map Collection
428 North Boulevard
Richmond, VA 23220
Established 1831.
Telephone: 804/358-4901.
Contact Person: Howson W. Cole, Senior Libn.
Staff: 1 professional (part time); 1 non-professional (part time).
Size: 10,000 maps; 100 atlases; 50 reference books and gazetteers; 5 serials (titles received).
Annual Accessions: 10 maps.
Area Specialization: Virginia.
Special Cartographic Collections: Jeremy F. Gilmer Confederate States Army Engineer Corps maps of Virginia, 1862–1865.
Classification System: LC.
Collections Cataloged.
Serves: students; faculty; employees; public. Mon.–Fri. 9 a.m.–4:45 p.m.; Sat. 9 a.m.–4:45 p.m. (Seats 20).
Reproduction Facility: photocopy; quickcopy.

669. VIRGINIA STATE LIBRARY
Archives and Records Division
Archives Branch Map Collection
12th and Capitol Streets
Richmond, VA 23219
Established 1828.
Telephone: 804/786-2306.
Contact Person: Anthony J. Gonzales, Head, Processing Section.
Size: 85,442 maps; 15 atlases; 1 globes; 20 reference books and gazetteers; 1 serials (titles received).
Annual Accessions: 200 maps.
Area Specialization: Virginia; southeastern United States.

Special Cartographic Collections: Board of Public Works—manuscript maps (ca. 400) relating to 19th century Virginia internal improvements (roads, canals, and railroads); Sanborn fire insurance maps of Virginia cities and towns, ca. 1886–1925 (2000 maps).
Dates: pre-1800 (25%); 1800-1899 (50%); 1900 - (25%).
Classification System: Dewey (modified).
Collections Cataloged. (90%).
Depository for: USGS (Topo.).
Serves: public. Mon.–Fri. 8:15 a.m.–5 p.m.; Sat. 8:15 a.m.–5 p.m. (Seats 39; 60 readers served per month).
Reproduction Facility: photocopy.
Publications: Many maps in the collection are described in E.G. Swem, comp., "Maps relating to Virginia . . . by E.G. Swem (1914) in the *Bulletin of the Virginia State Library,* 7, nos. 2 & 3 (1914). See also James W. Sames III, comp. *Index of Kentucky & Virginia Maps: 1562 to 1900* (Frankfort: Kentucky Historical Society, 1976). Manuscript maps (ca. 400) are described in *Board of Public Works Inventory,* compiled by John S. Salmon (Richmond: Virginia State Library, 1978).

Wise

670. CLINCH VALLEY COLLEGE
John Cook Wyllie Library
Wise, VA 24293
Established 1955.
Telephone: 703/328-2431 Ext. 255.
Contact Person: Rosemary P. Mercure, Head, Public Services.
Staff: 2 professional (part time).
Size: 1,600 maps; 65 atlases; 25 reference books and gazetteers.
Annual Accessions: 100 maps; 5 atlases; 2 reference books and gazetteers.
Area Specialization: Middle Atlantic States.
Subject Specialization: geology.
Dates: 1800-1899 (5%); 1900 - (95%).
Classification System: LC.
Collections not Cataloged.
Depository for: USGS (Geol.).
Serves: students; faculty; employees; public. Mon.–Fri. 8 a.m.–10 p.m.; Sat. 1–5 p.m.; Sun. 1:30–10 p.m. (Seats 300; 1,000 readers served per month).
Reproduction Facility: photocopy; quickcopy.
Publications: *Resources in Appalachian Studies in the John Cook Wyllie Library* (guide).

WASHINGTON

Bellevue

671. KING COUNTY LIBRARY SYSTEM
Bellevue Library
Map Collection
11501 Main Street
Bellevue, WA 98004
Established 1980/81.
Telephone: 206/455-6889.
Contact Person: Barbara J. Knopf, Reference Libn.
Staff: professional (full time); professional (part time).
Size: 1,839 maps; 28 atlases; 1 globes; 15 aerial photographs; 40 reference books and gazetteers; 1 serials (titles received).
Annual Accessions: 50–60 maps; 3 atlases; 10 reference books and gazetteers; 2 serials (titles received).
Area Specialization: Pacific Northwest.

Special Cartographic Collections: Washington State topographical maps; Green Trails maps; Snohomish basin maps.
Dates: 1900 - (100%).
Classification System: Dewey.
Collections not Cataloged.
Serves: students; faculty; employees; public. Mon. 12 noon–9 p.m.; Tues.–Thurs. 10 a.m.–9 p.m.;. Fri. 10 a.m.–5 p.m. Sat. 10 a.m.–5 p.m.; Sun. 1–5 p.m. (Sept.–May). (Seats 90; 33,000 (total for library) readers served per month).
Interlibrary Loan Available.
Reproduction Facility: photocopy; microform.

Bellingham

672. WESTERN WASHINGTON UNIVERSITY
Dept. of Geography and Regional Planning
Map Library
Bellingham, WA 98225
Established 1957.
Telephone: 206/676-3272.
Contact Person: Janet Collins, Map Curator.
Staff: 1 professional (full time); 9 non-professional (part time).
Size: 172,000 maps; 670 atlases; 55 globes; 50 relief models; 20,600 aerial photographs; 676 reference books and gazetteers; 9 serials (titles received); 4 microforms (no. of titles).
Annual Accessions: 3,500 maps; 20 atlases.
Area Specialization: Pacific Northwest; Alaska; Canada; Pacific Rim.
Dates: 1800-1899 (5%); 1900 - (95%).
Classification System: LC.
Collections Cataloged. (95%).
Depository for: DMA; NOS; NTS (Canada); USGS (Geol., topo.); NOAA; Washington State Dept. of Natural Resources.
Serves: students; faculty; employees; public. Mon., Tues., Thurs, Fri. 9 a.m–4 p.m., Wed. 9 a.m.–4 p.m. and. 6–8 p.m. (Seats 42; 500 readers served per month).
Reproduction Facility: photocopy; quickcopy.
Publications: *A guide to the WWU Map Library* (guide).

Cheney

673. EASTERN WASHINGTON UNIVERSITY
Department of Geography
Geography Map Library
Isle Hall
Cheney, WA 99004
Telephone: 509/359-2433.
Contact Person: David S. Anderson, Staff Cartographer.
Staff: 1 non-professional (full time).
Size: 10,000 maps; 20 atlases; 4 globes; 40 relief models; 15,000 aerial photographs; 20 reference books and gazetteers.
Annual Accessions: 100 maps.
Area Specialization: Pacific Northwest.
Subject Specialization: topography; aerial photography of N.E. Washington.
Special Cartographic Collections: Out of print U.S.G.S. 1:125,00 and 1: 62,500 Pacific N.W. (topographic); US.G.S. Geologic atlas folios.
Dates: 1800-1899 (1%); 1900 - (99%).
Classification System: by geographic areas.
Collections Cataloged. (50%).
Serves: students; faculty; employees; public. Mon.–Fri. 8 a.m.–12 noon, 1–4:30 p.m. (Seats 10; 20–30 readers served per month).
Reproduction Facility: photocopy; quickcopy.

Ellensburg

674. CENTRAL WASHINGTON UNIVERSITY
Library
Documents Department, Map Services
Ellensburg, WA 98926
Established 1962.
Telephone: 509/963-1541.
Contact Person: Ruth D. Hartman, Head, Documents Dept.
Staff: 1 professional (part time).
Size: 67,000 maps; 125 atlases; 3 globes; 1 relief models; 20 aerial photographs; 150 reference books and gazetteers; 10 serials (titles received); 75 microforms (no. of titles).
Annual Accessions: 3,000 maps; 12 atlases; 12 reference books and gazetteers.
Area Specialization: Washington (State); Pacific Northwest.
Subject Specialization: geology.
Dates: pre-1800 (1%); 1800-1899 (99%).
Classification System: LC.
Collections Cataloged.
Depository for: DMA; NOS; USGS (Geol., topo.).
Serves: students; faculty; employees; public. Mon.–Thurs. 8 a.m.–10 p.m., Fri. 8 a.m.–5 p.m.; Sat. 9 a.m.–5 p.m.; Sun. 1–10 p.m. (Seats 16; 60–70 readers served per month).
Interlibrary Loan Available.
Reproduction Facility: photocopy; microform.
Publications: *Purchasing maps of Washington, a popular guide* by Peter L. Stark.

Pullman

675. WASHINGTON STATE UNIVERSITY
Owen Science & Engineering Library
Pullman, WA 99164-3200
Telephone: 509/335-2671.
Contact Person: Barbara Parks, Supervisor B.
Area Specialization: Pacific northwest.
Dates: 1900 - (100%).
Classification System: .
Collections not Cataloged.
Depository for: USGS (Topo.).
Serves: students; faculty; employees; public;. Mon.–Fri. 8 a.m.–12 midnight; Sat. 8 a.m.–12 midnight; Sun. 8 a.m.–12 midnight.
Interlibrary Loan Available.
Reproduction Facility: photocopy; microform.

Seattle

676. SEATTLE PUBLIC LIBRARY
History Department
1000 Fourth Avenue
Seattle, WA 98104
Established 1959.
Telephone: 206/625-4894.
Contact Person: Marjorie R. Henry, Libn., Public Service.
Staff: 1 professional (part time); 1 non-professional (part time).
Size: 69,000 maps; 850 atlases; 3 globes; 30 relief models; 150 reference books and gazetteers; 12 serials (titles received).
Annual Accessions: 2,000 maps; 6 atlases; 3 reference books and gazetteers.
Area Specialization: Pacific Northwest.
Subject Specialization: topograhy; political maps; plat atlases; nautical charts.
Special Cartographic Collections: maps of Seattle and King County from 1875; maps of Washington (State, Terr.)

from 1854; maps of Wash. counties from 1905; Maps of American and foreign cities.
Dates: 1800-1899 (2%); 1900 - (98%).
Classification System: AGS (modified).
Collections Cataloged.
Depository for: DMA; NOS; USGS (Geol., topo.); U.S. Forest Service.
Serves: public. 12; Sat. 9; Sun. 4. (Seats 100 (History Dept. seating area) 1,100 readers served per month).
Reproduction Facility: photocopy; quickcopy.

677. UNIVERSITY OF WASHINGTON
Libraries
Map Section FM-25
Seattle, WA 98195
Telephone: 206/543-9392.
Contact Person: Steve Hiller, Head, Map Section.
Staff: 1 professional (full time); 4 non-professional (part time).
Size: 217,012 maps; 1,406 atlases; 39,164 aerial photographs; 4 serials (titles received); 2,116 microforms (no. of titles).
Area Specialization: United States; Pacific Northwest; Circum-Pacific region; Europe; East Asia.
Subject Specialization: geology; socio-economic studies.
Dates: 1800-1899 (1); 1900 - (99).
Classification System: LC;.
Collections Cataloged.
Collections not Cataloged.
Depository for: DMA; GSC; NOS; USGS (Geol., topo.).
Serves: students; faculty; employees; public. Mon.–Fri. 7:30 a.m.–5:30 p.m. (Seats 45; 1,000 readers served per month).
Interlibrary Loan Available.
Reproduction Facility: photocopy; quickcopy; microform.

Spokane

678. EASTERN WASHINGTON STATE HISTORICAL SOCIETY
Library
West 2316 First Avenue
Spokane, WA 99204
Established 1916.
Telephone: 509/456-3931.
Contact Person: Douglas A. Olson, Libn.
Staff: 1 professional (full time).
Size: 250 maps; 25 atlases; 1 relief models; 150 aerial photographs.
Area Specialization: Pacific Northwest; Washington state.
Subject Specialization: geology; history; trails.
Serves: public. Tues.–Fri. 10 a.m.–5 p.m.; Sat. 10 a.m.–5 p.m. (Seats 10).
Reproduction Facility: quickcopy.

679. SPOKANE PUBLIC LIBRARY
Documents Department
West 906 Main Avenue
Spokane, WA 99201
Established 1911.
Telephone: 509/838-3361, ext. 312.
Contact Person: Sharon Ufer, Documents Libn.
Staff: 1 professional (part time); 1 non-professional (part time).
Size: 6,000 maps; 75 atlases; 3 globes; 3 relief models; 1 aerial photographs; 170 reference books and gazetteers.
Annual Accessions: 150 maps; 5 atlases; 5 reference books and gazetteers.
Area Specialization: Pacific Northwest.
Subject Specialization: local history.
Dates: 1800-1899 (5%); 1900 - (95%).
Classification System: Dewey; Superintendent of Documents.

Collections Cataloged. ((atlases)).
Depository for: USGS (Geol., topo.).
Serves: public. Mon., Tues., Thurs. 9 a.m.–9 p.m.; Wed. 1–6 p.m.;. Fri. 9 a.m.–6 p.m. Sat. 9 a.m.–6 p.m. (Sept.–May). (Seats 90).
Reproduction Facility: photocopy; microform.

Tacoma

680. PACIFIC LUTHERAN UNIVERSITY
Mortvedt Library
Reference Department
121st & Park Avenue South
Tacoma, WA 98447
Telephone: 206/535-7507.
Contact Person: Susan McDonald, Reference Libn.
Staff: 2 professional (full time); 2 non-professional (part time).
Size: 15,500 maps; 150 atlases; 1 globes; 20 reference books and gazetteers.
Annual Accessions: 100 maps; 5 atlases.
Dates: 1900 - (95%).
Classification System: LC (atlases and books only).
Collections Cataloged. ((atlases only)).
Depository for: USGS (Topo.).
Serves: students; faculty; employees; public. Mon.–Fri. 8 a.m.–10 p.m. (Seats 25).
Reproduction Facility: photocopy.

681. U.S. GEOLOGICAL SURVEY
Project Office, Glaciology
1201 Pacific Avenue, Suite 450
Tacoma, WA 98402
Telephone: 206/593-6502.
Contact Person: David R. Hirst, Photographer.
Staff: 1 professional (full time); 2 non-professional (full time).
Size: 80,000 aerial photographs.
Area Specialization: western North America; Canada; Alaska; Ellesmere Island; and Greenland.
Subject Specialization: glaciology; glacier land forms.
Dates: 1900 - (100%).
Classification System: by glacier name.
Collections Cataloged. (50%).
Serves: students; faculty; employees; public;. Mon.–Fri. 9 a.m.–4:30 p.m. (10 readers served per month).
Reproduction Facility: photocopy; quickcopy.

682. UNIVERSITY OF PUGET SOUND
Geology Department
1500 North Warner
Tacoma, WA 98416
Telephone: 206/756-3129.
Contact Person: Dr. Stewart Lowther, Professor of Geology, Department Chairman.
Staff: 2 non-professional (part time).
Size: 20,000 maps; 100 relief models; 400 aerial photographs.
Annual Accessions: 1,000 maps.
Area Specialization: western United States including Hawaii and Alaska.
Subject Specialization: topography; geology.
Dates: 1800-1899 (1%); 1900 - (99%).
Classification System: local system.
Collections not Cataloged.
Depository for: USGS (Topo.).
Serves: students; faculty; employees; public. Mon.–Fri. 9 a.m.–5 p.m. (Seats 30).
Interlibrary Loan Available.
Reproduction Facility: quickcopy.

683. WASHINGTON STATE HISTORICAL SOCIETY
Library
315 North Stadium Way
Tacoma, WA 98403
Staff: 2 professional (part time).
Size: 5,000 maps; 25 atlases.
Area Specialization: Pacific Northwest.
Special Cartographic Collections: Buckmaster Collection of late 19th century maps of Pacific Northest, California, Alaska; Allen Collection—maps dating from 1511–1865 of the world, North America, Pacific Northwest.
Dates: pre-1800 (1%); 1800-1899 (19%); 1900 - (80%).
Classification System: local system (area classification).
Tues.–Fri. 9:30 a.m.–5 p.m.; Sat. 9:30 a.m.–5 p.m.
Reproduction Facility: photocopy.

Walla Walla

684. WHITMAN COLLEGE
Penrose Memorial Library
Walla Walla, WA 99362
Telephone: 509/527-5191.
Contact Person: (Mrs.) Marilyn M. Sparks, Documents Libn.
Size: 30,075 (est.) maps; 266 atlases; 1 globes; 3 relief models; 2,618 aerial photographs; 80 (est.) reference books and gazetteers; geography 16, geology 59 serials (titles received).
Area Specialization: Pacific Northwest.
Dates: 1800-1899 (8% approx.); 1900 - (92% approx.).
Classification System: local system.
Depository for: DMA; USGS (Geol., topo.).
Serves: students; faculty; employees; public. Mon.–Fri. 9 a.m.–12 noon; 1–5 p.m.; Sat. 9 a.m.–5 p.m. (No service available); Sun. 11 a.m.–5 p.m. (No service available).
Interlibrary Loan Available.
Reproduction Facility: photocopy.

WEST VIRGINIA

Beckley

685. NATIONAL MINE HEALTH AND SAFETY ACADEMY
Learning Resource Center
Box 1166
Airport Road
Beckley, WV 25801
Established 1977.
Telephone: 304/255-0451, ext. 266.
Contact Person: Stephen J. Hoyle, Libn.
Staff: 3 professional (full time); 2 non-professional (full time); 1 non-professional (part time).
Size: 5,300 maps; 50 atlases; 10 reference books and gazetteers.
Annual Accessions: 100 maps; 3 atlases; 4 reference books and gazetteers.
Area Specialization: United States.
Subject Specialization: geology; mining and mineral resources; topography.
Special Cartographic Collections: coal resource maps of the United States and selected foreign areas.
Dates: 1800-1899 (5%); 1900 - (95%).
Classification System: local system.
Collections Cataloged. (100%).
Serves: students; faculty; employees; public. Mon.–Thurs. 7 a.m.–8:30 p.m., Fri. 7 a.m.–5:30 p.m. (Seats 16; 250 readers served per month).
Reproduction Facility: photocopy.

Morgantown

686. WEST VIRGINIA (STATE) GEOLOGICAL AND ECONOMIC SURVEY
Library
Morgantown, WV 26507
Telephone: 304/594-2331.
Contact Person: Ruth I. Hayhurst, Libn.
Staff: 1 professional (part time).
Size: 3,567 maps.
Annual Accessions: 50 maps.
Area Specialization: West Virginia and contiguous areas.
Subject Specialization: geology; natural resources.
Depository for: USGS (Geol.).
Serves: employees.

687. WEST VIRGINIA UNIVERSITY
Library
Map Room
P.O. Box 6069
Morgantown, WV 26506
Established 1931.
Telephone: 304/293-3640.
Contact Person: Jo. B. Brown, Reference Libn.
Staff: 1 professional (part time); 2 non-professional (part time).
Size: 45,000 maps; 1 reference books and gazetteers.
Annual Accessions: 2,500 maps.
Area Specialization: Appalachia.
Dates: 1900 - (100%).
Classification System: local system.
Collections not Cataloged.
Depository for: DMA; USGS (Geol., topo.).
Serves: students; faculty; employees; public;. Mon.–Fri.8 a.m.–12 midnight; Sat. 9 a.m.–5 p.m.; Sun. 2–11 p.m. (Seats 6; 40–50 readers served per month).
Interlibrary Loan Available.

688. WEST VIRGINIA UNIVERSITY
Library
West Virginia Regional History Collection
Colson Hall
Morgantown, WV 26506
Established 1935.
Telephone: 304/293-3536.
Contact Person: George Parkinson, Curator.
Staff: 3 professional (full time); 5 non-professional (full time).
Size: 5,000 maps; 30 atlases; 1,000 aerial photographs; 3,000 reference books and gazetteers; 50 microforms (no. of titles).
Annual Accessions: 50 maps; 100 reference books and gazetteers.
Area Specialization: West Virginia; Virginia; Upper Ohio Valley.
Subject Specialization: coal; natural resources; railroads; waterways.
Special Cartographic Collections: Sanborn fire insurance maps—W. Va., 1880–1935; Kreps Map Collection—coal and mineral lands; mine interiors; Meadows Map Collection—Coal and mineral lands; mine interiors; ASCS aerial photo-maps of W. Va. counties, 1938–58; W. Va. county geologic maps.
Dates: pre-1800 (5%); 1800-1899 (45%); 1900 - (50%).
Classification System: local system.
Collections not Cataloged.
Depository for: USGS (Geol., topo.); W Va Geological Survey; W Va Dept. of Highways.
Serves: students; faculty; employees; public;. Mon.–Fri. 8 a.m.–5 p.m.; Sat. 9 a.m.–5 p.m. (Seats 30; 50 readers served per month).
Reproduction Facility: photocopy; microform.

Publications: *Guide to Manuscripts & Archives in the W. Va. Collection.* 1974 (new and used available in 1984) *W. Va. History; a bibliography and guide to research.* .

WISCONSIN

Appleton

689. LAWRENCE UNIVERSITY
Seeley G. Mudd Library
119 S. Lawe
Appleton, WI 54912
Established 1870.
Telephone: 414/735-6752.
Contact Person: Kathy Isaacson, Reference Libn.
Staff: 1 non-professional (part time).
Size: 1,000 maps; 50 atlases; 10 reference books and gazetteers.
Classification System: DMA.
Collections not Cataloged.
Depository for: DMA; USGS (Geol., topo.).
Serves: students; faculty; employees; public;. (Seats 2; 10 readers served per month).

Beloit

690. BELOIT COLLEGE
Col. Robert H. Morse Library
731 College Street
Beloit, WI 53511
Established ca. 1900.
Telephone: 608/365-3391, Ext. 481.
Contact Person: Ruth Williams, Head of Serials.
Staff: 1 part time non-professional (part time).
Size: 80,627 maps; 300 atlases; 2 globes; 50 reference books and gazetteers.
Annual Accessions: 300 maps.
Area Specialization: United States.
Subject Specialization: geology.
Dates: 1800-1899 (2%); 1900 - (98%).
Classification System: DMA.
Collections not Cataloged.
Depository for: DMA; USGS (Geol., topo.).
Serves: students; faculty; employees; public.
Interlibrary Loan Available.
Reproduction Facility: photocopy.

Eau Claire

691. UNIVERSITY OF WISCONSIN-EAU CLAIRE
Dept. of Geography
Simpson Map Library
Eau Claire, WI 54701
Established 1969.
Telephone: 715/836-3244.
Contact Person: Dr. Adam Cahow, Professor.
Staff: 1 professional (part time); 4 non-professional (part time).
Size: 120,000 maps; 250 atlases; 20 globes; 50 relief models; 2,500 aerial photographs; 500 reference books and gazetteers; 15 serials (titles received).
Annual Accessions: 2,000 maps; 20 atlases; 2 globes; 5 relief models; 250 aerial photographs; 50 reference books and gazetteers; 3 serials (titles received).
Area Specialization: United States; Canada.
Subject Specialization: topography.

Dates: 1900 - (100%).
Classification System: LC.
Collections Cataloged. (100%).
Depository for: DMA; NTS (Canada); USGS (Geol., topo.).
Serves: students; faculty; employees; public. Mon.–Fri. 9 a.m.–5 p.m. (Seats 30; 600 readers served per month).

Green Bay

692. UNIVERSITY OF WISCONSIN—GREEN BAY
Library
Government Publications
Green Bay, WI 54301
Established 1968.
Telephone: 414/465-2547.
Contact Person: Kathy Pletcher, Assistant Director.
Staff: 1 professional (part time); 2 non-professional (part time).
Size: 45,000 maps; 300 atlases; 1 globes; 1 relief models; 200 reference books and gazetteers.
Annual Accessions: 800 maps; 3 atlases; 5 reference books and gazetteers.
Area Specialization: Wisconsin.
Subject Specialization: environment.
Dates: 1800-1899 (5%); 1900 - (95%).
Classification System: LC; DMA.
Collections Cataloged. (75%).
Depository for: DMA; USGS (Geol., topo.).
Serves: students; faculty; employees; public. Mon.–Thurs. 8 a.m.–11:30 p.m.; Fri. 8 a.m.–8 p.m.; Sat. 9 a.m.–6 p.m.; Sun. 1–11:30 p.m. (Seats 32; 100 readers served per month).
Interlibrary Loan Available.
Reproduction Facility: photocopy.

Kenosha

693. KENOSHA COUNTY HISTORICAL SOCIETY
6300 Third Avenue
Kenosha, WI 53140
Established 1925.
Telephone: 414/654-5770.
Contact Person: Lois Stein, Libn.
Staff: non-professional (part time).
Size: 150 maps; 20 atlases.
Area Specialization: Wisconsin; Kenosha, Racine and Milwaukee counties.
Subject Specialization: local history.
Dates: 1800-1899 (85%); 1900 - (15%).
Serves: public. Tues. and Thurs. 2–4:30 p.m.; Sun. First Sunday of every month.
Reproduction Facility: photocopy.

694. UNIVERSITY OF WISCONSIN—PARKSIDE
Library/Learning Center
P.O. Box 2000
Wood Road
Kenosha, WI 53141
Established 1971.
Telephone: 414/553-2360, ext. 2167.
Contact Person: Barbara Baruth, Head, Technical Services.
Staff: non-professional (part time).
Size: 3,627 maps; 1 globes; 10 aerial photographs; 5 reference books and gazetteers.
Annual Accessions: 250 maps.
Area Specialization: Wisconsin and contiguous states.
Subject Specialization: topography.
Special Cartographic Collections: laminated city maps.
Dates: 1900 - (100%).

Collections not Cataloged.
Serves: students; faculty; employees; public. Mon.–Thurs. 7:45 a.m.–12 midnight, Fri. 7:45 a.m.–4:30 p.m.; Sat. 8:30 a.m.–4:30 p.m.; Sun. 12 noon–10:30 p.m. (10 readers served per month).
Reproduction Facility: photocopy.

La Crosse

695. UNIVERSITY OF WISCONSIN—LA CROSSE
Department of Geography
Map Library
La Crosse, WI 54601
Established 1965.
Telephone: 608/785-8333.
Contact Person: Jerry B. Culver, Associate Professor.
Staff: 1 non-professional (full time); 1 non-professional (part time).
Size: 12,000 maps; 12 atlases; 12 globes; 3,000 aerial photographs; 100 reference books and gazetteers.
Annual Accessions: 50 maps.
Area Specialization: Wisconsin; Minnesota; Iowa.
Dates: 1800-1899 (5%); 1900 - (95%).
Classification System: USGS state index.
Collections not Cataloged.
Depository for: USGS (Topo.).
Serves: students; faculty; employees; public. Unscheduled, but access available 8–4 p.m. (Seats 12; 20 readers served per month).
Reproduction Facility: photocopy.

Madison

696. STATE HISTORICAL SOCIETY OF WISCONSIN
Archives and Manuscripts
816 State Street
Madison, WI 53706
Established ca. 1854.
Telephone: 608/262-5867.
Contact Person: Michael Edmonds, Special Collections Libn.
Staff: 1 professional (part time); 1 non-professional (part time).
Size: 25,000 maps; 2,500 atlases; 1 globes; 3 relief models; 125 reference books and gazetteers; 9 serials (titles received).
Annual Accessions: 100 maps; 150 atlases; 10 reference books and gazetteers.
Area Specialization: Wisconsin; North Central States; North America.
Subject Specialization: history; land-ownership.
Special Cartographic Collections: Wisconsin bird's-eye views; Sanborn fire insurance maps of Wisconsin; official maps created by various branches of state government.
Dates: pre-1800 (15%); 1800-1899 (50%); 1900 - (35%).
Classification System: local system (expanded Cutter).
Collections Cataloged. (88%).
Depository for: USGS (Topo.).
Serves: students; faculty; employees; public. Mon.–Fri. 8 a.m.–5 p.m.; Sat. 9 a.m.–4 p.m. (Seats 32; 150 readers served per month).
Reproduction Facility: photocopy.
Depository for: USGS (Topo.).
Reproduction Facility: microform.
Publications: *Union List of Topographic Maps of Wisconsin* (1975); *Maps and Atlases showing Ownership in Wisconsin* (1978); *Maps in the Collections of the State Historical Society of Wisconsin* (brochure).

697. UNIVERSITY OF WISCONSIN
Cartographic Laboratory
Arthur H. Robinson Map Library
310 Science Hall, 550 N. Park Street
Madison, WI 53706
Established 1945 (renamed Nov. 4, 1982).
Telephone: 608/262-1471.
Contact Person: Mary Galneder, Map Libn.
Staff: 1 professional (full time); 4 professional (part time).
Size: 207,176 maps; 9 globes; 300 relief models; 133,545 aerial photographs; ca. 500 reference books and gazetteers; 22 serials (titles received); ca. 500 items microforms (no. of titles).
Annual Accessions: ca. 7,000 maps; ca. 1,300 aerial photographs.
Area Specialization: comprehensive.
Subject Specialization: comprehensive.
Dates: 1800-1899 (ca. 3%); 1900 - (ca. 97%).
Classification System: LC (modified); modified O.S.S.
Collections Cataloged. (100%).
Depository for: DMA; NOS; NTS (Canada); USGS (Geol., topo.); selected SuDocs.
Serves: students; faculty; employees; public;. Mon.–Fri. 8 a.m.–12 noon, 1–5 p.m. (Seats 8; 500 readers served per month).
Interlibrary Loan Available.
Reproduction Facility: photocopy.
Publications: *Union List of Topographic Maps of Wisconsin* (1975).

Milwaukee

698. MILWAUKEE PUBLIC LIBRARY
814 W. Wisconsin Avenue
Milwaukee, WI 53233
Telephone: 414/278-3000.
Contact Person: Carol Gordon, Map Libn.
Staff: 1 professional (full time).
Size: 120,000 maps; 2,500 atlases; 1 globes; 25–30 relief models; 650 reference books and gazetteers; 33 serials (titles received).
Annual Accessions: 2,500–3,000 maps; 30–50 atlases; 10–15 reference books and gazetteers; 1–3 serials (titles received).
Area Specialization: Milwaukee; Wisconsin; Great Lakes region.
Special Cartographic Collections: The Local History Room houses historical maps and atlases of local, state, and regional interest and a collection of over 1,000 Great Lakes nautical charts.
Dates: pre-1800 (1%); 1800-1899 (14%); 1900 - (85%).
Classification System: Dewey; DMA.
Collections Cataloged.
Depository for: DMA; USGS (Geol., topo.).
Serves: public. Mon.–Thurs. 8:30 a.m.–9 p.m.; Sat. 8:30 a.m.–5:30 p.m.
Interlibrary Loan Available.
Reproduction Facility: photocopy; microform.

699. UNIVERSITY OF WISCONSIN—MILWAUKEE
Golda Meir Library
American Geographical Society Map Collection
2311 E. Hartford Ave.
Milwaukee, WI 53211
Established 1852.
Telephone: 414/963-6282.
Contact Person: Christopher Baruth, Map & Imagery Libn.
Staff: 1 professional (full time); 2 professional (part time); 3 non-professional (part time).

Size: 396,000 maps; 6,500 atlases; 71 globes; 100 relief models; 98,000 aerial photographs; 1,800 reference books and gazetteers.
Annual Accessions: 8,000 maps; 150 atlases; 1 globes; 25 reference books and gazetteers.
Area Specialization: The Americas.
Dates: pre-1800 (1%); 1800-1899 (2%); 1900 - (97%).
Classification System: AGS.
Collections Cataloged.
Depository for: DMA; GSC; NTS (Canada); USGS (Geol., topo.).
Serves: students; faculty; employees; public. Mon.–Fri. 8 a.m.–5 p.m.; Sat. 8 a.m.–12 noon. (Seats 200; 100 readers served per month).
Interlibrary Loan Available.
Reproduction Facility: photocopy.
Publications: *Current Geographical Publications,* Sec. III— Selected Maps.

Milwuakee

700. UNIVERSITY OF WISCONSIN—MILWAUKEE
Map and Air Photo Library
385 Sabin Hall
3407 North Downer Avenue
Milwuakee, WI 53201
Established 1961.
Telephone: 414/963-4871.
Contact Person: Prof. James J. Flannery, Curator.
Staff: 4 non-professional (part time).
Size: 170,000 maps; 11 atlases; 5 globes; 75 relief models; 6,500 aerial photographs; 50 reference books and gazetteers.
Annual Accessions: 3,500 maps.
Area Specialization: Wisconsin.
Subject Specialization: urban studies.
Dates: 1800-1899 (2%); 1900 - (98%).
Classification System: LC.
Collections Cataloged. (98%).
Serves: students; faculty; employees; public. Mon.–Fri. 9:30 a.m.–4:30 p.m. (Seats 25; 350 readers served per month).
Reproduction Facility: photocopy.

Oshkosh

701. UNIVERSITY WISCONSIN-OSHKOSH
Department of Geography
Elmwood
Oshkosh, WI 54935
Established 1932.
Telephone: 424-4242.
Contact Person: Paul S. Jones, Student Assistant.
Staff: 1 non-professional (part time).
Size: 20,290 maps; 25 atlases; 3 globes; 160 relief models; 4,600 aerial photographs.

702. UNIVERSITY OF WISCONSIN—OSHKOSH
Department of Geology
Harrington Hall
Oshkosh, WI 54901
Telephone: 414/424-4460.
Contact Person: Norris W. Jones, Chairman, Department of Geology.
Size: 39,125 maps; 5 relief models.
Area Specialization: Wisconsin; Illinois; Minnesota; Iowa; Michigan; Indiana.
Subject Specialization: geology.
Dates: 1900 - (100%).
Collections not Cataloged.

Depository for: USGS (Topo.).
Serves: students; faculty. open on request. (Seats 2; 4 readers served per month).

703. UNIVERSITY WISCONSIN—OSHKOSH
Polk Library
Government Documents
Oshkosh, WI 54901
Established 1969.
Telephone: 414/424-3347.
Contact Person: Gerald Krueger, Government Documents Libn.
Staff: 1 professional (part time).
Area Specialization: Wisconsin.
Dates: 1900 - (100%).
Collections not Cataloged.
Depository for: DMA; GPO.
Serves: students; faculty; employees; public. Mon.–Thurs. 7:45 a.m.–10 p.m., Fri. 7:45–4:30 p.m.; Sat. 1:30–5:00 p.m.; Sun. 1:30–10 p.m. (Seats 75; 5 readers served per month).
Interlibrary Loan Available.
Reproduction Facility: photocopy.

Platteville

704. UNIVERSITY OF WISCONSIN—PLATTEVILLE
Karrmann Library
Government Publications and Maps
725 West Main Street
Platteville, WI 53818
Established 1964.
Telephone: 608/342-1758.
Contact Person: Margaret Hohenstein, Libn.-Government Publications.
Staff: 1 professional (part time); 2 non-professional (part time).
Size: 30,523 maps.
Annual Accessions: 622 maps.
Area Specialization: midwestern United States including Wisconsin; Iowa; Illinois; Minnesota; Michigan.
Dates: 1900 - (100%).
Classification System: local system.
Collections Cataloged. (100%).
Depository for: DMA; USGS (Geol., topo.).
Serves: students; faculty; employees; public;. Mon.–Thurs. 7:45 a.m.–12 midnight, Fri. 7:45 a.m.–10 p.m.; Sat. 9 a.m.–5 p.m.; Sun. 1–12 midnight. (Seats 20).
Interlibrary Loan Available.
Reproduction Facility: photocopy; microform.
Publications: Microfiche indexes.

Racine

705. RACINE PUBLIC LIBRARY
75 7th Street
Racine, WI 53403
Telephone: 414/636-9241.
Contact Person: Jill Hartman, Federal Documents.
Staff: 1 professional (part time).
Size: 1,000 maps; 120 atlases; 1 globes; 250 reference books and gazetteers.
Dates: 1900 - (100%).
Classification System: SuDoc.
Collections not Cataloged.
Serves: public. Mon.–Fri. 9 a.m.–9 p.m.; Sat. 9 a.m.–5:30 p.m.; Sun. Nov.–April 2:00–5:00 p.m. (5 readers served per month).
Interlibrary Loan Available.
Reproduction Facility: photocopy.

Stevens Point

706. UNIVERSITY OF WISCONSIN—STEVENS POINT
Geography-Geology Department
Map Center
Stevens Point, WI 54481
Established 1964.
Telephone: 715/346-2629.
Contact Person: William M. McKinney, Professor and Map Libn.
Staff: 2 professional (part time); 10 non-professional (part time).
Size: 98,100 maps; 45 atlases; 1 globes; 33 aerial photographs; 10 reference books and gazetteers.
Annual Accessions: 2,500 maps.
Area Specialization: Wisconsin; Portage County, Wisconsin.
Subject Specialization: topography; geology.
Special Cartographic Collections: Portage County Maps of 1866 (photocopies.).
Dates: 1800-1899 (0.1%); 1900 - (99.9%).
Classification System: local system.
Collections not Cataloged.
Depository for: DMA; USGS (Geol., topo.).
Serves: students; faculty; employees; public. Mon.–Fri. 9 a.m.–4 p.m. (Seats 6; 60 readers served per month).

Superior

707. UNIVERSITY OF WISCONSIN—SUPERIOR
Jim Dan Hill Library
18th and Grand Street
Superior, WI 54880
Established 1936.
Telephone: 715/394-8341.
Contact Person: Edward F. Greve, Reference Libn.
Staff: 1 professional (part time).
Size: 2,500 maps; 75 atlases; 1 globes; 30 reference books and gazetteers.
Area Specialization: Wisconsin.
Subject Specialization: geography; topography.
Dates: 1900 - (100%).
Classification System: AGS.
Collections not Cataloged.
Depository for: selected, GPO.
Serves: students; faculty; employees; public. Mon.–Thurs. 8 a.m.–10 p.m., Fri. 8 a.m.–5 p.m.; Sat. 12 noon–4 p.m. (winter), 10 a.m.–2 p.m. (summer); Sun. 6–10 p.m. (Seats 25; 12 readers served per month).
Interlibrary Loan Available.
Reproduction Facility: photocopy.

Waukesha

708. SOUTHEASTERN WISCONSIN REGIONAL PLANNING COMMISSION
916 N. East Avenue
Waukesha, WI 53186
Established 1960.
Telephone: 414/547-6721, Ext. 272.
Contact Person: Leland H. Kreblin, Chief Planning Illustrator.
Size: 700 maps; 790 aerial photographs.
Area Specialization: Southeastern Wisconsin.
Subject Specialization: large scale topographic maps; small scale planimetric maps.
Dates: 1900 - (100%).
Classification System: U.S. public lands survey system (township and range system).

Serves: employees; public. Mon.–Fri. 8 a.m.–5 p.m.
Reproduction Facility: Diazo.

Whitewater

709. UNIVERSITY OF WISCONSIN—WHITEWATER
Geography Department
Map and Reference Library
800 West Main
Whitewater, WI 53190
Established 1963.
Telephone: 414/472-1071.
Contact Person: Dennis M. Richter, Professor.
Staff: 1 non-professional (full time); 3 non-professional (part time).
Size: 32,000 maps; 37 atlases; 20 globes; 80 relief models; 9,300 aerial photographs; 1,300 reference books and gazetteers; 50 serials (titles received).
Annual Accessions: 500+ maps; 2+ atlases; 2+ globes; 2+ relief models; 200+ aerial photographs; 20+ reference books and gazetteers.
Area Specialization: Wisconsin; upper midwestern United States.
Subject Specialization: regional planning; environmental planning; urban studies; cartographic methods; water resources.
Special Cartographic Collections: U.S.G.S. folios, pre-1920's.
Dates: pre-1800 (0.5%); 1800-1899 (1.5%); 1900 - (98.0%).
Classification System: LC.
Collections Cataloged. (100%).
Serves: students; faculty; employees; public. Mon.–Fri. 1–4 p.m. (Seats 30; 375 readers served per month).
Interlibrary Loan Available.
Reproduction Facility: photocopy.

WYOMING

Casper

710. CASPER COLLEGE
Goodstein Foundation Library
125 College Drive
Casper, WY 82601
Established September 1945.
Telephone: 307/268-2371.
Contact Person: Rose Mary Malone, Western History Libn.
Staff: 1 professional (part time); 1 non-professional (part time).
Size: 3,573 maps; 74 atlases; 2 globes; 3 relief models; 8 aerial photographs; 31 reference books and gazetteers; 2 serials (titles received).
Area Specialization: western United States.
Dates: pre-1800 (less than 1%).
Dates: 1900 - (99%).
Classification System: LC.
Collections Cataloged.
Depository for: USGS (Geol., topo.).
Serves: students; faculty; employees; public. Mon.–Fri. 7:30 a.m.–10 p.m.; Sun. 2:30–10 p.m.
Interlibrary Loan Available. (restricted)
Reproduction Facility: photocopy; quickcopy; microform.
Publications: *Index to Maps in the Catalog of the Everett D. Graff Collection of Western Americana; USGS Index to GS topo maps: Wyoming, U.S., Alaska;* our own listing of historical maps—largely The West and Wyoming.

711. NATRONA COUNTY PUBLIC LIBRARY
307 East 2nd Street
Casper, WY 82601
Established 1910.
Telephone: 307/237-4935.
Contact Person: Kathleen Nowak, Earth Sciences Libn.
Staff: 1 professional (full time).
Size: 6,367 maps; 25 atlases; 1 globes; 2 relief models; 500 aerial photographs; 50 reference books and gazetteers.
Annual Accessions: 100 maps; 1 atlases; 2 reference books and gazetteers.
Area Specialization: Wyoming.
Subject Specialization: geology.
Dates: 1800-1899 (1%); 1900 - (99%).
Classification System: local system.
Collections not Cataloged.
Depository for: USGS (Topo.).
Serves: public. Mon.–Wed. 9 a.m.–9 p.m.; Thurs.–Fri. 9 a.m.–6 p.m.; Sat. 9 a.m.–6 p.m.; Sun. 2–6 p.m. (Seats 6; 20 readers served per month).
Reproduction Facility: photocopy.

Cheyenne

712. WYOMING STATE ARCHIVES MUSEUM AND HISTORICAL DEPARTMENT
Research and Publications Division
The Barrett Building
Cheyenne, WY 82002
Established 1952.
Telephone: 307/777-7518.
Contact Person: Jean Brainerd.
Staff: 1 professional (full time).
Size: 1,750 maps; 20 atlases; 20 relief models; 30 aerial photographs; 10 reference books and gazetteers; 5 microforms (no. of titles).
Area Specialization: Wyoming.
Subject Specialization: local history.
Dates: pre-1800 (10%); 1800-1899 (50%); 1900 - (40%).
Classification System: Dewey.
Collections Cataloged. (50%).
Serves: employees; public. Mon.–Fri. 8 a.m.–5 p.m. (Seats 8; 25 readers served per month).
Reproduction Facility: photocopy; microform.

713. WYOMING STATE LIBRARY
Supreme Court and Library Building
Cheyenne, WY 82001
Staff: 1 professional (full time); 3 non-professional (full time).
Size: 22,000 maps; 50 atlases.
Annual Accessions: 100 maps; 2 atlases.
Area Specialization: Wyoming.
Dates: 1800-1899 (2); 1900 - (98).
Classification System: local system.
Collections Cataloged.
Depository for: USGS (Topo.).
Serves: employees; public. Mon.–Fri. 8 a.m.–5 p.m. (Seats 12; 30 readers served per month).
Interlibrary Loan Available.
Reproduction Facility: photocopy.

Laramie

714. UNIVERSITY OF WYOMING
Coe Library
Documents, Maps, and Microforms Department
University Station, Box 3334
Laramie, WY 82071
Established 1907.
Telephone: 307/766-2174.
Contact Person: Jim Walsh, Maps/Documents Libn.
Staff: 1 professional (full time); 3 non-professional (part time).
Size: 96,000 maps; 150 atlases; 2 globes; 19 relief models; 400 reference books and gazetteers; 2 microforms (no. of titles).
Annual Accessions: 5,500 maps; 15 atlases; 40 reference books and gazetteers.
Area Specialization: Wyoming; The West; Rocky Mountain Region.
Dates: 1800-1899 (3%); 1900 - (97%).
Classification System: LC.
Collections Cataloged. (3%).
Depository for: DMA; NOS; USGS (Geol., topo.).
Serves: students; faculty; employees; public. Mon.–Thurs. 8 a.m.–10 p.m., Fri. 8 a.m.–5 p.m.; Sat. 9:30 a.m.–4:30 p.m.; Sun. 1–9 p.m. (Seats 30; 75 readers served per month).
Interlibrary Loan Available. (restricted)
Reproduction Facility: photocopy; microform.
Publications: *Map Projections: Newsletter/Acquisitions List of Coe Library's Map Collection.*

715. UNIVERSITY OF WYOMING
Geology and Geophysics Department
Geology Library
P.O. Box 3006, University Station
Laramie, WY 82071
Established 1959.
Telephone: 307/766-3374.
Contact Person: Josephine Battisti, Manager, Geology Library.
Size: 23,000 maps; 10 atlases; 2 globes; 1 relief models.
Annual Accessions: 100 maps; 1 atlases.
Area Specialization: Rocky Mountains.
Subject Specialization: tectonics; geology; gravity; stratigraphy.
Dates: pre-1800 (1%); 1800-1899 (2%); 1900 - (5%).
Classification System: local system.
Collections not Cataloged.
Depository for: USGS (Geol., topo.).
Serves: students; faculty; employees; public. Mon.–Fri. 8 a.m.–10 p.m.; Sat. 9 a.m.–4 p.m.; Sun. 12 noon–10 p.m. (Seats 75; 100 readers served per month).
Interlibrary Loan Available. (restricted)
Reproduction Facility: photocopy.

Sheridan

716. SHERIDAN COLLEGE
Griffith Memorial Library
Sheridan, WY 82801
Telephone: 307/674-6446, ext. 213.
Contact Person: Karen Mydland, Government Publications Coordinator.
Staff: 1 non-professional (full time).
Size: 7,994 maps; 19 atlases; 1 globes; 4 reference books and gazetteers.
Area Specialization: Colorado; Idaho; Montana; North Dakota; South Dakota; Utah; Wyoming.
Subject Specialization: topography; geology.
Dates: 1900 - (100%).

Classification System: Dewey book collection; checked in on state index maps.
Collections not Cataloged.
Depository for: USGS (Topo.).
Serves: students; faculty; employees; public. Mon.–Thurs. 7:45 a.m.–9:30 p.m.; Fri. 7:45 a.m.–5 p.m.; Sat. 11:30 a.m.– 4:30 p.m.; Sun. 3–8 p.m. (Seats 80; 8–10 readers served per month).
Interlibrary Loan Available.
Reproduction Facility: photocopy; microform.

Map Collections in Canada

ALBERTA

Banff

717. PETER AND CATHARINE WHYTE FOUNDATION
Archives of the Canadian Rockies
Map Collection
111 Bear Street, P.O. Box 160
Banff, Alberta T0L 0C0
Established 1968.
Telephone: 403/762-2291.
Contact Person: Mary Andrews, Librarian, Archives of the Canadian Rockies.
Staff: 3 professional (full time); 1 non-professional (full time).
Size: 2,000 maps; 14 atlases; 50 aerial photographs; 5 reference books and gazetteers; 1 serials (titles received).
Area Specialization: Canadian Rocky Mountains; western Canada.
Subject Specialization: topography; national parks; geology; soils; land use; forestry.
Dates: 1800-1899 (5%); 1900 - (95%).
Classification System: local system.
Collections Cataloged.
Serves: public. Tues. 10 a.m.–5 p.m.; Wed.–Fri.: 1–9 p.m.; Sat. 10 a.m.–5 p.m. (Seats 12).
Reproduction Facility: photocopy.

Calgary

718. GLENBOW MUSEUM LIBRARY
130 9th Ave. S.E.
Calgary, Alberta T2G 0P3
Telephone: 403/264-8300.
Contact Person: Len Gottselig, Chief Libn.
Staff: 1 professional (part time).
Size: 10,000 maps; 60 atlases; 75 reference books and gazetteers; 10 serials (titles received); 2,000 microforms (no. of titles).
Area Specialization: Western Canada; Arctic Regions.
Subject Specialization: Land settlement; transportation routes in Canadian west; 19th century Arctic exploration.
Dates: pre-1800 (5%); 1800-1899 (15%); 1900 - (80%).
Classification System: local system.
Collections not Cataloged. (classified).
Serves: students; faculty; employees; public. Mon.–Fri. 9:00 a.m.–5:00 p.m. (Wednesdays to 8:30 p.m.). (Seats 10; 25 readers served per month).
Interlibrary Loan Available.
Reproduction Facility: photocopy.
Publications: *Canadian West Discovered* (exhibition catalog).

719. UNIVERSITY OF CALGARY
Library
Map and Air Photo Division
Calgary, Alberta T2N 1N4
Established 1965.
Telephone: 403/284-5969.
Contact Person: Bob Batchelder, Map and Airphoto Librarian.
Staff: 2 professional (full time); 1 non-professional (part time).
Size: 90,000 maps; 1,800 atlases; 4 globes; 500,000 aerial photographs; 50 microforms (no. of titles).
Annual Accessions: 12,000 maps; 160 atlases; 5,000 aerial photographs.
Area Specialization: Canada; United States North America; Latin America.
Subject Specialization: topography; geology; geophysics.
Dates: pre-1800 (1%); 1800-1899 (5%); 1900 - (94%).
Classification System: LC.
Collections Cataloged. (100%).
Depository for: DOS (Gt. Brit); GSC; NTS (Canada); Canada Hydrographic Service.
Serves: students; faculty; employees; public. Mon.–Fri. 8:30 a.m.–5:00 p.m.
Reproduction Facility: quickcopy.
Publications: *Guide to the collection; Accession lists.*

Edmonton

720. ALBERTA ENERGY & NATURAL RESOURCES
Alberta Bureau of Surveying & Mapping
Map and Air Photo Reference Library
9945-108 Street, 2nd Floor, North Tower, Petroleum Plaza
Edmonton, Alberta T5K 2G6
Established 1976.
Telephone: 403/427-7417.
Contact Person: Alice S. Chen, Technologist (Supervisor).
Staff: 2 professional (full time); 1 non-professional (part time).
Size: 2,400 maps; 6 atlases; 1 globes; 604,000 aerial photographs; 200 reference books and gazetteers; 25 serials (titles received).
Annual Accessions: 28,000 aerial photographs; 2 reference books and gazetteers; 3 per month serials (titles received).
Area Specialization: Alberta.
Subject Specialization: Aerial photographs.
Dates: 1900 - (100%).
Classification System:
Collections Cataloged.
Depository for: NTS (Canada).
Serves: public. Mon.–Fri. 8:15 a.m.–4:30 p.m. (Seats 10; 250 readers served per month).
Reproduction Facility: quickcopy; Photolaboratory facility with 2 weeks turn around time.

721. ALBERTA RESEARCH COUNCIL
Library Services Department
4445 Calgary Trail South
Edmonton, Alberta T6H 5R7
Established 1950.
Telephone: 403/438-1666, ext. 309.
Staff: non-professional (part time).
Size: 5,000 maps; 25 atlases; 10 reference books and gazetteers.

Special Cartographic Collections: Alberta Research Council—geology, soils, groundwater; Geological Survey of Canada.
Dates: 1900 - (100%).
Classification System: None.
Collections not Cataloged.
Depository for: GSC.
Serves: employees; public. Mon.–Fri. 8 a.m.–4:30 p.m. (Seats 20).
Reproduction Facility: photocopy.

722. PROVINCIAL ARCHIVES OF ALBERTA
Cartographic Collection
12845-102 Avenue
Edmonton, Alberta T6H 0S3
Established 1963.
Telephone: 406/427-1750.
Contact Person: M. K. Aubrey, Manuscript and Cartographic Archivist.
Staff: 1 professional (part time).
Size: 13,000 maps; 31 atlases.
Annual Accessions: 700 maps; 1 atlases.
Area Specialization: Alberta and pre-1905 North-West Territories.
Dates: pre-1800 (5%); 1800-1899 (20%); 1900 - (75%).
Classification System: Duplex numeric for separate subject and geographic indexes.
Collections Cataloged. (95%).
Depository for: NTS (Canada); Alberta Bureau of Surveys and Mapping; Department of Transportation.
Serves: students; faculty; employees; public; Provincial government departments. Mon., Tues., Thurs., Fri. 9 a.m.–4:30 p.m.; Wed. 9 a.m.–9 p.m. (Seats 18 seats; 4 microfilm stations).
Reproduction Facility: photocopy.

723. UNIVERSITY OF ALBERTA
University Map Collection
Edmonton, Alberta T6G 2H4
Established 1966.
Telephone: 403/432-4760.
Contact Person: Ronald Whistance-Smith, Map Curator.
Staff: 3 professional (full time).
Size: 250,000 maps; 1,481 atlases; 7 globes; 700,000 aerial photographs; 334 reference books and gazetteers.
Annual Accessions: 12,000 maps; 60 atlases; 1,000 aerial photographs.
Area Specialization: Alberta; Canada.
Subject Specialization: topography; geology; soils; land use.
Dates: 1800-1899 (2%); 1900 - (98%).
Classification System: LC (modified).
Collections Cataloged. (95%).
Depository for: NTS (Canada).
Serves: students; faculty; employees; public;. Mon.–Fri. 8:00 a.m.–4:00 p.m.
Reproduction Facility: photocopy; quickcopy.
Publications: Accessions list.

Lethbridge

724. UNIVERSITY OF LETHBRIDGE
Department of Geography
4401 University Drive
Lethbridge, Alberta T1K 3M4
Established 1969.
Telephone: 403/329-2537.
Contact Person: Darla M. Young, Map Librarian/Cartographer.
Staff: 1 professional (full time).

Size: 35,000 maps; 225 atlases; 6 globes; 50 relief models; 6,500 aerial photographs; 250 reference books and gazetteers.
Annual Accessions: 3,000 maps; 25 atlases; 200 aerial photographs; 35 reference books and gazetteers.
Area Specialization: Alberta; Canada; United States; Polar Regions.
Subject Specialization: Canada history; climatology; geology.
Dates: pre-1800 (5%); 1800-1899 (10%); 1900 - (85%).
Classification System: AGS (modified).
Collections Cataloged. (90%).
Depository for: NTS (Canada); Canada Hydrographic Service.
Serves: students; faculty; employees; public. Mon.–Fri. 8:30 a.m.–4:30 p.m. (Seats 20–25).
Reproduction Facility: photocopy; photography.

BRITISH COLUMBIA

Burnaby

725. SIMON FRASER UNIVERSITY
W.A.C. Bennett Library
Social Science Division, Map Collection
Burnaby, British Columbia V5A 1S6
Established 1966.
Telephone: 604/291-4656.
Contact Person: Jack Corse, Geography & Map Libn.
Staff: 1 professional (full time); 1 professional (part time); 1 non-professional (full time).
Size: 70,000 maps; 1,500 atlases; 1 globes; 12,000 aerial photographs; 500 reference books and gazetteers; 4 serials (titles received).
Annual Accessions: 2,500 maps; 30 atlases; 50 reference books and gazetteers.
Area Specialization: British Columbia; Canada; western United States.
Subject Specialization: biogeography; geomorphology; climatology; economic resources.
Dates: 1900 - (90%+).
Classification System: LC.
Collections Cataloged. (98%).
Depository for: NTS (Canada); USGS (Topo.).
Serves: students; faculty; employees; public. Mon.–Fri. 9 a.m.–5:30 p.m. (Wed. & Thurs. to 9 p.m.); Sat. 11 a.m.–5 p.m. (Seats 30; 400 readers served per month).
Reproduction Facility: photocopy.

Vancouver

726. UNIVERSITY OF BRITISH COLUMBIA
Department of Geography
Map and Air Photo Centre
1984 West Mall
Vancouver, British Columbia V6T 1W5
Established 1950.
Telephone: 604/228-3048.
Contact Person: Rosemary J. Hadley, Map and Air Photo Libn.
Staff: 1 professional (full time).
Size: 74,990 maps; 160,996 aerial photographs; 160 reference books and gazetteers; 7,000 microforms (no. of titles).
Annual Accessions: 2,000 maps; 100–200 microforms (no. of titles).
Area Specialization: Canada; British Columbia; Pacific Northwest.

Subject Specialization: aerial photography; remote sensing.
Special Cartographic Collections: aerial photographs; remotely sensed images.
Dates: 1900 - (100%).
Classification System: Boggs-Lewis modified.
Collections Cataloged. (maps 10%, aerial photograph collection 100%).
Depository for: NTS (Canada); DOE Pacific Weather Center (Vancouver Airport Weather Maps).
Serves: students; faculty; employees; public. Mon.–Fri. 8:30 a.m.–4:30 p.m. (Seats 25; 750 per month readers served per month).
Reproduction Facility: photocopy.

727. UNIVERSITY OF BRITISH COLUMBIA
Library
Historical Maps & Cartographic Archives, Special Collections Division
1956 Main Mall
Vancouver, British Columbia V6T 1Y3
Established 1960.
Telephone: 604/228-2521.
Contact Person: (Miss) Frances M. Woodward, Reference Libn.
Staff: 1 professional (part time); 1 non-professional (part time).
Size: 24,835 maps; 450 atlases; 2 globes; 5 aerial photographs; 450 reference books and gazetteers; 10 serials (titles received); 550 microforms (no. of titles).
Annual Accessions: 200 maps; 10 reference books and gazetteers.
Area Specialization: British Columbia; Canada; Pacific Northwest; Arctic; America; world—pre-1900; Japan.
Subject Specialization: British Columbia and Canadian history; historical cartography.
Special Cartographic Collections: Howay-Reid Collection (British Columbiana; Canadiana); Rogers-Tucker Map Collection (Historical Cartography); George H. Beans Collection of Japanese Maps of the Tokugawa Era; University Archives; Cartographic Archives (maps from Historical Mss Collections, esp. B. C. industry & labour records).
Dates: pre-1800 (30%); 1800-1899 (40%); 1900 - (20%).
Classification System: Boggs-Lewis modified.
Collections Cataloged. (50%).
Serves: students; faculty; employees; public. Mon.–Fri. 8:30 a.m.–5 p.m. (between terms 9 a.m.–5 p.m.); Sat. 9 a.m.–5 p.m. during term. (Seats 30; 20 readers served per month).
Reproduction Facility: can be arranged.
Publications: Checklists of fire insurance plans; *Union List of Atlases* (1974 - OP); inventories to cartographic archives collections; cartobibliography of Greater Vancouver (in preparation).

728. UNIVERSITY OF BRITISH COLUMBIA
Library
Map Division
1956 Main Mall
Vancouver, British Columbia V6T 1Y3
Established 1949.
Telephone: 604/228-2231 or 6191.
Contact Person: Maureen F. Wilson, Head.
Staff: 1 professional (full time); 3 non-professional (full time); 1 non-professional (part time).
Size: 125,683 maps; 2,543 atlases; 11 globes; 1 relief models; 2,040 reference books and gazetteers; 29 serials (titles received); 10 microforms (no. of titles).
Annual Accessions: 3,000–4,000 maps; 100–125 atlases; 1–2 globes; 150 reference books and gazetteers; 3–4 serials (titles received); 2–3 microforms (no. of titles).
Area Specialization: British Columbia: Canada; Latin America; Pacific Rim.

Subject Specialization: topography; geology; mountaineering maps for Asia; facsimile town plans.
Special Cartographic Collections: Ogg Collection of city guides of England in the 1960s and 70s (most have city maps) 58 boxes.
Dates: 1900 - (98%).
Classification System: LC Books; Boggs-Lewis Maps.
Collections Cataloged. (100%).
Depository for: DMA; GSC; NOS; NTS (Canada); USGS (Geol., topo.); Australia Division of National Mapping; Canadian Hydrographic Service.
Serves: students; faculty; employees; public. Mon.–Fri. 9 a.m.–5 p.m.; Sat. 9 a.m.–5 p.m. (during Univ. sessions). (Seats 68; 360 readers served per month).
Interlibrary Loan Available.
Reproduction Facility: quickcopy; Canon 18x24.
Publications: *Selected list of maps added to the library. . . ; University of British Columbia Library Map Division* (information leaflet).

729. VANCOUVER CITY ARCHIVES
1150-Chestnut Street
Vancouver, British Columbia V6J 3J9
Established 1933.
Telephone: 604/736-8561.
Size: 1,000 maps; 50 atlases.
Annual Accessions: 10–25 maps; 1 atlases.
Area Specialization: Vancouver.
Subject Specialization: urban planning.
Dates: 1800-1899 (10%); 1900 - (90%).
Classification System: local system.
Collections Cataloged.
Serves: students; faculty; employees; public. Mon.–Fri. 9:30 a.m.–5:30 p.m. (Seats 40).
Reproduction Facility: photocopy; quickcopy; microform.

730. VANCOUVER PUBLIC LIBRARY
750 Burrard Street
Vancouver, British Columbia V6Z 1X5
Telephone: 604/682-5911.
Contact Person: Aileen Tufts, Acting Director.
Staff: 3 professional (part time); 3 non-professional (part time).
Size: 12,700 maps; 512 atlases; 2 globes; 20 aerial photographs; 385 reference books and gazetteers.
Area Specialization: British Columbia.
Subject Specialization: hydrography; land use.
Dates: 1900 - (100%).
Classification System: Boggs-Lewis.
Collections Cataloged. (50%). Mon.–Thurs. 9:30 a.m.–9:30 p.m.; Fri. 9:30 a.m.–6 p.m.; Sat. 9:30 a.m.–6 p.m.; Sun. 1–5 p.m.
Reproduction Facility: photocopy.

Victoria

731. GREATER VICTORIA PUBLIC LIBRARY
Arts and Humanities
735 Broughton St.
Victoria, British Columbia V8W 3H2
Telephone: 604/382-7241, ext. 33.
Staff: 1 non-professional (part time).
Size: 2,700 maps; 170 atlases; 25 reference books and gazetteers.
Annual Accessions: 100 maps; 5 atlases; 5 reference books and gazetteers.
Area Specialization: southern British Columbia; marine charts of B.C. coast.
Dates: 1800-1899 (4%); 1900 - (96%).
Classification System: local system.
Collections Cataloged. (7%).

Serves: public. Tues.–Fri. 9 a.m.–9 p.m.; Wed. 9 a.m.–6 p.m.; Sat. 9 a.m.–6 p.m.
Reproduction Facility: photocopy.

732. PROVINCIAL ARCHIVES OF BRITISH COLUMBIA
Library and Maps Section
Map Collection
Parliament Buildings
Victoria, British Columbia V8V 1X4
Telephone: 604/387-6516.
Contact Person: David R. Chamberlin,, Section Head.
Staff: 1 professional (full time); 1 professional (part time); 1 non-professional (full time).
Size: 25,000 maps; 210 atlases; 3 globes; 650 reference books and gazetteers.
Annual Accessions: 2,000 maps; 6 atlases; 25 reference books and gazetteers.
Area Specialization: British Columbia; northwest coast of North America; western Canada.
Subject Specialization: exploration.
Classification System: local system.
Collections Cataloged. (30%).
Depository for: NTS (Canada); Canadian hydrographic charts.
Serves: public. Mon.–Wed., Fri. 9 a.m.–5 p.m.; Thur. 9:30 a.m.–5 p.m. (Seats 4; 41 readers served per month).
Reproduction Facility: photocopy; quickcopy; microform.

733. UNIVERSITY OF VICTORIA
McPherson Library, Circulation Division
University Map Collection*
Victoria, British Columbia V8W 2Y2
Telephone: 604/477-6911.
Contact Person: Brian Turnbull, Map Curator.
Staff: 2 professional (full time).
Size: 78,500 maps; 320 atlases; 2 globes; 61,000 aerial photographs; 25 reference books and gazetteers.
Annual Accessions: 2,500 maps; 5 atlases; 1,500 aerial photographs.
Area Specialization: British Columbia; Canada; northern Europe.
Subject Specialization: harbors; geology; cities and towns.
Classification System: LC.
Collections not Cataloged.
Depository for: NTS (Canada); USGS (Topo.); Canada Hydrographic Service.
Serves: students; faculty; employees; public;. Mon.–Fri. 8:30 a.m.–5 p.m.
Interlibrary Loan Available. (restricted)
Reproduction Facility: quickcopy.

MANITOBA

Winnipeg

734. PROVINCIAL ARCHIVES OF MANITOBA
Historical Archives Division
Map Room
200 Vaughan St.
Winnipeg, Manitoba R3C 1T5
Established 1967.
Telephone: 204/944-3972.
Contact Person: Tim Ross, Cartographic Archivist.
Staff: 1 professional (full time); 1 non-professional (part time).
Size: 12,000 maps; 30 atlases; 1 relief models; 1,600 aerial photographs; 60 reference books and gazetteers; 4 serials (titles received).
Annual Accessions: 1,000 maps; 3 atlases; 3 reference books and gazetteers; 1 serials (titles received).

Area Specialization: Manitoba; Canadian West; Northwestern Ontario.
Subject Specialization: historical; cadastral; transportation; topography; government cartographic records.
Special Cartographic Collections: Dominion Lands Survey: homesteader maps and surveyors' original plans & field notes; Sectional Maps of the West: time-series topographic maps.
Dates: pre-1800 (1%); 1800-1899 (60%); 1900 - (39%).
Classification System: Boggs-Lewis.
Collections Cataloged. (20%).
Depository for: Manitoba Govt.
Serves: public. Mon.–Fri. 9 a.m.–5 p.m. (Seats 8; 55 readers served per month).
Reproduction Facility: photocopy.

735. UNIVERSITY OF MANITOBA
Department of Earth Sciences
Winnipeg, Manitoba R3T 2N2
Telephone: 204/474-8252.
Contact Person: Iva Cerny.
Staff: 1 non-professional (part time).
Size: 1,450 maps; 8 atlases; 1 globes; 15 relief models; 3,500 aerial photographs.
Annual Accessions: 100 maps; 200 aerial photographs.
Subject Specialization: geology.
Collections Cataloged. (90%).
Serves: students; faculty. Mon.–Fri. 9 a.m.–4 p.m.
Reproduction Facility: photocopy.

736. UNIVERSITY OF MANITOBA
Elizabeth Dafoe Library, Reference Services Department
Map and Atlas Collection
Winnipeg, Manitoba R3T 2N2
Telephone: 204/474-9844.
Contact Person: Hugh C. Larimer, Reference/Map Libn.
Staff: 1 professional (full time); 1 non-professional (part time).
Size: 75,000 maps; 1,250 atlases; 3 globes; 1 relief models; 275 reference books and gazetteers; 10 serials (titles received).
Area Specialization: Canada; United States; Latin America; Europe; Africa; southern and eastern Asia.
Subject Specialization: topography; geology.
Dates: 1800-1899 (1%); 1900 - (99%).
Classification System: Boggs-Lewis.
Collections not Cataloged.
Depository for: NTS (Canada); USGS (Geol., topo.).
Serves: students; faculty; employees; public;. Mon.–Thurs. 8:30 a.m.–10 p.m.; Fri. 8:30 a.m.–5 p.m.; Sat. 9 a.m.–5 p.m.; Sun. 1–10 p.m. (Seats 86; 125 readers served per month).
Interlibrary Loan Available.
Reproduction Facility: photocopy; quickcopy.

737. UNIVERSITY OF WINNIPEG
Geography Department
515 Portage Avenue
Winnipeg, Manitoba R3B 2E9
Established 1972.
Telephone: 204/786-7811, ext. 546.
Contact Person: Jeffrey M. R. Simpson, Map Libn.
Staff: 1 professional (full time).
Size: 40,000 maps; 20 atlases; 50 relief models; 10,000 aerial photographs.
Annual Accessions: 1,000 maps.
Area Specialization: Manitoba, Canada; United States; Europe.
Subject Specialization: topography; physical and cultural geography.
Special Cartographic Collections: Prairie Land Settlement Maps; International Boundary Maps of Canada (Historical).
Dates: 1900 - (100%).

Classification System: local system.
Collections Cataloged.
Depository for: NTS (Canada).
Serves: students; faculty; employees; public. Mon.–Fri. 9 a.m.–4 p.m. (Seats 50; 50 readers served per month).

738. WINNIPEG PUBLIC LIBRARY
Information & Reference
251 Donald Street
Winnipeg, Manitoba R3C 3P5
Established approx. 1969.
Telephone: 204/985-6450.
Contact Person: Eileen A. Nayda, Reference Libn.
Staff: 1 professional (full time).
Size: 1,000 maps; 75 atlases; 1 globes; 50 reference books and gazetteers.
Area Specialization: Manitoba.
Dates: 1900 - (100%).
Classification System: LC; Dewey.
Collections not Cataloged.
Serves: public. Mon.–Thurs. 10 a.m.–9 p.m.; Fri. 10 a.m.–6 p.m.; Sat. 10 a.m.–6 p.m.; Sun. 1–5 p.m.
Reproduction Facility: photocopy.

NEW BRUNSWICK

Fredericton

739. PROVINCIAL ARCHIVES OF NEW BRUNSWICK
P.O. Box 6000
Fredericton, New Brunswick E3B 5H1
Established 1971.
Telephone: 506/453-2661, ext. 24.
Contact Person: William R. MacKinnon, Jr., Archivist.
Staff: 1 professional (full time); 1 professional (part time).
Size: 30,000 maps; 60 atlases; 6 relief models; 50 reference books and gazettee. ; 5 serials (titles received).
Annual Accessions: 500 maps; 5 atlases; 5 reference books and gazetteers; 1 serials (titles received).
Area Specialization: New Brunswick.
Special Cartographic Collections: York—Sunbury Historical Society Collection—Central New Brunswick.
Dates: pre-1800 (10%); 1800-1899 (80%); 1900 - (10%).
Classification System: modified Public Archives of Canada.
Collections Cataloged.
Serves: students; faculty; employees; public;. Mon.–Fri. 8:30 a.m.–5 p.m.; Sat. 8:30 a.m.–5 p.m. (Seats 6; 40 readers served per month).
Reproduction Facility: photocopy; commercial photocopying.
Publications: Roger P. Nason, "Map Classification System, Provincial Archives of New Brunswick", 1974. (o.p.).

740. UNIVERSITY OF NEW BRUNSWICK
Harriet Irving Library
Map Room
P.O. Box 7500
Fredericton, New Brunswick E3B 5H5
Established 1969.
Telephone: 506/453-4752.
Contact Person: Elizabeth Hamilton, Libn.
Staff: 2 professional (part time); 2 non-professional (part time).
Size: 35,800 maps; 490 atlases; 3 globes; 100 aerial photographs; 95 reference books and gazetteers; 7 serials (titles received); 1 microforms (no. of titles).
Annual Accessions: 1,000 maps; 60–70 atlases; 20 aerial photographs; 3 reference books and gazetteers.
Area Specialization: Canada; New Brunswick; Maritime Provinces.

Subject Specialization: comprehensive.
Dates: 1900 - (100%).
Classification System: LC.
Collections not Cataloged.
Depository for: GSC; NTS (Canada).
Serves: students; faculty; employees; public;. Mon.–Fri. 8:30 a.m.–9:30 p.m.; Sat. 1–5 p.m. (Seats 6–12; 40 readers served per month).
Interlibrary Loan Available. (restricted)
Reproduction Facility: photocopy.

Moncton

741. UNIVERSITE DE MONCTON
Departement d'histoire-Géographie
Moncton, New Brunswick E1A 3E9
Telephone: 506/858-4069 or 4027.
Contact Person: Brian Keogh, Adjunct Professor.
Staff: 1 professional (part time).
Size: 5,000 maps; 10 atlases; 500 aerial photographs.
Depository for: NTS (Canada); Canada Hydrographic Service. Mon.–Thurs. 9 a.m.–5 p.m.

NEWFOUNDLAND

St. John's

742. MEMORIAL UNIVERSITY OF NEWFOUNDLAND
Queen Elizabeth II Library
Map Library
St. John's, Newfoundland A1B 3Y1
Telephone: 709/737-8892.
Contact Person: Alberta Auringer Wood, Map Libn.
Staff: 1 professional (full time); 3 non-professional (full time); 2 (students, Sept. to mid-April) non-professional (part time).
Size: 47,530 maps; 928 atlases; 2 globes; 46 relief models; a few aerial photographs; 479 reference books and gazetteers; 2 serials (titles received); 9 microforms (no. of titles).
Annual Accessions: 4,900 maps; 70 atlases; a few relief models; a few aerial photographs; 50 reference books and gazetteers; 2 or 3 microforms (no. of titles).
Area Specialization: Newfoundland.
Special Cartographic Collections: The Centre for Newfoundland Studies, a special collections division of the Queen Elizabeth II Library, contains a collection of approximately 250 early (pre-1900) Newfoundland, Labrador and St. Pierre and Miquelon maps.
Dates: 1800-1899 (2%); 1900 - (98%).
Classification System: LC (Maps will be classified beginning in 1984).
Collections Cataloged.
Depository for: NTS (Canada).
Serves: students; faculty; employees; public. Mon.–Thurs. 8:30 a.m.–10 p.m.; Fri. 8:30 a.m.–6 p.m.; Sat. 10 a.m.–6 p.m.; Sun. 1:30 p.m.–10 p.m. (Seats 32; 360 readers served per month).
Interlibrary Loan Available.
Reproduction Facility: photocopy; quickcopy; microform.
Publications: Contributor to the "recent acquisitions" listing in the Association of Canadian Map Libraries *Bulletin*.

743. NEWFOUNDLAND (PROVINCE) DEPARTMENT OF MINES AND ENERGY

Mineral Development Division
Publications and Information Section
95 Bonaventure Avenue
St. John's, Newfoundland A1C 5T7
Telephone: 709/737-3159.
Contact Person: Norman L. Mercer, Mineral Exploration Consultant.
Staff: 3 professional (full time); 1 non-professional (full time); 2 non-professional (part time).
Size: 3,000–4,000 maps.
Annual Accessions: 300 maps.
Area Specialization: Newfoundland; Labrador.
Subject Specialization: geology; geophysics, geochemistry; mining and mineral resources.
Dates: 1800-1899 (2%); 1900 - (98%).
Classification System: N.T.S.
Collections Cataloged.
Serves: students; faculty; employees; public;. Mon.–Fri. 9 a.m.–5 p.m. (Seats 3–5; 5–6 readers served per month).
Interlibrary Loan Available. (some)
Reproduction Facility: photocopy; microform.
Publications: List of publications on request
Established Mercer, Norman L.

744. PROVINCIAL ARCHIVES OF NEWFOUNDLAND AND LABRADOR

Colonial Building, Military Road
St. John's, Newfoundland A1C 2C9
Telephone: 709/753-9380.
Contact Person: Edward Tompkins, Map Archivist.
Staff: 1 professional (full time).
Size: 20,000 maps; 70 atlases.
Area Specialization: Newfoundland; Labrador.
Subject Specialization: architecture; engineering.
Serves: public. Mon.–Fri. 9 a.m.–5 p.m., Wed. & Thurs. 6:30–10 p.m. (Seats 25).
Interlibrary Loan Available. some
Reproduction Facility: photocopy.

NOVA SCOTIA

Amherst

745. MARITIME RESOURCE MANAGEMENT SERVICE

Information Division
Library
16 Station Street, P. O. Box 310
Amherst, Nova Scotia B4H 3Z5
Established 1972.
Telephone: 902/667-7231, ext. 30.
Contact Person: Margaret E. Campbell, Libn.
Staff: 1 professional (full time).
Size: ca. 150,000 maps; 50 atlases; 150 reference books and gazetteers; 50 serials (titles received); 200 microforms (no. of titles).
Area Specialization: Atlantic Region.
Subject Specialization: land use; planning and development.
Special Cartographic Collections: thematic map collection—Maritime Region; hydrographic map collection—Atlantic Region.
Dates: pre-1800 (5%); 1800-1899 (5%); 1900 - (90%).
Classification System: Boggs-Lewis.
Collections Cataloged. (80%).
Depository for: NTS (Canada); Canada Hydrographic Service.
Serves: students; faculty; employees; public. Mon.–Fri. 8 a.m.–4 p.m. (Seats 6+; 20+ readers served per month).

Interlibrary Loan Available.
Reproduction Facility: photocopy.
Publications: MRMS Regional Library Information Brochure; ACRIC Library Services & Information (guide).

Dartmouth

746. BEDFORD INSTITUTE OF OCEANOGRAPHY

Map/Chart Collection
Map Collection
P.O. Box 1006
Dartmouth, Nova Scotia B2Y 4A2
Established May 1981.
Telephone: 902/426-2397.
Contact Person: Wm. Kirk MacDonald, Assistant Supervisor Technical Records.
Staff: 1 non-professional (part time).
Size: 60,000 maps; 20 atlases; 3 globes; 20,000 aerial photographs; 30 reference books and gazetteers; 10 microforms (no. of titles).
Annual Accessions: 2,500 maps; 2 atlases; 2,000 aerial photographs; 5 reference books and gazetteers; 1 microforms (no. of titles).
Area Specialization: Arctic and Subarctic regions; North Atlantic; world oceans.
Subject Specialization: undersea cartography; coastal processes; living resources of the sea.
Dates: 1900 - (100%).
Classification System: LC.
Collections Cataloged.
Depository for: DMA; GSC; NOS; NTS (Canada); USGS (Geol., topo.); Canada Hydrographic Service.
Serves: students; employees. Mon.–Fri. 8 a.m.–4 p.m. (Seats 2; 20 readers served per month).
Reproduction Facility: photocopy; complete photo mechanical facilities available within Institute.

Halifax

747. DALHOUSIE UNIVERSITY

Macdonald Science Library
Map Collection
Halifax, Nova Scotia B3H 4J3
Established 1971.
Telephone: 416/424-3757 or 2384.
Contact Person: Susan Greaves, Map Libn.
Staff: 1 non-professional (full time); 1 non-professional (part time).
Size: 50,000 maps; 1,000 atlases; 3 globes; 11,500 aerial photographs; 500 reference books and gazetteers.
Annual Accessions: 3,000 maps; 50 atlases; 500 aerial photographs; 20 reference books and gazetteers.
Area Specialization: Nova Scotia and Maritime Provinces, Canada.
Subject Specialization: topography; oceanography; geology.
Dates: 1900 - (100%).
Classification System: LC modified.
Collections Cataloged. (100%).
Depository for: GSC; NOS; NTS (Canada); USGS (Geol., topo.); Canada Hydrographic Service; Nova Scotia Dept. of Mines.
Serves: students; faculty; employees; public. Mon.–Fri. 9 a.m.–5 p.m. (Seats 8; 150 readers served per month).
Interlibrary Loan Available.
Reproduction Facility: photocopy.

748. PUBLIC ARCHIVES OF NOVA SCOTIA
Provincial Map Collections
6016 University Ave.
Halifax, Nova Scotia B3H 1W4
Established 1974.
Telephone: 902/423-9115.
Contact Person: Garry D. Shutlak, Map/Architecture Archivist.
Staff: 1 professional (full time); 2 professional (part time); 1 non-professional (full time).
Size: 500,000 maps; 184 atlases; 3 relief models; 15,000 aerial photographs; 40 reference books and gazetteers; 4 serials (titles received); 50 microforms (no. of titles).
Area Specialization: Nova Scotia and the Maritime Provinces, Canada.
Subject Specialization: Nova Scotiana.
Special Cartographic Collections: Architectural plans of Nova Scotia firms or of Nova Scotia buildings. The collection is eclectic and includes buildings in Florida, North Carolina, France, etc.
Dates: pre-1800 (10%); 1800-1899 (25%); 1900 - (65%).
Classification System: AACR2.
Collections Cataloged. (75%).
Serves: students; faculty; employees; public. Mon., Tues., Thurs., and Fri. 8:30 a.m.–5 p.m.;. Wed. 8:30 a.m–10 p.m. Sat. 9:00 a.m.–6 p.m. every 11 weeks; Sun. 1 p.m.–10 p.m. every 11 weeks. (Seats 24; 75 readers served per month).
Reproduction Facility: photocopy; microform.

749. SAINT MARY'S UNIVERSITY
Geography Department
Map Library
Robie Street
Halifax, Nova Scotia B3H 3C3
Established 1974.
Telephone: 902/429-9780, ext. 334.
Contact Person: Benoit Ouellette, Cartographer/Map Libn.
Staff: 1 non-professional (full time).
Size: 20,000 maps; 22 atlases; 3 globes; 500 aerial photographs; 500 reference books and gazetteers.
Annual Accessions: 2,500 maps; 2 atlases; 50 aerial photographs; 30 reference books and gazetteers.
Area Specialization: North America; western Europe; Asia.
Subject Specialization: topography.
Dates: 1800-1899 (1%); 1900 - (99%).
Classification System: NTS index and regional indexing system for each country.
Collections Cataloged. (100%).
Depository for: NTS (Canada).
Serves: students; faculty; employees; public. Mon.–Fri. 9 a.m.–5 p.m. (Seats 10; 20 readers served per month).

Sydney

750. UNIVERSITY COLLEGE OF CAPE BRETON
Beaton Institute
P.O. Box 5300
Sydney, Nova Scotia B1P 6L2
Established 1960.
Telephone: 902/539-5300, ext. 346.
Contact Person: Dr. R. J. Morgan, Director.
Staff: 5 professional (full time); 1 professional (part time).
Size: 800 maps; 10 atlases; 20 aerial photographs; 2 microforms (no. of titles).
Annual Accessions: ca. 50 maps.
Area Specialization: Cape Breton Island; Maritime Provinces.
Special Cartographic Collections: 18th century maps of Cape Breton and Atlantic Canada.
Dates: pre-1800 (20%); 1800-1899 (50%); 1900 - (30%).
Classification System: local system.

Collections Cataloged.
Serves: students; faculty; employees; public;. Mon.–Fri. 8:30 a.m.–8 p.m. (4 p.m. in summer). (Seats 35).
Reproduction Facility: photocopy; quickcopy; microform.

Wolfville

751. ACADIA UNIVERSITY
Geology & N.T.S. Repository
Wolfville, Nova Scotia B0P 1X0
Established 1970.
Telephone: 902/542-2201, ext. 284.
Contact Person: Ian A. Austin, Curator.
Staff: 1 professional (part time); 1 non-professional (part time).
Size: 4,000 maps; 2 globes; 10 relief models; 8,000 aerial photographs.
Annual Accessions: 500 maps; 50 aerial photographs.
Area Specialization: Canada; world.
Subject Specialization: geology.
Special Cartographic Collections: Fletcher & Faribault Nova Scotia series.
Dates: 1800-1899 (1%); 1900 - (99%).
Classification System: AGS; geology maps by area and country.
Collections not Cataloged.
Depository for: GSC; NTS (Canada); USGS (Geol.).
Serves: students; faculty; visiting geologists. as required— daily between 9 a.m. and 5 p.m. (Seats 12; 100 readers served per month).

ONTARIO

Guelph

752. UNIVERSITY OF GUELPH, LIBRARY
Humanities/Social Science Division
Map Collection
Guelph, Ontario N1G 2W1
Telephone: 519/824-4120, ext. 3150.
Contact Person: (Mrs.) Flora Francis, Reference Libn.
Staff: 3 professional (part time); 3 non-professional (part time).
Size: 60,000 maps; 1,000 atlases; 1 globes; approx. 500 reference books and gazetteers; approx. 350 serials (titles received).
Annual Accessions: varies maps; varies atlases; varies reference books and gazetteers; varies serials (titles received).
Area Specialization: Canada; southern Ontario; Guelph; United States; Europe; Far East.
Subject Specialization: agriculture; climatology; economics; geology; historiology; hydrology; land use; population; soils; topography; transportation.
Special Cartographic Collections: Canadian fire insurance maps; Melby Collection of World War II maps for the Pacific area.
Dates: 1900 - (99%).
Classification System: LC.
Collections Cataloged.
Depository for: NTS (Canada).
Serves: students; faculty; employees. Mon.–Fri. 8:30 a.m.–9 p.m.; Sun. 12 noon–4:30 p.m. (Seats 600; 300 readers served per month).
Interlibrary Loan Available.
Reproduction Facility: photocopy.
Publications: *Map and Geography Selected Information Sources* (brochure); *General Information Sheet* (brochure).

Haileybury

753. NORTHERN COLLEGE
Haileybury School of Mines Library
640 Latchford Street
Haileybury, Ontario P0J 1K0
Established 1945.
Telephone: 705/642-3376 or 3356.
Contact Person: M. G. Taeger, Libn.
Size: 8,000 maps; 10 atlases; 50 reference books and gazetteers; 30 serials (titles received).
Annual Accessions: 400 maps; 2 reference books and gazetteers.
Area Specialization: Ontario.
Subject Specialization: geology; geophysics.
Dates: 1900 - (99%).
Collections not Cataloged.
Depository for: GSC; Ontario Mines Branch.
Serves: students; faculty; public. Mon.–Fri. 9:30 a.m.–9:30 p.m.; Sat. 10 a.m.–12 noon. (Seats 42; 350 readers served per month).
Reproduction Facility: photocopy.

Hamilton

754. HAMILTON PUBLIC LIBRARY
Social Sciences Department
Map Collection
55 York Street
Hamilton, Ontario L8R 3G9
Established 1950.
Telephone: 416/529-8111, ext. 253.
Contact Person: Miss Eugenia Repcyte, Co-ordinator Social Sciences Dept.
Staff: 1 professional (part time); 1 non-professional (part time).
Size: 2,613 maps; 310 atlases; 150 reference books and gazetteers.
Annual Accessions: 100 maps; 75 atlases; 10 reference books and gazetteers.
Area Specialization: Ontario.
Subject Specialization: topography; transportation; Ontario historical atlases.
Dates: 1800-1899 (5%); 1900 - (95%).
Collections Cataloged.
Depository for: NTS (Canada).
Serves: students; public. Mon.–Fri. 9 a.m.–9 p.m.; Sat. 9 a.m.–5 p.m.; Sun. 1–5 p.m. (Seats 50; 200 readers served per month).
Reproduction Facility: photocopy; microform.

755. MCMASTER UNIVERSITY
Lloyd Reeds Map Library, Room 137 BSB
1280 Main Street West
Hamilton, Ontario L8S 4K1
Established 1947.
Telephone: 416/525-9140, ext. 4745.
Contact Person: Mrs. Kate Donkin, Map Curator.
Staff: 1 professional (full time); 1 non-professional (full time); 2 professional (part time).
Size: 95,000 maps; 1,472 atlases; 6 globes; 10 relief models; 30,800 aerial photographs; 1,200 reference books and gazetteers; 4 serials (titles received); 200 microforms (no. of titles).
Area Specialization: Canada.
Subject Specialization: geography; history; geology.
Special Cartographic Collections: historic and contemporary maps of Wentworth County.
Dates: pre-1800 (1%); 1800-1899 (2%); 1900 - (97%).
Classification System: .

Collections not Cataloged.
Depository for: DMA; NTS (Canada).
Serves: students; faculty; employees; public. Sept.–Apr. 30: Mon.–Thurs. 9 a.m.–10 p.m.;. Fri. 9 a.m.–5 p.m.; summer: Mon.–Fri. 8:30 a.m.–4:30 p.m. (Seats 35; 4,000 except during summer readers served per month).
Interlibrary Loan Available.
Reproduction Facility: photocopy.

Kingston

756. QUEEN'S UNIVERSITY
Douglas Library
Map and Air Photo Library
Kingston, Ontario K7L 5C4
Established 1960.
Telephone: 613/547-6193.
Contact Person: Kathryn Harding, Senior Technician.
Staff: 1 non-professional (full time); 1 non-professional (part time).
Size: 85,000 maps; 800 atlases; 3 globes; 25 relief models; 25,000 aerial photographs; 250 reference books and gazetteers; 35 serials (titles received).
Annual Accessions: 2,500 maps; 30 atlases; 500 aerial photographs; 10 reference books and gazetteers.
Area Specialization: Canada.
Subject Specialization: history of cartography.
Dates: pre-1800 (1%); 1800-1899 (4%); 1900 - (95%).
Classification System: Boggs-Lewis.
Collections Cataloged. (95%).
Depository for: NTS (Canada); USGS (Topo.); Canadian Hydrographic Service; Canadian Aeronautical Charts;. Ontario Base Mapping (OBM)
Serves: students; faculty; employees; public. Mon.–Thurs. 9 a.m.–5 p.m., 7 p.m.–10 p.m.; Fri. 9 a.m.–5 p.m. Sat. 1–5 p.m.; Sun. 1–5 p.m. (Seats 55).
Interlibrary Loan Available. (restricted)
Reproduction Facility: photocopy.
Publications: *Queen's University Map and Air Photo Library* (brochure).

757. QUEEN'S UNIVERSITY
Douglas Library, Special Collections
Rare and Historical Map Collection
Union and University
Kingston, Ontario K7L 5C4
Established ca. 1900.
Telephone: 613/547-3030.
Contact Person: William F. E. Morley, Curator of Special Collections.
Staff: 1 professional (part time); 2 non-professional (part time).
Size: 900 maps; 75 atlases; 2 globes; 100 reference books and gazetteers; 6 serials (titles received).
Annual Accessions: 20 maps; 8 atlases; 10 reference books and gazetteers.
Area Specialization: Canada; North America; Kingston; Ontario.
Subject Specialization: discovery and exploration.
Special Cartographic Collections: About 400 4' × 7' photographs of rare maps (with slides to match), filed so as to serve as an index to the originals, thus relieving wear on the originals. Copies can be made as requested, from the slides.
Dates: pre-1800 (25%); 1800-1899 (65%); 1900 - (10%).
Classification System: Boggs-Lewis modified.
Collections Cataloged. (25%).
Serves: students; faculty; employees; public. Mon.–Thurs. 10 a.m.–9 p.m., Fri. 9 a.m.– 5 p.m. (Seats 25; 10 readers served per month).
Interlibrary Loan Available. (only by special arrangement)

Reproduction Facility: photocopy; microform; photography.

758. QUEEN'S UNIVERSITY
Geology Library
Map Collection
Kingston, Ontario K7L 3N6
Established 1950.
Telephone: 613/547-2653.
Contact Person: Mary Mayson, Senior Library Technician.
Staff: 2 non-professional (full time).
Size: 30,000 maps; 60 atlases; 1 globes; 2,000 microforms (no. of titles).
Annual Accessions: 500 maps.
Area Specialization: Canada.
Subject Specialization: geology.
Dates: pre-1800 (2%); 1800-1899 (23%); 1900 - (75%).
Classification System: local system.
Collections not Cataloged.
Depository for: GSC; USGS (Geol.).
Serves: students; faculty; employees; public. Mon.–Fri. 9 a.m.–5 p.m.; 7:30–10:30 p.m.; Sat. 2–5 p.m.; Sun. 2–5 p.m. (Seats 60).
Interlibrary Loan Available.

London

759. LONDON PUBLIC LIBRARIES AND MUSEUMS
Central Library
East 2 Reference Desk/London Room
305 Queens Avenue
London, Ontario N6B 3L7
Telephone: 519/432-7166, ext. 77 or 78.
Contact Person: Laura MacRae, Travel/Geography Libn.; W. Glen Curnoe, London Room Libn.
Staff: 5 professional (full time); 4 non-professional (full time).
Size: 1,200 maps; 150 atlases; 50 reference books and gazetteers; 10 microforms (no. of titles).
Annual Accessions: 50 maps; 10–15 atlases; 5 reference books and gazetteers; 1–2 microforms (no. of titles).
Area Specialization: North America.
Subject Specialization: topography.
Special Cartographic Collections: history and development of London, Ontario.
Dates: 1800-1899 (25%); 1900 - (75%).
Collections not Cataloged.
Depository for: NTS (Canada).
Serves: public. Mon.–Fri. 9 a.m.–9 p.m.; Sat. 9 a.m.–5 p.m. (Seats 75).
Reproduction Facility: photocopy; microform.

760. UNIVERSITY OF WESTERN ONTARIO
Department of Geography
Map Library
London, Ontario N6A 5C2
Established 1966.
Telephone: 519/679-3424.
Contact Person: Serge A. Sauer, Map Curator.
Staff: 1 professional (full time); 2 non-professional (full time); 3 non-professional (part time).
Size: 203,000 maps; 1,600 atlases; 8 globes; 550 relief models; 21,000 aerial photographs; 1,400 reference books and gazetteers; 24 serials (titles received); 650 microforms (no. of titles).
Annual Accessions: 9,000 maps; 100 atlases; 500 aerial photographs; 40 reference books and gazetteers; 50 microforms (no. of titles).
Area Specialization: North America; Canada; Great Lakes Region.
Subject Specialization: comprehensive.

Special Cartographic Collections: Great Lakes cartographic resource center (topo. and thematic maps, historic and current); Time series of Canadian topographic maps.
Dates: pre-1800 (1%); 1800-1899 (2%); 1900 - (97%).
Classification System: local system.
Collections Cataloged. (95%).
Depository for: DMA; GSC; NOS; NTS (Canada); USGS (Geol., topo.); Ontario Base Map (OBM).
Serves: students; faculty; employees; public. Mon.–Fri. 8 a.m.–8 p.m.; Sat. 10 a.m.–2 p.m. (Seats 32; 3,400 readers served per month).
Interlibrary Loan Available.
Reproduction Facility: photocopy.
Publications: *Atlas Collection, U.W.O. Map Library* (1983); *Theses and Undergraduate Reports* (1983); *Newsletter: Map Library; Map Library Guide.*

Ottawa

761. CARLETON UNIVERSITY
Library
Map Library
Colonel By Drive
Ottawa, Ontario K1S 5B6
Established 1966.
Telephone: 613/231-4392.
Contact Person: Barbara Farrell, Map Libn.
Staff: 1 professional (full time); 6 professional (part time); 2 non-professional (full time).
Size: 105,000 maps; 845 atlases; 8 globes; 50 relief models; 6,050 aerial photographs; 700 reference books and gazetteers; 7 serials (titles received); 25 microforms (no. of titles).
Annual Accessions: 4,000 maps; 40 atlases; 50 reference books and gazetteers.
Area Specialization: National Capital Region and Eastern Ontario; Canadian Arctic; Canada; U.S.S.R. and Eastern Europe; Eastern and Southern Africa; Europe; United States.
Subject Specialization: topography and land surface characteristics; area analysis; socio-economic analysis; urban areas; historical maps.
Special Cartographic Collections: Zaborski Collection: USSR and Eastern Europe.
Dates: pre-1800 (5%); 1800-1899 (10%); 1900 - (85%).
Classification System: Public Archives of Canada.
Collections Cataloged. (40%).
Depository for: DMA; GSC; NTS (Canada); USGS (Topo.).
Serves: students; faculty; employees; public. Mon.–Thurs. 9 a.m.–8:30 p.m.; Fri. 9 a.m.–5:30 p.m. (Seats 64; 600 readers served per month).
Reproduction Facility: photocopy; Blueline.
Publications: Intermittent selected accessions, subject and area lists for internal distribution only.

762. GEOLOGICAL SURVEY OF CANADA
Map Library
601 Booth St.
Ottawa, Ontario K1A 0E8
Established 1842.
Telephone: 613/995-4177 or 4151.
Contact Person: Tara Naraynsingh, Map Libn.
Staff: 1 professional (full time); 1 non-professional (full time).
Size: 125,000 maps; 300 atlases; 200 reference books and gazetteers; 200 microforms (no. of titles).
Annual Accessions: 2,000 maps; 10 atlases.
Area Specialization: comprehensive.
Subject Specialization: geology; earth sciences.
Dates: 1800-1899 (5%); 1900 - (95%).
Classification System: LC 10%.

Depository for: GSC; USGS (Geol.).
Serves: students; faculty; employees; public. Mon.–Fri. 8:30 a.m.–4:30 p.m. (Seats 10).
Interlibrary Loan Available.
Reproduction Facility: photocopy.
Publications: accessions included in accessions list of main library.

763. OTTAWA PUBLIC LIBRARY
Reference Department
120 Metcalfe Street
Ottawa, Ontario K1P 5M2
Telephone: 613/598-4008.
Contact Person: Alyson Pember, Library Assistant Specialist.
Staff: 1 non-professional (full time).
Size: 4,877 maps.
Area Specialization: Ontario.
Subject Specialization: topography.
Special Cartographic Collections: old maps of Ontario region.
Dates: pre-1800 (2%); 1800-1899 (8%); 1900 - (90%).
Classification System: UDC.
Collections Cataloged. (100%).
Depository for: NTS (Canada). Mon.–Thurs. 10 a.m.–9 p.m. (8 p.m. in summer); Sat. 9:30 a.m.–5 p.m. all year; Sun. 1–5 p.m. from mid-Oct. to mid-May. (Seats 100).
Reproduction Facility: photocopy.

764. PUBLIC ARCHIVES OF CANADA
National Map Collection
395 Wellington Street
Ottawa, Ontario K1A 0N3
Established 1907.
Telephone: 613/995-1077 or 992-0468.
Contact Person: Betty Kidd, Director.
Staff: 13 professional (full time); 12 non-professional (full time).
Size: 1,200,000 maps; 2,000 atlases; 15 globes; 2 relief models; 27,000 aerial photographs; 1,200 reference books and gazetteers; 70 serials (titles received).
Annual Accessions: 50,000 (varies widely) maps; 70 atlases; 2 globes; 75 reference books and gazetteers; 5 serials (titles received).
Area Specialization: Canada; North America; world.
Subject Specialization: comprehensive.
Special Cartographic Collections: Canadian series maps; *The Atlantic Neptune;* rare atlases; insurance plans and atlases; nineteenth century townland survey of Ireland.
Dates: pre-1800 (10%); 1800-1899 (15%); 1900 - (75%).
Classification System: Public Archives of Canada.
Collections Cataloged. (10%).
Depository for: DMA; DOS (Gt. Brit); GSC; NTS (Canada); USGS (Topo.); Deposit agreements maintained with many Canadian and foreign. governments
Serves: students; employees; public; government departments. Mon.–Fri. 8:30 a.m.–4:45 p.m. (Seats 15–20; 150 readers served per month).
Interlibrary Loan Available. Current foreign maps only
Reproduction Facility: photocopy; microform; Reader-printer copies.
Publications: "List of publications of the National Map Collection" available upon request.

765. UNIVERSITY OF OTTAWA
Morisset Library
Map Library
65 Hastey
Ottawa, Ontario K1N 9A5
Established 1968.
Telephone: 613/231-6830.
Contact Person: Aileen Desbarats, Map Libn.

Staff: 2 professional (full time); 3 non-professional (full time).
Size: 122,800 maps; 1,665 atlases; 14 globes; 15 relief models; 244,150 aerial photographs; 6,700 reference books and gazetteers; 58 serials (titles received).
Annual Accessions: 5,000 maps; 100 atlases; 6,000 aerial photographs; 500 (includes reports) reference books and gazetteers; 2 serials (titles received).
Area Specialization: National capital region; eastern Ontario; western Quebec; Yukon; Canada; western Europe; certain countries in Africa, South America.
Subject Specialization: geomorphology.
Dates: 1800-1899 (5%); 1900 - (95%).
Classification System: LC (for reference works and atlases); UDC (for maps).
Collections Cataloged. (Ref. atlases 100%; maps 20%).
Depository for: DMA; GSC; NTS (Canada); USGS (Topo.); Ontario Base Map; Canada Land Inventory;. Canada Hydrographic Service
Serves: students; faculty; employees; public. Mon.–Thurs. 8:30 a.m.–9 p.m.; Fri. 8:30 a.m.–5 p.m.; Sat. 11:a.m.–4 p.m. (Seats 20; varies from ca. 125-850 readers served per month).
Interlibrary Loan Available. Some
Reproduction Facility: photocopy.
Publications: *Map library; selection of recent acquisitions.*

St. Catharines

766. BROCK UNIVERSITY
Department of Geography
Map Library
St. Catharines, Ontario L2S 3A1
Established 1965.
Telephone: 416/688-5550, ext. 468.
Contact Person: Olga Slachta, Supervisor, Map Library.
Staff: 1 professional (part time); 1 non-professional (full time).
Size: 45,000 maps; 400 atlases; 3 globes; 48 relief models; 14,000 aerial photographs; 1,000 reference books and gazetteers.
Annual Accessions: 1,000 maps; 15 atlases; 100 aerial photographs; 100 reference books and gazetteers.
Area Specialization: Niagara Peninsula; Ontario; Canada.
Subject Specialization: topography; geology; hydrography; soils.
Special Cartographic Collections: Welland Canals 1825–1982; historical maps of Niagara Peninsula.
Dates: pre-1800 (1%); 1800-1899 (7%); 1900 - (92%).
Classification System: AGS.
Collections Cataloged. (90%).
Depository for: GSC; NTS (Canada).
Serves: students; faculty; employees; public;. Mon.–Thurs. 9 a.m.–7 p.m.; Fri. 9 a.m.–4 p.m. (Seats 20; 400 readers served per month).
Interlibrary Loan Available.
Reproduction Facility: mapograph.
Publications: *University Map Library, Dept. of Geography* (brochure); acquisition list.

Scarborough

767. UNIVERSITY OF TORONTO-SCARBOROUGH CAMPUS
V. W. Bladen Library
Special Collections
1265 Military Trail
Scarborough, Ontario M1C 1A4
Established 1971.
Telephone: 416/284-3183.
Contact Person: Ms. Loan Le, Special Collections Libn.

Staff: 1 professional (full time).
Size: 10,946 maps; 221 atlases; 1 globes; 1,679 aerial photographs.
Annual Accessions: 650 maps.
Area Specialization: Toronto; Ontario Province; Canada.
Special Cartographic Collections: wall map collection.
Classification System: LC (modified).
Collections Cataloged.
Depository for: NTS (Canada).
Serves: students; faculty; employees; public. Mon.–Thurs. 9 a.m.–10:30 p.m.; Fri. 9 a.m.–5 p.m.; Sat. 10 a.m.–5 p.m.; Sun. 1–5 p.m. (75–100 readers served per month).
Reproduction Facility: photocopy.
Publications: *Selected Recent Acquisitions* (Quarterly).

Sudbury

768. LAURENTIAN UNIVERSITY
Library
Map Collection
Sudbury, Ontario P3E 2C6
Established 1960.
Telephone: 705/675-1151, ext. 563.
Contact Person: Raymond Labbe, Technologist.
Staff: 1 non-professional (part time).
Size: 20,000 maps; 200 atlases; 1 globes; 100 reference books and gazetteers; 200 serials (titles received).
Annual Accessions: 850 maps; 10 atlases; 10 reference books and gazetteers; 10 serials (titles received).
Area Specialization: Canada.
Subject Specialization: topography.
Dates: 1900 - (100%).
Classification System: LC.
Collections not Cataloged.
Depository for: NTS (Canada).
Serves: students; faculty; employees; public. Mon.–Fri. 9 a.m.–4:30 p.m.
Reproduction Facility: photocopy.

Thunder Bay

769. LAKEHEAD UNIVERSITY
Geography
Map Library
Oliver Road
Thunder Bay, Ontario P7B 5E1
Established 1974.
Telephone: 807/345-2121, ext. 548.
Contact Person: Iain Hastie, Cartographer/Map Curator.
Staff: 1 professional (part time).
Size: 12,500 maps; 21 atlases; 2 globes; 4 relief models; 1,800 aerial photographs.
Annual Accessions: 300 maps; 1 atlases.
Area Specialization: Northern Ontario.
Subject Specialization: topography.
Dates: 1900 - (100%).
Classification System: Public Archives of Canada.
Collections Cataloged. (35%).
Serves: students; faculty; employees; public. Mon.–Fri. 9 a.m.–12 noon; 1–5 p.m. (Seats 8–10; varies readers served per month).
Interlibrary Loan Available.

Toronto

770. ARCHIVES OF ONTARIO
Map Collection
77 Grenville Street
Toronto, Ontario M7A 2R9
Established 1904.
Telephone: 416/965-4030.
Contact Person: John W. Fortier, Archivist, Government Records Section.
Staff: 1 professional (part time); 1 non-professional (part time).
Size: 30,000 maps; 183 atlases; 500,000 aerial photographs; 12 reference books and gazetteers; 360 microforms (no. of titles).
Annual Accessions: 500 maps; 3 atlases.
Area Specialization: Ontario.
Subject Specialization: historical maps of Ontario.
Special Cartographic Collections: David Thompson—exploratory surveys & boundary surveys; Thomas Talbot—land tenure; Canada Company—general and land tenure; John Graves Simcoe—late 18th century manuscript maps; fire insurance plans within province of Ontario.
Dates: pre-1800 (20%); 1800-1899 (40%); 1900 - (40%).
Classification System: AGS.
Collections Cataloged.
Depository for: NTS (Canada).
Serves: employees; public. Mon.–Fri. 8:30 a.m.–5 p.m. (Seats 6; 80 readers served per month).
Reproduction Facility: photocopy; quickcopy; microform.

771. CITY OF TORONTO ARCHIVES
City Clerk's Dept., City Hall
100 Queen Street West
Toronto, Ontario M5H 2N2
Established 1960.
Telephone: 416/947-7483.
Contact Person: Victor L. Russell, Manager, City of Toronto Archives.
Staff: 1 professional (part time); 1 non-professional (part time).
Size: 3,000 (approx) maps; 1,000 (approx) microforms (no. of titles).
Area Specialization: city of Toronto.
Subject Specialization: city of Toronto.
Dates: 1800-1899 (50%); 1900 - (50%).
Classification System: local system.
Collections Cataloged. (33%).
Serves: employees. Mon.–Fri. 8:30 a.m.–4:30 p.m. (Seats 15; 300 readers served per month).
Reproduction Facility: photocopy; microform.

772. METROPOLITAN TORONTO LIBRARY
History Department
Map Room
789 Yonge Street
Toronto, Ontario M4W 2G8
Established 1969.
Telephone: 416/928-5271.
Contact Person: Nancy Biehl, Map Libn.
Staff: 1 professional (full time); 1 non-professional (part time).
Size: 38,000 maps; 1,250 atlases; 1 globes; 350 aerial photographs; 1,100 reference books and gazetteers; 20 (directly on cartography) serials (titles received); 48 microforms (no. of titles).
Annual Accessions: ca. 1,500 maps; ca. 50 atlases; irregular aerial photographs; ca. 75 reference books and gazetteers; irregular serials (titles received); ca. 4 microforms (no. of titles).
Area Specialization: Canada; Ontario; Toronto.

Subject Specialization: road, city and topographical maps for world travel; historical maps of 19th century Toronto and Ontario.
Special Cartographic Collections: insurance plans for major Canadian cities and Ontario towns and villages.
Dates: pre-1800 (1%); 1800-1899 (9%); 1900 - (90%).
Classification System: Dewey.
Collections Cataloged.
Depository for: NTS (Canada).
Serves: public. Mon.–Thurs. 10 a.m.–9 p.m., Fri. 10 a.m.–6 p.m.; Sat. 10 a.m.–6 p.m.; Sun. afternoons from October to April. (Seats 50).
Interlibrary Loan Available. (restricted)
Reproduction Facility: photocopy; photography.
Publications: *Map collection in the Public Reference Library* (1923); *Gazetteers in Metropolitan Toronto Central Library* (1975).

773. ONTARIO MINISTRY OF NATURAL RESOURCES
Queen's Park
Toronto, Ontario M7A 1W3
Established 1972.
Telephone: 416/965-1352.
Contact Person: Nancy Thurston, Libn.
Staff: 4 professional (full time).
Size: 20,000 maps.
Annual Accessions: 1,500 maps.
Area Specialization: Ontario; Canada; United States.
Subject Specialization: geology; mining.
Depository for: GSC. Mon.–Fri. 8:15 a.m.–4:30 p.m.
Interlibrary Loan Available. (restricted)
Reproduction Facility: quickcopy.

774. ROYAL ONTARIO MUSEUM
Library
100 Queen's Park
Toronto, Ontario M5S 2C6
Established 1961.
Telephone: 416/978-3673.
Contact Person: Sharon Hick, Associate Libn.
Staff: 1 professional (part time); 1 non-professional (part time).
Area Specialization: Canada.
Subject Specialization: topography; geology.
Dates: 1900 - (100%).
Classification System: NTS or GSC numbering.
Collections not Cataloged.
Depository for: GSC; NTS (Canada).
Serves: students; faculty; employees; public. Mon.–Fri. 10 a.m.–4:30 p.m. (Seats 24; 4 readers served per month).
Reproduction Facility: photocopy.

775. UNIVERSITY OF TORONTO
John P. Robarts Library
Map Library
130 St. George St.
Toronto, Ontario M5S 1A5
Established 1964.
Telephone: 416/978-3372.
Contact Person: Joan Winearls, Map Libn.
Staff: 1 professional (full time); 1 professional (part time); 2 non-professional (full time); 1 non-professional (part time).
Size: 183,066 maps; 10,376 (includes reference books and gazetteers) atlases; 1 globe globes; 20 relief models; 205,283 aerial photographs; 45 serials (titles received); 24 microforms (no. of titles).
Annual Accessions: 7,000 maps; 400 atlases; 8,000 aerial photographs; 1 microforms (no. of titles).

Area Specialization: Toronto; Ontario; Canada; United States; Europe; Latin America especially Brazil.
Subject Specialization: comprehensive.
Special Cartographic Collections: Provincial government aerial photography 1952–1972; aerial photography for Toronto 1947–1983.
Dates: 1800-1899 (5%); 1900 - (95%).
Classification System: LC.
Collections Cataloged. (75%).
Depository for: DMA; GSC; NOS; NTS (Canada); USGS (Geol., topo.); Some Ontario government maps.
Serves: students; faculty; employees; public. In term: Mon.–Thurs. 9 a.m.–9 p.m.; Fri. 9 a.m.–5 p.m.; Summer: Mon.–Fri; Sat. In term: 9 a.m.–5 p.m. (Seats 48; 1,072 readers served per month).
Interlibrary Loan Available.
Reproduction Facility: photocopy; microform; slides.
Publications: Publications: *Climate: maps atlases and reference books in the Map Library, Rev. 1982; Map interpretation: an annotated bibliography, Rev. ed. 1980; Toronto Base Maps 1982; Toronto maps: maps, atlases and aerial photographs in the University of Toronto Map Library, Rev. ed. 1981;* (Brochures): *Aerial Photo Collection; 1983; A Guide to the Geological Maps and Atlases in the Map Library,* 1983.

776. YORK UNIVERSITY
Scott Library
Map Library
4700 Keele Street, Downsview
Toronto, Ontario M3J 2R2
Established 1967.
Telephone: 416/667-3353.
Contact Person: Janet Allin, Map Library Supervisor.
Staff: 2 non-professional (full time); 7 non-professional (part time).
Size: 82,000 maps; 3,600 atlases; 9 globes; 3,891 aerial photographs; 27 serials (titles received).
Annual Accessions: 3,000 maps; 300 atlases; 200 aerial photographs.
Area Specialization: Toronto; southern Ontario; Canada; United States; Europe.
Subject Specialization: physical geography; urban geography.
Special Cartographic Collections: Readings in Cartography (466 photocopied articles or reprints on mapping from geographical journals, historical journals, environmental studies journals); 1,701 maps on Slides; 133 Maps on Transparencies; 520 Base map collection (page size black and White)—520.
Dates: 1800-1899 (2%); 1900 - (98%).
Classification System: LC.
Collections Cataloged. (10% (maps)).
Depository for: GSC; NTS (Canada); USGS (Topo.); Canada Land Inventory; Canada Aeronautical Charts; Canada Hydrographic Service.
Serves: students; faculty; employees; public. Mon.–Thurs. 9 a.m.–10 p.m.; Summer Hours: 8:30 a.m.–4:30 p.m.; Sat. 12–5 p.m.; Sun. 1–6 p.m. (Seats 50).
Interlibrary Loan Available.
Reproduction Facility: photocopy.
Publications: Map Sources Directory (sold—price $10 Can); Bibliographies on the following topics—Cartography; Computer cartography; Climatology; Medical Geography; Middle East; Metropolitan Toronto; Metro Toronto outline maps; Remote Sensing; Rural Geography; Surficial Geology; Surveying; World Energy Resources; Map Library Information sheet.

Waterloo

777. UNIVERSITY OF WATERLOO
Engineering, Mathematics and Science Library
Waterloo, Ontario N2L 3G1
Established 1965.
Telephone: 519/885-1211, ext. 3520.
Contact Person: Diane Harding, Libn., Reference and
Collection Development Dept.
Size: 5–6,000 maps.
Annual Accessions: 500 maps.
Area Specialization: Ontario; Canada; North America.
Subject Specialization: geology; hydrology.
Classification System: LC; Some maps are titled.
Collections Cataloged. (50%).
Depository for: GSC; Ontario Geological Survey.
Serves: students; faculty; employees; public. Mon.–Fri. 8
a.m.–12 midnight; Sat. 8 a.m.–12 midnight; Sun. 1–12
midnight.
Interlibrary Loan Available.
Reproduction Facility: photocopy.

778. UNIVERSITY OF WATERLOO
University Library
Map and Design Library
Waterloo, Ontario N2L 3G1
Established 1965.
Telephone: 519/885-1211, ext. 3412.
Contact Person: Richard Hugh Pinnell, Head, University
Map and Design Library.
Staff: 3 professional (full time); 7 professional (part time); 2
non-professional (full time).
Size: 65,000 maps; 1,500 atlases; 3 globes; 25,000 aerial
photographs; 350 reference books and gazetteers; 35
serials (titles received).
Annual Accessions: 3,000 maps; 75 atlases; 1,000 aerial
photographs; 25 reference books and gazetteers; 1 serials
(titles received).
Area Specialization: southern Ontario.
Subject Specialization: topography; land use.
Dates: pre-1800 (0.5%); 1800-1899 (0.5%); 1900 - (99%).
Classification System: LC.
Collections Cataloged. (3%).
Depository for: DMA; NTS (Canada); USGS (Topo.);
Canadian Hydrographic Service; Ontario Geological Survey.
Serves: students; faculty; employees; public. Mon.–Thurs.
8:30 a.m.–9 p.m.; Fri. 8:30 a.m.–4:00 p.m; summer: Mon.–
Fri.; Sat. 1–5 p.m.; Sun. 1–6 p.m. (Seats 55).
Interlibrary Loan Available.
Reproduction Facility: photocopy.
Publications: *University Map and Design Library* (brochure).

Windsor

779. UNIVERSITY OF WINDSOR
Department of Geography
Paul Vandall Map Library
Room 51, Windsor Hall South
Windsor, Ontario N9B 3P4
Established 1969.
Telephone: 519/253-4232, ext. 2182.
Contact Person: (Mrs.) Rosaline Milks, Map Libn.
Staff: 1 professional (full time).
Size: 40,000 maps; 200 atlases; 3 globes; 25 relief models;
4,000 aerial photographs; 2,000 reference books and
gazetteers.
Annual Accessions: 4,000 maps; 6 atlases; 100 aerial
photographs; 25 reference books and gazetteers.
Area Specialization: Canada.

Subject Specialization: climatology; geomorphology
environmental sciences; urban studies; medical geography.
Dates: 1900 - (95%).
Collections not Cataloged.
Depository for: NTS (Canada); USGS (Geol.).
Serves: students; faculty; employees; public. Mon.–Fri. 8:30
a.m.–4:30 p.m. (Seats 25; 200 readers served per month).
Interlibrary Loan Available.
Reproduction Facility: photocopy.

PRINCE EDWARD ISLAND

Charlottetown

780. PUBLIC ARCHIVES OF PRINCE EDWARD ISLAND
P.O. Box 1000
Charlottetown, Prince Edward Island C1A 7N4
Established 1972.
Telephone: 902/892-3504, ext. 42.
Contact Person: N. J. de Jong, Provincial Archivist.
Size: 1,500 maps; 2 atlases; 2,000 aerial photographs.
Area Specialization: Prince Edward Island.
Dates: pre-1800 (8%); 1800-1899 (82%); 1900 - (10%).
Classification System: local system.
Collections Cataloged.
Serves: students; faculty; employees; public. Mon.–Fri.8:30
a.m.–5 p.m. (Seats 20; 225 readers served per month).
Reproduction Facility: photocopy; microform.

Summerside

781. LAND REGISTRATION AND INFORMATION SERVICE
Surveys and Mapping
120 Water Street
Summerside, Prince Edward Island C1N 1A9
Established 1973.
Telephone: 902/436-2107.
Contact Person: Brenton H. MacLeod, Map Libn.
Staff: 1 professional (full time); 1 non-professional (part
time).
Size: 10,715 maps; 10 atlases; 15,000 aerial photographs;
400 microforms (no. of titles).
Annual Accessions: 400 maps.
Area Specialization: Prince Edward Island; New Brunswick;
Nova Scotia.
Subject Specialization: metric line mapping; metric
orthophoto mapping.
Collections Cataloged.
Depository for: NTS (Canada).
Serves: students; faculty; employees; public;. Mon.–Fri. 8
a.m.–4 p.m.
Interlibrary Loan Available.
Reproduction Facility: photocopy; quickcopy; microform;
whiteprint.

QUEBEC

Chicoutimi

782. UNIVERSITE DU QUEBEC A CHICOUTIMI (U.Q.A.C.)
Bibliothèque
Cartothèque
555, Boulevard de l'Université
Chicoutimi, Quebec G7H 2B1
Established June 1974.
Telephone: 418/545-5453.
Contact Person: Richard A. Bouchard, Responsable de la cartothèque.
Staff: 1 professional (full time); 1 non-professional (full time); 1 non-professional (part time).
Size: 19,700 maps; 617 atlases; 1 globes; 5 relief models; 29,000 aerial photographs; 30 reference books and gazetteers; 5 serials (titles received).
Annual Accessions: 800 maps; 20 atlases; 1,500 aerial photographs; 3 reference books and gazetteers; 1 serials (titles received).
Area Specialization: Saguenay; Lac-Saint-Jean; middle northern Quebec.
Subject Specialization: geography; geology; environment.
Dates: 1800-1899 (2%); 1900 - (98%).
Classification System: Boggs-Lewis.
Collections Cataloged.
Depository for: NTS (Canada); Photocartotheque du Quebec.
Serves: students; faculty; employees; public. Mon.–Fri. 8:30 a.m.–5 p.m. (Seats 24; 400 readers served per month).
Reproduction Facility: quickcopy.
Publications: *Guide de la cartotheque Université du Québec á Chicoutimi; Répertoire Carto-bibliographique de la Région 02 et du Moyen Nord; Liste des acquisitions nouvelles de la carhothèque* (annual).

Montréal

783. BIBLIOTHEQUE NATIONALE DU QUEBEC
Service des Collections Spéciales
Secteur des Cartes
1700 Rue St-Denis
Montréal, Québec H2X 3K6
Established 1968.
Telephone: 514/873-4408.
Contact Person: Pierre Lépine, Responsable.
Staff: 1 professional (full time).
Size: 30,000 maps; 600 atlases; 6 globes; 10 relief models; 500 reference books and gazetteers; 5,000 microforms (no. of titles).
Annual Accessions: 3,000 maps; 10 atlases; 500 microforms (no. of titles).
Area Specialization: Province of Québec.
Dates: pre-1800 (3%); 1800-1899 (6%); 1900 - (90%).
Classification System: LC.
Collections Cataloged. (50%).
Depository for: NTS (Canada).
Serves: public. Tues.–Fri. 10 a.m.–4 p.m. (Seats 20; 30 readers served per month).
Reproduction Facility: photocopy; quickcopy; microform.

784. CONCORDIA UNIVERSITY
Dept. of Geography Annex Z205
Sir George Williams Campus
1455 de Maisonneuve Blvd. W.
Montréal, Québec H3G 1M8
Established 1967.
Telephone: 514/879-5885.

Contact Person: (Miss) Vivian Janes, Map Libn. & Geography Resource Coordinator.
Staff: 1 professional (full time); 1 professional (part time).
Size: 100,000 maps; 160 atlases; 6 globes; 10 relief models; 1,500 aerial photographs; 250 reference books and gazetteers; 3 serials (titles received).
Annual Accessions: 1,200 maps.
Area Specialization: North America.
Subject Specialization: land use and land capability in Canada.
Classification System: Boggs-Lewis.
Collections Cataloged. (50%).
Depository for: NTS (Canada).
Serves: students; faculty; employees; public;. Mon.–Fri. 8:30 a.m.–4 p.m. and by appointment. (Seats 20).

785. ECOLE POLYTECHNIQUE
La Bibliothèque
Cartothèque
C.P. 6079, Succursale A
Montréal, Québec H3C 3A7
Telephone: 514/344-4849.
Size: 38,000 maps; 30 atlases.
Annual Accessions: 2,000 maps; 5 atlases.
Area Specialization: Canada; eastern United States; France.
Subject Specialization: topography; geology. Mon.–Fri. 9 a.m.–10 p.m.; Sat. 9 a.m.–5 p.m.

786. MCGILL UNIVERSITY
McLennan Library, Department of Rare Books and Special Collections
Map Collection
3459 McTavish Street
Montréal, Québec H3A 1Y1
Established 1969.
Telephone: 514/392-4714.
Contact Person: Mrs. Carol Marley, Map Curator.
Size: 5,908 maps; 370 atlases; 4 globes; 248 reference books and gazetteers; 5 serials (titles received).
Annual Accessions: 120 maps; 5 atlases; 15 reference books and gazetteers.
Area Specialization: North America; Canada; Quebec; Montreal.
Subject Specialization: topography.
Special Cartographic Collections: W. H. Pugsley collection of early maps of Canada (49 16–18th century maps of parts of Canada; small collection of Yorkshire, England maps; topographical ephemera.
Dates: pre-1800 (50%); 1800-1899 (30%); 1900 - (20%).
Classification System: Cutter.
Collections Cataloged. (20%).
Serves: students; faculty; employees; public. Mon.–Fri. 9 a.m.–6 p.m.; Sat. 9 a.m.–12 noon. (Seats 3; 35 readers served per month).
Reproduction Facility: photocopy; quickcopy; microform.
Publications: *Catalogue of the W. H. Pugsley Collection of Early Maps of Canada* (1975); *Pre-Nineteenth-Century Maps and Atlases of Montreal in the Collections of the Rare Book Department of the McGill University Library* (1981); *Nineteenth Century maps and Atlases of Montreal . . .* (1951); *Twentieth Century Maps and Atlases of Montreal . . .* (1981; A Checklist of Canadian Immigration Atlases held in the Collections of the Rare Book Department of the McGill University Library (1983); A Checklist of Bluchette Maps . . . (1981); Pre-1757 Maps of Acadia . . .(1983); Maps of Ireland . . . (1973); A Preliminary Guide to Nineteenth Century Canadian Guide Books: A Survey of Holdings of the McLennan Library with an Historical Introduction (1982); Finding List for Guide books to North America published by the House of Appleton, held in McGill University's Department of Rare Books and Special Collections.

787. MCGILL UNIVERSITY
Map and Air Photo Library
805 Sherbrooke Street West
Montréal, Québec H3A 2K6
Established 1945.
Telephone: 514/392-5492.
Contact Person: Lorraine Dubreuil, Map Curator.
Staff: 2 professional (full time); 3 non-professional (part time).
Size: 146,500 maps; 644 atlases; 12 globes; 30,184 aerial photographs; 300 reference books and gazetteers; 10 serials (titles received).
Annual Accessions: 6,500 maps; 1,500 aerial photographs; 10 reference books and gazetteers.
Area Specialization: Montreal; Quebec; Canada; Latin America; Africa.
Subject Specialization: geology.
Special Cartographic Collections: fire insurance plans of Canadian cities.
Dates: 1900 - (100%).
Classification System: LC; Boggs-Lewis.
Collections Cataloged. (10%).
Depository for: DMA; GSC; NTS (Canada); USGS (Geol., topo.); Australia (topo, geol).
Serves: students; faculty; employees; public;. Mon.–Fri. 9 a.m.–5 p.m. (Seats 10; 240 readers served per month).
Interlibrary Loan Available.
Reproduction Facility: photocopy.

788. MUSEUM OF ST. HELEN'S ISLAND
David M. Stewart Library
P.O. Box 1024 Station A
Montreal, Quebec H3C 2W9
Established 1974 (approx.).
Telephone: 514/861-6701.
Contact Person: Elizabeth F. Hale (Mrs.), Libn. Consultant.
Staff: 1 professional (full time); 1/2 non-professional (part time).
Size: 400 maps; 30 atlases; 14 (16–18th centuries) globes; approx. 100 reference books and gazetteers; 2 serials (titles received).
Area Specialization: New World; world.
Subject Specialization: history as it relates to the end of the French Regime (i.e., to 1763).
Dates: pre-1800 (99%); 1800-1899 (1%).
Classification System: local system.
Publications: exhibition catalogs that include our major participation; *Frontenac Sous Louis XV St. Germain en Laye France 1980; Naissance de la Louisiane, North Archives Nat. de Paris 1982–83; Decouverte du Mon de XVI-XVIII siecle. St. Malo France May 1984* (forthcoming).

789. QUEBEC (PROVINCE) MINISTERE DE AFFAIRES CULTURELLES
Archives Nationales du Québec
Collection des cartes et plans
100, Est, Notre-Dame
Montréal, Québec H2Y 1C1
Established 1971.
Telephone: 514/073-3064.
Contact Person: Jean-Marc Garant, Archiviste-Cartothécaire.
Staff: 1 professional (full time).
Size: 268,000 maps; 70 atlases; 200 rolls aerial photographs; 18 reference books and gazetteers.
Annual Accessions: 5,000 maps; 1 atlases; 50 rolls aerial photographs.
Area Specialization: Montréal and region.
Subject Specialization: building inspection plans; land surveyors plans; architectural plans; engineering plans.
Dates: pre-1800 (2%); 1800-1899 (8%); 1900 - (90%).
Classification System: SAPHIR [archival structure system].
Collections Cataloged. (85%).

Serves: students; faculty; employees; public. Wed. 9 a.m.–4:30 p.m. (Seats 6; 18 readers served per month).
Reproduction Facility: photocopy.

790. UNIVERSITE DE MONTREAL
Département de Géographie
cartothèque
C.P. 6128, Succ. "A"
Montréal, Québec H3C 3J7
Established 1954.
Telephone: 514/270-6525.
Contact Person: Cécile Fugulin, Carthothècaire.
Staff: 1 professional (full time).
Size: 60,000 maps; 400 atlases; 1 globes; 25 relief models; 60,000 aerial photographs; 150 reference books and gazetteers.
Annual Accessions: 3,000 maps; 10–15 atlases; 2–2,000 aerial photographs; 5–10 reference books and gazetteers.
Area Specialization: Quebec; Canada; United States.
Subject Specialization: topography; geology; thematic maps.
Dates: 1800-1899 (2%); 1900 - (98%).
Classification System: NTS.
Collections Cataloged. (90%).
Depository for: NTS (Canada).
Serves: students; faculty; employees; public. Mon.–Fri. 9.am.–12 noon, 1:30–5 p.m. (Seats 30).
Reproduction Facility: photocopy.

791. UNIVERSITE DE QUEBEC
Institut National de la Recherche Scientifique
Carththeque
3465 Durocher
Montreal, Québec H2X 2C6
Telephone: 514/842-4191.
Contact Person: Christiane Desmarais, Cartothécaire.
Staff: 1 professional (full time).
Size: 27,500 maps; 35 atlases; 35 reference books and gazetteers; 15 microforms (no. of titles).
Annual Accessions: 2,000 maps.
Area Specialization: Montréal Québec; Province Montréal.
Subject Specialization: urban geography.
Special Cartographic Collections: Montréal: land use.—scale 1:1000, 1964–1983; fire insurance plans for the Province of Québec.
Dates: 1800-1899 (1%); 1900 - (99%).
Classification System: local system.
Depository for: NTS (Canada).
Serves: students; employees; public. Mon–Fri. 9 a.m.–5 p.m. (Seats 4).
Interlibrary Loan Available.
Reproduction Facility: photocopy; quickcopy.

792. UNIVERSITE DU QUEBEC A MONTREAL
Carthothèque
1255 Saint Denis
Montréal, Québec H3C 3P3
Established 1970.
Telephone: 514/282-4381.
Contact Person: Leon-Pierre Sciamma, Responsable.
Staff: 2 professional (full time); 2 non-professional (full time).
Size: 58,000 maps; 450 atlases; 1 globes; 328,000 aerial photographs; 6,000 reference books and gazetteers.
Annual Accessions: 4,000 maps; 20 atlases; 15,000 aerial photographs; 200 reference books and gazetteers.
Area Specialization: Quebec Province.
Classification System: system based on the S.N.R.C.
Collections Cataloged.
Depository for: NTS (Canada); Ministère Energie et Ressources; Ministère Energie Mines—Ressource. (Ottawa); divers autres ministères

Serves: students; faculty; employees. Mon–Fri. 9 a.m.–7 p.m. (Seats 115; 2,500 readers served per month).
Interlibrary Loan Available.
Reproduction Facility: photocopy.

Québec

793. ARCHIVES DE LA VILLE DE QUEBEC
350, rue Saint-Joseph Est, 3e étage
Québec, Québec G1K 3B2
Established 1924.
Telephone: 418/694-6372.
Contact Person: André Laflamme, Archiviste.
Staff: 1 professional (part time); 1 non-professional (part time).
Size: ca. 3,000 maps; 14 atlases.
Annual Accessions: 100–300 maps.
Area Specialization: Quebec city territory.
Subject Specialization: maps and plans produced by the city.
Special Cartographic Collections: surveying and architectural plans; town plans; public works plans.
Dates: pre-1800 (5%); 1800-1899 (45%); 1900 - (50%).
Classification System: local system.
Collections Cataloged.
Serves: students; employees; public. (Seats 12 (for all Archives purposes); about 30, for maps and plans readers served per month).
Reproduction Facility: photocopy; Photography.
Publications: *Guide la Cartothéque.* 1975 (not available).

794. UNIVERSITE LAVAL
Bibliothèque générale
Carthothéque
Québec, Québec G1K 7P4
Established 1964.
Telephone: 418/656-2002.
Contact Person: Yves tessier, Chef de la Carththèque.
Staff: 1 professional (full time); 3 non-professional (full time); 1 non-professional (part time).
Size: 93,162 maps; 2,178 atlases; 3 globes; 3 relief models; 126,194 aerial photographs; 600 reference books and gazetteers; 10 serials (titles received); 30 microforms (no. of titles).
Annual Accessions: 3,000 maps; 125 atlases; 500 aerial photographs; 50 reference books and gazetteers.
Area Specialization: Québec; Canada; northeastern United States; West Indies; France; French africa.
Subject Specialization: physical geography; demography; land use; regional development; historical geography; cartographic methods; school atlases.
Special Cartographic Collections: 3,500 old maps of New France and Québec; maps by Joseph Bouchette, 1774–1841.
Dates: pre-1800 (1%); 1800-1899 (3%); 1900 - (96%).
Classification System: LC (for atlases); Boggs-Lewis modified (for maps).
Collections Cataloged. (100%).
Depository for: GSC; NOS; NTS (Canada); USGS (Topo.); Canadian Hydrographic Service; Quebec Government.
Serves: students; faculty; employees; public. Mon–Fri. 8:30 a.m.–11 p.m.; Sat. 10 a.m.–5 p.m.; Sun. closed. (Seats 75; 1,600 readers served per month).
Reproduction Facility: photocopy; microform; optical enlarger-reducer.
Publications: *Catalogue collectif des atlas des cartothéques universitaires du Québec* (1976); *Carto-03: répertoire cartobibliographique sur la région de Québec* 1983); Bibliographic guides: *La Cartothéque* (1982); *Documentation cartographique sur le Québec* (1982); *La cartographie et la*

documentation cartographique (1983). *Cartologica* (1969–) quarterly accessions list.

Rimouski

795. UNIVERSITE DU QUEBEC A RIMOUSKI
Bibliothèque Générale
La Cartothèque
300 Avenue Des Ursulines
Rimouski, Quebec G5L 3A1
Established 1971.
Telephone: 418/724-1669.
Contact Person: Yves Michaud, Map Libn.
Staff: 1 professional (full time).
Size: 25,500 maps; 720 atlases; 5 globes; 4 relief models; 19,500 aerial photographs; 50 reference books and gazetteers; 10 serials (titles received).
Annual Accessions: 2,000 maps; 25 atlases; 1 globes; 1 relief models; 1,000 aerial photographs; 10 reference books and gazetteers; 2 serials (titles received).
Area Specialization: Lower St. Lawrence and Gaspesia Region.
Subject Specialization: topography; physical geography.
Special Cartographic Collections: all maps of B.A.E.Q. (Bureau d'Amérragement de l'Est du Québec).
Dates: pre-1800 (2%); 1800-1899 (1%); 1900 - (97%).
Classification System: Boggs-Lewis.
Collections Cataloged. (100%).
Depository for: GSC; NTS (Canada); USGS (Topo.).
Serves: students; public. Mon.–Fri. 8:30 a.m.–12 noon; 1:30 p.m.–5 p.m. (Seats 16; 150 readers served per month).
Reproduction Facility: photocopy.
Publications: *Information cartologique* (published occasionally).

Sherbrooke

796. UNIVERSITE DE SHERBROOKE
Service des bibliothèques
Cartothèque
2500 boul. Université
Sherbrooke, Québec J1K 2R1
Established 1970.
Telephone: 819/565-4507.
Contact Person: Diane Quirion-Turcotte, Préposée à la cartothèque.
Staff: 1 professional (full time); 1 non-professional (full time).
Size: 20,000 maps; 135 atlases; 2 globes; 1 relief models; 53,300 aerial photographs; 60 reference books and gazetteers; 1 serials (titles received); 3 microforms (no. of titles).
Annual Accessions: 2,500 maps; 12 atlases; 1,500 aerial photographs; 20 reference books and gazetteers.
Area Specialization: Québec (province); New England; general maps of the world and continents.
Subject Specialization: topography; geology; cadastral; land use.
Special Cartographic Collections: Cadastral maps of townships and counties dating from 1900 to 1950.
Dates: 1800-1899 (5%); 1900 - (95%).
Classification System: Boggs-Lewis.
Collections Cataloged.
Depository for: GSC; NTS (Canada); Quebec Ministère Energie et Ressources.
Serves: students; faculty; employees; geographers, engineers who are in private or public offices. Mon.–Fri. 8 a.m.–5 p.m.; Mon. and Tues. 6–9 p.m. (Seats 30; 700 readers served per month).
Interlibrary Loan Available.

Ste-Foy

797. ARCHIVES NATIONALES DU QUEBEC
Section des Cartes et Plans
1210, avenue du Séminarie
Ste-Foy, Québec G1V 4N1
Telephone: 418/643-8904.
Contact Person: Antonine Gagnon.
Staff: 1 professional (full time).
Size: 8,000 maps; 95 atlases; 3,800 aerial photographs.
Area Specialization: Province Québec.
Subject Specialization: plans d'architecture et plans d'arpenteurs cartes se rapportant à tous les aspects de la vie québecoise.
Dates: pre-1800 (10%); 1800-1899 (45%); 1900 - (45%).
Classification System: .
Serves: students; faculty; employees; public. (Seats 12; 30 readers served per month).
Reproduction Facility: microform; photography.
Publications: *Guide de la cartothèque* (1982).

Trois-Rivières

798. UNIVERSITE DU QUEBEC A TROIS-RIVIERES
Département des sciences humaines
C.P. 500
Trois-Rivières, Québec G9A 5H7
Established 1971.
Telephone: 819/376-5351.
Contact Person: Marie Lefebvre, Map Libn.
Staff: 1 professional (full time); 1 professional (part time).
Size: 33,413 maps; 185 atlases; 3 globes; 5 relief models; 44,615 aerial photographs; 1,372 reference books and gazetteers.
Annual Accessions: 3,600 maps; 20 atlases; 1,000 aerial photographs; 130 reference books and gazetteers.
Area Specialization: Canada; Québec; Mauricie-Bois-Francs region (Trois-Rivières).
Subject Specialization: topography; cadastral; political land use.
Dates: 1900 - (100%).
Classification System: Boggs-Lewis.
Collections Cataloged.
Depository for: NTS (Canada); Quebec Ministère Energie et Ressources.
Serves: students; faculty; employees; public;. Mon.–Fri 9 a.m.–4:30 p.m. (Seats 30; 350 readers served per month).
Interlibrary Loan Available.
Reproduction Facility: photocopy.
Publications: Liste d'acquisitions (interne).

SASKATCHEWAN

Regina

799. SASKATCHEWAN ARCHIVES BOARD
Mailing address: University of Regina; Street Address: 3303 Hillsdale St.
Regina, Saskatchewan S4S 0A2
Established 1945.
Telephone: 306/565-4067.
Contact Person: Margaret Hutchison, Staff Archivist.
Staff: 1 professional (part time).
Size: 7,763 maps; 9 atlases.
Area Specialization: Province of Saskatchewan.
Dates: 1800-1899 (4%); 1900 - (96%).
Classification System: In-house system.

Collections Cataloged. (85%).
Serves: students; faculty; employees; public. Mon.–Fri. 8 a.m.–5 p.m. (Seats 30).
Reproduction Facility: quickcopy.

800. UNIVERSITY OF REGINA
Faculty of Arts
Map Library
Regina, Saskatchewan S4S 0A2
Telephone: 306/584-4401.
Contact Person: Laura Ross, Map Libn.
Staff: 6 non-professional (part time).
Size: 25,000 maps; 150 atlases; 11 globes; 20 relief models; 18,000 aerial photographs; 8 serials (titles received).
Area Specialization: western Canada.
Subject Specialization: topography.
Special Cartographic Collections: topographical maps; aerial photographs.
Classification System: local system.
Collections Cataloged.
Depository for: NTS (Canada); USGS (Topo.).
Serves: students; faculty; employees; public. Mon.–Fri. 8:30 a.m.–4:30 p.m.; Sat. closed; Sun. closed. (Seats 20; 400 readers served per month).
Reproduction Facility: photocopy.

Saskatoon

801. SASKATCHEWAN ARCHIVES BOARD
Murray Memorial Building, University of Saskatchewan
Saskatoon, Saskatchewan S7N 0W0
Established 1945.
Telephone: 306/664-5832.
Contact Person: Lloyd Rodwell, Staff Archivist.
Staff: 1 professional (part time); nil non-professional (full time).
Size: 6,468 maps; 4 atlases.
Area Specialization: Province of Saskatchewan.
Dates: 1800-1899 (4%); 1900 - (96%).
Classification System: In-house system.
Collections Cataloged. (85%).
Serves: students; faculty; employees; public. Mon.–Fri. 8 a.m.–5 p.m.; Sat. closed; Sun. closed. (Seats 13; 8 readers served per month).
Reproduction Facility: quickcopy.

802. SASKATCHEWAN URBAN AFFAIRS
Community Planning Services
122-Third Avenue North
Saskatoon, Saskatchewan S7K 2H6
Established 1977.
Telephone: 306/664-5397.
Contact Person: Nicholas D. Hazen, Chartered Cartographer.
Staff: 1 professional (full time).
Size: 960 maps; 6 atlases; 1,000 aerial photographs; 4 reference books and gazetteers.
Annual Accessions: 96 maps; 100 aerial photographs.
Area Specialization: Saskatchewan Province.
Subject Specialization: urban planning.
Collections Cataloged.
Depository for: NTS (Canada).
Serves: students; employees; public. Mon.–Fri. 8:30 a.m.–5:00 p.m. (Seats 6; 25 readers served per month).
Reproduction Facility: photocopy; Diazo.

803. UNIVERSITY OF SASKATCHEWAN
Library
Government Publications, Maps, and Microforms
Saskatoon, Saskatchewan S7N 0W0
Telephone: 306/343-3141.
Contact Person: Andrew Hubbertz, Head of Government
Publications, Maps & Microforms.
Staff: 1 non-professional (part time).
Size: 29,000 maps; 700 atlases; 20 reference books and
gazetteers.
Annual Accessions: 500 maps; 60 atlases; 2 reference
books and gazetteers.
Area Specialization: Canada.
Subject Specialization: topography.
Dates: pre-1800 (1%); 1800-1899 (5%); 1900 - (96%).
Classification System: Boggs-Lewis.
Collections Cataloged.
Serves: students; faculty; employees; public. Mon.–Fri. 8:30
a.m.–5 p.m.; except summer: Mon.–Fri. 8:30–4 p.m.; Sat. 12
noon–4 p.m. (150 readers served per month).
Interlibrary Loan Available.

YUKON

Whitehorse

804. YUKON ARCHIVES
Box 2703
Whitehorse, Yukon Y1A 2C6
Telephone: 403/667-5321.
Contact Person: Charles Maier, Map and Government
Records Archivist.
Size: 3,000 maps; 200 atlases.
Annual Accessions: 300 maps; 30 atlases.
Area Specialization: Yukon Territory.
Special Cartographic Collections: plans of placer mining
dredges operating in Yukon.
Dates: pre-1800 (1%); 1800-1899 (39%); 1900 - (60%).
Classification System: local system.
Collections Cataloged.
Depository for: NTS (Canada).
Serves: public. Tues.–Fri. 9 a.m.–5 p.m. (Seats 25; 290
readers served per month).

INDEX

The numbers in this index are entry numbers, not page numbers.

A

Acadia University
751

Accession lists (University of Calgary)
719

Accidents in N.A. Mountaineering
461

Adams, Agnes
395

Adams, Virginia M.
314

Adirondack Museum Library
444

Aeonautical charts
499

Aerial photographs
371

Aerial photographs of Minnesota, 1937 to date
357

Aerial photography
See also Satellite imagery
96, 103, 131, 144, 150, 214, 319, 321, 377,
393, 457, 478, 547, 688, 700, 720, 726,
756, 782
Bibliography
214
Broward County, Florida collection
146
World War II Pacific Islands Collection
172

Aeronautical Charts
292, 384, 414

Agee (Rucker) collection of historical and regional maps
2

Agriculture
42, 50, 144, 338, 390, 455, 457, 538, 593,
624, 752

Aiken, Jean R.
579

Akron
University of Akron
Bierce Library
507

Alabama
Archives and History Department
5
Colleges and universities
University of Alabama
7, 8
Anthropology Department
6
Development Office, depository
3
Geological Survey, depository
8
History
2, 3, 5, 8

Alameda County
History
62

Alaska
Colleges and universities
University of Alaska
Elmer E. Rasmuson Library
11
Institute of Marine Science Library
12

Geological and geophysical maps and reports, depository
14
Geological and Geophysical Surveys Division
10
History
9, 10
Natural Resources Department
15
Geological and Geophysical Surveys, Division
14
State agencies, depository
13
State Libraries and Museum Division
13

Alaska Packers Association
13

Alaska photography collections: Old Alaska Mapping Photography; USGS Alaska Autopositives; Alaska High Altitude photography microfilms
9

Alberta
Colleges and universities
University of Alberta
723
Energy and Natural Resources Department
720
Provincial Archives
722
Research Council
721
Surveys and Mapping Bureau
Transportation Department
722

Albion College
327

Albuquerque
History
427

Albuquerque Public Library
427

Alexander, Elizabeth
149

Alfred University
441

Allen collection of maps of the world, North America, Pacific Northwest, 1511–1865
683

Allen County Public Library
218

Allen, Virginia
123

Allin, Janet
776

Alma College
329

Alten, Diana
563

American Alpine Club
461

American Alpine Journal
461

American Antiquarian Society
325

American Automobile Association
655

American Commission to Negotiate Peace
144

American Congress on Surveying and Mapping. Map Design Competition collection
143

American Map Collection
143

American Revolutionary War
422

American settlement collection
588

Ames Library of South Asia, pre-1900 maps of India and South Asia
357

Amherst College
296

Amling, Russell K.
354

Amoskeag Industries, Inc. collection of plot plans, street plans, industrial development plans
406

Amoskeag Manufacturing Co. collection: Merrimack River, Amoskeag Canals, Steet plans, profiles, plot plans, building plans
406

Andersen, Thomas K.
75

Anderson, David S.
673

Anderson, Joanne
80

Anderson, Verl A.
547

Andrews, Mary
717

Andrews University
James White Library
334

Annotated Mediagraphy of Old Maps in the KU Map Library
250

Antarctic collection
665

Anthropology
17, 414

Antioch College
532

Antiquarian map collection: Illinois, 19th century; Great Lakes area, 17th and 18th century; Eastern Europe and the Russian Empire, 16th to 19th century
198

Antiquarian maps
See Rare Maps

Appalachian State University
485

Archaeology
10, 17, 172

Archeology
273

Architectural plan collection of Nova Scotia firms and buildings
748

Architecture
See also Building plans
744, 789, 793, 797

Archivo General de Indias maps of Florida and the southeastern United States
149

ARCRIC Library Services and Information
745
Area analysis
761
Arizona
Colleges and universities
Arizona State University
22
Northern Arizona University
18
University of Arizona
Geology and Mineral Technology Bureau
24
University Library, Map Collection
25
Historical Society/Arizona Heritage Center
23
Mines and Mineral Resources Department
20
Museum of Northern Arizona
17
Arizona Library, Archives and Public Records Department
19
Arkansas
Colleges and universities
Arkansas State University
28
University of Arkansas
27
University of Central Arkansas
26
Armstrong, Dr. Helen Jane
150
Art
435
ASCS collection of aerial photo-maps of West Virginia counties
688
Association of Canadian Map Libraries Bulletin
742
Atlas and Map Acquisitions
43
Atlas collection (strong in Ptolemy and Ortelius)
217
Atlas collection, U.W.O. map library (University of Western Ontario)
760
Aubrey, M. K.
722
Auburn University
1
Augustana College
209
Aurora Public Library
185
Austin, Ian A.
751
Austin Peay State University
Felix G. Woodward Library
604
Australia
Division of National Mapping
depositories
British Columbia
728
Geological Survey
depository
374
Natural Development Department, depository
207
Topographical, geological depositories
787
Australia, depository
214
Australia, map depositories
58
Automobile Club of Southern California, depository
48

Ayers, Janet
202

B

Babson College
321
Backman, Lisa
298
Bahamas collection
153
Bailey, Alberta S.
27
Baird, Dennis
181
Baker, Grace E.
89
Baldwin, Janet
465
Ball State University
226
Baltimore
Enoch Pratt Free Library
284
History
295
Bangor Public Library
276
Barkdull, Margery K.
140
Barnaba, Eugenia M.
455
Barnett, LeRoy
344
Barnette, Donald
530
Barrettt, Buckley
76
Barrick, Susan
656
Bartlett, Eleanor A.
135
Barto, Steve
478
Baruth, Barbara
694
Baruth, Christopher
699
Base maps
438, 760, 776
Basic Information Sources: Maps (guide)
154
Batchelder, Bob
719
Bates College
Ladd Library
278
Bathymetry
93, 142, 173, 324, 495, 746
Battisti, Josephine
715
Baty, Laurie A.
288
Baumruk, Robert
190
Baylor University
Moody Library
633
Texas Collection
634
Bayr, Klaus
404
Bean, Cathie
221
Beans (George H.) collection of Japanese Maps of the Tokugawa Era
727
Beasecker, Robert
328
Becker, Ronald L.
416

Bedford Institute of Oceanography
746
Beil, Eloise
479
Bell, Marion V.
284
Beloit College
Col. Robert H. Morse Library
690
Belvedere collection of Baja California maps and books
82
Bemidji State University
350
Bennett collection of early survey maps of South Georgia
170
Bennett, Josiah, "The Cartographic Treasures of the Lilly Library" in *The Map Collector*
217
Benson (Kenneth R.) collection of forest maps Cedar City, Utah area
635
Berea College
258
Berens, John
346
Berg, J.
69
Bergen, John V.
205
Berkeley Public Library
31
Bernice P. Bishop Museum
172
Bernier-Feeley, Elise
316
Berthelsen, Barbara
456
Berthelsen, John F.
403
Biblical archaeology
414
Biblio: Collection Development Statement (accession list)
214
Bibliographies
Data bases
665
Bicycle maps
226
Biehl, Nancy
772
Biogeography
172, 725
Biography
545
Biography, Bostonians
299
Biology
17, 42, 529
Bird's eye view collection of Nebraska
394
Bird's-eye Views of Wisconsin Communities
696
Birmingham Public Library
2
Black, Anne
233
Blaeu (Joan) *Grooten Atlas*
162
Blair (Montgomery) collection of 19th century maps
143
Blakely (William A.) collection of printed maps of Texas, 1820–1890
634
Blazek, Inka
529
Blazquez, Dr. Carlos H.
151
Bloomfield

History
409
Bloomfield Public Library
409
Blust, Sandra
559
Board of Public Works Inventory Virginia
669
Boardman, Richard
571
Boatman, Mildred, *Maps in the St. Louis Public Library*
382
Bock, Jean S.
23
Boehm, Hilda
59
Boise State University
180
Boldrick, Sam
153
Bosse, C.D.R. Maurice
306
Bosse, David
333
Boston
History
299
Boston Athenaeum
298
Boston Stein Club Map Room
309
Bostonian Society
299
Bostonians, biographical material
299
Boswell, Roy V.
45
Bouchard, Richard A.
782
Bouchette, Joseph
794
Boundaries
74, 144
Bowdoin College Library
277
Bowling Green State University
509
Boyer, Jack K.
437
Brainerd, Jean
712
Bramucci, Nancy M.
283
Branner (J.C.) collection on geology and mining in Brazil 1848–1940
99
Brantley (William H.) collection of 18th and 19th century maps of Alabama and the Southeast
3
Brennan, Thomas G.
587
Brey, Francis
225
Bridgeport Public Library
116
Bridgewater College
Alexander Mack Memorial Library
652
Bridgewater State College
Clement C. Maxwell Library
305
Brigham Young University
Harold B. Lee Library
637
Brinkman, Dr. Leonard W.
609
British Battle Plans, Maps and Charts of the American Revolutionary War, 1775–1793
45
British Columbia

Colleges and universities
University of British Columbia
Geography Department
726
Library, Historical Maps and Cartographic Archives
727
Library, Map Division
728
History
727
Provincial Archives
732
British Ordnance Survey map collection
582
Brock University
766
Broken Hill Mine—Australia collection of reports and maps
99
Brooklyn
Historical Society
446
History
447
Brooklyn College, CUNY
445
Brooklyn Public Library
447
Brosky, Catherine M.
576
Browar, Lisa
476
Broward County, Florida
Aerial photography collection
146
Brown, Jo. B.
687
Brown, Regina A.
521
Brown University
John Carter Brown Library
588
Rockefeller Library
589
Sciences Library
590
Brownlee, Richard S.
371
Bruce, Robert K.
355
Brun, Christian. *Guide to the Manuscript Maps in the William L. Clements Library*
333
Bryan (J.P.) collection of printed maps of Texas, 1656–1900
634
Bryan, Vivian
647
Bryn Mawr College
555
Buck, Aileen
503
Buckallew, Fritz A.
534
Buckmaster clollection of late 19th century maps of Pacific Northwest, California, Alaska
683
Bucknell University
Ellen Clarke Bertrand Library
567
Buffalo
Buffalo and Erie County Historical Society
448
Buffalo and Erie County Public Library
449
History
449
Building plans
See also Sanborn fire insurance maps
61, 406

Inspection
789
Bumgardner, Georgia Brady
325
Burhans, Skip
206
Burke, E. Dawn
423
Burns, John
73
Burton Historical Collection of the Detroit Public Library
336
Business
131
Busse, Lawrence R.
360
Buthod, Craig
540
Butt, Paul L.
26

C

Cabeen, S. K.
464
Cadastral maps
See also Land ownership, Real estate
416, 512, 734, 796, 798
Cahow, Dr. Adam
691
Calgary
University of Calgary
719
Calhoon, William
122
California
Colleges and universities
California Academy of Sciences
82
California Institute of Technology
64
California Polytechnic State University
91
California State College
San Bernardino
76
Stanislaus
102
California State University
Chico
Geography Department
38
Meriam Library
39
Fresno
43
Fullerton
Geography Department, Map Library
44
Library Collection for the History of Cartography
45
Long Beach
Geography Department
51
Library and Learning Resources
52
Los Angeles
54
Northridge
61
Humboldt State University
29
San Diego State University
81, 81
San Francisco State University
Geography Department
87
Library
88
University of California
Berkeley

Bancroft Library
32
East Asiatic Library, Map Collection
34
General Library
36
General Library, Earth Sciences Library
35
Geography Department
33
Water Resources Center Archives
37
Davis
42
Irvine
47
Los Angeles
Geology-Geophysics Library
57
Map Library
58
University Research Library
59
Riverside
Earth Sciences Department
70
Library, Government Publications Department
71
Physical Sciences Library
72
San Diego
Central University Library, Map Section
48
Scripps Institution of Oceanography Library
49
Santa Barbara
93
Santa Cruz
96
Counties
89
Historical Society, Library
83
Historical USGS collection
87
History
39, 56, 62, 65, 73
Mines and Geology Division
30, 43, 52, 84, 99, 103
State agencies, depository
65, 73
State Archives
73
State Automobile Club, depository
48
State Lands Commission
74
State Library
75
California & Other Early Maps Illustrating the History of Cartography, 1375–1873 (O.P.)
45
California imagery collection
93
Camp, Paul Eugen
158
Campbell, Ina
409
Campbell, Margaret E.
745
Campbell University
Carrie Rich Memorial Library
486
Canada
Aeronautical charts
depositories
756, 776
Geological Survey, depositories in Canada
Alberta
719, 721
British Columbia
728

New Brunswick
740
Nova Scotia
746, 747, 751
Ontario
753, 758, 760, 761, 762, 764, 765, 766, 773, 774, 776, 777
Québec
792, 794, 795, 796
Toronto
775
Geological Survey, depositories in the United States
Alabama
8
California
29, 58, 69, 99
Colorado
105
Connecticut
119, 125
District of Columbia
137, 143
Florida
147
Illinois
197
Maine
279
Maryland
292
Massachusetts
307
Michigan
343
Mississippi
367
Missouri
374
New Jersey
423
New York
442, 456
North Dakota
504
Ohio
513, 514, 521, 531
South Dakota
601
Texas
624
Virginia
652, 664
Wisconsin
699
History
724, 727, 755, 794
Hydrographic Service, depositories
Alberta
719, 724
British Columbia
728, 732, 733
New Brunswick
741
Newfoundland
742
Nova Scotia
745, 746, 747
Ontario
756, 765, 776, 778
Québec
794
Land Inventory, depositories
New Brunswick
740
Ontario
765, 776
Land use, depositories in the United States
Michigan
338

National Topographic Survey, depositories in Canada
804
Alberta
719, 720, 722, 723, 724, 725
British Columbia
726, 728, 732, 733
Manitoba
736, 737
Maritimes
745
New Brunswick
740, 741
Newfoundland
742
Nova Scotia
745, 746, 747, 749, 751
Ontario
752, 754, 755, 756, 759, 760, 761, 763, 764, 765, 766, 767, 768, 770, 772, 774, 776, 778, 779
Prince Edward Island
781
Québec
782, 783, 784, 787, 790, 791, 792, 794, 795, 796, 798
Saskatchewan
799, 802
Toronto
775
National Topographic Survey, depositories in the United States
California
58, 61
Connecticut
119, 125
District of Columbia
140, 143
Florida
155
Illinois
199, 214
Indiana
233
Iowa
246
Maryland
292
Minnesota
357
New Hampshire
403
New York
463, 468
Ohio
513, 520
Pennsylvania
583
Vermont
644
Virginia
650
Washington
672
Wisconsin
691, 697, 699
Province administration maps
414
Provincial government aerial photography collection 1952–1972
775
Public Archives
National Map Collection
764
Canada Aerial photography
775
Canada Company collection of general and land tenure
770
Canadian series collection of maps
764

Canadian West Discovered (exhibition catalog)
718
Canals
406, 416, 424, 533, 560, 572, 594, 766
Canan, Julia
528
Caparros, Ilona
415
Cape Breton
University College of Cape Breton
Beaton Institute
750
Capone, Dr. Donald L.
147
Capps, Marie T.
484
Captured German prints collection of World
War II, Europe
144
Carleton College
359
Carleton University
761
Carlson, Cathy
666
Carlton, Dr. Don E.
617
Carnegie Library of Pittsburgh
576
Carnegie-Stout Public Library
241
Carr, Betty H.
405
Carrington collection of China trade maps
592
Carson, Kit
437
Carson-Newman College
606
Cartobibliography of Greater Vancouver
727
Cartographers
794
Cartographic and image-processing software
collection
564
Cartographic Archives maps from Historical
Manuscript Collections
727
"Cartographic Resources of the New York
Historical Society," *The Map Collections*
467
Cartographic Treasures of the Lilly Library in
The Map Collector
217
*Cartographie et la documentation
cartographique, la*
794
Cartography
9, 142, 564, 571, 665
History
2, 4, 45, 144, 195, 337, 347, 403, 468, 516,
727, 756
Methods and techniques
58, 196, 449, 468, 709, 794
Readings in cartography collection of articles
and reprints
776
Cartothéque, la
794
*Carto-03: répertoire, cartobibliographique sur la
région de Québec*
794
Carver, Larry
93
Case Western Reserve University
Sears Library
515
Casey (Albert E.) collection of maps from
Ireland, particularly from the Ordnance Survey
3

Cashman, John
445
Casper College
Goodstein Foundation Library
710
Casserly, Joan
86
Castle, Joseph D.
270
*Catalog of Aerial Photos in the Map Collection
of the University Library*
96
Catalog of Maps Mounted for Classroom Use
96
Catalog of maps, ships' papers and logbooks
660
*Catalogue collectif des atlas du des
cartothéques universitaires Québec*
794
*Catalogue of the W. H. Pugsley Collection of
Early Maps of Canada*
786
Catawba College
Corriher-Linn-Black Library
501
Cavagna collection of Italian maps
214
Cave map collection
377
Caves
377
Census
See also United States—Bureau of the
Census
240, 311, 501, 619, 654
Indiana
215
Census collection of reports from New Spain
to the King of Spain
619
Census dime file collection
564
Centre for Newfoundland Studies collection
742
Cerny, Iva
735
Chace, Laura L.
511
Chamberlin, David R.
732
Chandrasekhar, Ratna
305
Chang, Dr. Kang-tsung
504
Chappell, Barbara A.
664
Chattanooga-Hamilton County Bicentennial
Library
602
*Checklist of Bouchette Maps in the Collections
of the Rare Book Department of the McGill
University Library*
786
*Checklist of Canadian Immigration Atlases held
in the Collections of the Rare Book
Department of the McGill University Library*
786
Checklist of Fire Insurance Plans
727
*Checklist of Printed Maps of the Middle West
to 1900*
195
*Checklist of Printed Maps of the Middle West
to 1900: V. 12 Nebraska*
394
Chen, Alice S.
720
Chen, Robert
188
Cherry Hill map collection of Albany capital
district region
439

Chesapeake Bay
283
Chicago
Colleges and universities
University of Chicago
Regenstein Library
197
Historical Society
189
Chicago Public Library
Government Publications Department
190
Social Sciences and History Information Center
191
Christensen, Lynette
204
Christian, Gayle
164
Christian missions
469
Christmas, Garey
67
Christopher Newport College
Capt. John Smith Library
659
Church of Jesus Christ of Latter-day Saints
Genealogical Library
638
Churchill, Robert R.
645
Cincinnati
Colleges and universities
University of Cincinnati
Library, Geology Department
513, 514
Historical Society
511
Public Library of Cincinnati and Hamilton County
512
Cincinnati and Hamilton County collection of
old maps
512
Cities and towns
Names of Cities, Urban areas and geography,
Urban planning
55, 58, 86, 118, 132, 197, 226, 303, 345,
459, 459, 507, 543, 566, 594, 596, 634,
644, 654, 676, 733, 764, 796
Historic urban plan series
507
Japanese cities collection
34
Ohio
522
Citrus areas
151
City planning
See Urban planning
Civil War
See also Mason-Dixon Line
2, 160, 210, 484, 518, 572, 591, 666, 668
Battle map collection
292
Virginia battlefield map collection
651
Claremont Colleges
40
Clarie, Thomas C.
125
Clarion University of Pennsylvania
Carlson Library
557
Clark, Robert M.
392
Clark, Suzanne
644
Clark University
326
Clausen, Eric
506
Claypool collection—geologic maps
636

Clemson University
  Robert Muldrow Cooper Library
    593
Cleveland area plat books collection (origianl and microfilm)
    516
Cleveland Public Library
    516
Cleveland State University
    517
Climatological data collection for New England from 1896 to present
    324
Climatology
  See Meteorology
Clinch Valley College
    670
Coal
    131, 262, 688, 688
  Virginia map collection, 1840–1920
    651
Coal geology
    559
Coal resource map collection of United States and foreign areas
    685
Coastal processes
    746
Coasts
    634
Cobb, David A.
    214
Cobb, David Allan, *Vermont Maps Prior to 1900: An Annotated Cartobibliography*
    646
Coe Library
    714
Cohlan, Gladys
    132
Cole, Howson W.
    668
Cole, Orrin
    533
Colgate University
  Geography Department
    453
Collection for the History of Cartography
    45
Collection Guide
    214
Collection of maps published before 1850
    127
Colley, Dr. Charles C.
    615
Collins, Evron
    509
Collins, Janet
    672
Colonial period
    434
Colonization collection
    588
Colorado
  Colleges and universities
    Colorado State University
      112
    University of Colorado
      Colorado Springs
        106
      University Libraries
        104
    University of Southern Colorado
      115
  Historical Society
    107
  History
    107
  School of Mines
    Arthur Lakes Library
      113
Colson, Marcia
    16

Columbia University
  Lamont-Doherty Geological Observatory
    472
  Lehman Library, Map Room
    463
Columbus
  History
    522
  Public Library of Columbus and Franklin County
    522
Columbus College
  Simon Schwob Memorial Library
    166
Computer graphics
    564
Computer mapping
    58, 442
Concordia University
    784
Confederacy, Museum of
    666
Confederate imprints
    160
Connecticut
  Colleges and universities
    128
    Central Connecticut State University
      124
    Southern Connecticut State College
    Hilton C. Buley Library
      125
  Historical Society
    117
  History
    116, 118
  State Library
    118
Contour lake map collection of Indiana
    218
Contra Costa County Library
    66
Conway, James E.
    335
Cook, Kevin L.
    28
Coombs, James
    386
Cooper, Dr. John E.
    498
Cooper, Inez S.
    635
Cooper (Laurence C.) collection of maps of Glen Canyon, Colorado area
    635
Copeley, William
    401
Cornell University
  College of Agriculture and Life Services
    455
  John M. Olin Library
    456
  Remote Sensing Program
    457
Corsaro, James
    439
Corse, Jack
    725
Cosmography
    588
Cotten, Alice R.
    489
Council Bluffs
  Free Public Library
    236
Counties
    3, 89, 96, 197, 211, 214, 251, 257, 408, 459, 468, 634, 796
  Early New York county atlas collection
    453
  Indiana
    224

U.S. county highway map collection
    292
West Virginia
    688
Cox, Barbara
    640
Cox, Bruce B.
    376
Cox, Richard J.
    5
Crawford County Historical Society
    568
Crawford, Dr. Maria Luisa
    555
Creaser, John
    35
Crissinger, John D.
    649, 650
Crofut, Florence
    117
Crotts, Joe
    39
Cruse, Larry
    48
Cuba collection
    153
Culture
    267
Culver, Jerry B.
    695
Cunliffe, William H.
    144
Curnoe, W. Glenn
    759
Current Geographical Publications, Section III— Selected Maps
    699
Current Reference Sheets (Missouri, Land Survey Repository)
    378
Curtis, Gwen
    263
Cushing, John D.
    301
Cussins, Marcia
    377
Custer, Dr. Stephan G.
    390
Cyr, Paul A.
    313

D

Daily weather map collection from most countries in the world
    294
Dalhousie University
  Macdonald Science Library
    747
Dallas Public Library
    622
Dalligan, Alice C.
    336
Dallin Aerial Survey Company collection of aerial photographs
    131
Danforth, Susan L.
    588
Darbee, Leigh
    223
Dartmouth College
    403
Data Base describing map, aerial, photo, and space imagery holdings of federal state and non-governmental agencies
    665
Data bases
    665
Davenport, Janet
    397
Davis, Beverly
    490

Davis, Dr. R. Laurence
441
Davis, Harry O.
291
Davis, Michael E.
228
Dayton and Montogmery County Public Library
524
Dayton Museum of Natural History
525
De Muth, Phyllis
13
Dean, Grant T.
189
Decouverte du Mon de XVI–XVIII Siecle
788
DeGraaff, Jerome
551
Delaware
Colleges and universities
University of Delaware
Morris LIbrary
130
Historical Society
132
History
129, 129
State Agencies
129
State Archives
129
Delaware and Raritan Canal Commission
collection of early 20th century canal maps
416
Demography
See also Census, Population
240, 414, 564, 633
Denver Public Library
108, 109
DePauw University
Roy O. West Library
221
Derksen, Charlotte
99
Desbarats, Aileen
765
Descriptive List of the Map Collection in the
Pennsylvania State Archives
560
Desmarais, Christiane
791
Detroit Historical Museum
335
Detroit Public Library
Burton Historical Collection
336
History and Travel Department
337
Detroit Public Library's Map Collection
337
Developing countries, national atlas collection
145
Dewitt Historical Society
458
Dickerson, Karen
486
Dickmeyer, John N.
218
Dictionary Catalog of the Map Division of New
York Public Library
468
Dictionary Catalog of the Water Resources
Center Archives
37
Digital cartographic and imagery data
collection–Terrain models
564
Discovery and exploration
2, 4, 13, 59, 120, 144, 214, 253, 333, 392,
437, 518, 539, 549, 588, 615, 639, 641,
718, 732, 757, 770, 788

Early Pacific collection of printed maps
172
District of Columbia
Public Library
Georgetown Regional Branch Library
134
Martin Luther King Memorial Library
135, 136
District of Columbia real estate collection of
atlases 1879–1976
136
Dixon, Janet
27
Documentation cartographique sur le Québec
794
Dodd, Jack L.
603
Doherty, Joan
413
Dolgopolov collection of Russian, America and
Pacific exploration materials
13
Dominion Lands Survey collection
734
Domitz, Gary
182
Donahue, Harold
608
Donkin, Kate
755
Donnell, Marianne
156
Dow, Judith
342
Downey, Mary
367
Drake University
Cowles Library
238
Drew, Laurel E.
427
Dubreuil, Lorraine
787
Duffy, Mary Anne Burns
584
Dufour, Lydia A.
466
Dugan, Frank
453
Duke University
Perkins Library
492
Dulka, Michael
470
Duluth Public Library
352
Dunkle, William M.
324
Dunn, Barbara E.
177
Dunn, Elizabeth
241
Duong, Dr. Buu
652
Dupuy, Ernest J.
414
Dvorzak, Marie
358

E

Eaglesfield, Jean T.
309, 310
Earlham College
229
Early 20th century collection of central Oregon
city maps
543
Earth resources
See also Fuel resources
508

Earth sciences
49, 245, 266, 414, 601, 627, 664, 762
East and Cathay
45
East Orange Public Library
411
Eastham (Melville) collection of printed maps
dating from 1493 through the 18th century
143
Easton, William W.
207
Echols collection of Southeast Asia maps
456
Ecole Polytechnique
785
Ecological Characterization of Coastal Maine
279
Ecology
279
Economic geography
141, 520
Economic geology
57, 377
Economics
131, 267, 332, 500, 588, 725, 752
Edmonds, Michael
696
Education
496
Edwards, Anne
372
Eger, Stephany
434
Eighteenth and nineteenth century collection of
maps of Europe, Asia, Africa and the
Americas
98
Eighteenth century map collection of Cape
Breton and Atlantic Canada
750
Eidblom, Nancy C.
474
Eleutherian Mills-Hagley Foundation
131
Elgin Gail Borden Public Library
201
Ellis, Ed
230
Ellison collection of Trans-Mississippi West
217
Embers, Richard L.
250
Energy resources
See also Fuel resources, Gas, Oil, Petroleum
7, 114, 212, 776
Enggass, Dr. Peter M.
320
Engineering
142, 144, 457, 744, 789
Engineering geology
363
Engineering Societies Library
464
Engle, Monica
111
English, Cynthia
298
English Origin of the Americas, Maps & Charts
1486–1808
45
Enoch Pratt Free Library
284
Environment
692, 782
Environmental engineering
391
Environmental geology
365
Environmental planning
709
Environmental protection
343

Environmental sciences
779
Erchul, Comm. Ronald
658
Erie County
Buffalo and Erie County Historical Society
448
History
449
EROS Data Center Browse Files collection
93
Erskine-DeWitt manuscript collection of the
American Revolutionary War period
467
Erves, Tony
369
Essex Institute
James Duncan Phillips Library
318
Ethier, Patricia
362
European history
217
Evans, Lewis
214
Everard, Wayne M.
271
Exploration
See Discovery and exploration
Explorers Club
James B. Ford Library
465

F

Facsimiles of Portolan charts belonging to the
Hispanic Society of America
466
Faden (William) collection of French and Indian
and Revolutionary War maps
143
Fa:DIARESISgerstrom, David M.
104
Fair (Ethel M.) collection of pictorial maps
143
Fairchild Aerial Photograph Collection
103
Falco, Nicholas
460
Fall River Collection of maps circa 1850, 1880,
1820
315
FAO/UNESCO collection of soil maps of the
world
499
Farrell, Barbara
761
Farrell, Maureen
516
Faul, Carol
575
Field Museum of Natural History
192
Field studies
See Surveys
Fillmore (Millard) collection of 19th century
maps
143
Filson Club
264
Finding List for Guide Books to North America
786
Finkel, Kenneth
573
Fire insurance
See also Sanborn fire insurance maps
109, 571, 727, 752, 770
Canada
787
Collection of Iowa city and town maps
246

Québec
791
Fire insurance collection of atlases of
Philadelphia
571
Fire insurance maps of Iowa cities and
towns— A List of Holdings
239
Fisher, Dr. James
159
Flannery, Prof. James J.
700
Fletcher and Faribault collection of Nova
Scotia maps
751
Fletcher, Patricia
461
Flint Journal Editorial Library
339
Floods and flood control
57, 365, 369, 608, 665
Florida
Colleges and universities
Florida Atlantic University
S.E. Wimberly Library
146
Florida International University
152
Florida State University
156
University of Florida
University Libraries, Map Library
150
Yonge (P.K.) Library or Florida History
149
University of South Florida
Library, Documents
157
University of Southern Florida Library, Florida
Map Collection
158
University of West Florida
John C. Pace Library
154
Geology Bureau
155
History
149, 154, 156, 158
Florida Historical Society Collection of maps of
Florida
158
Flower, Eric S.
280
Flynt, Billie J., Jr.
497
Fogg, Larry
543
Forbes Library
316
Force (Peter) map collection
143
Forest and forestry
See also United States—Forest Service,
United States—National Forests
95, 181, 229
Forestry
229, 393, 430, 499, 635, 717
Fort Lewis College
111
Fort Worth Public Library
627
Fortier, John W.
770
Fortney, Mary
203
Forts
5, 594
Foscue (Edwin J.) Map Library
624
Foster, Theodore S.
508

Fouts, Dorothy
624
Fowler (Thaddeus) collection of panoramic
maps of American cities
143
Fox, Herbert S.
43
Fox, Prof. John F.
426
France
History
4, 131
Francis, Flora
752
Franklin County land ownership map collection
522
Frazier (Daniel B.) collection of 19th–20th
century manuscript maps of the Jersey shore
416
Free Library of Philadelphia
571
Freels, Dr. Edward T.
606
Freeman, Allen
410
Freeman collection of early maps of America
214
Freeman, H. Gera
97
Freier, Arlene
153
French in America
788
Froborn, Jerome B.
713
Frontenac Sous Louis XV or Germain en Laye
France
788
Frostburg State College
291
Fry, Roy H.
194
Fuel resources
See also Energy resources, Gas, Oil,
Petroleum
109, 114, 343, 343
Fugulin, Céile
790
Fuhri, Fiona
375
Fur trade
437

G

Gagnon, Antoine
797
Gail Borden Public Library
201
Galbraith, Marc
254
Galik, Simone
418
Galkowski, Patricia E.
590
Gallalee Cartographic Collection
4
Galneder, Mary
697
Gannon, Barbara
407
Garant, Jean-Marc
789
Garrabrant, William A.
412
Garrett (John Work) Collection
287
Gas
343, 536
Gaspari-Bridges, Patricia
421

Gaswick, Carolyn
327
Gazeteers in Metropolitan Toronto Central Library
772
Geib, Jerry
247
Geiger, G. E.
1
Gelfand, Julia
47
Gelpke, Richard
304
Genealogy
427, 446, 458, 478, 483
General Drafting Co., Inc.
410
General Land Office collection of original survey maps
540
Geochemistry
10, 385, 391, 559, 743
Geodesy
142
Geodetic control
9, 665
Geodetic diagram collection of Oregon and northern California
546
Geography
See also Biogeography, Economic geography, historical geography, medical geography, political geography, social-cultural geography
54, 86, 105, 106, 121, 170, 172, 188, 250, 332, 343, 354, 393, 409, 414, 501, 520, 595, 606, 654, 701, 707, 737, 755, 779, 782, 794
Geology
165
Human
564
Physical
564
Geologic manuscript map collection of Pennsylvania
559
Geologic Map Index to 7.5' and 15' Quadrangles of California, 1883–1983
39
Geological surveys, depository, other states and national (non-USGS)
Oklahoma
536
Geology
See also Coal geology, Engineering geology, Lunar geology
10, 14, 17, 18, 22, 25, 27, 30, 35, 39, 43, 49, 52, 57, 61, 64, 70, 72, 84, 86, 90, 99, 106, 110, 111, 113, 114, 115, 121, 126, 128, 155, 156, 161, 162, 166, 173, 180, 181, 184, 186, 187, 192, 197, 198, 201, 206, 207, 209, 212, 216, 222, 228, 229, 232, 244, 256, 258, 261, 262, 265, 266, 274, 275, 278, 285, 307, 310, 312, 317, 319, 322, 323, 324, 328, 332, 338, 341, 343, 344, 345, 346, 348, 358, 363, 363, 365, 365, 374, 376, 377, 380, 385, 389, 390, 391, 393, 395, 398, 400, 403, 419, 421, 425, 429, 430, 431, 439, 441, 443, 445, 450, 452, 453, 457, 462, 464, 472, 475, 481, 487, 492, 497, 498, 500, 501, 505, 506, 508, 514, 515, 516, 521, 525, 526, 528, 529, 531, 533, 536, 538, 540, 541, 544, 550, 555, 559, 571, 576, 582, 585, 595, 601, 603, 604, 605, 606, 607, 609, 613, 616, 618, 621, 622, 623, 624, 626, 629, 631, 632, 640, 643, 648, 649, 654, 664, 670, 673, 674, 677, 678, 682, 685, 686, 688, 690, 702, 706, 711, 715, 716, 717, 719, 721, 723, 724, 728, 733, 735, 736, 743, 747, 751, 752, 753,

755, 758, 762, 766, 773, 774, 777, 782, 785, 787, 790, 796
Geomorphology
60, 212, 559, 725, 765, 779
Geophysical investigation
365
Geophysics
60, 99, 173, 310, 363, 385, 391, 487, 500, 536, 559, 664, 719, 743, 746, 753
George Mason University
Fenwick Library
654
George Washington University
Gelman Library
137
Georgia
Colleges and universities
Georgia Institute of Technology
Price Gilbert Memorial Library
162
Georgia Southern College
169
Georgia State University
Pullen Library
164
South Georgia College
William S. Smith Library
167
University of Georgia
Geography Department
159
Libraries, special Collections Division
160
Science Library, Map Collection
161
Valdosta State College
170
West Georgia College
Irvine Sullivan Ingram Library
165
Historical Society
168
History
170, 602
Surveyor General Department
163
Transportation Department, depository
161
Geosciences
90
Geothermal resources
57
Gerencher, Dr. Joseph J.
554
Gettysburg College
Musselman Library
558
Geyer, Barbara
630
Gibbs Paige
315
Giefer, Gerald J.
37
Gilbert, Holly
505
Gilcrease (Thomas) Institute of American History and Art
539
Giles, Partricia
502
Gillispie, Jim
285
Gilmer collection of Civil War maps
484
Gilmer (Jeremy Francis) collection of Civil War Maps
668
Ginsburgs, Ida G.
574
Glacier land forms
681

Glaciology
442, 681
Glass slide collection of economic, political and cultural subjects of the world from 1900–1930.
332
Glassboro State College
412
Glenbow Museum Library
718
Glendale
History
46
Glendale Central Library
46
Globes
646
Goff (Dr. John H.) collection of southern place names and historic places
163
Gondra collection of maps of early Paraguay
619
Gonzales, Anthony J.
669
Goodman, Susan
419
Goodwin (William Brownell) collection, 1934–1949
118
Gordon, Carol
698
Gordon, Martha
322
Gottselig, Len
718
Government Publications: Information guide #14
88
Graff, William P.
425
Grand Ocean
45
Grand Rapids Public Library
340
Grand Valley State College
Zumberge Library
328
Gravity
57, 715
Great Britain
Directorate of Overseas Surveys, depositories in Canada
Alberta
719, 721
New Brunswick
741
Nova Scotia
747
Ontario
759, 764, 779
Prince Edward Island
781
Québec
792, 794
Directorate of Overseas Surveys, depositories in the United States
8, 29, 137, 147, 367, 423, 504, 583, 652
California
58, 67
Colorado
105
Connecticut
119, 125
District of Columbia
143
Florida
153, 155
Illinois
197, 208
Maryland
292

Massachusetts
307
Michigan
328
New York
439, 470
Ohio
513, 531
South Dakota
601
Virginia
664
History
4
Topography
350
Great Lakes Cartographic Resource Center
760
Great Lakes collection of nautical charts
698
Great Plains Journal
535
Great Plains, Museum
535
Greaves, Susan
747
Green, Richard S.
246
Green Trails map collection
671
Gregory, Rona
311
Greve, Edward F.
707
Grissom, Helen
654
Grout Museum of History and Science
248
Guelph
University of Guelph
752
Guide de la cartothèque
(Univertsite de Sherbrooke)
796
Guide for Readers-Map Library
250
Guide la Cartotheque (Québec. Archives)
793
Guide to Ball State University Libraries Map Collection
226
Guide to Boston and Vicinity Maps
303
Guide to Cartographic Records in the National Archives
144
Guide to Cartographic Resources in the MSU Libraries (guide)
338
Guide to Geo-Abstracts Syracuse University
481
A Guide to Locating Maps in the Sciences Library (Brown University)
590
Guide to Maps in Alcuin Library
351
Guide to maps in the CSU Library (Colorado State University)
112
Guide to Pennsylvania State University Maps Section
583
Guide to Research in Geography
43
Guide to the Alaska Packers Association Records, 1891–1970
13
Guide to the Cartographic Resources in the UVM Bailey/Howe Library
644
Guide to the collection (University of Calgary)
719

Guide to the Dolgopolov Collection in the Alaska Historical Library
13
Guide to the G. W. Blunt Library
123
Guide to the Manuscript Maps in the William L. Clements Library
333
Guide to the Manuscripts and Archives in the West Virginia Collection
688
Guide to the Map Collection of the UNC Geology Library University of North Carolina
487
Guide to the map room
507
Guide to use of geological survey maps (guide)
515
Guildi (Alan F.) collection of 20th century American road maps
416
Gunter, Pauline
11
Gustavus Aldolphus College
364
Gutgesell, Stephen
519
Gutiérrez-Witt, Laura
619

H
Haacke, Don P.
180
Haas, Mary
30
Hadley, Rosemary H.
726
Hagen, Carlos B.
58
Hale, Elizabeth F.
788
Hall, Vivian S.
262
Hallam, Cheryl A.
9
Halliburton (Richard) Map Collection
422
Hamblin, Alden H.
643
Hamilton College
450
Hamilton, Elizabeth
740
Hamilton Public Library
754
Hammond Incorporated
414
Hammond Report
414
Hammur, Deborah
459
Hampden-Sydney College
657
Hand-painted collection of 16th century maps of relaciones geográficas
619
Hanes, Alice C.
662
Hanover College
222
Hansen, Joanne
349
Hanson (Thorsten) Scandinavian map collection
209
Harbors
5, 733
Harding, Diane
777
Harding, Kathryn
756

Harris collection of Civil War maps
591
Harris, June C., Detroit Public Library's Map Collection
337
Harris, Maureen
593
Harrison, Orion
169
Harrisse (Henry) collection
143
Hart, Lyn
286
Hartford
Metropolitan District depository
117
Hartford Public Library
119
Hartjen, Charles F.
77
Hartman (Charles) collection of 18–20th century manuscript South Jersey property and tax maps
416
Hartman, Jill
705
Hartman, Ruth D.
674
Hartmann collection of Southeast Asia maps
456
Hartwig, Deborah
385
Harvard University
Geological Sciences Library, Map Collection
307
Pusey Library, Harvard Map Collection
308
Hassell, Robert H.
18
Hastie, Iain
769
Haug, Mary Ellen
106
Hause, Aaron
388
Hauslab-Liechtenstein collection
143
Hausler, David
62
Haverford College
563
Hawaii
Colleges and universities
Hawaii Institute of Geophysics
173
Universities of Hawaii
Manoa
178
Hilo
171
Historical Society
177
State Archives
174
State Library
175, 176
Hayhurst, Ruth I.
686
Hazen, Nicholas
802
Hedrick, David T.
558
Heidlage, Robert
374
Hein, Paul G.
438
Heisser, David C. R.
312
Hemispheric Mapping Program, depositories
181
Hemperley, Marion R.
163

Henry, Marjorie R.
676
Henson, Stephen
275
Hess, Elmer B.
231
Hick, Sharon
774
Hickcox, David H.
527
Higginbotham, Jay
4
Highways and roads
See also Streets
77, 153, 158, 191, 211, 226, 253, 289, 292,
335, 345, 349, 362, 410, 413, 414, 416,
424, 430, 549, 560, 596, 654, 655, 772
Pre-World War II collection of Maps
545
Hihn (Frederick A.) collection of 19th century-
late land ownership of Santa Cruz County
96
Hill, John Davis
398
Hillary (Edmund) Map Room
465
Hiller, Steve
677
Hills (John) collection
143
Hines (General John L.) collection of World
War I maps of the western front in Belgium
and France
143
Hirsch, Sarah
539
Hirst, David R.
681
Hispanic America map collection
459
Hispanic Society of America
466
Historical collection of original and
photographic copies of Oklahoma and
Southwest maps
535
Historical geography
794
Historical map collection of Niagara Peninsula
766
Historical maps collection
250
Historical Maps in the Richardson Archives.
601
"Historical Maps of Nebraska" by Ann Reinert
in V. 14 no 1 Spring 1983 of Nebraska
Library Association Quarterly
394
Historical Resource Center
599
Historiology
752
History
See also discovery and exploration, Rare
maps, Subheading Historical Society under
names of places, Subheading History under
names of places
59, 78, 105, 210, 250, 273, 286, 331, 414,
468, 534, 634, 636, 637, 732, 759, 776
Hobart and William Smith Colleges
452
Hoehn, Philip
32, 36
Hoffman (Frederick L.) collection of maps on
Mexico, Central America, South America
273
Hofstra University
454
Hohenstein, Margaret
704
Holobeck, Noel C.
382

Holtzendorff collection of early Georgia history
and geography
170
Hordusky, Clyde
523
Hotchkiss (Jedediah) collection of Confederate
Civil War maps
143
House, Dorothy
17
How, Sarah E.
57
How to Find a Map in PCL (Perry-Castaneda
Library)
620
How to Locate Maps, Charts, and Atlases in
Map Room. (guide).
442
Howard, Bill
261
Howay-Reid collection of British Columbiana,
Canadiana
727
Howe (Admiral Lord Richard) collection of 18th
century maps
143
Howitson, Brenda
302
Hoyle, Stephen J.
685
Hubbertz, Andrew
803
Hudson, Alice C.
468
Huges, Jean
79
Hughes, Cleo A.
612
Humber, Amy
458
Humboldt State University
29
Hummel (Arthur W.) collection
143
Humphreys (A. A.) collection of Civil War maps
and railroad maps of the 1850's
572
Hunt, Amoes
101
Hunter, Marian
199
Huntingfield Corp. collection of Maryland maps
1565-1891
283
Hutchinson Public Library
249
Hutchison, Margaret
799
Hydrographic map collection of Atlantic Region
745
Hydrography
See also Water Resources
6, 49, 142, 172, 232, 292, 293, 324, 423,
428, 603, 730, 745, 766
Hydrology
10, 60, 99, 115, 124, 209, 212, 319, 363,
365, 395, 445, 498, 500, 559, 636, 752, 777

I

The Iberian Origin of the Americas, Maps &
Charts A.D. 1513–1851
45
Ice, Diana Carolyn
471
Idaho
Colleges and universities
Boise State University
180
Idaho State University
Eli M. Oboler Library
182

University of Idaho
181
History
179
State Historical Society
179
Ilisevich, Robert D.
568
Illinois
210
Colleges and universities
Eastern Illinois University
188
Illinois Institute of Technology
193
Illinois State University
Milner Library
207
Northern Illinois University
199
Southern Illinois University
Carbondale
Morris Library
186
Edwardsville
200
University of Illinois
Urbana
Geology Library
212
University Library, Map and Geography Library
214
Urbana-Champaign
Illinois Historical Survey
213
University of Illinois Chicago Circle
198
Western Illinois University
205
County highway map collection, 1937–date
211
Highway map collection, 1921–date
211
History
213
State agencies, depository
214
State Geological Survey
186
Library, Map Room
187
State Historical Library
210
State Library
211
Transportation Department
186
Transportation Department, depository
205
Imaginary lands collection of maps
Counties
571
Index of Kentucky & Virginia Maps: 1562 to
1900
669
Index to Areal Geologic Maps of Missouri
377
Index to Historical Maps of Greater Los
Angeles
55
Index to Maps in the Catalog of the Everett D.
Graft collection of Western Americana
710
Index to Maps in the Graff Collection of
Western Americana
195
Index to Published Geologic Mapping in
Oregon, 1898-1979
550
Index to the Defense Mapping Agency-Army
Map Services Catalogs.
39

Index to Topographic Maps of Missouri
377
India
Geological Survey
depository
374
Pre-1900 map collection
357
Indian land
144
Indian lands
251
Indian maps
5, 253, 594
Indiana
Colleges and universities
Ball State University
226
Indiana State University
230
Indiana University
Lilly Library
217
Indiana University Geography and Map Library
215
Indiana University Geology Library
216
Indiana University - Purdue University
Fort Wayne
219
Indianapolis
225
Indiana University Northwest
220
Geological Survey, depository
226, 232
Historical Society
223
History
217
State Geological Survey, depository
216
State Library
224
Indiana University of Pennsylvania
564
Indians
223, 563
Industrial development
406
Industry
261, 406, 560
INFO 1-A List of Illinois County Atlases
214
INFO 2-List of Aerial Photographs
214
Information cartofogique (Université du Quebec)
795
Institute of Food and Agricultural Sciences
151
Insurance
See also Fire insurance, Sanborn fire insurance maps
131, 413, 764
Canadian cities
772
Ontario towns and villages
772
Insurance Library Association
300
International boundary collection of Canadian maps
737
International Boundary Commissions
144
Inventories to Cartographic Archives Collections
727

An Inventory of the Collections of the Middle American Institute: No. 4: Maps in the Library of the Middle American Institute; No. 3: Maps in the Frederick L. Hoffman Collection
273
Iowa
Colleges and universities
Iowa State University
234
University of Iowa Geology Library
245
University of Iowa Libraries, Special Collections Department
246
University of Northern Iowa
235
Geological Survey
243
Historical Department (State)
239
State agencies, depository
237
State Historical Society
244
State map depositories
246
State Planning Board
Works Progress Administration plans, charts, maps
234
Iowa State Library
240
Irrigation
37, 636
Irvine (James) Foundation Map Library
68
Isaacson, Kathy
689
Ithaca
History
458

J

Jacinto, Julia
40
Jackson (Andrew) collection
143
Jackson, James E.
82
Jacobsen, Lavonne
88
Jaggers, Karen
432
James Ford Bell Library
356
Janes, Vivian
784
Japanese collection of old maps
34
Japanese map collection
59
Jennings, C. W.
84
Jennings, Vincent
454
Jersey City Public Library
413
Jett, John
20
Johns Hopkins University
Milton S. Eisenhower Library
Government Publications/Maps/Law Department
285
Peabody Department
286
Special Collections Division
287
Johnsen, John H.
475
Johnson, Bruce L.
83

Johnson, Carol P.
351
Johnson, John L.
252
Johnson (John) manuscript collection of maps/surveys of northern Vermont towns, 1795–1842
644
Johnson, Joyce
208
Jones, Larry R.
179
Jones, Norris W.
702
Jones, Paul S.
701

K

Kahl, Barbara J.
548
Kaimowitz, Dr. Jeffrey H.
120
Kansas
Colleges and universities
Kansas State University
252
University of Kansas
250
Libraries, Kansas Collection
251
Wichita State University
256, 257
History
Pre-1900 collection of Kansas and midwest region maps
250
State Historical Society
253
State Library
254
Kansas City Public Library
375
Karpinski collection of American Maps from European collections
403
Karpinski collection of French archival depository maps
213
Karpinski Reproductions French Archive series of early American maps
516
Karrow, Robert W.
195
Kaschins, Elizabeth
237
Katz, Jane
287
Keene State College
404
Keeth, Kent
634
Keller (Frank) collection of maps on South America
273
Kelly, Ardie L.
660
Kelly, Michael T.
257
Kelso (William G.) collection of Jansson-Visscher maps of America
571
Kenamore, Jane
628
Kendall Collection Catalog
597
Kendall map collection
597
Kenosha County Historical Society
693
Kent State Unversity
528

Kentucky
  Colleges and universities
  University of Kentucky
    Geology Library Map Collection
      262
    MIK Library
      263
    Western Kentucky University
      259
  Commerce Department
    261
  Geological Survey
    263
  Historical Society
    260
  History
    259, 264
Keogh, Brian
  741
Kern County Library
  30
Kidd, Betty
  764
Kidd, Claren M.
  536
Kile, Barbara
  629
Kim, Bang
  598
Kim, Chi Su
  91
Kim, Dr. Soon
  219
Kimball, Bernice
  55
King County Library System
  671
Kinsey (Alfred C.) map collection
  215
Kipp, Judy
  167
Kit Carson Memorial Foundation, Inc.
  437
Kita, Arlene
  176
Klein, Robert
  242
Klein, Stephanie A.
  381
Klimley, Susan
  472
Kline, Sims
  148
Knecht, Bob
  253
Kneedler, Bill
  21
Knight, Rebecca C.
  130
Knopf, Barbara J.
  671
Koch, Donald L.
  243
Koellen, Joann
  352
Koepp, Donna
  108
Kohl (Johann Georg) manuscript copies of
  early maps of America
  143
Kraft, Nancy E.
  244
Kreblin, Leland H.
  708
Kreps collection of coal and mineral lands,
  mine interior maps
  688
Krick, Mary
  187
Krueger, Gerald
  703

Kruger collection of World War II—Pacific area
  maps
  484
Kruse, Rhoda E.
  78
Kuelrner, Irvin V.
  343
Kuennecke, Dr. Beund
  663
Kutztown University
  Rohrbach Library
    565

L

Labbe, Raymond
  768
Labrador
  History
    742
  Provincial archives
    744
Laflamme, André
  793
Lakehead University
  769
Lakes
  218, 330, 533, 698, 760
Lambert, Dennis K.
  578
Lamonte, Joyce
  8
Lancaster
  Mennonite Historical Society
    566
Land forms
  498
Land grants
  32
Land grants collection (original) of the Penns
  and the Commonwealth of Pennsylvania
  561
Land ownership
  See also Cadastral maps, Real estate
  96, 257, 416, 511, 522, 577, 577, 696
Land Registration and Information Service
  781
Land settlement
  718
Land surveys
  See Surveys
Land tenure
  770, 770
Land use
  39, 42, 59, 93, 319, 346, 373, 416, 430, 455,
    471, 508, 568, 603, 663, 669, 717, 723,
    730, 745, 752, 778, 784, 791, 796, 798
Landsat satellite data collection
  564
Landsat satellite imagery collection
  9, 25, 487
  False color composite scene collection of
  Montana
    393
Landsat-2 imagery collection
  93
Large scale collection of topographic maps
  708
Larimer, Hugh C.
  736
Larsgaard, Mary Lynette
  113
Larson, Frank
  10
Larzelere, David
  339
Lasher collection of Revolutionary War maps
  484
Lasker collection of antique atlases and maps
  476
Latin America History
  619

Laurentian University
  768
Lawrence University
  Seeley G. Mudd Library
    689
LéPine, Pierre
  783
Leahy, Palmyra
  495
Lee, Michael
  387
Lee, Tae M.
  440
Leen, Mary
  299
Lefebvre, Marie
  798
Lehigh University
  Linderman Library
    553
Leonardo, James S.
  238
Lessard, Elizabeth
  406
Lethbridge
  University of Lethbridge
  Young, Darla M.
    724
Leverenz, Paul M.
  49
Levorson (A.I.) collection of foreign geology
  540
Lewis, Alison M.
  155
Lewis (Meriwether) and Clark (William)
  collection of 13 manuscript maps
  143
Librarianship (maps)
  571
Lincoln
  210
Linda Hall Library
  376
Lindsey, Dr. David R.
  625
Lineback, Neal G.
  7
Lipchinsky, Z. L.
  258
Liste d'acquisitions (Université du Québec)
  798
Lithographic (bird's-eye) view collection of
  Michigan cities and towns
  347
Living resources of the sea
  746
Lloyd, Heather M.
  538
Le, Loan
  767
Lohrman, Fred
  626
London (Ontario)
  759
London Public Libraries and Museums (Ontario)
  759
Long Beach Public Library
  53
Long Island
  History
    446, 460
Long, John
  282
Loras College
  Wahlert Memorial Library
    242
Lord, A. C.
  569
Loring (David M.) Map Library
  209
Los Angeles

History
55, 56
Public Works Department
55
Los Angeles Public Library
56
Louisiana
Colleges and universities
Louisiana State University
266
Middleton Library
Archives and Manuscripts Department
267
Louisiana Room
268
Louisiana Tech University
Prescott Memorial Library
275
Southern University
John B. Cade Library
269
History
267
Louisiana State Museum
270
Louisville
Colleges and universities
University of Louisville
Ekstrom Library
265
Love Library Map Collection
396
Lowell, Barbara A.
330
Lowery (Woodbury) collection of maps of Spanish possessions in America
143
Lowther, Dr. Stewart
682
Loyola University of Chicago
E. M. Cudahy Memorial Library
194
Lozupone, Frank P.
142
Lucey, Jean
300
Lumber
331, 635
Lunar geology
87, 385
Lunar surface collection of satellite photo imagery
87
Lundquist, David
42
Luther College
Preus Library
237
Lybyer collection of Near East maps
214
Lyle, Robert W.
134
Lynch, Evangeline Mills
268

M

MacDonald, Laurie S.
44
MacDonald, William Kirk
746
MacKinnon, William R.
739
MacLeod, Brenton H.
781
MacRae, Laura
759
Mager, John G.
557
Magnetics
57

Mahoning River-Army Corps of Engineers collection-lake to River canal project maps, 1920
533
Maier, Charles
804
Maine
Colleges and universities
University of Maine
Orono
Raymond H. Fogler Library, Government Documents Department
279
Raymond H. Fogler Library, Special Collections Department
280
Historical Society
281
History
280
State agency publications
280
Malone, Rose Mary
710
Manchester City Library
405
Manchester Historic Association
406
Manitoba
Colleges and universities
University of Manitoba
Earth Sciences Department
735
Elizabeth Dafoe Library
736
Government maps
depositories
734
History
734
Provincial Archives
734
Mankato State University
354
Mann (C. Harrison) collection of late 1500's to late 1800's maps of America
654
Mann (J.S.) collection of land parcel maps, late 1900's
483
Manning, Lucinda
446
Manuel, Larry
133
Manuscript charts and archaeological survey collection
172
Manuscript collection of field notes of early state geologists of Michigan and Michigan lumber companies
331
Manuscript map collection from Richmond County Clerk's Office
478
Manuscript map collection of USGS geological field work
110
Manuscript Maps
See Rare Maps
Map Classification System, Archives of New Brunswick
739
Map Collection Resource Guide—University of Arkansas Library (guide)
27
Map Collection—maps of special interest
Syracuse University
481
Map Collections in the Public Reference Library
772

Map Library Guide University of Western Ontario)
760
Map Line (acquisitions list)
338
Map Projections: Newsletter/Acquisitions List of Coe Library's Map Collection
714
Map reading and interpretation collection of literature
583
Map Resources of Africa
150
Map Resources of Latin America
150
Map roll microfilm collection of current and historical USGS topographic, river survey, flood prone area and special maps
665
Map Sources Directory
776
Mapline (quarterly newsletter)
195
Mapping the American Revolutionary War
195
Mapping the Great Lakes Region: Motive and Method
195
Maps and Atlases: Information guide #20
88
Maps and Atlases showing Land Ownership in Wisconsin
696
Maps in Earth Science Publications
601
Maps in the collections of the State Historical Society of Wisconsin
696
Maps in the St. Louis Public Library
382
Maps of Connecticut by Edmund Thompson
117
Maps of Ireland in the Collections of the Rare Book Department of the McGill University Library
786
Maps of Michigan and the Great Lakes, 1545–1845...
336
Maps (a guide to the University of Chicago collection)
197
Maps relating to Virginia
669
Marathon Oil Company
114
Marine Environment serial atlas collection, 1963-1974
233
Marine sciences
See also Bathymetry, Hydrology, Lakes, Nautical charts, Oceanography, Rivers
233, 656, 676
Mariners' Museum
660
Maritime atlas collection
572
Maritime history
549, 588, 660
Maritime Resource Management Service
745
Marley, Carol
786
Marquette, Carl G., Jr.
512
Marquette County Historical Society
J. M. Longyear Research Library
345
Marshall, Douglas W., *Research Catalog of Maps of America to 1860.*
333
Marshall, Penny
510

Marshburn, Peg
90
Maryland
Colleges and universities
Frostburg State College
291
Towson State University
295
University of Maryland
Baltimore County
Albin O. Kuhn Library and Gallery
289
McKeldin Library
290
Geological Survey, map depository
285
Hall of Records Commission
283
Historical Society
288
History
286, 295
State road map depositories
289
Maryland Historical Society, *The Mapping of*
Maryland 1590–1914: An Overview
288
Maslyn, David C.
586
Mason-Dixon Line
572
Massachusetts
Colleges and universities
Bridgewater State College
305
Massachusetts Institute of Technology
Boston Stein Club Map Room
309
Rotch Library
311
Massachusetts Maritime Academy
Capt. Charles H. Hurley Library
306
Salem State College
319
Southeastern Massachusetts University
315
University of Massachusetts
Amherst
297
Boston
Library and Geography and Earth Sciences
Department
304
Historical Society
301
History
303
Institute of Technology
Lindgren Library
310
Panoramic view maps
302
State Library
302
Mastel, Debbie
50
Mastrogianis, George
293
Matanuska-Susitna Community College
16
Mattern, Joanne A.
129
Matteucci, Emily
622
Mauer, Linda
240
Maxwell, Barbara
137
May, Anne C.
604

May, Brian
463
Mays, Genease B.
610
Mayson, Mary
758
Mazzucchelli, Dr. Vincent G.
54
McBee, Martha
366
McCain, Margaret
281
McCauley, Philip F.
600
McClendon (George) collection of early maps
of Europe
617
McConnell, Edward N.
239
McCorkle, Barbara B.
127
McCracken, John R.
627
McCullough, Deborah
533
McDermott, Jack C.
378
McDevitt-Parks, Kathryn
85
McDonald, Susan
680
McDonnell, Michael
341
McGarvin, Tom
24
McGill University
787
McLennan Library
786
McGlamery, Thornton P.
128
McGuire, Laura H.
433
McKinney, William M.
706
McLean, G. Robert
531
McMaster University
Lloyd Reeds Map Library
755
McMullen, Glenn
651
McQuillan, David C.
596
Meadows collection of coal and mineral lands,
mine interiors maps
688
Mechanics' Institute Library
85
Medical geography
779
Medieval cosmography collection
588
Melby collection of World War II maps for the
Pacific area
752
Melhor, Prof. Wilton N.
232
Mellville Whaling Room
313
Memphis and Shelby County Public Library and
Information Center
610
Memphis State University
611
Mercure, Rosemary P.
670
Merriam, Dr. Daniel F.
256
Merritt, Floyd S.
296

Metallurgy
24, 358, 391
Meteorology
42, 153, 209, 294, 310, 324, 624 724, 725,
752, 779
Metric line maps
781
Metric orthophoto maps
781
Metropolitan Washington Council of
Governments
Metropolitan Map Center
138
Mewshaw, Dorothy R.
56
Miami
University of Miami
Geography Department, Map Library
147
Miami University (Ohio)
529
Miami-Dade Public Library
153
Michaud, Yves
795
Michigan
Colleges and universities
Central Michigan University
Clarke Historical Library
347
Library, Documents Department
348
Eastern Michigan University
349
Grand Valley State College
328
Michigan State University
338
Northern Michigan University Olson Library
346
University of Michigan
Bentley Historical Library, Michigan Historical
Collections
331
Harlan Hatcher Graduate Library, Map Library
332
William L. Clements Library, Map Division
333
Western Michigan University
Waldo Library
341
Department of Natural Resources
Depository
343
Geological Survey
Depository
343
History
331, 347
Library
342
Lumber companies, early field notes and maps
331
Natural Resources Department
Geological Survey Division, Library
343
Institute for Fisheries Research
330
Rural property inventories (1935-1940)
344
State Archives, History Division
344
State geologist, early field notes and maps
331
Microfilm
665
Microform collection of Connecticut bird's eye
views
128
Microform imagery
93

Micropaleontology
385
Middle American Institute
273
Middlebury College
645
Midland County Public Library
631
Midwestern United States
County and state atlas collection
214
History
213
Miles, William
347
Military College of Vermont
648
Military map collection relating to American
intervention in Russia, 1918–1919
331
Military maps
5, 23, 144, 144, 437
Defense mapping collection (worldwide
topographic maps)
56
German "captured" map collection of Europe
and North Africa
98
Milks, Rosaline
779
Miller, Carmen
66
Miller, G.
69
Miller, M. Stone
267
Miller, Mary B.
248
Miller, Michael
435
Miller, Rosanna
22
Millersville Unversity
569
Mills Atlas original survey collection
594
Mills, Constance A.
259
Mills, Dr. Annie E.
368
Milwaukee
History
698
Milwaukee Public Library
698
Mineral Resources
25, 32, 60, 84, 99, 187, 232, 262, 343, 358,
365, 391, 487, 536, 623, 635, 649, 664,
685, 688, 743
Mineralogy
385, 559
Mines and mining
15, 24, 32, 43, 52, 84, 99, 109, 113, 343,
464, 635, 685, 688, 743, 773
Collection of plans of placer mining dredges in
Yukon
804
History
23
Mine and claim maps and sketches collection
20
Virginia coal mine map collection, 1840–1920
651
Minn, T. H.
171
Minneapolis Public Library and Information
Center
355
Minnesota
Colleges and universities
Bemidji State University
350

Mankato State University
354
Saint Cloud State University
360
University of Minnesota
Duluth
353
Minnesota Geological Survey Library
363
O. M. Wilson Library
James Ford Bell Library
356
Treude, Mai
357
Winchell Library of Geology
358
Geological Survey, depositories
363
Historical Society
361
History
354, 357
Minnesota bird's-eye views
361
Minnick, Roy
74
Minot State College
506
Minton, James O.
25
Miquelon
History
742
Mishler, Catherine
449
Missions
23, 469
Mississippi
Archives and History Department
366
Colleges and universities
Mississippi State University
367
University of Mississippi
368
Geology Bureau
365
Agency list of Publications
365
History
366
Mississippi River collection of maps and
atlases, ca. 1880–1945
613
Mississippi River Commission
369
Missouri
Colleges and universities
Central Missouri State University
387
Southeast Missouri State University
370
Southwest Missouri State University
386
University of Missouri
Columbia
Geography Department
373
Geology Library
374
Elmer Ellis Library
372
Rolla
Curtis Laws Wilson Lbirary
379
Geology Library
380
Geological Survey
depository
374
Historical Society
381

Natural Resources Department
Geology and Land Survey Division
Geological Library
377
Land Survey Repository
378
State Historical Society
371
State map publications
386
States publications
371
Missouri D.N.R.—D.G.L.S. List of Publications
377
Mitchell, Marilyn Dean
249
Mobil Research and Development Corporation
623
Mobile Public Library
4
Moffat, Riley
637
Moline, Dr. Norman
209
Moline, Robert T.
364
Moncton
Université de Moncton
741
Monmouth College
Hewes Library
206
Monmouth County Library
423
Montana
Colleges and universities
Eastern Montana College
388
Montana College of Mineral Science and
Technology
391
Montana State University
Earth Sciences Department
390
University of Montana
393
Historical Society
392
History
393
State agencies, depository
392
Monterey Bay region
History
96
Montgomery County
Dayton and Montgomery County Public Library
524
Montréal
Colleges and universities Université de Montréal
790
Land use collection, 1964–1983
791
Moody, Marilyn K.
234
Moore, Evia B.
100
Moore, Jean
605
Moravian College
Reeves Library
554
Moreland, Virginia
396
Moreley, William F. E.
757
Morelli, Marcia A.
570
Morgan, Dr. R. J.
750
Morris Canal and Banking Company Collection
424

Morris, Mary Lee
433
Morris, Pamela A.
616
Morrisett, Elizabeth
391
Morse, Diana
525
Mosser, Donald M.
191
Mottler, Lee S.
172
Mount Holyoke College
320
Mountaineering
461, 728
Mounted wall map collection—world-wide
coverage
545
MRMS Regional Library Information Brochure
Maritime Resource Management Service
745
Museum of the Confederacy
Brokenbrough Library
666
Museum of the Great Plains
535
Mustonen, Karlo K.
636
Mydland, Karen
716
Myers, Christine
431
Myers, Richard
552
Mystic Seaport
G. W. Blunt White Library
123

N

Naissance de la Louisiane
788
Naraynsingh, Tara
762
NASA
See United States, National Aeronautics and
Space Administration
Nashua
History
408
Nashua Public Library
408
National Capital Planning Commission
Carto and Graphic Services Department
139
National Cartographic Information Center
9
National Geographic Society
Map Library
140
National Mine Health and Safety Academy
685
Natrona County Public Library
711
Natural Hazards
485
Natural history
82
Natural resources
See also Energy resources, Fuel resources,
Living resources of the sea
29, 93, 114, 343, 435, 455, 686, 688, 746
Nautical charts
142, 154, 305, 306, 315, 499, 660, 676, 698
Collection of 19th century Florida charts
158
U.S. National Ocean Survey Collection
292
Nautical charts collection of global oceans by
U.S. and foreign hydrographic agencies
49

Naval history
660
Navigation
123, 369, 603, 608
Nayda, Eileen A.
738
Nebraska
394
Colleges and universities
University of Nebraska
Lincoln
395, 396
Omaha
398
State Historical Society Library
394
State agencies, depository
394
Nelson, Charles
38
Nelson, Dennis O.
614
Nelson, Joyce
266
Neuendorf, Klaus
550
Nevada
Colleges and universities
University of Nevada
Reno
400
Mines and Geology Bureau
depository
400
State Library
399
New acquisitions list Virginia Polytechnic Institute
and State University
649
New Acquisitions/Cartographic (quarterly)
583
New Bedford
Free Public Library
313
History
314
New Bedford Collection of maps circa 1850,
1880, 1820
315
New Brunswick
Colleges and universities
University of New Brunswick
740
Provincial Archives
739
New Castle Public Library
570
New England
125
History
646
New England coastal charts and maps
324
New France and Québec collection of maps by
Joseph Bouchette 1774–1841
794
New Hampshire
Colleges and universities
Keene State College
404
County map collection
408
Historical Society
401
History
408
State Library
402
New Jersey
Colleges and universities
Glassboro State College
412

Trenton State College
426
Department of State
Archives and Records
Management Division
424
Environmental Protection Department
Manuscript Collection
424
Geological Survey
425
Collection of maps 1880s–1950s
424
Historical Society
417
History
411, 422
State documents
412
Topographic Atlas Sheet Series
425
New Mexico
Bureau of Land Management
430
Colleges and universities
Eastern New Mexico University
433
New Mexico Highlands University
432
New Mexico Institute of Mining and Technology
436
New Mexico State College
431
University of New Mexico
Geology Department
429
Zimmerman Library
430
Forest Service
430
Mines and Mineral Resources Bureau
430
Museum of New Mexico
434
State Library
435
New Orleans
Archives collection
271
Public Library
271
University of New Orleans
274
New York (state)
Agriculture and Markets Departments, depository
455
Colleges and Universities
New York State University
Buffalo
442
State University of New York
Albany
440
Binghamton
443
Geneseo
451
Oneonta
471
Plattsburgh
473
Potsdam
474
Stony Brook
480
Commerce Department, depository
455
Counties
453
Historical Society
467

History
446, 451, 478, 483
State Library
439
Topographic map collection
442
Transportation Department
438
New York (city)
459
Brooklyn Public Library
447
Colleges and universities
Brooklyn College
445
City College of New York
462
Public Library
468
Queens Borough Public Library
460
New Zealand
Geological Survey
depository
374
Geological Survey, depositories
82
New Zealand, map depositories
58
Newark Public Library
418
Newberry Library
195
Newfoundland
Colleges and universities
Memorial University of Newfoundland
Queen Elizabeth II Library
742
History
742
Mines and Energy Department
743
Provincial archives
744
Newman, Linda P.
400
Newman, Lisa A.
499
Newport Historical Society
587
News map collection, World War II
207
Newsletter: Map Library University of Western
Ontario)
760
Newsome, Walter L.
653
Newton, Robert M.
317
Niederer, Karl
424
**Nineteenth century collection of Illinois county
atlases**
211
**Nineteenth century collection of townland
survey of Ireland**
764
Nineteenth century county atlas collection
197
*Nineteenth Century Maps and Atlases of
Montreal in the Collections of the Rare Book
Department of the McGill University Library*
786
**Nineteenth century street maps for western
European cities and towns**
197
Nobles, Steven J.
541
Noga, Michael
99
Nolan, Martha D.
119

Nonack, Stephen
298
**Norden (Eric) collection of Swampland maps of
eastern North Carolina**
496
North America
History
788
Western explorations collection, pre-1850
549
North Carolina
Colleges and universities
Appalachian State University
485
East Carolina University
495
North Carolina Central University
James E. Shepard Memorial Library
493
North Carolina State University
Marine, Earth and Atmosphic Sciences
Department
500
Raleigh
D.H. Hill Library, Documents Department
499
University of North Carolina
Chapel Hill
Geology Library
487
Wilson Library, Maps Collection
488
Wilson Library, North Carolina Collection
489
Charlotte
490
Greensboro
494
Western Carolina University
491
Cultural Resources Department
496
History
488
Natural Resources and Community Development
Department
497
State Museum of Natural History
498
Superintendent of Public Instruction
496
North Dakota
Colleges and universities
Minot State College
506
North Dakota State University
503
University of North Dakota
Geography Department, Map Library
504
Libraries, Geology Branch
505
Northampton
History
316
Map Collection
316
Northern College
Haileybury School of Mines Library
753
Northwestern University
Grant Memorial Library of Geology
202
University Library
203
Norwich University
648
Noteworthy Maps & Charts A.D. 1513–1774
45
Notre Dame, University
227
Nova Scotia

Mines Department
depositories
747
Public Archives
748
Nova Scotiana
748
Nowack, Kathleen
711
Nuquist, Mrs. Reidun D.
646

O

Oakland
History
62
Oakland Public Library
62
Ocean floor photographs
324
Oceanography
29, 49, 114, 207, 310, 314, 324, 521, 746,
747
**Ogg collection of city guides of England in the
1960s and 1970s**
728
Ohio
Colleges and universities
Bowling Green State University
509
Cleveland State University
517
Kent State University
528
Ohio State University
Main Library, Map Library
520
Orton Memorial Library of Geology
521
Ohio University
Alden Library
508
Wright State University
526
County Atlases collection (original and microfilm)
516
Early Ohio collection of topographic maps
529
Historical Society
519
History
520, 533
Library depository
516
State documents
519
State Library
523
Ohio Wesleyan University
527
Oil
343, 536
Oklahoma
Colleges and universities
Central State University
534
Oklahoma State University
538
University of Oklahoma
536
Historical Society
537
Olbrich, William L.
633
Old Dartmouth Historical Society
314
Old Dominion University
661
Oliver, Dr. John
230
Olivet Nazarene College

Benner Library
204
Olson, Douglas A.
678
Olson, Gordon
340
Omaha Public Library
397
Ontario
Archives
Map Collection
770
Base Maps, depository
756, 760, 765
Colleges and universities
University of Western Ontario
760
Fire insurance plan collection
770
Geological Survey, depository
776, 777, 778
Government maps
depository
775
History
754, 770
Mines Branch, depository
753
Ministry of Natural Resources
773
Oregon
Colleges and universities
Central Oregon Community College
543
Eastern Oregon State College
547
Oregon Institute of Technology
546
Oregon State University
544
Portland State University
551
Southern Oregon State College
542
University of Oregon
545
Geology and Mineral Industries Department
550
Highway Division, depository
549
Historical Society Library
549
Stabilization and Conservation Service depository
547
state agencies, depository
544
State Library
552
Oregon State University Library Information Bulletin: Map Room
544
Organization of American States
Columbus Memorial Library
141
Ortelius
217
Oser, Anita K.
491
Otness, Harold M.
542
Ottawa
Colleges and universities
University of Ottawa
765
Public Library
763
Ottumwa Public Library
247
Ouellette, Benoit
749

Out-of-print collections of geologic and topographic maps
377
Ozanne (Pierre) collection of manuscript views and maps of the Revolutionary War
143

P

Pacific Lutheran College
Mortvedt Library
680
Pacific Northwest
History
679
Maritime and overland exploration collection, pre-1850
549
Pacific Northwestern United States
678
Pacific voyages and exploration collection
59
Paidle, Pamela
227
PAIGH depository
621, 622
Painter, Jaqueline S.
648
Paleontology
365, 385, 559
Palmer (William R.) collection of manuscript and published maps of the West
635
Palo Alto City Library
63
Palumbo, Kristine M.
114
Pamphlet map collection or California and the West.
59
Panama Canal Company collection
143, 144
Panoramic views of Connecticut
117
Papers (James Hall) map collection of historical geology
439
Pappas, Rise
428
Parcel maps
77
Parker, John
356
Parker, Peter J.
572
Parkinson, George
688
Parks
See also United States, National Parks
529
Parks, Barbara
675
Parmly Billings Library
389
Parsons, Kathy
379
Pasadena
History
65
Pasadena Public Library
65
Patents
566
Patrick, Stephen
607
Patton, Peter C.
121
Paulson, Edna
345
Paz, Guillermo J.
141

Peace
144
Pember, Alyson
763
Pennsylvania
Colleges and universities
Clarion University of Pennsylvania
557
Indiana University of Pennsylvania
564
Pennsylvania State University Pattee Library
583
Slippery Rock University of Pennsylvania
581
University of Pennsylvania Philadelphia
575
County atlas collection
571
Environmental Resources Department
Topographic and Geologic Survey Bureau
559
Historical and Museum Commission
Land Records Bureau
561
Archives and History Bureau
560
Historical Society of Pennsylvania
572
Historical Society of Western Pennsylvania
577
History
559, 562
State agencies, depository
561
State Library
562
Pennsylvania Maps and Atlases in the Pennsylvania State University Libraries by Ruby Miller
583
Peoria Public Library
208
Pepper, Jerold
444
Perdue, Bob
154
Perkins, Priscilla
329
Peroni, Patricia A.
567
Perry, Joanne
19
Peters, Sharon
639
Petersen collection of photostats of New England towns, villages, school districts from 1840–1875
128
Peterson, Margaret V.
46
Petroleum
53, 90, 114, 131, 262, 540, 621, 622, 631
Historical collection of petroleum industry in California
53
Petrology
385
Petrus, Robert
443
Philadelphia
Free Library of Philadelphia
571
History
563
Library Company
573
Library Company of Philadelphia
573
Philipson, Warren R.
457
Phoenix Public Library
21

Photo mosaic collection of USGS mapping photography
9
Photogrammetry
142
Photographic collection of rare maps
757
Photography
See also Aerial photography
9, 331, 673
Photolithographic copy collection of original land surveys of Michigan, 1800-1850
331
Photomaps
See Aerial photography
Physical geography
373, 776, 794, 795
Physical sciences
93
Pierrre, Sciamma Leone
792
Pierson, Robert
334
Pike, Kermit J.
518
Pinnell, Richard Hugh
778
Pintozzi, Chestalene
618
Piquette, Constance M.
393
Pittsburgh
Carnegie Library
576
Colleges and universities
University of Pittsburgh
Darlington Memorial Library
578
Hillman Library
579
Place names
172, 196, 583, 601
Plainfield Public Library
420
Plane, Daphne
64
Planetary maps
See also Remote sensing
319
Planimetry
438, 459, 608, 708
Planning and development
See also Urban planning
91, 745
Plat atlases
676
Plat books
186
Plat books collection or Kansas counties
257
Plat maps
144, 224, 257, 344, 516
Atlas collection for many Kansas and Missouri Counties
251
Original survey collection of Alabama
8
Pletcher, Kathy
692
Poage (Frances) collection of printed maps of Texas
634
Pocatello Public Library
183
Poe, Celia D.
488
Political geography
409, 442, 470, 494, 638
Political maps
27, 337, 676, 798
Pomona Public Library
67

Population
See also Census, Demography, United States—Bureau of the Census
240, 250, 633, 752
Portage Co. collection of maps of 1866
706
Portland
Library Association of Portland
548
Portland History (brochure)
548
Portland Public Library (Maine)
282
Portland State University
551
Portolan charts... descriptive list of those belonging to the Hispanic Society of America
466
Portsmouth
Naval Shipyard Museum
Marshall W. Butt Library
662
Portugaliae Monumenta Cartographica collection of Portuguese cartography
233
Posey, Merne H.
166
Potter collection of early manuscript maps of Narragansett, R.I.
592
Potter, Donald B.
450
Prairie land settlement collection of maps
737
Preliminary Guide to Nineteenth Century Canadian Guide Books
786
Pre-Nineteenth Century Maps and Atlases of Montreal in the Collections of the Rare Book Department of the McGill University Library
786
Pre-1757 Maps of Acadia in the Collections of the Rare Book Department of the McGill University Library
786
Price, Edward
561
Price, Patricia
173
Prince Edward Island
Public Archives
de Jong, N.J.
780
Princeton University
Geology Library
421
Rare Books and Special Collections
422
Proehl, Karl H.
583
Property
See Real estate, Cadastral maps
Providence Public Library
591
Ptolemy
217
Public lands
180
Public Record Office Map collection of Florida and southeastern United States
149
Public works
55, 793
Publications Brochure (Museum of the Great Plains)
535
Puerto Rico
Colleges and universities
University of Puerto Rico
585
Puget Sound, University of
682

Pugsley (W. H.) collection of early maps of Canada
786
Purchasing Maps of Washington, a Popular Guide
674
Purdue University
Geosciences Department
232
Libraries, Map Collection
233
Putnam (William C.) Map Room
57

Q

Quaker history
582
Quakers
563
Quarterly List of New Map Library Acquisitions (Ohio State University)
520
Québec
Aménagement, Bureau d'de l'est du Quebec, depository
795
Archives de la ville de Québec
793
Archives nationales du Québec
797
Bibliothèque Nationale du Quebec
783
Colleges and universities
Université du Québec
Institut National de la Recherche Scientifique, Cantothéque
791
Montreál
792
Rimouski
795
Trois-Rivières
798
Université du Quebec
Chicoutimi
782
Université Laval
794
Energie et Ressources, Ministère, depository
792, 796, 798
Ministerè de Affaires Culturelles
Archives Nationales du Quebec
789
Photocartotheque, depository
782
Provincial depository
794
Urban planning
793, 797
Queens Borough Public Library
459
Long Island Division
460
Queen's University
Douglas Library
Map and Air Photo Library
756
Rare and Historical Map collection
757
Geology Library
758
Queen's University Map and Air Photo Library (brochure)
756
Quirion-Turcotte, Diane
796

R

Racine Public Library
705

Radford University
663
Railroads
5, 131, 251, 253, 345, 371, 424, 560, 572,
594, 688
Ohio collection
522
Virginia map collection, 1840–1920
651
Raisz (Erwin) collection of personal maps and books
150
Rand McNally & Co.
196
Rare maps
2, 4, 34, 59, 98, 127, 149, 158, 172, 198,
213, 214, 217, 250, 283, 286, 308, 333,
357, 377, 424, 434, 468, 476, 478, 479,
535, 540, 558, 559, 619, 651, 676, 683,
750, 757, 786, 788, 794
Early map and atlas collection 1482–1850
118
Ray, Jean M.
186
Ray, Kathryn
136
Répertoire Carto-bibliographique de la Région 02 et Moyen Norde; Liste des Aquistions nouvelles
782
Real estate
See also Cadastral maps, Land ownership
109, 344, 416, 460, 468, 478, 577, 798
Baist's real estate atlas collection of Indiana
224
District of Columbia real estate collection of atlases 1879–1976
136
Reasoner, Lynne
68
Reclamation
50
Recreation
See Travel
Redlands
University of Redlands
68
Reeds (Lloyd) Map Library
755
Reeser, Gale D.
184
Regina
University of Regina
Map Library
800
Regional development
457
Regional planning
564, 709
Reich, Richard B.
220
Reichlin, Elinor
303
Reid, Ruth S.
577
Reinert, Ann
394
Reinert, Ann, "Historical Maps of Nebraska V. 14 no 1 Spring 1983 of Nebraska Library Association Quarterly
394
Remote sensing
See also Planetary maps
9, 93, 150, 319, 385, 564, 603, 665, 726
Remote sensing imagery collection
150
Rensselaer Polytechnic Institute
482
Repcyte, Eugenia
754

Repository Catalogue (Missouri, Land Survey Repository)
378
Resco, Carol
72
Research Catalog of Maps of America to 1860
333
Resources in Appalachian Studies in the John Cook Wyllie Library (guide)
670
Revolutionary War
403, 412, 484, 572
Rex, Heather
430
Reyes, Angeles M.
585
Reynolds, Betty
436
Reynolds, Kathryn
526
Rhode Island
Colleges and universities
University of Rhode Island
586
Historical Society
592
History
591
Rice University
Fondren Library
629
Richardson, Eleanor
597
Richmond Public Library
69
Richter, Dennis M.
709
Richter, E.A.
433
Ricks College
David O. McKay Learning Resources Center
184
Riddall, Margaret K.
33
Rieke, Judy
621
Ries, Linda A.
560
Ristow (Walter W.) map Christmas Card collection
143
Ritchie, Mary M.
318
Rivera, Diana H.
338
Rivers
See also Floods and flood control
5, 217, 228, 233, 345, 369, 406, 533, 613,
665
Rizza, Dr. Paul F.
581
Roach, Delbert
638
Roads
See Highways and roads
Roberts, Nancy
193
Robertson, Martha B.
273
Robinson Cris
613
Rochambeau (Comte de) collection of Revolutionary War maps
143
Rocky Mountain Fuel Co. map collection
109
Roderiguez, J. Hortensia
152
Rodwell, Lloyd
801

Rogers-Tucker Map collection of Historical Cartography
727
Rollin-Duffy, Karen
63
Rosenberg Library
628
Roshon, Sam
522
Ross, Laura
800
Ross, Tim
734
Rothenberger, James
71
Rothesay (Stuart de) collection or continental maps, ca. 1715–1840
59
Royal Ontario Museum
774
Ruger (Albert) collection of panoramic maps of American cities
143
Rural property inventory collection 1935-1940
344
Rush, Dorothy
264
Ruskell, Virginia
165
Russell, Victor L.
771
Rutgers University
419
Alexander Library
Maps and Microforms
415
Special Collections and Archives Department
416
Ryckman, Nancy B.
494

S

Sadler, Dr. Peter M.
70
Safley, Ellen Derey
632
Saint Anselm College
407
Saint Cloud State University
360
Saint Helen's Island, Museum
David M. Stewart Library
788
Saint John's University
351
Saint Joseph's College
Earth Science Department
228
Saint Louis Public Library
History and Genealogy Department
382
Saint Louis University
383
Saint Mary's University
749
Saint Paul
Public Library
362
Saint Pierre
History
742
Salem, Claudia
507
Salem State College
319
Salmon, John S. *Board of Public Works Inventory*
669
Salt Lake City Public Library
639

Sames, James W. III, *Index of Kentucky & Virginia Maps 1562–1900*
669
Samford University
3
San Diego
State University
81
San Diego County
77
San Diego Public Library
California Room
78
History Section
79
Science Section
80
San Francisco
History
86
State University
87, 88
San Francisco Public Library
86
San Joaquin
Stockton-San Joaquin County Public Library
101
San Joaquin County
depository
50
Historical Museum
50
San Joaquin Delta College
100
Sanborn fire insurance maps
143
Alabama
8
Alaska
13
Boston
311
California
78
Florida
150
Georgia
161, 164
Illinois
214
Indiana
215, 224
Iowa
239, 244
Kansas
251
Kentucky
263
Louisiana
268, 270
Massachusetts
302
Michigan
337
Minnesota
361
Missouri
372
Montana
392
Nebraska
394
New England (excluding Boston)
300
New Mexico
430
North Carolina
496
Ohio
528
Oregon
544

Pennsylvania
583
South Carolina
597
South Dakota
599
Texas
617
Utah
641
Virginia
669
West Virginia
688
Wisconsin
696
1880's to 1960's
61
Sanborn Fire Insurance Maps in the Map & Geography Library
214
Sang collection of early North America maps
186
Santa Ana Public Library
92
Santa Clara
Public Library
94
University of Santa Clara
95
Santa Clara County Free Library
41
Santa Monica Public Library
97
Saskatchewan
Archives Board, Regina
799
Archives Board, Saskatoon
801
Colleges and universities
University of Saskatchewan
803
Urban Affairs Department
802
Sass, Dr. Herman
448
Satellite imagery
See also Aerial photography
9, 25, 87, 93, 145, 150, 457, 487, 665
Sathrum, Robert L.
29
Sauer, Serge
760
Saunderson, Robert
31
Scammell, Harry D.
126
Scavenious collection of American Revolution maps
403
Schaffel, Dr. Simon
462
Scheckter, Stella
402
Schlesinger, Francis
304
Schmidt collection of Lewis Evans maps
214
Schneck, Ann
201
School atlases
794
School maps
70
Schoolfield, Dudley B.
623
Schoyer, George P.
520
Schroeder, Walter A.
373

Schumacher, *Index to Published Geologic Mapping in Oregon, 1898-1979*
550
Schwartz, Julia
157
Schwarz (Theodore Edward) Memorial Map Room
310
Scott, Virginia K.
2
Scripps Institution of Oceanography Library
49
Se Garden Därhemma map collection of Scandinavia
209
Seattle
History
676
Seattle and King County collection of maps from 1875
676
Seattle Public Library
676
Sectional map collection of the West (Canada)
734
Seiferth (Solis and Helen) cartographic collection
270
Seismology
60
Seldin, Daniel T.
215
Selected Atlases (by state) in the Atlas Collection Syracuse University
481
Selected List of Maps and Charts
608
Selected Recent Acquisitions (Quarterly)
University of Toronto
767
Sell, Dr. Betty
501
Selmer, Marsha L.
198
Settlements
539, 563, 588
Seventeenth and eighteenth century collection of rare atlases and maps
468
Sharp, Alice L.
107
Sheaves, Miriam L.
487
Shepard, Florence
408
Shepard, Paul
297
Sherbrooke
Université de Sherbrooke
796
Sheridan College
Griffith Memorial Library
716
Sherman (William T.) collection of Civil War maps
143
Sherwood, Arlyn
211
Shevchik, Zina
477
Shields, Sarah
667
Shippensburg University
Ezra Lehman Memorial Library
580
Shirley, David B.
348
Shirts (Dr. Morris A.) collection of manuscript maps of Cedar City, Utah
635
Shively, Donald H.
34

Shoemaker, Edward C.
537
Shorelines
293
Shupe, Barbara
480
Shutlak, Garry D.
748
Sigler, Judith
14
Simcoe (John Graves) collection of late 18th
century manuscript maps
770
Simon Fraser University
Bennett (W.A.C.) Library
725
Simon, Peggy
138
Simonetti, Martha L., *Descriptive List of the
Map Collection in the Pennsylvania State
Archives*
560
Simpson, Jeffrey M. R.
737
Skiffington, Frances W.
274
Skylab satellite imagery collection
9
Slachta, Olga
766
Slide map collection
776
Slippery Rock University of Pennsylvania
581
Slocum, Charlotte
326
Small scale collection of planimetric maps
708
Smiley, Gladys
515
Smith, Anne
168
Smith, C. Earle, Jr.
6
Smith College
317
Smith, Dirk A. D.
321
Smith (Sanderson) collection of early maps
(world coverage) 16th–20th century
479
Smith (T.R.) Map Collection
250
Smock, Mildred K.
236
Snaden, Dr. James N.
124
Snohomish Basin map collection
671
Social-cultural geography
332
Society for the Preservation of New England
Antiquities
303
Society of California Pioneers
89
Socio-economics
141, 677, 761
Sociology
267
Soils
5, 39, 42, 91, 99, 161, 341, 419, 499, 521,
528, 538, 594, 621, 622, 624, 717, 721,
723, 752, 766
Surveys
72
Soloman, Marvin
200
South Africa
Geological Survey
depository
374

South Asia
Pre-1900 map collection
357
South Carolina
Archives and History Department
594
Colleges and universities
University of South Carolina
Map Library
596
South Caroliniana Library
597
Secretary of State depository
594
State Development Board
595
South Dakota
Colleges and universities
South Dakota School of Mines and Technology
Devereaux Library
600
South Dakota State University
H. M. Briggs Library
598
University of South Dakota
I.D. Weeks Library
601
*South Dakota Topographic Maps and Selected
Place Names Index*
601
Southeastern United States Territorial
development
3
Southern Methodist University
624
Southern United States
History
163
Southwestern United States
History
25, 535, 538
Space science
414
Spain
History
4, 459
Sparks (Jared) collection of American
Revolution maps
456
Sparks, Marilyn M.
684
Spellman, Lawrence E.
422
Spohn, Richard A.
513, 514
Spokane Public Library
679
Spoor, Richard D.
469
Sprankle, Anita T.
565
Spreng, Dr. A.C.
380
Squier (Ephraim G.) collection of maps of
Central America
143
Standard Oil Company of California
90
Standards of Practice (Missouri, Land Survey
Repository)
378
Stanford University
Branner Earth Sciences Library
99
Cecil H. Green Library, General Reference
Department
98
*S(tanford) U(niversity) L(ibrary) Guide #21—
Map Collections*
98
Stansbury expedition
639

Stapley, Polly
451
Stark County District Library
510
Stark, Peter C.
545
Stark, Peter L., *Purchasing Maps of
Washington, a Popular Guide*
674
Starkey, J. Robert
411
State Atlases: An Annotated Bibliography
214
State map collection for 19th century
292
Staten Island
Historical society
478
Institute of Arts and Sciences
479
Stauffer, Michael
594
Stavec, Kathleen
417
Stefansson collection of polar and arctic
region maps
403
Stegall, Patricia
289
Stein, Lois
693
Steiner, Rodney
51
Stephens, Dr. John D.
564
Stetson University
DuPont-Ball Library
148
Stevens, Alan R.
665
Stevens, Irving
482
Stevens, Stanley D.
96
Stevenson, George
496
Stevenson, Marshall
295
Stewart collection of Jerseyana and the
Revolutionary War
412
Stewart, Henry
661
Stjernholm, Kirstine
115
Stockton-San Joaquin County
Public Library
101
Stout, Paul W.
226
Stratigraphy
715
Street map collection of various California,
United States and foreign cities and towns
86
Streeter, Agnes
595
Streeter, David
67
Streets
86, 153, 166, 197, 337, 406, 406
Strickland, Muriel
81
Strona, Proserfina
175
Structural geology
57
Structural geology map collection
377
Structure
358

Stuckenberg collection of early maps of
  Europe
  558
Sul Ross State Unviersity
  614
Sullivan, Dan
  115
Sullivan, Larry E.
  467
Sund, Cheryl
  110
Survey collection of unpublished information
  378
Surveys
  See also Boundaries
  5, 8, 14, 74, 77, 110, 132, 144, 163, 170,
    228, 239, 293, 331, 344, 365, 378, 460,
    483, 536, 540, 594, 644, 721, 734, 764,
    770, 789, 793
Sutherland, Johnnie D.
  161
Suzuki, Mabel
  178
Swamplands of eastern North Carolina, 19th
  century collection of Superintendent of Public
  Instruction maps
  496
Swan, Clark W.
  602
Swanson, Byron
  224
Swanson, Lynn
  363
Swarthmore College
  582
Swedish American Line
  209
Swem, E.G. Maps Relating to Virginia
  669
Swift, Michael
  61
Swinyer, Joseph G.
  473
Syracuse University
  Ernest S. Bird Library
  481
Syracuse University Libraries Information
  Bullentin—Map Collection
  481

T

Taeger, M. G.
  753
Takugi, Elda
  277
Talbot (Thomas) collection on land tenure
  770
Tamimi, Judith A.
  102
Tancock, James
  384
Taulman (Joseph E.) collection
  617
Taylor, Lynn
  109
Taylor, Maureen
  592
Teaching maps
  Wall map collection
  767
Technology
  131
Tectonics
  212, 262, 358, 715
Temple University
  Samuel Paley Library
  574
Ten Hoor, Joan
  265
Tennessee
  Colleges and universities

Austin Peay State University
  604
East Tennessee State University
  Sherrod Library
  607
Memphis State University
  611
Tennessee Technological University
  Jere Whitson Memorial Library
  605
University of Tennessee
  609
  Geology Division
  232, 606
  History
  602, 613
State Library and Archives
  612
Transportation Department, depository
  612
Tennessee River Collection of maps, ca. 1850–
  1930
  613
Tennessee Valley Authority
  603
  Map Sales
  608
Tennessee Valley Authority collection of
  planimetric maps
  613
Tessiere, Yves
  794
Texas
  Colleges and universities
  North Texas State University
  Willis Library
  625
  Sul Ross State University
  614
  Texas A&M University
  621
  Texas Tech University
  630
  University of Texas
  Arlington
    Library, Cartographic History Library
    615
    Library, Documents Department
    616
  Austin
    General Libraries, Barker Texas History Center
    617
    General Libraries, Geology Library
    618
    General Libraries, Nettie Lee Benson Latin
      American Collection
    619
    Perry-Castaneda Library
    620
  Dallas
    632
  El Paso
    626
Theatrum Orbis Terrarum facsimile atlases,
  1477-1776
  233
Thematic map collection of Maritime Region
  745
Thematic maps
  790
Thompson (David) collection of exploratory
  surveys and boundary surveys
  770
Thompson, Edmund, Maps of Connecticut
  117
Thompson, Gary
  452
Thompson, Richard F.
  174
Thurston, Nancy
  773

Tilden, Terry
  562
Time series collection of Canadian topographic
  maps
  760
Time series topographic map collection
  734
Tobin International Geological Map Collection
  618
Toledo
  Colleges and universities
  University of Toledo
  William S. Carlson Library
  531
  History
  530
Toledo-Lucas County Public Library
  530
Tompkins, Edward
  744
Tongate, John
  620
Tonge, Karyl
  98
Topographic and geologic map collection of
  U.S., Mexico, Central and South America
  49
Topography
  5, 6, 8, 22, 25, 26, 27, 30, 35, 36, 40, 46,
    47, 49, 51, 52, 56, 61, 64, 66, 67, 69, 70,
    76, 80, 84, 87, 91, 93, 95, 96, 106, 112,
    116, 124, 128, 130, 137, 142, 145, 146,
    147, 148, 152, 153, 155, 156, 159, 161,
    162, 166, 172, 173, 182, 183, 188, 190,
    196, 197, 198, 200, 206, 207, 208, 209,
    215, 218, 222, 227, 228, 230, 231, 232,
    233, 240, 243, 245, 247, 249, 250, 258,
    262, 265, 272, 274, 275, 282, 285, 292,
    293, 305, 308, 309, 312, 322, 324, 328,
    337, 341, 350, 352, 359, 364, 367, 370,
    372, 374, 377, 383, 388, 389, 390, 393,
    397, 398, 399, 400, 403, 413, 416, 419,
    421, 423, 425, 426, 429, 430, 431, 438,
    442, 445, 450, 454, 460, 473, 475, 477,
    481, 488, 492, 494, 495, 497, 498, 499,
    506, 508, 510, 513, 514, 515, 516, 520,
    523, 525, 526, 527, 528, 529, 531, 533,
    538, 540, 541, 543, 545, 552, 554, 555,
    557, 559, 565, 569, 570, 574, 576, 583,
    585, 586, 594, 596, 598, 603, 605, 607,
    608, 609, 611, 613, 616, 625, 626, 632,
    633, 634, 638, 643, 648, 654, 657, 658,
    659, 661, 663, 665, 671, 673, 676, 682,
    685, 691, 706, 707, 708, 716, 717, 719,
    723, 728, 734, 736, 737, 747, 749, 752,
    754, 759, 760, 761, 763, 766, 768, 769,
    772, 774, 778, 785, 786, 790, 795, 796,
    798, 800, 803
  Bibliographies
  697
Toponymy
  470
Toronto
  Aerial photography collection 1947–1983
  775
  City of Toronto Archives
  771
  Colleges and universities
  University of Toronto
  John P. Robarts Library
  775
  Scarborough
  V. W. Bladen Library
  767
  Metropolitan Toronto Library
  772
Totten, Stanley M.
  222
Tourist and road map file collection
  349
Town plans
  See Urban planning

Townsend, Peter
532
Townships
See Cities and towns
Towson State University
295
Trade maps
592
Trails
253, 437, 671, 678
Transparencies map collection
776
Transportation
See also Bicycle maps, Canals, Highways and
Roads, Railroads, Streets, Trails, Bridges
50, 78, 161, 162, 196, 197, 209, 226, 250,
332, 335, 344, 345, 390, 410, 422, 510,
519, 538, 568, 583, 634, 718, 734, 752, 754
Travel
97, 208, 250, 355, 414, 459, 510, 603, 671
Treacy, Hugh J.
659
Trenton State College
426
Trinity College
120
Trout, Frank E.
308
Tufts, Aileen
730
Tufts University
Wessell Library
312
Tulane University
273
Howard-Tilton Memorial Library
272
Tulsa
Colleges and universities
University of Tulsa
541
Tulsa City-County Library
540
Tung, Victor
41
Turnbull, Brian
733
Tutor, Kathryn
185
Tutwiler, Dorothea
420
TVA Maps—Map Catalog
608
*Twentieth Century Maps and Atlases of
Montreal in the Collections of the Rare Book
Department of the McGill University Library*
786

U

*UCLA Library Newsletter and Selected
Acquisitions*
58
Ufer, Sharon
679
Undersea cartography
746
Union College
477
Union List of Atlases
727
Union List of Topographic Maps of Wisconsin
696, 697
Union Theological Seminary
Burke Library
469
United Nations
Dag Hammarskjold Library
470
FAO/UNESCO collection of soil maps of the
world
499

United States
See also names of regions and states
Agriculture Department
Collection of U.S. 1930's and 1940's
144
Conservation Service Soil Surveys
279
Depositories
312
Air Force Academy
105
Army
207
Corps of Egineers
River charts
233
Corps of Engineers
418, 533
War College
556
Bureau of Indian Affairs
144
Bureau of Land Managements depositories
27
Bureau of the Census, depositories
27, 43, 52, 311, 396, 626, 654
Collection of district maps 1900–1960
144
Central Intelligence Agency
Foreign Countries map collection
654
Central Intelligence Agency, depositories
27, 105, 312, 520
Corps of Engineers
Collection of 19th century exploration, military
activities, engineering project maps
144
Culture
318
Defense Intelligence Agency
144
Defense Mapping Agency
Aeronautical Center
384
Historical and current map collection
665
Hydrographic/Topographic Center
Scientifc Data Department
142
Index
39
Defense Mapping Agency, depositories in
Canada
British Columbia
728
Nova Scotia
746
Ontario
755, 760, 761, 764, 765, 778
Québec
787, 792, 794
Toronto
775
Defense Mapping Agency, depositories in the
United States
688
Alabama
1, 7, 8
Alaska
11, 16
Arizona
22
California
29, 31, 36, 39, 40, 42, 43, 44, 48, 51, 54,
56, 58, 61, 62, 66, 71, 76, 81, 88, 93, 96,
98, 102
Colorado
104, 105, 108, 113, 115
Connecticut
119, 119, 122, 124, 125, 127, 128
Delaware
130

District of Columbia
137, 140, 143, 144
Florida
147, 150, 156, 157
Georgia
161, 162
Hawaii
172, 178
Idaho
181, 182
Illinois
186, 188, 190, 193, 197, 198, 199, 203, 205,
207, 214
Indiana
215, 219, 226, 227, 230, 231, 233
Iowa
234, 246
Kansas
250
Kentucky
263, 265
Louisiana
266, 269, 272
Maine
277, 279
Maryland
284, 291, 292, 295
Massachusetts
296, 297, 305, 308, 309, 310, 312, 315, 322,
324, 326
Michigan
327, 332, 337, 338, 341, 348, 349
Minnesota
350, 351, 354, 357, 359, 364
Mississippi
367, 367, 368
Missouri
372, 379, 380, 382, 385, 386, 387
Montana
390, 391
Nebraska
396
Nevada
400
New Jersey
419, 422, 423, 426
New Mexico
430, 431, 433
New York
439, 442, 443, 447, 454, 456, 463, 468, 471,
475, 480, 481
North Carolina
485, 488, 490, 491, 492, 493, 494, 495
North Dakota
503, 504
Ohio
508, 509, 512, 513, 516, 520, 528, 529, 530,
531
Oklahoma
536, 538, 541
Oregon
544, 545, 548, 552
Pennsylvania
555, 569, 571, 574, 575, 579, 581, 583, 584
Puerto Rico
585
Rhode Island
586, 589
South Carolina
593, 596
South Dakota
598
Tennessee
607, 609
Texas
620, 621, 624, 626, 629, 633
Utah
636, 637, 640
Vermont
644, 645
Virginia
650, 652, 653, 664

Washington
672, 674, 676, 677, 684
West Virginia
687
Wisconsin
689, 690, 691, 692, 696, 697, 698, 699, 703, 704, 706
Department of Interior
459
Engineer Corps, map collection of Virginia, 1862–1865
668
Federal Emergency Management Agency, depositories
27
Federal Insurance Administration
Flood, Hazard Boundary Maps
365
Fish and Wildlife Service
Ecological Characterization of Coastal Maine
279
Fish and Wildlife Service, depositories
New York
455
Forest Service
See also Forest and forestry, United States—National Forests
676
Forest Service
27
General Land Office
Collection of township plat and filed note maps
144
Geographic Survey
National Cartographic Information Center
Virginia
665
Geological Survey
California historical collection
87
Denver Library
110
Folio Atlases
207
Library
Menlo Park
60
Map roll microfilm collection
665
Map Series
365
National Cartographic Information Center
Alaska
9
National Wetlands Inventory
665
Open File Reports, microfiche depository
72
Out of print collection of topographic, geologic atlas folios
673
Project Office, Glaciology
681
Quadrangle map collection of area bordering Mississippi River
369
USGS Index to GS topo maps: Wyoming, U.S., Alaska
710
Water Resources Division
428
Geological survey collection of pre-1920's folios
709
Geological Survey, geological map depositories in Canada
British Columbia
728
Manitoba
736
Nova Scotia
746, 747, 751

Ontario
756, 758, 760, 762, 779
Québec
787, 792, 794
Toronto
775
Geological Survey, geological map depositories in the United States
Alabama
1, 7, 8, 154
Alaska
10, 11
Arizona
18, 22, 24, 25, 137
Arkansas
27
California
29, 35, 39, 40, 42, 43, 47, 48, 57, 58, 61, 64, 72, 75, 76, 80, 81, 82, 84, 85, 86, 91, 93, 96, 99, 100
Colorado
104, 105, 106, 111, 113, 115
Connecticut
119, 125, 126, 128
Delaware
129, 130
District of Columbia
137, 143, 144
Florida
147, 150, 153, 154, 155, 156
Georgia
154, 161, 162, 163, 166
Hawaii
176, 178
Idaho
180, 181, 182
Illinois
186, 187, 188, 190, 192, 197, 198, 199, 200, 202, 204, 205, 206, 207, 209, 211
Indiana
216, 219, 220, 222, 225, 226, 228, 229, 230, 231, 232
Iowa
235, 245
Kansas
250, 252
Kentucky
258, 259, 261, 262, 265
Louisiana
266, 269, 274, 275
Maine
276, 277, 278, 279
Maryland
284, 285, 288, 289, 292, 295
Massachusetts
296, 297, 302, 305, 307, 310, 312, 317, 319, 320, 324, 326
Michigan
327, 332, 334, 337, 338, 341, 343, 346, 348, 349
Minnesota
350, 351, 354, 358, 363, 364
Mississippi
365, 367, 367
Missouri
374, 376, 377, 379, 380, 382, 383, 385, 386
Montana
390, 391, 393
Nebraska
395, 398
Nevada
400
New Hampshire
402, 403
New Jersey
419, 421, 423
New Mexico
428, 429, 430, 431, 432
New York
439, 440, 441, 442, 443, 445, 449, 450, 452, 456, 463, 468, 472, 474, 475, 480, 481

North Carolina
485, 486, 487, 488, 490, 491, 492, 494, 500, 501
North Dakota
503, 504, 505, 506
Ohio
508, 509, 512, 513, 516, 525, 526, 528, 529, 530, 531, 532, 533
Oklahoma
535, 536, 538, 540, 541
Oregon
544, 545, 546, 550, 552
Pennsylvania
553, 555, 559, 567, 574, 575, 576, 581, 582
Puerto Rico
585
South Carolina
593, 595, 596
South Dakota
600, 601
Tennessee
258, 605, 607, 609, 612, 613
Texas
614, 618, 620, 621, 624, 626, 629, 630, 631
Utah
636, 637, 640
Vermont
644, 645, 647, 648
Virginia
652, 653, 664
Washington
672, 674, 676, 677, 679, 684
West Virginia
686, 687, 688
Wisconsin
689, 690, 691, 692, 697, 698, 699, 704, 706
Wyoming
710
Geological Survey Library
Reston, Virginia
664
Geological Survey, topographic map depositories in Canada
Alberta
725
British Columbia
728
Manitoba
736
Nova Scotia
746, 747
Ontario
760, 761, 764, 765, 776, 778
Québec
787, 792, 794, 795
Saskatchewan
799
Toronto
775
Geological Survey, topographic map depositories in the United States
Alabama
1, 6, 7, 8, 170
Alaska
11, 13, 15, 16
Arizona
18, 19, 22, 24, 25, 115
Arkansas
26, 27, 28
California
29, 31, 35, 36, 39, 41, 42, 43, 47, 48, 53, 54, 56, 57, 58, 60, 61, 62, 63, 64, 66, 67, 68, 69, 71, 75, 76, 80, 81, 82, 84, 86, 87, 88, 93, 94, 95, 96, 98, 99, 100, 101
Colorado
104, 105, 106, 108, 111, 112, 113, 115
Connecticut
118, 119, 119, 122, 124, 127, 128
Delaware
129, 130
District of Columbia
135, 137, 138, 140, 143, 144

Florida
147, 148, 150, 151, 152, 153, 155, 156, 157, 158
Georgia
161, 162, 164, 165, 167, 168, 170
Hawaii
101, 172, 176, 178
Idaho
180, 181, 182, 183, 184
Illinois
185, 186, 187, 188, 190, 192, 193, 194, 197, 198, 199, 200, 201, 203, 204, 205, 206, 207, 208, 209, 211, 212, 214
Indiana
215, 216, 218, 219, 220, 221, 222, 224, 225, 226, 227, 228, 229, 230, 231, 233
Iowa
234, 235, 236, 238, 241, 242, 243, 245, 246, 247
Kansas
115, 249, 250, 252, 253, 254, 255
Kentucky
258, 259, 261, 262, 265
Louisiana
266, 269, 272, 274, 275
Maine
277, 278, 279, 282
Maryland
283, 284, 285, 288, 290, 291, 292, 295
Massachusetts
296, 297, 298, 302, 304, 305, 308, 309, 312, 315, 316, 317, 319, 320, 323, 324, 326
Michigan
327, 328, 329, 332, 334, 337, 338, 340, 341, 342, 343, 346, 348, 349
Mid Atlantic states
135
Minnesota
350, 351, 352, 353, 354, 355, 357, 358, 359, 360, 361, 362, 363, 364
Mississippi
365, 367, 367, 368
Missouri
374, 375, 376, 377, 378, 379, 380, 382, 385, 386
Montana
388, 390, 391, 392, 393
Nebraska
395, 397, 398
Nevada
101, 400
New England
119
New Hampshire
403, 405, 407
New Jersey
413, 414, 419, 420, 421, 422, 423, 425
New Mexico
115, 428, 430, 431, 432, 435
New York
119, 125, 438, 439, 440, 441, 442, 443, 445, 447, 449, 450, 451, 452, 453, 454, 456, 459, 463, 468, 473, 474, 475, 477, 480, 481, 482, 483
North Carolina
485, 486, 487, 488, 490, 491, 492, 495, 497, 498, 499, 500, 501, 502
North Dakota
503, 504, 505, 506
Ohio
508, 509, 512, 513, 514, 516, 517, 520, 521, 522, 523, 524, 525, 526, 527, 528, 529, 530, 531, 532, 533, 570
Oklahoma
534, 535, 536, 538, 540, 541
Oregon
101, 542, 543, 544, 545, 546, 548, 549, 552
Pennsylvania
555, 559, 560, 562, 564, 565, 567, 569, 570, 571, 574, 575, 576, 579, 580, 581, 583, 584
Puerto Rico
585

Rhode Island
590
South Carolina
593, 595, 596
South Dakota
598, 600, 601
Tennessee
258, 604, 605, 606, 607, 609, 610, 611, 612, 613
Texas
614, 618, 620, 621, 622, 624, 625, 626, 627, 629, 630, 631, 632, 633
Utah
115, 636, 637, 639, 640, 642
Vermont
644, 645, 647
Virginia
650, 652, 653, 654, 656, 657, 658, 659, 661, 663, 664, 669
Washington
101, 672, 674, 675, 676, 677, 679, 680, 682, 684
West Virginia
687, 688
Western United States
54, 60, 112, 680
Wisconsin
689, 690, 691, 692, 695, 696, 697, 698, 699, 702, 704, 706
Wyoming
115, 710, 711, 713, 715, 716
Geological Survey, topographic sheets
Historical maps
544
Government Printing Office, depositories
19, 36, 150, 178, 197, 211, 214, 246, 337, 386, 396, 433, 435, 449, 468, 481, 531, 538, 600, 622, 650, 703, 707
District of Columbia
137
Missouri
370
History
4, 9, 318, 412, 459, 544
Colonial period
270
Library of Congress
143
Military Academy Library
484
Mississippi River Commission
369
Nation Ocean Service, depositories in the United States
Texas
620
National Aeronautics and Space Administration
Aerial Film Library
150
Reconnaisance photography
9
National Archives and Records Services
Cartographic and Architectural Branch
144
National Cartographic Information Centers, Co-affiliate
19
National Forests
95, 499, 529, 544
Collection of Maps pre-1930
181
National Ocean Service
Map Library
292
Maryland
293
National Ocean Service, depositories in Canada
Nova Scotia
747
Ontario
760

Toronto
775
National Ocean Service, depositories in the United States
Alabama
8
Arizona
22
Arkansas
27
California
29, 36, 39, 48, 49, 53, 56, 58, 93
Colorado
105
Connecticut
127
Delaware
130
District of Columbia
143, 144
Florida
150, 154, 156
Georgia
161, 162
Idaho
180
Illinois
186, 197, 199, 203, 207, 214
Indiana
215
Iowa
234, 246
Louisiana
266
Maine
279
Maryland
284, 292
Massachusetts
302, 304, 306, 308, 315, 324
Michigan
328, 332, 337, 341, 342, 346, 348, 349
Minnesota
354
Mississippi
367
New Jersey
422, 423, 425
New Mexico
430
New York
438, 439, 442, 443, 468, 471, 480
North Carolina
488, 495
North Dakota
504
Ohio
509, 512, 513, 514, 516, 520, 528, 531
Oklahoma
538
Oregon
544, 545
Pennsylvania
575, 579, 583
Tennessee
613
Texas
621, 626
Utah
636
Vermont
644
Virginia
652, 656
Washington
672, 674, 676, 677
National Oceanic and Atmospheric Administration
294
National Oceanic and Atmospheric Administration, depositories
Georgia
169

National Oceanographic Survey, depositories in
Canada
British Columbia
728
Nova Scotia
746
Québec
787, 792, 794
National Oceanographic Survey, depositories in
the United States
Colorado
113, 115
Connecticut
119, 125
District of Columbia
137
Florida
147
Hawaii
178
Michigan
328
Texas
624
Wisconsin
697
National Parks
459, 529, 717
Soil surveys
341
State Department
International Boundary Commissions and
American Commission to negotiate Peace
Collection
144
Superintendent of Documents, depositories
312, 697
United States Counties
See Counties
United States History
See also Civil War, Revolutionary War
144, 518, 572, 591
University campus maps
226
University Map and Design Library (brochure)
University of Waterloo
778
*University Map Library, Department of
Geography* (brochure, Brock University)
766
Urban areas and geography
128, 164, 197, 761, 776, 791
**Urban land utilization collection of Virginia
localities, ca. 1886–1925**
669
Urban planning
See also Cities and Towns, Industrial
development
31, 50, 77, 93, 138, 139, 162, 251, 308, 311,
344, 364, 406, 422, 455, 457, 459, 481,
485, 565, 566, 583, 700, 709, 728, 729,
779, 793, 802
City plan collection from all cities, especially
from last 100 years to the present
58
Facsimile town plans
728
Historic urban plan series
507
Québec
797
Urness, Carol
356
U.S. National Fisheries Service Map Collection
13
User Guide to Government Documents
611
Utah
Colleges and universities
Southern Utah State College
635
University of Utah

Marriott Library, Science and Engineering, Map
Collection
640
Marriott Library, Special Collections
641
Utah State University
Merrill Library
636
History
641, 642
State geological surveys
637
State Historical Society
642
Utah Field House of Natural History
643
Utica Public Library
483

V

Valdosta State College
170
Valentine Museum Library
667
Valparaiso University
231
Van Balen, John
601
Vancouver (British Columbia)
City Archives
729
Public Library
730
Weather maps
726
Vanderbilt University
613
Vassar College
Geology Map Library
475
Library, Special Collections
476
Vegetation
39, 42, 161, 321
Vellum chart collection
143
Vermont
Colleges and universities
University of Vermont
Bailey/Howe Library
644
Historical Society Library
646
State Libraries Department
647
*Vermont Maps Prior to 1900: An Annotated
Cartobibliography*
646, 646
Vestal, Charles S.
53
Vick, Timothy D.
359
Victoria
Greater Victoria Public Library
731
University of Victoria
733
Vierich, Dick
72
Virginia
Colleges and universities
University of Virginia
Alderman Library
653
Virginia Military Institute
658
Virginia Polytechnic Institute and State University
649
University Libraries
650

University Libraries, Special Collections
651
Historical Society
668
History
651, 669
Institute of Marine Science
656
Mineral Resources Division, depository
649
Public Works Board, 19th century manuscript
maps
669
State Library
669
Vos, Larry A.
255

W

Wadsworth, William B.
Geology Department
103
Waide, John
383
Wake Forest University
Z. Smith Reynolds Library
502
Walker, Barbara J.
162
Wall charts collection of teaching maps
70
Walsh, Jim
714
Walstrom, Jon. L.
361
Walter, Diana L.
212
Waltz, Mary Anne
481
Wang, Paul
92
Warkentin, Katherine
580
Warner (Langdon) collection
143
Warrantees
566
Warren, Lola N.
290
Warrington, David
217
Washington
Colleges and universities
Central Washington University
674
Eastern Washington University
673
University of Puget Sound
682
University of Washington
677
Washington State University
675
Western Washington University
672
Historical societies
Eastern Washington State Historical Society
678
Washington State Historical Society
683
History
676
Natural Resources Department, depository
672
State Department of Natural Resources
depository
672
Washington, D.C.
See District of Columbia

Washington State and territorial map collection from 1854
676
Washington University (Missouri)
385
Wason, collection of China and East Asia maps
456
Water resources
See also Hydrography
37, 59, 343, 365, 373, 428, 616, 624, 664, 709, 721
Waterloo
University of Waterloo
Engineering, Mathematics and Science Library
777
Map and Design Library
778
Waterways
See also Canals, Lakes, Rivers
130, 688
Watts, Kit
334
Weary, Richard L.
556
Weber, Robert
546
Wedig, Eric
611
Wegner, Mrs. LeRoy
631
Weirather, Linda
389
Weiss, Stephen C.
636
Welland Canals map collection
766
Wellesley College
322
Wells, Elizabeth C.
3
Wells, Stephen G.
429
Wesleyan University
Earth and Environmental Sciences Department
121
Science Library
122
West Chester University
Francis Harvey Green Library
584
West Florida historical map collection
154
West Virginia
Colleges and universities
West Virginia University
Library, Map Room
687
Library, West Virginia Regional History
Collection
688
Geological and Economic Survey Library
686
Geological Survey
depository
688
Highway Department
depository
688
History
688
West Virginia History; a Bibliography and Guide to Research
688
Western Reserve Historical Society
518
Western United States
217, 539, 710
History
393, 635
Western United Stats

History
641
Whaling
313, 314
Whetstone, Susan
642
Whistance-Smith, Ronald
723
Whitman College
Penrose Memorial Library
684
Whittier College
103
Whyte (Peter and Catharine) Foundation
717
Wichita Pubic Library
255
Wichita State University
257
Wick, Constance
307
Wight, Susan
276
Wihbey, Francis R.
279
Wiler, Linda
146
Wilkins, Eleanore
60
Wilkinson, Patrick J.
235
Williams College
323
Williams, Paula
535
Williams, Richmond D.
131
Williams, Robert G.
12
Williams, Ruth
690
Williams, Sheryl
251
Williams, Sue W.
655
Williamson, Sue
582
Willingham, J. Robert
370
Willingham, Robert M.
160
Wilmington Institute Free Library
133
Wilson (James) collection of globes
646
Wilson (John) original survey collection for map
594
Wilson, Maureen F.
728
Windheuser, Christine S.
145
Windsor
University of Windsor
779
Winearls, Joan
775
Winn, LaVerne
278
Winn-Dixie Map Library
7
Winnipeg
University of Winnipeg
737
Winnipeg Public Library
738
Winroth, Elizabeth
549
Winter, Mary
260
Winters, Christopher
197

Wisconsin
Cities and towns—collection Bird's eye views
696
Colleges and universities
University of Wisconsin
Cartographic Laboratory
Arthur H. Robinson Map Library
697
La Crosse
695
Eau Claire
Simpson Map Library
691
Green Bay
692
Milwaukee
Map and Air Photo Library
700
Oshkosh
Geography Department
701
Geology Department
702
Polk Library, Government Documents
703
Parkside
694
Platteville
Karrmann Library
704
Stevens Point
706
Superior
Jim Dan Hill Library
707
Whitewater
709
University of Wisconsin, Milwaukee
Golda Meir Library
American Geographical Society Map Collection
699
History
693, 698
Southeastern Wisconsin
Regional Planning Commission
708
State Historical Society
696
Witchita State University
256
Witzig, Fred
353
Wobus, Reinhard
323
Wohlsen, Theodore O., Jr.
118
Wolter, John A.
143
Wood, Alberta Auringer
742
Woodblocks
34
Woodland, B. G.
192
Woodley, Carolyn
365
Woods Hole Oceanographic Institution
324
Woodson, Ernest L.
442
Woodward, Frances M.
727
Woodward (Joseph H.) collection historical and regional maps
2
Woolpy, Sara
229
World Bank
145
World Bank report map collection
145

World IMW series
414
World War I
144
World War II
144, 207, 277, 484
World War II collection of Japanese maps
508
Wright, Janet K.
183
Wright State University
526
Wuest, Anna H.
500
Wyoming
Colleges and universities
University of Wyoming
714
Geology and Geophysics Department
715
History
712
State Archives Museum and Historical
Department
712

State Library
713

Y

Yale University
Geology Library
126
Sterling Memorial Library
127
Yale University Library Information Leaflets:
The Map Collection
127
Yeaman, Ruth R.
641
Yellowstone original map
389
York, Henry E.
517
York University
Scott Library
776
Yorkshire, England map collection
786
York-Sunbury Historical Society collection
739

Yoshinaga, Tsugio
447
Youngstown and Mahoning County Public
Library
533
Yukon
Archives
804

Z

Zahner, Jane
170
Zartman, Geraldine
15
Zeager, Lloyd
566
Zenthe, Andrea J.
139
Zipp, Louise S.
245
Zoellner, Alan
657
Zoning
522

Geography and Map Division
Special Libraries Association
Map Collections in the United States and Canada, 4th edition
Directory Questionnaire

PLEASE TYPE OR PRINT

Map library name and address:

Institution: [1A]_____

Dept. or Library [1B]_____

Division or Map Coll. [1C]_____

Street: [1D]_____

City: [1E]_____ State: [1F]_____ Zip: [1G]____

Date map library was established: [2]_____

Phone number (area code and extension): [3]_____

Name/title of person in charge of map coll:
Name: [4A]_____
Title: [4B]_____

Number of persons employed in map library:

Full time	Part time
Professional [5A]_____	[5B]_____
Non-Professional [5C]_____	[5D]_____

Size of collections:

	Total	Annual Increment
maps [6A]_____	[6I]_____
atlases [6B]_____	[6J]_____
globes [6C]_____	[6K]_____
relief models [6D]_____	[6L]_____
aerial photographs [6E]_____	[6M]_____
reference books and gazetteers [6F]_____	[6N]_____
serials (titles received) [6G]_____	[6O]_____
microforms (no. of titles) [6H]_____	[6P]_____

Major geographic area specializations: [7]_____

_____

Major subject specializations: [8]_____

_____

Special cartographic collections (characterize contents of each): [9]

_____

_____

_____

Chronological coverage of the collections (% of holdings):

Pre-1800 [10A]_____   1900 [10C]_____

1800-1899 [10B]_____

Classification system: LC [11A]_____ Boggs-Lewis [11B]_____ AGS [11C]_____

Dewey [11D]_____ DMA [11E]_____

Other [11F]_____

CONTINUED ON BACK

Are the collections cataloged?   Yes [12A]_____   No [12B]_____   % [12C]_____

Map depository for:

DMA [13A]_____   NTS (Canada) [13E]_____

DOS (Gt. Brit.) [13B]_____   USGS (Geol.) [13F]_____

GSC [13C]_____   USGS (Topo.) [13G]_____

NOS [13D]_____   Other [13H]_____

Collections open to:

students [14A]_____   public [14D]_____

faculty [14B]_____   other [14E]_____

employees [14C]_____

Hours of service: Weekdays [15A]_____

Sat. [15B]_____Sun. [15C]_____

Seating capacity of reading area: [16]_____

Average number of readers served per month: [17]_____

Are materials available for interlibrary loan? Yes [18A]_____   No [18B]_____

Reproduction facilities:

Photocopy [19A]_____   Microform [19C]_____

Quickcopy [19B]_____   other [19D]_____

Map library publications, including catalogs, guides to the collections, lists of publications, bibliographies, etc. (please attach sample copies): [20]

_____

_____

_____

_____

Please recommend other map collections in your area you feel should be listed in the Directory:

_____

_____

_____

Return completed questionnaire to:

Directory Revision Committee
Geography and Map Division   _____
Special Libraries Association   Name of person completing form
235 Park Avenue South
New York, New York 10003

                                       _____
                                       Title   Date